GHOSTS
OF
DUNKIRK

Patrick Gibbon

First published in paperback 2013 by
Patrick Gibbon

Copyright © 2014 by Patrick Gibbon
The moral right of the author has been asserted.

Every effort has been made to acknowledge copyright holders and obtain their permission.
If any have been inadvertently overlooked,
the publisher will be pleased to correct the oversight at the earliest opportunity.

Every effort has been made to verify all material published in this book.
If the reader discovers any error or glaring omissions in this book,
please contact the author at
email: ghostsofdunkirk@talktalk.net
and he will be only too happy to correct the inaccuracy or add such facts
where possible at the earliest opportunity.

To learn more about this book, add your own information or interact
please visit the author on **FACEBOOK** at
www.facebook.com/ghostsofdunkirk

A CIP Catalogue record for this book is available from the British Library

ISBN 9780992795504

Picture Credits
Grateful consideration and thanks is acknowledged for
permission to reproduce the following illustrations:

Picture reference 22: Bundesarchiv, Bild 183-H01758, Foto: o.Ang. 1 1938
Picture reference 31: Hulton Archive/Archive Photos/Getty, Image No: 2695884

Ghosts of Dunkirk is a true story of an ordinary, patriotic young Englishman who, like thousands of others, preferred to leave the safety of his protected employment in England in order to fight for his king and country.
His battalion was sent only partially trained, unprepared and ill-equipped to France in order to halt and repel the all-powerful Nazi war machine,... like innocent lambs to the inevitable slaughter.

This book is dedicated to Dennis Minter and all the young heroes of the BEF (British Expeditionary Force) sent overseas in the spring of 1940 in order to halt the cancerous spread of Hitler's Nazis across Europe and the free world.
In particular, it is especially devoted to all those left behind after the evacuation of Dunkirk on 4th June 1940, who either died or were captured, destined to spend the next five long years in PoW camps across Germany and occupied Europe.
Hailed at the time as a monumental victory, the reality of the aftermath of Dunkirk told a very different story...
a story of forced marches and torturous transportation into captivity, of slave labour, malnutrition and starvation, brutality, beatings and murder, culminating in the horror of the 3 month 'Death March' from January to April 1945.
These men were forced at gunpoint to walk through one of Europe's worst winters of modern times, without adequate clothing, food or shelter.
How so many of them survived is almost beyond comprehension.

DUNKIRK

In the newspapers and newsreels of the day,
the evacuation was heralded as a successful, heroic adventure.
However, in private, even Churchill acknowledged that Dunkirk was 'the greatest military defeat for many centuries'.
Historians have since called the public image of the evacuation which was portrayed in Britain as 'the necessary myth' – essential to maintain the morale of the nation during the darkest of days, but with scant regard for the actual truth.
Dunkirk was a hollow victory, snatched from the jaws of a monumental defeat.
The situation should never have arisen and is a lesson from history.

Winston Churchill

During Churchill's famous 'we shall fight them on the beaches'
speech to The House of Commons on 4th June 1940, he described
Dunkirk as 'a miracle of deliverance' and went on to say:
"we must be very careful not to assign to this
deliverance the attributes of a victory.
Wars are not won by evacuations."
But there was a victory of sorts within this deliverance.

Captain Sir Basil Henry Liddell Hart
(1895 - 1970)
English soldier, respected military historian and leading inter-war theorist
once wrote:
"The German generals of this war
were the best-finished product of their profession - anywhere."

Dennis Minter
1919 - 2012 and counting
English Private, 2nd/7th The Queen's Royal Regiment
said of the above:
"Sadly, that's what we were up against!
It was a shambles,... a bloody disaster."

PREFACE

2nd/7th THE QUEEN'S ROYAL REGIMENT,
12TH (EASTERN) INFANTRY DIVISION, PART OF THE BEF,
AS OF 9th MAY 1940
GENERAL OFFICER COMMANDING-IN-CHIEF:
GENERAL THE LORD GORT

When sent to France in April 1940, the 12th consisted of:
> 35th Infantry Brigade
> 2/5th The Queen's (Royal West Surrey Regiment)
> 2/6th The Queen's Royal Regiment
> 2/7th The Queen's Royal Regiment
> 36th Infantry Brigade
> 5th Royal East Kent Regiment
> 6th The Queen's Own Royal West Kent Regiment
> 7th The Queen's Own Royal West Kent Regiment
> 37th Infantry Brigade
> 6th The Royal Sussex Regiment
> 2/6th The East Surrey Regiment
> 7th The Royal Sussex Regiment

The 12th (Eastern) Infantry Division was a division raised by the British Army during the First World War.

The Division was reformed as a second line Territorial Army formation just prior the start of the Second World War. As such it contained mostly half-trained units, some of whom had not even fired their rifles. In April 1940 the 12th (Eastern) Infantry Division under Major-General R. L. Petre, along with the 23rd (Northumbrian) Division and 46th (North Midland) Divisions, were sent as pioneer units to France to undergo continuing training and labour duties. They were all totally ill-equipped and didn't even have their signals, Royal Artillery or administrative units with them.

When Nazi Germany invaded France and the Low Countries on 10th May 1940 only *every third battalion of the 12th Infantry Division had completed a week's training.* Not surprisingly, these innocents suffered heavy casualties during the Battle of France and the subsequent disastrous retreat and evacuation from Dunkirk. As a result of its high proportion of casualties and the failure of many to be brought home, the decimated 12th Infantry Division was disbanded on 11th July 1940.

HOW THIS BOOK CAME TO BE WRITTEN

My name is Patrick Gibbon. It was not until early 1997 that I first got to know Dennis Minter, just after the death of Ruth Messingfeld, my mother-in-law, who died that year. Dennis became her partner after the premature death of her first husband, George Osborne. My wife, Angelika (daughter of Ruth and George Osborne), wanted to make sure that Dennis was not forgotten and began to invite him around for regular meals. Over countless dinners, he would tell us tales of his life during the war and his subsequent years as a PoW in Europe. So many and varied were these stories, that I recognised the potential tragedy of allowing them to die with him.

In 2004, I suffered a serious road accident which eventually gave me the analeptic reason and subsequent time in order for me to write this, my first book. Over the course of the next seven years began the long, slow process of teasing every last drop of information from him and digitally recording them over countless cups of coffee at the kitchen table. What amazed me was his phenomenal memory and recollection of detail. However it was the authentication of these recollections, the time line and chronological order of events that proved to be the most challenging aspect.

I have tried as best I can to verify the happenings and to ensure the accuracy of this document as both Dennis and I would like this book to be a serious record of a little known story, an unsung and largely forgotten tragedy that befell over 41,000 British troops after Dunkirk. It was just one event, often buried amongst an ocean of facts and information that chronicles the worst global conflict in history to befall our world - The Second World War.

1919
Day 1

Dennis Henry Minter
Born in Woking in the county of Surrey
on 1st December 1919, just one year
and nineteen days after the Great War ended.
I suppose you could call him a war baby.

THE BEACH AT DUNKIRK

25th May 1940

Somehow, our blistered, long-suffering feet carried us up the last sand dune. The sight that presented itself to us could not have been imagined, only dreamt of, for this was the stuff of nightmares. The full spectacle of the final disastrous chapter of our battle for France was revealed before us. A national disaster was culminating here on the beaches of Dunkirk.

Despite the sun beating down mercilessly, our arrival at the beach was to be no seaside picnic. On both sides, the seemingly endless sands stretched as far as the eye could see. Blemishing this once peaceful seashore were thousands upon thousands of figures, defeated brothers-in-arms huddled in groups or wandering alone or in pairs amongst the debris of abandoned possessions, a vast army of ants on a bed of sugar. Amongst all of this, extended snake-like lines of men, two or three abreast, twisted and buckled, flowing away from the dunes, meandering across the broad stretches of sand and into the sea beyond, their ends like snake heads dancing on the waters. Small boats, some no bigger than rowing boats, bobbed around them on the gently swaying waves. Men scrambled awkwardly aboard whilst other boats laden with despondent troops sped away back out to sea, towards the ships that waited patiently a short distance off-shore. If they were lucky, to carry them home or to place them on board ship that were destined to be attacked and sunk by the persistent attacks from Goring's Luftwaffe.

So this was our evacuation point, our exit ticket from a calamitous seven weeks in France. Even in my exhausted state, I could see this withdrawal was a task of monumental proportions.

Further out to sea, a ship lay forlorn on its side, its deck facing the shore. It lay too far out to see it in more detail, whether Royal or Merchant Navy. It reminded me of a film I had once seen at our local cinema in Walton, of a majestic elephant that had been killed by a trophy hunter. This sight was just as sad.

A mile away and to our right, dense grey smoke rose, drifting lazily skywards. Dotted above, tiny crosses circled, darting too and fro through the smoke before diving down towards the port that sat uneasily below. From its midst, sudden balls of fire erupted, quickly turning to a mass of billowing cloud followed by the boom of distant explosions.

This was Dunkirk and it looked like hell on earth.

We staggered the last few paces away from the dunes towards the sea, before collapsing en masse onto the soft sand, joining other bands of exhausted despondent soldiers scattered about. We were utterly drained but the words fail to describe our true physical and mental condition. None of us could be bothered to even talk. Had we not been so enfeebled, we might have been more aware of the distant hum that was fast approaching from our right.

The throbbing rattle of cannon fire finally alerted us to the deadly problem from above, as the Messerschmitt 109 unleashed a hail of deadly projectiles. We had nowhere to hide and all we could do was pray. The roar of its Daimler-Benz engine was deafening as it flew low overhead, still firing in quick bursts. My head was buried so deep, I could taste the sand. As soon as it flew past, we sat up and looked about.

"You men, don't just bloody sit there, dig in if you don't want a red hot German shell up your backside," a sergeant screamed.

Behind him, a never ending procession of dejected soldiers, French, Belgium and British, spilled out from the dunes.

Instantly we set to work and dug, using our hands and helmets as though our very lives depended on it, which of course they did. We had barely started when we heard it again. A second Messerschmitt followed, racing along the beach towards us, cannons ablaze, seemingly hell bent on our destruction. We ducked behind our hastily built sandcastle but this time I was able to watch the aircraft approach. The pilot was flying just above the water towards the men queueing for the boats. Those on shore and on the water's edge dived to the ground whilst those in the deeper waters could only stand and wait. The aircraft's cannon fire found its mark, sending soldiers flying backwards into the water. They were sitting ducks. Those at the front of the wavering line standing shoulder deep could do nothing but wait their turn to be dragged aboard. Every attack made them scramble up more urgently than ever.

All around, waiting troops lay on their backs with rifles raised skywards desperately trying to shoot down the aircraft, whilst others fired from a prone or kneeling position. Volley after volley was fired but on this occasion, to no avail.

Freddy, Herby, Tommy, Charlie, Bill and I immediately scrambled up and frantically dug again, chucking the excavated sand to the sides of our pit. In the distance, from the heart of Dunkirk, came the 'boom' of a tremendous explosion. A shell had landed on target, hitting a fuel dump or ammunition store. Flames, glowing cordite and deadly shrapnel raced upwards before rearing off to the sides, falling back to earth in a perfect arc. We could only watch helplessly as another Luftwaffe squadron crossed the shoreline and headed out to sea, towards the flotilla of Naval ships awaiting orders to sail back to England, fully laden with their precious human cargo. And all about, the air was filled with the smell of exploding munitions, burning buildings, oil, blood, fear and death.

However, our Messerschmitt's airman wasn't satisfied with his first sortie. As we dug, we watched as he turned and came in again, this time low over the beach. He seemed to weave from side to side, spraying his cannon fire from left to right. More shells pounded the beach until the lines of fire found batches of intended victims, of desperate allied soldiers lying in its murderous path.

What had we walked into? 'Out of the frying pan and into the proverbial fire' sprang to mind. Probably like everyone else, I was petrified, for we were all so exposed.

The Messerschmitt, now content, its murderous purpose appeased, sped on climbing almost vertically as it headed towards Dunkirk before banking sharply to the right and heading inland. We heaved a collective sigh of relief. Now, the terrible cries could be heard above the background clatter, the screams of men in agonising pain from their horrific injuries. After every attack, the all too brief silence was absorbed and replaced with the background noise of distant gunfire and shelling from Dunkirk.

By now, the Luftwaffe squadron had reached the first of the Naval ships and commenced its attack. Dive bombers whined as they started their fall, releasing their deadly cargo before checking their descent. The first aircraft missed the target and climbed once more to escape the anti-aircraft fire that rose steadily from the ship's guns. No sooner were they out of the way than the second wave of bombers initiated their attack. Its first bomb also missed, overshot the ship and exploded in the water on the starboard side, sending a column of water skywards. As I held my breath, the next aircraft took the plunge, dispatching its more accurate bomb. Luck had finally run out for all those on board as the angel of death sped towards the ship. She was a sitting target to the swarm of enemy aircraft. We watched, utterly helpless as the deck exploded. Hot on its tail, the following aircraft came in for the *coup du grâce*.

Another explosion resulted and with that, an almighty third explosion sealed the fate of the ship. With its back broken, it was torn apart. Glowing smoke seemed to billow from it's whole length. It begged the question 'how could anybody have survived the resulting fireball?'

I turned and stared at the others who did likewise. No words were necessary. The horror, fear and tragedy of this war of ours seemed never ending.

Finally darkness descended and an orange glow lit up the night sky above the beleaguered port. Like Calais just days before, Dunkirk had become a raging inferno, Hades on earth, and I pitied those within as I sank back into the retained warmth of the sands wondering what the hell I was doing here and why had I volunteered when I could have been at home, sitting safely behind my drawing board back home in dear old Blighty. Before I had time to reflect more, I fell into the heaviest of sleeps that comes with fear and total exhaustion, dreaming the dreams of recalled memories, of my youth and work colleagues and of times gone by when this war seemed an impossibility after the Great War. THE WAR that was meant to mark the end of all wars.

· · · § · · ·

1934

FAREWELL TO MY CHILDHOOD

As a fourteen year old, I was unconcerned during these troubled times. Whilst the world's economies were still clawing their way out of the Great Depression, I learnt of events from my father's newspaper. A comical fascist by the name of Hitler had succeeded in becoming leader of Germany; the elected Chancellor of Austria had been assassinated and whilst the King of Yugoslavia was on a state visit to France, yet another liquidator ended his life with a bullet. Next door, Spain was on the brink of a genocidal civil war and on the other side of the world, China was teetering on the edge of a precipice as communists fought nationalists for supremacy over untold millions. News from America that the famous aviator Charles Lindberg was coming to live in Britain seemed to upset my mother dreadfully as she related to us the tragedy of the Lindbergs' kidnapped baby, murdered the previous year. But as oblivious as I was to the consequences of these occurrences, my father constantly reminded my mother that the world was indeed a troublesome place.

My recollection is so clear for it was the year that I left school. Father had risen through the ranks and was now a police superintendent, a proud and respected member of the establishment *(see picture reference 6)*. Each evening after tea, he would end the day by religiously reading his police reports in total silence, displaying the appropriate gravitas that his paperwork deserved. This was followed by a slightly more animated reading of the daily newspaper, which often led him to comment accordingly to my mother. Regardless of whether the news was sombre or frivolous, his remarks were made with equally grim emphasis. He could best be described as a man of sullen humour. I was fourteen and because of his daily bulletins, I was increasingly made aware of the slowly unfolding crises that were enveloping our world.

Cyril, my eldest brother, was growing up rapidly but there were increasing testosterone-fuelled, head-butting confrontations filling our house as the tension between the posturing generations grew ever more frequent. At the time, Cyril was courting and his present girlfriend was a large, jolly girl called Kathleen *(see picture reference 7)*. She lived close by in Weybridge and was not the prettiest of girls but kind and chubby. Personally, I couldn't understand what Cyril saw in her, that is, until one day...

I was rummaging through the saddle bag of his bike, looking for a spanner with which to fix my wheel, when unexpectedly I found something half hidden, wrapped up in a brown paper bag. Being of an enquiring nature, I looked inside. In an instant, the reason for Cyril's fascination with Kathleen became all too apparent. An opened packet of condoms stared back at me. Wow! And to think that her name, Kathleen, actually means 'pure maiden'. But I was impressed with Cyril, my brother, having sex! The lucky devil!

This was at the very heart of the grating friction between him and our increasingly irate father. Once tea was over, Cyril always disappeared as he sought to pacify his lust induced hormones, eventually creeping into his own bed around midnight. With the advent of summer, he would remain out 'til one or two o'clock. His cavorting eventually proved his undoing for mother couldn't sleep until Cyril was home safely tucked up in his bed. If mother couldn't sleep then neither could my father, and if he couldn't sleep he became extremely irritable. Needless to say, the following morning raised voices were always evident over the breakfast table. One such morning it all came to a head, culminating in an almighty row that must have been heard in the next county. I listened from the top of the stairs for a while, smiling, as my father gave Cyril a severe tongue lashing. I think rival siblings of our age are often like that, sometimes pleased when the other is on the receiving end of a tongue-lashing for a change. When I eventually came down to breakfast, I could see my father's face distorted by anger. As I entered the kitchen, he exploded once more, staring daggers at the man that was no longer his son, but my bad brother. Finally, he bellowed without warning.

"I've had enough of you. At the weekend, I want you to pack your bags and get lodgings. You're out."

Cyril looked shocked whilst I quietly laughed, revelling in his discomfort and bad news, and that was my fatal mistake. My father's head spun round and his angry eyes locked onto mine.

"And as for you, you can pack your bags as well and go with him."

My mouth fell open. I was shocked and deeply hurt. I looked first at him and then at my poor mother. I saw in her face that she dare not offer me any support for fear of contradicting my father, whose cerebral veins were on the brink of erupting whilst she was on the brink of tears.

I turned to my father. "What, me? Why me? I haven't done anything."

"Henry, please, he's only fourteen," pleaded my shocked mother *(see picture reference 9).*

In a flash, he turned to her, his face purple with rage.

"And I was only twelve when I left school and got a job," matter closed. *(see picture reference 1)*

There was no arguing with my father. Once he had said something, it was cast in stone. We knew enough of his character to not even attempt to argue our cause, even if we could find the courage. Soft he certainly wasn't, and when he shouted, it shook you to your core. In response to my feeble protestations, he bore into my eyes

"I know you haven't. Just call it a preventative act. I'm getting rid of you before you do."

And that was that. At the weekend, both Cyril and I were out. At only fourteen years of age, my childhood came to an abrupt and unexpected end. It seemed unbelievably harsh, unjust even. After all, I was innocent of any wrongdoing. In the space of a few moments, I was homeless and in desperate need of employment. At least my brother Cyril was three years older than me and more able to cope with the harsh realities of adult life in the 1930s.

Without assistance I found employment with Vickers Aviation, whose factory was situated on the site of the famous Brooklands race track at Weybridge. My next priority was to find lodgings which I soon did, conveniently in Elmsgrove Road, Weybridge, at the back of the Post Office in the High Street, so I could easily walk to work. After paying for my lodgings, I was left with pennies. How I managed to exist was down to frugality and a miracle of fiscal management.

During my earlier adolescent years, playtime often involved battles against either the Germans or the American Indians, depending on what films had recently been screened at the local cinema. Memories of the Great War were still fresh in everybody's minds and everyone knew somebody first hand who still bore the horrific physical or mental scars and deformities of battle. The books and short comic style stories that I loved as a child were mostly related to that war and the magnificent bravery of our servicemen fighting against the evil Hun. It was real boys stuff, heroes and villains, good against evil, us against them. In particular, the pilots of the Flying Corps, forerunner of today's Royal Air Force, were the modern day equivalent of Knights in Armour - Knights of the Skies, defending our homeland against the barbaric Boche. These Knights were our heroes of the day. For me, tales of ground troops fighting in the trenches did not fire my imagination as much, for the naked reality of that war was too festering a sore to expose and examine, best kept under wraps, too horrid to relate. Sometimes I was a flying ace, soaring into the skies in my glamorous biplane, attacking the infamous Bloody Red Baron. Then, I was a cowboy in the Wild West, mowing down the hostile Indians with a US cavalry Gatling gun, or I was a brave Tommy in the Great War, defending my position against overwhelming hordes of fearsome but foolhardy German infantry advancing towards my trench.

On the first day of my first full-time job, I was assigned to the Erecting Shop inside a huge hangar within Brooklands, one of two to three hundred other men and boys. Many of these great characters were ex-Air Force, men from the First World War. Such was my enthusiasm for my new job that every morning I would spring up out of my bed and rush to be at the factory early, but it was the people and atmosphere that I enjoyed more than anything. Everybody was good to me and most helpful. During tea breaks, the men would tell me their stories and experiences of the Great War, tales both funny and exciting, whilst others were exceedingly tragic. Their vivid descriptions of trench life and the carnage of that war were almost beyond belief, and often a far cry from the sanitised versions that I read. But at every opportunity I would relive their war through their words and eyes. That Vickers factory was where I spent the best days of my early adult life.

I was set to work under the watchful eye of a man called Tom Peacock, the armourer. Tom was a short, stocky man whilst I was tall for my age. Satirically, he called me 'Titch'! Tom's job was to test the Lewis machine guns. The disc-shaped, ring-mounted magazine would hold 97 rounds of .303 ammunition. Every day we would open the wooden crates that contained the grease-coated guns. I soon grew to love the smell of gun oil. My task was to remove the surplus grease and test fire them, prior to final installation on the aircraft. The firing was, without doubt, the most exciting aspect of my job.

In the middle of the famous oval Brooklands race track, the company had built a short firing range. At the far end of the range, a thick pile of sand bags lay against a high wall of wooden rail sleepers in order to absorb the spent bullets. Once I had cleaned the guns we would carry them to the range and fire off ten rounds whilst Tom sat in the shadows with his fag, cup of tea and newspaper. Once satisfied that the gun had the potential to kill the enemy and not explode in the face of a far more valuable serviceman than myself, I would move onto the next. It was exhilarating and once behind the weapon, I was in heaven, acting out my warlike fantasies.

It was fortunate that my particular Lewis machine gun was fixed with a narrow operating angle to prevent an over-enthusiastic operator, such as myself, from mowing down some poor unfortunate racing car driver on the track beyond. The work, if you can call it that, was pure pleasure. I loved every part of it and it was to fuel a lifelong passion with firearms and shooting. I spent those first six months of my working life with Tom before I was moved on to advance my experiences.

My second placement was in the machine shop and by comparison, it was dull and I hated every second. I was trained to operate one of the hundred small capstan machines. Each operator was given a hexagonal 'bar' or 'barrel' of differing sizes from which to make bolt nuts. Picking out a bar, drilling it, tapping it and cutting it up into pieces soon proved mind-numbingly boring. To a young chap like me, the monotony and drudgery of my employment on a production line was slowly stifling me. After two months of this tedium, I could stand it no longer. Word reached me that a factory at Hersham was taking on labour. I applied to the Hackbridge Electrical Construction Company and much to my delight, was successful. I was now working the same number of hours as at Vickers and being paid thirty shillings a week - five shillings more than my basic wage at Vickers, but with additional overtime on Tuesdays and Thursdays. I was over the moon and flush with my new found wealth.

~ 1935 ~

In March 1935 it was with a certain amount of sadness that I learnt that I would be seeing even less of my dear mother. Father had been promoted yet again and posted to Leatherhead and mother had to uproot all over again. Although I had been living independently for a while now, I felt the pain of separation from her once more.

· · · § · · ·

PROSPECTS

1936 ONWARDS

Sixteen is a difficult age, stuck precariously between two worlds, as the chrysalis, metamorphosing into maturity. I met a girl called Irene Maker, who briefly became my first girlfriend. But after an eternity lasting two weeks, I was ready to move on to another distraction and her name was Florry Haughton. For me it was lust at first sight. She had the largest chest I had ever seen on a young girl and it was something to behold. It was her main attraction (and possibly her only one). I realised that I was following in my brother's footsteps but had the comfort of knowing that I could no longer be thrown out of *my* home. When I found time from work and college, which was not often, I would cycle to Florry's parents' house and politely ask the same question.

Even as I approached their house, I could feel the fear, like dampness rising through my bones. Even the front door appeared gloomy and hostile as it regarded me with repugnance. With each approaching footstep, my determination was being tested, my inclination pulled one way and then the other; to knock or to wait until the bile started to burn my arid throat; to flee or to stay; to return to the uncomplicated safety of childhood or to follow this strange new desire that was igniting this wondrous appendage between my thighs.

I prayed that her mother would answer.

"Good evening Mrs. Haughton. Do you know if Florry would care to come out with me?"

But as time went by, it was her father who always happened to 'greet me'. He was never able to hide his total dissatisfaction with my every fibre. He would stare intently with no warmth or hint of kindness and scrutinize my inner being for the slightest indication of wrong-doing, refusing to address the obnoxious globule that presented itself on his doorstep. He would stare at me until I felt like crawling into the nearest crevice to join the other low life that dwelled under the rocks. If he managed to refrain from slamming the door in my face, he would turn his back and speak to those inside, those more worthy than I.

"THAT BOY's here,... AGAIN."

Turning once more to face me, he looked straight into my eyes and beyond, searching for the reason for my existence before spitting the words he had such difficulty saying.

"Florry,... HE wants to know if you want to go out with him?"

There would follow another dreadful pause, designed to drive the last nail of discomfort into my already wretched body.

Not bothering to turn away as he addressed his daughter, the inquisitor's stare bore into me, his eyes never leaving me for a second.

"Well,... are you going to?"

"Yes Dad, tell him I will be down in a moment."

At that point, her father would always confront me, sticking his big, fat, powerful face aggressively into mine. With only a hair's width between us, he would address me with an openly exposed threat of malice.

"... and YOU, young man, bloody well watch your step and watch what you get up to or you'll have ME to contend with,... GOT IT?"

To emphasise the point, his bony finger prodded my chest in time to his words.

As soon as Florry and I had put enough distance between us and the interrogating eyes of her protective father, Florry and I would hold hands and head off to our 'nid d'amour', (French always sounds so romantic, don't you think?). Throughout the summer of 1936 my apprenticeship into manhood cautiously and nervously advanced. I still saw Irene but my driving lust was centred on Florry and I was having the time of my life.

Fear can be a great deterrent to the amorous advances of a young man and consequently this emotion must be regarded as one of the best contraceptives in the world. My contemporaries and I were, for the most part, too afraid to have full sex. Every time I thought of the lust-driven act, the terrifying image of Florry's father's stern face pressing into mine killed my ardour stone dead. My fears were very real; retribution from protective fathers and elder brothers; pregnancy out of wedlock and finally; the crippling financial consequences of such a pregnancy. And if that wasn't enough to make you choose celibacy, there existed the 'Breach of Promise Law'. Just as The sword of Damocles hung threateningly over the head of Dionysius II of Syracuse, likewise, this ancient act of parliament hung over any man foolish enough to offer marriage as a means of satisfying his lust. As far as cicil law was concerned, any such declaration amounted to a verbal contract of 'intent to marry'. If you subsequently changed your mind and withdrew your offer you could be said to be in "breach" of that promise and subject to litigation for damages by the girl and her family. Believe me, mistakes - you dare not make them! Who would have thought that the path from boyhood to manhood could be so worryingly burdensome?

For the first few weeks we simply enjoying walking out together until one particular sunny afternoon. We had taken a walk down to the grassy pastures adjacent to the river with a simple picnic, away from prying eyes. After the food was eaten, we lay back on the tartan rug, staring up at the few clouds that refused to move on, hanging like balls of sheep wool on a barbed wire fencing. I was telling Florry about a western I had seen at the local cinema in Walton - 'Roaming Wild'. Cowboy Tom Tyler starred and Florry was telling me that she thought him quite a handsome man. I turned towards her, surprised that she could possibly have found an old man such as him, 'handsome'. Her eyes were shut so I raised my hand and plucked a long strand of grass with seed pods swelling its end. With great care, I brushed her on the very tip of her nose. She swatted the bothersome thing. I lifted the grass and once more and again she attempted to brush it aside. The third time I pushed the pod up her nostril and watched as she jumped up, spitting and snorting through her nose whilst jumping up and down, believing that some huge flying insect was beginning its quest to eat its way into her skull. How I laughed before the penny dropped. She giggled before lying back down. I turned and kissed her nose. She looked up into my eyes and I bent forward to kiss her lips. We each closed our eyes. Not sure why, but it seemed automatic, the instinctive thing to do.

The sound of my beating heart could have been heard by a deaf person. I was probably clumsy, I certainly felt like a blundering octopus as I kissed her, my hand slowly, nervously journeyed across her smooth tummy and slowly upwards towards its mythical goal. Any moment I expected her hand to land on mine, to stop the advance. So far, so good. Maybe she hadn't noticed, 'slowly Dennis, slowly'. Stupid me, of course she's noticed, you fool, is she dead? Then, sudden awareness of her heart pounding like mine, confirmed that she was still alive. She must be excited too,... she was enjoying this as much as me. That gave me the confidence to creep forward to the final assault on her womanly mounds. I raised one finger and felt the swelling. A current surged through my body from my finger tips directly to my groin. I was on fire.

I grew bolder and oh so gently, covered her breast with my hand, touching her nipple. I thought that I had died and gone to heaven. Young ladies in those days didn't seem to wear bras. I was not sure if the reason was just a case of not wanting to, not being able to afford to, that it wasn't fashionable or that it was all too embarrassing to buy them in the shops. But according to my brief survey of the local girls, there did seem to be a lack of this particular undergarment.

With regards tutoring in the blundering art of love-making, I was lucky enough to be able to draw upon the experiences of my elder brother and as time progressed, on the advice of the older men at my place of work.

Now, condoms were an issue for all young lads like me. Even if you never got the opportunity to use them on a date, it was more reassuring to feel them in your pocket and know that you were at least prepared. If you were brave and could pluck up enough courage, you could even buy some. But unlike today, there were no such items as condom vending machines strategically placed in every public convenience and pub toilet. You dare not go to your local chemist either, for sure enough, behind the counter of every local chemist would be a woman serving and such a purchase would be far too embarrassing. Added to that, in all probability the woman behind the counter would probably know either your parents or the parents of your girlfriend. To ask these fearsome judgemental counter staff for birth control protection was a recipe for murder,... your murder.

There was only one other person to whom a young man such as myself could turn to if you were consumed with this irrepressible passion and his name was George Elliott, the local barber. If you needed condoms, you could go to his establishment and follow a well-established protocol.

"George, give us three off the top shelf please," was the acknowledged phrase.

By pretending to be well versed in the ancient art of love-making and discreetly handing over your hard earned cash, followed by a knowing nod of the head, a wink of the eye or a tap on the side of the nose, you were well on the way to achieving your objective and finally escaping from a potentially embarrassing situation with the minimum of humiliation and without actually using the word 'condom'.

Oh yes, sex was safe in my day because you usually couldn't get it AND it was expensive to a young man on lowly wages, so I was destined to remain a virgin for quite a while. But such limits to our sexual behaviour made each little indiscretion so much more exciting. A kiss was thrilling but a fumbling exploration up a jumper was positively sensational. That was the norm and we were all happy with the situation, probably more so than the youth of today.

With my newly-acquired job at the Hackbridge Electrical Construction Company, it made sense for me to move back to Hersham. I easily found convenient lodgings at No. 37 Claremont Close, a road adjacent to the factory *(see picture reference 39)*, enabling me to roll out of bed in the morning and be at work within minutes. The owners, Mr. & Mrs. Thompson, were a kind and religious couple. Mr. Thompson spent his working week at the Vickers plant in Weybridge and all their Sundays were spent at the chapel.

I began my work on the factory shop floor and laboured enthusiastically and happily until one Friday afternoon in early November, when I was called to the main office on the top floor. The prospect of being summoned by the works manager caused butterflies in my stomach as it had never happened to me before. Convinced of some wrong-doing, I wondered what I had done, for guilt was always sitting uncomfortably at the back of my conscience. After a considerable time waiting patiently, I was called in. I entered his large office and from behind his paper-littered desk he offered me a seat. That was promising. He looked and sounded stern as he questioned me about my work and ambitions for the future. I gave the appropriate answers and this seemed to please him. Finally, he informed me that I had been singled out in order to be trained as a draughtsman if I so wished. Having feared bad news I was instantly relieved that I still had a job, then surprised and finally delighted at the prospect. This meant a considerable advancement in terms of my skills development and would eventually lead to a huge increase in my earning power. For once in my short life, I had landed on my feet and come up smelling of roses - or so I thought, for I had yet to learn that nothing is ever certain, and certainly not for long.

The following Monday morning, I arrived at the drawing office and was shown to my new place of work, which was a tall stool in front of a large drawing board. As I sat down and contemplated my new surroundings I was left alone for a while, when a rather frightening thought suddenly struck me. Such was my joy and eagerness to be trained in a new craft that I had not actually done my homework and now found myself with a headache. My lodgings cost me twenty-two shillings and sixpence a week. My wages had plummeted to a meagre seventeen shillings and six pence a week as an apprentice draughtsman. It didn't take a genius to realise that, financially, I was in deep trouble and in anyone's language, this was a recipe for disaster. No amount of clever fiscal management this time was going to balance this discrepancy. My smile of smug satisfaction at landing the apprenticeship was instantly wiped off my face as I deliberated on my shocking realisation.

How was I to make ends meet?

The simple answer was - I hadn't a clue!

Nearly all the men in the drawing office at that time were from the north of England, for in those days unemployment had decimated the regions, forcing men to move to the south to seek work. Just in front of my desk sat an older man who was the senior draftsman. His name was Freddy Mills *(see picture reference 40)*. He seemed a very kind chap and whilst making small talk on my first day, he noticed the glum look on my face.

In his broad Yorkshire accent, he enquired "What's the matter with you, young'un?" (From that point on, he would insist on calling me young'un). I lifted my sorry head and explained my dire predicament to him in fine detail. He listened intently with a look of deep concern, mulling over my situation for a few minutes before looking back at me with a broad smile on his rugged face. He had a solution.

"That's no problem, young'un," he said. "I tell you what we'll do. We will raffle your wage packet each week."

With that, he went to the other twenty-nine men in the office, related my story and arranged it all. From then on, all thirty of them, including Freddy, paid a shilling each week for a raffle ticket and every Friday, pay day, the numbers were all put into a hat and the winning ticket drawn out. I then handed over my unopened wage packet to the winner and Freddy Mills handed me back the thirty shillings he had collected. Freddy and his colleagues kept this up for two long years until my money went up to meet that sum. It was one of the most endearing memories that sustained me throughout my life, for they were truly a great bunch of people.

> *Europe and the world in general was filled with grief and turmoil and on the brink of disaster. Stalin and his particular band of communists were having troubles with Trotskyites and various other factions. Civil unrest never seemed far away from that troubled country. Franco's Nationalist Fascist Party was still engaged in the bloody battle with the communists whilst idealists from all over the world were flocking to fill the ranks of both opposing sides. Spain was being used as a testing ground for a huge experiment in ideology and the innocent civilians were paying a terrible price. Italy's Mussolini, with grandiose plans to recreate the Roman Empire, had ruthlessly attacked the poor and backward African state of Abyssinia using 20th century weaponry against spears and shields. In the Far East, Japan was slaughtering Chinese civilians in a war of unparalleled aggression and brutality. Suddenly, the world around me was becoming an increasingly dangerous place to be.*

During tea breaks, my work colleagues would gather together to chat, tell jokes and discuss the news events of the day. More often than not our conversation centred on a man who was never out of the newspapers, a man my father had often spoken about. His name was Adolf Hitler.

Seemingly, he was causing quite a stir. Through him, Nazi Germany was threatening the delicate balance of peace and power within Europe. In March 1938, this dictator had 'peacefully' invaded Austria with the apparent support of the Austrian people.

"You mark my words young'un," Freddy Mills would say whilst wagging his nicotine-stained finger, "there's another war coming before very long, you mark my words."

His words rang in my ears and would come back to haunt me in the years ahead.

Our Prime Minister at the time was Neville Chamberlain. Not many of us thought he was worthy of the job. He was not a particularly good leader, a 'bit of a wet blanket' was how the lads put it (often adding some swear words to emphasise the point).

It was at this time that my employment at Hackbridge was suddenly cut short. By the beginning of October 1938, business at the factory was bad. There was a considerable drop in new orders coming in from the Government and other customers and the outlook was grim. Rumours were circulating of lay-offs and redundancies and on the morning of 31st October 1938, upon arrival at the factory, I was handed two envelopes. The small cream-coloured envelope had my name typed on the front. To receive company letters was most unusual. I opened the first and was shocked to read that I was being made redundant after three glorious years of training. I felt as though I had just been punched in the stomach. With that, I opened the other letter addressed 'TO WHOM IT MAY CONCERN'. This contained my references, a brief outline of my service record with the company and a short, favourable overview of me - and that was it.

Worry and despair engulfed me. There was no severance package in these dark days and all I had to live on was my unemployment money. I was on 'the dole' and my spirits hit rock bottom. I think it was about eleven shillings and six pence. It all added up to a considerable shortfall between my income and outgoings.

When I returned to my lodgings, I entered the house filled with worry, dragging my spirits along the floor behind me. The gloomy hallway now took on a more sombre atmosphere than ever and even the wonderful sound of Mr. Thompson playing the piano, did nothing to lift my resolve. I found Mrs. Thompson in the kitchen preparing the supper. She turned towards me but I couldn't bring myself to raise a smile.

"Dennis lad, what's the matter, you look dreadful?"

She sat me down at the kitchen table whilst I related my sorry tale. Her face showed a gentle concern as my financial problems unfolded and she disappeared into the front room to fetch her husband. Within a minute they both returned and sat either side of me.

"Sorry to hear of your bad news Dennis, that leaves you in a fine pickle, doesn't it." Sympathy oozed from his face.

Out of pure Christian kindness, they allowed me to stay on, only taking ten shillings of my dole money, which meant that I had to survive on one shilling and six pence a week and my promise that I would repay the arrears once I had secured new employment.

I felt utterly relieved that my immediate problem had been solved but overall, I was short of money, having even less to spend on my all too important social life. But I did have a new girlfriend to soften the blow, introduced to me by way of my benefactor and friend at Hackbridge, Freddy Mills. Freddy was courting a local girl, the oldest of three daughters of a wealthy local businessman by the name of Ben Stanley.

> *Ben Stanley originally started with only a simple horse and cart, ferrying people and transporting goods, gradually expanding his business. After the First World War and the advent of motorised transportation, he replaced his horses with motors and established a large and hugely successful coach company in Hersham.*

Freddy introduced me to her younger sister, a jolly girl called Josephine. We took an instant liking to each other and started to date. Such was her upbringing that as soon as she was able, she had been taught to drive, a rare privilege unavailable to ordinary people such as I. Whenever she could, she would borrow her father's car and drive over to meet me. The vehicle was a big Armstrong Siddeley model with a running board along each side and would not have looked out of place on a Hollywood gangster's film set. After picking me up, she would drive off somewhere secluded and spend many a happy summer's evening kissing and cuddling on the back seat. During these sessions, I tried my best to improve my knowledge of biology and my understanding of the fairer sex on the luxurious black leather seats. Meanwhile, with the stigma of being unemployed and short of money, each weekday, I made a point of cycling around the area, desperately canvassing for work at any place I passed and work of any description.

After a month of frantic searching, I was offered a job at Thompson and Taylor Motor Mechanics. They operated from an extensive site on the Brooklands site at Weybridge.

> *Former World Land Speed Record holder Malcolm Campbell built his first shed here in 1926. It was here that his successful 'Blue Bird' racing and world record-breaking cars were often*

kept, displayed and built. The building which survives today as part of the Brooklands Museum, was used by him as an office, workshop and showroom until around 1935. It was then taken over by leading motor engineers Thomson and Taylor as a workshop and showroom specialising in Alfa Romeos and Railton cars.

Thompson Taylor looked after cars for the ERA, the English Racing Association, also based at Brooklands. All of their cars were painted a deep green which eventually was to become known as the British Racing Green. I was overjoyed to be back at work again and earning a much-needed wage and to return such a famous racing location doubled my enjoyment. Throughout the day, racing cars thundered around the track whilst in the skies above, the almost continuous drone of amazing flying machines was more than I could have hoped for. As well as the aircraft which were assembled and tested at the Brooklands factories, there was also a Flying Club and a School of Flying. Both club and school used the old De Havilland Gipsy Moth biplanes as their work-horse and during break times, I would pop out to watch them come and go, with their distinctive yellow moth emblems on the sides. On landing, they would bounce heavily along the runway before finally coming to a belated halt. Often, these old flying machines would bounce with such ferocity that the serious danger of running out of runway would force them to push their engines into full throttle and take to the skies once more, thus avoiding a fatal encounter with a huge hangar.

When I first commenced work on the Brooklands site way back at the beginning of 1934, Vickers had no new bombers and were still manufacturing the famous old Vickers Vimy bomber aircraft from the Great War. This was almost the same model that first flew the Atlantic in June 1919. My early job was to clean and test fire their Lewis machine guns, the only form of defence for the old biplane. In front of the tail wings, set into an oval wooden frame covered with only a thin plywood skin, was set a cylindrical container into which stood the rear gunner who operated the Lewis gun. The sides of the cylinder came over his waist, which meant that the whole of his upper body was exposed to the elements. Only a couple of thin 3mm plywood sections separated him from a hail of enemy bullets. I shudder to think just how cold it must have been; the wind chill factor alone would have been horrendous. The aircraft operated with another exposed gunner in the very nose of the plane, and a pilot and navigator side-by-side in the middle. There was no form of wired communication between all the crew; they just had to rely upon hand signals and a prayer. But at least their air conditioning was excellent!

> *This highlights just how ill-prepared England was for war in those far-off days. Back in 1934, our fledgling British Air Force was still producing and flying antiquated, wooden-clad open bombers, left over from the last war. Re-armament was off the political agenda.*

And so I joined the drawing office at Thompson Taylor. My initial excitement soon wavered as there was only one other member of staff working with me, a senior draughtsman by the name of Mr. Beacham. He was very reserved and not prone to idle conversation or flippant jest. Our job was to produce the drawings for spare parts of the racing cars. Each car belonged to their owner/driver. We looked after a car belonging to Billy Cotton, a band leader of repute, and also a Riley Imp and later an R2B for a foreign dignitary and legendary racing driver, Prince Bira of Siam. We would often watch the rich and famous battling it out on our track in gladiatorial fashion.

However, there was one other aspect to my job that was considerably more exciting. Once repairs and modifications had been made to a car, they had to be road tested before being allowed to race again and that was down to Alan, the test driver, and me. At a certain point along the race track a series of white lines had been painted. The test driver had to lap the track at 60 mph, then at 80 mph and finally at 100 mph. At these high speeds and on touching the line, he would apply his brakes and come to a halt as soon as was possible. This is where I came in. As all the cars were single-seaters, the company had constructed a small wooden crate for me to sit in, a bit like my mother's home-made bicycle trailer, definitely a Heath Robinson construction. The box was attached to the side of the test car. On the front of the box, a crudely-made wind deflector had been fixed, but because of my height this allowed me no protection from both rain and wind. Adding to my woes, the driver's own windscreen deflected everything from him onto me. I was often soaked through and always freezing cold after being blasted by the elements as well as being permanently numb from the waist upwards. That was not the only problem for me for the track was uneven in many places.

With the high banking all around the track and an imperfect surface, the car would bump along at high speed and my backside felt each and every lump. After several laps of the track and whilst crossing the painted stripe on the road, Alan would hit the brakes and the car would come to a screeching halt. That was my cue to jump out but, to be more accurate, I should really say that I fought my way out of the cramped box, desperately trying to unfold my lanky legs. Armed with my trusty chain measure, clipboard and pencil, I would proceed to record each of the stopping distances.

In spite of the boredom of the drawing office and the cold and rain, I never complained and considered myself the luckiest person alive. Life was good again and I was getting my fair share.

The world-famous Brooklands race track was also home to another celebrated aircraft manufacturer, Hawker Aircraft Limited. Planes such as the Hawker Fury, a biplane and forerunner to the acclaimed Hurricane, were built at their factory in Kingston, Surrey, some twelve miles away. Upon completion, they were transported by lorry to Brooklands with their wings folded back against the fuselage. Upon arrival at the aerodrome, the aircraft were brought inside the compound to Hawker's huge assembly shed where their wings were unfolded and inspected before being sent on their inaugural test flight. Near to the assembly shed, straddling the internal race track, stood a massive clock supported on two great arms. Once in the air, the pilots would fly in low above the track and dive down almost touching the clock with their wheels.

The lack of work at the Hackbridge factory was short-lived. With the impending troubles across the channel, government orders for new generators finally came flooding in. Soon they were recruiting again and I was back in the drawing office once more, with my friends. That first Friday, we celebrated my return and I staggered back from the pub just before 1.00am. The Thompsons had a noisy gravel drive leading to the back door. Anxious not to wake them, I walked on the thin strip of grass next to the wall. As quietly as only a drunk can, I negotiated the stairs to my room. As I opened my door, a sweet voice called to me.

"Goodnight Dennis."

I turned to see their daughter, a seductive sixteen-year-old who had taken a shine to me. She was a sweet temptress with all the innocence of youth. Recalling the old adage, '*never shit on your own doorstep*,' she was strictly off limits. No matter how late I was, she always waited to say good night. If only...

During the mid '30s, no factories appeared to be working to full capacity or on overtime in preparation for war. On reflection, I regarded it as criminally negligent, given the war clouds that were slowly but surely gathering over Europe. My brother, Cyril, was a key worker at the Hawker factory in Kingston and likewise, there was no flurry of activity and no burning the midnight oil to increase production. England seemed to be just plodding along, whilst the German war machine was working to full capacity, producing and stockpiling state-of-the-art machines of war.

~ NEWSPAPER REPORTS ~

My political views were shaped by my father, his newspapers, my friends and work colleagues and the common consensus was that war with Germany would inevitably come.

I will always remember the newsreels of the day at the cinema on 30th September 1938, showing Neville Chamberlain landing back in England after his return from the famous Munich meeting, waving that ridiculous piece of paper in front of him, the new Anglo-German accord, declaring 'peace in our time'. We all hoped and prayed that the declaration really was true but I think Chamberlain was the only one who actually believed the words of Herr Hitler.

Six days later, Hitler's troops walked into Czechoslovakia and that small country became the second to be swallowed up by the fast emerging Nazi beast.

But still, at least we had peace in our time!

Churchill for the main part was nowhere to be heard. After Hitler and the Nazi Party gained power in Germany in 1933, Churchill sensed the danger and became a leading advocate of our own re-armament to counter the threat from the newly-emerging, re-armed Germany. He was politely critical of Chamberlain's government's policy of appeasement. Unfortunately he was in the minority and regarded as a political pariah, as I recall. His warning message was neither popular with the newspapers nor with the government and he was regarded by most politicians from all three main parties of the day as a warmonger. The mighty news barons of Fleet Street seemed reluctant to report his knowledgeable speeches and articles or to take his words seriously. If we hadn't had a man as tough and determined as Churchill waiting in the wings, we might never have gone to war and we might well have capitulated to Hitler, just as France was eventually to do.

When the daily newspapers did cover stories of Hitler's supposed re-armament, the reports were usually played down and his armaments denounced as being only 'paper tanks' and for the camera's eye only. It was all propaganda. Whether these 'paper tanks' were a deliberate ploy, leaked by the Germans to the foreign press in order to hide Germany's growing might or newspaper articles released by the Government, pandering to the peace lobby within parliament and the politicians who were against re-armament at any price, I will never know. Initially the government just wanted to believe that Hitler only had limited desires of German enlargement. This view of mine stemmed from one such newspaper report in the mid 1930s, a report that stuck in my mind and one which I was to recall after the fall of France. At that time many nations had military parades in order to show off their might. They would invite foreign defence attaches to observe, to impress both them and their own people. The Germans were still governed by the 1918 armistice agreements and officially were not allowed to build up their defences beyond a certain point. On this particular occasion, I recall the papers were full of pictures of a German military display with accompanying armoured cars. Some papers and newsreels carried the story that the tanks and armoured cars were actually just ordinary civilian vehicles with plywood or cardboard outer skins to make them look like armoured vehicles†.

---

† *In Hugh Sebag-Montefiore's brilliantly researched book 'DUNKIRK-Fight to the Last Man', he alludes to this, saying 'some British propaganda suggested that Germany was passing off cardboard mock-up tanks as the real thing to make their Panzer divisions appear more powerful than they really were'.*

In reality, they WERE the real thing and Germany WAS secretly stockpiling armaments. Likewise with their Air Force and, to a lesser extent, their Navy. The complicated bluff paid off. The general public bought the dangerous lie that the Germans had little in the way of equipment.

~ THAT LAST SUMMER HOLIDAY ~
1938

My days at Hackbridge continued, with me happily enjoying both work and ambience. Two work colleagues became good friends, Cyril Plumbridge, whose father was the manager of our local Co-op in Hersham, and 'Flicker' Johnson, so-called because he was a pretty good football player and could flick the ball with great ease into the corner of the net. Both were older than me, but I was the tallest.

At best, we could only afford one week's holiday a year and considered ourselves lucky. During the year we would save a few pence here and there until we had scraped together enough for our one week summer spectacular. For the second consecutive year we elected to return to Cliftonville in Kent, on the Isle of Thanet, but this year 'Flicker' brought a friend with him, a short Scottish chap called Joc Macavoy. The previous summer we had stayed at a B&B with an elderly lady, Mrs. Ellis, a widow. Her husband died fighting in the First World War and she supplemented her meagre pension by renting out a couple of rooms.

Earlier in the year, we had contacted Mrs. Ellis by letter and booked the accommodation for the week. We were in great spirits as we travelled across country by train. On arrival, Mrs. Ellis greeted us as though we were her long lost sons, hugged us and showed us up to our rooms. Before leaving each morning after breakfast, she would ask what time we would return so that she could have our supper ready, but it was a complete waste of time for we always stumbled back several hours late, under the influence of a beer or two. As she opened the front door, she would give us a look of slight annoyance, but we doubted that she really meant it. We were her boys and she loved having us to stay. She kindly remarked that her house was alive when we stayed and fell quiet when we left.

Every morning, we dressed to impress in our dapper clothes. We thought we were so suave, and surely a catch for any young lady. We would either go swimming at Cliftonville Lido or catch the bus to Margate and spend the hours enjoying ourselves in 'Dreamlands', a huge funfair and an extraordinary place in which to over indulge in fun, day and night and of course there was the additional attraction that the place was teeming with girls.

For a special treat, we had taken a ferry trip the previous year, across the channel to Calais, my first ever trip abroad. The pleasurable experience had convinced us all that we should repeat the journey and on the last Thursday of July, just after dawn, we caught the early morning bus to Margate. The day was already sunny and warm as we walked to the booking office to buy our tickets. We sailed aboard the 'The Royal Daffodil', an old paddle steamer. According to the postcards that were for sale on board, she had seen active service in The Great War, playing an important part in a famous raid on the Mole at Zeebrugge in 1918.

However, this morning, she had sailed down the Thames from Tower Bridge Pier in London, docked briefly at Southend to pick up more passengers before steaming on to Margate where we boarded before sailing to Calais. Immediately we made our way to the bar, where we settled back with a pint of beer to celebrate. With the sun, sea, clear blue sky and the exuberance of youth, life seemed perfect on that day so long ago.

After disembarking at Calais, we exchanged as much money as we had on the black market, at the unofficial rate, and received 180 francs to the pound as opposed to the official rate of 120. Rumour had it that the French public suspected that the war was coming. They were anxious to 'stash' the more stable and attractive English pound rather than their own currency. Upon our return, we would officially exchange our francs back into pounds and make a little profit from the transaction.

We walked and soon came upon a large church or cathedral in an open square. In front of the building stood a wonderful bronze statue, green with corrosion in places, the heads and shoulders splattered with bird droppings. It stood on a raised stone platform surrounded by a low, elaborate wrought iron work balustrade. The actual statue consisted of six rather downcast figures, all men, young and old, dressed in sack cloth with bare feet. Round their necks hung the rope of a hangman's noose - a haunting yet intriguing image. I was fascinated and felt compelled to learn more.

> *I discovered that the work of art was called 'The Burghers of Calais' (Les Bourgeois de Calais) and was one of the most celebrated works by the famous sculptor Rodin. Completed in 1888, it serves as a monument to an event way back in 1347, during the 'Hundred Years War' between two old adversaries, England and France. England's Edward III, after the victorious Battle of Crécy, laid siege to Calais. Philip VI of France ordered*

*the city to hold out at all costs. After being under siege for over
a year, Philip still refused permission for the city to surrender
but starvation eventually forced it to parley for surrender terms.
Edward finally offered to spare the people of the city if any six of
its leaders would surrender themselves to him, presumably to be
executed. Edward demanded that they walk out almost naked, each
wearing a noose around their necks and to be carrying the keys to
the city and castle. Eustache de Saint Pierre, one of the wealthiest
leaders, was the first to volunteer and five other burghers soon
followed suit. They stripped down to their breeches. Saint Pierre
led this envoy of emaciated volunteers to the city gates and it was
at this moment, this poignant mix of defeat, heroic self-sacrifice
and the facing of their imminent mortality, that Rodin captured in
these figures, which are scaled somewhat larger than life.*

*But don't shed a tear for the six brave Frenchmen. Apparently,
King Edward spared them all upon the request of his queen.*

I asked a passer-by to take a photo of the four of us. We opened
a pack of cigarettes and posed whilst smoking, just to look the part.
(see picture reference 10)

Having satisfied my thirst for a token piece of French culture and
history, we found a bar. After some more liquid refreshments and a
little something to eat, we went in search of the less cultural centre
of the city, the seedy cafe district that we had discovered the year
before. The port of Calais was littered with so-called café regions
and the lads were eager to return, for they had certain activities on
their dirty little minds, for the previous year, they had employed the
services of 'female companions'. Last year, I had waited outside in the
street, kicking my heels until they had finished what they came to do.
However, this year, they all made it clear to me that I was to receive
my introduction and initiation into the wicked ways of the flesh.

Eventually, we rediscovered our cafés and stood outside in the
street whilst Reg and the other two nagged me into overcoming my
reluctance and embarrassment. I was to enjoy myself at all cost and
offer up my body onto the altar of lust. Eventually I caved in, although
I was shaking nervously. For some reason the lads didn't like to go
into the same café together to 'do their business', so each chose a
separate establishment in the same road. I watched as they went in
before smoking yet another cigarette, allowing me to pluck up enough
courage to take my turn and walk to my café, where I paused. I stood

for a minute of two, looked intently at the door, then drew a deep breath whilst drawing heavily on my cigarette, laying my trembling hand on the door handle. I entered with considerable foreboding. Inside was gloomy and uninviting. Opposite the door were chairs on which sat four 'ladies', waiting, bored out of their minds. Smoke hovered in the stale air, merging with the dirty ceiling. One lady attempted a half smile and, as she looked the least frightening, I walked towards her. Before I could say anything in my extremely bad French, with just a hint of an accent, the lady stood up and broadened her smile to one of over-exaggerated glee. She gently and seductively spoke to me but I couldn't understand what she was saying. She steered me towards the bar. The barman uttered something and they both looked at me, so I assumed I was meant to buy a drink. She had a wine and I had a beer. After five minutes of embarrassing silences broken by nervous conversation that neither of us could follow, she took my hand and led me upstairs to a room with me in tow, like an errant child. At the door, she stood aside to let me pass. Once inside, she closed the door, pushing it shut with her bottom. She eyed me up and down whilst my heart pounded. I swallowed hard and was momentarily struck dumb. I turned away from her stare. Ahead stood the intimidating centre of our attention,... the bed.

Apart from this important tool of the trade, the room was scarcely furnished with only dirty curtains hanging from a wire, a bedside table, lamp and a wooden chair. From the ceiling hung a single dull bulb without a shade. The wallpaper was well past its prime, clinging desperately in places to the old walls. In the far corner of the room stood a small wash basin decorated with brown stains and a multitude of chips.

"Trente francs monsieur" (30 francs).

I nodded in the affirmative, trying desperately to look as though I was an old hand at this sort of business.

Her smile was now gone. My 'lady', having secured my patronage, now looked jaded and past caring and just as eager as I to complete the whole squalid affair as quickly as possible. She beckoned me over to the basin, pointed to my crutch and indicated that I should release myself and give it a wash in the basin. I was so embarrassed that I pretended that I did not understand, so madam pulled me over, undid my flies and took it out for me. She took hold of the soap and ran the water before lathering it briskly in both hands. I almost pulled away for the water was cold. She then proceeded to give it a thorough wash, working up a rich lather. By this time, and in spite of the cold water, I had become aroused, excited and fully charged. Within seconds I was spent, all over her hands and into the basin.

"Oo là là!" she exclaimed, shaking her head from side to side whilst tutting. "Oo là là!"

And that was it. My partial sexual initiation.

I cleaned myself, replaced my flaccid member and hurriedly left. I was so utterly relieved that it was all over, but, a little smile of satisfaction crept over my face. Outside, I could hear Flicker shouting for me to hurry as we had to make our way back to catch the return ferry. I ran down the stairs and into the road outside. They congratulated me on the success of my admission into the sordid but extremely likeable world of sex.

We ran all the way back along the uneven cobbled street, laughing all the way. We only just made it in time for the boat's departure. The temperature was still warm so we returned to the bar for another pint of lukewarm beer and sat down on some spare seats. By now, Reg could hardly contain his curiosity.

"Well tell us then, Dennis, was it good?"

Damn! I was too uncomfortable to tell them what had really happened, preferring to fabricate a little and be vague with the exact details.

"Wow! That was good,... that was very good."

They slapped my back and we burst into fits of laughter.

As expected, we all had an amazing and memorable time and returned to work refreshed, with tales to tell of our exploits over endless cups of tea in the works canteen.

·   ·   ·   §   ·   ·   ·

1939

THE YEAR THAT CHANGED THE WORLD . . .
FOREVER

*With war clouds gathering over the continent we decided that it might
be prudent not to return to Mrs. Ellis' B&B for our annual love trip to
France. With Calais now firmly off the agenda, we booked a week in
Clacton. Had I known what fate had in store, I might have made more
frivolous use of my leisure time and savoured every second of those last
few months of peace.*

Springtime, and like the thousands of other people in the south
east of England, my parents took delivery of an Anderson
Shelter, a prefabricated hut named after the then Home
Secretary, John Anderson. Made from 14 corrugated iron sheets
bolted together, it was buried as much as possible in the ground for
added protection against aerial bombardment. If the general public
were still in any doubt as to the gathering war with Germany, then this
act alone drove the impending nightmare home.

Today was 28th April 1939. It was a Friday and that meant one
thing, pay day. I was due to meet up with my present girlfriend,
Josephine, so I needed some money for a drink or two. When I got
in to work, most of the drawing room staff, including my three close
work mates, Percy Studwick, Peter Birch and Alan Hores, were
already there. They were gathered round Freddy Mills' drawing board
and all wore a serious expression.

"Morning chaps," I called out in my usual happy manner.

"What's wrong, has somebody died?"

All was quiet. They looked up, but only Freddy Mills spoke as he peered over the top of his spectacles, his manner most grave.

"Things are looking serious, young'un. Government's just announced a call-up of all young men over nineteen. Conscription's in."

Mixed feelings came flooding over me of both fear and excitement. I looked over his shoulders and read the headlines.

"Told you, young'un, war won't be long coming now."

It seemed to me there was hardly a working day went by that didn't start with a gathering of us over an office newspaper to read and discuss the day's bleak headlines. Only last month we thought that war would be declared after Hitler's 'peaceful invasion' of poor Czechoslovakia but Chamberlain and the western powers seemed to let him get away with it once more. Since then we had joined with France and signed a Mutual Assistance Pact with Poland, pledging to come to Poland's aid in the event of a Nazi invasion as that country seemed to be his next focus of attention. Finally, Freddy stumbled upon some good news in his paper.

"Well lads, at least the Spanish Civil War has finally come to an end."

That evening, Josephine managed to get the car. We drove to a local pub and had a drink before driving off to a secluded spot for a much-needed kiss and cuddle.

Spring soon gave way to what was to become a glorious summer. In the drawing office, a surge of government orders required a corresponding increase in production. We were working like Trojans with unlimited overtime. Tangible excitement hung in the air, caused by the threat of hostilities, which seemed to release a heightened sense of enjoyment and devilment in us young ones, for we had no responsibilities to speak of and no children to worry about and no sons who would become the soldiers of tomorrow. The older members of staff however, were far more solemn and rightly so, considering what experience they had of the last war and the inevitable destruction and loss of life that would result from the next.

My love life was still virginal but wonderful, filled with naughty, enquiring innocence. We revelled in that last hot, hazy summer of peace.

Friday nights saw me flush with my week's wages, which at the time were thirty shillings basic plus overtime. This Friday night was pub night. Peter, Karl, Cyril Plumbridge and I met up and went off to our favourite watering hole, the Kiwi pub at the top end of the High Street in Walton-on-Thames, (so named because of the New Zealand troops stationed nearby during WWI). Peter, an old school friend of mine, now worked alongside his father as a carpenter just a few miles away on the other side of the Thames, making film sets and the like at Sound City Film Producing and Recording Studios before it became British Lion Studio Company Ltd. Now it is known more famously as Shepperton Studio. Cyril and I had been friends and drinking partners for a couple of years. Inside the pub, the atmosphere was thick with the chatter of customers enjoying themselves, eager to forget the ever present threat of war. We joined the buzz and laughter for the whole evening before being kicked out at closing time. These were happy days.

An almighty shock came to us all late in August when the papers released news that the two arch enemies, the Soviet Union and Germany, had signed a non-aggression treaty. This was a staggering revelation to us all as the two autocrats, Stalin and Hitler, had always appeared as sworn ideological enemies for as many years as I could remember. News of the alliance between them made no sense to any of us and it gave us all something else to speculate and worry about.

I had been at work since 8.00am and it was time for our mid-morning break. We gathered in groups as usual around several drawing boards scattered throughout the office and chatted while we drank our mugs of tea. The drawing office double doors suddenly swung open, sending both crashing against the walls on either side. Percy Studwick burst through in a state of obvious excitement. He stopped just inside the office. He stood breathless and had that look of a man with something important on his mind before addressing us all.

"I've just heard on the radio. Germany has invaded Poland at daybreak this morning."

· · · § · · ·

THE INEVITABLE DECLARATION
WAR

3rd September 1939

All of us living through these troubled months before the invasion of Poland will never forget the Prime Minister, Mr. Chamberlain, the appeaser who left our country woefully unprepared for a war, a war that a blind man could see coming.

My recollection of that September 1939 is as clear today as it was then. It was a gloriously warm, sunny Sunday morning, two days after Germany had crossed the border into Poland and set free the rabid dogs of destruction that would transform Europe into hell on earth. Church bells were ringing, as they had done from time immemorial across the rolling Surrey countryside as I cycled to Leatherhead to see my parents, arriving at their house just before 11am.

My mother opened the door and although she greeted me with her usual warm hugs, I sensed an underlying concern. My father was sitting in the lounge with his ear to the radio. He nodded a curt greeting, absent of a smile as he was too engrossed in what the BBC reporter had to say.

"Looks grim son," was all he could manage as he nervously combed his fingers through his big moustache. Mother and I entered the room together and sat down, listening intently. A BBC spokesman announced that the Prime Minister was about to address the nation.

Dead on 11.15am he began his now famous broadcast:

"I am speaking to you from the Cabinet Room at 10 Downing Street. This morning the British Ambassador in Berlin handed the German Government an official note stating that unless we heard from them by eleven o'clock, that they were prepared at once to withdraw their troops from Poland, a state of war would exist between us. I have to tell you now that no such undertaking has been received, and consequently this country is at war with Germany.

"You can imagine what a bitter blow it is to me that all my long struggle to win peace has failed. Yet I cannot believe that there is anything more or anything different that I could have done and that would have been more successful.

"Up to the very last it would have been quite possible to arrange a peaceful and honourable settlement between Germany and Poland, but Hitler would not have it. He had evidently made up his mind to attack Poland whatever happened, and although he now says he put forward reasonable proposals which were rejected by the Poles, that is not a true statement. The proposals were never shown to the Poles, nor to us, and although they were announced in the German broadcast on Thursday night, Hitler did not wait to hear comment on them, but ordered his troops to cross the Polish frontier next morning. His action shows convincingly that there is no chance of expecting that this man will ever give up his practice of using force to gain his will, and he can only be stopped by force.

"We and France are today, in fulfilment of our obligations, going to the aid of Poland, so bravely resisting this wicked and unprovoked attack on her people. We have a clear conscience, we have done all that any country could do to establish peace. The situation in which no word given by Germany's ruler could be trusted and no people or country could feel safe has become intolerable. Now we have resolved to finish it, I know you will all play your part with calmness and courage. At such a moment as this the assurances of support that we have received from the Empire are a source of profound encouragement to us.

"When I have finished speaking, certain detailed announcements will be made on behalf of the Government. Give these your closest attention. The Government has made plans under which it will be possible to carry on the work of the nation in the days of stress and strain which may be ahead of us. These plans need your help. You may be taking your part in the fighting services or as a volunteer in one of the branches of civil defence. If so, you will report for duty in accordance with the

instructions you have received. You may be engaged in work essential to the prosecution of war, or for the maintenance of the life of the people in factories, in transport, in public utility concerns, or in the supply of other necessaries of life. If so it is of vital importance that you should carry on with your job.

"Now may God bless you all, and may he defend the Right. For it is evil things that we shall be fighting, against brute force, bad faith, injustice, oppression and persecution, and against them I am certain that Right will prevail."

Both my parents were in a sombre mood for the remainder of the day, with mother worried for our overall safety. Being young, I was far from gloomy with no real understanding of the terrible repercussions of war, unlike my father and his generation who had fought in the last Great War.

During the evening, the King in turn made his broadcast on the radio to the nation, including this announcement to his subjects.

> *"We can only do the Right as we see the Right, and reverently commit our cause to God."*

The following day, I passed the newsagent's in the village on my way to work. The news board outside the shop simply stated:

'WAR DECLARED - OFFICIAL'

As I entered the drawing office there could be no doubt as to the only topic of conversation. I joined Percy, Peter, Alan and Freddy Mills to talk it to death before Sid Hurn, the chief draughtsman at Hackbridge, gave the whole office a pep talk from the management about how we were all now to do our best and to work that much harder for the war effort. The country was relying on us, as well as our troops. We started work later that day in earnest. Concentrating was difficult, for my mind was overactive with thoughts as to the future.

The unreal 'Twilight War', as Churchill called it, slowly unfolded almost unnoticed over the course of that glorious Indian summer. How much easier it all would have been for the world if our government and the governments of Europe had not been negligent for so long.

At the outbreak of war, engineering draughtsman like myself were regarded as essential to the war effort and classified as being in a 'Reserved Occupation', so it came as no surprise that some two months later, Sid Hurn assembled us all once more for another of his increasingly convened pep talks. Again, he outlined the importance of our work and told us that we were all to be given the option to apply for this 'Essential Reserved Occupation Category' and handed out the relevant forms for us to complete before urging us to work even harder for the country. As soon as it was tea break, my three closest friends, Percy, Peter and Alan and I gathered together to discuss this much anticipated development. We were fired up, filled with patriotic fervour and the blissful innocence that youth afforded us. Within ten minutes we were all in full accord,... there was no way on God's earth we were going to miss out on the greatest adventure of our lives. I was a healthy, basically fit and able-bodied young man, brought up on a diet of The Great War, with tales of courageous battles against the German hordes, of protecting our motherland from the warmongering barbarians. We were green fledglings, wet behind the ears, just starting out in life, keen, unbelievably patriotic, resistant to injury and positively immune to death. We were agreed, to join the armed forces and fight for our country would be our greatest adventure. I was excited and energised by our decision and felt such a strong bond with my friends. We would live forever. We could never die for death was something of which we had no concept and therefore had no fear of.

What could possibly go wrong?

The final reason for my decision was that I had become increasingly bored with my work since the outbreak of war. I had just acquired my first draughtsman's qualification and was soon to start another more advanced course at Kingston, where I was to study for my Higher National Certificate. The thought of continuing with my work at Hackbridge, cycling the ten miles to college and back three evenings a week to study through cold, wet winter nights before returning to my lonely lodgings to start homework before bed, whilst my friends and fellow countrymen were defending ME from the Nazi tyranny, filled me with dread. To be honest, I could have shaken Hitler's hand.

That same November day, we collected the paperwork that would exempt us from service in the armed forces and handed them back to Sid Hurn, uncompleted. We would no longer be cosseted in the safety of our drawing office, undertaking work of so-called vital national importance.

In reality, we really were vital. The frantic surge in orders was due solely to the long overdue realisation by the government that as soon as proper hostilities commenced, power stations across the country would become prime targets for German bombers. Consequently, our factory was given contracts to manufacture unlimited numbers of mobile electricity generators to maintain the power supplies to the factories, hospitals and all the important government sites in just such an event.

Later that same day, Sid Hurn spoke to the four of us alone. He was disturbed by our decision to enlist.

"Are you sure you boys don't want to apply for your deferment?" he asked in a concerned manner that was really quite touching.

He tried his best to talk us out of it but we were adamant. We all wanted to go, indeed, needed to go. Life was now going to become exciting and nothing was going to change our minds - well nothing except possibly Lana Turner, the blonde Hollywood pin-up, sitting naked on my lap, begging me to make love to her rather than go. For a hot-blooded young male such as I, that might just do it.

For us all, avoiding the war could have been so simple. In the days that followed, it was now just a matter of waiting patiently for our call-up papers to hit the doormat.

~ CALL-UP FINALLY COMES ~
November 1939

We all received our letters from the War Department during that same week, instructing us to report for enlistment three days after my 20th birthday, to a Territorial Army address in Guildford. Our beautiful Indian summer had long gone and the weather outside was now bitter. In fact, it was preparing itself for the coldest winter I could ever recall. Within days of receiving my letter, I awoke with a thumping headache, a fever and aches in every part of my body, including places that I didn't know existed. I was aware that 'something' had been coming on for the last twenty-four hours, but now I felt like death. My landlady was concerned enough to called for the doctor to visit and, after taking my temperature and a brief examination, he summarised his thoughts.

"Mr. Minter, I'm sorry but the Army will have to wait, you have contracted influenza."

I barely heard and couldn't care what I had, I just wanted to die quietly. Unable to join up in my present bed-bound state, my doctor wrote a letter to the War Office explaining my predicament and, consequently, a week or so later I received a twenty-one day deferment before being required to attend for enlistment. But my friends had no such excuse. Percy, Peter and Alan went off to war together without me whilst I lay suffering in my bed, too ill to move. I was jealous and saddened at being left behind. Already our dream of the joint adventure and of fighting together had just fallen apart.

Lady Luck must have turned her blind eye to them as they joined the services that day, recklessly handing over their young souls to The Gods of War. Percy Studwick went into the Air Force. When he received his papers, he was informed that he was needed by the rapidly expanding bomber command and was instructed to attend an RAF training camp. They had recently taken delivery of new twin engine bombers and Percy was to train as a tail gunner of all things, in one of the newly-formed bomber squadrons. Peter Birch had no choice either and was sent into the Royal Navy. Finally, Alan Hores was sent to joined The Royal Engineers.

Their 'great' adventure had begun but sadly and tragically, all going their separate ways, and without me.

~ BIRTHDAY MISERY ~
1st December 1939

It was my birthday. I awoke late with a fever and my body still aching as I shivered amongst saturated sheets. Whilst the temperature outside plummeted, my landlady fought to keep me warm with hot water bottles and a coal fire burning constantly in my room. I passed a miserable morning feeling sorry for myself and drifted in and out of a troubled sleep. Just after midday I was awoken by a knock on my bedroom door. Before I could muster enough strength to respond, my landlady announced to me that I had a visitor and opened my door.

"Hello Dennis," a sweet voice meekly spoke from behind my landlady, who now stood aside. It was my girlfriend, Josephine. I was so delighted to see her. She entered the room. My landlady smiled and closed the door behind her, leaving us alone, turning a blind eye to the rule common to all young men in lodgings.

'NO YOUNG LADIES ALLOWED IN GUESTS' ROOMS'.

I assumed that my landlady thought that in my state of ill health, nothing remotely untoward was going to happen. We chatted for a while but I just lay there, grateful for her company. After telling me all her news she delved into her bag and produced a small parcel neatly wrapped in brown paper. I attempted to sit up but failed and simply smiled as best I could as she wished me a happy birthday. Josephine lent forward to kiss me but I reluctantly suggested that she keep her distance as I was still a breeding ground of germs. I unwrapped her gift to reveal a small hinged black box. My mouth dropped open in surprise for inside was a beautiful gold wrist watch.

"Joe, what can I say, it's wonderful. Thank you so much."

I slipped it onto my wrist and held out my arm to admire it. It really did look most grand.

"Joe, you've spent too much money."

"Oh Dennis, don't worry, it's also a little going away present,... it was only five guineas."

Five guineas! That was a king's ransom to me, but she seemed most insistent, so I could hardly refuse it. The manner in which she had dismissed my understandable concern at her spending 'ONLY five guineas' amused me for it represented almost three weeks of my wages. My existing watch was old and worn by comparison and I was absolutely thrilled to bursting point with this one.

She talked easily and I for the most part, listened. I was not aware of the passage of time. As it grew dark outside, she finally announced that she had to leave and blew me a farewell kiss from the door. I was alone once more but at least I was happier. As lovely as Josephine's visit was, her unexpected call had exhausted me. No sooner had I heard her depart through the front door, I instantly fell asleep, still wearing my new gold watch.

I virtually slept my way through the next week, missing out on my usual joyous Christmas, whilst I slowly recovered my strength. Despite losing a considerable amount of weight I eventually recovered and my doctor finally pronounced me fit enough to die for my country.

Two days later I left my bed to enlist.

· · · § · · ·

1940

THE TWILIGHT WAR

The rail station at Walton-on-Thames was close enough to my lodgings for me to walk. I caught the train to Guildford but as I sat back in the carriage, I felt strangely detached from the bustling world around me. Everything had already gone wrong. It was not meant to be like this at all. My three friends and I should all have joined up together, stayed together, fought together side-by-side, looking after each other, doing brave deeds like our comic book heroes, fighting the evil Hun and sharing the thrill, the laughter, the fear, the danger,... but the reality of the killing aspect and of death hadn't entered my head.

As the train rushed on by, pulling on urgently down the line, I looked out of the grubby window at the bare, bleak countryside. Angry-looking clouds were gathering overhead. A storm was approaching.

Our 'Great Adventure' no longer seemed such a good idea to me and the thought of facing a war on my own was beginning to look less and less attractive. My journey time was short, only six stations down the busy Waterloo to Portsmouth line. As well as civilians like myself, the train was packed with soldiers, airmen and naval personnel. Inside, the carriage was humid and smoky but above all, loud. Whilst some seemed to be in high spirits, others sat in isolation reading the gloomy news that filled the broadsheets with war as the headline story.

A sailor tried to console his girlfriend, offering to wipe away her tears with his hankie. What little make-up she wore was leaving tiny flowing rivulets etched on her pretty flushed cheeks. On the other side of the carriage, three soldiers burst into laughter as the fourth related tales of his encounter with a 'lady of the night' the previous evening in some sordid pub in Soho, a conversation more suited to the confines of their barracks than the delicate ears of the females on board but for me, it was an amusing distraction.

A business man in overcoat and bowler hat appeared oblivious to all around him, heavily engrossed in his newspaper.

A naval rating whispered something to a young lady. From her coy and modest manner, I assumed that she was a stranger to him and his forward behaviour did not sit easy with her. She edged her body away from him, as far as the seated passenger on her right would allow, and tried to ignore him. His failure to read her obviously negative body language may well have been due to the previous night's alcohol that still befuddled his brain.

My eyes returned to the window and the drab landscape of various shades of grey. I had never felt so utterly alone, a friendless alien. I was yet to discover the comradeship that binds one soldier to another, a platoon to a company and so on within an army.

Queasiness gripped my stomach, I felt sick for a brief moment. Was I only now facing a previous unaddressed fear as to the horrors of the war that awaited me?

~ MEDICAL ~
5th January 1940

As I climbed out onto the platform at Guildford station, the full chill of that January day hit me, not a crisp fresh blast but as wet cold fingers invading my body. A fast train sped by on the other side of the platform on its way to Waterloo. The sudden rush of wind knocked a trilby hat off the head of an elderly gentleman. A soldier ran to save it before it fell onto the rails. A kindly act that went some way to warm my fears and trepidation.

I left the station and walked along Portsmouth Road to the junction, turning left into the High Street before crossing the bridge that spanned the River Wey. Here the late morning air was ice cold, paining my exposed ears. A clinging mist idly wafted across the icy surface of the waters below. I quickened my pace and walked briskly up the steep, ancient cobbled street. As I neared the top of the hill, I heard a bell chime twelve times. On my left, I passed under the old clock that jutted out over the High Street from the Elizabethan Guildhall. It was indeed midday and I was early, but no matter. Passing the Tunsgate I finally arrived, slightly out of breath after my recent illness. At the top of the hill on the right-hand side I saw the Methodist Church Hall that had been converted into a recruitment centre. Outside, a line of young men from all walks of life patiently queued in the freezing conditions. For the most part they looked uncomfortable and apprehensive. Quietly, I joined the back of the queue and gradually shuffled forward until I was under cover from the hall. Apart from the occasional sound of strained laughter coming from three men, few in the queue seemed in any mood for idle chitchat, so we smoked and sluggishly moved from foot to foot in order to stay warm.

Inside the hall stood rows of roughly-constructed semi-cubicles, only serving to define an area without according any privacy to those inside. In each cubicle were wooden desks, behind which sat expressionless men in uniform, seeking answers to mundane questions before recording the information on piles of buff-coloured, official-looking forms. The room was abuzz with the sounds of monotone voices and gentle movements.

Our line slowly inched its way along some predetermined path, meandering past the rows of desks. Finally it was my turn. At the first desk I came to, I was asked to produce my letter from the War Office requesting my attendance. The soldier asked me to confirm my name and details. A note was duly taken before I was ordered to proceed.

The next set of desks were manned by medical personnel. This was where I was to receive a series of thorough obligatory examinations. First, my eyesight was assessed using the usual card of ever decreasing-sized letters. I passed with flying colours but the next assessment was of more concern to me. I knew that I was fit enough to fight, except for one minor detail that I was all too aware of. I had an ear problem. All my life I had suffered with mastoids. This could potentially disqualify me from entering the armed services, so I had to think quickly to get over this hurdle. Desperate as the military were for men, my hearing defect was enough for them to reject me for combat duty at this early stage in the war. I faced the medical examiner, who was taking meticulous notes of any problems and failings and ticking boxes, for they needed to make sure that, at the end of your service life (assuming that you survived that long), you left in the same condition as when you joined. If you did not and you were discharged with a medical condition, you might be eligible for a costly disability or war pension. Therefore, anything and everything untoward was spotted and recorded.

Making sure that he had the corresponding paperwork, the medical examiner rose from his desk to examine my ears. The test was simplicity itself. I had my back towards him as the doctor asked me to cover my right ear with my right hand. Then he examined my left ear, which was my fully-working one. He then started his stop watch and held it nearby before whispering a few words in my left ear. I then responded, telling him what I had heard.

"Fine," he replied.

He then turned to his desk and recorded the results. Meanwhile, I turned round to face him and he asked me to do the same with the other ear. So I covered the same ear again, but to him it looked as though I was covering up the other ear. In his eagerness to get through the line of men behind me, he had not noticed and passed me as having A1 hearing in both ears. I was so pleased with myself, I could have shouted.

The next medic placed a cold stethoscope against my chest. Because of the deception of my last test, my heart was still pounding as he listened intently. But at least it was pounding and it was rhythmical, so I passed.

My lungs too were given the all-clear.

The foot doctor was much impressed with my most ordinary of feet. Likewise my dentist, with not a filling in sight, gave me yet another pass.

By now, we had shed most of our clothing, carrying it as we progressed towards the end of the hall. There was no heating so we shivered. At the penultimate set of desks, I was told to drop my pants.

I had already seen what was in store for me as I watched others ahead. Privacy was not a luxury the forces recruitment Officers believed in. I now stood naked in a hall full of 200 men whom I had never seen before today. I had never exposed myself so brazenly to anybody before since I had stopped playing with my Dinky toys. The doctor looked at me just as nature had intended, noting that I could cough when requested, that my testicles danced accordingly and that my back passage was clear. He turned to complete his notes and dismissed me. I was now at the final stage and could dress myself once more.

The last staff member was the 'careers' Recruitment Officer. He began with his first question.

"If you were to be accepted into the armed services, which service would you wish to join?"

The Army was my first reply, adding, "I would like to join the Grenadier Guards as that was my father's old regiment."

I then gave my second and third choice. The consultation process was a farce. On reflection, his interview seemed twisted and rather cruel, for the system took no heed of anyone's answers. Regardless of whatever anybody said, you were sent into whichever branch of the services needed men at that particular time.

That afternoon, I realised my now wavering ambition. I was passed as being fit and ready to join His Majesty's Armed Forces.

The following day saw me back at Hackbridge. It was all so unreal as I sat at my drawing board that morning, trying to work as though nothing had altered. Percy, Peter and Alan had already left to join their respective units. We had been the ones to set our wheels of fortune in motion and now my course was set, on an unstoppable roller-coaster ride that would lead me to the battle-weary fields of Europe.

~ WINTER's MISERY ~
First Week of January 1940

Within a week my landlady handed me the letter, the ink stamp on the envelope confirming that it came from the War Office. She showed no signs of leaving my side, taking on the role of a concerned mother. I hurriedly tore the letter open. It contained my letter of acceptance into the Army with details of where and when I was to report for active service. I was instructed to join the 2nd/7th Battalion, The Queen's Royal Regiment.

We both smiled nervously, but mine was a hollow smile. I was due to leave in just over a week's time. By now, I was feeling more than a little apprehensive, having to make my journey alone. Included in my letter from the War Office was a printed warrant authorising my free train journey to where I was to enlist, at a place called St. Leonards-on-Sea, near Hastings, on the Sussex coast.

By this time, the government had introduced food rationing. Being a hearty eater, rationing directly affected my stomach. Butter, sugar, bacon and ham were all suddenly restricted and could only be bought on production of your ration book.

I met up with Josephine two days later to say our good-byes. She collected me in her father's car and drove into the countryside before stopping at the quiet location that we had found a while ago. We talked, then kissed and cuddled for the last time. Much as a condemned man might be allowed a splendid last meal, Jo allowed me to touch her ample breasts but we went no further. On the fateful eve of my departure, I appreciated my reward but unfortunately, sex remained strictly off the menu.

Eventually, she drove me back to my lodgings and we made our last good-byes. A tear overflowed and made its slow journey to the edge of her mouth. I pulled her to me and whispered words of comfort that I thought I should say.

"Don't worry Jo, I'll be fine. I have no intention of getting shot. I will keep my head down and out of trouble, I promise."

As if I had any control over my destiny! Even I was left unconvinced as the last of my assurances left my quivering lip. I opened the door to leave but Jo reached across into the glove compartment and retrieved a small package. I smiled shyly and took her gift.

"Thank you, shall I open it now?"

"No, please wait and open it when you get inside."

Standing alone on the cold pavement in front of my landlady's house, I waved her goodbye, her black car slowly pulling away. I watched her until she turned the corner and was gone. I wondered if I would ever see her again.

I turned to open the front door of the Victorian semi-detached house. Fortunately for me, my landlady was out for I wasn't in the mood for small talk. I climbed the stairs to my room and removed her present from my coat pocket. Just as her birthday gift had been, this was similarly wrapped. I sat on the edge of my bed and carefully opened it. Jo had given me the customary gift of a loved one to a soldier leaving for war, a small pocket bible.

The following night was my last as a civilian. It was a rather sedate affair, tinged both with apprehension and an underlying excitement, an eagerness to get started and move forward. At the pub I met up with friends for farewell drinks before walking back on my own. I lay curled up in my bed and finally realised that my childhood was at an end. As I tried to sleep, my mind was full of thoughts of tomorrow, of service life, of battles to be won, of brave deeds to do, but thoughts of the unimaginable horrors of a war that I was about to face were gnawing away at the back of my mind.

~ FAREWELL ~

The following morning I emptied my room, placing a few very personal possessions that I intended to take with me into the army and packing all my other belongings into a small suitcase. It did not take me long. I said my good-byes to my landlady, shook her hand and thanked her for looking after me so well.

I strapped the case onto my bike rack, doing so with a heavy heart. The impending excitement of going to war was at best, muted. I climbed onto my bike and rode away.

Although I had cycled to my parents' house a hundred times before, the journey had never seemed longer. Ice on the roads made the going treacherous. When I arrived at 83 Copthorne Road, Leatherhead, my mother was there to greet me in her usual way.

"How are you, ducky?" she asked as she reached up to give me one of her big hugs. I bathed in her warmth. She took my hand and pulled me in. We chatted in front of the open fire over endless cups of warm, sweet tea and cakes. When my father eventually returned from work, I looked at the clock above the mantel place and realised that it was time to leave. My mother caught my eye and looked at me, tears welling in her big, bright eyes. She could control herself no longer and burst into floods of tears, hugging me as she wept.

"I'll be alright mum, don't worry about me," I said, trying to put on a brave face. But in reality I was dreading leaving. I DIDN'T WANT TO GO. I wanted to stay, to be at home again with my mum. Although I had been kicked out by my father some five years ago, I had never been far away from my mother and friends. Now I was off to war. I had to tear myself away from mother's warm embrace for it was time. I turned to my father waiting behind me.

"Ready son?"

I simply nodded. We left the house together. The grey clouds above were darkening above the snow-covered streets. This winter had all the makings of a bitter one and had I not been leaving, the child within me would have loved this weather.

Father and I walked the short distance to the railway station, but it seemed like miles for father was a man of few words. The silence, although uncomfortable, was to be expected for my father didn't talk a lot even when we were children.

At the end of every working day he would arrive home, have his dinner and bury his moustache in his police reports. My brothers and I were typical young lads but after father came home, the air of frivolity and happiness seemed to leave the house as he sucked in all the brightness and replaced it with gloom. Mother would mildly 'tick us off' each time we made any noise. She would raise her index finger to her lips and 'shush' us. "No noise children, your father is trying to work," and then wink, and briefly the sunlight would re-enter.

On arrival at the station, I produced my travel warrant. Father explained that he was seeing me off so he was allowed onto the platform with me to wait. The train was running late because of the bad weather. We stood together in the winter gloom, lost in our own thoughts, waiting. A blackout was in full force as the threat of German bombing was ever present. I was freezing as the icy wind blasted down the long platform. I buried my head into my coat and pulled my scarf tighter around my neck.

I heard the train long before I saw it, chuffing to itself in the dim distance. The engine passed on by in the dark, the smoke from its funnel illuminated by the fire from within. As the carriages screeched on by I tried to peer inside, through the darkened windows, for any spare seats. When the train finally hissed to a halt, I moved forward towards the nearest door and climbed aboard. The door slammed shut behind me with a heavy, muffled thunk. I turned and pulled down the sliding window, lent forward and stuck my head out just as the guard blew his whistle. My father was looking up at me. If he was sad, he certainly wasn't going to show it. For him, expressing such an unfamiliar emotion was a weakness.

Father offered me his huge powerful hand and immediately I was taken back to my childhood, to my earliest memory of him carving the Sunday roast, slicing the meat for mother, muscles rippling on the backs of his mighty hands.

His first job at twelve was not in his home town of Dover (see picture reference 5), but 200 miles away in Birmingham, as an apprentice motor trimmer and upholsterer in the fledgling automobile industry. He secured digs at No. 214 Ladywood Road. Tirelessly and without question he laboured there for nine tough years in order to support the family, sending every penny he could spare back home to his mother and her eight other children. Day after day with no weekend breaks or holidays, he worked. Armed with a hammer, sheets of leather and a mouth full of tacks, his job was to stretched the hide using his hands and secure the material to its wooden frame, hour after hour and year after year. Such physical work so early on in his life resulted in him developing the muscular hands that were his hallmark.

We shook hands and I bade him farewell, prompting him to finally break his silence.

"Look after yourself son, and don't forget the family name," was his thinly-veiled warning.

'Whatever you do son, don't let me down and shame me,' was his meaning. And that was it. I will never forget those last few words to me. I might get shot, lose a limb, be killed by a Nazi bayonet thrust through my guts. Of all the things that he could have said, he chose those words. His words were utterly impersonal. The whistle blew and with the hiss of steam, off I went to my war.

I was pleased to find myself in an empty compartment. Inside, the gloomy carriage was damp, filled with the stale air of previous passengers. With the smell of coal and steam in my nostrils, I lit a cigarette as the train slowly journeyed towards London. The windows were grimy and misted over. My hand squeaked against the glass as I cleared a patch, allowing me to stare out through the jet black window at the wintry countryside, catching the occasional glimpse of a twinkling light in the distance. House tops, gardens and trees passed by in various shades of grey under a flat sky of nothingness. The clatter of the wheels on rail was soporific and my mind soon drifted into a troubled place, somewhere between sleep and consciousness and thought of my father and his cold farewell, wondering who bade him farewell when he left for his war some twenty-two years previously.

I don't believe I had either a particularly good or bad early life. For the most part my brothers and I were left to our own devices, growing up in the cold shadow of our imposing father. We all thought it normal and we survived our childhood without any mental scarring - or did we? Father was a tall, imposing, powerful man with an exceedingly wide and flamboyant handle-bar moustache, as was fashionable at the time. I don't have many fond memories of him and would go so far as to say that I didn't really love him as such, for he was not that sort of man.

Father always had one burning ambition, to join the Police Force. However, for some reason that I never did quite understand, it had to be the Surrey force. In the early 1900s, one of the necessary stipulations was that all applicants had to be over six feet one inch tall. For my father, this was no problem for by the time he was eighteen, he had reached the required height. At that size, police constables of the day were intimidating figures, and with their helmets they were giants. Respect came with the size and the uniform.

As soon as he reached his twenty-first birthday, my father applied and on 4th April 1912, he was accepted at Guildford into the Surrey Police Force, earning the princely sum of £1 3s 4d a week, less than a farm labourer. But for him the wage didn't matter, the job was everything. He loved every aspect of it and took to his new occupation like a hawk to flying. He worked tirelessly, studying every evening in his bid to climb up the promotion ladder as speedily as was possible.

His career plan was briefly interrupted by the tragedy of the First World War. Prior to 1916, the British Army was filled by volunteers, but the wholesale slaughter of troops on the battlefields of Europe meant that there were insufficient numbers to fill the boots of the war dead, hence conscription was introduced in 1916. Those in the police were usually exempt from the services but by 1918 even he was called up to serve.

The nucleus of our new group was the local Territorial Army Unit and we were there to make up the numbers before emerging as a full battalion. Then I saw the main building and headquarters that I had been ordered to report to, The Westgarth Hotel *(see picture reference 17).* By the time I stepped inside, I was bitterly cold and nervous. To top it all, my feet and trousers were soaking. Having been an office worker for the last few years, walking up these steep roads had made me realise just how unfit I really was. As it was so late in the day, I assumed that I was probably the last to arrive, so I was surprised to see twenty others standing before me. The harsh weather was playing havoc with all methods of travel and many men had become lost or trapped in transit. I was met by a soldier with two stripes on his arm. My uniformed host did not strike me as being over-friendly.

The date was 17th January 1940.

Once we were checked in, our small group of raw recruits were taken outside once more to another building, shown upstairs to rooms that were stripped bare, devoid of everything, even a carpet. Inside my room, five others like me were sitting or lying back on the bare floorboards. This was to be my 'comfortable' billet for the duration of my training.

I was handed two woollen army blankets by the orderly, which kept me neither warm nor comfortable throughout that long first night.

Morning it may have been, but it was still dark. An NCO burst into our room, shouting at us to report to yet another building up the road. We were being directed to our tailors. It was obvious that the Army had taken over most of the buildings in the road. We slid our way to the boarding house that had been converted into a Quarter Masters Stores. Upon entering, we were confronted by another steely-looking Corporal. When my turn came, he looked at me, cast his eyes from my head to my toes before mumbling something, presumably estimating my clothes size or, by the expression on his face, he could have been uttering a curse. He turned, grabbed a pile of clothes and thrust them at me. That was me kitted out. If items had been too long or too short then tough, we would just have to get on with it. The amazing thing was that the Corporal was almost 100% correct in his estimations.

And that was how I officially became a vital and important member of His Majesty's Armed Forces and an integral part of the 2nd/7th Battalion, The Queen's Royal Regiment.

The uniform felt truly awful. Amongst the pile I found that I had been given two pairs of vests and pants made from wool. They were dreadfully itchy. I now realised what a monk had to go through when performing penance, wearing only sackcloth and ashes. Fortunately for us all, the Army fitters took slightly more scientific care with regards to our footwear. I was asked my boot size! I was then handed the hardest lumps of leather that had ever graced the backside of an African elephant. Clearly, the NCO read my expression. With hands held behind his back, he sauntered over to me, bending forward slightly and whispered words of advice in my shell-like ear.

"Son, in the Army, soldiers don't wear the boots in to fit their feet, they wear the boots until their feet take on the shape of their boots!" I half smiled nervously at him, but I could see no humour in his eyes. He wasn't joking and I wish he hadn't been so right. The following day saw us all limping around within hours of forcing our blameless feet into the unforgiving leather. Blisters became as common as our hair on the barber's floor.

Once in uniform, we were ordered to pack our civilian clothes into a bag which was sealed, addressed and labelled 'On His Majesty's Service', before being sent off to our nearest and dearest for the duration of the war.

"Get those bloody boots cleaned" was the first order that we received from one of the rather bad-tempered NCOs. Now I was confused, for they were clean, they were brand new but we soon discovered what he meant. The toe cap had to be mirror finished. Apparently he wished to see his face in them, but I could just as easily have told him how ugly his mug was! This was achieved with the help of black shoe polish, spit and the back of a heated spoon.

Next, we were each handed a rifle, a relic of the First World War, a .303 Lee-Enfield to be precise, still covered in wonderful smelling gun grease, which resulted in his next order.

"... and get that gun cleaned up an' all, and don't drop it or you'll have to pay for it. Got it?"

As you can appreciate, we were already learning to hate this particular NCO.

That evening, amidst the background babble of muted voices and cutlery scraping on china, we ate our mediocre food in the cold makeshift canteen. Suddenly one of the recruits on the adjacent tables read aloud from his well-thumbed newspaper.

"Christ almighty! Did you know that the Thames at Westminster froze over last night? No wonder my testicles were on the floor this morning."

We burst out laughing, glad to have the freezing conditions confirmed.

Maybe the Sarge' will now turn the heat up in my bedroom," responded another wag.

"Not until hell itself freezes over," came a sarcastic response.

From another, "it was so cold when I was walking down Piccadilly, I saw pickpockets sticking their hands in strangers' pockets just to keep them warm!"

Tables were banged and tears of laughter flowed.

These frequent but brief interludes of hilarity kept our spirits up in the face of rough woolly clothes, uninteresting food, uncomfortable nights and sleep deprivation sleeping on the floor with relative strangers through one of the coldest winters in living memory.

Those first few days of training at St. Leonards were the coldest and bleakest that I had yet experienced. Little did I realise that this was but a foretaste of things to come.

The snow lay knee deep on the ground and even though the households had removed what snow they could from their own frontage, ascending and descending the mountainous roads of St. Leonards was dicing with broken bones. Our living conditions and training were nothing like I had anticipated and we seemed as far away from becoming a fearsome killing machine as I could ever imagine.

For the duration of our grounding, we only ever had our two blankets to sleep with without even the luxury of a simple mattress. Each morning we awoke shivering and aching, but without me realising, this was the start of a toughening-up process that was to be vital to our survival in the years ahead. Unfortunately, none of us appreciated this at the time.

Within days, we had learnt 'The Three S's' (Shit, Shower and Shave),the vital morning requisite for every British soldier, before going down to receive the mainstay of the British Army, our mug of steaming hot tea. This was prepared for us by our highly-trained team of chefs, who were to look after our culinary requirements for the first few weeks of our army life. Each morning in the kitchen, the tea was 'cooked' in a massive copper pot, a huge cauldron. After our tea was served, the cauldron was re-filled with water and porridge was prepared for breakfast. If for some reason porridge was off the menu, we were given slices of bread with bully beef on top.

Lunch always seemed to be a boiled stew of some description, and for supper, yes, you've guessed it, boiled stew. If the cooks could boil it, we had it. But at least the food was consistent - consistently awful. A trained monkey could have prepared better food, but monkeys were in short supply these days as most were being trained as Officers. That cauldron was the most used piece of equipment in the British

Army at the time and later I would see that it was the ONLY piece of equipment in the British Army that was evident at the outbreak of hostilities.

Lance Corporal 'Bloody' Ryan was our particular section leader at St. Leonards. He was a cocky little sod, and like a lot of cocky little sods he suffered with a serious case of 'Little BIG Man Syndrome'. Being a former Territorial, he had probably only been in the regular Army a few days longer than us, but he thought that this gave him the right to act like an arrogant, know-it-all little bastard. To summarise, we weren't too fond of him.

As a trainee squaddie I was paid a relatively paltry amount for my troubles. My outgoings were nonexistent so I wasn't concerned at the amount, but what did annoy us all was a listed deduction on our pay slips that appeared under the heading of 'STOPPAGES'. Bearing in mind that we slept on the floor with a couple of army blankets, with no furniture in our so-called 'barrack rooms', in a bleak old boarding house, the Army had, in their infinite wisdom, decided to deduct four shillings a week for possible damage to barrack property. It was unbelievable. It was daylight robbery when the only damage caused was by our chattering teeth grinding away on the wooden floorboards as we slept.

Four days into my training, the weather took another turn for the worse. Conditions were severe and newspapers announced that a record -23°C had been recorded at Rhayader, Powys, in Wales, during the previous night of 21st January 1940.

Amongst our band of recruits was a young chap who stood out. His name was Roy Gough, a young man in his mid twenties. Unfortunately, he did not 'stand out' for any of the right reasons. Gough was tall and built 'like a brick shithouse'. He was huge. In civvy street, he had lived on the coast with his mother in New Haven, Sussex, only twenty miles away. How Gough had managed to get into our Surrey-based battalion was a conundrum, but I was pleased he had been allocated to us. Goughey, as we called him, had been employed on the docks since his early teens, where his job was to unload timber from the ships. At work he would wear a jacket with leather patches across the shoulders because of the huge slabs of timber that he was required to carry. His work was seasonal, from early spring to late autumn, when ships were able to sail through the ice-free Baltic with their holds laden with wood from the pine forests of Scandinavia. He was hugely powerful and yet gentle and kind, possessing a childlike simplicity in life. Goughey had an endearing habit of calling everybody 'old mate', including NCOs and Officers. Unfortunately, this endearing quality was not well received by either group. No matter how many times he was reprimanded for using the term he just couldn't stop and, as a consequence, it did not take too long for him to be brought up before the Commanding Officer in overall command of the battalion, Lieutenant Colonel Girling. Girling was an austere looking Officer with dark, deep set eyes. When Goughey was brought before Girling, he was ordered to explain himself, which he did admirably. However, the somewhat bewildered Lieutenant Colonel didn't take too kindly to being addressed as 'old mate' either. For his sins, poor Goughey was locked up for two weeks in a military prison or Glasshouse, as it was known. Upon his release, the military police Sergeant was genuinely thanked by Goughey in his usual, unintentionally disrespectful but friendly manner.

He said "thanks old mate," and offered to shake his hand.

We howled with laughter when we heard. How he escaped being slung straight back in I don't know, but I think it's safe to assume that by then, they had all but given up on him.

Goughey had a second problem that made him stand out from the rest of our platoon. When he walked, marched or ran, he moved like a great lumbering gorilla, through no fault of his own. That was just how God created him, a big, friendly, oaf. His long, powerful arms refused to co-ordinate with his lower limbs, often swinging forward with his corresponding leg. That meant it was impossible for him to march in step with the other thirty of us in our platoon, causing considerable confusion to those who marched beside him (more commonly known in military circles as 'Tick-Tocking'). The poor drill Sergeant went ballistic at every parade. But no amount of screaming into his ear or bullying could change this, for his body simply refused to do what came naturally to others.

Apart from his size, Goughey had another physical characteristic that rather alienated him from the others, as far as the Army was concerned. He had huge feet. They were far in excess of size fourteen and, as such, the Army could not provide him with standard issue boots. As a result, the paymaster gave him a 'boot allowance' so that he could wear his own.

The final endearing quality of dear old Goughey was that he refused point blank to eat army food. He simply couldn't stomach it (as if another source of irritation were needed). When ordered directly to eat what he was given by an ill-tempered Officer or our manic Sergeant (who was always driven to distraction by Goughey's obstinate antics), it had no impact on him whatsoever. He would simply but politely decline to eat it.

"Sorry old mate, I just can't 'cos I will be sick."

For sustenance, Goughey paid the local milkman to deliver pints to him every day. For food, he would pop down to the local baker's and buy their special version of a meat and gravy pie. There was actually no solid meat left in it, having been cooked for so long. The meat would disintegrate to form a thick but appetising jellied gravy, and it did taste wonderful. Goughey existed on this diet for the duration of his training.

The Officers and NCOs may have hated Goughey but we loved him, for in his innocence, he made a mockery of all our superiors.

During the days and weeks that followed, weather permitting, we trained on the streets around our billets, which wasn't easy for every road in St. Leonards sloped at 45 degrees. It seemed that 'flat streets' had not yet been invented in this town and with the compacted snow and ice, our winter parades were a complete and utter shambles. By now, our daily routine had been established, and after a spell of inspection and compulsory drilling on the slopes, we would undertake some more drilling.

Then one morning, the pattern changed. We were to commence 'killer' training. Lance Corporal 'bloody' Ryan was in charge of us and we lined up for bayonet practices. Straw-filled dummies were placed in the middle of the road to represent our unlikely passive victims. By this time, any locals who were just passing by or who needed some sort of entertainment at our expense would form a line on the pavement and watch the best free show in town. The spectacle of us, the cream of English youth, lined up and threatening a poor, defenceless, straw-filled sack swinging from a makeshift gibbet whilst, one by one, we surged forward like wild banshees, intent on slaying the inanimate focus of our attention, was a show not to be missed. Every so often, the peace and quiet of that suburban street would be shattered by our vocal Sergeant Major. He was an old reservist from the Great War, a proper soldier intent on transforming us from nancy office boys into feared killing machines. As was the case on all the streets in St. Leonards, it was proving to be an uphill struggle and the ice made the run almost impossible.

"Right lads, give them what for.... now... CHAAAAARGE."

At that point, each of us in turn would run up the hill towards the dummy, screaming as loudly as our considerable embarrassment would allow and certainly not as if our lives depended on it. We tried to instil some terror into the rather docile sack, but even 'he' was having none of it. By the time we had run up that hill and reached the dummy, we were out of breath and barely able to tickle the 'enemy's' straw-bloated stomach with our cold steel, let alone tear out his dry guts. As often as not, all we could muster was a dry wheeze.

Our Sergeant would watch, unable to hide his disappointment and annoyance, before screaming. At random, he would confront us and depending on whether there were ladies present amongst the crowd of onlookers, he would verbalise his frustration in differing ways.

"Call yourselves bloody soldiers? What's the matter, have you shit yourself Sonny?"

We were always embarrassed at being screamed and belittled in front of the ever watchful eyes of the local civilians, who at this point were usually in hysterics. I wondered if they slept well in their beds at night, knowing that we were there, in strength, to protect them and the country from the dreaded Hun just across the Channel. We felt that we were simply the entertainment and for them, it was far cheaper and considerably more fun than paying at the local cinema to watch the latest Laurel and Hardy film. If our audience took time to reflect upon the quality of our training and ultimately, our ability to keep the Hun at bay, I am sure that they would have emigrated.

On 27th January, the worst storms in living memory hit Britain. The country virtually ground to a halt. The following day we heard, via the soldier's grapevine, some serious news that may have had grave consequences for my stomach; we were dangerously low on supplies of our amazingly bland army rations. Fortunately, word reached us that a truck filled with our essential supplies had left Tenterden in Kent, some twenty miles away, in the early morning on 29th January in an attempt to re-supply us. But our glee was short lived. News came that the truck had become stuck in snow drifts at Northiam, halfway between St. Leonards and Tenterden. By now, everyone in our company was eagerly following the progress of our supplies. By late afternoon, a relief truck was dispatched to the rescue but it too became trapped at Brede, a mere five miles up the road. That evening we ate the last of our supplies. The following morning we awoke to the best of news.

A Bren gun carrier had been dispatched to tow them all out of trouble. Using its half tracks to full advantage, it successfully managed to free the trapped vehicles. I heard my stomach heave a sigh of relief, saved from a potentially disastrous situation. That night a prayer of gratitude was said by all, except for young Goughey, 'The Pie Man', who couldn't give a toss!

As we bade farewell to January, February heralded the arrival of *slightly* better weather - sleet instead of snow. Consequently, we were taken on more and more route marches into the surrounding area but usually ended up at the local park. Once there, we were ordered to dig. March and dig, march and bloody dig. We had all heard of 'Digging for Victory', but after a solid week we seemed no nearer to our ultimate goal of being turned into the 'killing machines' that would send shivers down the spines of Hitler and his cohorts. By now, we were the finest hole-diggers in the British Army.

On these outings, our chefs would usually accompany us, complete with our best friend, Captain Cauldron. They kept us going with tea. Mugs of it were liberally handed out throughout lunch, accompanied by two great slabs of bread in the guise of a sandwich. Where the filling had gone to, nobody knew. Then to work once more.

To break the monotony, our kind, caring NCOs varied our work pattern and, in the afternoon, we were allowed to fill in the holes that we had just dug!

During the following month of March, we were forever having medical inspections of one sort or another and the doctor's orderlies took every opportunity to insert huge needles into us. Supposedly, they were our inoculations but I wasn't convinced, for the orderlies seemed to take a great pleasure in their work.

One morning came a pleasant surprise, a break from hole-digging. We were taken off in army trucks on a little jaunt and were allowed to take a companion with us, our Enfield .303 rifle. We ended up at a firing range, where we were instructed in some basic safety procedures before having the targets pointed out to us, in case we were in any doubt. By now, the rain had returned and the wind lashed at our faces, stinging our eyes. It was time to retire under cover for the more intimate introduction to our weapon. We gathered around a table and were shown the stripped component parts of the rifle, its name and purpose and how to dismantle, clean and reassemble it. Finally the function of the rear sights were explained and how to set the range correctly. Only then were we taken back outside to fire our little beauties. The wind had dropped considerably and the rain no longer battered us from its previous near horizontal angle. Instead, it drizzled. We were made to lie on the soaking ground, before further instructions on holding the Enfield in the correct firing position. Our target's range was given and we adjusted our sights accordingly before finally being allowed to fire a single round. Bang! For the first time in all my weeks of training, I came alive and began to believe that I actually was a soldier. After more brief instructions we continued and I fired off my remaining nine rounds. Each of my bullets was on target and high scoring. I am sure the instructor would have been happy if only one single piece of lead had hit the mark, but my grouping surprised even him. I was the top man of the day and it felt great. How I loved every second of my limited time behind that rifle.

Prior to me joining the Army, I had been a member of a local Rifle Club. Not wanting to appear boastful, I was good, having won several competitions. But the other men had never seen a gun before, never mind fired one. This was the first of only two visits that we ever made to the firing range during our not-so-intensive training. But no matter, for at least we could dig!

We were never schooled in any strategies of warfare. No hugely beneficial camouflage techniques, no tactics involving enemy engagements, nothing except polishing toe caps, drill, marching and, above all, digging!

It appeared to us all that the outbreak of war had taken the weak and negligent Mr. Chamberlain by surprise. As far as our limited troop training was concerned, it was woefully inadequate. Preparations had been criminally neglected at best. If only Churchill's words had been heeded. Had he been given free rein a few years earlier, as we had often discussed in the works canteen, things might have been significantly different. Hindsight is a wonderful thing.

~ TRAINING CONTINUES IN FRANCE ~
9th April 1940

Since the invasion of Poland in September of last year, Russian troops had invaded Finland. After bitter fighting and an initial humiliating rebuff, Russia finally overwhelmed the small heroic state and Finland was crushed under the weight of the Soviet hammer. But more importantly to us,

Germany had unleashed its war machine, invading Denmark and Norway. Denmark succumbed without much trouble within the day but Norway was a much harder nut to crack and, according to the papers, the fighting was fierce.

For the last three months, all we had done was to parade, march and dig our way through Churchill's 'phoney war', but increasingly, whispers began to circulate of a possible posting. On Wednesday 13th April, we were ordered to collect extra kit from the stores and our rifles, each stamped with the date of 1918; the long bayonet in its scabbard worn on the left side, which was more like a sword; a small side pack by the bayonet; five ammunition pouches, water bottle; our multi-purpose dixie tin with handle, used for eating and drinking from, and shaving and other less mentionable things. We filled our back packs with our greatcoat, cape/groundsheet, spare underwear and socks but no blankets. These were to be left behind, supposedly for the next batch of trainee soldiers, poor buggers! New blankets would be issued on arrival. Our greatcoat and groundsheet were enough protection against all that Mother Nature would be throwing at us in the months ahead. After a full inspection by our Commanding Officer, Major Carr *(see picture reference 15)*, he completed the paperwork by signing our pay books to confirm that we had been issued with all our kit.

> *Dennis was about to join The BEF (British Expeditionary Force) in France. The General Officer Commanding-in-Chief was General the Lord Gort. Just before the start of the Second World War The 12th (Eastern) Infantry Division was reformed as a second line Territorial Army formation. As such it contained mostly half trained weekend units, some of whom had not even fired their antiquated rifles. In April 1940 the 12th Infantry, along with the 23rd (Northumbrian) Division and 46th (North Midland) Divisions, were sent as pioneer units to France to undergo further training and performing labour duties. They were all ill-equipped and did not have their signals, Royal Artillery or administrative units with them.*
>
> *Along with 2/5th Battalion, The Queen's Royal Regiment (West Surrey), 2/6th Battalion, The Queen's Royal Regiment (West Surrey) and 2/7th Battalion, The Queen's Royal Regiment (West Surrey), these formed the 35th Infantry Brigade.*

The following Sunday began with the peal of church bells ringing through the crisp, clean spring air. The date was 21st April 1940. We paraded early in the road outside our billet and waited patiently for our NCO to address us.

"At 05.00 hours tomorrow, you will assemble with full kit. You will be leaving here so make sure you have everything relevant with you," he barked with his usual contempt. For ten minutes, he continued issuing orders for the day but nothing of any real importance, and I found my mind wandering off to another place as his monotonous voice droned on. My mind was busy with thoughts of glorious battles, explosions that couldn't harm me, comradeship and celebrations of victories, all based upon cinema films, newsreels and boyhood stories.

I came crashing back to earth as the NCO brought us to attention and a senior Officer, who was unfamiliar to me, took over the proceedings.

"Men. Tomorrow we leave. Your destination is at present a secret for obvious reasons. Tell no-one of your arrangements, not even girlfriends and family. We leave at 06.00 hours. Good luck men."

Finally it had come through from above, orders that we were off. Destination unknown and supposedly to continue with our training.

I was writing my last letter to mother before embarkation.

"Don't know about you chaps, but I don't know whether to be excited or scared about tomorrow," I muttered.

I could see nervous half smiles all around, just as Lance Corporal 'bloody' Ryan entered the room.

"Come on girls, get a bloody move on, there's a war on. Pack your handbags and get outside. Nice day for some exercises," and slammed the door.

"Do you know what Dennis, when I get to France, I'm going to put a bullet in Lance Corporal 'bloody' Ryan."

We nodded and laughed. The rest of our day was spent in talking it to death, speculating and preparation whilst trying to ignore the knot that was slowly developing in my stomach.

To get up so early is always a shock to the system, but by now we were accustomed to it. By 06.00 hours, we were on our way. We marched the short distance down to the railway station in the still morning air. On the distant horizon, a warm glow was nurturing the new dawn.

When we arrived, there was barely an inch of space to be found. Save for a few; the sick, the unsuitable and some administrators to tidy up after our departure, the whole battalion was there, officers and men. We were allowed to relax a little, but strict discipline was called for. We were instructed to conduct ourselves correctly at all times and even loud voices were to be frowned upon.

The first train arrived shortly before 09.00 hours, but it was full in no time and I, along with the other half of the battalion, waited for the next train, some two hours later.

Meanwhile, cigarettes ensured that we were kept sufficiently occupied. With my mind consumed with endless hours of drudgery and training in the town, I hadn't even been aware that spring had come. England had never looked so beautiful, cased in the rectangular wooden frames of the carriage windows. The train journeyed slowly across the south coast amidst breathtaking scenes as the early morning sun bathed the hills and fields with gold. New leaves swamped the trees and fresh shoots filled the neat green fields. Blossom adorned the hedgerows as our progress continued unabated. Familiar station names flashed by in a blur as we journeyed westward. There was to be no stopping for this troop train. We passed the time happily enough, chatting amongst ourselves but despite having been together for four months and bonding as a unit, British reserve meant that we were still relative strangers to each other.

Our train pulled into Southampton station shortly after one o'clock. I'm sure we all shared the same thought. Southampton meant a port and a port meant ships. We must be going to France to join the British Expeditionary Force (BEF), for that was the rumour on everyone's lips. Everywhere was a hive of activity as we spilt out onto the platform before marching off towards the docks. Over the heads of our marching column, a single black funnel slowly came into view. As we neared I could see that it was a steamer, the S.S. Tynwald *(see picture reference 19)*. She was a peacetime ferry steamer that had been commandeered for the war effort. She was moored up on the quayside, waiting patiently for her disparate travellers, full of every emotion from nervous, frightened through to cocky and excited. Troops were already milling aboard on her upper decks, the first train load of troops from our battalion.

At the quayside, all was calm, organised and a bustling hive of activity. Our group of 300 to 400 men were ordered aboard the steamer and with the minimum of delay, we embarked. Our fully-laden khaki line marched up between the ropes of the gangplank. The operation was carried out swiftly and with military precision, as was to be expected. Below deck was already bursting to capacity, which meant that we were allowed to stay on deck, thank goodness. I much preferred the fresh air.

It was a glorious spring day. The sun was shining and the sea was like a gently billowing tent top as the S.S. Tynwald slipped her mooring and slowly edged away from the quayside, just after four in the afternoon. I leant over the side with the rest of the men and watched, waving a last farewell gesture to anybody in the small crowd who happened to be watching. As the ship's fog horn sounded its farewell, I had no idea when I would see dear old England again, if ever. I watched the docks and warehouses slip on by as we moved out into the deeper channel and my heart was filled with the conflicting emotions that had troubled countless generations of servicemen bound for overseas. The excitement that our adventure was now beginning in earnest was tinged with the sadness of leaving my home and my dear mother.

But I had no fear. Don't get me wrong, I wasn't trying to be brave, on the contrary. Until now, I hadn't the slightest notion how fearful it was all going to become in just a short time hence. After all, we were only going to France to continue with our training.

We didn't sail far that evening, anchoring just off shore in Southampton Waters. In the following hours, we were joined by four other commandeered vessels of different descriptions, along with two Royal Naval ships as our escort, before our little convoy raised anchor and slowly inched its way out to set sail.

Under cover of darkness we steamed south-east, across the Channel. With the throb of the engine vibrating through the deck and the rhythmic swell of the vessel, I soon fell asleep.

The crossing was smooth and peaceful and you could have been forgiven for thinking there was no war; that is, until we neared our destination. As we approached the French coast, those of us on deck could hear the distant thud of an explosion. On the horizon, smoke drifted lazily skyward, above or near Le Havre. From across the sea the distant sound of sirens could be heard. Word spread that the port might be under German attack. Fortunately for us all, our small convoy decided that it was prudent not to go any further, so we cut engines and waited a few miles off shore. As we bobbed up and down in the calm waters, I sat back on deck once more, facing the backdrop of war and closed my eyes. Recollections of the last time I had travelled to France in that happy summer of '38 came flooding back. How very different it all was then.

I awoke as the new dawn was about to break above the coast of France, the distant cry of seagulls having disturbed me. During this short wait, we were fed a simple breakfast, courtesy of the ships crew. After an hour or so and no repeat of the explosions of the evening before, the ship's engines slowly whirled into life and we steamed uneasily into Le Havre harbour. In the distance, thin patches of smoke still rose from somewhere near the port. It's hardly surprising that we all felt apprehensive after what we had witnessed the previous day.

We moored on the jetty and disembarked with more than a sense of urgency, fearful of an air raid or bombardment. Le Havre looked unscathed but I couldn't help thinking that we was sticking our young heads into the jackal's mouth.

~ FRANCE ~
23rd April 1940

Le Havre appeared chaotic, with army and naval personnel moving around with urgency. Ships loaded with troops and supplies nestled on the quayside, as personnel rushed to unload their cargo. The bustle was breathtaking.

Once we had disembarked, I had only one thing on my mind - my bowels. It was imperative for me to find a toilet. I joined the ranks of the desperate and queued for my first encounter with a French loo. I smelt the building even before I saw it. Upon entering the truly foul interior, I saw a long row of cubicles in front of me. When I opened the first available door, I was surprised to see that there was no actual toilet as such to sit upon, just a hole in the floor. Disappointed, I queued again and went to the next cubicle, but it was exactly the same, nothing but a hole. So this was normal? Secondly, there were no locks, only two vertical handles fixed to the back of each door for me to hold onto whilst squatting with my trousers round my ankles and my backside hovering in mid air over the stinking abyss below. I then had to pray that my aim was good and true!

Whilst I attended to my needs, I prayed that some other desperate soul would not try to gain entry at this precise time, for with one hefty pull on the door, the unsuspecting person was likely to yank it open with me clinging on, thereby flinging me out across the floor in front of him, with my backside exposed for all to see.

My first unfavourable encounter with the 'toilettes françaises' system did nothing to impress me and my opinion did not alter as time went by. From the dockside, we were taken to a large customs shed where we were fed a decent hot meal. Whilst queuing and then eating, I saw 2nd/6th Battalion of The Queen's with us, swelling our total number to over twelve-hundred men. The huge open place echoed with the conversations of so many, all eager to express their feelings and worries. To date, we had not been told anything officially but another rumour was circulating that we were heading for a training camp to enable us to continue with the efforts of His Majesty's Government to transform us into the efficient fighting force that was sure to defeat Hitler. Overall, our spirits were high and general morale amongst us was good, believing that Britain would defeat Germany just as they had done in 1918.

The plan seemed to be to get us out of the port as soon as possible. Trapped like maggots in a tin and not knowing if the port would come under enemy fire again, I was in full agreement for it would be the greatest misfortune for any of us to be killed the same day as landing on foreign soil.

Quickly we assembled into some kind of order and marched directly to the railway yard. The French train was there, ready and waiting for our onward passage.

We journeyed on, painfully slowly at times. Over four hours passed before we arrived at a place some eighty miles east of Le Havre just north of Cambrai. After disembarking, we marched through the pleasant French countryside until we came upon a hastily established military camp in the Abancourt area that was to be our new home for the foreseeable future. Inside the camp perimeter, there were row upon neat row of standard circular grey/green British Army bell tents, each with a centre pole and guide ropes radiating out from their tops. From a distance, they looked like rows of children's cup cakes. Every tent could accommodate about twelve men. However, there didn't seem to be enough of them to house the sudden influx of twice as many men than had been expected and conditions were very cramped.

By the time we settled in, it was almost dark as we arranged ourselves as per the Army instruction manual. The tents and procedure had barely changed since Napoleonic times. Each man started by leaning his rifle up against the central pole and lightly securing it with a spider rope. We then lay down, with our feet facing the central pole and our heads towards the outer flaps of the tent. We were as the spokes of a wheel, with our kit by our heads. When it was warm we could lift and tie up the tent flaps, and when cold or windy, let them down to be secured to the ground with pegs.

Those with me in the tent were in a good mood. We were bonding as only those in the services can. We joked and reflected upon the day's incidents. I shut my eyes, and in that moment before succumbing, I happily recalled the last time I was in France just over a year ago. I smiled as I pictured myself with 'Madam Oo là là' before sleep finally engulfed me.

~ 24th April ~

Why does wake-up call come so early? It was a truly miserable morning, the sky was overcast and it had just started to drizzle. Here we were, a couple of hundred miles from home, and there to greet us was our old friend Captain Cauldron, ready with our first brew of the day. After a very wet morning parade came breakfast. Some mornings, our talented chefs would treat us to local sausages but today our meal consisted of a huge lump of bread and a chunk of bully beef. It was almost reassuring for us homesick lads that the food was just as bad as it had been in St. Leonards.

During the day came the news that tomorrow we were to start our real training in earnest. It pleased me that we would now commence genuine soldiering and the art of warfare. Until then, we were given jobs around the camp, although anything we did was hampered by the ever increasing heavy rain. Within twenty-four hours, the campsite was a quagmire. With the now torrential rain, we could achieve nothing, so for the next three days we trod water and waited. Living conditions inside the tents had become a nightmare for there was no flooring and the ground under us was awash. On the second day, Tommy Grigg, a London wag who seemed capable only of speaking humorously, made an announcement.

"Hey lads, I think it's time to build that f***ing Ark."

It seemed a reasonable proposal, given the circumstances.

A rather unpleasant aspect of camp life was the totally inadequate toilet facilities but on reflection I wish that I had appreciated them more, for later I was to regard these facilities as grand by comparison.

On the third day of perpetual rain there was a highlight, PAY DAY. I queued with the other ranks and within minutes my greatcoat was sodden, its weight increasing by the second. Eventually, I was handed the princely sum of 75 French francs.

On the morning of the 27th, the skies had finally exhausted their once plentiful supply of water, allowing our training to commence. They called it basic training and you had to be there to realise just how basic it was. The commencement of training in the art of soldiering and warfare was to take the familiar form, marching... and digging! More trenches to dig out every morning but this time we didn't fill them in afterwards. I think they were actually defensive trenches. Marvellous! I was assured that the Germans would have packed up and gone home if only they had known what awesome trench-diggers they were about to face.

After a week of digging, our Officers decided that it would be expedient for infantry, such as us, to practise shooting. Some of the young men that I was now with were actually afraid of their weapons as they had never fired a gun before. Even though they had been given instructions on how to dismantle it, clean it, parade with it and hold it, there were some who were physically afraid when the gun was fired. I would watch as they curled up their faces in a dreaded grimace, closing their eyes and turning their heads in anticipation before releasing the bullet with the resulting almighty bang. The rifle would recoil and hit them square in the shoulder, causing painful bruising. For intended infantrymen, this behaviour was worrying!

Officially, we were not in France as combat troops, but as trainees and pioneers, digging, building defences and mending roads, which was just as well, for we had little or no equipment to train with. Our Commanders divided us up into groups and gave us grand names such as 'Mortar Platoon', 'Machine Gun Platoon' and the like, but we simply didn't have the equipment to go with the title. The closest any of us got to a mortar or a machine gun was actually hearing the name.

I was placed into the 'Stretcher Platoon' and we were the lucky few, for we actually had stretchers to practise with. However, I was a little perturbed at my appointment. Considering that I was already a crack shot and marksman, I rightly regarded myself as slightly misplaced and under-used. I couldn't help but question the wisdom of my seniors up to and including Commander-in-Chief, Lord Gort.

I was paired with a lad two years older than me. His name was Freddy Laws *(see picture reference 31)* but for some reason best known to himself, he was sometimes referred to as Bert, after his father. Although of average height, he was broad and muscular with bright, sandy-coloured hair and full of life. We seemed to click. This particular day was his birthday and his mother had sent him a cake a few days earlier. When our company was ordered out on a march in full kit, Freddy and I took the stretcher. To make the exercise more realistic, our sadistic corporal ordered us to carry a couple of sandbags covered with a blanket. We marched with full kit. Our sergeant, a seemingly pleasant enough chap, must have got out of bed the wrong side, for after every mile, he made us run for ten minutes. Soon we were exhausted.

After eating a hastily prepared meal, Freddy uncovered his little surprise hidden between the sand bags on the stretcher, the birthday cake. Our little band of brothers polished it off, washed down with a cup of tea.

Fortunately I wasn't a stretcher-bearer for long. Once the NCOs and Officers had been reminded several times that I was actually a crack shot, that old oxymoron - military intelligence - swung into action and I was transferred from the stretcher-bearers to the Bren Gun Carrier Platoon within HQ Company. Apparently, this word 'Carrier' referred to a small, lightly-armoured tracked vehicle, only capable of carrying two men - a driver and an operator, the type of vehicle that had come to the aid of the stranded supply truck during the bleak winter of three months past. The operator, me, would fire the Bren gun mounted on the front of the vehicle. I was pleased to be re-deployed and was really looking forward to my placement with some degree of excitement. However, I soon discovered that there was one slight problem,... we had no Bren gun carriers! In fact, I had not even clapped eyes on one during all of my training, but at least I had fired 28 rounds of ammunition from a Bren gun,... once, so I considered myself fortunate.

You had to be in France in the spring of 1940 to believe and understand the utter chaos within the British Army. Sometimes you could taste the desperation, despair at the lack of planning and worry about the lack of reliable intelligence. Of course, we were so far down the chain of command, we had no idea as to what the generals and politicians at home were planning and plotting, but from what little I saw, I don't think they did either.

By the end of April, our schooling in the ancient art of warfare continued to elude us, whilst, unbeknown to us, the unstoppable Nazi war machine was just completing its meticulously crafted plans.

> † *As April turned to May, there were 394,165 British soldiers in France. 235,000 made up the main fighting force and 17,000 of us trainees and pioneers were supposedly well on the way to join the main force when the time came. 80,000 were employed in the perilously inadequate lines of communications and others were serving in HQs and supporting roles.*

~ OFF DUTY ~

During the days, our mood drifted like the tides, ebbing from highs to inevitable troughs of unhappiness, as with the weather. But this was still an adventure, albeit a slowly unfolding one.

When not training we grabbed every opportunity to leave camp,... but not before the customary lecture on the dangers that we faced. Not from the threatening Hun to the north-east but from something much closer to camp, the 'French Ladies' and the readily available variety of diseases that were on offer, out there in the wonderful world of sin.

That evening, turned completely off by all the talk of venereal disease and the painful treatments that we would have to endure if we succumbed to the wickedness of the flesh, Freddy and our little band cadged a lift to a café into the local town. There we could indulge our taste buds and buy a decent meal with our wages or just get merry but nothing too outrageous. Once inside the café the first thing we noticed was the hostility of the locals, seeming to resent our presence. I found this rather surprising, expecting them to be at least pleased, if not grateful for our being there, but resentful? To me, it made no sense.

As the evening wore on, we discovered that those warnings of unprotected sex were wasted on us, for there were no girls to consort with and no romance to be found. But it wasn't all bad for without such distraction, we ate, smoked, exchanged jokes and relaxed whilst gradually succumbing to the effects of the local wine. Our French 'patron' mixed the vinegary liquid with a little sugar to make it more palatable to 'les Anglais'.

---

† *Source: Dunkirk, The Men they Left Behind by Sean Longden.*

Freddy Laws came from Nottingham and this troubled my inquisitive nature.

"Hey Freddy, how the hell did a northerner like you end up in the Queen's Surrey Regiment?"

Freddy laughed, " northerner?...huh!... a midlander if you don't mind, you ignorant southerner, and the answer is they needed a real soldier, so here I am."

We chuckled.

"Did they ask you which regiment you wanted to join when you enlisted?"

"Yep! At school, I once read a history book about the Gordon Highlanders." His eyes were ablaze with enthusiasm. "It was full of paintings of great battles. Stories of India, fighting the Afghans, Egyptians and sailing up the Nile to save General Gordon in Khartoum. As a kid, I fought in every one of those battles,... should have got a bleeding medal,... so I asked, extremely politely and kindly, if I could join the Highlanders? The bastard NCO told me it was fine and made a note. And that's how I ended up here with you lot, you lucky band of misfits."

We all laughed,... having shared a similar experience.

We soon learnt why we were resented by our allies, the French soldiers; it was over our pay. Whilst we were receiving about eleven francs a day, they were only being paid one franc a day. Understandable, but hardly our fault. However, we were still being taken for an expensive ride by our Army paymaster, for the legalised theft as 'barrack room stoppages' were still being deducted from our wages. Our barracks now consisted of army tents on the bare ground. What was there to damage, the grass?

As the weeks in France progressed, our consumption of the local French beverage increased accordingly. To us, it was dirt cheap and took you to where you wanted to go. Armed with bulging wage packets, we could choose to spend the whole damn lot if we wished, unlike the poor 'soldat français'. But there was little to spend our money on. The food in the cafés was good but you could only eat so much, so we turned even more to drink. Once we got used to the plonk, the patron moved us on to 'Absinthe', a potent aniseed-flavoured drink which hit the spot every time and took us to another place, a place that we really didn't want to go. The down side to all this was the following morning, for after drinking anything, we became drunk all over again. Drinking had developed into a major problem and was not well received by the Officers and NCOs. I suppose that a parade ground full of drunks was not ideal. As a consequence, we were banned from drinking the evil spirit. Shame!... but that order probably saved our livers.

~ GRACIE FIELDS CONCERT ~
First Week of May 1940

In early May 1940, Gracie Fields left the safe shores of England with her accompanist Harry Parr, returning once more to France and Belgium to entertain troops of the BEF.

The first I knew about her tour was one morning when we were milling around camp whilst off duty. We were approached by a Corporal, who asked us if we wished to attend her concert in Lille. Most of the men jumped at the offer. Personally, as a 42 year old, Gracie Fields did not set my loins on fire and I would have preferred to revisit the cafés. But, not wanting to miss out on free tickets plus the opportunity to escape camp, I jumped at the chance.

By mid-morning there was a group of about sixty men gathered and waiting on the parade ground. As soon as our transportation arrived (courtesy of our CO) we leapt aboard and left in high spirits.

After a relatively long and arduous journey to Lille, our driver delivered us to the doors of the venue where upon we had to wait a couple of hours before being allowed to enter the huge, decorative concert hall where Gracie was to perform. Once inside, we found the hall packed to the rafters with British soldiers, all in splendid mood, if not slightly the worse for drink.

Prior to her arrival in France, Gracie had been ill and was still recovering from a spell in hospital. When she eventually took to the stage, we saw no signs of her ill health and the place erupted with the cheers of thousands. It was electrifying and took a while for the outburst to subside so that her performance could begin. She sang all the favourites and her loving audience joined in. Halfway into her act Gracie chose to sing what was arguably her most famous song, 'The Biggest Aspidistra in the World', but sung it with a twist by changing a few lines, with an unflattering mention of Hermann Goering, Joe Stalin and how *'they were going to string up old Hitler from the highest bough of the biggest aspidistra in the world'*.

That was enough for everybody to burst into tumultuous applause all over again, threatening to bring the roof down. After countless encores, she bade us all a big farewell and blew us a thousand of her trademark exaggerated kisses before waving us a final goodbye. We cheered until our throats went dry and our hands hurt and even I applauded.

It turned out to be a good evening and we returned to camp tired, a little merry and very happy.

> *Known only to a few for security reasons, Gracie Fields toured the BEF camps throughout northern France during the spring of 1940. After staying at a small private hotel in the town of Arras, about halfway between Lille and Amiens, she finished her tour and left incognito under cover of darkness to return home. Two days later, the hotel she had stayed in was the target of a lone bombing raid by the Luftwaffe and her bedroom was reduced to ruins.*
>
> *By this time, Gracie had already come to the attention of the Germans because of her outspoken songs aimed at Hitler and his cronies and was regarded by them as a part of the 'war industry', therefore making her a legitimate target. Albeit belatedly, it seemed as though the Germans may have targeted her personally, but we will never know. She did return home safely and continued doing her bit by entertain the troops overseas for the duration of the war.*
>
> *Throughout early May, our battalion continued with 'training' and general labouring work in the area around Abancourt, assisting French engineers with defence preparations and minor guard duties.*

· · · § · · ·

THE FOUR HORSEMEN ARE UNLEASHED

10th May 1940

hether there already existed a tangible atmosphere throughout the camp or perhaps the presence of high-ranking Officers moving from place to place with unaccustomed urgency created the tension, I am uncertain, but morning parade was different today. After the usual routine we were addressed by our Major, which was unusual in itself and his speech sent my heart pounding. He began in a solemn tone.

"Men, at dawn this morning the German Army crossed over into Belgium and Holland. The much anticipated invasion has begun."
He continued, assure us that we were not in the thick of it but must prepared for the possibility.

"Stiff opposition from the combined weight of the French and BEF forces will prevail and halt the German advance in its tracks, of that I am certain. Your immediate task is to continue with your training whilst our forces do their bit. That is all."

"Fall out," bellowed the Sergeant Major.

This news would change everything for us and most of Europe and the consequences would spread like wildfire around the globe. I was dumbstruck. The apocalyptic destruction of mainland Europe had finally begun in earnest.

We were all anxious for news but news was hard to come by. There were few newspapers and no official information filtered down from on high. Although we were close to the now active German,

Belgian and French borders, we continued to be kept in the dark as to the progress of the fight, of defeats and possible victories.

Shortly after, news followed of Chamberlain's resignation, news which was enough to lift our spirits but when we heard that Churchill had been appointed Prime Minister we were elated and a three cheers went up.

~ ABANCOURT ~
11th May 1940

We had always been led to believe that the formidable 'Maginot Line' made the invasion of France nigh on impossible. Those fortifications were now sidelined by Germany invading through Belgium and the Ardennes forest and the news shocked us all. That day, we talked it to death, each giving his educated (or not-so-educated) opinion as to the reasons and the eventual outcome of this action, but we all knew what it meant. The farcical tranquillity of the 'twilight' or 'phoney war' was finally smashed on that day in May and the world was ill-prepared.

The German Army was sweeping through those lightly defended countries and heading straight for the softer underbelly of France. And guess who was sitting in that soft underbelly, waiting?

Despite the frantic activity of the BEF and allied forces, nothing seemed to dramatically change for our untrained battalion. Senior Officers came and went with an urgent spring in their step, but for us, our ill-conceived training schedule remained.

For a few, life was about to change forever. I finally received recognition from the Army for being a good marksmen and therefore of some additional benefit to the war effort other than a 'digger of holes'. Little did I know just how desperate the situation was and from now on, how confusing and deadly our war was about to become.

~ THE FIGHT BEGINS IN EARNEST ~
12th May 1940

Two days after Hitler unleashed his cancerous plague of death over the neutral countries of western Europe, my company within the 2nd/7th Battalion of The Queen's was called out after morning parade.

Our senior Officer was Major Carr, a man of average stature and in his late forties, sporting a grand moustache. He seemed a nice enough sort but only time would tell. Our platoon Sergeant ordered us to gather our full kit and issued us with 50 rounds of ammunition before we clambered into the waiting trucks which were a mishmash of both army and commandeered civilian lorries. To see how ill prepared we were didn't fill me with a great deal of confidence. By eight o'clock we were off, destination unknown. As we drove through the first French village, we were greeted by a most pleasant sight. The local inhabitants rushed out waving at us, thrusting food and drink into our hands as the truck slowed to a walking pace. They shouted 'Berlin or bust' and 'Hooray for the British' and cheered as we passed on by. I felt elated by this adulation but the truth was, as of yet, we had done absolutely nothing to deserve their praise.

The sun looked favourably upon us as we journeyed on, a far cry from the terrible winter of only a few months ago. Had it not been for the war raging across western Europe, we could have been excused for thinking that we were out for the day on a charabanc. There was no let-up in the intermittent waves of French civilians who were heading in the opposite direction to our battalion.

Our journey took most of the morning, and after an hour or so we crossed over the River Somme, whose name for us all was synonymous with the infamous bloody battles and dead of the last war.

As we drove on through the peaceful, lush countryside, my mind wandered back to recall the stories of strife and heroism of previous generations of British soldiers. High above, a squadron of large bombers flew accompanied by smaller fighters.

"Ours or theirs?" someone asked.

"Some poor sods will soon find out," was the cryptic reply.

We endured several hours of bum-numbing travel in the back of our trucks before eventually arriving at our destination, a place we would often return to as we journeyed across northern France and beyond by train, truck and shank's pony. A place too small to appear on most maps but known to many a British soldier in times of war, a place called F***knowswhere!

Some amongst us thought that this jaunt was still part of our training, as indeed it should have been, for we still had no experience to draw upon and everything to learn. We piled out of the trucks, the metal studs on our boots grating and clattering as we jumped down onto the road. I cast my eyes over the surrounding countryside.

"So this is what F***knowswhere looks like?" I muttered.

> *What I didn't appreciate at the time was that at this early stage in the land war, the German advance through Belgium and France towards the Channel ports and Atlantic coast had been so rapid. Our position, and that of thousands of trainee troops like us, was untenable right from the outset and would rapidly develop into a full-scale rout. I am not sure that even the Officers knew what was going on. Lacking effective modern communication systems or reliable intelligence as to the enemy's position and strength, our own situation was already hopeless.*

So now we marched. As I did so, I thought of the consequences if any of us got separated from our superiors. We would certainly be in dire straits, for none of us had been shown how to navigate with a map, even if we had one. Only the Officers possessed a compass and none of them had taken the bother to inform us of our overall 'global' strategy. We were clueless chicks following our mother hen.

From behind, 2nd Lieutenant Mumford came running by to catch up with the Major at the head of our column. Mumford was a tall officer, thin and rather weedy with a stern yet feckless look about him. From what I had seen of him, he didn't fill me with confidence. I did not care for him much.

I assumed that we were in no immediate danger so I wore my much cooler forage cap rather than my steel helmet. We marched as squads of 12 men in single file along the side of a narrow cobbled road, heading deeper into the surrounding countryside. Shortly after leaving we came upon a British photographer.

"Give us a smile lads," he shouted, "pretend you're enjoying this." He took several pictures of us whilst the wags amongst us laughed and shouted back at him.

"Did you get my best side, mate?"

"Show the picture to my missus will you, she thinks I'm on a bleedin' 'oliday."

"We'll see you in Berlin."

> *A short while after that picture was taken, my father was reading a copy of a magazine he subscribed to, 'The War Illustrated', dated 7th June Issue No. 40. He came across a picture of 'British troops in the northern war area marching towards the battle*

zone'. *He studied the picture and thought he recognised me in my forage cap. Because of his occupation, he was able to pull a few strings and find information that other lesser mortals couldn't. He contacted the magazine and obtained a copy of the photo, dated 12th May 1940. (see picture reference 20).*

~ 1940's COMMUNICATIONS... BRITISH STYLE ~

To maintain communication between platoons and companies, our part of the British Expeditionary Force did not rely on a speedy modern communication system, unlike our enemy. We had no radio. For the most part, we relied on tried and tested methods perfected through the centuries and last used in the previous war. We used runners, soldiers who ran between army groups with messages of the lightning war that was unfolding and changing around us, sometimes for miles. Even before the exhausted messenger had arrived at his destination, his information was usually outdated. But some argued that runners were, at least, a slight improvement on carrier pigeons, but I wasn't so sure.

Our company employed such a man, a skinny private who was our best runner, thereby attempting to maintain perilously frail communications with the chain of command up to HQ, wherever they were.

~ OUT OF THE FRYING PAN AND INTO THE MIRE ~
12th May, later the same day

I hadn't a clue what we were doing, why or where we were save for the fact that we were a long way from our camp at Abancourt. Herby, our Medical Officer's orderly, was marching alongside me.

"I don't know Dennis, who is the bright spark that gave me a rifle and pointed me in the direction of the enemy?"

'Ah, that's military intelligence, they know what they are doing."
We had only been in the army a few months and already we were all so cynical.

Herby seemed most indignant. "Yes but it's ridiculous,... do you know that I have never even fired this thing before?" as he indicated with a sideways nod of his head to his First World War rifle.

"Don't worry mate, you're not alone, neither have I."

We laughed, but in reality I was shitting myself.

I think we were now playing 'Hunt the Hun' or, most probably, 'Run Rabbit Run', but what did I know?

The afternoon delivered more glorious sunshine but it was stinking hot, causing our bodies to drip with sweat. I itched under my woollen uniform as we marched towards a battle proven enemy.

Although we thought that the enemy was still a long way off, at every turn in the road or over the brow of each hill, I half expected to meet the elusive Germans head on. Occasionally we would catch a glimpse of allied or German aircraft flying overhead, but no sight of enemy ground forces, thank God, only the continuous sound of distant artillery and machine gun fire. Neither had I seen any allied tanks or artillery. Our helmets were our only form of defence against attack and officially, if we wanted to don them, we had to obtain permission from an Officer. Likewise, we were informed that in times of fighting, we must return all spent cartridges if we wished them to be replaced.

> *To this day, I am still embarrassed to even contemplate that such antiquated regulations were still in force at the time.*

We marched along twisting tracks and country roads with tall poplar trees either side, offering us some shade from the unrelenting sun but only partial cover from the airborne enemy. I was brought out of my self-imposed trance by an order to halt and rest for ten minutes whilst the officers and sergeants gathered around a map, deep in discussion. I wondered if we were lost.

I lay in the shade of an overgrown hedge full of lush green shoots. The early summer flowers were everywhere and the air was filled with the buzz of insects engrossed in nature's work. Briefly, we dozed, smoked or chatted, enjoying those few precious moments of relaxation under that peaceful azure blue sky.

The sharp crackle of rifle and machine gun fire broke the peace of that late spring day. It appeared to be coming from behind us. 2nd Lieutenant Mumford *(see picture reference 14)*, our platoon Officer, gave the order for us to enter the field on the other side of the hedge. Whilst the others remained where they were, our platoon, led by Major Carr and Mumford, advanced up the incline towards an elevated wood. As quickly and as quietly as possible, we moved forward. I felt so vulnerable until reaching the protection of the woods, without having come under any direct fire.

~ WE ENTER THE WOODS ~

Inside my chest, my heart was pounding. I couldn't believe it, we were still only raw recruits, still under trained and about to face the enemy. What the hell were our officers thinking? Once under cover of the trees I felt safer and we followed the Major, carefully making our way through the trees towards the sound of gunfire. Without warning an explosion occurred; we were under attack. It was the first time that I had ever been on the receiving end of a bombardment, and until the day I die I will never forget the gut-wrenching terror of that assault. The unbelievable noise was painful as it reverberated through my head. I ducked as every explosion burst around me, unaware that by doing so, it was already too late to avoid the flesh-tearing consequences of any flying shrapnel. I had never been so scared.

Within only days, the Germans had smashed their way through the inadequate allied defences with breathtaking speed and efficiency, but we still hadn't a clue where we were in relation to them.

Our carefully controlled walk was replaced with a frantic crouched run. As I rushed through the woods carrying my Bren gun, my number two, laden with the ammunition box, trailed behind me. I dived for ground cover, falling flat on my face. A mortar bomb exploded nearby. I attempted to force my body into the hard earth, out of harm's way. The almighty, ear-splitting eruption shook the ground. Despite the ringing in my shattered ears, I heard a ghastly and inhuman noise, shouts then screams from ahead and in front of me. The sound of other explosions continued but all I could focus on was the pained scream that filled the space between each blast. We ran forward once more for those were our orders.

Without warning, I stumbled upon the source of the animal-like cry as soon as we entered the clearing, a clearing made possible by the shell that had landed some thirty seconds earlier. A soldier, one of ours, was propped up against a tree. He was just sitting there, screaming then whimpering. His face was contorted with either pain or terror, his teeth bared to the cordite-filled air in a horrifying grimace. No blood appeared on his face, for it was clean, save for the tears that ran down his young cheeks. After each single breath and scream, he would look down and bleat uncontrollably.

I had stopped moving forward but my number two almost crashed into me as he blundered onto the scene. He too looked straight ahead at the screaming trooper. My eyes left his grief-stricken face and drifted down his torso in an automatic search of his body. My horror-driven scan of his frame stalled as I reached his waist. He had been hit, wounded by shrapnel which had torn through his uniform and sliced his belly open. His intestines were spilling out and he was cradling the wet, sticky mass in his blood-soaked hands. He was in shock, not knowing what to do. We had no stretcher-bearers and no other support. As a unit, we were on our own. To witness such a horrific injury shook me to the core. I was both clueless and powerless to do anything as I froze in terror. And all this brief while, time was now standing still. Sounds had ceased whilst others from my company ran past in slow motion. Momentarily, I had fallen into a bizarre parallel world devoid of noise and time. I was rudely spat back into the reality of my surroundings as another deafening explosion became the prelude for the next bombardment. Hell broke loose once more.

This latest onslaught was even more intense. My number two and I left the wounded man and ran forward to join the others. I flung myself amongst the thick of my comrades, who had already gone to ground. In a brief respite from the noise of battle, I heard a more familiar sound. An Officer came crawling through the undergrowth towards us. Much to my relief, Major Carr emerged through the bracken and late spring flowers that littered the woodland floor. With his pistol held tightly in his right hand, he hurriedly joined our group. Before the next shell landed, he shouted at us abruptly.

"I want one volunteer."

I believe there has always been an unwritten rule amongst the ranks in any army - NEVER volunteer,... so naturally, no-one did.

Then the Major re-phrased his question. "Who is the best shot?"

The others immediately pointed to me. My years of membership in my local rifle club had assured me of this claim to fame. The Major didn't bother to wait for confirmation from me; time seemed to be of the essence.

"What's your name soldier?"

"Minter, sir, Private Minter."

"Leave the Bren gun with your number two. Take his rifle," he ordered, nodding to the man next to me. "Make sure it's loaded and follow me, we've got some work to do. The rest of you, wait here, understood, and don't panic!"

Easier to say than to do!

He took a rifle for himself from the nearest man and nodded to me whilst placing his pistol back in its holster. He turned and we both crawled along the ground through the undergrowth, back in the direction that he had come from. Ground cover was still quite dense, so we were reasonably well concealed from the enemy, wherever they were.

The mortar fire and ensuing noise of the explosions continued about us, causing more injuries, for the enemy was managing to pinpoint our position with increasing accuracy.

Major Carr and I eventually came upon a building deep in the wood. The small cottage was probably a gamekeeper's lodge. The pitched roof was steep and tile clad. A chimney stack penetrated the roof on the nearside of the house. Almost hidden from view in the angle formed by the roof and stack we could see two Germans soldiers. They were artillery 'spotters'. One was holding his field binoculars up to his eyes, surveying the results of the devastating mortar fire, whilst the second German relayed information and firing instructions back to the gunners by way of his radio.

The Major whispered in my ear.

"You take the one standing and I'll take the one sitting down."

"Fire when I do."

I nodded my understanding but I was as nervous as hell, for this was my first engagement and the first time I had fired at a living soul. We estimated the distance to be a hundred yards and adjusted our sights accordingly before I took up my firing position. I carefully aimed my rifle. My hands trembled slightly as I tried to take aim. The Major, on the other hand, seemed calm, having plenty of experience to draw upon. I thought of my rifle club practices, relaxed my grip, lowered my rifle, closed my eyes for a second or two and breathed slowly, calming my nerves, telling myself that this was just a rifle competition and resumed my position. I was now composed.

We both aimed for their hearts.

"Ready?" Carr whispered.

"Yes sir," I replied and we gently squeezed the triggers.

The crack of our single rounds was almost in unison. Carr's sitting target was knocked backwards against the roof and lay where he fell, a clean kill. My target slumped and then slowly slid forward before tumbling off the roof onto the ground below. As soon as he landed we both jumped up and ran to where he lay. Unfortunately for both him and I, my victim was still alive and groaning. He looked even younger than me. My aim had been a bit too low, wounding him an inch below and left of his heart. Now I was so close to him, the shooting that had been so detached a moment ago was now personal. I couldn't help but feel sorry for my enemy, even guilty for what I had just done. There was no hatred, just an unexpected sadness and regret. I wished that I had not been so keen to rush forward to inspect my 'kill'. Next to his body lay his binoculars. As I stood above him, the Major bent down and retrieved the valuable item.

"Come on Minter, lets move."

I looked at my German and bent down to unbutton his blooded jacket to see what I could do. I pulled open his tunic and saw his life blood pumping rhythmically from his open wound. His body jerked as he coughed weakly. His face was contorted with pain. A crimson trickle appeared in the corner of his mouth and began its leisurely passage to the base of his ear.

"Mutter, mutter, ich komme nicht Zu Houzen". (Mother, mother, I shall never come home). "Shuss mich, shuss mich noch mal, bitte, bitte!" (Shoot me, shoot me once more, please, please!)

That was the first time I heard a German speak. I felt so utterly helpless, not knowing what to do as I knelt by his side, watching as his life slowly ebbed away. With his lungs filling with blood, he wheezed and spluttered through to his last desperate breath. A red spatter sprayed my sleeve and the back of my hand. For a few seconds I knelt beside him and witnessed his release from this violent world. His demise hit me hard. My stomach was in turmoil and I felt utterly sick.

I was brought racing back to reality as more rounds exploded. I was alone. It was time to leave my victim. The Major had crept off, back to his men without me, believing that I was following him. He didn't hang around and neither should I, so I hurriedly turned back, desperate to re-join my squad. By the time I found them, I felt a different emotion, more a feeling of elation I suppose, as the adrenaline was still pumping round my body. After all, I had just killed one of the enemy and I had got away with it. I was still alive and unhurt. I had been blooded. My first kill and things would never be quite the same for me again. It made me realise just how effortless it is to slay someone with a gun, in times of peace or war.

The daylight slowly began to retreat into the western horizon and things quietened down. The Germans did not usually like fighting during the hours of darkness and neither did Major Carr, thank

God. Once we were well clear of the other side of the woods, not wishing for his band of inexperienced young soldiers to blunder into the hidden enemy in the dark, he ordered us to dig in for the night, making ourselves as safe and comfortable as possible. But little foxholes were not for us. We were required to build great trenches, just like in the First World War. I think we must have dug up half the countryside whilst we travelled the length and breadth of northern France.

What rations were available were distributed and we ate a small meal of bread and bully beef and for pudding, we smoked. It had been one hell of a day. The image of our wounded comrade with his guts blown open continuously drifted in and out of my mind. I hoped to God that a medic had found him.

Sentries were posted with each of us taking it in turn to be on watch, two hours on and four hours of rest. The quiet that followed allowed me to fall into an exhausted sleep under the shelter of the woodland canopy until it was my turn on duty.

I awoke to the sweet sound of the dawn chorus. The world appeared at peace, and luckily for us it had been a dry night. Our company quietly arose. A thin blanket of mist hung over the marshy ground that surrounded us. Using his newly-acquired binoculars, Major Carr spotted a château in the distance and decided to head for it. We were immediately ordered to move and continue with the game of 'Hunt the Hun' or whatever it was we were meant to be playing, but I couldn't help thinking that it was us who were the hunted. Unlike stories and pictures of the First World War, fought in thick mud and shell holes, our localised encounters were being fought in what I assumed were the virgin woods and fields of the Somme, green and lush and as yet largely unscathed by the new warmongers. But as I crossed the ground and thought of the chronology, I realised that over twenty years had elapsed since the last terrible slaughter had been played out on this blood-soaked soil, enough time for nature to have at least hidden the scars and heal the worst of the wounds of war.

· · · § · · ·

~ THE CHÂTEAU ~
13th May 1940

Following the lead of our Officers, we cautiously approached the château. The Major sent our Sergeant and two men forward to reconnoitre. Five minutes later, they returned to say that the place was unoccupied so we advanced to the front of this picturesque building, its mellow stone and brick walls allowing it to melt into the landscape. It stood four stories high, with windows set into the steep, ornate tiled roof. Short spires topped each of the circular towers. No standard or colours flew from the flagpole. The gravel drive curved gently around to the front of the building before sweeping into a longer drive that disappeared through huge wrought iron gates to the road beyond. An equally impressive stone wall surrounded the château.

The Major and platoon Sergeant walked up the steps to the heavy, grey, wooden door and it came as no surprise to any of us that it was locked. Swiftly, they disappeared around the other side of the building whilst we watched and waited.

"France" was the best anybody could come up with.

Before long, the sound of sliding bolts and dry metal emanated from the front door before our smiling Major and sombre Sergeant materialised. All appeared satisfactory. Following the all-clear we were summoned in.

The decorative interior reflected grand days of yesteryears. The lack of dust and debris suggested that the château had only recently been vacated. Some furniture was present but obvious large gaps indicated that probably the best and most valuable pieces had been removed to safety.

Because of his strength, our blundering but lovable clown Roy Gough. had been given the task of carrying the cumbersome anti-tank rifle. Despite its name, the rifle was incapable of inflicting any damage whatsoever on the heavily-armoured German panzers. However, this was the most powerful weapon in our company's miserable arsenal. Once the château had been thoroughly checked, we set about securing the building. Observers were placed at every strategic window and door. As for me, I was assigned to the hall with Goughey and six others. The Sergeant gave orders for us to move the massive oak dining table into the hallway, which took ten of us to move and place against the closed front door. The heavy letter box was propped open and the anti-tank rifle was laid onto the table.

Its two support legs were pulled down and the end barrel of the gun was pushed up to the open letter box but not actually through it. Goughey was ordered to use it only when instructed to, if and when the need arose. Meanwhile, food stocks had been discovered in the large kitchens. Fortunately for us, the Major decided that cautious cooking would be allowed and a meal was prepared for us hungry souls.

We took it in turns with guard duty and used what washing and toilet facilities there were to full advantage. After recent experiences, this was like being in a five-star hotel.

Towards midday, lookouts on the upper floor shouted from the upper landing. The tone was one of desperation.

"Major, large column of German tanks sighted at the front."

I was taking my rest turn and rushed to the window. Sure enough in the distance, a convoy of panzers were visible, passing swiftly along the road at the end of the château's long drive. Immediately we were put on full alert, ordered to be quiet, stay calm and take up positions. This included Goughey, who clambered awkwardly onto the solid dining table that had been dragged in front of the main door.

He took up his firing position, stuck the end of the rifle through a gap in the door and brought his eye to bear down the long barrel and onto the drive beyond.

"Gough, where's your bloody ammunition?" uttered the Sergeant in his shell-like ear.

"Oh yes, sorry, old mate,... put it somewhere."

The Sergeant was barely able to control his temper as Goughey fumbled in his pockets.

"Ah, got it, old mate," and produced his magazine containing the miserly five rounds of 'anti tank' ammunition.

It was a joke, facing a squadron of enemy tanks with a bloody pea-shooter and five peas! The exasperated Sergeant turned away towards us and reminded us not to open fire until ordered to do so. Clearly we were no match for this armoured column or anything other than a small scouting troop. I crossed my fingers and hoped that they would just drive on by.

We waited as the first tank sped past the end of the drive. In the distance, the tank commanders could be seen with their upper bodies poking out through the turret doors, enjoying the clean spring air. The next five tanks passed without incident but a smaller, less powerful light-armoured vehicle suddenly peeled off from the main column and started to make its way up the long drive, towards the château.

"Shit!" came a muffled muttering.

"QUIET that man" came the swift response.

Our Sergeant calmly whispered reassuring words to us. We were to remain hidden from view, still and quiet and hopefully the driver would just look and drive away.

As the vehicle reached the main gates, my heart mirrored my concerns and pounded accordingly.

The Sergeant spoke. "Remember you lot, just hold your fire and stay hidden." He pulled his face away from the window and withdrew behind the full length crimson curtain.

The light tank drove towards the château's main door before turning twenty yards in front of us so that the vehicle's left side was facing us. It came to a jolting halt on the loose gravel drive. Slowly two German soldiers jumped out, whilst a third remained half in and half out, stretching his cramped legs. The two Germans took a few paces towards the château before stopping. The Commander was wearing a soft field cap at a slight angle and a black blouse. He turned to face the other before offering him a cigarette. I watched spellbound with my heart beating madly out of control. He withdrew his lighter, cupped his hands and lit both before drawing heavily on his. They both turned to face the château once more and took a few more steps forward. They talked casually to each other, their conversation muffled. By now, they were close enough to make out the gold star and Swastika pinned under the eagle on their chests. Any closer and we would be able to smell what he had for breakfast

Every one of us held our breath, patiently waiting in absolute silence for them to finish their cigarettes and rejoin the column. Such were their numbers that they were still thundering past the gate. The soldier on the right withdrew the cigarette from his mouth and, with the same hand, pointed up towards the top of the building, possibly identifying the white face of a petrified British soldier on the upper floor, whose nose was pressed hard against a pane of glass, too terrified to move, or, more likely, he was admiring some part of its fine architecture, for it was a truly splendid building.

Inside the chateau, nothing stirred, not even the fleas in my hair and all I could hear was the sound of my blood pulsating through my ears. You could have heard a moth pass wind...

The next occurrence came out of the blue.

BANG!

It was as if time itself stood still. The unexpected discharge shattered the fragile silence and reverberated throughout the building. All eyes turned to Goughey who had accidentally pulled the trigger, firing his anti-tank rifle. I turned back to look out of the corner of the window in the unrealistic hope that the two Germans had not heard his gun go off. Some hope. It was as if the whole world had suddenly gone into ultra slow motion. If they had been deaf and had not already heard the initial explosive ignition of the small ballistic missile, they could not fail to be alerted as Goughey's shell 'pinged' and bounced off the tank's armour plating. Momentarily, both Germans looked at the front of the building before, almost simultaneously, throwing their unfinished cigarettes to the ground and jumping back on board their vehicle. The driver had already sunk back to the controls and the tank's engines exploded into life. It jerked forward unsteadily, turned and raced back down the drive, disappearing behind a cloud of exhaust, dust and gravel.

"GOUGH!", screamed the Sergeant, "What the f*** did you do that for, you bloody idiot." He could barely contain his understandable anger as the Major came running down the marble staircase.

"Sorry, old mate, it just went off," was his simple but honest answer. If it hadn't been so serious, I would have died laughing.

"Sergeant!" the irate NCO bellowed, "call me bloody SERGEANT! I am not your old mate. Do you hear me, do you understand you useless, incompetent..."

"Sorry, old mate, sorry... I mean ..." Goughey stuttered and never finished the sentence.

"Blimey Sarge, look at this, there's another Jerry tank heading this way," shouted Stoker, one of our platoon members. Now everything ran in 'fast forward'. The Major moved to look. Sure enough, the tank was now heading through the gates, where it jolted to a halt on the gravel drive. By now, most were just watching the drama unfold.

"Sergeant," bellowed the Major, "Get the men down and out the back... NOW!"

"Sir", he shouted, racing up the stairs shouting orders as he went to the dumbstruck men.

Goughey's mouth fell open. He looked bemused as I rushed to my window by the door. What I saw next sent my sphincter into spasms. The tank, having retreated some fifty yards, came to a halt. Slowly and mechanically the tank's turret swung round and lowered its powerful barrel. It looked to be pointing directly at me.

"Shit! I cried, "they're going to fire!"

I threw myself on the marble floor and covered the back of my neck with my hands as I felt the chill of the stones against my cheeks. I assumed that everybody had followed suit, except for the one person that I could not take my eyes off - Goughey. He just stood to the side of the front door, waiting for the message to sink in.

BOOOOOOOOOOOOOM!...

The explosive ignition reverberated through my ears as the tremendous blast caused the main door to splinter into a thousand pieces. The noise was deafening in the confines of the cavernous marble hall. I cowered and felt wooden debris falling on top of me. I looked up, coughing from the dust that filled the foyer. Where the door had stood a few moments ago, scattered wood and wreckage littered the hall. Unbelievably, the shell had not exploded on impact with the door but had simply atomised the upper section, pushing the heavy table back a pace or two. The shell had hurtled down the empty corridor, travelling the full width of the château, before bursting through the rear glass doorway and exploding in the relative safety of the garden beyond.

I turned to see our lovable Goughey, still prostrate on the table, somewhat overwhelmed. His hair and face was covered in dust and fragments. Miraculously, he appeared to have escaped unscathed as the shell had flown over him. If he had been sitting up, the shell would have taken his head off.

"Right, everyone out the back NOW!" bellowed the Major.

We didn't need telling twice. Dear old Goughey swung his ungainly legs off the table and seized his heavy rifle. To the thunderous sound of two-hundred metal-studded boots smashing into wooden flooring and flagstones, we evacuated the building in seconds, through the now open rear doorway. And how we ran. We made for the protection of the nearby trees and huge shrubs where we were able to disappear from immediate view. We did not stop until we were well clear of the château. Thankfully, without infantry support, the Germans were unable to follow, so for now, we were safe.

· · · § · · ·

~ SECOND ENGAGEMENT ~

With the château incident literally behind us, we pressed on and finally arrived at an isolated road junction, somewhere near a fuel depot. Apparently, this had always been our objective but God knows how we had found it. Our platoon was placed in a commanding position on the brow of a small hill overlooking the junction, with the cover of thick woods behind us. The remainder of the company was dispersed accordingly. We got stuck in, digging our defensive trenches whilst the Sergeant did the rounds, inspecting our handywork. From behind, I heard him.

"You digging that pit for a hippo, private? Didn't they train you to dig a bloody trench?"

In view of our training, I couldn't help but laugh at the irony

"Deep and narrow son, deep and narrow." He spoke softly but with absolute authority and walked on.

After posting guards we settled down. With the platoon well dug in, our Sergeant did the rounds once more to examine our defences, telling us to place logs and bushes on the ground in front for additional camouflage and cover. His name was Sergeant Hawkes. I had a growing respect for this old soldier.

Despite the hot day, temperatures plummeted under the clear night sky. I tried to sleep curled up on my groundsheet, wrapped in my greatcoat. It proved to be an uncomfortable experience. When it was my turn for guard duty, I draped my groundsheet tightly round me like a cloak for additional warmth. Although it wasn't a full moon, the cloudless sky allowed enough light to illuminate the countryside. With my borrowed rifle at the ready, I kept watch on the valley below for any signs of movement and soon found myself chuckling as I recalled poor old Goughey's calamitous *faux pas*. How lucky we were to have escaped unscathed. If that tank shell had exploded in the hallway,... I brushed aside my dice with death.

The sudden screech of an owl focused my attention once more on my guard duties. A few minutes later, through a growing patch of mist in a hollow to my left, I caught sight of movement. I brought my rifle to bear down on the area in question, straining my eyes but whatever it was had stopped dead. An eerie scream filled the night air and the object moved forward, clear of the early morning mist. It stopped and screamed once more, craning its head forward. Bloody fox. I smiled and relaxed once more.

Night gave way to the new dawn and I was alerted to activity in the pale, misty fields below. Quietly, I informed the others on either side. Slowly advancing across the dew-covered meadow before us, a column of a hundred or so German soldiers emerged from the milky blur, heading directly towards us. They were still some way in the distance but not far enough for my liking. However, this was not what the Major had envisaged, for the Germans were meant to be using the road, where our ambush would have maximum effect.

They moved forward in small groups in a wide spread, perfectly trained and looking every part the effective soldiers that they surely were. As they progressed, I saw two men laying cables behind, presumably for their field radios. Momentarily, I was spellbound, as though watching a documentary in the cinema, a film unfolding like clockwork before me, with text book efficiency. I felt strangely divorced from the reality of the impending action.

New orders were passed along our line from mouth to mouth. We were to wait for the Germans to come closer. I handed back the rifle and checked my Bren gun, releasing the safety catch as quietly as I could, almost afraid to breathe for fear of alerting the enemy. Meanwhile, Josh, my newly appointed number two, opened the ammunition boxes and retrieved a few additional magazines in readiness. Now we waited. All I could hear was my thumping heart, working overtime. I fumbled in my pocket for my cigarettes in the hope that one would steady my nerves, placed it in my mouth and passed another to my number two. Just then, a stone landed in our trench. I looked up to see Sergeant Hawkes scowling at me. He raised his two fingers to his lips and shook his head, indicating that there was to be no smoking. I timidly replaced the cigarette and returned the packet to my pocket whilst Josh stuck his behind his ear for a later date. In the cold, clear morning air, I supposed that even a single puff of white tobacco smoke would relay our hidden position to a watchful enemy. How ill trained we were for this deadly task.

I could clearly make out an Officer below, field glasses in hand, scanning the gentle hill ahead. Our hill. In spite of our camouflage cover, we had been spotted. He pointed and orders were given and the enemy prepared for action. They had come as close as was prudent and were forming themselves into battle formation. Light field artillery and mortars were brought forward and trained on us. Within seconds, they had commenced their bombardment. The order came to return fire and the sharp crackle of rifles spitting lead filled our ears. I immediately fired off two magazines but the distance was too great to do any real damage. In the back of my mind was the realisation that I had to conserve my ammunition as it was unlikely to be replenished any time soon, for at that moment we were operating as an isolated group.

The German mortars were beginning to find their range. Further over on my left, another section was dug in. They received two direct hits, at which point our Officer decided that for us untrained troops to remain in our present positions, facing artillery, would be suicidal as we had no means of either defending ourselves or destroying them. We were ordered to fall back into the cover of the woods behind and then to peel off to the side.

Josh stuck to me like glue. He was burdened with heavy ammunition cases as we cleared the edge of the wood and entered the field beyond. At first glance it looked clear of the enemy so we all made a dash for it. We were crossing open ground, making for the next thicket of cover, when a shell burst just behind me. I heard the explosion and then a cry. I instinctively ducked and momentarily stumbled before regaining my balance and turned to see that Josh was down. Hit by the blast, he never stood a chance, lying where he fell, silent and motionless. What remained of his right leg had come to rest three feet from his body, whilst the other lifeless limb clung to its host by the threads of his trousers. More shells were bursting all around and small arms fire was beginning to crackle away. For a second or two, my mind was in turmoil as I stared at his still and bloody body. He was surely dead and if not, soon would be through loss of blood. Another explosion shook the earth. I turned away and just kept running, following the others to escape the bombardment, leaving what was left of Josh where he lay. I made it to the cover of the next clump of trees. The eight or nine of us threw ourselves to the ground before quickly re-grouping and continuing.

I had survived. Unfortunately, Josh hadn't. Not only had I lost him but most of my ammunition as well. He had certainly died instantly, or so I wanted to believe, becoming yet another statistic of war. I could not face the thought that I had left him for dead. I had only known him a few days since leaving Abancourt and I didn't even know his surname.

It took us over three hours, taking a wide circular route behind the hill for several miles before linking up with the Major and the rest of the company. They too were retreating ahead of the German advance. I would have liked to boast that our navigational skills had resulted in us finding them again but no, it was sheer luck. On hearing our brief report, Major Carr seemed genuinely saddened at the loss of Josh. That evening, we were debriefed and the facts were recorded accordingly.

Our feet were beginning to suffer for the ground we had covered was, for the most part, wet, marshy bog land which had thoroughly soaked our boots. Painful blisters had already formed.

~ 14th May ~

The following morning, a new number two was appointed to me, Private Fred Hammond. I took an instant liking to him. In addition, some much needed ammunition was found.

We had only been on the move for a few minutes when we became aware of heavy armour. We heard the metallic clatter of their tracks before actually seeing them. To our great relief, they were French. I could only liken them to great lumbering dinosaurs. Black clouds of diesel belched from their backsides. Their guns looked powerful enough but they seemed incapable of anything that resembled speed. Instead, they trundled along the road at a brisk walking pace, causing us to cough wildly as they slowly passed us by. I had no idea what they were doing. I watched as they thundered up the road, only to return some time later. None of us ever saw or heard them engaging the enemy.

By now, the skies above seemed to be dominated by German fighters and bombers. I could see neither French nor allied planes. We either didn't have any, there simply were not enough and otherwise occupied on missions elsewhere or they had been destroyed. The Germans seemed free to swoop down as and when they saw fit, strafing the roads and bombing any activity that they deemed a target.

Unfortunately, the roads were fast filling with civilians, often headed in the opposite direction to us, further hindering our movements. The German Luftwaffe seemed to regard these civilians as legitimate targets too, which was indefensible. More often than not, our platoon kept off the roads as much as we could, preferring to use the open fields and only walking the roads when there was no alternative, but the Luftwaffe ensured that we spent a lot of time diving into the roadside ditches. Fortunately, we lost no more men.

~ GOODBYE FRED ~

We entered a small French village. It was deserted, the occupants having wisely fled from the advancing Germans. We took up defensive positions using the empty buildings for cover. We were not privy as to whether the order came down from on high or was the sole decision of the Major but to find ourselves under the protection of these buildings was an unaccustomed luxury for us. The houses did not appear to have been looted and inside was relatively clean and orderly. However, all that was about to change.

Hawksey distributed us throughout the buildings. Fred and I took up a position in one of the upper bedrooms with a commanding view over the countryside behind the house. I dragged a table over to the window and positioned my Bren gun accordingly whilst Fred got a few magazines from the ammo box. We were as ready as we could ever be.

Every so often, our motherly Sergeant Hawkes did the rounds to check on us. Fred and I didn't have the slightest notion as to where the Germans were, so I thought it best to say something.

"Sergeant, which way will the Germans come?"

"That way son, that way," smiling and pointed out through the window, "but they may decide not to play by our rules, so if they don't then you just tell the referee, 'cos that just ain't British son, ain't British at all!" God, if only life was that simple.

We watched, waited, chatted and smoked and, if we thought about it long enough, terrified ourselves with thoughts of our next encounter. Fred was a young, inexperienced recruit just like me. He insisted on telling me everything there was to tell about himself, and despite our British reserve a friendship rapidly developed.

Without any warning a small group of German infantry, probably a reconnaissance party, advanced towards us, as had been predicted. The casual manner of their approach suggested they were unaware of our presence. As they had done the decent thing and arrived from the correct direction, we were able to engage them and play the deadly game of battle. Having waited until they were well within range, someone fired the first shot, allowing us to commence rapid fire. The surprised enemy responded in kind and still advanced but when my Bren gun opened up, they fell to ground. I was firing in intermittent bursts, five or so rounds a time, having no idea if I was on target or not until they made a hasty retreat. I counted five bodies as they withdrew back from whence they came. Both Fred and I felt relieved, elated even at having driven them back. He slapped me enthusiastically on the back.

"Well done Dennis, that's the way to do it," he laughed.

Our little victory was celebrated with a cigarette whilst retrieving the spent magazines and reloading them. Each magazine was designed to hold 28 rounds of .303 calibre ammunition. However, if you insisted on cramming the full number into the magazine they were very likely to jam the gun. To avoid this potentially lethal malfunction we always under-loaded or removed a couple of rounds from those already prepared.

We waited until mid-afternoon for the German return. Field artillery opened up and unfortunately, the accuracy of their gunners was excellent. Our building took an immediate direct hit, smashing into the window's lintel and causing an ear-shattering explosion right above our heads. The noise was unbelievable as shrapnel and debris rained down on us. For a brief moment I was in shock. It took a few seconds for me to realise what had happened.

I was still alive and remarkably unscathed.

With the help of my helmet, I had survived once more. I coughed heavily, my lungs filled with masonry dust and cordite as I staggered back away from the hole in the wall. As soon as the smoke cleared, I saw Fred. He was lying face up on the floor behind me having been seriously wounded in the forehead by a lump of flying masonry and propelled back into the rear of the room. His face was white from the dust which made his open bloody wound appear horrendous. He was in a terrible state. Initially I believed he was dead, but when I found his pulse I discovered that his heart was still beating. I made him as comfortable as possible, pulled out a field dressing and bandaged over the grievous wound on his forehead, just above his eyes. Before I had time to finish nursing him, the firing recommenced. The German infantry had returned. I rushed back to the window and recovered my Bren gun. It too was covered in debris but appeared undamaged. I picked it up and hurriedly positioned myself behind the pile of rubble on the bedroom floor and commenced fire on the advancing line.

All the while, the artillery continued with its deadly work.

The exchange of gunfire persisted for the next hour whilst I ran from house to house trying to avoid the accurate shelling and secure a safer firing position. As evening approached, the fighting gradually subsided and the order came for our platoon to withdraw. By now, we were managing to do this quite well. Those of us still alive were in full agreement, for to stay much longer would be suicidal as it was only a matter of time before tanks would be called in to clear us out.

Before I could leave, I had something to do. I returned to the house where Fred had been injured. He lay there barely alive and I was convinced he would not survive the night. With the assistance of another, we gently picked him up and carried him down into the cellar of a nearby house. Others gathered, bringing with them the seriously wounded from our company, those considered too ill to evacuate. This was common practice when cellars were available, offering the injured at least some protection from the fighting above ground in the hope that later they might be found by our own side or, if not, by the enemy as they passed through.

However, such actions were always fraught with danger, especially if the German troops were anything like us. Amongst our limited arsenal, we possessed one type of weapon in abundance. Grenades, crates full of them. Any soldier who was given the unenviable order to clear a building of enemy troops would usually throw a grenade or two into the cellars. It was easier and certainly safer to do so than risk your life by entering them, but obviously this was a murderous policy for any occupants, be they soldiers or, regrettably, civilians.

I felt dreadful as I now had to abandon Fred and leave him to his fate. As I climbed the steps back to the ground floor, I thought that was the last I would ever see of him. It also occurred to me that being my number two carried with it a high risk of death!

After the war I was stationed at Shorncliff for a short while, waiting to be demobbed. One morning, I was given a message by one of the guards that I was wanted at the gate house. I hurried down and, to my great surprise and delight, Fred Hammond was there waiting for me, accompanied by a St. Dunstan Nurse. He was blind in both eyes, a tragic legacy of that explosion. The medical staff had patched him up but couldn't save his eyesight. The scars were all too apparent but he was surprisingly well, considering. I requested and was given permission to take the rest of the day off, so Fred and I headed off into town. He seemed to have plenty of money on him and had mastered the art of identifying his notes. By using his fingers as a rule, he placed each note width-ways between his digits and measured how wide they were against the first two, thereby gauging its denomination – the shortest being a ten bob note, the largest a pound. It was marvellous to see that he was adapting.

We soon found a pub, and over a pint or two he related his tale.

We had been relatively near the French/Belgian border at the time of the engagement. As we pulled out that evening, some of the villagers came back to their houses. When he and the other wounded were found, they were taken on to Brussels and ended up at a military hospital, The Berkendael Institute, where the famous nurse Edith Cavell had worked during the First World War. It later became a Red Cross hospital where they nursed both allied and German wounded. After a considerable time spent there under the care of the conquering Germans, Fred was transferred to a PoW camp before finally being repatriated with the assistance of the Swiss and the Red Cross. Given his injuries, his survival was nothing short of a miracle.

~ BRITISH TO THE CORE ~

We spent the night at a farm where we were fed by the owner, which was fortunate for we were ravenous and only had our emergency rations left. Supplies of food in any war zone can be a problem. Our lines of communication and supply had already reached breaking point. All around, there was an abundance of farms and villages that must have been stocked with food, but such was the discipline of our British Army that it was strictly forbidden for any Officer or NCO to sanction the wholesale theft or looting of supplies, even if we were starving. In these circumstances, our Officers would pay for the food with battalion cash. A few days earlier, one of our Officers had to organise a whip round amongst the men for some francs to enable him to legitimately buy our bread, but somehow I couldn't imagine the enemy being burdened with such qualms. To shop like this in a war situation struck me as being far too civilised and somewhat surreal.

By now it was generally accepted that we were incapable of effectively engaging the enemy and our rather disorganised retreat was gathering pace. The Major had somehow acquired transportation for our return journey back to the battalion in relative luxury. They were still encamped at Abancourt, on the other side of the

Somme. As we hurtled along the road, five British tanks passed us going in the opposite direction, if you could call them tanks. They were known as whippet tanks, being lightly armed with a machine gun mounted on the turret. They had minimal armour plating, which allowed any panzers to turn them into scrap metal with ease.

During our long and often arduous drive we passed through village after village still occupied by hearty or foolish French civilians, reluctant to desert their homes. We were no longer greeted by shouts of "Vive l'anglais!" I could not understand why they now chose to spit on us as we passed, screaming insults.

"English pigs!" they shouted.

Was it possible they knew that they were already defeated and that Britain was about to desert them and abandon them to their fate? How circumstances and attitudes had changed in only a matter of days.

~ CHRISTMAS COMES EARLY ~
FRENCH AERODROME
15th May

After days of seemingly aimless marching across the French countryside, our weary feet appreciated the drive. Occasionally, we could hear the distant thunder of war, but we remained unscathed. As we journeyed, we chatted freely and enjoyed endless cigarettes as we peered out through the open flaps of the canvas-covered truck as civilian traffic hurriedly passed by in all directions.

Still believing that we were to return to the battalion, I was surprised when we swung off the main road and drove up to a French military airfield, at Cambria-Epinoy. Along with my platoon, I was ordered out and told to exchange my Bren gun for a rifle. As the trucks drove off, Sergeant Hawkes made contact with the Armée de l'Air (French Air Force) authorities. Before long, he returned and proceeded to outline our objective in the briefest of terms - we were simply there to guard the airstrip.

Immediately, we set about digging in around the perimeter. The airfield was very active, and over the next two days we watched as a Groupe de Chasse (Fighter Group) of Dewoitine D.500 and Bloch MB.150 fighter aircraft came and went, supposedly to engage with the common enemy. The anti-aircraft guns dotted around the perimeter never saw action as the airfield itself wasn't attacked whilst we were there, which pleased us all.

For the next two days, we simply enjoyed the peace and quiet, catching up with our overdue ablutions, nursing our feet and soaking up the warmth of the French spring. But the distant, thunderous explosive sounds were a constant reminder of a war that was never far from us.

There was one particular aspect of our new posting that really did appeal to us. When off duty, we ate in the canteen with the French and whilst on guard duty they brought us food in our perimeter dugouts. Our diet had improved tremendously in both quality and quantity, courtesy of the Armée de l'Air, the best we had eaten since joining the Army, but that wasn't difficult.

Between meals, we had time to roll up our sleeves, sunbathe and relax. As a consequence of this 'soft living', our spirits soared, much like the aircraft that went into battle each morning. At the end of each day however, I was saddened as we counted in fewer and fewer returning planes. They were obviously taking a terrible hammering from the Luftwaffe. After the last sortie of the third day, I heard the now familiar drone of a lone fighter engine. It was the first of the returning Groupe de Chasse. As it neared, I could hear the splattering and coughing of the engine and saw a grey line of oily smoke trailing behind. A siren was sounded and a fire-tender and ambulance sprang into action, heading towards the runway. With some difficulty, the shell-riddled fighter bounced and screeched along the concrete before coming to a tortured halt. During flight the wind had suppressed the fire, but at standstill the single engine burst into flames as the firemen raced towards it. The pilot could clearly be seen struggling in his cockpit as flames began to lick against the half-open canopy. He must have been terrified. Miraculously and in time, a brave firemen risked his life and clambered up onto the wing. After frantic efforts, he managed to release the hood and drag the pilot out whilst others dealt with the encroaching fire. Both must have suffered serious burns.

Of the twelve fighters that left just a short while ago, only three came back, all peppered with cannon. They were no longer a viable fighter squadron. The last two aircraft to return refuelled with some urgency and took off once more, never to return. I muttered a silent prayer and wished them God speed, hoping that they were not shot from the skies.

Shortly afterwards, French trucks and vehicles of all descriptions left the airfield in convoys until finally we were once more alone. For once this was no bad thing, for in their haste to leave the French left considerable quantities of supplies. We now had food in abundance along with cigarettes in their thousands, more than enough to guarantee a lifetime of lung disease. As for us, we were like children in an abandoned sweet shop. Quickly, we emptied our packs of what we considered to be unnecessary items. Summer was upon us and it was hot so I, for one, discarded my greatcoat. Officers and senior NCOs were nowhere to be seen to berate us for committing such heinous crimes, so bugger the consequences. Others did the same, without a thought as to their possible use sometime in the uncertain future. We all knew that our existence was far from certain but we assumed that we would all be back in England by the time summer turned to autumn. Our only thoughts were of our immediate, more basic needs and invariably they were for food and ciggies (but not necessarily in that order). By the time we had finished, our packs were bulging. Christmas had come early this year and we were loving it.

At dusk, as if from nowhere, a 30 cwt. British Army truck arrived with instructions for us to return to Abancourt. Hawksey gave the order and we piled in, sure in the knowledge that with our back-packs filled, we could now eat and smoke ourselves silly over the coming days.

~ TURN AND TURN, AGAIN ~
17th May 1940

It was the night of 17th May 1940 when we arrived back at Abancourt camp. We were lucky to have made it for, if the rumours were anything to go by, the surrounding countryside was crawling with isolated packs of fast-moving German panzers. Most of the battalion were sleeping and had been doing so for a couple of hours as our trucks came to a halt. We had only just climbed out when the chilled night's silence was rudely interrupted by the battalion's bugler. As they had all been trained to do, bleary-eyed men staggered forward to gather on the parade ground. My old friend, Bert Laws from Nottingham, was in HQ Company, like me. Briefly, we greeted each other before forming up into our separate platoons. We were given just twenty minutes to get ready to leave with full kit and equipment.

113

With apprehension knotting my stomach, we were on the move once more with no idea as to where we were going. Whilst Officers and men hurried by, we joined the queue to be re-issued with emergency food rations, field dressings and our promised fifty rounds of precious .303 ammunition. But when it came to my turn, my rifle was taken from me and I was issued with a brand new Bren gun, along with a new number two to carry my ammunition and reload my gun. I couldn't help but wonder how long his life expectancy would be now. We were appointed to what was comically known as 'The Bren Gun Carrier Platoon', despite the distinct lack of 'carriers'. However, those in command didn't seem to worry about such trivialities. All this new equipment and sudden movement made me conclude that things were grave. Instead of going home as we hoped, it was obvious we must be destined for battle. It wasn't only my battalion leaving, the whole camp was on the move, including our fellows from the 2nd/6th Battalion of The Queen's and other regiments. When I saw our combined numbers preparing for the off, standing neatly en masse, I felt a wonderful sense of pride and quiet exhilaration at our impending departure. Impressed by our sheer weight of numbers and cocooned within this throng of brothers in arms, I felt encouraged and safe. After all, I was no longer a naive young recruit having just experienced three days of armed conflict.

Thankfully, I was still blissfully unaware of the vast and unstoppable German war machine that was heading our way.

Waiting impatiently, we talked incessantly amongst ourselves. I looked over the heads of others. Bert caught my eye so we moved closer. He too was part of HQ company.

"Good to see you again. Have you heard anything?"

"Well me and Girling have just been talking about what to do next, so I gave him my advice,... to send me home as a runner."

We both laughed.

"I haven't a clue where we've been these last few days. Traipsing all over the place like headless chicks."

"Same here mate. I felt like a target at the fair with Jerry taking pot shots."

"Rumour has it that we are all going home."

"Hmm!" I replied, "let's hope it's true and not just wishful thinking."

"We didn't stand our ground once,... just turned and ran I'm glad to say. What the hell are we doing here anyway?"

"Good question!"

"Didn't some buggering Officer tell us we were only here to continue with out training?"

I was sure that every other soldier with me that night was filled with differing degrees of trepidation, although we did our utmost to hide it. Even though we were standing outside in the open air, warm and fresh, the gentle night breeze was filled with the sweet smell of tobacco as a thousand cigarettes lit up the night sky. I wouldn't have been surprised if an Officer had screamed at us to observe the blackout.

Shortly after midnight, with adrenaline surging through my veins, I took my position amongst the several thousand men from both battalions and marched out of camp to the town's railway station. We were on our way. Although deprived of sleep since arriving back at camp, I had at least managed to doze in the truck.

We arrived far too early at the station and had to wait until morning for the train to arrive. An assortment of Officers stood about on the platform but then somebody pointed out that our Commanding Officer, Lieutenant Colonel Girling *(see picture reference 16)*, was amongst them, also waiting to board. His dark, sunken eyes and moustache made him an instantly recognisable figure.

At 9am precisely, the train departed.

As soon as I was able, I made myself comfortable and slept as best I could. As soldiers, we had all learnt to grab forty winks whenever the opportunity presented itself.

Around 1pm, our train pulled into the town of Abbeville, wheels screeching on rails of tarnished iron. However, we didn't disembark but waited as Officers hurried back and forth from the station buildings, seemingly without purpose. Meanwhile the locomotive hissed with impatience and huffed in protest, waiting for those at the upper end of the chain of command to voice their orders and animate the driver and his charge. At this point, it appeared that all communications with HQ (wherever they were) were non existent or that intelligence was so out of date due to the lightning speed of the German advance, that confusion reigned supreme. Finally, a decision was taken. Everybody climbed back on board and the train's heavy wheels skidded as if on ice before finding some sort of purchase and gradually pulling its massive weight out of Abbeville.

Our journey grew increasingly tedious and my stomach began to growl in protest as we trudged through the French countryside at an urgent pace. The repetitive clatter of wheels on rail gaps and the rhythmic flashing of the sun's rays through the overhanging trees had a soporific effect, sending me into a trance-like state. I dozed off once more and dreamt of home and soft apple blossom.

The 60 mile journey was completed without stops and we pulled into the town of Lens, gliding to a halt under a huge metal and glass roof, reminiscent of London Waterloo. I was impatient to leave the confines of the train and stretch my legs and hopefully feed my complaining stomach, for I was famished. As was usual, the Officers alighted first. With a cigarette hanging from my mouth, I waited by an open window for the order to disembark; by now fresh air was at a premium inside the smoke-filled carriage.

That's when I heard the noise.

Instantly I knew what it was but I didn't know whose it was until we heard the tone and change in the aircraft's pitch, just before pandemonium erupted. Accompanied by the unmistakable whine, the Stuka swooped down from the hidden skies towards our stationary train. Instinctively I ducked, as we all did, trying to burrow down onto the floor of the carriage. Bodies fell onto each other, including mine, as I heard and felt the vibrations of the first explosions. There may have been two aircraft, but I couldn't be certain. Having dropped what bombs they had, they turned for a second run. This time, they strafed the train itself, sending a hail of cannon shells hurtling earthwards towards us. The loud implosive sound of shattering glass filled my ears, followed by tinkling shards of glass as they cascaded down followed by the explosive impact of the larger panes, shattering into a million splinters as what remained of the glass roof finally came into deafening contact with the platform below.

As quickly as it began, the attack was over and silence returned once more. Gradually we stood up and somebody began to laugh, which had the effect of lightening the tension a little. Without awaiting further orders, most of us automatically jumped off the train to confirm what had happened, see the damage and to be free of our enclosed mobile coffin. The bombs had avoided the train completely, landing amongst the station buildings. However, some of the carriages at the front and back had been hit by cannon fire from the aircraft. By sheer luck, my battalion was allocated the middle of the train. The 2nd/6th Battalion were in the front and rear sections that had taken the brunt of the attack. I could only stand and watch as their casualties were carried from the war damaged carriages. Those still on board were ordered to disembark immediately and form up outside to await further orders, which were not immediately forthcoming. By now I was ravenous, but I had managed to find and retrieve my back pack, which was still stuffed with French Air Force booty. I opened a tin and tucked in. It's funny how, after a spell of danger, the basic needs to eat and smoke completely overwhelm you. More generally, rations were eventually found from somewhere and distributed, after which a thousand cigarettes were lit.

Whilst we ate, an inspection of the train was made. When it was deemed to be rail worthy, we received orders to return, not all the way back to Abancourt, but to a station that we had already passed through, Abbeville. It appeared that Military Intelligence was at work again! Someone had got their wires crossed and we should not have journeyed to Lens in the first place. I could not help but remember the old adage - 'the left hand doesn't f***ing know what the right hand's doing'.

I grabbed a seat quickly this time, sat back again and tried to relax and at the same time pray that the bombers would not return for another turkey shoot. We waited until midnight for the train to pull out of what remained of Lens station. By travelling under cover of darkness we prayed that the German pilots would all be tucked up in their beds.

The line of carriages eventually shuddered into motion. The first part of the journey back took almost four hours and I awoke to the now familiar sound of metal on metal as we screeched to a halt on the outskirts of a town, just before dawn. Foolishly believing that finally we were about to get off this damn train, I was sadly disappointed. In the near distance came the sound of explosions. The town was under attack from German bombers.

"Bloody hell, not again," someone shouted, "the bombers must have followed me here."

"That bastard Hitler's got it in for me!"

We responded with nervous laughter, half expecting to be targeted at any minute.

I looked out through the window and saw the name painted on a board and remembered my father once talking about this place, the town of Arras. He had been here at the end of the First World War when hardly a building had been left standing, such was the destructive power of persistent German and Allied bombardments.

The town fell into enemy hands, only to be captured and recaptured time and time again. Having been rebuilt, this once historic medieval town was being destroyed once more. What a bloody waste!

As we waited for the attack to finish, we watched the sunrise before moving off.

Once through Arras, we continued throughout that long day with an occasional brief stop here and there. Just as the sun readied itself to set in the colourful evening sky, our train came to a grinding halt in the middle of 'F...knowswhere'. Surrounded by fields and woodland, the order was given to disembark. With no platform, we jumped from the carriage with full kit. Well over a thousand of us stood down alongside the train. We had stopped at a road/rail crossing. All around in the half light was peace and tranquillity as birds hurried themselves to their resting places before nightfall. The air was pleasantly warm as we formed up into columns and marched off in near darkness. But to where?

At times, our progress was hindered as we passed through lines of desperate refugees on their way to anywhere. After an hour, we came upon the village of Vauchelles-Les-Quesnoy, just to the east of Abbeville, in total darkness. A halt was called and we were split into small sections and ordered into whatever buildings could be procured from their civilian owners and told to grab some sleep. The accommodation was just a roof over our heads, but that was enough. We had food, cigarettes and each other, were in a relatively quiet war zone and alive, so after the recent traumas, I was happy. We might not have slept at all had we known that just a few miles away, the German 6th Panzer Division had taken Doullens.

I didn't even have time to sink into my dream! We were woken even before the evasive dawn. All was utter chaos and confusion. From what I could gleam, all of the 2/5th as well as the 2/6th and 2/7th battalions were here in the immediate area. For a fact, we were the worst armed in the whole division having only 3 Bren guns and 5 rather pathetic anti-tank rifles in each battalion and still using First World War .303 rifles. And now we were preparing to engage the enemy? It beggared belief.

Orders were barked, officers and men ran - headless chickens sprang to mind as thousands of us prepared to move. Some headed east towards Ballencourt, whilst others went south towards the Somme and west towards Abbeville.

You could taste the panic.

THE BRIDGES OF ABBEVILLE

Daybreak, 20th May 1940

mongst our company of odds and sods from all walks of life was an older, regular soldier whom I liked and admired for he was fair, trustworthy and knowledgeable, almost a father figure. He name was Sergeant Hawkes, aka Hawksey, whom I have already mentioned. Because of his presence, I felt less scared for our immediate future.

Along with others of HQ Company, our Carrier Platoon and one other received fresh orders, to rapidly move west into Abbeville. I was in 1st Platoon commanded by 2nd Lieutenant Mumford and Sergeant Hawkes. Sergeant Hooper was in command of 2nd Platoon. Together, we were Freddy Laws, Herby Davies, dear old Goughy, Tommy Grigg, Charlie Turner, Arthur Fullerton and two Londoners; Norman Shearsmith and Bill Westaway, Norman Tidey from Cuckfield, Alfie Day and Jeff Hatch both from my village of Hersham, Bobby Underwood and Alfie Smithers from nearby Chertsey, Phil Luscombe from Devon, Lewin Smart from Wandsworth, Ronny Drayton from Newmarket, Ivor Gumbrell, Johnny Hamon, Tommy Read, Charlie Lloyd, C. Payne, Loche, Timmy Jakeman, Day. Then Reggy Prowse, Ernie Francere, Stan Dukes, Sid Laver and Norman Gosling, all from Southampton, Charley Jago and Gerald Gear from Salisbury, Charlie Head from Brighton and a few others making a total of thirty-eight. An Officer had miraculously managed to commandeer an army truck, so although cramped, we travelled in relative luxury.

The strategic importance of Abbeville was that it had several bridges over the River Somme and was the last major town before reaching the English Channel. Our instructions were to hold two central bridges, one on the Doullens road and the next bridge to the north against capture or destruction by advancing Germans, thereby enabling thousands of French and allied troops to retreat across the Somme to the perceived safety of their lines north of the Somme. We were to set up defensive positions on and around the bridgehead. The German High Command were equally anxious to seize as many of these bridges as possible from allied control before the Allies had time to destroy them and thereby halt the German advance. Both sides had a vested interest in our crossing points.

Daybreak threatened on the horizon as we reached the outskirts of Abbeville, right in the middle of a heavy bombardment. The defence of the town was being seriously tested by the Luftwaffe. Over the noise of our truck's engine we could hear the sound of the Junkers bombers circling above, unleashing their cargo of death on the defenders below. The Germans seemed to have unhindered command of the air. My stomach was already in knots and as I scanned our group of nervous warriors, their faces did nothing to calm my nerves for I saw through their jokes and forced smiles. Needing a change of scenery, I stood up to look out through the gap above the lorry's cabin. I saw it before hearing the unmistakable whine, a German Ju-87 Sturzkampfflugzeug flying low, following the line of our road as it rapidly headed straight towards us. The vision of death screaming closer was neatly framed by the truck's canvas. It was as though I was watching a slow motion movie at my local cinema, 'The Palace' in Walton. The pilot couldn't possibly reduce his altitude anymore because of the close proximity of the houses on either side of the road.

And then his cannons opened fire, spitting their lethal hail of death towards us. Without warning, our driver swerved and slammed on the brakes, screeching to an abrupt halt a quarter of a mile or so before the bridge, with the driver shouting frantically.

"Get out!" he bellowed at the top of his voice.

As the truck began a frantic turn on a sixpence, we fell out onto the road. By the grace of God alone, we somehow avoided the cannon shells by a whisker as they peppered the canvas cover of our lorry before hitting the road below sending shattered cobble stones flying skywards. We dropped into the cover of the doorways of the houses and shops on both sides of the road. Our driver didn't hang around and the next thing I saw was our truck racing off. Instead of waiting for us he disobeyed instructions and shot away, and with it our only fast means of returning to our battalion. His instinct for self-preservation was to be our undoing.

As soon as the air raid was over, we picked ourselves up and, led by Sergeant Hawkes, moved forward towards the river in search of our bridges. On arrival, we split into two sections. We remained where we were, whilst Bert and his platoon walked along the north bank to the adjacent bridge. Mumford and Hawkes quickly established our defensive positions. By this time and unbeknown to us, the whole BEF was almost encircled, with the German 12th Army to the north-east and the despondent French forces to the south retreating towards us, ahead of the 2nd Panzer-Division, poised to take Abbeville.

Within minutes, we were entrenched and for a brief moment on that sunny May morning, you would be forgiven for thinking that all was well with the world. As I looked down at the river, sunlight danced on the tranquil waters. As the Somme slowly meandered its way to the open sea some twenty miles to the north west, I was mesmerised by a pair of kingfishers diving for food. In that brief instant, I found it difficult to believe that we were in the middle of a war.

A shattering series of explosions redirected my attention. I positioned my Bren and left it pointing across the bridge towards the town and waited. It's funny what you focus on after staring down the barrel of your gun for an age. You can't help it, your mind wanders and you start to notice insignificant details in the landscape to alleviate the boredom. On the river bank opposite, a two-storey building stood to the left; its lower floor was at river level whilst its first floor door opened onto the road at bridge level. On its wall, an advert for Ripolin paint faced me. Above the name was a white silhouette of a man and some wording, but all I could read were the words 'création de' for a shell had burst through the wall and obliterated the first words, leaving a ragged, gaping hole in the loft space.

When the next air raid came, I looked up into the clear sky to witness the line of dive bombers dropping out of the blue towards us. Often, their clusters of six bombs would fall in their wake before exploding in quick succession. They were following the river on the north side, our side.

"Take cover lads, they will be wanting to hit us but leave those bloody bridges intact."

On Sergeant Hawkes' instructions, I grabbed my Bren gun and cowered behind a fallen tree trunk, praying. Whilst I and Bill Westaway (my new number two) sheltered on one side of the trunk, Hawkes hid on the other. He saw my confusion and popped his head over.

"It's to limit the odds of a total wipe out son,... if the bomb hits near to one side of this tree trunk, then only one of us will get it."
It made perfect sense, simple tactics taught to us by experienced regulars, priceless knowledge to us raw recruits.

"Count 'em in lads," he screamed above the whine of the planes.

"Count 'em in?... is he bloody mad, just tell me when they've pissed off," muttered Bill as he covered his neck with his hands and kissed the dirt.

As they fell, I froze. Frightened seems such an inadequate word to describe my feelings, a word more suited to a child's bad dream. I felt the first impact and started to count them,... two,... three,... four. They were coming our way. Five burst with deafening destruction, far too close for comfort. The ground beneath us reverberated. I knew there was one more to follow. I pushed my body into the ground itself and waited for lady luck to decide my fate. Bang on time, the sixth eruption occurred,... safely on the other side of me.

Up above, the dive bombers circled, banked sharply right and turned before heading back towards us, cannons blazing. Time to get our heads down again. The cannon shells followed the line of the bridge, pounding the cobbles but veering off towards us. They too failed to find their intended targets.

At the end of the raid I noticed old Sergeant Hawkes' face coming into view, looking at us from around the end of the tree trunk.

He laughed as though he hadn't a care in the world.

"Don't worry lads," he casually said, "I had heavier rain than this when I was in India."

Hawkes had served there before the war as a regular enlisted soldier. He had no idea how reassuring and comforting it was to have a figure of authority like him saying this to us, as young recruits. It helped us get through the bombardment. Such calm behaviour was inspirational. For the most part, the platoon was unharmed and still intact and, miraculously, so was our bridge. I felt strangely elated, happy even. We had survived another day.

As soon as the raid was over, I picked up my gun and repositioned myself, pointing the Bren's barrel across the bridge and down the main road directly into town.

"Bill, grab a few more magazines will you?"

He was new to this job. I thought it prudent to ask him a question.

"Have you ever fired or loaded a Bren before?"

"Well not since my christening,... of course I bloody haven't,... can't tell one end from the other."

"Hmmm! Now's a good time to learn."

So much for our less-than-perfect training. I gave him a quick demonstration and let him practise a few times. We were now as ready as we ever would be.

It was early afternoon as we listened to the discordant tumult of war creeping ever closer. Past the Ripolin building, I scanned the row of shops on the other side of the river. Within a few minutes, we all seemed to notice crouched figures creeping towards us, keeping in the shadows of the buildings and darting into doorways. German infantry were cautiously heading our way.

"Shit Den, I feel like a sitting duck."

I was too engrossed to reply.

There now followed one of the most thrilling moments of my army life. I had not felt like this since my first encounter with a gun, at my first job in 1934 when Tom Peacock, the armourer at Brooklands, allowed me to test those old Lewis machine guns. In my protected position and a target of troops before me, my mouth felt so dry. I carefully re-adjusted the sights of my Bren, lifted up the stock and tucked it well into my shoulder. My finger rested on the trigger whilst my other hand steadied the gun above the stock. I took careful aim and waited until I was sure that many of the Germans were in range. It was time.

I gently squeezed the trigger, opening fire with a long burst. As the first soldier fell, my targets jumped back against the wall. I continued firing, sweeping the street, first down the left-hand side and then up the right side. The shop windows exploded to the sound of splintering glass. Whoever and whatever got in my path was peppered with bullets. I released the whole magazine. Within seconds, Bill replaced my spent magazine and I continued to spray the road with death. It must have put the fear of Christ in them. Those not hit disappeared from view.

All too soon, my second magazine was empty and a third was inserted. I was ready. But just as suddenly as it had started, this particular skirmish ended without any return fire. It was quiet once more. As I scanned the scene ahead, I counted only four bodies in the road, but nobody standing. We waited a while. It seemed likely that the other Germans had left, hopefully believing that the bridge was too heavily protected to engage us without additional reinforcements. We left the safety of our positions and moved cautiously forward, watching for any signs of the enemy. There were none. We reached the first body slumped against the wall of a building, blood seeping from his chest wound. He was young, just doing his job, following orders,... just like us.

Although there were no signs of the other Germans, it was obviously unsafe to linger amongst the dead and damage of the surrounding shops so we hurriedly ran back to our positions. Another cigarette was needed and I noticed my hands shake as I struck the match. I felt both relieved that our brief clash was over for the time being and exhilarated.

We waited whilst Sergeant Hawkes checked for casualties amongst us. Our first cigarette was followed by a second.

"I tell you Dennis, this ain't good for my young nerves."

"Your nerves Bill?... just look at these!" I replied whilst offering up my outstretched hand, still shaking.

Between the intermittent explosions, acrid smoke and the angry crackle of timber filled the air as bombed buildings nearby were consumed, their flames reaching an intensity that would ignite adjoining buildings. Ethereal clouds of smoke and ash drifted across the road, blurring my vision.

An hour passed and still no sight of the enemy. Strange sounds drifted towards us. I nudged Bill, deep in the land of nod. As the minutes ticked by, the sound of boots on cobbles grew louder. Sergeant Hawkes ran from across the other side of the road and dropped down behind our log.

"Brace yourselves lads but hold fire till you can smell the sauerkraut."

Thirty seconds later, a column of troops turned a corner and came into view. After only days in action I had often regarded our own men's appearance as a bit rough, but one needed to witness this horde of sad humanity first hand to appreciate the look of despair and defeat on their faces. A wave of thousands were heading our way. They were an utter shambles, the walking dead. They carried few weapons, if any, most having been abandoned along the way. They were not British but allied troops. For some reason I had been expecting a smart and well presented French Division, marching in formation with rifles slung over their shoulders, still a recognisable fighting force. How wrong I was. Hawksey sprang up to confront the line that did not stop. He engaged one of their Officers and after the briefest of exchanges, he stood aside to allow the column to continue unhindered. A kaleidoscope of colours passed by, native French troops, colonial black and brown troops, Moroccan, and Senegalese with their bright blue-tailed jackets and loose-fitting pantaloons, topped with bright red turbans. If German snipers had been present they would have delighted in such clear targets.

This dejected rabble looked more like the civilian refugees we had seen on every road across northern France rather than a once proud fighting unit from the largest army in Europe. On the way they had obviously been looting from their own countrymen, for instead of weapons many were carrying a vast array of items. Some were so heavily burdened with booty they pushed hand carts to ease their efforts, whilst others used wheelbarrows and anything else they could muster. So much for discipline and the rules of war. They were thrown into mass panic as another bombardment began and aircraft screeched overhead. They ran, hopped and pushed onwards across our bridge. Nearly thirty minutes elapsed before the last man finally crossed to the south bank, heading out of town, over the last bridge to the rail yard beyond and onwards to the next French line of defence.

More bombs fell and shells pounded into the smouldering ruins as the gunners searched out the unscathed buildings of ancient Abbeville. Smoke choked my lungs. At that moment, the 2nd Platoon were making a dash along the riverside road towards us led by Sergeant Hooper, crouching low and dodging shrapnel. As soon as they arrived, Mumford did a roll call. Locke was missing and Mumford ordered Jakeman to follow him back to the bridge to search for him. Meanwhile Hawkes had heard and then seen a Panzer dash across a crossroads ahead whilst my eyes were drawn to movement downstream on the next bridge. Instantly I recognised the square helmets. I could see the column of infantry darting across the river.

Locke had taken refuge in a shelter and as soon as Mumford returned with him, he decided that our situation was untenable against the overwhelming and utter superiority of the enemy forces. To stay was to risk the certain death of our inexperienced untrained group. We had no instructions to blow the bridge, and without suitable explosives it was impossible to do so anyway. I watched as he and

Hawkes quickly discussed the situation. Our HQ, the battalion and hope lay some miles northwest, uncertainty and terror lay south. Reluctantly, they took the decision to abandon the bridge and to a man, we were only too pleased to leave.

"Right men, we are going to make a dash for it and try to get back the way we came to HQ," said Mumford, pointing with his outstretched arm. "Sergeant Hawkes and I will lead and Sergeant Hooper will guard our rear. We will halt at each road junction and assess the situation. Keep into the side of the building as we move. Keep low and watchful. Lets move out. If anybody gets separated, keep heading back following the Doullens Road but watch out for the enemy who may be advancing down or across that route into Abbeville. Good luck and let's go."

Quickly and quietly, we re-grouped and set off. We moved rapidly, following the cobbled road, aware that we might very well be travelling parallel with the German column who had just crossed the Somme or crossing the path of the Panzers. Hawkes relieved me of my Bren and exchanged it for his rifle and instructed me to carry the heavy boxes of ammunition with my number two. We threaded a stout pole through the handles of the boxes and lifted the dead weight between us before following.

Our progress was slowed by the earlier bombing raid, for many of the roads were blocked with debris. Soon we came across buildings ablaze. The flames were so fierce I felt that my face was on fire. Safe passage through the narrow street became impossible. Although Mumford was with us, Sergeant Hawkes seemed to be in overall command and instructed us all to go back in order for us to find an alternative route. Hurriedly, we set off in an easterly direction following the south-easterly course of the river. We were hampered by more burning buildings and two lorries burning fiercely hindered our desperate retreat.

The bombardment ceased as suddenly as it had begun and soon we were sharing the road with scores of frightened refugees, eager to escape before the bombers returned. It was difficult for our platoon to stay together whilst avoiding the crowds of mainly women, children and the elderly. The civilians were in a state of confusion, running in all directions. We passed a bloody scene where a bomb had recently detonated. Several bodies of women and children lay dead, their bodies still smouldering. Some were eager to learn where the Germans were and therefore avoid them but we could be of no help to them anymore, having seen Germans on both sides of the river. In their eyes I could see the panic simmering just below the surface.

As we neared the outskirts of Abbeville, we heard screams ahead and the crowds scattering. Sergeant Hawkes grabbed hold of my shoulder and threw me towards a side entrance and bellowed at us to take shelter in the yard beyond. As we flung ourselves against the wall, we heard the sound of motor vehicles and watched as a pack of fast moving motor cycles with side cars roared past, the mounted machine gun of the side car passenger trained on the road ahead. Silently we waited until they passed. My heart was pounding. Hawkes popped his head round the corner as civilians surged back onto the road.

"Ok lads, let's get moving."

We had been walking for an hour when Charlie Lloyd suddenly appeared, having caught up with me.

"Hey Den," he said, slightly out of breath. "I've just seen Mumford back there."

His news was hardly earth-shattering so after a returned glance, I stared straight ahead again and carried on walking. Charlie was obviously bursting to tell me more so he carried on regardless of whether I was interested or not.

"Mumford just stopped and,... well... collapsed at the side of the road. He didn't fall exactly, just slowly sank into a sitting position, cradling his head in his arms and burst into tears. He was out of control, it was weird. Sergeant Hawkes just stood over him, watching."

Now I was interested, for Mumford was our Officer in command. Without stopping, I looked at Charlie enquiringly.

"Bloody hell Chas, what happened?"

"I could see them both clearly. Hawksey was talking to him like a father to an errant child. Mumford slowly lifted his head to look at Hawksey, tears streaming down his face."

"What was wrong with him, was he wounded?" I asked.

"Not as far as I could see," Charlie replied. "For a few seconds they stared at each other, both waiting for the other to say something. Then Hawkes calmly and deliberately slapped him hard across the face."

"Bloody hell, he could be in trouble for that," was my only comment.

"I know, but there was no response from Mumford at all, he just took it. I don't know if he was in shock, scared or what but Mumford didn't seem to know what was happening."

"So what happened then?"

"Hawkes took the Lieutenant's pistol from his holster and then quickly caught up with us again," replied Charlie. "He left Mumford where he was, just sitting by the side of the road."

"Christ, that's weird." I answered. Striking an Officer was rather frowned upon amongst the higher echelons of the army. I wondered if I could be nosey, brave or stupid enough to bring the subject up with Hawksey later in the day, for of all the NCOs in our battalion, he was the most approachable.

We were now several miles away from Abbeville. Having been fortunate in avoiding the enemy so far, we continued over the well-worn cobbles. The numbers of refugees on the road had fallen, which meant we could move more quickly. By now, my arms were tiring and felt like dead lumps of meat. I tripped, nearly dropping the heavy box of ammunition, so we all stopped for a brief moment of rest.

Before long, we stumbled upon a British supply dump, hastily abandoned and left open. Hawkes walked through the gate and we followed. Once inside, he tore open boxes and spilled out cigarettes and emergency rations of food onto the floor. With great haste, we grabbed handfuls of the supplies on offer before rejoining the road and continuing our retreat.

The peace-shattering sound of gunfire surprised us all. It appeared to be coming from the isolated collection of farm buildings immediately ahead. We dived for the cover of the hedgerows and in our haste, Bill and I abandoned the box of ammo in mid air, letting it crash onto the cobbles. Fear and mayhem sent troops and refugees scattering in all directions, their screams only adding to the tension created by the crackling sounds of sporadic bursts of machine gun and rifle fire.

~ RUN AND HIDE ~
Late in the day, 20th May 1940

By now, our platoon was spread out along the road, taking shelter against the hedgerows. Believing the enemy to be concealed amongst the farm buildings ahead, Sergeant Hawkes and others edged forward to reconnoitre, keeping their heads down below the level of the hedges.

Those of us remaining waited nervously. Seconds seemed to take minutes to tick by as the firing continued in short bursts. I held my rifle at the ready just in case, but couldn't make out what was going on. Then we heard the rumble, the unmistakable clatter of motorised tracked vehicles advancing towards us on that cobble-stoned road. As I peered out over the top of the drainage ditch and looked up the road towards the direction of the sound, my worst fears were realised. From around a bend in the road came the ubiquitous Krauss-Maffei SdKfz, the Germans' half-tracked troop carriers towing light artillery weapons, followed by a whole German column. My pulse quickened.

"Shit," was my instant and only reaction.

There was another loud burst of gunfire, which I recognised as being another Bren. I raised my head above the ditch, giving me a worm's eye view of the unfolding drama. The half-tracked carrier veered off the road as the occupants ducked for cover. From behind, another vehicle lumbered then jerked awkwardly into view. I saw its barrel before I saw the main body of the vehicle. It was a light German tank. This was serious and the odds were overwhelmingly stacked against Hawkes and the men. From behind, I heard a rustle of activity. As I turned my head, I saw the backside of a fellow soldier disappear through a hole in the hedge into the field beyond. I tapped the boots of Bill, lying in front of me, and called to him.

"Come on, let's get out of here."

The hedge to my left looked thick and impenetrable, so I crawled backwards to where the other had been. By the time I reached the gap, the next soldier in line was already pushing his way through. With my heart pounding, trying to burst its way out through my chest, adrenaline had taken over my bodily functions. I cast a last quick glance towards Hawkes and the enemy column just as the loud explosion tore through the air. I pulled my head and neck down deep into my shoulders in an instinctive reflex action as a grenade exploded. I turned away to see that the soldier in front of me had cleared the hedge. I now had a chance to break through and, gripping my rifle tightly, I pushed forward on all fours into the hole. I felt as cumbersome as a rampaging elephant as I tried to hurry myself through with my uniform, webbing and packs seeming to catch on every branch and bramble. Halfway through, I came to an unexpected abrupt halt. Someone had caught me. Whoever it was held me firm. I could go no further. Gunfire seemed to echo all around me as I frantically tried to tear myself free, blindly pulling with all my might against the invisible hand that held me so powerfully. Sweat rolled freely from my brow and down through my eyebrows. I was held in its vice-like grip.

Through the opening, I could just see the others who had made it through, scrambling across the field, keeping tightly to the hedgerows.

Without warning, everything around me stopped, no sounds came to me. My efforts crept at a snail's pace, real time ground to a halt. I felt a stabbing pain in my side.

I slowly turned to confront my captor.

But he wasn't there.

Expecting to see a dagger thrust into me, I saw the end of my sheath-held bayonet sticking into the ground, causing the hilt to dig into my side as I struggled. My expression changed from one of fear to utter consternation. There was no hand on my webbing, no-one holding me by the collar, no German soldier trying to wrench me back, forcing me to return to the road to face a prisoner's fate. It took a moment for me to realise that it was my webbing that was holding me captive. It had become snared on a stout branch. How stupid I had been. In that instant, the sounds of battle rushed back into my ears and time returned to normality. It seemed as if I had been trapped for an eternity, but in reality it had been seconds. I twisted to free myself and lunged forward into the open field beyond. I was free. I half picked myself up and blindly followed the others, whom I counted as four. I glanced back to see Bill emerging through the gap, Knowing that my life depended on speed and eager to rejoin them, I sprinted towards the woods at the edge of the field, not stopping until I reached the sanctuary of the trees. I soon crashed into them hiding in the undergrowth. Lungs bursting, I dropped to the ground and turned back to face the road. Seconds later Bill fell amongst us. Only now could I feel the sweat soaking my whole body. My hands were shaking uncontrollably. Raising my head, I adjusted my twisted helmet, breathed deeply until my heart slowed itself and let out a long sigh of relief. I had made it and I was still alive.

"What do we do now?" came the obvious question from someone to anyone... but nobody answered.

Lying flat about me were Freddy, Herby, Tommy, Charlie and Bill, all breathing heavily.

To confirm our escape had gone undetected, we crawled back to the edge of the wood. Nobody had pursued us and the shooting had stopped. Our comrades had been easily overrun and now their soldiers were milling amongst our boys in the process of disarming them. From our slightly elevated position we could see individual British soldiers taking advantage of any distraction and running across the open fields on the opposite side of the road to us. Some were spotted and a half-track kicked into action, belching diesel fumes as it accelerated after them, smashing its way through a gate and giving chase. There was never much likelihood of the Brits reaching the distant woods. After a short burst of machine gun fire, more as warning shots than a killing volley, most stopped, turned and raised their hands high above their heads, but one made it to the safety of the woods to disappear amongst the trees beyond. In the distance, I heard German voices barking orders to their new captives. There appeared to be no casualties but we had no way of knowing for sure, or what had happened to Sergeant Hawkes and the other members of the platoons who had initially engaged the enemy. I felt sorrow for their plight, but I also felt relieved that I had managed to escape and at least now we had a chance of finding the rest of the battalion and reaching home.

Amongst our lucky band was one of our corporals, Herbert Davies, but we called him Herby. He was one of the good guys and was the medical officer's orderly. Still fighting for breath, he finally managed to speak.

"That was too bloody close for my nerves," he wheezed in a whisper, even though we were too far away from the enemy to hear.

"Did you see what happened to poor old Hawksey?" Freddy enquired anxiously, but it was more of a statement than a genuine question.

Tommy Grigg, the oldest of our gang of six, broke the silence.

"No, what happened?"

He paused. He was flushing with fear, relief and adrenalin, relishing the knowledge of his precious secret. He took another deep breath before continuing.

"As soon as the column came into view, Hawksey fired at the troop carrier with the Bren. Then the tank came forward. Bloody German poked his head out of the tank and chucked a stick grenade at him."

"That must have been the explosion I heard, was he OK?" I asked.

"Dunno mate."

"Poor sod, I liked him," was all I could think of saying.

"Did anyone else get hurt?"

"Dunno mate, I didn't hang around long enough to find out."

He smiled in relief and we smiled back.

We waited a while longer, discussing our options and deciding to continue in the same direction heading northwest but to keep off the roads for the moment and travel using the cover of the surrounding woods. Quietly creeping away from the scene of the skirmish we continued for a few miles in what remained of the daylight. Fearful of stumbling into other Germans in the advancing darkness we looked around for somewhere to spend the night. We soon came upon an isolated farm and, at a safe distance, argued as to what we should do next. Without the directions of Officers or NCOs, our new found freedom left us hesitant. Initially, we looked at Herby for advice.

"Hey! he said defensively, don't look at me, I am only a medic, what do I know about soldiering?"

Everything about the place was reassuring and with no sign of the enemy. Anxious to stop the dithering, Tommy Grigg, the eldest amongst us, broke the uncertainty.

"Come on, let's take a butchers."

We unslung our rifles, crouched and cautiously crossed the field towards the farm. I felt nervous in our exposed position, my senses strained to breaking point. I exhaled loudly as we reached the comparative safety of the single-storey stone dwelling without incident. Freddy was feeling bold and decided on direct action, simply walking up to the front door and politely knocking. There was no answer so he knocked again. By now, we had all found the courage to join him and huddled around in a semi-circle. Freddy turned to look at us, shrugged his shoulders and took hold of the door handle. It opened easily. Inside was dingy but quiet. No light, sound or smell could be detected so very carefully he crept inside and whispered a general greeting to anybody who might have been listening.

"Hello?"

There was no response. We checked all the rooms to discover that the farm house was deserted, and by the look of the place the owners had left in a hurry, taking what little they could carry. Relieved, I put my rifle down and lit a cigarette, relaxed a little and went back into the kitchen we had just checked. By now, I was starving and soon found some bread, dried fish, jams, jars of pickled fruits, several bottles of bitter white wine and a pitcher of milk, which still smelt fresh. My stomach gurgled with happiness. I took my cigarette out of my mouth and called to the others in a sing-song manner.

"Guess what I've found,... supper's ready boys!"

They all came running. We sat in the cool kitchen and ate the lot. I was not in the mood for any of the wine; to me it tasted foul but the others enjoyed it. With no-one to lecture us on soldierly conduct, we dispensed with the need for sentry duty, deciding instead to kip down together and make the best use of the two beds. It was comfort heaven, especially after the turmoil of the last nine days. Within minutes I fell into a deep slumber, the like of which can only be achieved through the exhaustion that comes after terror.

In the ensuing confusion across the whole of northern France, our group of six was now to be officially regarded as 'missing in action'. It was the dawn of 21st May 1940.

~ OUR ORGANISED RETREAT DESCENDS INTO A ROUT ~
22nd to 24th May

Many months later, I spoke to Alfie Evans, a Private from one of our sister battalions, the 2/5 Battalion Queen's Royal Regiment who had been shipped out to France with us. He was able to tell me what fate had befallen their battalion:

"On 18th May the whole Battalion was force marched to a small village called Ballencourt. The following day we were told to prepare to meet the enemy. That's when the bloody Germans bombed us. The planes came from nowhere; there were bodies everywhere. Later on, we made contact with them and exchanged fire. They had Panzers and artillery with them whilst we only had rifles and a couple of Brens. Soon we were forced back but were eventually surrounded and taken prisoner by an SS. Tank Unit. Whilst marching away, we literally stumbled across a French horse-drawn supply column which had been attacked on the road. All the black colonial drivers were lying dead by the roadside or still in their wrecked wagons, their dead horses almost blocked the road. They were torn to pieces,... it was like a butcher's yard."

We awoke from our slumbers, dazed but rested. It was strange to wake up of our own accord without the 'gentle encouragement' of our dear Corporals bellowing into our ears or the battalion bugle calling us to muster. But then, the extent of our plight hit home. After the briefest of greetings and no food, we set off, following the agreed plan of yesterday, heading north-west whilst staying clear of main roads as much as was possible. Another day passed. We had only just started again when we were forced to cautiously join a quiet road and moved as speedily as our legs could carry us. Before long, we came to a junction where we met a group of British troops from various regiments resting by the roadside and smoking. We greeted each other cheerfully but none were from 2nd/7th The Queen's.

Tommy mouthed our quandary.

"Do any of you know where we should be going?"

Being the oldest, he seemed to have taken unofficial charge of our band of not so merry men. Collectively, they shrugged their weary shoulders and each took out cigarettes and lit up. A chap from the 5th Battalion Green Howards piped up.

"I haven't a clue, mate. It's utter chaos around here and nobody seems to know anything." He exhaled smoke from deep inside his body. I remember thinking how tired and dirty he looked.

We told them what had happened to us and how we had become separated from our battalion and almost captured after our flight from Abbeville. They, in return, responded with a similar sorry tale.

"We're heading back towards the channel coast. Might be able to make it back to Blighty from there."

"Same here," I said, "bound to meet up with some others on the way."

At this stage, I was still hoping to rejoin my unit, but there seemed to be safety in numbers so we joined forces and marched off together. We now numbered nineteen.

Within a short space of time, we found ourselves amongst a small group of local French civilians who managed to return my questioning smile. I approached an elderly man in their party who possessed a huge white moustache, tinted with a dirty nicotine yellow around his mouth. Recalling a few suspect school French phrases and an even more suspect accent, I managed to put together an excuse for a sentence.

"Where are the English soldiers?".

"Fumée, fumée" was his short answer.

You're not having my smokes mate, was my immediate thought. Maybe he didn't understand my French? With that, he pointed across the flat countryside ahead towards the distant horizon. I hadn't noticed the plumes of dense black smoke slowly drifting towards the heavens. The direction was northwest, the direction we were intent on going.

~ APPROACHING DISASTER ~

We no longer needed to use the sun as our only source of navigation, for now we could rely on the smoke for a bearing. For the next two days, we managed to dodge sporadic mechanised German troop movements and at the end of each day, we found accommodation in houses or farm buildings. By now, we knew that a total disaster was unfolding around us. Every mile, our numbers increased with both British and French. Whenever we could we exchanged information and received so-called 'news'. True or false, we never knew for sure, but the overall tone was consistently depressing. The Germans were unstoppable and successfully pushing the Allies back. I knew we were running for our lives. All signposts seemed to point towards Calais and a place that we had not heard of before. Its name was Dunkerque (Dunkirk).

Over Calais, a sinister plume of grey smog hovered ominously, dirtying the otherwise clear blue sky, and this was the direction in which we were heading? But regardless, we just continued to go with the flow. With every step I was becoming increasingly weary, thirsty and hungry. All I wanted to do was to return to my home. My childlike dream of a heroic wartime adventure had not materialised. The harsh reality of war was now crystal clear and not in any way glamorous. I thought of my dear old mother, my girlfriend and close friends sitting comfortably back home, and my workmates who were safely at their drawing boards. I rightly questioned the wisdom of my decision.

And still the sun continued to beat down on us relentlessly.

Every so often, I would reach a very slightly elevated position where I was able to look towards that distant horizon. The columns of black smoke were increasingly evident, accompanied by the rising thunder of distant explosions. None of us seemed to question the folly of heading towards this tumultuous war zone.

The roads were becoming more congested with every mile. Thousands of troops like us and civilians were joining our swollen ranks of destitute refugees, fleeing the advancing enemy. Cartloads of treasured possessions, some pulled by horses, others pulled by hand, struggled on by, increasing the already chaotic situation. Men, women and children of all ages, carrying whatever possessions they could, moved in an endless stream along the highways, a heaving mass of dejected humanity. Their presence was slowing our crawling advance to the coast until I remembered that this was no advance, it was a retreat.

It did not take long for our newly amalgamated force to become separated, then diluted and finally lost amongst the mass of other road users. Although we from the Queen's tried to stick together, we were constantly joined by concerned French families, elderly peasants, French soldiers or fellow Brits, all equally eager for information.

We were barely sleeping, trying to reach the perceived safety of the coast as quickly as possible.

On the morning of the third day, artillery shells exploded nearby. I didn't know if it was us who were the intended target but I wasn't going to wait around in the open to find out. The screams of civilian refugees filled the air, only to be drowned out by another series of explosions. I dived for cover but there was precious little available, save for the shallow ditches on either side of the road filled with their dubious contents. A minute passed and all was silent once more - silent from the bombardment, that is. In its place, other noises drifted through our ranks, slowly increasing in volume; the haunting sounds of babies crying, of moans and complaints amid the background commotion of a thousand bodies picking themselves up, along with their precious carts and possessions and returning to the Calais road. Along the way, I witnessed both Officers and men openly weeping by the roadside, emotionally in tatters, unable to continue. Both fear and defeat gripped them. I assumed that some of these Officers had abandoned their men to their fate. Others lay collapsed, hiding deep within their own terrified minds, curled up in a state of shock. In the main, these very few Officers were the exception. The vast majority were still doing their duty and leading their men to wherever they were instructed to or wherever they thought best. Military operations are different now, but in 1940 the Officers were the only ones who really knew the full picture, passing down information to the NCOs on a 'need to know' basis. I and my fellows, trainees in the art of war, were at the very bottom of the information ladder and needed to know sod all, making us even more reliant on the Officers and Sergeants for our survival. We were only trained to blindly follow orders, their orders, with no thoughts of our own.

At what point our column changed direction I had no idea. Instead of heading into Calais, we had diverted towards another destination, towards a place called Dunkirk.

On the fourth day, I became aware of vehicles. I do not know when I first noticed it for it happened gradually. At first, there were just a few, then scores,... then hundreds and thousands. Vehicles of all kinds, military staff cars, trucks, jeeps, tanks, motorbikes and armoured carriers, ambulances, commandeered civilian lorries along with artillery and guns of every description littered the whole area. During all my time in France, I had never seen so much mechanised equipment. Amongst this dumped debris of war, I saw a Bren gun carrier, the vehicle I had been assigned to but never actually seen. Ironic, given the circumstances. The carrier was now beyond any conceivable use to me or my fanciful Bren Gun Unit. I paused momentarily as I thought of my friend and number two, Fred Hammond, whom I had sadly abandoned, injured and barely alive, in a cellar some days ago. He would have been delighted had he been able to see these carriers. But none of this equipment was moving anywhere. None was parked neatly in regimental fashion, it had just been unceremoniously discarded. The scene was surreal, thousands upon thousands of tons of valuable ordnance left wherever there was space, by the roadside or in the fields. The closer we got to Dunkirk, the more I saw. In places, there was barely room enough to squeeze past. We trampled over the debris of abandoned clothing and blankets, boxes pulled from the vehicles and forced open, the contents strewn across the road. Whatever could be looted, was looted and all about was chaos and the litter of a defeated army. Drivers were leaving engines running in an attempt to burn the remaining fuel or by adding sugar or sand to seize up the engines. Small organised squads of troops clambered over vehicles with their heads buried under open bonnets, ripping out important parts to immobilise them and puncturing fuel tanks. Many were burning furiously, billowing out great plumes of acrid smoke from their blazing tyres. Similarly, guns were being smashed and spiked to put them beyond the use of the Germans. Tanks with their tracks destroyed were in evidence. The message was clear. The British Army was abandoning all its equipment, the action of a defeated army, of which I was a member. The assured soldier that had joined up some four months earlier, ready to fulfil the brash oath and give Hitler that bloody nose was long gone and the bloody nose was ours.

In a clearing to my left, I saw an abandoned Vickers Mk.E light tank with its stubby little gun. I watched as a sapper dropped something inside its open turret before jumping down and sprinting away. As he cleared the tank, a deep blast sent debris flying skywards as the interior of the tank exploded. My eyes followed the blast. In the distance, a Stuka was heading straight towards us, its infamous 'whine' causing instant panic. I looked along the road to see our ragged column of displaced souls magically divide and fall to the sides. It was like witnessing the biblical parting of the Red Sea. The aircraft had no bombs hanging from its underside but this did not stop the pilot from issuing another form of death and destruction. Its two wing-mounted cannons erupted into life, spitting shells into the crowd. The pilot spat his ammunition along the line before climbing once more and banking away to the east. I was relieved he had no further interest in us. Seemingly, his attack was just for the hell of it and we grudgingly resumed our foot-slogging haul.

We came upon a road junction which was a scene of considerable chaos. This was the Dunkirk perimeter, a defensive position drawn on a map. A crude but effective roadblock had been positioned, consisting of two smashed vehicles placed across the road opposite, their wheels destroyed. Armed British troops were arguing with French civilians, trying to guide them along another road. Likewise, I watched as French soldiers were ordered to take a different route, to a beach specifically set aside for them. The defenders were not allowing any civilians or non-British troops, vehicles or large equipment of any sort beyond their barrier. Now it was our turn to face the British Corporal standing in our way.

"What's up mate, what's going on?" I enquired, pleased at last to be presented with someone who might just know what was happening.

"They're evacuating us back home. Keep moving and just follow the others down onto the beach and await further orders," he replied hurriedly, standing aside to usher us through whilst other guards gave similar instructions or sent others on their way.

Only rifles and small arms were being allowed through, so we kept ours for as far as we knew, failure to carry your weapon was still against military orders.

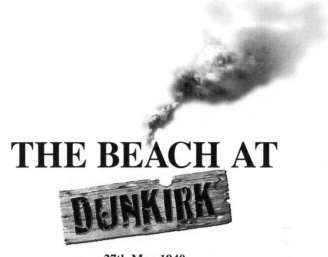

THE BEACH AT
DUNKIRK

27th May 1940

Between 20th and 25th May, the German Army had advanced swiftly south of the Somme to the Atlantic coast whilst another army had advanced north of the river. Calais was surrounded and cut off, seeming to take the brunt of the German offensive.

The Dunkirk perimeter had compressed into a long bulging corridor, some sixty miles long and holding. The only aim was to keep the enemy at bay and far enough away from our men gathering in the town and on the sands either side so as not to be in range of the advancing German artillery, dreaded panzers and eventual capture.

When the authorities realised their plan to withdraw and evacuate the British Expeditionary Force from France, they chose Calais and Dunkirk as exit points along with lesser known embarkation points from Normandy to the Bay of Biscay .

On the 26th the evacuation began, but by the 27th, German forces finally captured Calais and with it thousands of allied troops. Their focus now turned towards Dunkirk and the long narrow corridor and the remainder of the BEF. At first, non-combatants, sappers and engineers, pioneers, motor transport sections, the wounded and medical staff were evacuated. The perimeter was manned by combat troops, both French and British and they were up against crack German forces well equipped with both artillery and tanks, flushed with recent success and the smell of impending victory. Holding that defence perimeter was becoming increasingly difficult by the minute and the defenders were paying a terrible price.

uddenly I remembered where I was as I awoke with a jolt, I was still in hell. How we had managed to sleep through the noise as battle raged over Dunkirk was beyond me.

God, it was hot today. Just above the surface of the sand, images shimmered in the heat. We had made ourselves as comfortable as possible by removing boots and socks. After our few days in battle, followed by our rapid retreat through woods and wetlands and without the benefit of washing facilities, our poor feet had paid a price. Like everybody else, our feet were in a poor state, filthy, smelly, damp and blistered. They really appreciated being freed from the confines of my boots and I massaged life back into them once more.

"Hey Herby, take a look at my feet will you? I think they need a bit of loving care."

"No fear mate, not getting near your plates, probably catch something really nasty."

"Thanks Doc, so much for your loving medical care," I replied as he tried to wave away the smell.

I walked to the water's edge and soaked my feet again in the sea. In the blistering heat of the day, my washing had dried easily,... and so had my mouth. Now my tongue felt like a boxer's jockstrap. I ducked my head in the cool water and rinsed my mouth before returning to the dubious safety of our fox hole. There was nothing any of us could do now except wait.

The peace didn't last long, for in the distance the next wave of dive bombers was rapidly approaching. Three Stukas this time fell from the sky to release their payload of death. I turned over, ducking down as low as I could into our hide. I knew what to expect, having been on the receiving end of these war machines before. They had devices fitted near the tops of their main undercarriage leg fairings that acted like sirens, so that when they dived to attack their targets they made their characteristic terrifying whine, designed specifically to intimidate and unsettle their victims, which they did to great effect.

I watched them come and ducked as I saw the flash of cannon. A light hail of sand fell about me, but fortunately that was all. I ducked again as another Stuka did its worst. Afterwards, the three aircraft turned and flew along the beach with front cannons ablaze as they screeched over our heads. Rifles opened fire once more in another valiant attempt at stopping their turkey shoot. Initially terrified, I knew how comparatively safe the beach was for us in contrast to

Dunkirk itself. Up till now, only one bomb had been dropped on our stretch and much of the blast and resulting shrapnel was absorbed by the sand, minimising the spread of its destruction as we lay there, defenceless. The main blast travelled skywards, carrying with it columns of sand. We were more likely to suffer from sand in our eyes than from shrapnel injuries. Of course there were casualties, scores of unfortunate men killed and wounded, but you had to be pretty unlucky to receive a direct hit. It was the aircraft's cannons that were causing most of our injuries. The strafing was lethal and for those who were hit, medical assistance was very limited. In the skies above, we saw no allied aircraft capable of stopping this onslaught; the Luftwaffe seemed to be in total control. Out at sea, time and time again waves of enemy aircraft attacked the ships, big and small, heading to and from Dunkirk, trying bravely to ferry away what remained of the BEF, French and Belgium armies.

As well as a lack of medical supplies, there was also a dearth of food and water. All we could do was wait and suffer, hungry and parched under a murderous sun. I lay back in our little crater with the others feeling utterly exhausted and all I wanted to do was sleep for a thousand years.

Too soon, sleep left me as the sound of more explosions greeted us. On this our second day, having rested, we joined one of the long queues but by mid-day, we still hadn't moved and our evacuation back to 'Dear Old Blighty' seemed as elusive as ever. Out of the blue, a motor launch approached the head of our queue and we all looked on as soldiers waded shoulder deep in the water towards it. As the boat swung around and came to rest side-on to the head of the waiting queue, the men surged forward, eager to clamber aboard. Within a minute, the little vessel was fully loaded but still more tried to climb in as the boat listed to the side, overwhelmed by more desperate men eager to be rescued. The raised voice of someone in command came drifting across the water.

"Stop,... stop,... there's no more room..."

But still they tried. All seemed chaos. Then we heard a shot ring out quickly followed by another.

"Get back or I will shoot."

Slowly, order returned and the over-loaded boat began to move forward and then turn towards the horizon.

"We'll be back, just hang on," were the last words we heard.

We all watched, waiting, as the craft gently made its way towards a large naval ship moored further out to sea. Our evacuation back to England had finally begun.

Carnage soon returned to the beaches as another air attack left us reeling. Wounded men lay where they fell, cared for as much as possible by medics or whoever was on hand. For the seriously wounded, there was little anybody could do for them, for without hospitalisation, their chances of survival were slim... at best. They and the bodies were carried up the beach and laid in front of the dunes, their faces covered with whatever was to hand.

Away from the beaches on the perimeter defences there were problems developing. The evacuation was meant to include equal numbers of British and French troops. Apparently, too few of the French were being evacuated and they were furious. This contentious issue caused the French high command to refuse to man the perimeter unless the British evacuated their troops in equal numbers. The defence perimeter was compressing and developing so many leaks it resembled a sieve rather than a container, as troops surrendered or were killed in action. I had witnessed the behaviour of many French soldiers over the last couple of weeks and I was not impressed. Like us they could smell defeat, but unlike us, their paper thin morale had evaporated and discipline amongst the rank and file was woeful. They already seemed resigned to their defeat.

On the third day, we received long-awaited but totally unexpected orders. The Germans were increasingly likely to break through at any moment thereby threatening the ongoing evacuation, unless those holes in our defences could be plugged. Increasingly, British Commanders were pulling 'combat' troops off the beaches in order to bolster defensive positions on the line. Although our small platoon was now separated from the rest of our battalion, our shoulder flashes indicated that we were from the Queen's, a known infantry battalion. Unfortunately for us, nobody knew that we were just trainee recruits, pioneers and not practised combatants. As we stood waiting in the queue, I noticed someone walking towards us. From his peaked cap, I knew that he was an Officer. He looked to be a man with a purpose. In his wake, several men followed him. As he approached, he stopped every so often to speak to soldiers. After a brief chat, some stood up and followed him whilst others remained. Eventually, he reached us and saw our insignia. The Officer in question was a Captain, looking unshaven and exhausted, with dark bags under his sunken eyes. Even though he looked on the point of collapse, his manner was positive.

"Right lads, follow me. I have a job for you."

The six of us just looked at each other, bewildered.

"But sir, we are waiting to be evacuated," protested Freddy.

Our thoughts precisely, we couldn't have said it better.

"Look men, we all want to get back to England as soon as possible, but at this moment, I need you with me."

He spoke kindly but forcefully and orders are orders, so we did as we were told and all six of us followed. What remained of our platoon combined with others that he had just acquired brought our numbers to about twenty. We mounted the dunes and walked along the coast road away from the beach, a mixed bunch of misfits from differing regiments. Even Herby, our Medical Officer's orderly, who had been with us since the bridges of Abbeville, was press-ganged into service, which was crazy for he had never fired a gun in his life.

Shortly after leaving the beach, we arrived at a supply depot that was packed with army munitions and goodies. A steady stream of soldiers were to-ing and fro-ing. I had grown accustomed to my Bren gun and ever since Sergeant Hawkes had 'borrowed' it, I felt almost naked without it. I mentioned to the Officer that I had been in a Bren gun platoon and was an 'ace' shot, so he acquired one for me and appointed a pleasant enough man from Birmingham called Duggy to be my new number two. We all collected ammunition boxes. A Corporal handed an anti-tank rifle and some of its .55 calibre ammunition to Freddy whilst the others were finally offered the elusive, brand spanking new .303 rifles still smelling heavily of gun grease. We all rejected the offer of Sten guns, having had no training in their use; besides, they were not as accurate as a rifle. The Captain was becoming increasingly agitated, searching the skies above for enemy aircraft.

"Hurry up men. We have got to get moving."

We strapped on additional ammunition pouches and filled them too. Our Officer took one of the Stens and a bag of grenades; I assumed he didn't have much regard for his pistol.

"Right lads, anybody require any cigarettes, I have plenty here." Like a magician in front of a party of kids, he delighted us by producing a large box full of them.

"Any water Sir?"

"Over there and take these emergency rations too."

I was tempted to ditch the box of ammo and replace it with the Weights and food but common sense prevailed. Needless to say, we took advantage of the Officer's kind gesture and filled whatever space we had left with them. He filled in a form and signed some paperwork, presumably a receipt for the guns and ammo. I laughed at the time-wasting bureaucracy, but however desperate the situation, time had to be found for the bloody paperwork.

Once outside, we quickly resumed our march. From every direction we could hear the sounds of warfare whilst smoke rose relentlessly from all points of the compass. Everywhere, we saw allied soldiers moving in all directions, some marching with purpose whilst most just wandered, without.

We had only just started to move again, away from the coast, when I looked skyward. By then, we could all hear the approach of aircraft.

"Take cover," shouted the Officer.

We didn't really need telling for we were already there, having dived headlong into the side of the road. The peace around Dunkirk never lasted more than a few moments. Cannon strafed the road and tarmac fragments and stones spat out in all directions. I covered the back of my head with my hands as usual, a futile gesture, but instinct dictated my actions as the grit and dust fell over me. The shells landed too close for comfort but still missing us.

The lone fighter only made the one pass and sped on its way in the direction we were heading, probably to refuel and rearm before resuming his action in the Dunkirk theatre. Having suffered no casualties we continued. After a mile or two, the Captain took out his map and compass and studied them for a while with the Corporal, whom he had in tow. Duggy, my new number two, took out a packet of cigarettes and offered me one.

"Thanks mate," I responded, and we sat down on our ammunition boxes. During our march, they had grown heavier by the minute and the relief of freeing our arms was delicious. We lit up and enjoyed the fumes that filled our lungs.

"Didn't think we would see any more fighting, did you mate?" he uttered casually. "I thought our next stop would be Southampton docks."

Duggy held his ciggie between thumb and second finger, examining its ragged end whilst releasing a perfect smoke ring. In the near distance came the sounds of more muffled explosions. The overcast sky was dotted with blue patches.

"Right men, gather round," barked the Officer, who beckoned us to join him by an upturned cart that he was using as a table. We gathered round. His map was unfolded and facing us. He had been holding his unlit pipe in his mouth, out of habit and for comfort more than anything. He withdrew it and drew an imaginary line on the map. Our briefing had begun.

"Roughly, this is our defence line. We are here, by this road that we have just marched along. Jerry is here in strength..." Again, he pointed at the map and then to the countryside behind him and behind our covering buildings.

"...and seems to be pushing infantry through these marshy areas. We don't believe that they would risk their tanks on this terrain, but just in case, we have the anti-tank rifle."

'Fat lot of good that will be!' I thought, as he paused for breath. I had seen that woefully inadequate weapon in action just a few days ago and I could only liken the rifle to using a pea-shooter on a slab of concrete.

"Our job is to stop Jerry here."

He affirmed his point by stabbing the air with his pipe in a firm downward movement.

"We are to hold them for as long as possible. Every hour is vital so we keep Jerry occupied and pinned down. By doing so, it means that more of our chaps can get away. We'll get our turn later." He looked around at us, reassuringly.

"Any questions?"

I was staggered. I had never had a proper briefing before and had certainly never been put in the picture like this.

"What if we can't hold them sir, what then?"

I looked to my left. The question was asked by our Medical Officer's orderly. He was some ten years older than me and we were all eager for his answer.

"If all fails, then we fall back. We just passed a hamlet," he replied, pointing back along the road, "head for there and hold that new position. But let's just try and hang on here men, is that understood?" asked the Captain assertively.

"Remember, every second gained means another man home."

We nodded. "Yes sir," came the rather muted response.

"When will our turn come Sir?"

"Don't worry, soon enough,... soon enough." He looked sincere.

We took up positions amongst a row of derelict single-storey cottages with the Officer instructing us as to how to prepare our defences. We knocked through a hole here and there and filled in larger openings with stout kitchen tables, cupboards and whatever else was available. An old mattress was found which was used to fill a gaping hole. Duggy came rushing in with news of his find, a well in the garden. After almost two days without water, we gulped heavily from it before taking the opportunity to fill our water bottles and then prepared ourselves for the inevitable arrival of the enemy.

It was late in the day, and within an couple of hours of settling in I was jolted into action by a loud explosion. Without warning, we came under attack. German forward observers or scouts had probably seen us hiding in the buildings. Mortars opened up, the softening-up process had begun before the inevitable infantry attack. Then it really started. I thought I saw Germans in the distance. I gripped my Bren and readied my trigger finger, resting my free hand on the stock to steady the gun. I looked down the sight. The distance was about right, I had judged it well. The advancing German soldiers were finally within range. Slowly, I squeezed the trigger and it burst into life.

Although uncertain of my targets in the dwindling light, I swept the area where I had just seen the enemy, first one way and then back again. The others opened up with a volley of sustained rifle fire. Now their infantry returned fire and we began to take hits as bullets peppered the buildings, hitting the cottage walls and shattering what remained of the glass windows. Outside, a pile of dry grass or reeds had caught alight and wafts of smoke began drifting across our field of vision. Tracer bullets sped towards our positions and debris rained down upon us from the roof above.

Every time my magazine emptied, Duggy did his job.

Spotting the enemy through the smoke and reed beds was practically impossible now. It was then that the mortars opened up once more, soon finding their target. Our building took a direct hit. The encounter felt serious for us press-ganged and under-trained soldiers but our basic survival instinct clicked in, managing to swamp the utter terror that was in danger of engulfing us.

Suddenly the wall and windows were blown away, the explosion virtually destroying the cottage. It all happened so quickly and unexpectedly that the shock left me stupefied, unable to fully comprehend what was happening. I was knocked sideways and my hearing was impaired from the deafening blast. I tried to stand but my movements were cumbersome and time became distorted as if we were swimming through treacle. What was left of the daylight burst through the gaping hole in the roof and where the wall had once stood, whilst dust and smoke choked the air. I saw Duggy lying by my side, covered with broken pieces of brick and mortar. Blood covered his battered face and his jaw was ripped open. He was dead, killed instantly. Four of our new comrades also died in that one explosion and the remainder suffered injuries of one form or another. On the other hand our band of six miraculously emerged pretty much unscathed, apart from cuts and bruises. Although I was proving to be a survivor, it did cross my mind that I might be jinxed, having sadly lost yet another of my Bren assistants.

Having taken the brunt of the explosion, what remained of the wall offered little protection. Gun fire was raining down upon us as we helped the walking wounded stagger out of the ruin. The adjacent buildings seemed to have fared a little better and returning rapid fire from inside indicated that at least some of them were still alive. We quickly found alternative cover and continued with the increasingly desperate task of 'holding' the Germans back as best we could. I resumed rapid fire with my Bren, all too aware of my dwindling ammunition and it wasn't long before the fighting stopped. Fingers crossed, we had held the Germans at bay, possibly believing that we were a stronger force than we actually were.

With darkness upon us, I found the others and they helped me carry Duggy's body out to the side of the road. Somebody found a old curtain which we draped across him. It was a sad moment for us.

I was pleased to be amongst a group of like minded souls for our situation did not seem quite so terrifying. Our Officer moved cautiously amongst us and chose Herby and Bill to return to the supply depot for more ammunition whilst we grabbed what rest we could, knowing that dawn would bring with it a fresh onslaught.

As usual, we took it in turns to stand guard. We ate what rations we had left and drank from our bottles as the well was now destroyed. We rested on the floor of our ruin. During the lull, I found my cigarettes and felt something hard and flat. It was my bible. I kissed it and replaced it safely in the left breast pocket of my tunic, shielding my heart. I remembered a story of a soldier in the trenches whose life had been saved by his bible, blocking a German bullet from entering his heart. Although not superstitious, it couldn't do any harm to be cautious, could it? Freddy and Tommy were sitting, watching me.

"What are you two heathens laughing about?" I asked, feigning indignation.

"Blimey,... sorry Father, please forgive us our sins."

Tommy could be a sarcastic bugger and Freddy had to join in too. "Na! He's a Bishop at least. Should have spotted his halo long ago."

"My girlfriend Josephine gave it to me just before I joined." I recalled her face and remembered her warm, sweet, gentle lips.

Continuing, I chastised them, mockingly. "And don't think I will let you two into heaven if I end up there before you bunch of savages. I have connections in high places you know."

"Well get bloody connected right now and get us out of this shit hole will you?"

If only.

Flush with ciggies, I tossed them a couple. I drew deep and long. They helped, as always, in times of stress. We talked and joked repeatedly for even in these tense times, I tried never to lose my sense of humour, for often it was the only thing that kept me going.

After a while, the two men returned, pushing a battered pram loaded with ammunition. Now we could fight another day.

"Well done men, that should do us."

At dawn, we watched and waited for the attack to recommence. Even though the smoke had gone, the German infantry would still be difficult to see amongst the reeds and their stubborn refusal to make a suicidal head-on frontal assault on our positions was hindering our best intentions to shoot the bastards. But we were thankful that the Officer was right about one thing - the marshy conditions were keeping the Panzers at bay.

As if from nowhere, a motorcycle squad with sidecars, armed with mounted machine guns was spotted approaching, along the exposed unmade road that ran past our position. Within seconds, our Officer was amongst us, telling us to hold fire until they were within effective range. I took aim, waited until such time that a single shot rang out before releasing a burst of fire. I don't think I hit the lead bike but the sound of my Bren firing was enough to stop them in their tracks. At that point a volley of rapid fire opened up to our left. Whoever they were, their fire was more accurate, hitting the second bike crew. With shots continuing from both sides, tyres screeched and engines groaned as the others turned rapidly. The lead machine gunner fell forwards in his side car whilst another driver fell from his bike. In a desperate panic, his gunner scrambled into his position and attempted to take control but was hit by another hail of bullets. He too collapsed to the ground. By now, those not hit sped away, kicking up clouds of dust. Now facing the wrong way, they were unable to return the fire. Keeping their heads down, they sped away, soon disappearing from view. Five hit that we could be sure of.

As soon as they had disappeared, a Sd.Kfz.222 light armoured car suddenly appeared as if from nowhere, tentatively probing our position. I looked across to my right towards the adjacent outbuilding some twenty yards away and watched through the gaping hole in its side. I could see by his torn trousers and hastily tied bandage around his calf that our Corporal had been wounded in the leg. He took the 'pea shooter' (the not-so-trusted anti-tank rifle) from Freddy and despite his wound it was the Corporal who now opened fire with the weapon. The first round, as expected, seemed to make no impression at all. The second did hit but failed to stop the vehicle, but unfortunately alerted the tank gunner to his exact location and that of his useless weapon. The armoured car stopped and the 20mm gun barrel spun round into a firing position.

"Shit", I cried, "here we go again."

It was time to leave.

I don't know if the Corporal got off another round but, at that moment, the firing commenced. I saw the smoke released from the barrel and then the deafening sound of the explosion before I had time to move a muscle. That was the last I ever saw of both the Corporal and the Officer. Their shelter erupted as the shell impacted. I instinctively ducked but still felt the force of the hot burst. Another shell followed, repeating the chaos. With the appearance of the armoured car, we were all but defenceless and our ammunition practically exhausted. Confirmation came that the Captain and corporal were both dead and under the new leadership of a more experienced soldier, our band of six and a few remaining others crawled away, falling back towards the hamlet, as instructed, to continue the battle. This pattern of fight, retreat a few yards and regroup was repeated throughout the remainder of the day, and every time we retreated we would come into contact with other small units of the defending forces and hastily re-established the next defensive position. By now, we had no idea who we were fighting alongside, with no time for introductions. I was now fighting side-by-side with total strangers. Hunger was not an issue for food was the least of my concerns. However, lack of drinking water was.

149

Had Dennis still been with the main body of his battalion, he might have been reminded that today was the glorious 1st June, a Regimental Day and very special in the history of the Queen's regiment. It dated back to 1794 when the regiment was acting as marines during the Battle of 'The Glorious 1st June' against the French Navy. The regiment was embarked on board five ships of the line - HMS Queen Charlotte (Admiral Lord Howe's flagship), HMS Russell, HMS Defence, HMS Royal George and HMS Majestic. The regiment's gallant conduct contributed to the victory and it was honoured accordingly. Today would have been his first chance to experience the celebrations had he not become lost at war.

The following day, we found ammunition in abundance, abandoned by our troops in their rush for the beach. I emptied the bullets from the rifle clips and physically reloaded them into my Bren magazines whenever there was a lull in the fighting.

I picked up a piece of paper lying on the ground. It was a leaflet printed in French and English, dropped by the Germans and calling us to surrender. It simply read:

> *'British Soldiers! Look at this map: it gives your true situation!*
> *Your troops are entirely surrounded - stop fighting!*
> *Put down your arms! (see picture reference 18).*

I tried not to dwell on it's not-so-hidden message and at least we now had some toilet paper.

Our struggle continued for the next two days. Each day, we were squeezed into a smaller narrower corridor leading into Dunkirk. A week ago I had never heard of the place, but now it seemed to be the epicentre of my whole world. We were all exhausted, hungry and thirsty and struggled to remain positive. But sooner or later, I knew we would be withdrawn and taken back to England, just as that now dead Officer had promised. That thought kept us going. In reality there was little time to think or predict tomorrow's outcome. Fighting, fear and adrenaline afforded little respite.

During the night of 3rd June, we crawled deep into a depression in the ground. I covered myself with my groundsheet and amongst the sound of constant explosions, fell asleep until it was my turn to keep watch.

That night, some 50 ships managed to take on board 38.000 French troops and evacuate them to England.

Later, Dennis was to hear tales of a few shameful Army Officers who tried to force themselves onto the waiting ships. Naval Petty Officers, equipped with Smith & Wesson side arms, were apparently given instructions not to allow Officers on board unless they were accompanied by their men. Those who tried were threatened with drawn pistols. If they persisted or became violent, they were shot. These often inexperienced well educated men from a higher social standing than their subordinates, men from a privileged background but without the necessary practical qualifications of leadership, were now found wanting in the hour of need.

But their dishonourable behaviour was not unique. He had previously witnessed soldiers too, driven to drink or reduced to a state of panic and hysteria who also fought to jump queues to make good their escape and force themselves onto the waiting ships. The trouble was that each and every one of them would liked to have boarded as soon as possible, but order had to be maintained for the greater good of us all.

Had Dennis been on the beaches of Dunkirk early that morning, he might also have heard the persistent calls from General Alexander from the deck of his motor launch, calling for all remaining stragglers to come forward to be rescued back to England as he made his much fabled last tour of the beaches to ensure that all had been evacuated.

Whilst he and many more were still fighting, there were others who had abandoned all hope and would not be found. Having first looted drink, they then lost themselves in an alcoholic mist of oblivion amongst the cellars and ruins of Dunkirk.

· · · § · · ·

IT'S  OVER

4th June 1940

We had been on the perimeter during the first three days of June. The defence line was still a few miles from Dunkirk but it was disintegrating and falling apart at every seam. My only surprise was that we had managed to hold the enemy at bay for so long, but at that time I had no idea that the Germans had been ordered to refrain from completing a full assault on Dunkirk on the instructions of their high command.

We were never sure how news spread through the BEF, but somehow information did seep down through the tenuous chain of command to us privates at the bottom of the heap, especially bad news. For the most part, it was accurate.

Today was 4th June 1940. Dawn had crept over the horizon a few hours earlier, when the earth-shattering news came to us that the evacuation was complete.

"It's over chaps, every man for himself."

I was dumbstruck. We had been fighting like hell these last few days, trying as best we could to hold the Germans so that others could make their escape back home to England. I had tried my utmost to do my bit and had been promised that when our turn came, we would be withdrawn and taken home. Now suddenly it was all over? I and my comrades had been abandoned and left to rot. I felt angry and bitter and in my tormented mind, I ranted and raved like a child. How could our own country do this to us? It was so utterly unfair. The safety of England was only twenty-four miles away across the Channel but it might just as well have been a million miles. How could the high command in London have reached such a decision knowing full well that so many of us were still fighting? I wanted to scream out loud.

"NO IT'S BLOODY WELL NOT ALL OVER, I'M STILL HERE!"

† *Nearly 400,000 of my comrades were lucky enough to have been evacuated back to England. Of course this was wonderful for them and, in the long term, vital to the survival of Britain itself. But for thousands like me, news of our abandonment was devastating. One estimate indicates that the British Army left behind 2,500 guns, 84,500 vehicles, 77,000 tons of ammunition, 416,000 tons of supplies and 165,000 tons of petrol, with 68,000 soldiers killed or taken prisoner.*

†† *Another staggering estimate quotes approximately 28,000 men of the BEF killed and almost 40,000 men marched into captivity, 2472 guns, almost 65,000 vehicles, 20,000 motorcycles, 416,000 tons of stores, over 75,000 tons of much needed ammunition and 162,000 tons of petrol.*

Later that same morning, I was pleased to stumble upon the other five from the Queen's. We were overjoyed to see each other and shook each other's hands. Freddy smiled and spoke.

"Been hiding up somewhere have you Den whilst we do all the work?"

"Looks like the bastards have abandoned us," but I was too angry for his or anyone's jokes.

Tommy spoke quietly, "Yer! we heard the same thing."

We stood in a circle, smoked what ciggies we had left and tried to find something to be pleased about, some light at the end of a bloody long and dark tunnel.

"Well guys, we're still alive," was Freddy's contribution, said with a strained half-smile.

Another scrap of an order was passed down the line to us lowly, worthless, sacrificial lambs. Someone shouted.

"Split into small groups and head south... and good luck."

---

† *Source: 'Dunkirk, Fight to the Last Man' by Hugh Sebag-Montefiori.*
†† *Source: 'Dunkirk, The Men they Left Behind' by Sean Longden.*

Good luck?... thanks you f***ing bastards.

This was not what we were promised. We had ONLY been sent to France to continue our training. We were not prepared for this. We were still raw recruits yet we had done more than should have been expected of us. We could give no more. It was now our turn to be evacuated, to be sent home. You promised,... you bastards. It's not right, it's so unfair. I can't do this,... I want to go home.

I wanted to scream and cry, but I was also so incensed I felt like killing someone.

Now, we were truly on our own.

† *The Miracle of Dunkirk - Hitler's 'Halt Order' of 11.42hrs, 24th May 1940:*

By the time Hitler issued his 'Halt Order" of 24th May, the evacuation had already began. 27,936 men who were not central to the functioning of the BEF had already been evacuated back to England. General Paul von Kleist's Panzers were only 18 miles from Dunkirk when he received the incredulous order to halt, countermanding Wehrmacht's Commander-in-Chief, General Walther von Brauchitsch's order to take Dunkirk.

This was to the amazement and immense frustration of commanders like Kleist and General Heinz Guderian, the genius of modern armoured warfare,

The planned coup de grâce that could have entrapped the entire northern Allied force was over-ruled, giving the Allies a vital breathing space to strengthen the perimeter and begin the exodus from the beaches of Dunkirk.

Kleist later commented with regret that the English had managed to escape his trap which he had so carefully laid, "only with the personal help of Hitler."

He went on: "There was a channel from Arras to Dunkirk. I had already crossed this channel and my troops occupied the heights which jutted out over Flanders. Therefore, my Panzer group had complete control of Dunkirk and the area in which the British were trapped. 'The fact of the matter is that the English would have been unable to get into Dunkirk because I had them covered. Then Hitler personally ordered that I should withdraw my troops from these heights."

Later, when Kleist met Hitler on the airfield at Cambrai (probably Epinoy which Dennis had guarded a month earlier), he alone had the courage to mouth the words, "a great opportunity had been lost at Dunkirk.

Hitler replied: "That may be so. But I did not want to send the tanks into the Flanders marshes – and the British won't come back in this war."

Indeed the ground around the Dunkirk pocket was not ideal for tanks and the infantry did need time to catch up, considering the startling amount of ground the Panzers had crossed.

Furthermore, the flamboyant Luftwaffe chief Hermann Göring, eager for a slice of the glory, confidently but foolishly promised that his Luftwaffe could destroy the pocket without any need for the Wehrmacht to do much more than conduct mopping-up operations afterwards. †

Thank God there were some fools amongst the military elite of the Nazi war machine. Had Hitler listened to his Generals such as Kleist or Manstein, over 440,000 members of the BEF trapped in France and Belgium would have been slaughtered or captured, leaving Britain undefended against a Nazi invasion, a frighteningly realistic prospect in the summer of 1940.

---

† *Source: Andrew Roberts' book, 'The Storm of War: A New History of the Second World War'.*

CAPTURE

BITTER RETREAT AND RUN

Some of my battalion were lucky and successfully evacuated back to the relatively safe shores of England. The evacuation that became known as 'The Miracle of Dunkirk', happened because of the stupidity of Hitler and the unstinting bravery and sacrifice of both French troops as well as the heroic British units fighting on the Dunkirk perimeter, allowing so many to be taken off the beaches.

The fearsome sounding Stuka dive-bombers and the Messerschmitt fighters would have done a lot more damage had it not been for the Spitfires, the Hurricanes and the Defiants. RAF Fighter Command lost some 60 pilots in these actions over Dunkirk and many more planes. But when Winston Churchill addressed the House of Commons, he reminded the gathered members that: "We must be very careful not to assign to this deliverance the attributes of a victory. Wars are not won by evacuations."

But it would always be known as 'The Miracle of Dunkirk'. The nine days of Dunkirk stopped what was a disastrous campaign becoming an even bigger tragedy of more epic proportions that would have left our shores utterly defenceless.

ggrieved as I was, the news was hard to digest, but the only thing that I did have to digest. I kept going over the same thought; how I too might have made it back to England, what would have happened if we had not become separated, or if I had not been sent to Abbeville. If only I had not been such a good shot and had stayed a stretcher-bearer... who knows? But even if I had been successfully evacuated, I would have eventually been shipped over to Africa or the Far East with the remains of my battalion to continue the long struggle for freedom against the axis powers. I may have endured the perilous journey and subsequent battles to eventually survive the war, or died in the struggle. All was speculation; there were no answers or solutions, only fear of the immediate future.

I cursed that lorry driver who had abandoned us to our fate; cursed the government who had catastrophically neglected our armed services before the war; cursed those who had thrown me and thousands like me into the thick of a conflict with only four months of woefully inadequate training; cursed Lord Gort, our Commander-in-Chief of the British Expeditionary Force in France and Belgium for his failings and whilst I was at it, cursed the whole stinking world.

By now, our band of six were bewildered, shocked, disappointed, totally demoralised and I am not afraid to say, scared. Even I had lost my sense of humour. I had no idea which way to go and quite honestly at that point, I didn't give a toss. Gunfire and shelling continued over Dunkirk as German infantry continued to press forward along with the others. But we hid and cautiously moved forward, towards the Germans for we had nowhere else to run to.

Small bands of enemy passed on by as we watched from the protection of abandoned vehicles, ditches, walls, woods and out-buildings. We kept off the roads at first, as seemingly endless motorised divisions were still advancing along these thoroughfares. We found shelter on the first night in an old barn at the edge of a field, hidden from the road. But it was a short uneasy sleep, for the horrors of the last few days replayed in my mind, over and over again. The melancholy soon set in as I sadly reflected on my fallen comrades and fellow members of the Queen's who had perished beside me. I pictured them lying there where they had fallen, their young bodies torn apart by another war. No time for burials, no time to mourn. They had all died alone, forgotten warriors in another foreign field with no loved one, relative or friend to lament at their passing and recite a prayer over their graves, for we had not the luxury of time.

> *5th June 1940, this was the day that three German Panzer Corps launched their 'Fall Rot' (Plan Red), their final attack on The Somme area.*

Well before dawn and under cover of darkness we continued southwards. At daybreak, we came to a road that cut across our path and fed into another road heading from north to south. As we crossed, my heart missed a beat. Wearily, moving in the same direction was a line of British troops. We ducked down behind a hedge to talk.

"Why not join them?"

"We are better off on our own, we can hide more easily."

"But we can move quicker."

"They might know something!"

"Why don't we ask them and then decide if we want to join them or not?"

And that seemed to be the best option, so we unanimously agreed and did just that. As we merged in with their numbers, nobody seemed to take any notice, just a slow cursory glance before resuming their downward stare.

"Excuse me mate, where are you heading for."

The reply was hardly reassuring. "Don't ask me, I ain't got a bloody clue!"

"But who's in charge?"

The soldier looked at me with an expression that said it all. "Don't ask me, I ain't got a bloody clue!"

We mingled and sought answers, any answers but there were none to be found. In short, nobody had the faintest idea.

We decided to stay with them for a while until we came across another route that appealed to us. In the meantime, we blindly followed the rest of the khaki line of thirty miserable beings, quiet and subdued in their own thoughts. Somehow we felt safety in numbers.

I became increasingly aware of the heavy Bren gun that I was still carrying. The thought crossed my mind that I had lost most of my remaining magazines, and without continuous ammo my gun was pretty useless. Anyway, apparently 'it was all over'. I looked at it for a brief second before tossing it aside into the ditch by the side of the road. Only Charlie noticed as the others were too immersed in their own despair.

"Don't blame you!" he said and smiled at me.

"Yer!... well,... what's the point in keeping it?"

In its place, I picked up an Enfield .303 rifle that was lying amongst the litter of war from our dejected army in retreat. I checked it out before resuming my disheartened trudge southwards to that well known place, F...knowswhere in the middle of Never Never Land.

I was but a tiny speck amongst droves of individual pockets of defeated allied troops, wandering aimlessly across the flat plains of north-west France without a clue, only some half-cocked idea that somewhere to the south lay our salvation.

We had been marching a few miles when we happened to stumble upon a blazing building. It was a former British NAAFI. In front of it stood a British Sergeant and stranger to us all. He was a big, jovial chap, carrying out boxes of goods and dumping them on the ground, safe from the destructive licking flames. There was food of every description, along with drink and fags - anything that could be of use to anybody the Sergeant was saving. As we passed, he beckoned us over and offered us what lay there.

"Come on lads," he shouted, "grab whatever you like. It's going to burn anyway and now the fight's over, it's a shame to let the Germans get their filthy hands on this lot."

I instantly became that kid of my dreams that was locked inside an abandoned sweet shop. I hadn't eaten for three days, but strangely I did not feel particularly hungry. But seizing the opportunity, I grabbed handfuls of cigarettes and a large container of 24 Cadbury's chocolate blocks. I ripped one open and stuffed it into my mouth. It was soft in the warmth of the day but tasted wonderfully smooth, sweet and satisfying. We felt compelled to keep moving and reluctantly left, carrying off as much as we could manage. After another few miles, I became increasingly weary. Greed had got the better of me and my chocolates box was becoming a burden. I stopped in the road, dropped the box at my feet and pushed as many bars as I could into my pockets and pouch, leaving the rest for whoever followed on behind.

If only I had been a bird soaring skywards on that summer's day, like a hawk with his discerning eye, I might have seen them coming...

We had been walking for miles in the heat of the day, making our way down a tarmac road. It was a typically long, tree-lined avenue, synonymous with the French countryside. The only man-induced sound to disturb the peace of that summer's day was the clatter of boots on tarmac. Soon we saw the civilian refugees streaming towards us. As they neared, they shouted.

"Boche, boche!" they cried, along with a deluge of other words. Of course we all knew what 'boche' meant but we didn't speak enough French to understand the rest, so we just kept on going, passing them by on the other side of the road. We had no idea where they were coming from or going to and soon they disappeared, becoming part of the distant landscape.

There was an urgency in our step now, to get as far away as possible from the war zone. By now we were spread out along a country road, all walking at different paces but our band of six just stayed behind the leading squad. Up ahead, we began to hear a sound. At first, it was just an indistinguishable rumble but seconds later we could discern the worrying sound of those caterpillar-tracked vehicles. Either side were raised grass covered banks topped with thick impenetrable hedgerows with no gaps,... we were trapped. Ahead, the road veered round to the right. We all stared straight ahead and waited, frozen to the spot, trapped. My heart missed a beat. From around the corner came a German light-armoured vehicle followed by troop-carriers full of Germans.

"Shit!" Freddy muttered, and I had to agree with him.

It was a horrifying repeat of what happened days ago, when we had managed to escape capture on the retreat from Abbeville. It had all happened so quickly that we just stood and watched as they came towards us,... just as a single shot rang out. We all dived for cover in our eagerness to escape any return fire. I didn't know who fired the shot, probably a knee-jerk reaction by one of us out of fear, but as I looked ahead I could see the mass of vehicles. They came to a halt whilst the light-armoured vehicle continued to approach us cautiously before coming to a halt, its machine gun at the ready.

Since mobilisation and leaving Abancourt camp, I had experienced one prevailing emotion above all others. Fear. This manifested itself in a more obvious physical manner by playing havoc with my bowels. I knew that I was not the only one. All the roadside ditches to and from Dunkirk and across northern France and into Belgium must have been flowing with human waste, from troops and fleeing refugees. Before we had time to do anything, the armoured vehicle jerked forward a little, bellowing out dirty clouds. In perfect English, the Commander in the turret shouted.

"Stand up Tommy."

I was lying face down, staring into the dirty soles of yet another soldier's boots inches from my nose. It was strange what thoughts flashed through my mind in times like these. I recalled that I had not shaved for days, that my hair was overgrown and uncombed, that my uniform was covered with dirt and filth and that I was still a virgin and had yet to live my life. But for now my only desire was to keep my head down and not move a muscle. If I stood up I feared the Germans would immediately open fire and I was not about to hand in my resignation to 'The Survivor Club' just yet. Nobody else moved, so the Commander barked out another order, with added impatience.

"If you don't stand up now, I will throw a grenade amongst you."

What should I do? Caution is always the better part of valour, so I continued lying there, waiting until the man in front of me stood up. If there was to be any shooting, I would much prefer somebody else to test the German's aptitude for killing. When the first man up ahead stood up and didn't receive a bullet for his troubles, we all followed, slowly surfacing with our eyes locked firmly onto the Officer's.

"Throw down your weapons," he shouted.

To the combined untidy clatter of our .303s hitting the road, we were joined by German infantry, running and then clustering around him, their rifles at the ready. We stood still, waiting. The Officer climbed out with his pistol drawn to be joined by another member of his tank crew. He walked casually but purposefully amongst us, disarming a few men before approaching me. In the same impeccable English, he looked me up and down before speaking. He was not unduly aggressive or threatening.

"Give me your knife Tommy."

What? I didn't have a knife... And my name's Dennis, not Tommy, he's behind me. I was scared, confused and my pulse was racing.
I simply stared back with a rather vacant expression of bewilderment. My mind was in turmoil. What did he mean? He looked at me before moving to my side, reached forward and behind and then pulled my bayonet out from its sheath. I didn't say it, but thought it.

'Please don't stick that in me', I quietly pleaded. He then turned to the side of me, bent forward with my bayonet and stuck it into the ground, blade first. I was relieved that the incident had passed and I was still alive.

Turning now to my fallen rifle, he picked it up and walked with it to a nearby tree, raised it behind his shoulder and smashed it against the trunk, breaking it across the small of the butt, before throwing it to the ground. Whilst this had been going on, the other German troops surrounded our group, disarming us and quickly searching for hidden weapons but taking nothing of our personal possessions. All of us were now standing with our hands in the air as ordered, waiting. The Commander then climbed back on board and issued instructions to us, pointing with his outstretched hand.

"Just keep walking in that direction and you will be alright."

He then spoke a now classic line that I was to hear quoted many times over, as though the Wehrmacht were told to utter the words to their vanquished foe, taught in anticipation of the victories that were to come.

"For you Tommy, the war is over."

The Germans drove off in the opposite direction, for their work was far from complete. They still had an already beaten army to subdue and capture. More half tracks followed. Then from behind, a whole German armoured division.

We set off walking along the road as the seemingly endless line of vehicles thundered past. The tanks had their turret doors open with crew and support staff sunning themselves on the tops of the vehicles, making the most of the dying rays from the late afternoon sun. For them, it looked like a public holiday. They seemed to be in great spirits, and why shouldn't they be? After all, they had all but beaten the two most powerful nations in Europe and were looking every bit the conquering heroes. Likewise, the infantry were taking full advantage of the calm, casually resting on their transportation whilst watching us with fascination as they drove on by. One clever sod rose up from tank top and gave us the Hitler salute as he passed, much to the delight of his comrades.

We continued to walk with our arms raised for as long as we could before they tired, feeling like lumps of lead ready to drop off. Inevitably, through sheer fatigue, our arms fell down by our sides and we were comfortable, for a short time at least. Without warning, the peace of that summer's day was broken as a trigger happy German fired a quick burst of gunfire over our heads, shouting and gesturing with his gun for us to raise our arms skywards once more, to continue our humiliation.

We had been marching into captivity for about an hour-and-a-half. Every so often, we passed stationary groups of Germans. They were watching our progress, relaxed but with guns at the ready, just in case. The wide, sweeping, open fields on either side of the road made escape rather suicidal under the circumstances but like many others, I fleetingly toyed with the idea of running. However, after weighing up the pros and cons, I decided that I was too shattered and dispirited to even attempt it. In any case, the countryside was swarming with more trigger-happy German troops, so what was the point?

Our band of six came upon an open German Mercedes staff car parked lazily at the side of the road in front of an opening. Inside the car were four Officers. Some were sitting, others standing. They watched as we approached. One Officer indicated to us to halt and beckoned us over. It was not easy to cross the road for the continually moving column of German tanks and support vehicles was in no mood to stop for us. Eventually, a small gap appeared in the traffic so we darted across to where they waited. Once more, in almost perfect BBC English, the senior Officer spoke.

"Who are you and what are you doing?"

Tommy, being the oldest, answered and then all the Officers started to speak to us in turn, in English. We told them our short story of where we had been fighting and where we were captured and chatted for a while. I was surprised at their interest and concern. As we approached their open staff car, my eyes were drawn to the food and a crate of wine on the back seat. They had been having a productive looting spree on their way through France for I doubted they had been 'shopping' as such, and here they were enjoying a pleasant picnic, basking in the glory of imminent victory. My eyes were popping out of my head and all I could think about was their food. I was famished. As if reading our minds, the senior Officer suddenly offered us food; bread, cheese and wine to drink whilst we talked. It was as if the war didn't exist. Their unexpected kindness heightened my respect for these front-line soldiers of the Wehrmacht.

But all too soon, the pleasantries were over. They had to continue conquering whilst we had an inescapable date with our destiny, assisted by our newly appointed guards who were gathering about us like vultures around a carcass.

~ LATER THAT SAME DAY ~
A GREAT GERMAN GENTLEMAN
5th June 1940

It was late in the day and our numbers were interfering with the smooth passage of the German column. We were immediately ordered off the road into a field, for nothing was going to stand in the way of the conquering German advance. Soon the field was crowded with prisoners. German soldiers moved amongst us and stripped us of our military attire such as helmets and ammunition pouches and searched for any remaining weapons. I slumped down just inside the gate, lay back on the long, lush grass and closed my eyes, basking in the remaining warmth of that summer sun. Our predicament contradicted the illusionary peace of that June day. Within seconds I nodded off but was soon disturbed by strange sounds, voices in a foreign tongue. I opened my eyes and sat up on one elbow looking around. Nearby, I saw another group of German Officers.

The three of them were walking freely amongst us without a care in the world. The most senior Officer, who I later understood to be a Commanding General, was accompanied by his entourage and armed guards. Slowly they made their way towards me, occasionally stopping on the way to point at a soldier and talk amongst themselves. His accompanying Officers both wore peaked caps, but he wore a simple forage cap. His uniform was more casual, more like battle dress, whereas his Officers appeared more formal. His top tunic carried collar flashes with gold leaves and insignia of some sort. Between the collars hung an Iron Cross, which impressed me greatly at that moment. Beneath this, he wore another more elaborate cross, pinned through his tunic. On his broad shoulders sat decorative epaulettes. Above his right breast pocket he wore the German eagle and swastika, and on his left breast pocket hung another Iron Cross. Jodhpurs tucked neatly into his mirror-shiny black leather boots which completed his dress. He had a presence about him that commanded respect. This must be an important man. He looked impeccable. To my dying day, I will always carry this image of him in my mind, such was the impression that he made upon me.

When he eventually reached me he looked down at me, not disparagingly but as a Commander to one of his men.

"Stand up boy," he ordered briskly. He also spoke in perfect English.

To me he looked elderly but he was probably in his early to mid-fifties. He stood tall, about six feet, looked powerful and had closely-cropped silver hair visible under his cap. I remember his strong, bent nose and interesting, kind eyes. He looked every bit the archetypal Prussian Officer and nobleman. I did as I was ordered and stood to attention. He looked almost regal. Even his guards looked as though they had just come off the parade ground. I wondered what I must have looked like by comparison, stinking, sweaty, untidy, dirty and unshaven. Why he singled me out of all the other prisoners I have no idea, but he did. It might have been because I looked the youngest of my group or because of my long, striking blonde hair. I expected him to interrogate me but instead, he smiled and talked to me in a kind and gentle manner.

"What do you think about the war, soldier?"

I responded as best I could, aware that I had to be polite to this high-ranking Officer, but I was aware that my friends and a host of other prisoners were all intently focused on me, listening to every word that was being said and to what I was about to utter. Somehow, I had to be respectful and a bit bolshy at the same time so as not to lose face with my mates. I felt like a child in front of the headmaster.

> *If you know a little of English history and art, you may recall a famous painting by William Frederick Yeames, depicting a small boy dressed in fine blue clothes who happened to be the son of Charles I. The youngster is depicted standing in front of his inquisitors, the Roundhead Parliamentarians, with his young sister in tears behind him. His inquisitors are all staring at him intently from behind a desk, asking him to betray his father by telling them where he was hiding. In front of this powerful German, I now felt as that small child must have felt.*

After a few minutes of light-hearted conversation, the Officer smiled broadly and asked me another question.

"When do you think the war will be over?"

By now, I was feeling more relaxed and with that came increased truculence.

"It will be years," I replied, never realising what a prophet I was.

"How come, when we have the whole British Army here?" as he swept his outstretched arm across the landscape, "...in our hands?" he retorted, raising up his hand in front of my face before slowly closing it into a tight clenched fist.

"No," I said, "you've only got the conscripted part of our army here. You have yet to meet the regular British Army."

Little was I aware that the German Army had all but wiped the floor with the very best of our troops, and now Britain had virtually no professional army at home, in reserve. Also, we had lost most of our ordnance, for I had witnessed the tonnage of guns and vehicles abandoned by our retreating forces.

He gave me a knowing half smile. "Do you realise that we will soon be in London?"

His eyes bore into me. He was reading me and knew I had no answer. He turned to his fellow Officers, who were all smiling sympathetically, then addressed one of his soldiers, speaking to him in his own tongue. With that, he walked away. I watched him as he continued his meanderings amongst us before returning to his vehicle at the entrance to the field. His driver, a young-looking Sergeant, held open the door of the small, unassuming vehicle as the Commanding General climbed into his Kübelwagen (the German Army's equivalent of an American jeep), followed by the other Officers.

The soldier whom he had just spoken to approached me.

"Come with me", he said in German.

Freddy Laws stepped forward to confront the guard.

"Where are you taking him?"

I could tell that the German didn't like the tone of his voice but he did nothing. I was escorted into the field on the opposite side of the road as the General and his entourage drove away. I was feeling very uneasy, not knowing what to expect. I knew that I had been totally respectful to him, but I had also argued against him. All eyes were fixed on me. I had the feeling that I was being led away to face some sort of punishment. They took me to a small barn in the middle of the adjacent field. One of them opened the door. I had no idea what to expect but as the door swung open, I saw the Tirailleurs Sénégalais inside.

> 'Tirailleurs Sénégalais' were West African colonial army troops from Senegal, Algeria, Tunisia, and Morocco who fought for the French, making up some 9% of their army. These colonials were treated badly even by their own side, often and openly regarded as mere cannon fodder by their generals. They did however, have a ferocious, bloodthirsty reputation. Their scant regard for human life, including their own, made them formidable fighters, almost suicidal.

I did not know what to make of it, as to why these black troops were either imprisoned or being given shelter in a barn. However, such was the nobility of this German Officer, it was just conceivable that he really was showing kindness and respect to them as well, although, from the Germanic racist standpoint, the likelihood seemed remote. The guard explained to me in sign language and German that the Officer wanted me to have shelter for the night and I was to go in, but he smiled as he spoke. This apparent act of 'kindness' by an enemy Commander to me, an ordinary British soldier, troubled me as I entered. However, there was a problem. The Sénégalais did not want me and immediately protested loudly to the German, holding their noses as they shouted.

"Odeur infect, enlever, enlever!" ("Foul smell, remove, remove!").

Even I with only schoolboy French could understand - *I smelt?* What a cheek. I was both mortified and embarrassed. But the German would have none of it and went in amongst them, bashing them with his rifle butt and shouting before finally threatening them with the barrel. Grudgingly they quietened down, allowing the guard to leave and lock the door behind him. Minutes ticked by. Then I noticed it. Never mind them thinking that I smelt, for in the warm confines of that wooden barn these Sénégalais reeked. Their combined stench was terrible. The result was that they moved down to the far end of the barn, as far away from me as possible, leaving me completely on my own at the opposite end, by the door. Initially I was relieved to be left on my own but now, I began to wonder if these troops would beat me up or even murder me as I slept. Fortunately they did neither. Gradually I relaxed and sat down with my back against the wooden boards to the side of the door. I faced them for I wanted to keep tabs on my potential assassins. I felt the warmth of that fading summer sun radiate through the thin wooden boards. I was bewildered for this was all so far removed from my cosy little life back home in Surrey. Eventually, I had to close my eyes and I fell into a deep, exhausted sleep, my head full of the life-changing recollections of what had occurred on this awful day.

The summer dawn came early. I opened my eyes. The barn was peppered with so many holes that sunlight streamed in. The Sénégalais were a hive of activity. Using kindle, matches, water and a pot, they had made a fire on which to boil a tin of water. Into this, they placed leaves of nettles, dandelion and daisies acquired by reaching out through the many small gaps in the old barn. They beckoned me over, smiling as they did. I joined them as one tried to communicate with me but to no avail. In spite of my 'awful smell' they made me welcome, and when the concoction was brewed, it was passed around and I was given a share. It was not great but it was wet, warm and, one assumes, had a trace of nourishment.

I had learnt a valuable lesson from the Sénégalais - if you are hungry enough, it is possible to eat the wild vegetation that surrounds you and who knows, one day in the future, that knowledge might even save my life

~ THE MARCH CONTINUES ~

After 'breakfast', the door was flung open, allowing daylight to flood the barn. I was ordered back onto the road once more but the colonial troops were not. The door was locked behind me.

The guard shouted for me to join the column of prisoners that were already clogging the road whilst I looked about expectantly. But my friends were nowhere to be seen. Concerned, I ran forward, searching amongst the faces in the crowd. I had no idea how long a head start they had on me. I turned around but was stopped from going back to search amongst those still trying to leave the fields. Were they ahead or behind?

We numbered well over a thousand and the long khaki line stretched ahead and behind. Shouting came from all around; the frustration of our guards was evident in their hurry to get everybody moving but all I could think of was the loss of my friends. Apprehension knotted my stomach.

As I passed on by, I could see mounds of our steel helmets and army equipment littering the meadows where we had spent the night, baggage abandoned by us prisoners on the instructions of our captors,... another humiliating reminder of our bitter defeat.

In the fields I spotted troops who appeared in need of medical attention. Since our capture, the condition of our wounded had obviously worsened. Many were unable to restart the gruelling journey so they remained where they lay in the hope of being treated by German medics. We had only just begun to move when I focused on a lone British wounded soldier to my right. Leaning up on one elbow, he watched as we walked on by. An irate German soldier saw him and shouted something before he unslung his rifle and ran towards him. I had no idea as to his intentions but given the tone of his voice, I feared that he might harm him. Fortunately that morning, a German Officer was travelling with our column in a small, open-topped staff car. He saw what was happening and ordered his driver to stop. He stood up with his hand gripping the top of the windscreen whilst removing his Luger pistol from his holster. As the guard ran towards our wounded comrade, he fired two shots into the air and shouted to him. The guard stopped dead in his tracks, replaced his rifle and walked back to rejoin the column. The Officer may have shared my concern and given him the order that he was to be left where he lay for the medics to deal with.

This was yet another surprising act of kindness that seemed at odds with my preconceived perception of the German character. Of those front-line Officers and combatants that I encountered in those early few days, the civilised rules of war seemed to prevail.

It's a strange aspect of war that opposing troops tended to treat each other with respect, despite the fact that before the cessation of hostilities, both were hell-bent on trying to kill each other. Afterwards, prisoners are taken and victors confront the vanquished, both knowing that the other was only following orders and doing their duty. In the main, all parties were managing to maintain that mutual respect. Of course, I do not include those who were unfortunate enough to come up against the SS troops, who were fast developing their awesome and terrifying reputation. Later, I came to know that it was amongst the noncombatant German guards that we found those most likely to inflict cruelty and war crimes upon us captives.

> *Memories of those German career Officers whom I had met, entered my mind and I found myself comparing them with our counterparts. The German Officers appeared to beat the British Officers hands down in terms of overall appearance and modern training. Even in the heat of that summer, the immaculate General who had spoken to me a few days earlier had his jacket buttoned up all the way, his back was as straight as a rod of iron. You could not fail to be impressed by his stature, his staff and the whole German Army. To me, the Germans had put the disastrous methods and howling mistakes of the First World War behind them, re-written the training manual of modern warfare and then studied and practised it at every level. Having invented this new warfare, they implemented it to perfection.*
>
> *This war was their war and fought on their terms.*
>
> *At the outset of hostilities, we British were sad amateurs by comparison and in war-torn Europe, the French didn't even warrant a rating and I considered their Officer Corps to be beneath contempt.*

The drudgery of our march continued throughout that day. The roads were less busy; only two convoys of supply trucks passed by, forcing us to take evasive action in the fetid ditches. We marched with no break, my mind still in a daze. As dusk approached, we came upon a farm in the middle of nowhere. Our guards halted our column and investigated the main building to find it still occupied by the French farmer. We were packed tightly into the surrounding buildings, barns and stables whilst those unable to find cover made themselves as comfortable as possible in the farm yard.

Having failed to find anything to eat, we fed off our emotions of worry and fear whilst our hungry, dirty bodies expressed absolute weariness. However, I did manage to find shelter inside the barn. As I sat on the straw-covered floor, a Captain entered the barn.

"How are you men coping?" he enquired, seemingly genuinely concerned.

"Not too bad Sir, could do with a cuppa though."

The men sniggered.

"I wish I could arrange that for you all. Look men, I know you are going through a tough time and I don't know how long this will last, but when we get to wherever the Germans are taking us, things will settle down and conditions will improve. Just hang on in there, we are all in this together and we can get through this."

We listened and did take some comfort from his words.

"Are there any sick amongst you?"

"My feet are killing me Sir and they smell something 'orrible."

We all laughed again, including the Captain.

"I can assure you that mine are no better," and he was probably right.

"One more thing men, before long, we will all be thoroughly searched. If you have anything of value, sentimental or otherwise, may I suggest that you take steps to conceal it somehow, so that it is not found. Trust me, they will take anything they want and there is little I or anybody else can do to stop them."

He stood up straight and adjusted his cap.

"Well try and get some rest, you are going to need all your strength in the morning. Good-night men."

With that, he left. I watched him as he went to the next group and squatted down amongst them. He was obviously trying to keep our spirits up and it did help; any act of kindness helped.

I still had several hundred French francs and my gold watch

given to me by my girlfriend Josephine, neither of which I wanted to lose. One of the guys in the barn had a small pocket knife, which I borrowed. I made a tiny slit in the epaulette of my tunic and very carefully slid the folded notes inside. My gold watch was a bit more of a problem but I managed to conceal it inside my sock and gaiters. Thereafter, I quickly slid into a deep but troubled slumber, not waking until dawn.

~ THE GENEVA CONVENTION ~

It might be of interest to read a reference to the Geneva Convention. It refers to several treaties agreed upon by the international community regarding the fair treatment of prisoners of war, civilians in war-afflicted countries and the treatment of the injured, signed before the start of the Second World War.

(The principles of the Convention can be read on page 588).

~ NEVER TRUST A FRENCHMAN ~

The third day of our captivity was sweltering and I had a thirst to match. My woollen shirt felt hot and itchy. I carried my top tunic and rolled my sleeves up as far as they would go but the sweat was still pouring down my spine. Our guards were making no effort to find water or food for us, but as we walked through yet another small French village, I saw a bucket of water in the porch way of a small cottage. With no guards watching, I made a dash for it. The water looked clean and fresh so I drank a huge amount of it as quickly as I could. Like bees to a honey pot, others came running over, which caused the Germans to take note. A guard shouted then fired into the air whilst running towards us. I had already had my fill so I let someone else take it and ran back to the column. I looked back and watched as the men continued to drink from the bucket right up until the moment that the guard knocked it from their hands to the ground and then proceeded to beat all those around with his rifle butt. He could easily have allowed each man to drink. So much for my *premature* heightened respect for these 'front-line soldiers', the 'bastard' in them was beginning to surface.

We eventually came to the French town of Béthune. From what I saw, it appeared relatively unscathed by the war, a mixture of old town with narrow, cobbled streets and contrasting industrial modernity all around. At its centre we passed a beautiful belfry, the likes of which I had never seen before. The locals were out in force with German troops amongst them, jeering at our meandering line of wretchedness making its way into internment. To increase our very public humiliation, a news photographer with a film camera stood on an open truck, recording our suffering.

Our march continued until we arrived at a stark set of buildings in a small town. We halted at the perimeter of the complex with its high, un-scalable walls. A plain but substantial solid gate was the only visible form of entrance. It looked like a prison but was, in fact, a jute factory. German soldiers stood guard on either side of the heavy double gates, which were unceremoniously pushed open for us with some difficulty before we were ordered through under the ever-watchful eyes of the armed and threatening sentries. I was astonished at what I saw beyond: thousands of prisoners of war crammed within the confines of the factory walls, British, French, Dutch, Belgian. It was like the League of Nations. Up until now, Officers, NCO's and enlisted men alike had marched together, suffering in the same way, but as our horde descended on the old factory, Officers were separated from us, politely ushered away and escorted out of sight. That was the last I saw of our Officer Corps for a couple of years.

As we entered, each of us was searched, just as had been predicted the previous night. Everything of 'value' was taken, money, watches, rings, soap, pouches and webbing. When they searched my pockets, my Players' Naval Cut cigarettes were confiscated, but finding nothing else of interest the soldier turned his attention to my watch. Fortunately, not the gold watch from Josephine which I had hidden, but my old cheap one. He instantly relieved me of that and, having no further use for me or my lack of worthy possessions, he ordered me through with the flick of his thumb into the courtyard beyond. So much for another fanciful clause of the Geneva Convention!

Once inside, my first thought was to go in search of my friends, not an easy task as the compound was extensive and the buildings numerous. An underlying odour of hemp hung within the confines of our impromptu prison. It probably did us all a favour as it helped mask the wretched stench of us, the great unwashed. I walked amongst them, my head flitting from left to right and back again. Some were sitting whilst others slept where they fell or just stood about whilst others exchanged tales with anybody who had the strength to listen.

My search was proving to be futile.

As far as I knew, none of us had been provided with food for two days or more and my stomach expressed its dissatisfaction,... and still the Germans did nothing to provide us with nourishment. By the mercy of God, water was available from an outside tap and in constant use as a never ending line of us satisfied our murderous thirst.

Day sank slowly into an oppressive night as I abandoned my search for my five friends. As I settled down I felt horribly isolated, alone amongst a crowd of a thousand. The surrounding walls were high and no breeze reached us thereby retaining the sweltering heat of the day.

The following morning, word rapidly spread that those of us with French francs could go to the back of the compound to another gate, where French civilians were ready to aid us, waiting to take our money and buy bread for us. To hungry men, this seemed a life saving idea and I was thankful that there were such kind folk willing to help us, especially as no other food was forthcoming. I decided to spend my way out of famine. Finding what privacy I could, I carefully removed some of my hidden francs and went in search of the back gate. It was a strong wooden construction with both vertical and horizontal cross members at regular intervals, which made it easy to climb. Once on top, the large semi-circular gap was blocked with vertically-placed iron bars about five inches apart, thereby foiling any attempt at escape or break-in. A few French civilians were gathered on the other side, all male. I manoeuvred myself and caught the attention of one of the waiting Frenchmen.

"Du pain, du pain" ("Some bread, some bread"), I shouted, waving my francs at him. The Frenchman nodded his understanding and waved back, holding up two fingers.

"Deux cents francs, Deux cents francs," he shouted.

Two-hundred francs! a king's ransom and daylight robbery,... but my stomach was reluctant to argue. He indicated for me to throw him my money. I scrunched the notes into a ball and threw it at him. Using sign language, he pointed to his watch and then towards some shops before leaving, smiling as he left. He didn't even count it, I thought him a trusting fellow. Along with all the others, I waited,... and waited,... and waited. I seethed with anger as it dawned on me that he would not return. How could I have been so naive as to think that he would. None of our French shoppers returned. Now I was seething with anger, still hungry and closer to broke than I had been an hour earlier. Today I had learnt a lesson... never trust a Frenchman.

We were kept in this insanitary, overcrowded holding pen for another day whilst other PoWs were gathered and brought in to join us. By now, my crotch and armpits were itching and I was constantly scratching but gave it little thought.

Things improved for us the next day,...slightly. Without warning, it started to rain bread! The Germans began tossing loaves over the walls into our compound. Within was utter mayhem. Struggles ensued and it was a case of dog-eat-dog and survival of the fittest. In the bitter fist fights that followed, I managed to grab my share of bread, enabling me to keep body and soul together. The Germans would have realised the consequences of their actions and must have enjoyed watching our humiliating behaviour. With my share hidden and stuffed under my tunic, I moved away from the chaos.

On the third day at Béthune, the gates were flung open once more and over three thousand of us poured out. Our guards took up their positions on the outside of the column at regular intervals of about twenty yards apart. It wasn't long before we were joined by more PoWs, converging from every direction whilst proceeding towards the south-east. With our increasing numbers I couldn't see how the Germans would possibly be able to feed us, and in the days and weeks ahead I resigned myself to the constant companionship of hunger. Hour after hour, we kept on. When I got the chance, I would ask a friendly-looking guard the question that I was to ask a hundred times more.

"How much further 'til we get there?"

I always received the same reply.

"Oh, just a little further, just a little."

They lied. We knew nothing and were told nothing. It was like being back in the British Army, but slightly more worrying.

Whilst some guards walked with our slow, bedraggled column, others took a less tiring form of transport. They wisely 'acquired' bikes, horses, carts and wagons from the civilian population, taking it in turn to rest whilst travelling in style.

We neared Lens and I recalled my last visit here on 17th May, just after the invasion of France, when we were bombed in the station.

Suddenly a woman dashed from her house with a bucket of water and put it down on the road. A prisoner ahead grabbed it, becoming lost in the seething crowd. I wasn't near enough to benefit from this kind act and fortunately for her, no guard saw her. On another occasion, somebody threw broken chunks of bread into out midsts, causing a riot. It was chaos as we fought for a portion. Order was only restored when guards fell amongst us thrashing wildly about us with their rifles. I managed to grab a piece but suffered a bruised back for my troubles.

I wearily reached the crest of a small incline and gasped at the sight that confronted me. I stopped momentarily to absorb it, causing others to bump into me. I could now see how long this column of ours was. The line of prisoners stretched ahead for mile upon mile into the distance. I slowly turned around, only to be confronted by a similarly depressing scene, but it was the sheer size that left me dumbstruck and no matter how much I stared, I could not take it in. I was somewhere in the middle of a huge khaki serpent slithering on its belly across the French countryside with no visible head or tail. It looked as though the Germans had captured the greatest numbers of enemy troops in the entire history of the world.

At each gruelling day's end, we were herded into any field to spend another night in the open. The only thing I had to be thankful about was that it was not winter. Escorting us were several small military vehicles fitted with four-barrelled heavy machine guns, designed for use against enemy aircraft attack. The barrels rotated as the gun was fired. By placing these vehicles at the corners of each field along with our foot guards, the Germans were assured of retaining most, if not all of us. Used against unarmed personnel on the ground, these vehicle-mounted weapons were an excellent choice by our captors to discourage any brave or suicidal prisoners from futile escape attempts.

~ BACK HOME IN ENGLAND ~
Thursday 20th June

It was an ordinary day in mid-June 1940. My mother was only one-hundred-and-fifty miles away (as the crow flies), busying herself with her house work, trying not to think about the war and the dangers that I might be facing. She was failing miserably. After Dunkirk, she had been praying to hear from The War Office after the return of so many troops from France, hoping that I had been one of the lucky ones to have made it home. As each day passed, her hopes faded.

At mid-morning the postman arrived. Mother was standing in the hallway and saw them drop onto the floor, landing with an almost inaudible flutter on the doormat. By now, she was getting used to her most recent letters being returned to her, stamped with the worrying wording;

> 'Return to Sender - Undelivered for reason stated - Not with Unit - ADDRESS NOT KNOWN.

Today as was usual, she prayed that she would not see a brown envelope amongst the post for by now, relatives of service men in France were receiving the dreaded letter from The War Office, informing them that regretfully, their son had been killed in action. As she cautiously searched amongst the batch of correspondence from The Surrey Police HQ to my father, there were two letters to her, one from an old neighbour in Hersham and another, in a cream-coloured envelope. She heaved a sigh of relief and took them into the kitchen to carefully open with a knife as my father hated so see letters torn open. The postmark showed that it had been posted in Northumberland. The address on the front was hand-written. Inside was a single sheet of cream-coloured lined paper, neatly scribed in pen. It was a letter from a Captain Brian Owen of the 2nd/7th Battalion The Queen's Royal Regiment, her son's regiment, now based in Haydon Bridge, Northumberland. It read as follows:

> *Dear Mrs. Minter,*
>
> *As you see from the address above we have now returned to England, but I am afraid we lack many of the people we originally started with. We were involved in action with the Enemy on 20th May and at the time of writing (16th June 1940) I regret I am unable to give you any news of your son, who is now posted as missing. We have reason to believe that many of his fellows have joined other forces or maybe become prisoners and therefore I hope you may hear something from your son himself. This letter is not an easy one to write and I can only offer you the sympathy and good wishes of the Battalion in your worry.*
> *Signed*
> *Brian Owen, Capt. O.C. HQ.*
> *(see picture reference 21)*

Had I been able to contact her, I would have reached into her tormented mind to say to her:

"Don't you worry Mum, it will take a damn sight more than this war to get rid of me."

The letter brought little comfort and only added to her worries. Countless sleepless nights and anxious days later, mother was close to tears when she saw another letter on her doorstep. This time it was an official small brown envelope. She studied it for ages, too petrified to open it. The envelope was marked 'On His Majesty's Service', posted on 24th June. Her little heart began to pound. She felt faint and sat down in the kitchen, staring with ashen face before finding the courage to open it.

> *Sir or Madam,*
> *I regret to inform you that a report has been received from The War Office to the effect that*
> *(No.) 6093969*
> *(Rank)....Private*
> *(Name) ....Dennis Henry MINTER*
> *(Regiment) .....2nd/7th The Queen's Royal Regiment*
> *was posted as "missing" on 21.5.40.*
> *The report that he is missing does not necessarily mean that he has been killed, as he may be a prisoner of war or temporarily separated from his regiment. Official reports that men are prisoners of war take some time to reach this country, and if he has been captured by the enemy it is probable that unofficial news will reach you first. In that case I am to ask you to forward any postcards or letters received at once to this Office, and they will be returned to you as soon as possible.*
> *Should any further official information be received it will be at once communicated to you.*
> *I am, Sir or Madam, Your obedient Servant,*
> *Signed: Officer in charge of Records*

Mother burst into tears. There was nobody home to comfort her.

During those summer months, over 40,000 such letters were being received by family, friends and loved ones of fellow servicemen 'missing' in action. For the next week, not knowing if I was alive or dead, they hoped upon hope that I was unharmed and indeed, a PoW, for even that was better than the other option. However, within her own mind, she was somehow preparing for the worst. It was hell for her but I never knew what effect it was having on my unemotional father!

A week later another official postcard from the Army Field Service arrived. It was signed by me and sent from Stalag XXA at Thorn. It was impossible to include any additional details. By way of deleting standard preprinted sentences on the card, all information was kept to the barest minimum. She was only able to gleam the following:

'I am quite well. Letter follows at first opportunity'.

The information was as cold as that and although short and to the point, at least she now knew that I really was alive.

Several days later, another card arrived, this time from The Geneva Red Cross informing her that I was a PoW in Germany, adding in hand-written pen that:

'He is well'.

Both had taken over a month to travel across war-torn Europe, which wasn't surprising. My mother was to patiently wait another four months before receiving any further news from me.

~ A SURVIVOR'S PHILOSOPHY ~
WAS NEEDED

We foot-slogged south west through Douai, then south to Bapaume and north west to Cambrai before turning south west again towards La Capelle. It was as though we were being sent through as many highly populated places as possible in order to show us off to the local civilians in order to humiliate us even further, in spite of the Geneva Convention. Every town and village on the way seemed filled with locals and Germans, hell bent on spitting, throwing rotten vegetables and shouting abuse at us.

"England kaput!"

Some sang songs, our songs,... with a bitter twist.

"Hey Tommy," one screamed, "we're gonna hang out your washing on the Siegfried Line, have YOU any dirty washing TOMMY dear?" before bursting into laughter and pointing at us.

Many took photos, capturing our misery for the photo album. It was hell and utterly soul destroying and made increasingly worse by the fierce heat of the day. I knew I must be stinking by now for I could smell the stench of my neighbours. My uniform was so uncomfortable to wear as sweat ran down every part of my body.

We must have looked a pitiful bunch by now. Gone were our new uniforms, for we were now covered in mud, shit and filth from head to toe. Finger nails blackened with filth, every line on the palms of my hands was filled with dirt. My hands resembled those of a navvy that no amount of scrubbing would remove.

Because of the heat, there were those in the column who had been captured without their battle dress tops and shirts and suffered from chronic sunburn. To protect themselves from the relentless rays of the sun, many had acquired curtains or floral patterned dresses to cover themselves. Others had raided civilian wardrobes and stolen jackets or raincoats, male or female which made our procession of captives a pretty motley looking collection of despairing humanity.

Thoughts of every kind continuously drifted in and out of my head for there was nothing else but the pain of defeat to keep it occupied. But I have never been one to roll over and give up in times of adversity and so it was on this occasion as I, along with thousands, endured our plight. I would talk to myself in an attempt to raise my flagging spirit.

"To hell with them, they won't get the better of me, I WILL keep going. After all, one day, this WILL be over and it WILL all end, it's bound to and I want to be there when it does."

I obviously didn't know when or even if the war would ever end, but that was what I had to keep telling myself.

It became my mantra and it sustained me throughout the war, even in my darkest hours. My simple philosophy applied in the short term as well. During that march, my common sense told me that eventually we would get to the end of the day. Likewise, we would finally reach our destination. We had to,... or we would all end up in bloody China!

Today was one of continuous heavy rain and my uniform was soaked. I shook uncontrollably in the cold morning mist that shrouded the field where we had slept. After only an hour of walking, I could feel the blisters forming on the insides of my red raw thighs and my feet were in agony.

I am happy to report that our German guards were sharing some of our misery. The fact that they were becoming increasingly irate as each day passed was a good indication that they were as fed up with being on this march as us, when they might have preferred to be facing death on a battlefield somewhere.

Since our capture, hunger had been our closest companion. The only time I stopped thinking of food was when I was thinking of a long, cool, refreshing glass of clear, wonderful water, or a cigarette. Either way, it was torture!

For the most part, the landscape was flat. Occasionally our column would pass over a slight incline, which would allow one to marvel at our vast line of captives, like ants, snaking and meandering across the never ending panorama. From such a vantage point, I would witness a sudden surge of khaki swarm out into an adjacent field as hungry men, hell-bent on finding anything to eat, swept through a farmer's crop. Shots would ring out as guards attempted to regain control of their charge. When I eventually reached such fields I found them almost decimated; the locusts had left little. I thought I might fare better if I was at the front of the column, then I would have first pickings, but there wasn't any beginning or end to our khaki mass that I could see.

The Germans had the devil's own job trying to watch over us all the time and survival was now the only game to be played so I too had to take risks. I kept my eyes glued to my surroundings during the long haul for anything that I could eat or make use of. If I saw anything growing such as fruit, unripe or otherwise, or vegetables not already plundered, I took the opportunity, dashing out of line, stealing and rejoining the column. By now, I and every other famished soul who wanted to live was doing the same. Then I would remember my Senegalese friends in the barn and try to search out the plants in the hedgerows that I could eat. Without fire and water the nettles were out of the question, but the dandelion leaves, daisies and even grass were edible to a degree, and an option that I often had to resort to.

We passed a field full of French and Belgium prisoners resting in the warmth of the sun whilst receiving food from German field kitchens. We hadn't had one meal provided for us by our captors and now we British were forcibly excluded from joining them. This happened time and time again, too many occasions to be an oversight. It must have been systemic discrimination against us British for some reason, which did nothing to enhance my feelings towards the Germans or our so-called French allies.

On the third day after the jute factory, the rains had sought to maximise our miserable condition. We rose to a damp and wretched day. As we stood about in a sodden meadow in the cool morning air, a mist of vapour steadily rose from the body of men, their clothing soaked to the core.

Another day, and so began our interminable trek towards the unknown. Not long after, I approached a very suitable house. It looked promising. As I neared, I readied myself, turning and looking about me. With no guards watching I dived into the garden of the house. It looked deserted and the door was locked. In one swift movement, I kicked it in and was inside. I made straight for the kitchen and rifled through the cupboards, searching for anything that might have been left behind that could be eaten. I was in luck. There was a stale half loaf of bread in the cupboard, a warped lump of something that looked like cheese and a tin with no label. All were in my tunic within seconds and I was outside in a flash. I waited behind a wall until a guard walked past before jumping back to join the others. A fellow PoW noticed me rejoin.

"Any luck mate?" he enquired eagerly.

"Place had been picked clean." I lied easily for I didn't know the man and he was in no more need of my scant meal than I.

I picked up my pace to lose myself amongst the throng ahead. As life was uncertain, I began eating the bread straight away breaking off small pieces whilst keeping the loaf hidden under my tunic. The contents of the mystery tin would wait until nightfall. There were no repercussions for me on that occasion.

The next likely 'shopping' opportunity was a farm. If our guards heard or saw us in action they were sure to follow, of that I was certain. This time, we were not so lucky. By the time I saw the place and jumped through the hedge and into the house, it was already full of marauding prisoners, pillaging at high speed. This time, we were spotted. Guards followed, bursting in through the front door. It was pandemonium. We played cat and mouse with them for a few seconds whilst they shouted and screamed, firing their rifles into the ceiling. We grabbed what we could and nipped out of the back door to rejoin the others before we were caught, all in the space of twenty seconds. I nonchalantly took my place before daring to look back over my shoulder, just in time to see three armed guards burst back onto the road, looking backwards and forwards for any sign of us thieving PoWs. I turned away and smiled with my heart racing. I do not know what they would have done if they had caught us; possibly shot us or roughed us up with their rifle butts. Who knows, but I was pleased not to have been found out.

"That was bloody close," I sighed to one of the other more successful foragers who returned a hearty grin.

I looked about me, but I could see nobody I knew. I was still alone but I still hoped to meet up with them at some point, but when? More often than not, I found nothing on these sorties as countless others before me had already been there. Hunger is a formidable motivator and it was always worth the risk of a look.

Still no sight of my mates. Today, I toyed with the idea of escape and of repeating my successful getaway after the bridge at Abbeville incident. I could have easily stayed hidden after diving into a farm building or nipping behind a hedgerow until nightfall. With hunger gnawing away inside of me, it seemed an attractive idea initially, but what then? The British Army had gone home, albeit without us, and we were still surrounded by the might of the German Army. I had no idea if they were still fighting the French or whether they had capitulated. I was a naive twenty-one-year-old enemy soldier, alone on foreign soil, unable to speak the language, with no idea as to where to go or how to get home. Roaming the country, I ran a serious risk of being shot by the trigger happy enemy. I had no weapon, no map and no hope. I had seen the change of attitude of the once-friendly French civilians towards us British and knew not if they would be helpful or hostile to escaping PoWs. With few positives and contemplating the mass of negatives, it made no sense for me to try. It was safer and easier to stay and do nothing for a while and see what happened. After all who knows, it might all turn out for the best anyway, for what did any of us know at that stage, so early in the war? Things might have been different for me if I had still been with my platoon leader, old dependable Sergeant Hawkes. Even though I was surrounded by thousands of my fellow countrymen, to all intents and purposes, I was alone.

With the sinking of the setting sun, we were ordered off the road for the night. God, I was itching.

As soon as I was settled, I quietly took out a large, flat rusty nail from my pocket that I had found lying at the side of the road and removed the tin that I had found. With the aid of my boot, I eventually tapped in the nail many times and tore open a hole big enough to get at its contents, which turned out to be sardines. I picked them out and enjoyed every morsel before sucking out the very last drop of oily juice.

British soldiers were issued with emergency rations that consisted of a piece of dense, hard chocolate. We were not supposed to eat it unless we had gone without food for forty-eight hours. Mine had gone into my aching stomach long ago. On this particular day, after marching in silence all morning, my stomach ached with hunger. I kept wishing that I had kept my ration for just this moment.

We passed another deserted French house with its front door partially open. I took my chance and dashed into the two-storey building and raided the larder. Unfortunately, all I found was an old jar with the remains of some suspect jam at the bottom, but I shoved my dirty fingers in and scooped out every bit of it, licking my fingers clean. It tasted heavenly. Within a minute I was back in line.

That night we spent another miserable time in the open, but this time it rained and the cold seeped into my core. My feet were aching like never before and all I could think of was taking my boots off and soaking my weary feet in a tub of hot, soapy water in front of an open fire. Now my natural exuberance momentarily deserted me and I was feeling miserable and alone.

Fortunately, the following day was warm and bright. My clothes began to dry and the sweet, pungent smell of dirty sweat and wet wool rose from my uniform. We passed a field in which vegetables were growing. I scrambled through an opening and raced into the field, along with a plague of locusts that now descended upon the crop. This particular farmer was growing peas that had not yet ripened. I grabbed as many as I could, tearing the pods from the plants before stuffing them into my tunic top. There was only a hint of the young peas beginning to swell inside the pods, but that was of no consequence to a hungry man. As I walked, I ate the lot, pods and all. They were sour but crisp and tender, satisfying my hunger and filling my shrunken belly.

At the day's end, in yet another field full of weary allied souls, the ground was soon contaminated with the waste of men, for dysentery was creeping through our ranks. By now, the actions of our guards left me in little doubt as to their potentiality for cruelty. Often the guards degraded us by preventing anybody from stopping to answer the urgent call of nature by forcing us to march on and defecate in our trousers whilst walking. Today I watched as one British Sergeant, squatting by the roadside, was forced at gunpoint to stand and move again. As he stood he was unable to stop himself going. The total humiliation of this fellow human being was complete.

The incident took me back to my childhood at Hersham. I was thirteen at the time and worked delivering prescriptions and medicines for old Mr. Wright, the local chemist. He provided me with a delivery bike that had a large wicker carrying basket mounted over the front wheel. Each Saturday morning I would pop in early to collect the deliveries and load up the bike. During my first few weeks, I had observed the pharmacist dispensing lengths of special liquorice from a drawer below the counter to poor patients who were unlucky enough to be suffering from constipation. This particular morning, Mr. Wright was in the back office attending to an urgent matter when my mischievous spirit whispered in my ear that it needed an outing. Checking that the coast was clear, I quickly pulled open the drawer and stole a handful of sticks and stuffed them into my short's pocket before returning to my bike to await Mr. Wright's return.

The following Monday, I took my stolen booty to school. During mid-morning break, I cut up the liquorice into portions and handed them out to a few specially chosen classmates in the playground, an act of uncharacteristic generosity to my unsuspecting enemies. They were very appreciative,... initially that is. Within half-an-hour of returning to the classroom, the results were devastatingly hilarious as the chosen few took it in turns to make a beeline for the toilet. However, one unfortunate couldn't make it and visibly revealed his backside and humiliation to us as he walked out through the classroom doorway.

It was not easy for me to control my laughter then, but now this treatment of our boys filled me with rage.

With my thirst and hunger came exhaustion and I collapsed into the long grass. I stared up at the star-studded sky and decided that it had the makings of a dry night. I rolled over onto my side in order to remove an uncomfortable stone when I saw a soldier sitting down in his underpants just a few feet from me. He was a lot older than I, probably in his early forties, with three stripes on his arm. At first, I thought he might be 'attending to the call of nature' until I righted my head and saw that he was merely sitting whilst holding his trousers in his hands, intently examining them. I was intrigued. As there was nothing else to occupy my mind, I continued to watch. His trousers were inside out and slowly he passed them through his busy fingers before stopping, pressing his head forward a little, scrutinising what was before him and then doing something that I couldn't quite see before continuing the process once more. After a few minutes, I could control my curiosity no longer.

"Excuse me Sergeant," I politely interrupted, "but if you don't mind me asking, what are you doing?"

He stopped and lifted his head to me. He had a tough old face, looked tired but easily managed a wry smile.

"I'm looking for lice son, bloody lice,... and killing the buggers!"

I pulled a face in revulsion at the thought.

"Lice, how did you catch those?" I innocently replied.

Looking straight back at me, his smile broadened before he openly laughed. I felt silly as though he was mocking me.

"I bet if you dropped your trousers right now son, you would find a whole army of the buggers living inside," he calmly suggested, nodding his head as if inviting me to do just that.

I was shocked at his suggestion for I knew that I was not some filthy tramp so I couldn't have lice, could I?

"Look son, the Sergeant continued, "I was in the last war and within days of being in the trenches we were covered with the little blighters. I would bet my life that we are all crawling with them."

That was it. I sat up, thought about it for a moment and then looked down, imagining them writhing about all over me and instinctively began to scratch, as indeed I had been doing for a while now. I took my trousers off to discover that he was right. I felt sick for they were everywhere, tiny greyish little bugs, feeding off me. I looked down into my pants and, to my horror, discovered that they were there too. Although initially self-conscious, I forgot my modesty and spread my legs. I could see them deep in my crotch.

"You'll get used to them son. Had 'em in the last war. They'll be your closest buddies and stick to you like glue 'till this war's over. You'll be inseparable."

His head rolled back as he roared with laughter, as did his mates, who joined in the hilarity.

"In the last bash we had 'em then, the size of cockroaches. All you need do is squeeze the buggers between your finger nails like I'm doing. Make 'em pop. You won't ever get rid of them but you may be able to keep them under control."

I immediately started the unpleasant task of crushing them.

As they popped they gave off an unpleasant smell.

"You can also burn 'em with a flame if you like," he continued, "but it can be bloody dangerous on your thatch if you know what I mean."

With that, he looked down towards his own crotch and belly-laughed.

"Oh, just one more thing son, they'll be in your armpits as well as your head," he chuckled, "anywhere you have hair son, anywhere."

He chuckled once more but I didn't. I was disgusted.

"Great" was all I could manage. No wonder I had been scratching since leaving camp. It was bad enough being on starvation rations without having to share what little my body had with a swarm of stinking parasites.

My waking hours and disturbed nights had developed into an unending wretched pattern of dejected misery. Every day and night was the same. I tried to maintain my sunny disposition as much as possible, finding humour in the most unlikely of places whilst we marched, hungry, thirsty and scratching our way across northern France. God, I was missing my companions.

Every one of those long days seemed to be hot during that summer of 1940. My thirst was relentless, constantly tearing at my parched throat. Outside many of the French houses, the civilian occupants still maintained the age-old custom that extended back throughout history in times of war of placing water in containers for their soldiers as they passed by. I remember my father telling me that this practice existed during his service days of the last war and he had welcomed it on many occasions. Prior to our capture, however, we were expressly forbidden by our own Officers from drinking their water for fear of contracting some bug or illness. How things had changed in such a short time. Now, whenever we could, we would try to take full advantage of these offerings. Getting the runs at some time in the future was not now a sufficient deterrent to a man dying of thirst.

The criminal neglect of us prisoners by our guards was shameless. They knew we had no option but to live off the land in order to survive, so when I saw their violence towards our boys, pushing them away from troughs of valuable drinking water before kicking them over, I was incensed. How I loathed them for their lack of compassion. All I could do was ask myself 'why'?... but could find no answer.

On very rare occasions, the Germans did feed and water some of us, but so infrequently as not to matter. I still liked to believe that this neglect may have been due to the sheer weight of numbers of unexpected allied prisoners, but I am not sure. Their pathetic efforts were a spit in the ocean. Once, they set up a kitchen of sorts and offered us some questionable 'soup' with a lump of hard, mouldy bread. The bread was not a problem but the soup was for we had no mess tins, having had them confiscated by the Germans, so we had nothing to put the soup into. During one afternoon, we passed through a French town. Our guards found a bakery and took all the bread. As we passed by, the Germans casually hurled the loaves at us, at intervals. More fighting ensued and the strongest ate. Most of us didn't really know who we were marching with and there was little loyalty or respect between us. Without the presence of Officers or NCOs to maintain order, we fought for whatever was hurled at us. If somebody else caught the loaf, it was best to make a grab for it anyway, and at least snap the end off and shove it in your mouth before continuing the struggle for more. That way, at least you got something. Initially I had difficulty behaving like an animal, but such survival tactics became commonplace in those early, lawless days.

By now, I was developing quite a tan (although how much of my tan was dirt, I wasn't certain) andy hair was bleached almost white blonde under that scorching sun. It seemed like months had passed since our capture but in reality, it was only a couple of weeks. I had given up counting the days.

Eventually, our column shambled past yet another signpost but I barely gave it a second glance. It simply read Luxembourg. Stamps, my stamp collection,... of all the things to pop into my head, that was a random thought and the only thing that I knew about this place, it produced stamps! And still we marched.

Dusk unhurriedly turned to darkness. Prompted by starvation we set about searching for anything to eat, looking through sacks, wooden boxes and the chicken runs, but to no avail. As we passed the main farmhouse, the light from inside one of the rooms caught my eye. It was full of German Officers seated round a large wooden table. Sitting amongst them I could not help but notice several men in British Officer's uniforms. I was surprised and instantly recognised one of them who was very much enjoying the company of the Germans whilst sharing their meal. It was 2nd Lieutenant Mumford. Obviously he had survived his apparent breakdown and been captured.

The unpalatable sight of him eating whilst we went hungry angered me and left a bitter taste in my mouth, but obviously not in his.

† *2nd Lieutenant J A B Mumford, Queen's Royal Regiment eventually ended up at Oflag VIIb, PoW. Camp, Eichstätt, Southern Germany.*

~ LUXEMBOURG AND ON INTO GERMANY ~

Another day had passed. I looked forward over the heads of the others in our long, twisting line and followed the herd into Luxembourg. What now, I wondered, what now?

It came as news to me that Luxembourg had been overrun by the Germans. When did that happen? Few of us, if any, had read a newspaper or heard any news on the radio since leaving for the front. We obviously knew of the invasion of Belgium and France, but I suppose this tiny country had been forgotten. Knowing only from my school days that Luxembourg had postage stamps for me to collect and was a very small principality somewhere in the heart of Europe, lodged uncomfortably between France and Germany and often fought over by both its more powerful neighbours, I turned to a fellow.

"Luxembourg. I wonder if they put up a fight."

In a broad Scottish accent came his reply, full of pent-up anger.

"I hope it were more 'a fight than those f***ing Froggies put up."

He was from the Seaforths and had nothing but contempt for our French allies, having fought with them and seen just how badly and, in his opinion, shamefully they had performed.

Luxembourg was so small, with practically no army to speak of. The Nazi war machine would have taken the country before breakfast. I wondered what else had happened across Europe since the invasion in the west and who else had fallen under the Hun's oppressive jackboot.

† *Luxembourg was unable to maintain its policy of neutrality when on 10th May 1940, Nazi Germany invaded at the same time as the Netherlands, Belgium and France and occupied the country, due to its strategic location on the invasion route into France. In contrast to the First World War experience, Luxembourg was*

† *Source: www.forces-war-records.co.uk/search.asp*

treated as a Germanic territory and informally annexed to an adjacent province of the Third Reich in 1940.

A government in exile based in London fought alongside the Allies, sending a small group of volunteers who participated in the Normandy invasion. After its integration, even the very name ceased to exist; from then on the country was called: 'Gau Moselland', (Moselle country district). The Nazis then set about to 'Germanize' the country. German law was imposed and the use of their native language was forbidden. Slowly a reign of oppression and terror befell the country until the allied liberation in September 1944.†

We tramped the length or breadth of little Luxembourg without seeing much of the locals. They were keeping their heads down whilst we staggered through into Germany before finally arriving at the ancient Roman city of Trier on the banks of the river Moselle.

Here, our guards seem to relish the task of parading us past the crowds of jeering civilians mocking us as we dragged our feet along the cobbled streets. Few of us escaped the spit. None of us had the will or tenacity to hold our heads high and meet their angry gaze, such was our total demoralisation. We were made to walk past the dark foreboding triumphal gates, just as the slaves of ancient Rome would have been made to do some two thousand years ago.

I felt like weeping. We had foot-slogged for sixteen days, some 300 miles, right across northern France, through Luxembourg and into Nazi Germany. Momentarily I was staggered by our accomplishment and prayed that we had finally reached our journey's end.

The sight ahead left me aghast. A concentrated sea of scruffy, pitiful prisoners, crammed into every open space across the sprawling goods yard and beyond only highlighted the scale of our defeat. Some were contained in an enormous barbed wire compound next to the rail yard whilst others were directed to whatever space was available. Our numbers amounted to thousands.

Like every other captive who had endured this march into captivity, I felt crushed, overwhelmed, dirty, exhausted and dizzy with dehydration. My heart sank and I could not find the slightest trace of humour to sustain me in my present situation.

---

† *Source: www.luxembourg.co.uk., web site of the Grand Duchy of Luxembourg.*

All around were allied soldiers of differing nationalities but mostly British, Belgian and French. I walked amongst them for a few minutes until I found a rare piece of unoccupied ground, onto which I collapsed. I was so thirsty that it hurt to swallow what little spit I could muster. Beautiful, clear sparkling water, nature's vintage champagne, nectar of the Gods, trickling forth, fresh and pure from a bubbling spring, chilled by a mountain glacier! It was torture, but it was all that my body would allow my brain to think of. The sun was doing its best to increase our suffering on what would normally have been a beautiful day. I wished to be back on holiday with my mates, sipping cold beer in a café in old Calais before the war.

It came as no real surprise that the Germans had still not made provisions to supply us with the most basic of human needs, let alone food. Fortunately, my stomach was shrinking nicely, and with it my hunger pains, so finally I had something to thank God for.

But nothing could relieve my pain of thirst.

> *At that point, Dennis sat back in his chair in my kitchen and burst into laughter. "God, was I thirsty then," he reiterated with a chuckle. "Do you know Pat, it makes me laugh. You can't go anywhere these days, into town, on any street in summer or winter, without seeing somebody clutching their expensive bottle of designer mineral water, costing more than bloody petrol, in case they should die of thirst,... as though water wasn't available?"*

Eventually word spread that water was being provided from huge troughs located around the yard. The presence of armed German troops in substantial numbers prevented a riot and there was no mad assault on the watering holes, just impatient but orderly queues. We drank like animals. Once I had satisfied my thirst, I rested, only speaking when somebody else spoke to me, too weary and dejected to really bother. Everyone wanted to know the same thing.

"Where are they taking us?"

There was no accurate answer, only a million speculative guesses. I could not help but wonder if we were headed for that unpopular destination yet again, you know,... that place called 'F***knowswhere'?

Countless thousands of muted men lounged around, nervously awaiting their fate, whilst the yard and its periphery were a hive of noisy activity; seemingly never ending lines of goods trains trundled through, heaving under the colossal weight of German armaments; men feverishly transferring cargo onto army trucks; engines spitting into activity, grinding their protests as they pulled away from the rail yard, commencing their forward journey into war torn France.

I lay down, removed my boots and examined my painful feet. Covered in dirt and sweat, they stank. Open sores, blisters, long painful toenails, fungal infections - they were not a pretty sight. My crutch and armpits itched and every part of my skin that was in contact with any other part was agonising. Like every other PoW, I was physically and mentally exhausted and an emotional mess.

I closed my weary eyes and rested, the clatter from the wagons - metal banging against metal, shunting wagons and the clang of wheels reverberated through the vicinity. Shrill whistles of pressurised steam being released from waiting locomotives pierced the summer air at irregular intervals. Yet in spite of it all, I easily slipped peacefully into unconsciousness and dreamt.

> *The sounds took me back to the very earliest memories of my childhood. I was three or four years old, curled up safely in my bed at home, with visions of my mother kissing me good-night as she tucked my sheet and blankets tightly around my body, trapping me in my warm cocoon of love and safety. I recalled the same comforting distant noise coming from the large goods yard at Woking, the clanging and clunking sound of the train carriages and wagons bumping together as they were shunted around the goods yard throughout the night. How secure I felt then and how I wished to be that child once more.*

My wonderful dream was violently interrupted by the harsh sound of loud voices in a foreign tongue rising above the background clatter and interference, accompanied by the ferocious barking of dogs. I had to force my eyes open to confront this sweltering bedlam before me. This present nightmare contrasted deeply with the vanished recollections of my youth. All about, I sensed the tangible threat of repressed, pent-up violence that gnawed away in the pit of my stomach.

To add to the tumult, church bells rang out their songs. I stood up and noticed crowds of people gathering on the outside of the perimeter wire. Most were dressed in their fine clothes, probably on their way to the church service, if that was still allowed in Hitler's Germany. Whilst some paused for a moment before continuing on their walk, most stood watching. I understand that curiosity is a human condition that we are all prone to and the sight of this beaten army of allied troops was of obvious interest, but what followed was not. Those nearest to the wire were spat upon, shouted at and insulted. Even women and children were joining in, pointing and laughing at us. We were worse than caged animals in a zoo. A middle-aged couple were looking at me. I thought that the woman looked troubled, even concerned and such was my lack of pride that I attempted to look forlorn and innocent, hoping that they might take pity on me and give me some food, but to no avail. Being humiliatingly viewed like beasts only added to our sense of degradation. Such treatment of PoWs was in direct contravention of the Geneva Convention but so was the forced march, the brutality, the lack of medical care and absence of food and water. What was one more infringement amongst the ever growing catalogue of violations?

What an ignominious beginning to my internment!

We stayed where we were overnight and through into the late hours of the following day, drifting in and out of sleep whilst trains came and went. Just after 4pm, armed guards and their dogs moved systematically amongst our section shouting.

"Aufstehen, schnell, schnell."

Even though I did not understand German yet, the inference was clear. Our waiting was over and it was time to leave. I was kicked in my arm as I lay on the ground, reacting too slowly for the German's liking. Along with hundreds of others, I was herded towards a waiting goods train that seemed never ending. A motley collection of dirty brown, deep dingy blue, grey and green-painted wagons made up the line of rolling stock, fifty to sixty wagons long. Their sliding doors were already open, waiting invitingly to receive us. I felt so relieved at the thought of giving my feet a well-earned rest and journeying on by train.

There were no platforms as we know them from which to embark. The first PoWs at the wagon doors were ordered in, clambering up as best they could. Once inside they leant a helping hand to their fellows, which quickened the boarding procedure. All the while, chaos and confusion filled the air as the German guards screamed for us to hurry. Their mad rants and the snarling barks of their Alsatian dogs, straining their leather leashes to breaking point in their excited and charged state of canine aggression, created a threatening and intimidating atmosphere.

> *God! How I hated Alsatians. I was eleven years old at the time, living in Hersham. My father had just passed yet more exams, resulting in his promotion to Inspector. One of his Constables was a young man called Coote, who lived next door to us with his wife. The other occupants of their home were their five-year-old son and PC Coote's Alsatian police dog. They were a good family. One summer's day their little boy was playing with the dog, chasing him around the back yard as he often did, pulling at his tail, climbing onto his back for a ride and generally teasing him. Without warning, the dog's temper snapped. He'd had enough and turned on the boy. With its powerful jaws, it made a grab for his tiny neck and ripped his throat open, killing him instantly. Such was the tragedy that there was obvious sadness at the station and throughout the small community. As for me, it was the first death I had experienced and it affected me greatly.*

It was then I saw them boarding. I was beside myself with joy and my spirits soared. I saw them nearly one-hundred yards to the left helping each other climb into one of the wagons. Freddy, Herby, Tommy, Charlie and Bill. I shouted at them, waving frantically and then I bellowed at the top of my voice amid the background babble.

"Freddy, Freddy, it's me, Dennis."

I called again,... and again.

Eyes bore into me from all directions.

Eventually, he did look up. He'd heard me, hadn't he? I made one more desperate effort to attract his attention, jumping and hollering like never before.

"Freddy," over here."

He seemed to be looking in my direction but I couldn't be sure. A rifle butt was raised in his direction and he was forced to retire into the darkness of the carriage.

· · · § · · ·

ONE 'HELL' OF
A RIDE

2nd June 1940

Today, the prospect of eighty PoWs being crammed into a space big enough to carry forty men or ten horses might be regarded as a serious breach of health and safety issues, but in 1940, it was common place for those unfortunate prisoners of Nazi Germany.

My heart sank as the door slid across the opening and they disappeared from view. Momentarily, I felt deflated but realised that if I managed to board this train, I was sure to find them at our final destination. Urgently, I pushed and excused myself forward. The guards stood in pairs by every wagon door, waiting for any excuse to bellow and menace us at gunpoint, counting each man in as we boarded to maximise the train's payload. In case we were unsure as to the urgency of our boarding, the occasional goon would raise a rifle butt and aim it indiscriminately at the back of any unfortunate PoW who was too slow. Nobody turned to confront such action for nobody dared. We had already learnt blind obedience. Those behind, like me, were kept moving, pressing forward along the line until we reached a wagon that could accommodate us. I saw a stencilled notice in French, roughly painted on the side of each wagon. Its message is probably engraved onto the memory cells of every one of us allied prisoners. '40 Homme, 10 Cheval' ('40 Men, 10 Horses'). If the wagons were good enough for horses, they were certainly good enough for PoW scum like us.

Any illusion of travelling to our onward destination in grand Pullman style was shattered. Half pulled, half shoved, I clambered aboard the waiting wagon and felt relieved at making it. Once inside, I immediately noticed the odour, strong but not unpleasant. It was the smell of coal, which sadly reminded me of home and the coal fires at my mother's house.

Between the mass of closely packed bodies, I was able to see the floor beneath my boots. Evidently the wagon had last been used to carry coal and the space had not been swept. I was pushed further inside. As we shuffled back, the coal residue was crushed even finer, filling the wagon with cough causing particles that entered our lungs. I fought my way deeper inside and jostled to get as close as possible to the carriage wall. As the last man entered, the claustrophobic conditions immediately became apparent.

The wagon's door was sliding. I took a last look at the sunlight before I heard it slam shut and the heavy metallic 'clunk' as the lever-lock engaged. We were now trapped, entombed. The muffled slow slide and 'clunk' was repeated along the line as each door was closed to the outside world. Within minutes of being in the filthy hell hole, the coughing fits reached a crescendo as the fine dust particles did their worst.

Minute by minute, the interior temperature rose rapidly and our train remained motionless under the hot summer sun, worsening our already dreadful situation. Each and every one of us baked in that sweltering oven. How long we stood there I could not recall for I was already beginning to feel faint and, in my vague, semiconscious state, my mind wandered, seeking oblivion, unaware to the passing of time.

Whilst at school, I grew to love history. The wonderfully rich stories of the British Empire were still fresh in my mind. As I stood up in that sweat box, fighting for limited space and air, my thoughts returned to one story that epitomised our current plight, the infamous 'Black Hole of Calcutta'.

During the rush by the British East India Company to expand their business empire throughout India, the local ruler, Siraj ud-Daulah, the Nawab of Bengal, took umbrage at their plans to colonise his lands. He laid siege to the British forces at Fort William. The fort was eventually captured in 1756 and the survivors, 123 British and Anglo-Indian soldiers and civilians were held captive overnight in a tiny dungeon. Conditions were unimaginably cramped and, as

a consequence, a large proportion of them died from suffocation,
heat exhaustion and simply from being crushed to death. The story
became legendary and the dungeon became known as 'The Black
Hole of Calcutta'.

This was our 'black hole' and it was hell on earth.

My thirst was all-consuming. I stuck my tongue out and caught a droplet of sweat as it trickled down the side of my face. It was salty. As soon as my eyes grew accustomed to the gloom, I cast a look around at my fellow occupants. I could only see heads. I saw no-one that I recognised, which was hardly surprising but disappointing nevertheless. In the gloom we looked a bloody mess, differing multi-coloured military head gear, dishevelled, lanky, long hair and weary, sunken eyes.

In each of the four corners of the wagon were four small rectangular openings, 30mm x 100mm to be more precise. Their position high up near the roof made observing our surroundings difficult unless you were seven feet tall. Although it would have been impossible for anybody to escape through these narrow gaps, even for us in our emancipated state the ever-cautious Germans had stretched barbed wire across the gap. These four vents were our only source of fresh air and was totally inadequate in the increasingly stifling heat. Spears of light pierced the wooden walls and ceilings through the tiny holes and cracks of the tired rolling stock. I could see the airborne coal dust swirling in the choking air. It never seemed to clear, for every time someone moved their feet they would disturb the thick layer of grime once more.

It seemed like an age had passed before I heard the angry hissing of the train's steam exhaust and muffled shouting of our guards as our wagon suddenly lurched forward, crashing into the buffers of the one in front. I fell onto the men behind and then in front of me as they uttered muffled curses. The carriage jumped forward again and we tried to steady ourselves. Slowly and awkwardly, we crawled away.

'Hell' was on the move and our oven had become an insufferable sauna. Amongst the occupants of my wagon there was no question of 'Well, old chap, I have had my turn at the air vent, please, let me stand aside so that you can take your turn.' The very opposite was true. It was "Piss off,", "f*** off" or a French, Belgian or Dutch equivalent, followed by a bony elbow fight as the combatants jostled for space, position and clean fresh air.

We travelled all that night, stopping occasionally for no obvious reason. With so many differing nationals in the wagon conversation was difficult, even if anybody could have been bothered to talk. I tried to sleep standing up, wedged as I was between flesh and wood. Despite being weary and weak through heat exhaustion, it was impossible to rest whilst we remained standing. As night wore on, the temperature inside dropped from unbearably sweltering to just plain hot. The smell of coal dust was replaced by others that were less pleasant.

Some how, we managed to survive the night and dawn did break whilst we proceeded onward. The mood in the carriage remained tetchy to say the least. The men were increasingly impatient with their immediate neighbours, especially if they were foreign to them. During the night, some of the occupants had urinated. We didn't have the luxury of a toilet on board or even a bucket, so one could only go where one stood. I couldn't tell if any of them had bothered to undo their flies or if they just urinated in their trousers. I was not revolted by the prospect of such things any more for I was almost beyond caring, but I did offer up a little prayer that the persons next to me would have no need to defecate!

My God, the carriage was stinking. If there was an up-side to this interminable heat, it was that we were fast becoming dehydrated which translated to less pissing. Added to that we had not eaten for days, so as the hours went by there was a decreasing chance of anybody passing much more than empty wind, thank God, except those unfortunates with diarrhoea, who could soon die through lack of fluids.

There was no improvement in our predicament as the day progressed. Shortly after ten, the train ground to its first halt of the day. Inside, the air was already stifling, but within minutes of being stationary the temperature shot up. Without warning, one of our number fainted, causing a much needed distraction from our agonising circumstances. He wasn't the last. Others were pulling themselves up to one of the four small gap 'windows' to view our surroundings which held no real interest.

Every time we came to a halt, the same thing happened as we ground into yet another siding and waited. After an hour, we heard another train steam on by in the opposite direction. Once it had cleared the track we began to move once more and rejoined the main line. Those lucky enough to be near the openings strained their necks in an attempt to breath the un-fetid air.

We journeyed on for two hours more in silence, too weary even for anger. Early in the afternoon we drew into yet another siding, falling upon each other as we came to an abrupt shuddering halt. Everyone was flung forward, causing the coal dust to become airborne once more, followed by the coughing. Suddenly, the volume of differing languages increased as tempers rose along with the temperature, before subsiding just as rapidly as they had flared, and the mood returned to a sort of normality.

Minutes ticked by. I could hear metal on metal, sliding and strange knocking sounds in the distance. Outside came sounds of increasing activity as those nearest to the high openings pulled themselves up to see. One of our boys was able to see what was happening outside and gave us a brief commentary amidst the unfamiliar noises gradually getting closer and closer. German guards were walking alongside the train. I closed my eyes for a moment as I stood, trying to doze to pass the time, retreating into my inner self.

"One day, this will all end," I chanted softly, "one day."

With a jolt, my slumber was disturbed. I opened my eyes in a daze, momentarily unable to remember where I was, just as the wagon door was flung open. Sunlight came bursting through the opening. Immediately, I shut my eyes in a spontaneous reflex, blinded by the brilliance. Inside was a sauna. I turned to face the opening to see what was happening. We had now been locked in for twenty-four hours and I thanked God that it was over. Through the gaps between the prisoners, I could see our guards standing with their rifles unslung, at the ready. Another was holding back a fierce Alsatian, barking wildly in frenzied excitement.

And then it hit us.

We were violently knocked backwards towards the other side of the wagon and onto others as water exploded all over us. After the initial shock, I realised what a wonderful thing this was. I opened my mouth and caught the water, drinking in desperate gulps. In the open doorway stood a guard with a fire hose in his hand. I could have kissed him. He was directing the jet of water into the wagon, spraying everything and everybody with it. Those at the front took the full force and had to turn their backs to avoid its stinging power. The conscientious guard even made sure that those around the corners of the wagon got their fair share of water as well. He drenched the roof of the wagon too, which then fell in torrents onto our heads. We drank what we could although it was not easy, given the sporadic spraying. All was well until the guard aimed the water onto the wagon's floor. By now the coal dust had turned into a black slurry and his actions caused the muck to spray up and over us. Bearing in mind that the floor had been used as a toilet, this added to the distress of being covered with the foul slurry. However, the more we were drenched in water, the more the filthy mess was washed overboard, flowing backwards, cascading out through the gaps in the woodwork to the ground below.

The heavenly dousing lasted thirty seconds before the water was turned off and the guard moved on to the next wagon. Our door was slammed shut and we were plunged into gloom once more. I felt water dripping on my head so I turned my face upwards and caught the droplets that continued to fall from the wagon's ceiling. In the coming heat of the day, our clothes would soon dry out and that would be a waste of this precious liquid so I turned my attention to my sodden uniform, sucking the water from the sleeves. This had been our first 'drink' for two sweltering days. As meagre as it was, it came at a crucial time and was a life-saver.

As soon as the Germans had finished 'washing us', we resumed our agonising journey. By now, the atmosphere had become more amiable.

"The goon could 'ave scrubbed my back for me."

We managed to exchange a few jokes, making light of even this sorry situation.

However, there were some amongst us who were not faring so well. As the second day wore on I watched others, albeit a few, moan constantly, bringing those around them down to their desperate level. Others, more pitifully, sank deeper into despair, collapsing to the floor and sobbing uncontrollably. They were giving up, losing what little dignity they still had left and their will to carry on, to fight for survival and ultimately to live. To me, it was understandable for we were all individuals with vastly differing family histories and relationship problems, all with differing levels of breaking point, some with more to lose than others. It is easier to cope with any hardship if you know when it will come to an end but when there is no apparent conclusion in sight, it is much harder. Added to that was the fear that we all harboured - what was awaiting us at the end of our journey?... and that uncertainty was unnerving. For some, it was all too much.

And still there was no sustenance of any kind, no food or water other than our shower, but the subsequent reduction in human waste in our wagon was evident and most welcome. For those still cursed with diarrhoea, I prayed that they were still wearing their army-issue gaiters around the base of their trousers and over their boots, so that whatever near solids they were passing would hopefully be contained in their trousers. This child-like vision made me chuckle aloud, as I looked about me, wondering whose trousers were ballooning.

I wondered,... was I losing my sanity?

"I don't think so," I reassured myself out loud, "it's your way of coping Dennis."

Shit! Now I really was talking to myself and I couldn't stop laughing.

"One day, this will all end," I chanted softly, "one day."

Eyes studied me, probably thinking '*there goes another nutter*!'

The minutes dragged on by and turned into hours. Then the hours lingered painfully, stagnating in time and resisting all attempts to move on from day into night. How was it possible for time to stand so very still? Had the all-powerful German war machine under Hitler even managed to harness the movement of the sun and delay its demise?

The train journeyed on relentlessly towards its undisclosed destination in the closing heat of another suffocating day, with frequent stops and starts, standing aside to make way for the more important armaments of the Third Reich.

Night finally came but there was no respite for our train as we continued on through the long hours of darkness.

When day three inexorably arrived, we were still moving. Inside, it felt as though a madman had turned off the air conditioning and cranked up the central heating. I couldn't possibly think of adequate words to describe my total despair and despondency.

"Today..."

I started to repeat my mantra, but for the first time I had trouble both finishing it and believing it. As I uttered the words under my foul breath, they sounded both hollow and ludicrous.

"One day, this will all end, one day,"...some hope,... oh please God, make it stop,... I can't stand it,... it's too much,... I promise I will never swear again,... I will go to church every day when I get home,... I will dedicate my life to looking after the sick,...I will give away all my worldly goods to the homeless,... I will become a monk and serve you till the end of time,... I will rule the world and make everybody rich and give them all the food and drink that they will ever need and banish all illness from the planet,... nobody will ever die and I will build a brand new better world without wars or suffering,... IF ONLY YOU WILL STOP THIS MISERY".......

I waited to see if those few spoken words had made me feel any better. They didn't. Prisoners rubbing shoulders with me gave me a blank stare, either trying to understand my mutterings, questioning my sanity or both, but at that precise stage I couldn't really care what they thought of me. I had ceased caring after the first night in our hell hole. My mind drifted from sleep to depressing thoughts to questions and conundrums, from quandaries to blank spaces that held no solutions. What if the Germans had no place for us and we were to be condemned to a lifetime in this damnable place, until our last gasp of life was boiled from our dehydrated bodies?

My consciousness played on whilst my body stood motionless, waiting. Suffice it to say my mind was in turmoil. There was nothing that I could do to stop the misery continuing.

From the other end of the wagon, someone was sobbing once more whilst a fellow Brit swore loudly for no apparent reason.

"He's dead," I heard someone say and another muttered something in French. Others tried to move his body into a more upright sitting position, presumably to take up less room. I felt no shock or remorse, just surprise that only one had died and a feeling that I was glad it wasn't me.

Around midday, I raised my hand and wiped the filthy sweat from my forehead with the back of my hand. I licked it before it evaporated, eager not to be robbed of the precious moisture.

We screeched to a slow halt on rails as dry as the walls of my agonising mouth. In the distance we heard the now familiar sounds and waited impatiently with increasing anticipation. After what seemed like an eternity, the wagon door was finally opened. Even before the hose was turned on, I opened my parched mouth in readiness and the welcome dousing began all over again. I drank as much as I could but unlike yesterday I didn't turn away from the full force of the water. Instead, I cupped both hands against my chin in front of my open mouth, closing my eyes as a stinging torrent blasted my face and sucking whatever water fell into my filthy hands.

Doors open, water on, soaking, water off, doors slammed and away. Momentarily I granted myself that rare moment of pleasure as the heavenly liquid hit me, ignoring the discomfort and filth that was my world. Surviving this journey was the only goal. After all, I had already endured three days, to withstand another day or so of suffering wouldn't be impossible for me to bare, would it?

This torturous pattern combined with the hunger, heat and exhaustion did not end until the closing hours of the fourth day, when we slithered our way into a marshalling yard, brought to our attention by the information spotters at the four observation holes. We had not stopped before at any place of this size. As soon as the train pulled in we heard the footsteps outside, running up and down the length of the train. Within minutes, orders in German were shouted and the doors opened. The daylight came flooding in and I had to shade my eyes against the burning glare.

"Raus,...... aussteigen,...... schnell."

Those nearest the door of the wagon jumped down onto the ground to be 'greeted' by the guards, who had their rifles pointing ominously at us. The dogs were there too, bearing their teeth and barking wildly, excited as we disgorged and collapsed onto the ground below. These guards were different from those who had travelled with us. They were smarter and cleaner looking so I assumed they were stationed at our new point of arrival. After four days of relative silence, all was now noise and mayhem. Why did these goons have to scream and shout all the time? Alas, a rhetorical question, for I already knew that their threat of violence and intimidation was going to be standard practice from now on, so I'd better get used to it.

As far as I knew, nobody had escaped and the full complement of us PoWs arrived at our intended destination, if you included the dead prisoner. We left the stranger there.

I stumbled as I hit the ground after standing with my legs locked for so long, and collapsed,... most of us did. We were given no time to compose ourselves, our German guards made sure of that. Somebody grabbed me by my arm and helped me to stand.

"Thanks," I uttered.

As my head gradually cleared, I remembered my friends and I began to push forward through the sea of prisoners in the now frantic search for them, for having found them, I was desperate to make contact.

'Please, please let them be there. I think they were six wagon lengths away,... could have been eight though.'

"Excuse me,... excuse me,... can I get through please,..."

"What's your hurry mate, got a hot date?" someone uttered.

"... excuse me please,..."

'Sixth wagon,... where are they?... must be somewhere around here,...'

"... excuse me, can I come through,..."

'Eighth wagon,...'

I was beginning to panic, they all had their backs to me. The surge of prisoners was flowing away from the wagons,...

"TOMMY, FREDDY,..."

Faces turned, it was them. I could have cried.

"Dennis, where the hell have you been?

The smiles on their dirty ugly faces matched mine. I had never been so pleased to see anybody before.

There was no time for protracted greetings. Barely able to move at all, we must have looked a sorry sight. Now we were shouted at, pushed and butted into a long column with typical German efficiency and great impatience. Within minutes, we were herded into some sort of order. No amount of persuasion could have made us dig any deeper into our resources of strength and determination, for there was none to be found. We staggered and shuffled our way out of the yard onto the open road without the slightest idea as to where we were. Some were too ill to continue and had to be left where they lay, their fate unknown to us. Somehow we marched regardless of the pain and difficulty. Our band of six were like all the rest, in a desperate and pitiful state, too tired to talk at all.

In the distance, I saw a sign with a single word painted on it.
THORN.

· · · § · · ·

STALAG XXA

THORN 5th June 1940

The hour was late afternoon as over a thousand of us marched away from the immediate vicinity of the marshalling yard at Thorn, escorted by our new German guards and a handful of agitated dogs. I had no idea as to where Thorn was. It sounded Germanic so I assumed that we had been transported to somewhere in their heartland.

The fresh air and the sunlight smelt and felt unbelievable. To be free from that damnable train was indescribable. You would have to experience such desperation to understand what it meant to have survived those conditions. I was surprised that we had the strength to walk at all. I wondered how many had died on that train.

I looked about me as we walked along the cobbled streets of the ancient city; at the people, the houses, countryside, the trees and sky, watched as birds soared freely, just as nature intended. I too shared the joy of their freedom, envious of their liberty.

As if from nowhere, a senior NCO came to the fore and tried to lick us into some sort of order. Their pride had not diminished, even if ours had.

"Left, left, left right left,..."

Somewhere a spirited soul shouted, "F***OFF."

For men who had stood for so long, I was amazed that we moved at all, let alone marched. Some even managed to pick themselves up and march like soldiers with their heads held high, thumbs up, arms swinging and with whatever shreds of dignity they could muster, but they were in the minority. We 'rebels' found it difficult to comply with what we regarded as a ridiculous show of pride after what we had been through, seeing our dead strewn across the roads of northern France and the horror inside those squalid cattle trucks. And so we, a pile of stinking filth and abandoned hope, shuffled and staggered, blinking under the blinding glare of a sun that we hadn't seen for days. The lame and sick hopefully followed on as best they could. After what appeared to be a painfully long haul, a group of two-hundred men at the front suddenly veered off down a side road led by their guards. I wondered where they were going. When my section of the column reached their turning, I looked for them but saw nothing for they had already disappeared round a bend in the road. Then again the same thing happened until it was the turn of my section. We peeled off and left what remained of the column, walking onwards, final destination unknown.

The area around Thorn was very flat so walking was comparatively effortless. We passed built up areas before finally reaching what looked like a medieval castle of all things, surrounded by a dry moat. Crossing over the bridge and through the main gate, I cast my eyes upwards to take a closer look at the imposing building. Above the large, impressive arched entrance was an inscription carved into the key stone. It simply read 'Winfred von Kniprode'.

We passed through the main entrance into a circular-shaped inner courtyard before being ordered to halt. I believed this to be a 'dulag' (Durchgangslager) or transit camp through which POW's passed for processing before being distributed to more permanent abodes in the surrounding district. Each and every one of us was thoroughly searched in turn. Since my arrival at the jute factory near Béthune, the only possessions that had not been stolen from me were my army-issue side pouch containing my toothbrush (with no toothpaste), my razor, a brush and comb, my bible and, still hidden, some French francs and Jo's gold wristwatch. When my turn came, I could not help feeling slightly amused as the German guard stuck his hands into my trouser pockets. Considering what squalid conditions we had endured during our hellish four-day train journey, I was glad the goons were handling this unpleasant job of searching our stinking, filthy clothes. I hoped they did not wash their hands afterwards and caught something really nasty, including my crotch lice.

We were separated by nationalities into smaller groups and led away through doorways that surrounded this central courtyard and taken to what could only be described as cells if you wished to be generous, or dungeons if you wanted to be factual. The six of us were amongst a group of thirty British soldiers who were shoved into the next available chamber. Under the brick-vaulted ceiling, it was stark. I took a second to cast my eye over our new surroundings before the door was slammed shut. We were contained prisoners once more.

Almost as one, we band of six reunited friends dropped down onto the cold, worn flag stones, with a scattering of straw for bedding. We were utterly done in. The throbbing pain in my limbs reminded me that we had literally been on our feet for the last four days. I collapsed, lay flat out and heaved a sigh of total exhaustion. Although the floor offered little in the way of comfort to our weary limbs, just to take the weight off our legs and rest was enough. We were silent for some time, too much pain, too much had happened and still fearful of our future.

"That was some train ride; not the best holiday I've ever been on."

Somebody sniggered.

"Dennis, now tell us what you've been up to after ditching us for the high life with your new German mates," demanded Herby who looked dreadful and had lost a lot of weight.

"Yer, we thought they were taking you away to shoot you for facing up to that Jerry officer," interrupted Freddy.

I spent the next few minutes filling in all the gaps, including my stop in the jute factory.

"We were there,... found a cosy little spot in the shade at the back of the factory, sorry we didn't see you mate."

"I tried looking for you," I continued, "but amongst so many identical khaki lads,..." I pulled a despairing face,... "no chance."

Charlie looked serious. "We tried to hang about, waiting for you to be released, but the guards wouldn't have it and made us move. Sorry mate, we couldn't do anything about it."

We exchanged a few words with the other inmates, but few were in the mood for conversation.

"Anybody know where we are?" said one.

"I saw the name 'Thorn' on a sign at the rail yard," I replied. We all looked round with blank expressions. Nobody seemed to know where in Europe Thorn was. For the next half hour my friends and I chatted easily and smiled a lot but tiredness soon got the better of us and one by one, we succumbed to exhaustion.

† Thorn (now Toruń) is an ancient city in northern Poland, on the Vistula River. Founded by the Teutonic Knights, it is one of the oldest cities in Poland. The medieval old town is the birthplace of the astronomer Nicolaus Copernicus, a town rich in history.

Thorn is surrounded by a ring of forts, having been built by the Prussians at the end of 19th century to defend their western borders.

After the invasion in 1939, Polish PoWs were held in the forts. It was rapidly converted, becoming Stalag XXA. It also served as a transit camp for the surrounding district, forwarding men on to camps such as Stalag XXB at Marienburg.

In June 1940 additional forts were reclaimed, cleaned out and added to the camp to accommodate British soldiers. In all, the camp was a complex of fifteen to seventeen forts. The first to arrive were 403 from the disastrous Allied campaign in Norway. Later about 4,500 arrived from Dunkirk and subsequently from the British 51st (Highland) Infantry Division (World War II) captured at St. Valéry-en-Caux. In 1941 and 1942 Soviet prisoners arrived. At its peak there were 10-20,000 prisoners in the camp. However many were located in sub-camps. The camp was over-run by the Soviet Army on 1st February 1945. †

I have no idea how long we slept but eventually, the door was opened. We were ordered out and shown into a larger bare room where we formed a single file watched over by our guards. One was standing in front of a barrel. He handed us his metal container as we filed passed, filled with brackish water. I saw that you had to be extremely quick, for as soon as the guard handed it to you he would snatch it back to refill it and pass it on to the next man. Anticipating his next move, I took mine in both hands, drawing back slightly and gulping down every last drop before the irritated German stretched forward to snatch back his precious container. The cold liquid felt refreshing and soothing as it slid down my throat and my first proper drink since boarding the train to hell.. It almost choked me in my haste. The best champagne in the world couldn't have tasted better.

---

† Source: http://www.gps-practice-and-fun.com/stalag-20a.html & Wikipedia.

I moved onwards to the next German but he was no happier. Considering that they were winning the war, it seemed strange that they appeared so miserable. If it had been me, I would be as happy as a bear with a honey pot and rejoicing, advertising our success with a great self-satisfying smile. This German handed me a chunk of heavy black bread *(see picture reference 36)*. Armed with this most welcome fare, we were ordered back to our cell, where I promptly sat down with my back against the cool wall and slowly ate, chewing each small mouthful over and over again, relishing every single morsel and crumb. To a starving man, this was a veritable feast and the first actual 'meal' that the Germans had given to me since my capture.

Given our recent travelling conditions, we spent our first night in comparative comfort, for I was horizontal and, given the stone flooring on which we lay, relatively snug. To top it all, I had something in my belly, albeit small. The following day we were taken to a building where we had our heads shaved, our remaining rags steam heated and our bodies sprayed with something pretty vile in the hope of de-lousing us. Afterwards, we were confined to our cell where our situation slowly improved, and with that improvement, our spirits rose an two inch above rock bottom.

Each morning, we were taken to a stone clad room, at the end of which was a long stone ledge. This was our toilet. Even after my meagre meal of bread and water, I needed to go. Moving forward, I unbuttoned my trousers as I walked. Out of curiosity, before positioning myself, I had to look over the ledge to see what I was exposing my backside to. Below was a dark void. How deep it went I couldn't see, but it stank. Now confident that my bottom was not in immediate danger, I positioned myself over the edge and did my business. None of us were embarrassed anymore, that emotion had been torn from us long ago. We looked at each other, smiled and then burst into laughter at the comedy of it all. I suppose we should have shown more respect for the historic medieval toilet that generations of noblemen had been using since its construction. God only knows what was at the bottom of the deep, black pit and I hoped that we would not have to be the ones to clear out this particular latrine. I assumed that *'in ye olden days',* the offerings would have dropped into the surrounding moat which had dried up long ago.

After our ablutions, but without the luxury of washing, we were taken back to the watering room to be presented with a metal container to replace our dixies. They were standard army-issue but I didn't know which army, for unlike ours they were circular. We ate from it, drank from it, shaved in it, pissed in it and lived out of it. Using it for the first time, I collected my coffee but had never tasted anything like it before. It was called '*ersatz*' coffee (*meaning artificial or substitute*), a German concoction made from roasted acorns or barley, depending what was available at the time. Apparently, they had been drinking it for years since the importing of African or American coffee beans had become economically difficult and logistically impossible. It was not good but needs must and I soon acquired a reluctant acceptance of its taste as there was no other choice to be had. After we had collected the 'coffee', another German handed out the loaf to share and counted five of us through before handing over another. On the table was a communal knife, which was guarded. Each loaf had to be shared and divided into five equal parts. We all crowded round the 'cutter' to watch and see that he was scrupulously fair in his work and that no-one received a crumb more than the other.

Back inside our cell, we propped ourselves up against the perimeter walls and passed the day getting to know the others a little better. At first, we exchanged stories of our capture and when that avenue was exhausted it came as no real surprise that the topic of conversation moved on to food; our best meal, best cook, favourite food, favourite cafe, best food that mum cooked, best food that you cooked, best food that you could possibly dream of and what we were going to eat as soon as we got home. Happy thoughts, but thoughts that were to painfully dominate our thinking for almost every single day in the years to come.

It took another day before the Germans were better able to organise matters by bringing in that friend of the common soldier, the field kitchen, consisting of a large cylindrical metal pot that was heated from below. Each evening, this was filled with water and into it the 'chef' threw anything that he could lay his hands on, mostly vegetable matter in the form of potato peelings, swede peelings, turnip peelings, turnip tops. In fact, any leftovers from the German's tables, slowly stewed with a dash of total disregard. It was thin but it was wet, warm and apparently, it contained a tiny trace of nutrients.

On the fourth day I allowed myself to believe that the worst was over and things were 'on the up' at last. That feeling didn't even last the morning as depressing news finally filtered through from the jubilant guards. France apparently, had surrendered and Germany was now in control of western Europe. Britain was alone and so were we.

Herby almost spat the words out. "Bloody French, bet they couldn't wait to put their hands up."

Nobody disagreed with him for we had all developed a strong dislike of both the French military and civilian population.

Now feeling utterly miserable again, we were led out room by room into the warm, open courtyard for the next stage of our processing, with one side bathed in sunlight and the other standing in shadow, rather like Europe at that point in time. Smiling armed guards stood around the castle walls, watching. On the opposite side to me were several Germans sitting down in front of tables with various pieces of equipment. A line of other PoWs had just finished being attended to, whatever that implied, so we moved forward, formed an orderly queue and waited our turn. The most senior NCO present was the Gefreiter (Corporal), a middle-aged man and slightly overweight with the standard issue German grumpy expression. Intimating with an upturned hand, waving his fingers back and forth impatiently, he beckoned.

"Nächster".

One by one, we were called forward. The first task was to issue us with our official camp number which was recorded against our name. A guard inserted a piece of lead-like rectangular metal into a machine, adjusted a dial, pulled a handle and gradually stamped a number onto it. I had officially become PoW No. 6161 *(see picture reference 26).*

The German handed it to me with instructions that it should be worn at all times. I now felt as though I had officially become a insignificant fragment in the malodorous Nazi establishment and I didn't like it one bit.

The next part of our registration process involved us having our photograph taken. We stood with our backs against the castle wall, onto which was hung a plain sheet. I was then handed a black board, onto which the camp name had already been scribed - Stalag XXB – and below it, No. 6161.

One click and all was recorded for the Nazi files.

At the next table, a German fiddled with his paperwork just long enough to make his point as to who was in control. He looked up and spoke but from my position, I could not hear what was being said. Several of my cell mates had already been processed and another line of fellow PoWs was slowly emerging from one of the courtyard doors. I glanced at each of them in turn for a familiar face but to no avail.

The Gefreiter then asked a series of questions in his native tongue and pidgin English.

"What is your trade?"

Hang on a minute! Having been given every detail that the Geneva Convention required, this guard's questions were now venturing beyond the military permissible limit. Before we were sent to France, we had been fully instructed as to what we were allowed to say to the enemy in the event of capture. The bottom line was that we were certainly not allowed to tell them anything that might be of the slightest use. As petty as it may sound, your trade was one such piece of information. If we were set to work by the Germans, as was permitted under the Convention, we were not allowed to be placed into any useful occupation that would allow the incumbent German national to be released from that job, thereby freeing him to join the services and thereafter aid the enemy's war effort. By revealing your trade, this could allow them to place you in that useful and forbidden employment.

Under this almost comical interrogation, Bill gave a good, considered answer and simply replied.

"Labourer."

Whether this was true or not, his answer was duly noted. It was now our very own lance corporal, Herby Davies and he too replied.

"Labourer."

Then came the turn of our jester, Tommy Grigg. When the trade question was put to him, the wag gave a different answer.

"I am a lamp-lighter."

The Gefreiter looked up, slightly taken aback.

"A lamp-lighter?" he repeated questioningly.

All the men behind could hear and smiled accordingly. Now it was my turn. I stood in front of the Gefreiter.

"Trade?"

With a blank expression, I looked straight at the German.

"Assistant to the above."

How we stopped convulsing into fits of laughter, I do not know. Tears were already beginning to well up in my eyes as the Gefreiter diligently noted the reply. Too busy trying to control his laughter, Charlie couldn't think of an outrageous or witty retort so he followed the others and was recorded as being a simple labourer, but behind him was our more adventurous man, Freddy Laws, and he gave a cracking reply in his Nottinghamshsire accent.

"I am a cross-country runner."

This time the Gefreiter did look up, no doubt surprised at yet another different and unexpected answer. Stifled sniggers and slight ripples of laughter could be heard down the line. He must have heard for suddenly, without warning, came a thunderous bang as the Gefreiter, with his eyes bulging, brought his clenched fist crashing down onto the table, causing the surrounding guards to wake up and spring into a state of alert but unsure what to do. Some even unslung their rifles. After a day of constantly entering meaningless, useless and fictitious trades, the Gefreiter finally snapped.

"What is the matter with all you British?" he roared. "No wonder you are losing the war. You are all unskilled. You are all stupid."

As if to emphasise his point, he thumped the table once more. It was like watching a Charlie Chaplin film and we loved every comical scene. This was my greatest moment of hilarity since being taken prisoner, and after the horror of the train what therapy! Our new found 'bolshy' attitude was slowly developing as we continued to recover and rediscover our very British sense of humour.

> *Dennis sipped another mouthful of his Nescafe Gold Blend coffee. "Honest to God Pat, as sure as I am sitting here, labourer, lamplighter, assistant to the above and cross-country runner, and the German wrote it all down."*
>
> *Dennis had to stop a moment. He couldn't carry on with tears rolling down his face, his laughter sounding like Mutley, the cartoon dog. He couldn't continue for several more minutes.*
>
> *"I die with laughter every time I recall what happened that day. It might not sound so very funny to you as I speak, but if you had been there and been through what we had just been through, I am sure you would have wet yourself too."*
>
> *Dennis stopped his story for the day as he went on to recall a few other reminiscences before returning home. He had a 'hot date' that night. At 90, he was off to Walton with one of his ladies for a dance evening, as he did every week.*
>
> *"Got to keep active as long as possible," he said with his usual gaiety. I wished him well and arranged to continue with his story the following Thursday.*

After we had finished the interrogation, we moved to another desk where two men sat. From the table in front of them hung a large piece of paper with a symbol clearly visible with a name printed underneath, 'Comité International de la Croix Rouge, Genève', the International Committee of The Red Cross, a friend to every captive soldier.

Bill Westaway and Herby Davies were the first of our batch to be called forward. Unlike our previous inquisitors, these gentlemen introduced themselves.

"Our task is to inform your families that you are alive and being held as PoWs in Germany.

By his side, stood an austere looking German officer who eyed us with smouldering indifference.

By contrast, the Swiss official smiled and continued politely.

"What is your PoW Number,... what is your family name,... forenames,... where and when were you captured?"

They both replied and to the last question, eventually answered,

"Abbeville, 20th May?" which was meticulously recorded.

"Next," bellowed the officer.

"What is your rank,... 'father's name,... mother's name,... address, so that they can be informed of your situation. Now where were you captured,... date of capture,...?"

We trusted these men and took them to be whom they professed to be, from the Red Cross. But to be honest, none of us lot had a clue as to dates and the whereabouts of our capture and Bill Westaway told them he didn't know.

The gentleman from Switzerland needed an answer to his every question, so he scribed an answer for us, an answer that he had been given previously. - 'Abbeville, 20th May'. That was good enough for we really couldn't care less. The others did likewise and still he recorded 'Abbeville, 20th May'.

I slipped my identity tag into my trouser pocket, for I had no means of hanging it around my neck.

The Red Cross sent the card and notified my family that I was well and a PoW at Stalag XXA (and what I believe was sub-camp 3).

As you can imagine, my mother cried with sheer joy upon reading the above news and that I was at least alive. She was also supplied with a forwarding address so that she could write back to me and keep in touch throughout my internment. Two days later, we were pleased to be handed another card and pencil so that we could write home. We knew that we had to be careful not to give anything important away, so the letter that I wrote was devoid of detail:

Dear Mum, Dad and Frank,

"I am well and a prisoner of war."

I then dived into a lengthy paragraph in which I asked for food, food and then for more food. It must have read like a shopping list before rationing. A big fruit cake, loaves of bread, steak and kidney pie, bread pudding with loads of currants, biscuits, etc., etc., etc., and boxes of cigarettes. I wrote little else. When I had finished, I placed it in the post box and waited.

Upon reflection many months later, my whole attitude changed. I imagined my poor mother reading the letter and I felt ashamed. I had not told her what had happened to me and I did not ask her about how she or the family were. I had only been interested in myself and my stomach. She would have deduced that I was starving. (Likewise, the German censor of letters probably did too.) My mother would have been terribly upset at the realisation of my plight.

When I finally returned home, I was so pleased to hear that this particular letter never reached her, which made me believe that the camp censor must have taken one look at it and decided that by asking for all that food, I was implying that I was being starved. That would have put the Germans in a bad light so my letter probably went straight into the bin.

After morning coffee, I was surprised to hear that we were to gather all our possessions and prepare to move out. The surprise was that they had given time to gather up our possessions for mine was only my side pouch with contents and my newly issued dixie, so packing did not take me too long. Once outside, I was delighted to see the Germans had laid on some transportation.

"Jerries must be getting soft in their old age," was Tommy's comment accompanied by chuckles from us all.

It was yet another sweltering summer's day. The sweat was running down our backs as we marched once more on to the next stage of our internment. Before long we arrived at a grass clearing the size of four football pitches, bordered by woodlands. Large white Bell Tents had been erected in long, neat rows. Crude wooden watch towers defined the rectangle perimeter. For the time being, we were without the barbed wire. The place had all the hallmarks of being hastily erected. We were 'checked in' and processed by another miserable-looking

German NCO before being unceremoniously cajoled into one of the large tents. I was surprised to see that inside there was nothing except a hundred or so other men and the long grass that had been happily growing before this particular invasion. What followed next was much scratching of heads as we wondered what to do. Where exactly were we and was this to be where we would rot for the duration of the war, for again, we were told nothing. That in itself was reassuring, for it was just like being back with the British Army in northern France.

By midday the interior heat and humidity of the tent had become unbearable under the relentless summer sun. Disorganisation reigned and, as a result, we received nothing in the way of food and drink. When I awoke after a restless night's sleep, I stood up, only to fall straight back down again. My head was spinning as though I had just got off a merry-go-round. I fell to the ground and lay there for a while, feeling sick and weak. I had succumbed to the lack of nourishing, healthy food and adequate liquid. The next time I tried, I took longer about it and stood up gradually. This time I managed to stay upright.

Outside, we were paraded, counted and led off to a recently delivered field kitchen. Hooray! Coffee was brewed and black potato bread was handed out. Even this small gesture did the trick, with my body immediately benefiting from what few nutrients the meal contained.

That evening, the German chefs managed to boil up some water and toss in a few old ingredients, the usual collection of dirty vegetable peelings and bits of fat, leftovers from the German's table, to create a hot, wet, smelly something-or-other.

Such was the new found generosity of the Third Reich that by the end of the second day we were issued with two blankets, second hand of dubious origins and certainly not clean. By day three, life inside that tented camp was becoming particularly boring. We spent most of our days sleeping which was good, regaining a little of our strength after the gruelling journey on a starvation diet. We looked for anybody that we might know amongst the prisoners and searched desperately for anything to smoke. I was dying for one, but so was everyone else.

· · · § · · ·

~ CALAIS ~
A TALE OF WOE

I have no idea how truthful their stories were but from what I have since read, it all seems horribly likely that these events did happen as described to me, with such understandable bitterness, at Stalag XXA and subsequently at Stalag XXB.

Our tented camp was receiving influxes of prisoners on an almost daily basis. As each new batch arrived, it was only human nature to search amongst them in order to determine if they were regimental comrades or friends from home, quiz them for news, ask for smokes and listen to their stories. I talked to one such private from The Queen Victoria's Rifles, but I forget his name. He and his mates described in bitter detail how he had been captured.

His battalion sailed from Dover in convoy, destined for Calais on 22nd May 1940 to help bolster the crumbling defences around the besieged town. As they neared the coast off Calais, they could all see that the port was being bombarded by the Germans. A low black cloud of acrid smoke covered the town. According to what this soldier had been told, the captain of their ship radioed a message back to London informing them of the dangerous state of affairs that existed. He requested further instructions, questioning the wisdom of delivering the troops into such hopeless danger. The message that came back to the ship's Commander was a bitter disappointment to them all. He was ordered to dock immediately and for the troops to disembark and defend the port. In the shallows offshore, smouldering hulks of ships lay lifeless, half submerged in the surrounding seas. As they landed, artillery shells and bombs were pounding the town. Buildings everywhere were ablaze. There was chaos at the quayside as his battalion had to force their way into the town past French troops and naval personnel desperate to escape in the opposite direction.

"I don't mind telling you mate, I was as scared as hell. I hadn't a clue what was going on or what we were meant to do. It was my first taste of fighting."

Then came an order to literally run and seek shelter in the many sand dunes just outside the harbour area where they received their baptism of fire. When they eventually reassembled, they were split up into smaller units and ordered to join the fight with the French against the encircling German Army. Unfortunately, within only four days of arrival, his platoon was ordered to surrender and by the following day, 27th May, the remainder of his battalion were either killed or captured. Those newly arrived troops went straight into a hopeless situation and into captivity. Many had already succumbed to wounds from artillery and rifle fire. He was taken prisoner without even firing a single shot, by the overwhelming, all conquering Germans. He went from ship to shore, just to join the swelling ranks of British PoWs across northern France and Belgium.

The men I spoke to were very bitter and could not understand or forgive their Generals for ordering them into a suicidal situation when there was no hope of them winning or escaping.

What a bloody shambles and a suicidal waste... or so it seemed to them and to me.

~ HOLLAND ~
ANOTHER TALE OF WOE

Within days, I came across another group of men who had a similar tale to tell. It was a sunny afternoon as I sat down for a chat with two guards over a smoke or two. Both tales demonstrated the selfless sacrifice and the sheer professionalism of the British soldier throughout history. Ordinary men and women in the service of their country who, when ordered to do a job, did it without question, even though they knew it might be futile and almost certainly result in their death.

I cannot recall their names as I soon lost contact with them.

This is their tale.

As was expected by the intelligence services in London, German forces invaded Holland on 10th May 1940 under the rather ridiculous pretence of saving them and their neutrality from the warmongering British and French forces.

On hearing the news, Churchill put his contingency plan into operation. A British torpedo-boat destroyer, HMS Hereward, and a troop ship left for Holland shrouded in secrecy. The naval personnel on board were joined by a mixed contingent of regular soldiers taken from remaining

Guards regiments still in England. They numbered about 650 Irish and Welsh Guards plus a contingent of Royal Marines. On 13th May 1940, they were moored alongside the Hook of Holland quay, waiting. Troops were dispatched to secure the harbour and safeguard the route into the port. Whilst the Germans began their final assault, a small convoy of cars ferrying Queen Wilhelmina, the infant Crown Princess Beatrix and other members of the Dutch royal family sped to the quayside. They were the first to arrive. The second convoy also managed to get through unscathed, carrying Prime Minister De Geer and most members of the Dutch cabinet. Finally, lorries loaded with inconspicuous-looking crates were delivered to the quayside and rapidly loaded on board.

Heavy air raids on the small area defended by the British forces resulted in many casualties, who were rushed to the local hospital. Without sizeable reinforcements, the continued onslaught rendered their position untenable. Reinforcements were not possible and on 14th May, the Guards signalled to a waiting naval ship. The remaining forces were evacuated and returned to Dover.

All Dutch forces were ordered to cease fighting and the country fell under the heel of the Nazi jackboot. However, as a consequence, the wounded were not so lucky and fell into the hands of the conquering Germans. The valiant Guards and Marines were effectively sacrificed in order to save the lives of the royal family and high-ranking Dutch officials.

As we chatted, they angrily questioned the wisdom of such a sacrifice. Their anger was understandable as they had seen their comrades die, but such was their job. Were their lives worth less than the rescued Dutch elite? I'll leave you to judge. As for my opinion and the opinion of those who sacrificed themselves on that mission, that is the price every soldier risks when doing his duty.

But this timely act saved the officials from falling into the hands of the Nazis, allowing them to form the nucleus of a Dutch government in exile back in England.

Unknown to us at the time, or to any of the ordinary populace, the ships had also brought back the total Dutch gold reserves and emptied Amsterdam, the diamond capital of the world, of many millions of pound's worth of precious gems, thereby depriving Nazi Germany of untold wealth for its greedy and costly war machine.

So was it a price worth paying after all?

History must be the final judge.

~ WORK BEGINS ~

Within days of our arriving at the tented camp on the outskirts of Thorn, the once lush grass had died away and we were left with a thin covering of dry, broken straw on top of the hard, baked earth. This was our only mattress. Night times were bearable for it was not too chilly and at least we were under cover. But these conditions did nothing to stop my itching. In fact, it was getting worse, it seemed that my lice were back.

During the three months that I was there, the camp developed rapidly. Whilst barbed wire fences were completed, the first job for us PoWs was to build a simple open latrine. This consisted of a long, very deep pit in the ground with a raised board across its full length. Onto this, one would perch oneself. Without the luxury of supplied paper, it was an unpleasant experience. Those without had used their hands before wiping them on the filthy plank. It was that simple. During that hot summer of 1940, the open pit stunk and foul scraps of soiled news paper blew across the camp.

With little to occupy us, we festered in our confinement, bored to death, for there was no joy or satisfaction in being idle for days on end. Eventually, volunteers were called upon to form working parties. Such was the dullness of my situation, I jumped at the opportunity.

"Den, you are forgetting the golden rule, never, ever volunteer for anything," Bill advised me.

"Come on chaps, anything is better than rotting here and who knows what we may find?" I argued.

"May I suggest 'hard bleeding work' is what we'll find," was Tommy's answer.

I managed to talk the others into coming with me and what a relief to escape the boredom and explore the opportunities in the world around us. For a while, we were 'employed' filling in the holes in the road. On other occasions, I was sent down to the local goods yard to unload items ranging from wood and coal to food from the goods wagons that were continuously arriving. One morning, we were assigned a delicious and heaven sent task. I thought I had died and gone to heaven. As the doors were opened, I saw rolls of delicious, appetising, great, fat, sweet- smelling yummy bread. Hundreds and thousands of them. En masse, our work gang started to salivate and immediately my mind went into overdrive to work out how I might relieve the Germans of a loaf... or two, as did the minds of every other PoW assigned to the wonderful but cruel job of unloading those delicious, appetising, great, fat, sweet-smelling yummy hunks of heaven.

We formed ourselves into a 'chain gang' from the wagons to the trucks which were waiting as close to the carriages as possible. We quietly chatted amongst ourselves as to how to liberate some bread before going into action. Our eyes were everywhere. At first, the Germans watched us like hawks, but as time dragged on, they became increasingly bored and relaxed their guard,... just enough. As soon as they turned away for whatever reason, a nod was given or a wink received and the person who had just handed over his tray to the next chap in line took a loaf and slid it into his trousers.

If the goons were watching too closely, we 'made' a loaf fall off onto the ground. This infuriated the guards, who would scream and shout at us with such pleasantries as "Dummheit" or °Dummkopf". Of course, they didn't pick up the dirty rolls, so they stayed there until we picked them up later, often kicking them under a piece of wood or a rail to hide them before popping those down our trousers too. At the end of the shift, every well-hung member of the work party was packing more inside his trousers than he had been that morning as we made our way back to camp. The extra rations helped us to stay healthy, but also, knowing that we had 'got one over' on our hosts sent our spirits soaring.

As summer turned to autumn, the nights got progressively cooler and our stay in those tents became increasingly more uncomfortable.

~ MEANWHILE, BACK HOME ~
22nd October 1940

Since receiving the last official notification from The War Office some four months ago, my mother had been dreading the arrival of the next letter to fall through the door. On the morning of Tuesday 22nd October 1940, she came out of the kitchen and noticed another official brown envelope in front of the door, this time marked from The War Office, Infantry Record and Pay Office, Ashford, Middlesex, and written on 17th October 1940:

Madam,
I have to inform you that a report has been received from The War Office
to the effect that your son is a Prisoner of War at Stalag XXA, Germany.

Camp No.: 6161. Should any other information be received concerning him, such information will be at once communicated to you.
Instructions as to the method of communication with Prisoners of War can be obtained at any Post Office.

'Could have told you Mum, I take a lot of killing!'

It was difficult to imagine how the Germans could possibly make our rations any more boring - ersatz coffee for breakfast, nothing for lunch and what was comically referred to as soup at the end of each and every day served with a lump of black bread. But sometimes those sneaky Germans would confuse and excite us by mixing things up a little and giving us this watery broth for lunch and nothing at night.

It was with a certain relief when, on the last day of October 1940 along with hundreds of other British PoWs, I received what we thought was good news. Morning parade was as usual, and then we waited for any orders of the day. But the orders never came. Instead, we were told to grab our ersatz, pack our belongings and move out. Tent by tent we assembled in our column until instructed to march. We followed the same route as when we arrived, returning once more to the marshalling yard where a train was waiting. We were immediately cajoled into clambering aboard those terrible cattle wagons all over again.

"Climb aboard quickly."

The guards never stopped shouting and their rifle butts came into action periodically, just for the hell of it. I was surprised that nobody seemed to count how many of us boarded, but presumably it didn't matter. As on my previous trek from Luxembourg to Thorn, the Germans packed us in tightly. However, this time the weather was much colder, so although hot inside the temperature was not an issue. As we were all British and spoke the same language, we were more understanding and respectful of each other plus we had been here before and knew what to expect.

It was late in the day before the train pulled out and we found ourselves once more on the move. We travelled overnight, making slow progress, stopping and starting to make way for more important freight moving in both directions. We were still travelling the next morning before coming to a halt at midday. Unbeknown to us, we had crossed over the border from Poland into East Prussia and arrived at our final destination. The signs outside read 'MARIENBURG'.

STALAG  XXB

MARIENBURG
1st November 1940

𝒜 chilling and drizzly reception awaited us. Our spirits were as damp as the weather. In spite of everything we had been through, an NCO tried to get us into shape and to march as British soldiers, upright and with pride. Unfortunately for him, we were in no mood to be browbeaten by one of our own.

"F**k off," came the universal reply.

As we journeyed through the edge of town, Charlie asked a general question.

"Any idea where we are?"

"I saw a sign back there that read Marienburg,... that's all I know."

"Sounds like somewhere in Germany," commented Herby.

"Well there's a surprise," commented some sarcastic bugger.

"Does it matter?"

"No."

Further response was not forthcoming from anyone so we dropped our brief conversation, for we were all pretty miserable. Towards mid afternoon, we took a right-hand turning off the road and onto a muddy track. As we continued I could see huts dispersed amongst the pine trees to the left, some distance ahead. The closer we got, the clearer it all became. In front, I could see a barbed wire gate, sentry box and a solitary hut, clearly visible. We had arrived. The trek from the marshalling yards at Marienburg hadn't taken too long, for the distance was about four miles. The sign on the tall, simple, wooden and barbed wire gate revealed what was to become our final destination. We had arrived at Stalag XXB.

> † *I was soon to discover that this camp had been created during the 1914-1918 war for the purposes of housing Russian PoWs, and it looked like it. Having been abandoned for some twenty-six years, it had been hastily brought back into service in 1939/40 to accommodate the vast numbers of unexpected allied prisoners captured during the invasion of France and the Low Countries and full scale rout of their armies that summer. As far as I was concerned, I wish the Germans hadn't gone to so little trouble to re-open it. It was established in a quarter of Marienburg called Willenberg (now Wielbark) for the housing of NCOs (non-commissioned officers) and privates. Territorially, it was subordinate to Danzig Province of West Prussia (District XX).*
>
> *It was situated in the Willenberg forest, on a high slope of the Nogat River, to the south of Malbork just off the Malbork-Stuhm (now Sztum) road. It formed part of today's municipal cemetery. The camp administration was housed in the timber barracks to the south west of the main entrance amongst the pine trees. The biggest number of prisoners was registered on the 1st July 1944: altogether there were 32,477 prisoners registered. Inside were 10,577 French, 9,324 British, 5,708 Soviet, 6,081 Italian, 470 Belgian, 315 Yugoslavian and 2 Polish prisoners.*
>
> *STALAG XXB Marienburg consisted of*
> *Willenberg main camp: fluctuated between 10-15,000 prisoners at any one time*
> *The three main sub camps where numbers always fluctuated:*
>   *Krolow (now Królewo): 300 prisoners*
>   *Gdingen (now Gdynia) - about 1,300 prisoners*
>   *Danzig (now Gdańsk) - about 600 prisoners*
> *and numerous working parties spread throughout the surrounding countryside.*

The camp appeared grimmer than our expressions. A lone guard, wrapped in his warm overcoat buttoned to his chin, left the comfort of his cosy-looking guard house to check the paperwork.

---

† *Sourced from: http://www.starymalbork.pl/stalag/ramka3uk.html*
http://en.wikipedia.org/wiki/East_Prussian_plebiscite

Others soon joined him. I shivered whilst we waited and wrapped my arms round my upper body for protection against a sudden cold blast, a foretaste of the approaching winter. We had a long wait whilst we were searched yet again. After so many searches, it was difficult to believe that we still had any items of value hidden about our person. Eventually the paperwork tallied to the satisfaction of the guards. I marched with a horrid sense of foreboding, through the gated entrance that was set at an angle to the wired perimeter, into the compound and onward, to the massive barren central area. Our processing was going to take a while. With a depressing resignation I looked around at this bleak encampment that had been carved out of the surrounding woods. Defining its boundary were the tall double barbed wire fences with coiled barbed wire between, forming a huge almost rectangular compound. Positioned on the outside of three corners were the wooden watchtowers, with others interspersed along the boundary. Each tower was manned by one or two German guards with machine guns and search lights, enabling them to deliver a hail of withering gunfire when and where it was needed. Inside the fence was a single wire running around the camp, one metre high. I was soon to learn that this was known as the 'death wire' or 'dead line'. Any PoW who dared to cross over or under it stood the real possibility of having his young life cut seriously short - whatever the circumstances. When our turn came to be processed, we were ordered to show our Stalag identity tags and camp number and were checked off. Like the deteriorating weather, our welcome was far from warm.

All the NCOs, including our friend Herby were separated from the rest of us and taken to one of the old wooden huts that ran along the far end of camp perimeter. As for us lowly enlisted men, we were split up and counted into squads of a set number. I couldn't believe my misfortune when a guard stopped me from moving forward with Freddy *(see picture reference 31)*, Tommy, Charlie and Bill and pushed me in another direction, forming another squad. I must have looked like a lost puppy as I stared across at the others on that wet winter's day. I could see their sad reluctant acceptance of the situation on their faces, but there was nothing that we could do to stop our separation.

Once they had gone ahead, it was my squad's turn. We walked past a row of old blackened wooden huts (which I later learnt were occupied by the 9,000 French PoWs already ensconced), towards a series of humps which were cut into a raised bank in the ground behind and ran the length of the left hand side of the camp. As soon as our squad reached the required number of men, we followed. As we passed along the line, I noticed the depressions in the ground at the front of each mound and a door. I realised what was in store and I was horrified. Winter was almost upon us and a thin peppering of frost already lay in patchy depressions on the ground. With our wholly inadequate clothing, our 'new' accommodation was to be these filthy holes in the ground. The Germans called them 'Erdehütte', the translation of which was literally 'earth hut'.

Trying to thwart the approaching clouds of depression, I tried to make light of our grim situation.

"I think it best at this precise juncture, not to complain to the management as to the inadequate accommodation," I muttered to my closest companion in my best BBC voice, managing to grin at the same time. At that precise moment I could still joke, for I had not yet been inside or experienced my first night.

~ THE ERDEHÜTTE ~

This was no ordinary camp as I understood it. This particular site had been designed by a sadistic madman. Previous persons unknown had dug out a series of large trenches in straight rows. Each trench was about five to six metres wide by twenty-five metres long and just over a metre deep. The excavated earth had been piled up to form a low wall around the trench. Over this, a simple triangular-shaped framed roof construction had been built and covered with wooden slats. Finally, the remaining earth from the excavation was piled back up over the roof, completely covering the construction. Since then, grass had grown over the soil-covered roofs, making them difficult to see from a distance. These earth and wooden mounds resembled animal sets and were only suitable for beasts. However, they were now to become our living quarters.

This alone was bad enough but the reality was about to get worse. Outside, it was already getting dark. I was amongst the seventh batch ordered into the next available so-called 'hut'. With trepidation and weariness, I approached the mound. The eleven men before me descended the three steps down into the 'devil's arsehole' as one of our number immediately christened them. I followed. With each step I took, my heart sank. As soon as I walked into the pit of despair, the grim reality hit me like a bludgeon and my remaining good spirits drained from my soul into the hard earth floor.

"One day, this will all end," I chanted softly to myself, "one day."

Inside, was almost total darkness. The interior smelt damp, cold and earthy. Nobody can begin to imagine what it was like inside these hovels. It was like stepping back in time to the stone age. Surely we were not expected to live in these holes? There must be a mistake, this must be just temporary. Yes, that's it, a temporary holding bay until they transferred us to the more suitable huts above ground that I had seen earlier.

By now, I had decided that these pits were even unfit for animals. The only means of ventilation was through the one door and at the very far end, the smallest of windows. The single source of artificial light was from a lone electric bulb hanging down from a cable hooked over a beam in the roof. It only illuminated the immediate surrounding area; the peripheral areas of the hut remained in depressing, dank, gloom.

All hope of this being only temporary accommodation ebbed away with what I saw next. Running down either side of the hut were our bunk beds in two rows, twenty down each side. In total, each Erdehütte seemed to house forty men. There was barely room to squeeze into or turn around between each row of bunks. I was pushed further in and randomly took possession of a bunk. It was just inches above the hard dirt floor. I sat on the edge of it, my backside coming into hard contact with its unyielding wooden slats, for there was no mattress. A voice from the front door area of the hut announced in English that just outside the door was a large bucket for us to pee into. How thoughtful!

As I lay back on my bunk. I felt the bitter cold and dampness seep through to my body. A German guard appeared silhouetted in the doorway, rifle slung over his shoulder, and slammed the door shut. We were entombed. I could hear the lock engage, making my mind race as I went over all that had happened that day. I tried to imagine what the future held in store for me now that I was on my own. Was this to be my fate for the remainder of the war? And how long was that to be? The German Army had made such an immense impression on me that I felt certain England would be incapable of ever liberating us. Moving from the previous summer's sweltering discomfort under canvas at Thorn to the misery of this winter hell hole, I realised that I had jumped out of the frying pan into the very bowels of a subterranean hell. To top it all, we had no food.

Bearing in mind that outside the temperature was bitter, within the hour of being entombed, the temperature in our hovel had risen considerably. Lacking adequate ventilation, the reality of one-hundred men generating heat and stale, moist breath inside our tomb, allowed temperature and humidity to increase with every passing minute. To have succumbed to the effects of carbon dioxide poisoning would have been a blessed relief from the hell of that first winter. The huts had previously housed Polish PoWs who had just been released, as Poland was now a crushed nation. I expect their labours were needed on the outside. I felt twangs of envy and sadly wondered just how long Britain could continue the fight alone and how long I would be kept here.

By morning, the air inside was fetid and beyond description. My body was clammy with my sweat and that of a hundred others. When the door was eventually unlocked and opened, I almost tripped over others in my desperate rush to be outside and breathe freely. I burst into the cold morning air, such was my eagerness to rid myself of every stinking particle of the night's Erdehütte breath that I inhaled too often, too deeply and too quickly. I almost keeled over. I had to steady myself against the door whilst those behind me pushed past.
At our first morning parade, we were 'welcomed' by Commandant, Oberst (Colonel) Bollman †. His welcoming speech only served to increase my present sense of helplessness and isolation as I studied this chubby well presented officer in his warm coat.

> † *Commandant, Oberst (Colonel) Bollman: I contacted the German authorities but was told that the records of the camp had been destroyed in the last few months of the war, along with the records of PoWs. Eventually, I did find the reference to Bollman in a document entitled "The Red Cross Report on the Inspection in Marlbork of 22/23 November 1940' (see page 590).*
> *In addition, according to Sean Longden's book 'Dinkirk, The Men They Left Behind', Oberst Bollman was ultimately responsible for the shooting and deaths of eighteen men, and a further twelve men wounded, under his watch.*

"Welcome to Stalag XXB. You are prisoners of the Reich here in Prussia."

The translator then went on to convey to us the utter stupidity of attempted escape. By informing us as to where we were, it made any thought of absconding seem completely futile. He continued with more rules and regulations for us to adhere to and explained the purpose of the 'death wire' whilst I kicked my heels to combat the chill that was seeping through my boots. The Officer and his translator seemed to talk for ages so I wrapped my arms around my freezing body as he droned on. Within half an hour, my ears were stinging as we stood around on that chilly winter morn. The vast majority of us were hopelessly under-dressed in our short army tunics. Many of us were now paying the price for foolishly abandoning our coats.

"Nice introduction Jerry, now piss off," came a mumbled uttering from my left. That broke the ice, so to speak, and smiles emanated briefly. Unfortunately, a guard who understood English happened to be standing behind him. From nowhere, he produced a cosh of some description and brought it smashing down on the side of his head. We just stood in shock whilst the unfortunate prisoner lay where he fell until Commandant Oberst Bollman had finished and we were dismissed. This was an intimidating introduction to Stalag XXB, and one that made a lasting impression

Given my PoW No. 6161, I assumed that I was amongst the first batch of many British PoWs to be interned at Stalag XXB over the next four years. However, there were others already there. Immediately after parade, I found my friends, including Herby' and toured our new surroundings. On the opposite side of the camp to us, I could see a row of wooden huts that seemed to stretch from one end to the other. Diagonally opposite and just to the right side of the entrance ran another line of huts. In total, I counted some 40 huts; these housed the French and Belgians. They appeared to have made themselves pretty comfortable, leaving us the far less inviting Erdehütte hovels. The end hut of their row and closest to the entrance was designated 'The Medical Block'.

Set just inside the entrance and slightly to the left and close to the left boundary fence was 'The Cookhouse and Stores with 'The Boiler Room' attached. The Cookhouse was run and staffed by the French, who also seemed to be in charge of every desirable job in the camp. Although we were meant to be allies, the presence of the French in the camp initially caused a lot of resentment. Almost to a man, we all had a tale to tell of French betrayal, obstruction, cowardice, lack of leadership, resentment, desertion, collaboration and finally, capitulation. To top it all, we had heard through the grapevine that their new Vichy government was now working closely with the Nazis, so one could easily see why they were not universally liked and because of my personal experience at Béthune, they were definitely not to be trusted.

"They were no bloody good in the last war so why should they be any different this time round," was Freddy's scathing comment.

None of us argued. To see them so happily ensconced and pally with the Germans made our blood boil. The French, not to be outdone, hated us just as much and as far as they were concerned, for equally valid reasons.

Behind the cookhouse was a prison within a prison, a small barbed wire enclosure containing one small hut. Prisoners awaiting trial were housed here, those who had stolen anything, having sex with German women whilst working out of camp and a long list of punishable offences.

We were made aware of a small brick building under construction, apparently the punishment block for more serious offences such as attempted escape and not wearing your PoW disc. We would soon come across gloating guards who would indicate the repercussions of our potential offences by holding up their fingers in front of their eyes and looking through them, thereby imitating 'behind the prison bars'.

~ A VERY PUBLIC CONVENIENCE ~

Framed by the surrounding barbed wire and miserable accommodation was a vast central open expanse of sandy mud, some 200m x 100m in size. Known as 'The Parade Ground' its primary use was for twice daily inspections, roll calls and lectures from our German hosts.

That first morning, I made my first visit to the latrines. Situated on the far side of camp between The Red Cross Store and the first French hut, they were about as far away from our hut as you could imagine. My first time was a most unpleasant experience. Even in the chilled November morning air, my nose started to twitch even as I approached. There were no cubicles of any kind, just a long single log suspended over the stinking pit. I joined the others already balancing over the precipice and tried not to look down into the stinking magma. Once outside, I looked about for the washing facilities? I wasn't sure that I had found them yet, for all I saw was an exposed outside trough with a few taps spaced along its length.

I went behind the latrine area and looked out through the barbed wire to the fast flowing river beyond. Cut into the steep sandy bank was a dirty looking trench that ran from the latrine down to the brown waters below.

The white of winter was now falling. We had nothing to do and nothing to occupy our minds during those first few weeks. The colder it got, the less time we could spend outside, which depressingly meant more time in our hovel. As each day drew to a close, I dreaded being locked in our appalling burial chamber. Within days, varying degrees of depression began to infect us all. Those most seriously affected seemed to be abandoning the will to live. Hellish conditions in the huts combined with the cold, miserable weather, short hours of daylight, inadequate food, isolation, a thousand miles from friends and loved ones and, to all intents and purposes, we were forgotten. Who could blame any living soul for becoming depressed? I also hated being separated from my friends.

I didn't think that conditions could get any worse, but they did. Once the door of the erde hütte was locked nobody could get outside to use the piss bucket. If anyone needed to go during the night, they had no option but to pee on the dirt floor. The stench of ammonia that rose from the urine-soaked ground was so intense that at times I could taste it on the back of my throat. No matter how much we used the latrines before lock-up, there was always somebody who needed to urinate during the lock-in. These piss pots were emptied every morning by the 'Jankers Squads' made up of PoWs on punishment duty. They would arrive in pairs, and with the aid of poles threaded through the bucket's rope handles the men would lift them onto their shoulders and transport the stinking buckets and foul contents to the latrines for disposal. They often left a trail of the pungent liquid as the suspended bucket gathered momentum, swinging from side to side. Fancy footwork was needed by them to avoid wet boots and trousers as they navigated their treacherous route.

· · · § · · ·

~ RED CROSS INSPECTION ~
Stalag XX B Malbork (Marienburg)
Visitation 22nd to 23rd November 1940

I was able to find the Red Cross Report on the Inspection of Stalag XXB for 22/23 November 1940. When I showed the report to Dennis, he was only able to manage a half-hearted smile, adding:

"It seems to me to be so criminally negligent of the Inspectors to ignore the obvious and take the offered selective evidence of the Germans at face value. I was never asked my true opinion as to our living conditions by any of them. Before each visit, we were warned as to the consequences of speaking out of turn to the Inspectors and what would happen 'if we told any lies'."

The Inspectors were always accompanied by a German officer.

> *Author: I have only included the report's conclusion here, which paints a very different picture from the reality. The full text translation can be seen on page 590 which makes for interesting reading, so please do. The 1941 Report and the 1942 Reports follow on. They give a factual snapshot of the conditions 'presented to them' within the camp and indicates just how easy it was for the Germans to fool the Inspectors.*

> † *Report Conclusions: Everything suggests that the conditions in the camp, some already completed, will be perfect. Food is good and possibly corresponds to the tastes of the prisoners. They themselves are happy. In turn, when it comes to clothing, especially underwear, it seems that there are still some gaps. Dennis looked aghast when I first showed him this report.*

"I can't believe it, so many lies," was Dennis' only comment

~ MY BIRTHDAY ~
1st December 1940

Four weeks had passed since our arrival. I have no idea how I knew but I awoke knowing that it was a special day,... my birthday. To make matters worse, it was my 21st. I should have been at home with my family and loved ones, out on the town with my mates, celebrating.

---

† *Source: The Geneva International Red Cross Archives*

I was now officially a man, a full adult in the eyes of the laws of England, and where was I? A thousand miles away in some God-forsaken country, a captive of Herr Hitler, held by the strongest, most powerful army that the world had seen since the Roman Empire some two thousand years ago. I spent my birthday clearing snow from one of the many roads around Marienburg and to make matters worse, I was unable to work with my mates who were assigned to another work party. With only a tin of morning coffee and a hunk of bread, pangs of hunger clawed at my stomach all day. Maybe it was because today was my birthday and my stomach should have been stuffed with the best grub that my dear mother could cook. I should have been home, being spoilt rotten. I tried to banish such distressing thoughts from my mind, but no matter how hard I tried, it was impossible. I was a lonely prisoner destined to fill pot holes in the roads until the ends of time in a far-off land. I was utterly despondent and couldn't even manage a smile, which was unusual for me.

Once I got my back into digging, I built up a bit of a sweat and the cold was no longer a problem, only the work was. Gradually my pace increased along with my anger until I was shovelling like a demon, directing my understandable rage at the stone chippings, hurling words of hate and vengeance at my captors - under bated breath, of course.

As darkness descended I felt shattered. We formed up into our column and started the hike back to camp. When we walked through the gates, a bigger wall of depression hit me. After our meagre meal of black German bread and the now familiar dish water, I felt no better and shoved the bread into my pocket for later. I swallowed the vegetable leftovers before it got cold and whatever else our German-supplied French 'chef' could find to minimise the bland taste and quality of a woefully inadequate birthday banquet. My feelings of despair and isolation were increasing by the second. With my hands shoved deep into my trouser pockets, I ran back to my billet. Christ it was cold, how I wished that I still had my greatcoat. I cursed my rash stupidity.

Once inside my tomb, I stood at the side of my bunk. It felt like a bitterly cold evening and most seemed to have had the same idea. The only thing I wanted to do was to climb into my bunk and hide, hoping to find some solace, safety and security. The top bunk was empty so I placed my 'valuable' piece of bread on it until I was ready. Still fully dressed, boots and all, I lifted the blanket and climbed in, shifting down under my cover before lifting up my arm to the bunk above to retrieve my bread. I felt nothing except for the blanket. I moved my hand, first up, then down its length. Still nothing. I sprang up out of my bunk in a panic. Although the light was dim, I could clearly see the top of the bunk above mine. There was nothing there, save for the dreary, thin army blanket stretched over the upper bunk. My bread was gone. I had only taken my eyes off it for a brief moment. Now my heart was pounding. Was this some sort of a joke, a game, albeit a sick one? Bread was the most valuable of items and important if you wanted to stay alive. I looked on the floor on either side. Nothing. I checked everywhere again. Nothing. I shouted out, demanding to know its whereabouts and for its return.

"Where's my bread?" I bellowed.

There was silence. Suspicion immediately fell on the two men either side of the upper bunk, men that I knew but they both remained silent, shrugging their shoulders and denying all knowledge.

"Dunno mate, wasn't me."

"You sure you had it?"

"Course I'm sure, it was on this bloody bunk."

I shouted again, my anger growing with each breath.

"Who's f***ing nicked my bread?"

Silence.

Voices further away asked, "what's wrong?" and "what's up mate?"

I explained angrily, demanding its return but to no avail.

Nothing. It was gone.

The thief, anxious not to get caught, had probably swallowed the evidence as soon as he had stolen it and now there wasn't anything to find. I was gutted. My shock turned to depression and now murderous intent. I lay back down on my bunk, clenching my fists and grinding my teeth, shaking with rage and with evil, vile thoughts racing through my troubled mind. Who had taken it? Was it so-and-so in the next bunk? I looked at those around me once more, wondering and then wanting to smash their faces in. If I had known who the thief was, I would literally have beaten his face to a pulp. I could do absolutely nothing and this dawning sense of injustice took me to the depths of despair so I closed my eyes.

Here I was, on my 21st birthday, half buried in a stinking, sweaty grave, hungry, angry and on my own. I withdrew into myself, hating everything and everyone around me. I closed my eyes even tighter and felt the first soft trickle rolling down the side of my face.

I actually began to cry.

I cried for my loss.

I cried for my plight, my loneliness and isolation.

I cried for my missed birthday and the hunger pain in my stomach.

I cried for my former life in England.

But more than that, I cried for my mum.

I wanted her again. Once more, I wanted to be her little boy cuddling up to her, resting my head on her warm, comfortable lap, to be held in her arms, those reassuring, comforting arms again. I wanted her protection, but above all I wanted to feel and know her love.

I wept as quietly as I could all evening, wondering if I would ever see my family again. I cried and cried until there were no more tears to shed. I simply wanted to die.

> *The birds were singing in the garden outside. The sun was shining and Dennis was warm and comfortable. There had been peace in western Europe for three generations. At ninety years of age, he was nearing the end of his long life. As he related this sad and possibly most desperate episode in his life, he recalled it as if it was only yesterday. Tears welled in his eyes all over again. He cried as he recalled the events and deep emotions in his troubled mind as, momentarily, he returned to that terrible place and day, 1st December 1940, when the world was on the brink of Armageddon.*

This was the lowest point in my whole life that I had ever experienced. My throat ached and my body jerked uncontrollably with every stifled surge of self-pity and tears. I wanted to cry out and wail aloud, to scream about my desperate situation, but I couldn't and sobbed into the sleeves of my tunic. I needed to kill,... anybody but I also wanted to die. Then, as suddenly as it had started, my crying stopped.

I had no more tears to cry.

I had finished.

I can't recall how long I lay there but afterwards, my whole body, mind and soul felt drained and empty. Whilst I lay there, my sorrow slowly cooked and as it did so, sorrow turned to hate, blind and uncomplicated hatred.

I hated the bastard who had taken my bread.

I hated the men next to me.

I hated everyone in my shitty pit.

I hated all the PoWs.

I hated the German Army and the whole f***ing German nation.

I hated Sergeant Hawkes for deserting me.

I hated my government for abandoning me without adequate training in a foreign land.

I hated the whole bloody, stinking human race.

Bastards, each and every one of them.

The hours dragged on by as I was unable to sleep. It was at some point in the early hours that something happened to me, something life-changing. I can only describe it as a turning point and the defining moment of my captivity. I had never felt like this before, never experienced such despondency, and knew that I had reached beyond rock bottom. I was only one stage away from giving up and inevitable death.

So that was it. I realised that it was time to draw a line and face this reality. From now on, I was going to look after myself. Me and me alone. Sod the whole world. I was going to learn from this experience and it was going to make me stronger. From now on, my life only existed in the here and now.

I had no former life.

I had no family.

I had no home.

My home was here.

There was nothing else.

Since my captivity, nothing else outside existed.

This was my life now and I was to live it day by day.

Tomorrow did not exist either, only today.

Freedom and hope did not exist.

Take every day as it comes afresh and deal with it. From now on, every morning that I woke up, I was going to say "Thank you, another night that I have survived and today is a new dawn. Live it."

I was going to get through this. I had no idea how long the war was going to last, but somehow I was going to survive.

"One day, this will all end," I chanted softly, "one day."

· · · § · · ·

~ WHATEVER I COULD FIND ~

This first winter in captivity was long, harsh and seemingly relentless. From December of 1939 to the end of our first month of training, I had experienced one of the worst and coldest British winters on record. But nothing could have prepared me for this. For most of the time, we hibernated inside our stinking hovels, like animals, whilst the full force of an Arctic winter raged outside. By now, we were bug-ridden, smelly and permanently hungry and dysentery was making an unwelcome return. Whilst the deep snow lasted there was nothing to do in the camp, for at this point in time there was still no organised internal camp structure for us inmates, and with too much time to do nothing, depression was sitting heavily on everyone's shoulders.

Then one day, fortune (if you can call it that), came my way. Marienburg and the surrounding roads were covered under tremendous snow drifts and help was urgently needed. When press-ganged volunteers were called for, I offered my services. Such was my desperation at being entombed in those hell holes that even hard labour was preferable to burial. However tough the working parties were going to be, I felt that my chances of surviving my imprisonment would increase outside the wire and that was where I felt my destiny lay. Inside, there was only stagnation, depression and a slow death.

By now the ground seemed to be permanently covered with this deep white blanket. I didn't let it bother me. Every day I would sweep away the covering and search out items that could serve me. Dead grass, leaves and rags were always welcome, and in no time at all they provided me with a soft mattress on which to sleep and insulate me from the cold. I would keep my eye on the guards whilst they were smoking, ready to pounce whenever they threw away their cigarette butts or even their discarded crusts of bread.

Today, whilst clearing the roads, I started to chat with the man working alongside me. He was a Londoner from Camberwell and his name was Alfred Evans from the 2nd/7th Battalion of the Queen's Royal Regiment. He had been captured trying to reach Dunkirk. We exchanged information as always, searching for anything that we had in common, home location or friends. In true British fashion, it wasn't long before we began to talk about the weather.

"I didn't know it could get this cold in Germany," I complained.

"Germany? We should be so lucky. You're miles out mate. You're in the heart of bloody Poland," he replied glumly.

I couldn't believe it, so far away from home and in the far-away country that brought us into the war in the first place!

At this point, there was a commotion. A PoW swore at a guard but unfortunately, the German understood his meaning or the tone only too well. A fracas ensued before the guard brought the incident to a quick conclusion by clouting him with his rifle butt across his face, breaking his front teeth. That was unlucky for the British prisoner involved but lucky for me. During the rumpus, I saw something fall from the German's coat pocket. As soon as I could, I moved across. It was almost hidden in the snow so I discreetly popped it into my trouser pocket before I was seen. Once back at camp, I retrieved it. It was a parcel carefully wrapped in grease-proof paper. Inside was his lunch, two slices of precious bread with two thick slices of sausage meat between them. I drooled with every tiny mouthful, for I wanted to make this last forever. All in all, a good day's work.

Anything could be and probably would be of use to me, so I kept my eyes and ears open. I was now a 'chancer' and beginning to learn the game of survival. Now I was more positive that I was going to endure this war. As for the Germans, I would keep tally of the score, for ultimately I wanted that score to be settled.

Every day, my hatred of the German nation grew and so did my craving for the cigarettes that were in extremely short supply. In desperation, I found dry leaves buried under a piece of wood in the snow. I stuffed a load in my pocket, and as soon as I returned to my hell hole, I began. I took out the bible that Joe had given me and looked at it for a short while before tearing out the first page. Initially, I was dubious about spoiling the holy book, but I was sure that under these dire circumstances, He who sits on high would forgive me. The paper was very fine and seemed ideal. I crushed the dry leaves and rolled it up, lit it, inhaled and coughed several times. Best Virginian tobacco it most certainly wasn't but I inhaled anyway, again and again. Not great but better than nothing.

~ CHRISTMAS 1940 ~

There were no warm, comforting, roaring fires for any of us during our first Christmas in captivity, unless you were French. They still occupied the wooden huts, and as I watched wisps of thin smoke rise from the single chimneys, I grew even more envious of their comparative comfort. I refused to allow myself to recall what I had been doing that previous year, for what was the point? Neither the past nor the future existed, only today.

It was Heiligabend Nacht, the night before Christmas, a time for celebration and the giving of presents across the German nation, but not for us. Under foot, the snow crunched as I strolled outside on that cold Christmas Eve before lock down. My spirits were low and I wanted to be completely alone so I didn't go in search of Freddy and the others. Everything around was covered with winter's white veil as I neared the camp gate. The deep blue-black night sky was littered with countless stars and the moon was shining down from above, unhindered by clouds. Everywhere was immersed in a subdued, radiated light courtesy of Mother Nature. The only source of artificial illumination came from the floodlights mounted high on either side of the gated entrance and the German compound outside the gates.

How grand and romantic that now reads, seventy years later, for my mind has allowed me to forget the worst of the pain that filled those days.

I was drawn to the gates by the presence of people and sounds, for in the stillness of that winter's night the soulful tones resonated across the parade ground. This sound was different, one that I had never heard before, and anything that broke the tedious boredom of camp life had to be fully investigated. My ears led me towards the camp entrance, where I was confronted by a wonderfully strange and mystical sight. Outside the camp gate, just to the right of the road, stood a group of twenty guards. They were standing to attention in their warm boots, long winter coats and forage caps. Each was wearing a pair of canvas covers over his boots stuffed with straw, good insulation from the cold. Four rows of five men, bathing under the powerful floodlights. By contrast, the area behind and to the sides of them retreated into the deep blackness of night. Standing in front, facing the men, was a lone German. To the left of the gate, a young, broad fir tree grew, no more than fifteen feet tall. From its branches I could see decorations of some description hanging in isolated splendour, presumably placed there by the guards.

At a given signal from the leading German, they started to sing. And how they sang, in perfect, beautiful harmony. God! They were more than good, they were excellent. The sound of Stille Nacht, Heilige Nacht (*Silent Night, Holy Night*) drifted effortlessly over the camp on that lonely Christmas of 1940. I recalled that this carol was written by a German composer over a hundred years before. I didn't want to like it for it was German but I couldn't help it. How could a nation of ruthless bullies be capable of such wonderfully divine yet effortless melodies? As their song drifted across the camp, other PoWs joined me. This first song was followed by *O Tannenbaum, O Tannenbaum (Oh Christmas Tree, Oh Christmas Tree)*, to the rousing tune of *The International*. I looked on and tried so hard to keep to my oath, to forget my past life and not to recall my childhood Christmases, but it was impossible and tears began to form. I wiped my eyes with the back of my hand and looked about me and there was not a dry eye in the house. To a man, we were all thinking of home and our loved ones. In my saddened state and despite everything that I had promised myself, I pictured my mother's face smiling at me.

I was ten years old and we had just finished eating our Christmas lunch, huge amounts of wonderful rare roast chicken, roast potatoes, Yorkshire pudding, brussels sprouts, bread sauce and mum's delicious gravy, washed down with a beer for the men and ginger beer for us children.

More tears welled in my eyes.

I was sitting on a dining chair. My mother and brothers were there, along with Uncle Harry and Aunt Maude, Uncle Charlie and his psychotic 'barking' Armenian wife, Mary who always carried a knife tucked into her apron. Father was in his armchair looking grumpy as usual, like some miserable Dickensian character. He didn't especially like company. We were gathered round the fireplace and I leant forward to give it a poke, just to watch the sparks fly up the chimney. As I did so, I farted. Everybody looked at me. My happiness now turned to horror for I recalled the look on my austere father's face. He was not amused and I was too petrified and embarrassed even to say sorry. In normal times, we would have all laughed at my indiscretion, but in front of visitors it was a hanging offence, even for a ten-year-old.

The memory still burns within me. The only difference now is that I laugh as I recall my dastardly crime.

How strange. I had not recalled that event before now. Briefly, my tears turned to laughter as I saw the funny side. My mind returned. I could see my whole family gathered round, laughing, chatting, opening presents and taking it in turns to make the toast in front of the open fire. More tears welled up in my eyes and my heart ached.

"One day, this will all end," I chanted softly to myself, "one day."

The Germans finished and the deafening sudden silence brought me crashing back to the reality of the day. In the oppressive quiet that followed, my attention turned to the woods behind the singers. Coming from amongst the trees, from the guards' accommodation block, another sound drifted our way across the snow, through the pine trees. It was the sound of raucous laughter and merriment. At least someone was having a good Christmas Eve!

By now, the freezing night air was chilling me to the bone. I still had no greatcoat and I cursed once more.

I will never forget that Christmas scene to the end of my days, such a picture of normality amidst such misery. We were acknowledging a traditional Christian celebration that was almost two-thousand years old, stretching across the divides of war, that brought two opposing countries together for a common reason. Much like those soldiers on the western front in the first Christmas of the First World War, who joined hands on Christmas Day, exchanged gifts and played that historic game of football before returning to their trenches and resuming the carnage. Our Christmas Day was unlike any that I had ever had. It was just another day with no presents and no Christmas dinner from our Camp Commandant. The similarity between him and Dickens' character Scrooge did not escape me; he gave us nothing, not even a hot toddy over a roasting log fire or a hog roast. However, grudgingly, he did allow us the day off from our laborious snow-clearing. That night, as I lay in my bunk, buried in my foul-smelling hole, I tried desperately not to let my mind wander back to Christmases past, but without success.

I was back in my bedroom, staring at the woollen sock at the end of my bed, waiting to see Father Christmas deliver my presents. My eyes grew heavy until I fell asleep. When I awoke early on Christmas Day, a pillowcase full of presents hung in its place. Inside were nuts, an orange and apple, chocolate and a few toys. I loved Christmas; fabulous lunches, Christmas puddings with hidden silver three-penny pieces for my brothers and I, etc.

After breakfast, we would open our presents with mother. Father was usually at the police station, even on Christmas Day. During the afternoon, we would sing carols accompanied by mother on the concertina and even father would join in for he had a good voice. Such happy days.

By this time I was in tears, sobbing gently under my blanket for fear of being heard. I couldn't show weakness, not here, not now.

Boxing Day simply brought more of the same, the same shit that we had endured since our arrival in this God-forsaken place. The visit to the latrine revolted me more than usual, the foul pit terrified me for fear of slipping off my precarious perch. Over the period that was laughingly referred to as the festive season, everything that I did and everywhere I went left me feeling utterly despondent. I just wanted to curl up and die. Not even the company of Freddy and the others could pacify me and bless them, they did try.

· · · § · · ·

1941

Letter Bearing Sad News

The new year came, just as Christmas had done, without so much as a celebratory fart. New Year's Day's arrival was heralded by an unbelievably cold, miserable morning, much like any other during our painful Polish winter, but I was surviving. Seven long, torturous months had passed since my capture and I was still alive. I had to be positive,... I had to,... didn't I?

"Today was another day and this was a new year. I will survive," I muttered, eager to convince myself, for the alternative was to court hopelessness and ultimately death.

Conditions inside our squalid warrens were worse than ever. Our universally collected crutch lice and bed bugs made us scratch our skin, causing their bites to quickly turn sceptic and fester, oozing puss, as did the smallest of wounds. Coughs and respiratory problems were as common as our multiple boils. Their spread through each hut was unstoppable. With our immune system so weak due to our poor sanitation and living conditions, combined with an inadequate germ infested diet, everybody continuously suffered with gastroenteritis and the like. But in our overcrowded hovels, the most worrying aspect to us all was the diphtheria outbreak, eventually prompting the Commandant to order mass inoculations over a three week period.

I found Freddy and the others, finished my morning coffee and managed to join the same work party. Thick snow still smothered the frozen ground, making our march something of an hilarious spectacle.

To summarise the weather conditions, Bill made an announcement.

"It's as cold as a witch's tit."

"Never actually felt one Bill, but I'll take your word for it."

We staggered off, but given the difficult conditions, our march into town was more like an outing of the blind stumbling over an obstacle course. Few had coats and the morning air was beyond bitter. I turned up the collar of my tunic against the chill wind. After an hour's struggle, we entered the gates of the marshalling yard at Marienburg. This was where we were to work for the next few months, returning each night to our hellish pits at Stalag XXB.

Whilst waiting for the locals to organise themselves, we stood chatting. I raised my head and sniffed the frozen air. The heavenly smell of tobacco wafted under my nostrils. I looked at one of the older, uglier guards drawing heavily on his freshly lit ciggie. I stood patiently watching as the red and grey burn ring travelled slowly down the length of his white cigarette. Oh, if only. I needed one so badly, or even just a puff would do. I casually shuffled over to him, cupping my hands as I blew into them. When I reached him, I nodded.

"Guten Tag," I politely said and smiled.

I looked pathetically into his fat German face, hoping to appeal to his fatherly instincts, staring at his beautiful cigarette and drooled. I smiled again and raised my two fingers to my lips.

"Tipna?" I simply said, which is what the guards used to call a cigarette end.

He turned to face me, looked straight at me and smiled warmly. He removed his half finished ciggie from his mouth, showing it to me and raising his eyelids, nodding slightly, indicating his understanding. I was euphoric and edged even closer. He took a deep, slow, long final drag. I could see the burning tobacco embers race along towards his mouth as he enjoyed his last puff. He took hold of the cigarette and waited a few seconds, watching the butt held between his thumb and second finger. Slowly, he exhaled loudly, blowing the delicious smoke into my face. In the cold of the morning air, it looked as though his whole mouth was on fire as clouds of tobacco smoke and mist belched forth, engulfing me. He held his hand out, offering me the last of his cigarette. I smiled in appreciation and lifted my hand to take it from him, but he dropped it to the ground before me, watching my eyes as he did so. It landed in the snow-trampled ground between us. Deliberately, he smiled broadly, lifted his boot and crushed it, grinding it into a soggy brown mess before laughing.

Funny, very funny. In my seething anger, I turned and walked away with their laughter ringing in my cold ears.

"One day,... one day!"

The Polish overseer and civilian workers were now ready for us. We were handed heavy implements which consisted of sledgehammers, long three foot chisels, pickaxes and shovels. By now, I had acquired some rags to wrap around my hands and fingers as make-do gloves, but still scant protection from the iron tools that were so cold as to 'burn' my fingers, or so it felt.

We walked over the rails to a section of track away in the middle of the yard and were given our task for the day, which was to dig a trench at right angles to and underneath the rails for the purpose of allowing the Germans to lay new cables and telephone wires without disrupting the trains. In case I did not already know, I was about to learn just how cold it can get on the plains of central Europe and why we had been given the sledgehammers and long chisels. Although we were standing on soil it was like solid concrete, frozen to a depth of two or more feet. This was as deep as we were required to go, so the frost may have penetrated even deeper. After half an hour labouring, the cold was no longer a problem as we were building up quite a sweat, but the effort was killing us. None of us had really worked hard for six months. Our rations had been at starvation level and now we were undertaking hard manual labour, but at least we were being regularly fed.

Progress was painfully slow, but the deeper we went the softer the ground became, or so I was told by the Poles. Personally, I suspected that it was hard all the way through to the Earth's core. We were not allowed a break that day so we worked continuously and, at times, I felt dizzy and so weak that I feared I would topple over. When the working day finally ended, I muttered a silent prayer. I was weary beyond words and in pain with the effort of staying awake. As soon as I collected my soup and bread, I ate it and ran back unsteadily to our cold earth hovel. I fell into my uncomfortable bunk feeling sick from exhaustion and placed my hands behind my head as a pillow. My knuckles scraped against the cold dirt walls behind me, feeling the droplets of ice particles caused by our condensed breath. In spite of the stench and sweat of the enclosed tomb, I slept the sleep of the dead, an appropriate simile for each night after lock-in as I felt as though we were being buried alive.

The following day, my body was brutally quick to wrench my mind back from my slumbers and out-of-body dreams straight back into the nightmare of today. Slowly I came to and remembered my mantra, repeating it with a smile.

"Another night that I had survived and today is a new dawn."

Roll call came to a grinding halt for the numbers made no sense to Fritz. Sometimes, I would swear when a few of my fellow PoWs sabotaged the count in the cold of winter, I wish they wouldn't. Another recount was ordered before the meticulous Germans were satisfied that no-one was missing and we were finally free to collect our rations. In addition there was a bonus, for today we received post from home and I collected a letter. I instantly recognised my mother's writing. I was over the moon and carefully tore it open.

Dear Dennis

How are you ducky?

She went on to say how sorry she was to hear that I was a PoW but how glad they all were that I was alive and well. There followed general updates on the family with news of my brothers and the family digging for victory. In one of my previous letters to mother, I had asked her to keep in contact with the parents of Percy Studwick, Peter Birch and Alan Hores. In the last paragraph, she had some disturbing news about one of my three friends. She had received news from Percy's mother that his plane had been shot down and he had died. I was shocked and saddened.

After the war, I went to see Percy's family to give them my condolences and learn what I could of his fate:

After his first tour of duty in 1940, Percy was given home leave and returned to see his family and friends. According to his family, he was quite happy and wishing to get back into action as soon as possible. However, after his second tour, he returned a completely different man, his spirit broken, a shaking shadow of his former self. He was tearful at the prospect of returning to his squadron and even contemplating going AWOL, for during the most recent bombing raids he had been involved in some terrible sorties amid heavy flak from anti-aircraft guns and relentless pursuits from enemy fighters. The trauma was clearly taking a massive toll on his fraying nerves, which was affecting his whole personality and former sunny disposition. He was on the brink of a total breakdown. They commented that it was almost as if Percy knew his next and third tour would be his last. And so it was.

Within the hour, we were back at the marshalling yard with every muscle in my back and arms aching. There had been a severe ground frost overnight and most of our good work of the previous day seemed wasted. The clods of broken earth had frozen together again, forcing us to smash it up once more. What would normally have taken one week to complete in the summer took us five or six weeks. It was hard, soul-destroying work and I was finding it difficult at times to be cheerful and just as difficult to convince myself that this indeed was 'truly character-building work'. I smiled again at my ridiculous plight but carried on talking to myself and repeating my mantra and laughing. I wondered if I was beginning to lose the plot.

Tonight, what I thought impossible happened, our food got worse. The cold stew was barely cooked. Swimming in the watery juice, hard lumps of rotting blackened foul potatoes stared back at us. Slime covered cabbage stalks bobbed up and down amongst the globules of fat. It was truly foul, made from the worst of ingredients but such was our hunger, all but the most fussy of individuals pushed it down their throats.

The following day saw a slight change in our work pattern. We were needed two kilometres further up the line on a section that needed repairing. When we got there, we had an unexpected break and gathered in a small group whilst we waited for delivery of rails to be brought from the depot. God, I was desperate for a cigarette.

Johnny Cairns from East Finchley began by telling us a story about a particular favourite pub of his that served the best jellied eels in the whole of London. (Food stories were always very popular in the camp.)

"The first time my f***ing mates and me found it was when we was f***ing walking down f***ing Muswell Hill on my f***ing birthday. We was f***ing pissed. We turned the f***ing corner and saw this f***ing geezer..."

Just then, one of our guards, a fairly decent man by their standards, casually walked towards us, the thumb of his gloved hand stuck behind the sling of his rifle on his left shoulder. He stopped behind us, head bent forward, listening intently to our conversation. He spoke very little English but was evidently wishing to add a few words to his limited vocabulary.

Johnny Cairns from the East End of London continued with his story.

"...come staggering out of this f***ing pub, spilling his f***ing beer all over the f***ing road with his f***ing..."

"Tut, tut, tut," the Kraut suddenly muttered, "tut, tut, tut."

Johnny Cairns stopped in mid-stream to see what he was tutting about. We all turned and watched as the German shook his head from side to side in a disbelieving, disapproving manner before speaking.

"Why English immer (always) say 'f***y, f***y, f***y' all time?"

I creased up, trying desperately hard not to laugh. The poor Kraut, eager to improve his understanding of the spoken English language, had clearly chosen the wrong tutor. He had come to the conclusion that there were hardly any other words in the English language to learn other than the words 'f***', 'f***ing' or 'f***y'.

He turned and walked away confused, still shaking his head from side to side whilst I laughed 'til my face hurt. I had never questioned it before, but it must have seemed mystifying to outsiders as to how some servicemen could swear continuously when in each other's company. Apart from a show of manly prowess, I don't know why it is but it happens, and probably in most armies and all-male environments across the globe. However, as soon as we leave our masculine domain and move amongst the fairer sex, everything changes and Neanderthal man is packed away to reveal 'the gentleman' who converses without the need to use expletives. All very strange.

Back on the tracks, our tunnelling continued until out task for our arrogant masters was completed.

~ SUICIDES ~
February 1941

As strange as it may sound, as the weeks dragged on, I began to realise how lucky I was not to have a strong emotional attachment with a steady, loving girlfriend who was dependent on me, or an equally loving wife and child. All around me I could see the pain and hurt on the faces of those men who were torn from their nearest and dearest, enduring the agony of separation and in their absence, the fear of losing their lover to another man. Many tormented themselves with such thoughts as to what was happening to them at home and slowly, it was tearing them apart.

Snippets of news began to trickle through from outside sources, but mainly from the guards. I'm sure this suited the Germans, whom we often suspected of spreading rumours about the defeat of Britain, supposedly in the sadistic knowledge that this would break our morale and increase our suffering. By now, word had reached us that the Blitz over England was in full progress. It began on 7th September 1940 and lasted 76 consecutive nights with London and the main industrial cities of England taking a hammering from the German Luftwaffe, the like of which had never been seen before. London, along with Coventry (which was almost razed to the ground), Plymouth and Liverpool to name but a few, being particularly targeted. Harrowing times for all concerned but particularly for those PoWs whose wives and children lived in those heavily populated areas. Their suffering was often immense, with no knowledge as to whether their families were alive, injured or dead. Hence my relief at being free and single without emotional ties. This concern and uncertainty, coupled with the understandable depression that we all felt at being incarcerated underground in a German PoW camp a thousand miles from home, lacking comfort, suffering appalling weather and inadequate food and clothing, was often all too much for some to bear.

To make matters worse, there was one more factor that often dealt a death blow to an already dispirited PoW, something utterly evil. There were those at home who deemed it necessary to make matters more intolerable for those captives. To me, they were worse than the bloody Germans and deserved to rot in hell for all eternity for what they did, knowingly and with malice and intent.

By now, we were beginning to receive mail from home, which in itself was wonderful. It was important for us all. Soon, this would be followed by packages from our loved ones and wonderful Red Cross parcels that were to become a lifeline to PoWs throughout Nazi- occupied Europe. In early 1941, letters from family, wives, lovers were all that PoWs had to look forward to, thereby keeping hopes and dreams alive for there was no other way of maintaining a link with home. When we received letters, all we wanted to read was good news, for we had more than enough of our own misery. In any case, it was kinder not to be told the bad, for what could we do to help or to resolve the situation? If we knew of their suffering we would only suffer with them, adding to our existing worries, and if we told them ours, then the reverse would be true. Most just needed to keep in touch, to receive a card full of pleasantries, of good things, of the ordinary everyday events that were continuing so reassuringly in our absence. Knowing that normality still existed back home and that they were alive and missing us was enough, but for some, this didn't happen.

Leading up to the start of hostilities, this conflict was no different from practices that had gone on throughout the history of warfare. Thousands of servicemen married their sweethearts in a last, desperate act before leaving for war. In 1939, the number of marriages soared to 459,000 as couples rushed to wed. Often, these young men married girls whom they had only just met and fallen in love with. Of course, this meant that they had not had time to really get to know and understand their partners and form that deep, lasting bond necessary for a couple to stay together in the long term. There just wasn't the loving loyalty or trust between couples that comes with time, and unfortunately for some prisoners, it didn't take long for those 'Dear John' letters to drip feed into camp.

We had just finished morning parade and the unexpected delivery of mail from home was being distributed. We tended to get excited at this point, hoping to receive a letter from someone, but on the other hand trying not to get too excited,... just in case. Amongst the crowd I saw one such poor soul from our 'dirt warren', receive a letter from home. His name is not important, but he typifies thousands of captives who were in exactly the same situation all over the war-torn world. The letter was not from his wife or loved one but sent by a so called 'well- wisher' and read as follows:

> *'Dear John',*
> *I don't mean to bother you unnecessarily, but I could not help but notice that I often see your wife with a Canadian*† *soldier. I think they are sleeping together as he always stays overnight. I don't like to tell you but I think you should know.*
> *Signed, yours sincerely,*
> *A 'friend'*

† *When I left England for France, back in the spring of last year, England was already awash with Canadian and Commonwealth soldiers, servicemen who had come over, often as volunteers, to fight in support of the country that they still considered to be their Motherland. Volunteers even came from the fledging free state of Ireland, a decision that went against the orders of the*

then government who wished to remain neutral and not assist England in any way. These Irishmen served bravely alongside us, in a struggle that they saw as a fight against fascism and not as treacherous supporters of the old colonial enemy. Upon their return to Ireland, they were shamefully punished by their authorities and banned from employment and social support.

Can you imagine the devastating effect that letters like these were having on the morale of those unfortunate PoWs recipients? This fellow in question was only twenty-three years old. Immediately, his already rotten world collapsed around him. He was distraught and inconsolable, nobody could comfort him. Within a week, he was dead. Suicide.

In my opinion, those so-called concerned 'friends' and neighbours were the filth of the earth .

I suspect that the person I literally 'bumped into' a few weeks later was another poor devil who had received just such a letter from another sincere 'friend'.

It was still dark as I made my way to the washroom on that freezing winter's morning and it was snowing still. I was so glad that I still had my army boots and not the clogs that many PoWs were now forced to wear. Morning parade was about to take place so I had to be quick. Just prior to the first snow of winter, we had hastily constructed some walls and a roof to partially shelter the washing trough. Inside was total darkness. All well and good for a blind man but I was stumbling about like a drunk as I made my way to the metal trough that ran the length of the building. Following the sound of the water dripping from the ever-running taps made navigating a lot easier. In order to remove the smell and taste of the Erdehütte, I leant forward to wash my face in the icy water. The top of my head suddenly hit something hard. Not expecting anything to be there I raised my hands to investigate. I felt a pair of army boots. I recoiled, slightly taken aback. I moved forward again to confirm my suspicions. It was indeed a body, hanging from the rafters of the hut. Another suicide by hanging, fast establishing itself as the preferred method of choice. I was later to learn that the pitiful PoW had used his army belt for the task.

Another victim of an insidious 'Dear John' letter?

I hurried to the morning parade head count and immediately reported the death to one of the senior NCOs. The failure of a PoW to attend a parade, even a dead PoW, would upset the Germans' paperwork and we would be subjected to endless recounts until his body, dead or alive, had been accounted for.

He was just one of the many PoWs who couldn't hack the appalling existence inside Stalag XXB, one of the many who chose this successful but tragic method of escape. All the time I was at that parade, freezing, jumping from foot to foot, thrashing my arms from side to side to keep warm, the only thought that came to me was 'One day, you utter bastards.' I clenched my fists.

~ FROM PIT TO SHED ~
March 1941

On 22nd June last year, the French government signed the Armistice forced upon them by a victorious Germany, effectively ending their war. One-and-a-half million French soldiers became prisoners overnight. Those captured during the early days of the war were interned just like their British, Dutch and Belgian counterparts, throughout Germany and Poland. Now that there was 'peace' between France and Germany, I suppose the French PoWs were no longer regarded as much of a threat, unlike us British. As soon as the weather improved, many were being transferred to other camps or destinations unknown, whilst others remained in Stalag XXB. Consequently, some of their treasured wooden huts became vacant and we were given the best news so far, permission to leave the squalor of our Erdehütte and take up occupancy.

It took me no time at all to gather up my all too few personal possessions and move. I tried to move in with Freddy and the others but I was too late. They had been moved the previous day and there was no space in their 'new' hut. The abandoned huts were pretty dirty, but walking inside for the first time was good and I smiled with delight. It was over three months since my 21st birthday, when one of my neighbours had stolen my bread. I had not forgotten that one of them was the thief so I still mistrusted all the old occupants of my Erdehütte. For us PoWs, there was only one thing lower than stealing from your fellow prisoners and that was betraying a fellow to the Germans.

Previously, upon entering our old hovels, I would shut my eyes and try to hurry myself to sleep in order to blot out the horror of our underground pigsties. Now I felt as though I had been released from a tomb. The old wooden huts were a homely palace. As the lights were turned off, I allowed my eyes to close and recall the terrible collective stench of diarrhoea, stale urine, farting, burping and vomit that could not be disguised by the ever present background smell of noxious breath, sweating bodies in reeking clothing, stale cigarettes and dampness. Now all that was confined to history, but just by recalling the horror of that foul interior I felt nauseous. I could even taste the bile rising within me.

"See," I said to myself, "that Officer who had tried to console us back in June 1940 was right, things will get better."

I slept well that night. No more tears and no more nightmares. Things might finally be improving. By comparison to our pit, our newish accommodation was light and airy and, most importantly, above ground. However, to put it into some sort of perspective, under any other conditions these wooden huts would have been a disgrace.

Most of us had yet to catch sight of our Camp Commandant, which meant that we could not search him out to thank him for upgrading us to 'The Ritz'. Over the next few days, many of the old huts were filled in and those remaining were sectioned off from the rest of the camp with a double barbed wire fence. As soon as this was done, other recent captives of the Nazis took up residency - the Russians, with whom we were forbidden to fraternise,... on any account.

Our 'new' huts each housed about 100-120 men. There were no partitions inside, each hut being one big open space. Down both sides of the hut and across the back were two continuous wooden platforms, just like wide shelves and deep enough for us to stretch out on. Along the exposed ends of the shelves a plank was nailed to stop us from falling off, I guess. All the way round vertical posts supported the shelves. This time, I made sure I took a top bunk, which was always a wise thing to do. I climbed up and slid back. Dirty mattresses filled with crushed straw had been left by the previous occupants, and although I could not see them I knew that they had not taken all of their lice and bed bugs. There was probably a space of about a foot between myself and the fellows on either side but an even smaller gap between myself and the lice. The space between the two rows of bunks on either side was about six feet, which served as the central pathway from one end of the hut to the other. In the middle of the hut was a single pot-bellied stove with its chimney poking out through the pitched roof. In the depths of the Polish winters to come, we would try to maintain a fire in the hut but this would prove to be difficult, for the

Germans did not provide us with regular supplies of fuel, be it their poor quality brown coal, coke or wood. At best, we were given about 15kg of coal per hut per day to burn, which was a joke. More often than not it was kept alight by the efforts of scavengers like myself. In the months ahead, those of us who were out on working parties would steal anything that was combustible to smuggle it back into camp after our shift. This allowed the solitary burner to stay alight and continue to heat our huts through most of the bitter winter nights.

The stove also had other uses. Any of us who were lucky enough to find some food, such as a potato or turnip, whilst out could cook it. Nobody usually shared their food in those early days, for the one good reason there was never enough. It was the law of the jungle: whoever found it, ate it.

The only other piece of furniture in the hut was a long, plain, wooden table with two benches either side, capable of sitting about fourteen men at one given time.

During darkness, the hut was illuminated by a single light bulb hanging from the rafters. Its electricity supply was centrally controlled by the Germans and we had no say as to its timing. The light was switched off at nine o'clock every night, and with no other lighting available we usually ended up going to bed. However, within days, the 'inventors' within the camp got to work. Using whatever was at his disposal, one of the lads invented the 'Margarine Lamp'. This was simply constructed from any old tobacco tin, into which was placed some boiled-down animal fat or margarine. To serve as a wick, a piece of old string was coated in the fat before being placed and supported inside the tin. Hey presto! We had ourselves a 'Margarine Lamp'. It couldn't compete with the Thomas Edison light bulb but it helped.

There was one more wonderfully liberating change to the drudgery of life at Stalag XXB that I was truly thankful for. The door to our hut was left unlocked at night time, which meant that we no longer had to pee on the floor. It doesn't take much to please a deprived prisoner of war.

> *Dennis and I finished his story telling and recording for the day as he had an appointment to keep. Each week, he helped out at his local Community Centre.*
>
> *"I've got to dish out the food at the Centre today and help serve the old folks," he laughed.*
>
> *"How old are you now Dennis?" I replied, laughing at his*

insistence in calling those younger than himself and whom he was helping "the old folks".

"Ninety'ish, but I don't feel it. I will never give in, and the day I do you will know that I am dead." He laughed again.

When Dennis returned home after the war, there was an obvious abundance of war films, many portraying PoW camps with tales of brave escapes and heroic deeds.

"I would chuckle at the show of utter luxury."

During the showing of the 'Great Escape', the prisoner huts were depicted as being crammed full with all sorts of personal items, pictures, stationery, clothing, food, musical instruments, even large pianos, darts, the list goes on and on. However, those huts and camps were for Officers and not for the likes of us, the common soldier. We lived as paupers and were expected to work, but Officers were exempt from such menial tasks and they lived a life of comparative luxury and privilege. One day it would be good to see a film made that genuinely depicted the harsh reality of what life was really like for the ordinary soldiers in a PoW camp, where the only break from our hum-drum boredom was the enforced hard labour that we had to undertake. Dirt, filth, cold, hunger, suicide and fear were the realities we faced every single day."

~ MAFIA OR POLICE? ~
March 1941

Moving into the old, vacated wooden huts during our first spring seemed to herald other changes in the camp that were mostly for the better. We would talk more at night time and socialise, liberated by the move, the space and light. I wondered if my new surroundings were beginning to soften my hard stance against my fellow hut mates, a position that I had broadly maintained since the pilfering of my precious bread.

I soon found myself talking about that theft and much to my surprise, I discovered that I wasn't alone. My revelation prompted others around me to reveal their experiences. There were many victims of crime in the camp and pilfering was rife. All had a tale to tell, if not of theft from themselves then theft from others that they knew. My experience was just the tip of a huge and nasty iceberg.

Just below the troubled surface, a systemic crime wave was rife within the camp and it was becoming an increasing problem for us all.

Of course, 'purloining' in itself was not necessarily a bad thing and one had to separate 'bad thieving' from 'good thieving'. For instance, if anybody stole from their fellows, it went without saying that it was a despicable act, and if they were caught, then God help them (but I hoped God wouldn't). However, we all accepted that it was right and proper to steal from the Krauts. I had nothing but admiration for these particular career thieves at Stalag XXB who played an important role in keeping the wheels of commerce well and truly greased with German produce. Without their assistance, I am sure many more PoWs would have died, particularly during that first winter.

The camp authorities were not really interested in our internal problems. As far as they were concerned, as long as we obeyed their rules, did what we were told, worked when ordered to and did not escape then they were happy. We could do what we liked to each other as long as it did not affect the smooth running of the camp. For many in the camp, law and order had already broken down and the law of the jungle was the dogma by which we lived. From the very beginning, we had allied ourselves with others of a similar disposition into groups or tribes, be they from former regiments, nationalities or regions within Britain, or just friendships already established. Their purpose was for mutual protection as well as support. After my 21st birthday and my subsequent vow to myself to become an island, to look after number one and sod the rest of them, I knew my attitude was changing. I too needed allies more than ever, as we all did, to watch our backs and, there was safety in numbers. In addition, I was a naturally gregarious person and I needed people and friendships just as much as food in order to survive.

Disputes between prisoners were commonplace. Just like me, nearly all of us were constantly suffering from nicotine deprivation, making us tetchy to say the least. We were also plagued with hunger, fatigue, were too hot, too cold, infested with parasites, often in pain, missing our loved ones and, if that was not enough, we were sexually frustrated. In fact we were often in a heightened state of perpetual grumpiness, likely to explode at the drop of a fart. Consequently, fights occurred on a daily basis and it was not pretty. These fights usually ended in a knockout situation, with the 'survival of the fittest' law prevailing and the winner had the right.

There were cases of bullying and intimidation surfacing, increasing reports being bandied around of emerging gangs, protection rackets and of ne'er-do-wells generally making life difficult for certain prisoners if they did not relinquish certain items of theirs or do what they were told.

Before our capture, it had been instilled in the British soldier to follow orders issued by his superiors, from the Officer corps down, without question. In a modern, effective army this had to be the case, following a strict military code that was the unquestionable law. Since we were now incarcerated without that corps and with no recognisable internal authority to maintain control and uphold the law, the internal structure was falling apart. In disputes that occurred, of which there were many, he who shouted the loudest and could hit the hardest was the victor. This led to fear of those who practised this methodology. Each group of nationalities within the camp governed themselves separately and had their own leader. It has often been said that in times of strife, a natural leader will emerge, and at Stalag XXB that is just what happened. Some said that our particular man was given the task by the elusive Camp Commandant. Others, that he sought the position because there was nobody else who could restore order. There were even some who said that he crowned himself 'The Boss' in order to control the rackets in the camp. Who knows but I suspect it was just sour grapes and camp gossip on their part.

Our 'natural leader' was a man by the name of Charles McDowell, known as Charlie.

> † *He was born in Glasgow to James McDowell and his wife on 27th January 1907. He was a Sergeant Major in the Gordon Highlanders, Service No: 2872464 and one of the many brave soldiers captured at St. Valéry-en-Caux on 12th June 1940. He was processed at Stalag XXA on 10th July 1940 and transferred to Stalag XXB on 7th November 1940. PoW No: 17403*

He came with impressive credentials to the vacant position of camp leader. For a start he was one of the senior NCOs and naturally able to control men. Secondly he came from Scotland, which in itself was not necessarily impressive until you understood that he came from Glasgow and the Gorbals area of that city. To survive there, let

---

† *Source: International Committee of the Red Cross Archives..*

alone thrive there, you had to be a particularly tough individual, which leads me to the third point in his favour. He was an ex-professional boxer and his massive fists were deadly weapons and he would use them to devastating effect on anyone who dared to disagree with his decisions and square up to him.

Finally, his last and probably his most impressive credential was his daunting body of powerful muscle. Nobody messed with Sergeant Major Charlie McDowell and remained standing long enough to tell the tale.

> *McDowell was only one of many Scottish soldiers within Stalag XXB, covering most of the glorious, historic Scottish regiments such as the Black Watch, the Seaforth Highlanders, the Gordon Highlanders and many more.*

His aides were his close friends and fellow Glaswegians were his assistants, with whom he had lived, drunk and fought with before ending up here in the middle of Poland. I suppose it was only natural that he surrounded himself with a staff taken from this exclusively Scottish circle, a mixed bunch of hangers-on and sycophants.

From that point on, he and his cohorts took over the morning parades and internal running of the camp for the Krauts. Orders, directives, instructions, requests and information were all passed down from the Germans and filtered through McDowell to us. At first, there were no problems. It was good to finally have somebody in charge whom most respected and would therefore obey. Prisoners who had difficulties, who had been victims of some crime or who were the subject of intimidation, unfair treatment or bullying could go to McDowell for help and he made it his business to remove the problem. He would gather whatever evidence was necessary to establish blame and then approach the 'defendant' for a little chat. Usually, his little chat would resolve the issue.

Initially however, there were a few who did not take kindly at suddenly being told what to do, even if they were obviously in the wrong. Some challenged his authority, and particularly those who were from a similarly tough background, seeing themselves as tough pretenders to his new crown. If they were boxers, of which there were many in camp, it became a testosterone struggle and resulted in a gladiatorial battle between the two men. In all my years at Stalag XXB, I never saw or heard of Charlie McDowell ever losing a fight.

Consequently, he maintained his position at the top of the pile, even if it was a pile of shit.

It didn't take many months before resentment slowly crept in and spread through the camp at this new state of affairs. By the summer of 1941, our new Scottish administration were being referred to as 'The Scottish Mafia' or 'McDowell's Mafia'. As many of his staff came from the very deprived and notoriously tough Gorbals area of Glasgow, they were also known as 'The Gorbals Bullies'.

The problem was that somebody had to police the camp at this internal level. If it had not been McDowell, then somebody else would have had to be appointed, with or without the added muscle. McDowell and his staff were privileged, being exempt from work, just like Officers. This was not unique, for all NCOs were exempt, a fact that didn't sit well with the other prisoners. Many felt as though they had been let down by their Officers and those in overall command of the BEF, which was why we had been captured in the first place. Our NCOs were part of that command structure, so blame for our situation was also laid squarely at their door.

It did not take long before rumours of corruption began to circulate, but I never experienced any wrongdoing by the McDowell gang. In the main, I was satisfied that he was the right man for the job, precisely at the right time and he became a charismatic and well respected figure.

~ COCK OF THE ROOST ~
March 1941

The last scruffy, grey remains of winter snow were stubbornly resisting the advance of spring and the ground outside the huts was reverting to mud. It was still bitterly cold, particularly at night, causing the mud to freeze into awkward, misshapen lumps that made walking difficult. For many, spirits were still as low as the temperatures outside.

Our Celtic Führer McDowell, to give him a more unflattering nickname, was aware that morale inside the camp was slowly sinking into the quagmire and he needed ideas as to how to turn things around. In a bid to lift our spirits, he decided on the obvious choice of activity, a 'cock competition'. Frowned upon by the intellectual elite, it seemed to catch the imagination of the whole camp. News spread like a dose of the pox and it was advertised. Improvised, hand-painted posters attached to the hut doors were placed and the event was given the snappy little title of 'The Biggest Cock in the Camp Competition'.

For some unknown reason, it was our hut that was chosen to host the event, where my newly acquired friends, Bert Stupples, Jimmy Farrington, Johnny Dunbar and I were billeted. It was to be held during our rest day, but none of us four volunteered.

"If I do," boasted Jimmy, "I would walk it. Best leave it to someone who needs the accolade."

"So you've got a small willy then?" said Bert amid hoots of laughter. Spectators we definitely would be.

On the elected day, our hut was bursting to capacity and beyond with crowds gathering at the windows. Everyone who could get inside entered with huge grins on their faces. It was a success even before it began. McDowell called the audience to order and explained the not-too-complex rules. He had amassed some twenty or so volunteers. Each volunteer had two helpers. Today, they might even be referred to as 'fluffers'. Behind closed curtains - consisting of our blankets strung up from the rafters - their job was to accompany their charge and assist him by 'chuffing him up'. In other words, to excite him so that he was as stiff and rampant as possible.

In our hut was a guy called Skipper, and he was given the task of making a measuring instrument. He had whittled a stick into a ruler and marked it off in inches along its length. Skipper's task was quite simple. As each volunteer came out in front of the audience, he would measure each person's member as it was presented to him, on the table, in full view of us all.

As the first 'member' entered the arena and offered his erect tool to Skipper, the whole place erupted. The event was run like a noble boxing match with its rules and accompanied by a hilarious running commentary. It was the funniest thing that I had ever seen in my life. With tears running down my cheeks, I could barely breathe with laughing.

"Six and a quarter inches," came the response from Skipper, followed by hearty applause and a cheer, followed by more laughter and much patting of backs.

The official 'recorder of length', who was sitting next to Skipper, duly recorded his name and impressive details before moving on to number two.

"Next!" Skipper cried.

"Hang on a second, not quite ready," came the reply from behind the curtain. "Just needs a bit more work."

Again, the hut burst out laughing as we patiently waited, offering up a slow hand clap to hurry him along. The next PoW came out from behind the modesty curtain. The commentator now spoke in racing terms as the contestant came to the bench.

"And now Rampant Rod enters the paddock. Quite a nice stud this one. Trained under Lady Chatterley and has delighted the crowd on Lady's Day ever since. Wearing the pink and red colours of his owner, Private Plonker is a magnificent beast, standing two hands tall. He only appears to have one eye but that doesn't seem to have held him back. Once he is in the box with his blinkers on, I am sure he will come out a conquering stallion."

There was uproar and the crowd was loving it. The atmosphere in the smoke-filled hut was wonderful as number three came out to an equally comical reception. His length was recorded to another round of applause.

"Impressive," I thought, but still seventeen more to go.

By the time we were halfway through the competition, we had reached the giddy heights of seven-and-a-quarter inches. The next PoW waiting behind the curtain was a guy called Konk Forest. He was great buddies with a PoW who went by the nickname of Granny Ellis. They were older, long-serving regular soldiers in their late thirties.

When Konk eventually emerged with his member proudly at the ready, a gasp went up from those in the front audience.

"F*** me!", "Bloody hell!" and "Oh my God!" were just some of the more repeatable comments.

Everybody tried to get a better look, those at the back standing on whatever and whoever they could. He did not acquire his name by accident for his tool was shaped like a huge battered old Cuban cigar tin or, as one person put it, "like Big Bertha's gun case".

It was almost as wide as it was long and I could not see how any woman could accommodate such a monster. It was the most peculiar member that I had ever seen and, oh boy, it was ugly. Konk Forest was like thousands of other wartime soldiers in as much as he had the great misfortune to have contracted a particularly nasty venereal disease, gonorrhoea. Not once but twice, with all the unpleasantness and pain that went with it. The treatment was as bad as the disease itself and poor old Konk had that old instrument of torture, the 'barbed umbrella', inserted into his urethra, whereupon his insides were given a good scraping for their sins. One would have thought that having this done the once would have put him off unprotected sex for life, but twice? If this had been a 'cock width' competition, then

Konk would have won by a length, pardon the pun. He would even have had trouble fitting his most peculiar member into the width of a Gold Flake tobacco tin, such was its girth. As he lobbed it onto the table, it hit the deck with a thump. Aghast! Everybody strained to get a better view. Skipper's face was distorted with a look of disgust and fascination. He seemed to be reluctant to get near the damn thing but managed to get a reading without actually touching the beast.

"Not bad, but not good enough I'm afraid... seven and a half inches... by... seven inches," shouted Skipper.

The hut exploded, the laughter almost brought the roof down and could probably be heard in Berlin. From then on, the proceedings became more boisterous and descended into total farce with cocks being 'chucked' onto the table from all directions. Big, small, thin and thick. It was all extremely 'slapstick'. In the end, we hadn't a clue who had the longest and who the outright winner was but it didn't seem to matter anymore. To stop the potential problem of people in the audience dying of heart failure, the prize was given to a private from the Rifle Brigade, simply because he made us laugh the loudest when he couldn't get his impressive member into a cylindrical cigarette tin capable of holding fifty cigarettes. Now that was impressive.

The whole event was a tremendous success. McDowell had done what he set out to do, he lifted our spirits and improved morale. He was hailed as a bit of a hero and talk of the competition lasted for weeks before making it into the annals of camp legend.

~ MARCH AND COUNTER MARCH ~
March 1941

The day was dry at last, which made a change. It had been raining solidly for three days and my clothes were still damp. The parade ground was a quagmire. As we waded our way along that well-trodden road towards Marienburg, I heard them before I actually saw them - a column of German soldiers striding towards us.

I hate to admit it but when German soldiers march, they do so superbly. I couldn't help but marvel as they passed us in formation of three abreast. The immaculately turned out squad was led by a German NCO at the head of the column. As soon as he was about twenty paces away from us, he suddenly bellowed at the top of his considerably powerful voice, "Drei, Vier..." ("Three, Four...") and burst into song. Right on cue, they all started up, seeming to know, as if by instinct, which song to sing. They continued to march on past, giving us a show of their superiority, reciting a song that they had been taught from day one of joining the German Army. It sounded good, great even, to us British. It served as a morale booster to their ranks and kept waning spirits high, of that I am sure.

When we had to foot-slog anywhere we also marched well, as though we were still under the command of our Officers. We were a match for any army, even if we were not quite so well turned out. As the Germans neared, we too thrust our chins up, chests out, thumbs in line down the crease of our trousers (if there had been one), swinging our arms up and pointing ahead, horizontally and in complete unison. I can honestly say that of all the nationalities in the camp, we British were the only PoWs who did march, and march properly, wherever we went. It was a case of discipline and honour.
As you can imagine, their parade ground-strutting and showing off needed to be addressed, for apart from showing off, they liked nothing more than to destabilise and confuse us as we marched past them.

We soon got the hang of their tactics and developed a counter measure that was to become our standard ploy, and it worked to great effect. As this particular lot approached and passed beside us, our squad leader shouted in German so that they could hear.

"Change step!" and then "Left, right, left", making sure that it was the opposite to their steps.

This had the desired effect, buggering up their marching pattern completely, throwing them into chaos for a few seconds. It probably sounds childish but on occasions, I have seen German squads virtually collapse in on themselves, tripping up before they angrily regained their stern composure. Their NCO went berserk, screaming at his troops out of sheer embarrassment at having been humiliated. Quickly, they composed themselves and continued as though nothing had happened. We fell about laughing. It was our way of getting our own back and restoring a little bit of pride in ourselves over our 'Lords and Masters'.

Deep down, I believe that the Germans respected us for our marching skills and our discipline in the face of such adversity. Unlike us, the French, Belgians, and later the Italian soldiers, would just amble along looking utterly dejected, with no pride or discipline. I also believe that the Germans respected our spirit. Other nationalities seemed to cave in and do what they were told without any protest.

The British spirit was somehow different, more obstinate and rebellious to foreign authority. For instance, this trait of ours would manifest itself on numerous occasions, playing dumb at every opportunity, pretending not to understand their simple orders and then watch, as the Germans erupted with rage, screaming and stamping their jackboots through sheer desperation.

~ I NEEDED AN ANGLE, A NICHE ~
April 1941

With the improving weather, it was now time for the Germans to put us to work in earnest. More working parties were being sent out in all directions from our camp, some returning every evening whilst men on other parties were never to be seen again, spending the whole of the war in factories, farms, mines and the like in the surrounding countryside.

It did not take me long to realise that if I was to survive being a guest of Herr Hitler, somehow I was going to have to create a niche for myself. Although I was not well versed in the wicked ways of this world, I had been kicked out of home at the tender age of fourteen and forced to fend for myself. As much as I loved my dear mother and her warm embrace, I was totally independent within days, which put me in good stead. Above all else, it taught me that in order to survive in these uncertain times, I could not rely on anybody else but myself. There might be others who came and went in my life, who one might call upon for help and support and that was all to the good. But if there was one certainty in my life it was that if I didn't look out for myself, no other bugger would and above all, I wanted to survive this stinking war.

One morning, my chance came to create such a niche after a particularly lengthy parade with roll call lasting four re-counts. Time wise, I would estimate it took two hours for the numbers to tally with the Germans' paperwork. Freddy and my friends had already left on another work detail and I was left with the others from my hut. Afterwards, Fritz shouted at us in German.

"I want thirty men out here now!"

Another guard barked, "Who is the engineer?"

As usual, nobody replied. To volunteer for anything was never a good idea at the best of times, let alone to volunteer your services for something unknown. Under these circumstances, dumb insolence was the best response and something we did rather well. This had two benefits: it did not land you with the terrible disappointment of foolishly volunteering for a miserable work detail and, more importantly, it really pissed off Fritz.

I had been in captivity for nearly a year. I am proud to say that contrary to German belief, I did possess a brain cell and during that time I had begun to understand the language of my captors - hardly conversational German, but I had become a dab hand at understanding barked orders and giving the correct answers. Virtually every time a guard tried to address us, a desperate expression of forlorn hope, tinged with expectant, inevitable disappointment and subsequent anger would appear on their square-headed faces. Today a tall, irritated guard stormed over to our group, bellowing as he went.

"Wo ist der Dolmetscher?" ("Where is the interpreter?")

The response was as before, dumb indifference, but the germ of an idea came to me. Could this be my PoW career opportunity? I casually raised my arm and took one step forward.

"Ich bin der Dolmetscher." ("I am the interpreter.")

The guard's look of irritation faded and was replaced by one of surprised relief. He informed me that he wanted thirty men immediately to work in the town. I turned to the men, and in my best sarcastic but polite, English, in a manner more befitting an Officer, I explained what was required of us and that was how I got the job!

I was pleasantly surprised and from the expression on the faces of my fellow PoWs, so were they. From that day on, I was sought after to make my 'stupid Englander pig' companions understand the requirements of our lords and masters. With the job came a *certain* respect from the Germans, who now regarded me as 'not quite such a stupid Englander pig'. As a result, on rare occasions, the guards 'kept me sweet' with the occasional cigarette.

I now had a vested interest in acquiring as much of the German vocabulary as possible to advance my new vocation, in the hope that I would benefit more at the hands of my captors.

· · · § · · ·

~ THE INTERPRETER ~

Now established as the German interpreter, I quickly discovered a parallel niche. When we arrived at the yard we were met by a Pole, our civilian overseer. Before we began our labours, the overseer needed to identify the interpreter, for although German was now the official language of Poland, most Poles had still to master it. Our knowledge of Polish was nonexistent and this, combined with our unwillingness to communicate when on a work party, led to all sorts of totally foreseeable problems created by us belligerent PoWs. For example, if we were instructed to dig a deep, long trench over there, we would dig a shallow, wide hole somewhere else. The Polish overseer would be disgruntled and the guards would shout, but usually at the Pole, for after all we were 'stupid Englander pigs' with no trade skills and not a brain cell between us. Naturally the Pole requested the interpreter and, in turn, the guards pointed to me, saying "Die grosse Blonde" ("The big blonde"). So that day I also became the Polish interpreter, without grasping a single word. With understandable difficulty, using a mix of German and mime, the Pole managed to make himself understood to me. I passed the information to the others who found the whole process laughable, for by then, they had deciphered the Pole's mime all by themselves. I heaved a sigh of relief for not failing on my first day.

That day, the work was done correctly, to a fashion. By way of thanks the Pole slipped me a loaf of bread that I later shared with some new friends from my hut, Bert, Jimmy and Johnny. Already, my new occupation was paying dividends and I realised that to some extent this gave me the upper hand, for if I was not looked after I could act dumber than usual and 'accidentally' instruct the men to do something silly or cause my fellow PoWs to become unco-operative, resulting in low or nil productivity, thereby upsetting the Germans. The overseer certainly didn't want to get on the bad side of the Krauts, for even a lowly soldier had the authority to administer arbitrary punishment and ultimately held the power of life and death over the likes of him and the civilian populus.

Sometimes there was no friendly Polish overseer, with just our guards to tell us what to do. On those occasions we would reluctantly do what we were told to do,... eventually. However, we tended to do it our way and follow instructions literally and to the letter, purposefully showing no initiative and not applying one ounce of common sense, thereby sabotaging any task we were set. (years later, our unions would call this 'Working to Rule). It was a game, balancing our stubbornness and good humour with our desire to escape a beating.

At the rail yard, one particular cocky little German guard with ideas above his lowly station was really annoying us. We had been digging trenches for weeks and knew what to do. This dim son of a Boche bitch started pushing us around, demanding that we did what he told us to do and 'dig ze hole' his way, pointing to the ground in front of him. He was quite insistent, and instead of allowing us to continue, as we had been doing without him, he wanted us to know that he was 'the boss'.

"Ausgraben, Dummkopf," he finally barked, pointing aggressively at the ground in front of him.

"Mit ja antworten, mein Führer," replied one of our group. We all smiled, looked at each other and instinctively knew what we were going to do. So we started to dig whilst he stormed off, presumably in triumph, satisfied that finally we were doing what he had told us to do. The trouble was, he didn't say he wanted the hole to join up with the main trench and he didn't say in which direction the hole was to go, or how deep he wanted it dug. Consequently, we dug a f***ing great, deep trench some eight feet deep. It was wide, not in line and running at right angles to the main trench and started to undermine the rail tracks on both sides. It was exactly where he had pointed to and we had done his bidding. When he returned, Fritz went berserk. His face turned crimson and he spat in temper, with little pools of foaming phlegm gathering in the corners of his mouth. He brandished his rifle, pointing it at us in broad, sweeping movements. We did nothing but stood where we were and waited for the storm to blow over. Eventually it did and we spent the remainder of the day filling it in and making good whilst our guard accepted that we British were inherently stupid and incapable of change.

An alternative strategy was to perform our allotted task so badly that it completely failed to achieve its intended purpose, so we would not be asked to do such a task again. We loved the game. The purpose was rebelliousness, for the sole pleasure of infuriating our captors, which had the corresponding effect of raising our morale. We hoped that whatever bad work we did had the additional effect of hindering the German war effort as much as we could manage with as little personal risk to us as possible. All's fair in hate and war.

~ RED CROSS PARCELS ~
April 1941

Article 372 of the Geneva Convention stated that: 'Prisoners of war shall be authorised to receive individually postal parcels containing foodstuffs and other articles intended for consumption or clothing. The parcels shall be delivered to the addressees and a receipt given.' A wonderful statement of intent, but in reality, many were not delivered.

With winter barely past, March waved us goodbye and April burst on the scene with blue skies and the promise of summer to come. We began to hear tales of Red Cross parcels that were destined to be coming our way. It was alleged that they were full of wonderful foods, chocolates and desperately needed cigarettes.

There was nothing as yet to separate this particular day from all the other previous boring days and I took no particular notice as I, along with several others, was pulled out after morning roll call for a work party. The Krauts had laid on an army truck for us, which was highly unusual. The driver took us on the by now familiar road into Marienburg. Upon arrival at the rail goods yard, we climbed out. The driver then manoeuvred his vehicle before joining a line of other German Army trucks already parked, waiting.

Behind them sat a freight train comprised of goods wagons, onto which bold, hand-painted Red Cross markings had been painted on the roofs and sides, supposedly to minimise the risk of being bombed by enemy aircraft. Immediately our guards started to shout, ordering us to start unloading. Wagon doors were flung open, revealing a solid wall of neatly stacked brown boxes. I was ordered up inside whilst the rest formed a chain from the wagon to the truck. The distinctive red cross in the top right corner and the words British Red Cross printed boldly in the middle made me happy.

"Hey lads," I shouted, barely able to control my excitement, "it's Christmas."

Bert was next in the receiving line. "Which one's got my name on it. I'll have it now."

"Schnell!" screamed the annoyed guard, eager to get back to his cosy billet.

We had almost filled the covered truck in only a short time when the guard ordered us to stop and climb back in. I could not fail to notice that we had only loaded a couple of hundred of the boxes and you did not have to be a genius to realise that two-hundred parcels did not mathematically divide very well into the thousands of men inside Stalag XXB. Some were going to go very short.

Back at camp, we were left at the gate whilst the lorry disappeared from view to leave us all wondering if we would ever see the inside of just one of the elusive Red Cross parcels. We immediately relayed the news and within minutes, word had spread throughout the camp. However, it took several days for some of the boxes to even make their way inside the camp and it was left to Charlie McDowell and his gang of Scotties to organise the distribution of the contents, on a hut by hut basis. Our hut of a hundred men received one box. We drew lots for the divided contents. Inside each brown cardboard box were about fourteen precious items, ranging from tea, tins of ham and stew to lumps of cheese, jars of marmalade, dry cubes of marmite and a box of fifty real English cigarettes, Woodbines, Weights or Players. These were most highly prized. Overall, this was a bitter disappointment and seemed even less than I had initially calculated, which led me to question where the remainder had gone - to McDowell's gang or to the pilfering Germans?

The inside of McDowell's hut was plush by comparison to ours, the lower ranks. It was always full of those little extras that people like him 'acquired'. His hut was physically split into two halves, their quarters at one end with an interior door to the camp 'sick bay' in the other half. Every camp had their fair share of sick and injured prisoners and we were no exception. Leg and feet ulcers were a common ailment, along with diarrhoea, which left untreated could lead to dehydration, total lack of energy and eventually death. It was fair and just that the first parcels were given to any seriously sick PoWs via the Scotties but, over time we all had our suspicions that not quite all of the full quota of remaining parcels were finding their way to us. I guess that is what happens, given the 'dog eat dog' mentality that often prevailed in camps.

The arrival of a life-giving parcel was a highlight in the awful life of a PoW, and conversely their failure to arrive was the greatest of disappointments. Initially, the early consignments were drip-fed to us and a single one had to be shared between so many PoWs that often one cube of Marmite or a lone McVitie and Price biscuit would have to be shared between two people or was decided by lottery. Gradually throughout 1942 and into 1943, the numbers increased. We shared one parcel between four and then one between two before finally, by late

'43, we reached a rare and short period where we received a Red Cross parcel each. By then, we were rich beyond compare to all previous and subsequent years in captivity, but from then on, it all went steadily downhill.

~ MA MINTER'S BOYS ~

By the time we had completed the arduous task of trench-digging and cable-laying I knew all the PoWs in my work squad, but there were three particular men with whom I clicked and by now, we had formed a lasting friendship. I have briefly mentioned them before. Their names were Bert Stupples *(see picture reference 32)*, Johnny Dunbar *(see picture reference 33)* and Jimmy Farrington *(see picture reference 34)* .

> *Bert Stupples came from Ramsgate and had an unfortunate and very noticeable cyst on the side of his nose.*
> *Jimmy Farrington was another Glaswegian and had joined the famous Gordon Highlanders 1st Regiment, just one of the regiments that formed the brave 51st Highland Division. He was well acquainted with Sergeant Major Charles McDowell.*
> *The bulk of the BEF had been evacuated from Dunkirk, but the 51st Highland Division was charged with recapturing the Abbeville bridgehead on the Somme. The attack on 4th June resulted in heavy casualties. The Germans launched a counter-attack the next day, out-flanking the Allies, trapping the 51st Highland Division and elements of the French 9th Army Corps. They withdrew to the coastal town of St. Valéry-en-Caux. Major General Fortune, Commander of the 51st, asked that they be evacuated on 11th June. The Germans had other ideas and were determined to stop another Dunkirk and four whole divisions were thrown into the attack to prevent an evacuation. Despite a fierce allied defence, the 7th Panzers (commanded by General Major Erwin Rommel) soon held the cliff-top ground overlooking the port and harbour, allowing them to bombard the encircled defenders with deadly accuracy. Open evacuation by the Navy was impossible. The Highlanders were conducting a desperate defence against advancing Germans while trying, without success, to eject the 7th Panzers from their dominating positions.*

The night of 11th June was the Highlanders' last chance to evacuate,
but Fortune was unable to contact the ships waiting off-shore.
The dense fog combined with German mastery of the skies and
devastating bombardments from the Panzers and German shore
batteries had delayed the Navy's rescue attempt. By 12th June,
it was too late to save the Highlanders, who fought so bravely at
St. Valéry-en-Caux.

Whilst elements of the 51st were still counter-attacking, the
French surrendered. Having exhausted their ammunition, Fortune
realised that his position was hopeless and his men would be
slaughtered. On behalf of what remained of the battered British
regiments, he surrendered and, as a result, Jimmy was amongst
many of those brave men sent to Stalag XXB.

Johnny Dunbar was the fourth member of our band. He came from
somewhere in the Midlands. He was at least ten years older than
me and when he wasn't laughing, had a most severe expression
on his face.

In spite of the promise I made to myself not to get involved
and only look after number one back in the awful winter of 1940, I
found it an impossible stance to maintain. I came to realise I needed
people, needed their comfort, support and comradeship to survive in
this harsh environment and this was now paramount to my survival.
My mates from the Queen's were my initial bedrock and fortunately,
in the spring of '41 I met three others, Bert Stupples, Jimmy
Farrington and Johnny Dunbar. Working closely together every
day, our friendships blossomed until an *almost* unbreakable bond
developed between the four of us that endured for the duration of our
time in the camp.

As time went by, we looked after each other in whatever way we
could. My increasing ability to speak German, and Polish to a greater
and lesser extent, was rightly seen as a strength. This enabled me to
search out and mix with the civilian Polish workers and eventually
trade, buy, barter and sell. When not trading I would resort to good
old-fashioned thieving from the Germans for anything I or my friends
could use, with food and cigarettes at the top of the shopping list.
Because I would do this for them, and my ability to look after the
'boys', just like their mothers back home, I was known as the mother
provider of my group and I was given the nickname of 'Ma Minter'.
Polish civilians would sometimes work alongside us, for often they

had been doing the job before the German occupation. These civilian workers would act as advisers to the 'Dolmetscher' (the interpreter, who was me). Supposedly, I was now 'important' in the not-so-grand scheme of things.

~ WORK ON THE COAL WAGONS ~
April 1941

After completing the cable-laying and a very brief return to boring life inside camp, we were delighted when the Germans found us other work to keep us occupied and out of mischief. Perish the thought of being idle for a moment longer! In any case, I wasn't going to remain within our grim camp any longer than was absolutely necessary.

After morning roll call and 'coffee', Bert, Jimmy, Johnny and I volunteered for outside work. Never sure what to expect in these circumstances, I wondered what was in store as we formed ourselves into our rows of three and marched back down towards Marienburg. Turning off before the town we ended up in the rail goods yard once more. I could hardly believe it, dreading the thought of more back-breaking trench-digging and wishing we had not been so keen to volunteer. As we entered, goods trains were moving in all directions. The yard was a hive of rail activity. We were taken over to a waiting goods train that was carrying coal and we were given the task of shifting the lot. To this purpose, we were handed our shovels and simply told to get on with it in that very German manner - screamed orders and the threat of the rifle butt.

~ QUICK WAS GOOD ~

This work was tough and the most back-breaking that I had ever done. We worked in two shifts; the first started at six in the morning until two in the afternoon with the second from two 'til ten and, each week we would alternate shifts. At the start of either shift, we were formed up into pairs and each pair given one wagon of coal to unload. As the sides of the wagon were swung open, the high pile of coal spilled out onto the platform. That was our cue to get stuck in. We worked together in pairs opposite each other, coordinating our actions, shovelling the coal away from the wagon. As it cleared, we moved inside, each taking half the truck. Each pair worked to a rhythm complementing each other's moves. There were no breaks. Save for standing upright for a brief moment in order to straighten our backs. We worked until the wagon was finally cleared. After the first gruelling day's shovelling, it came as no surprise to see huge blisters on my hand. I winced with pain as I squeezed a blister, watching as the liquid trickled down my palm, washing away some of the coal dust as it flowed. I wondered if the Germans might provide us with gloves on the morrow then smiled at the stupidity of the thought. Our work meant that at the end of our shift, we were absolutely filthy and our already dirty uniforms were now beyond respectability, covered with the oily coal dust. It got everywhere, and after two days we pleaded and pleaded again until we eventually got a result.

On the afternoon of the third day, at the end of the early morning shift, we received three surprising rewards. Firstly, we were each issued with a precious bar of rough soap and escorted to a squat little building, inside which were the showers. We did not need telling twice. From then on, at the end of each shift, we were allowed the luxury of a shower, a proper, glorious, body and soul cleansing shower. The washing block was provided for the German workers and we were delighted to be allowed to use the same facilities - and doubly surprised when we discovered that the water was actually warm. I can hardly describe how strange and satisfying this simple facility was. I literally bathed in the pleasure and took the opportunity to wash my crotch, underarms and hair again and again,... and then my underpants and anything else that I was wearing.

After the shower came our second reward, another uniform. They were not new by any means, but clean and free from coal grime and grease. From where the Germans acquired these British outfits I had no idea and I did not dwell on the question for too long, but I was pleased to note that as I dressed I could find no suspicious bullet holes. We left the old ones hanging from hooks for us to change back into at the start of the following day's shift.

Finally came our third reward. Due to the physically demanding aspect of the work, the Germans wisely gave us what they called 'Schwerarbeiter ration' or 'Arbeitskommandos' (manual workers ration). Effectively this was an extra food, usually given to us mid-way through our shift, a thick hunk of bread and a piece of something on it. It might be a massive dollop of thick, tasty pork fat or a slice of thick sausage meat. I really didn't care what it was, as long as we got it.

After work, we would be marched back to camp, exhausted but fed and washed, and often with goodies pilfered from our captors hidden amongst our clothing. Although our labours were absolutely gruelling, they were the most rewarding to date.

~ ROMANCE WAS IN THE AIR ~

The natural order for us internees was that we were prisoners held captive by the all conquering Germans who were our guards. They did what they had to do and for the most part, we were coerced into complying in order to survive and endure the remainder of the war whilst submitting to the minimum of force and unpleasantness.

Once we had finished our toilsome work, it was not unusual for the guards to turn a blind eye to our wanderings whilst the others laboured to complete theirs. They knew that in reality, there was nowhere for us to run to, for escaped PoWs in British uniform would have stuck out like a sheep amongst a pack of wolves. Secondly, to travel on any form of transport, you needed a 'Reisenschreibarbeit' or 'Reisendokument' (travel papers/documents) dated for that day. Added to that, the daunting realisation that we were stuck in the middle of Poland, a thousand miles from home, indicated the enormous difficulty of escape and reaching home. Apart from a few intrepid escapees, most of us were resigned to our fate.

One day, two of our work party fell ill and reported for sick parade. They were replaced by two who had never worked with us before. Each teamed up with another more experienced man, fortunately not with me. After only a short time, they really struggled. Whilst their more experienced partners surged ahead clearing their half of the truck, the two replacements became slower and slower. My buddy and I had worked well together that day and we were the first to empty our wagon. Our gang was fast, even under such tough conditions; any new labourer took time to develop his rhythm, muscles and his stamina. By the time the rest had finished, the novices still had a ton to shift. The impatient guards, eager to return to camp as soon as possible, responded with anger, shouting and intimidating them, as was their way.

"English pigs!" they shrieked, which was one of their most popular terms of endearment.

However, on this occasion their slowness gave me an opportunity that I took full advantage of, freedom to go exploring and see what I could find. I had already noticed a huge construction built amongst the rails, several hundred metres away. I had already seen people entering and leaving the building, but more importantly, amongst their numbers I had noticed a number of women, a rare sight for us. I turned to my buddy and told him I was going for a walk round to see what I could 'find' and wander over to the building to investigate. When I got closer, I saw that it was an engine turning and maintenance shed. About eight rail tracks converged on it in both directions. Fearing that entering the building might be 'VERBOTEN' (forbidden) I cautiously strolled inside. My eyes lit up at the sight of so many Polish girls, who were busy cleaning the engines and rail carriages. There were a few men amongst them but they busied themselves with their engine maintenance. I sauntered over to the girls and attempted to communicate with them in a mix of pidgin Polish and German. Most seemed to be able to speak at least some German so I managed to make myself understood. One girl amongst them caught my eye and I directed most of my conversation towards her. After fifteen minutes, I became concerned as to the passing of time so I left the girls and went to speak to the men. One of my hut mates had a gold fountain pen. Like many PoWs who had such expensive but trivial items that were now useless except as 'currency', they were eager to exchange them for more pressing needs, items such as food and cigarettes. He had asked me to trade it. I found a Pole who was interested, so I hastily arranged another meeting with him to complete the exchange.

Hurriedly, I returned to my work party just at the right moment. The guards were impatiently waiting by the side of the last wagon to be unloaded, not happy at being delayed for so much longer than usual, but such was the problem when introducing novice slave labour.

As soon as they finished, we collected our Schwerarbeiter ration. This time it was topped with a sweet, delicious fruit jam and the sweet taste was wonderful. That done, we walked over to the shower block. By now, my work uniform was heavy with the sweat of toil and coal dust, with not a hint of khaki visible, and it deserved a wash. I did not even bother to take it off but walked fully-dressed into the showers and washed it as best I could with the hard, gritty Kraut soap. A vile-looking black slurry containing sweat and body filth collected on the shower floor before the slowly flowing grey effusion drained reluctantly into the dark drain hole. That day I had worked the morning shift and in the heat of the afternoon, I hung my heavy woollen uniform on nails to dry. By the following day, it was as dry as a bone, which was a reflection on the sweltering spring temperature rather than adequate drying facilities.

This new found pride in my cleanliness had its foundations in my vanity, a desire to look more appealing to my new Polish lady friends, for even a miserable, lowly PoW such as I was still capable of this mortal sin.

The next day, I was eager to see my girl again and I was going to make sure I did. Such interludes were a distraction to my plight and one small way of retaining a modicum of normality in this horrid world that we found ourselves in. On the way to the yard, I reminded my work mate of my 'date' and we both worked our socks off to ensure that we finished early. As soon as the last lump of coal left my shovel, I almost ran to the turning shed, unhindered. I was so delighted to see my girl and made a beeline for her. Her smile met mine and I felt a surge of delight. Despite our different languages, we talked easily. She giggled as I tried to explain myself in German, English and hand gestures. For the very first time her countenance and youthful disposition allowed me to forget that I was a PoW whilst a world war raged across the globe. This was the start of my first romance with a Polish girl and my first female contact since leaving home in the spring of 1940, and I was loving it. Her name was Stacia, short for Anastacia and she was beautiful, young and sweet. We chatted, smiled and laughed, just as young romantics do. However, time was short. As I said goodbye, I turned and found my Polish contact with the two long loaves of bread and cigarettes and, as agreed, made the exchange. I hid them in concealed pockets, especially sown inside my trousers before returning to the others for the march back to camp.

Shifting coal in the rail marshalling yards went on all through that blossoming spring, as did my flourishing romance with Stacia, and on into the oppressive summer.

One particularly glorious, sunny day, Stacia and I decided to take a brief walk, away from the turning shed in search of some privacy. We crossed the open tracks to a grassy embankment on the far boundary of the yard. It sloped up steeply to end amongst some trees on the other side of the security fence. We climbed for a few metres before stopping to lie down, side by side in the long grass. We were almost hidden from view, or so we thought. It was not long before mutual passion reared its inevitable rampant head and we were locked in a strong, amorous embrace. Unbeknown to us, above and on the other side of the security fence was a footpath hidden from view. By this time we were completely oblivious to the woman who had suddenly appeared on the path. I was the first to see her, and I was petrified. I instantly rolled over to cover Stacia's face whilst burying mine in her hair, trying to hide our identities. I whispered to her in an attempt to make her understand what was happening as we lay there, frozen to the ground. My heart was pounding in my bony chest and my stomach was protesting, albeit quietly. I continued to watch the casual observer out of the corner of my eye as she stared down at us. The thirty seconds seemed more like thirty minutes as she watched before turning her head away to continue on her stroll along the path. I was concerned for us both, fearing that she would report us. What the crime would have been I wasn't certain, but I was damn sure that the Germans would have both a crime and punishment ready and waiting for us. As soon as our voyeur was out of sight I jumped up, pulling Stacia after me, and ran. Holding on to her hand, we hurried back to the turning shed. Once safely inside, we flung ourselves against the inside wall to catch our breath. My heart was pounding so much, I thought it would burst. I poked my head around the side of the door to see if we had been followed and heaved a sigh of relief. I turned to Stacia and smiled. We both burst out laughing, causing me to find the courage to kiss her gently on the lips. I pulled away and we stared into each other's eyes before touching noses and laughing once more. What relief. We relaxed against the wall, still holding hands. But it was time to go so I bade her farewell, hurriedly returning to the others, happy and content. The guards hardly noticed me and seemed unconcerned. If they sensed anything, they said nothing but if they could have read my thoughts, I would have been locked up. With no repercussions, we survived to kiss another day. Maybe the female 'observer' was a moralist who disapproved, or an irrepressible romantic content to watch two young people in love in such troubled times, for life had to go on. We will never know. Although the incident did frighten me I vowed to take more care, if not for my own sake then for Stacia's.

The following day was another scorcher. The shirts were off and sweat was glistening on our bodies. I stood up to arch my spine and shoulders backwards to gain a moment's relief from the aches and pains of my overworked body. I looked over the side of the wagon at a passing train which was filled to capacity with fresh, clean German troops. They were travelling as we had back in the summer of last year, in cattle wagons, but that is where the similarity ended, for they were no more than 40 troops to a wagon. They travelled with the doors open whilst relaxing on a bed of clean, fresh straw. Some slept whilst others smoked, content to watch the world go by.

By now, Stacia's fellow workers knew that I was her 'boyfriend' and they always greeted me with a friendly smile. Stacia and I decided that it was wiser to sneak away into the relative safety and privacy of the carriages than risk being seen outside. Inside were plush passenger-carrying coaches, unlike the wagons that had transported us on our hellish journey across Germany into Poland. At each end of the carriages was a flat, open viewing platform encompassed by an elaborate safety rail. From this platform, metal steps allowed passengers to climb up and thereby gain entrance. Once inside, Stacia and I could hold each other, caress and kiss. That was all we ever did and was enough for me. We were both virgins and more than happy to simply embrace. For me, to feel the warmth of a loving female held close against my body was heaven. The memory of her embrace will stay with me until the day I die. After being treated no better than an animal at times, Stacia made me feel alive and human once more, offering me a glimpse of a future, of prospects, expectations and, above all, hope. She gave me something to live for. At the most we only ever had half an hour together, but I had never been happier since leaving England.

Work on the coal wagons was unrelenting, incredibly tough and demanding slavery. We kept the Krauts satisfied and they, in turn, remained tolerant of us, turning a blind eye to our occasional dealings and minor transgressions, The guards' main priority was always to get back to the comfort of their barracks as early as possible, thus avoiding the sheer boredom of watching us building coal castles.

With each passing day, my knowledge of Polish and German increased, as did my reputation as a 'trader' within the camp. All PoWs craved the two most important commodities in our life, food and cigarettes and they became the currency of the camp. On the other side of the wire, the Poles had plenty of bread but were very short of clothes. PoWs would hand me their unwanted items to trade outside and I took the agreed commission of 25% in the form of bread or cigarettes. Commerce was flourishing, and happily I was in the thick of it and helping my chums at the same time.

INVASION
OF THE USSR

22nd June 1941

Herr Hitler must have thought that June was the perfect month for his
Army to have its first major outing since his victory over France.
If we had not been prisoners in a foreign land, slaving away on meagre
food rations, it might have been a splendid June for us as well, at least
as far as the weather was concerned.

The clock showed five. I had been on the early morning shift and had just collapsed onto my bunk for a well-earned rest. I was shattered. As I dozed, the door unexpectedly burst open and a short, serious-looking man burst into the hut. I vaguely recognised him. His name was Sammy Newton *(see picture reference 28)*. Complete with his big, thick bottle spectacles and neat ginger moustache, he seemed excited. I was to learn later that 'Little Sammy', as he was known, was an educated man and had been a proofreader before the war on a newspaper called The Reynolds News. He was an insignificant man really, and would have continued to pass completely unnoticed in our camp had it not been for one small thing. Sammy had found his own niche within the camp: he was 'The Teller of the News'.

Hidden somewhere within the camp was a clandestine radio. Each day, someone would listen to the BBC World News service and all interesting or significant bulletins were related via Sammy throughout Stalag XXB, even to the French. As soon as he stormed into our hut, we knew that he was bursting with news, fresh from the radio, news of major importance. With no need of notes, he began.

"Excuse me everybody, I have some news," he announced, rather out of breath.

Although he was always enthusiastic, this day he seemed positively fit to explode, such was the burden of his communiqué. Some of the men were sitting at the table, busying themselves with books, letter-writing or playing cards. They did not bother to lift their heads, continuing with their activities. Sammy was not amused, for he thought that what he had to say was of such significance that it deserved everyone's full attention.

He waited. Nothing. He forced an irritated cough, and when that didn't work he was less subtle.

"Excuse me, this is bloody important!" he bellowed impatiently.

With that, the 'naughty' PoWs gave each other a glance that mocked their apparent rudeness. They were all ears. Now it was his turn. He paused for a moment for dramatic effect, to emphasise the importance of his recital, and then he spoke in a loud but sombre tone.

"Germany has invaded Russia."

Now that did catch everyone's attention. Usually, whatever Sammy had to report was only of mild interest and only served to underline the setbacks that were befalling us British and our allies. However, they were still one of the highlights of our boring existence. At times, I wondered if the radio actually existed at all because his news was often devoid of specific details that we craved for. But even if it was all a figment of Sammy's fertile imagination, it did give us the feeling of being 'kept informed' and in touch with home and the outside world. As far as I knew, Sammy never left the confines of the camp, so I assumed that the radio was real or how else would he have found out about the invasion?

This story was news, big news. I could not help but wonder if Hitler was now mad, or was this just further proof of his awesome conquering power? Then I started to speculate if it would prolong our incarceration in this hell hole or, dare I speculate, shorten it? Had Hitler bitten off more than he could chew and would now choke on his audacious act? Was the combined might of Britain, the Dominions, her Allies and now the USSR enough to defeat Hitler and be his eventual downfall? At this point in time, we didn't even know if America had joined the war, but if they had I was sure that Sammy would have been the first to tell us.

We talked about the news for a long while and over the next few days efforts were made to 'pump' the German guards for anything that we could glean. There were a couple of them whom I suspected of being almost human, and the following day, as soon as I saw one of them, I asked for information. He along with most of the guards seemed more than happy to confirm that the Wehrmacht had indeed invaded Russia.

"Russia is now finished," he said. "Germany will smash the Bolshevik once and for all. In a week, we shall be in Moscow."

He smiled and walked away, giving nothing else away except an extremely broad grin that I wanted to knock off his arrogant, square head. The following day I saw the other 'friendly' guard and approached him at the rail yard. Likewise, he confirmed the reports, telling me that they were a thousand kilometres inside Russia and that it would soon be over. He added that their panzers had destroyed hundreds of Russian tanks. I thought that one-thousand kilometres into Russia was a hell of a lot of territory in a few days, but after our experience in France, nothing about the Wehrmacht's capabilities and their Blitzkrieg war surprised me anymore.

"How many German tanks were destroyed?" I asked, flippantly.

"Vier Panzer,... vier Panzer und bald Moscow" ("Four tanks, four tanks and soon Moscow") was his gleeful response. "This will be a great victory for our country."

"Four tanks my arse Fritz!" was my mumbled uttering.

The Polish civilians at the marshalling yard were usually a better source of news. They hated the Germans as much as the Russians and were very kind and hospitable to us British, their allies, even if we did not manage to or were incapable of going to their assistance when Hitler invaded. If there was any news to tell us, they certainly would. They had to listen to the German broadcasts on their radios, which was propaganda from start to finish. If they chose to listen to the broadcasts of the BBC or the Allies and were caught, they would face harsh and swift justice, resulting in them being sent to a concentration camp or even to their deaths.

However, in spite of the ever present threat, many patriotic Poles did tune in to the BBC.

· · · § · · ·

~ THE SEAFORTH HIGHLANDERS ~
RE-IGNITE OUR PRIDE
Late June 1941

I was relaxing one hot afternoon, smoking a rare English cigarette whilst leaning back against the side of my hut. The unmistakable tone of the bagpipes accompanied by the sound of singing drifted across the canp. A squad of the Seaforths came into view, parading across the empty, dust-covered ground in front of the huts. Their song paid homage to the regiments that made up the Highlander Divisions.

I'm Geordie MacKay of the H. L. I. *
I'm fond of the lassies and a drappie forbye,
One day when out walking I chanced to see,
A bonnie wee lass wi' a glint in her ee'
Says I to the lassie 'Will you walk foe a while?
I'll buy you a bonnet and we'll do it in style,
My kilt is Mackenzie o' the H. L.I.'
She look'd at me shyly and said wi' a sigh.

Chorus
A Gordon for me, a Gordon for me,
If ye're no a Gordon ye're no use to me.
The Black Watch** are braw, the Seaforths*** and a'
But the cocky wee Gordon's the pride o' them a'.

I courted that girl on the banks of the Dee,
I made up my mind she was fashioned for me,
Soon I was a' thinking how nice it would be
If she would consent to get married to me.
The day we were wed, the grass was so green,
The sun was as bright as the light in her 'een,
Now we've two bonnie lassies who sit on her knee,
While she sings the song she once sang to me.

Chorus"

* *Highland Light Infantry*
** *Famous Scottish Regiment in the British Army (allowed to wear kilts)*
*** *Another famous Scottish Regiment, now inactive. At one time there was a Gordon Highlander Regiment. This song pays homage to them all*

Their marching was impeccable and their singing inspirational as they strode past, led by two pipers. They did a tour of the camp and it brought a tear to most who heard it. At every hut, they received a tumultuous applause. Boy, I felt elated and proud that day.

~ EAST & WEST ~
DEATH AWAITS IN BOTH DIRECTIONS

My friendship with Stacia continued to flourish and by now, I actually looked forward to the march to the rail yard. Unfortunately, I could only ever see Stacia whilst on the morning shift. My Polish was improving and likewise, so was her English. I longed for her company. We laughed and loved in equal amounts and our meetings were a tonic in my otherwise wretched life.

Since the invasion of Soviet Russia, we had noticed increasing numbers of bright-eyed and bushy-tailed German soldiers passing through on their way eastwards to the new front. The stream of trains, armaments and troops seemed relentless.

Our suffering under the constant summer sun was relentless, beating down on our backs as we continued with our exhausting labour. We were two hours into the morning shift when a train loaded with troops pulled up alongside us. To a man, those still awake eyed us with a mix of indifference and derision. They were relaxed and in good spirits and morale amongst them seemed high. One wagon stopped directly opposite me, two rail lines away. I was working with Johnny.

"Hey Tommy, England kaputt!" shouted one soldier, who was smoking and relaxing in the open doorway with his left leg dangling over the side. He was laughing and by now, so were his colleagues. Their chortling filled my ears as the train jumped into movement again, its metal buffers hitting into one another. Their brief stop was over.

"England kaputt, England kaputt!" he repeated in a singsong manner, which was followed by a wagon load of merriment, "We will give your love to your girlfriend, don't worry."
As the train pulled away, I locked eyes with him, smiled and raised one finger.

"Eine woche, eine woche," (One week, one week) I bellowed. "Sie werden wieder mit einem Arm, einem Bein, wirst du zurück sein. (You'll be back with one arm, one leg, you'll be back)."

As if to emphasise the point, Johnny pulled his leg up behind him and hopped briefly on the other. Now it was our turn to laugh.

Sure enough, throughout July, trains returning from the Russian front began to pass on through Marienburg on their way back home to their beloved Fatherland. The wagons no longer carried the fresh-faced innocent troops of yesterday, but only the smashed and battered bodies of those who had suffered and survived at the hands of the defending Russians. The bandages on every soldier told their own tale and now, the sound of laughter was nowhere to be heard. Neither Johnny nor I felt the need to respond or retaliate to their sounds of silence, pain and suffering.

But in the opposite direction, trains continued to clatter their way towards Russia laden with supplies, munitions and troops, at all hours of the day and night. Marienburg could not have been busier in those weeks after the invasion.

Towards late summer, other trains began to appear carrying another type of cargo, a cargo of human misery. These trains were guarded not by the Wehrmacht who had escorted us across Europe, but by more sinister troops clad in uniforms bearing the symbol of the SS or Totenkopf. Every time a train passed through, we would halt what we were doing and watch, disturbed at what we saw. These wagons had their doors bolted shut like ours had been. Dispersed amongst the train were wagons carrying the SS. They watched us menacingly. Sometimes their trains would stop and on other occasions they continued on to their own hellish destination.

Today, one such train did come to a halt. For hours it sat there under the blazing sun. There was no attempt to feed or water the unfortunate occupants and I only had to recall my own terrible experience to appreciate just how awful their conditions must be. From inside we could hear soft moans and bleating noises that grew louder as time passed. Out of every small, barbed wire-covered window hands and arms waved weakly or hung limply in mid-air. We could stand the cries no longer and several of our party stopped work. We moved towards their train and Bert picked up our own bucket of water to give to them, although how precisely we were going to pass it into the enclosed wagon was another matter. Immediately, our own guards rushed forward with rifles raised.

"Stop! Get back to work,... *NOW*" screamed the guard.

Upon hearing the commotion, the SS guards took an interest, readying themselves to move if they had to. As for us, we stopped and did nothing. Bert replaced the water bucket and we reluctantly resumed our work. It was uncomfortable to hear their helpless cries and to do nothing. The Nazi bastards didn't even douse them with cold water as they had done with us. Two hours crept by before the train rolled forward again and the poor passengers continued on their way. Our own guards now relaxed. One of them, who spoke a little English, beckoned me, the interpreter, to him. I half expected a telling-off but instead I received an explanation.

"You must not do this," he began. "You will tell the others, do not go to those trains. It is forbidden. The SS will shoot you next time... and us. You will not go near them, ever,... is that understood?"

His mood was deadly serious, his anger controlled but real. I was not yet fully aware of the terrifying reputation of the SS troops or the mass murders that were being committed in the concentration camps across Europe, but to hear that they would shoot their fellow countrymen for not controlling us left us in little doubt that they would regard our lives as totally expendable.

My face was one of dumb insolence, which eventually infuriated our guard. Not satisfied, he called us all together and repeated his order.

"You will not go near them. You will not talk to them. You will not give them food and you will not give them water. You will give them nothing, NOTHING. IS THAT UNDERSTOOD? Anyone who disobeys will be shot. Is that understood?"

Nobody responded.

"DO YOU UNDERSTAND?" screamed the guard, brandishing his rifle and removing the safety catch, demanding a response.

"Yes," we replied, quickly and loud enough for him to hear. My eyes were downcast. Only then did the guards relax.

"Get back to work," he bellowed. By the look on his face you could see that he was still seething.

We did as we were instructed and tried to ignore the trains. We never had any idea who the poor unfortunates were, if they were Russian dissidents, Jews, political prisoners or any number of categories that did not fit neatly alongside the Nazi state, but it was safe to assume they were innocents.

~ RATS ~

The main camp of Stalag XXB was sited just outside the town of Marienburg, right beside the banks of the River Nogat that flows from the River Wisla in the south-west to the Baltic in the north-east.

The barbed wire fence at the back of the camp stopped short of the river. After that, there was an area of grass before the ground fell away, down the sandy bank to the water's edge. Under normal circumstances, this would have been an idyllic location for a holiday home, with a view to match. But these were not normal times and with Stalag XXB sited so close to the river, its location brought problems. Rats,... and they were huge.

During the previous winter months, whilst we had existed in those abominable huts, rats had not been an issue. In fact, I never saw a single one. I suppose it was too cold, but since the arrival of the warmer weather they were multiplying at a phenomenal rate. Location, riverside, time of year and the presence of open latrines must have all contributed to the general appeal of the camp to our furry little friends. We were informed that they were water rats, just like Ratty of Toad Hall from The Wind in the Willows. But whatever type of rat they were was of no concern to me or the occupants of Stalag XXB, for a rat is a rat, is a dirty, filthy rat.

The first night it happened was during the summer of 1941, at around ten. The lights were switched off and the huts were plunged into darkness, to be turned on again at five in the morning, heralding the new working day for those on the early shift. Lights out was the signal for the fun to begin. From one end of the hut came a loud cry, a cry not of pain but of surprise tinged with childlike fear. From somewhere, a plague of rats literally crawled out of the woodwork. They were jumping over us, running the full length of the bunks. At first I was startled by the scream.

"What the bloody hell was that?" someone shouted.

When I moved in, I was unfortunate enough to get the bottom shelf of bunks. As I lay there in the dark I unexpectedly felt the occupant next to me shift as he wriggled about. Something had landed on top of him and then scurried across his blanket before launching itself at the next person in line - me. Then another came and another until the whole hut was in uproar. I really did wonder what the hell was going on.

And then I screamed.

"Some bastard thing's just bitten me on my bloody nose!" I cried.

By now, matches were being struck whilst others lit their 'margarine lamp'. A horrific swarm of disgusting rats was revealed, scampering around everywhere. The rodents didn't appreciate the light or the threat and use of violence as boots hurtled through the air but failed to find their intended targets. Just as soon as they had arrived, they scuttled back into the darkness from whence they came, leaving a death toll of one rat, clubbed to death by a proud hunter.

~ SICK PARADE ~

The following day, I had to endure the discomfort of a developing septic nose. It may have looked comical to others, but to me it was increasingly painful. By the following evening, I could feel my nose actually pulsating with every heartbeat. I was in so much pain I couldn't sleep.

The following day, I joined the ranks of the sick. As was usually the case, scores of prisoners presented themselves in an effort to see the camp doctor, a Polish medic on this occasion. He had been given half a hut as a surgery. Because of our living conditions and lack of proper nutritional food, the camp always had its fair share of sick. The seriously ill were transferred to Marienburg hospital, where they either survived treatment and returned to camp or simply died. Within the camp itself, dysentery, diarrhoea and ulcers were commonplace and in my time there, I had the misfortune to suffer all of the above.

When it was my turn to see the doctor, I was surprised at the equipment in his surgery, or to be more precise, the lack of it, for there was none. You would have had to be a blind person not to have noticed my septic, ulcerated nose, pulsating away like Rudolf the Red-Nosed Reindeer, but I pointed it out to the doctor just in case. The doctor possessed a poor bedside manner and appeared bored out of his Polish mind. He looked closely at the open wound and touched the edges, which made me wince, before turning to a shelf behind him. On it were two items, a large glass tub containing massive white tablets and another glass tub containing a thick white paste. Although a difficult choice, the doctor chose the latter and placed it on his consultation desk. He then took an old sheet of newspaper from his drawer and tore off a piece. Into it, the doctor scooped up a wad of the white paste and deposited it in the centre of the paper, telling me to spread some on my nose each day. Consultation and treatment over.

It took two weeks for my nose to healed. Whether the ointment helped or hindered the healing process only 'the great surgeon in the sky' would know.

~ STILL MAKING US RATTY ~

Within a week or so, the problem with the rats had increased to plague-like proportions. Every night, the *sing-song* cry would go out.

"Here they come."

With that, we would quickly pull the blankets over our heads or get up and try to smash the little buggers with our boots. The lower sleeping shelf in the huts became known as 'The Rat Run'. I was still on it for nobody above wanted to swap positions. I would have preferred to be on the top shelf, known as 'The Bug Run', or even the middle shelf, known as 'The Flea Pit', but relocation was not an option.

Our first point of call was to Charlie McDowell. He in turn raised the problem with the Germans, who continued to do nothing, but when the rodent army eventually expanded their empire and discovered the accommodation huts of our conquering heroes on the other side of the wire, well, that was a conquest too far. Action now had to be taken, thank God, for sleeping in the huts was not only a nightmare... but dangerous.

With total annihilation as the goal, rat poison was the solution, to be used in large doses.

Our huts were built on short brick pillars, which meant that there was a space under each hut. This is where the Germans placed the poison. Within days it did its job and we were seeing more and more of them fall victim to the deadly chemicals and less and less in our huts at night. The poison had the dramatic effect of causing their stomachs and intestines to blow up, to such an extent that their little feet could no longer touch the ground. They resembled bizarre grey/brown rugby balls with a pinkish string at one end. They would eventually roll over and expose their bloated bellies, so distended that their dark brown fur was not thick enough to cover their expanded pink skin. They would just lie on their backs, waving their little legs about until they died.

Now that alone would have been fine had it not been for the fact that it was the height of summer. Under the blazing sun, their bodies began to decompose. Within the day, they simply exploded and emitted the most pungent, God-awful stench you could ever imagine - and there were hundreds of these evil stink bombs 'popping off' all over the camp. That year was not good for either the faint-hearted or those with a sensitive nose.

~ A LAUGH AT THEIR EXPENSE ~

Prisoners like me were always looking for ways to brighten up our days and nights. This usually involved having a laugh at the expense of a more placid German guard.

Down at the rail yard, we were shovelling coal as on any other day. We had our shirts off as usual and were building up a head of steam. I was desperate to see Stacia again and I needed to trade with the Poles, so I had to finish early. A guard came over to replace the one who had been watching over us. When two guards normally met each other, they would greet each other with an outstretched arm salute and a 'Heil Hitler'. As they did this, we would give them the fingered 'V' sign and mumble 'F*** him' (meaning Hitler), just loud enough for other PoWs or civilians to hear, but not the guards. We even did this in front of particularly friendly guards who were known to be pro-Germany but anti-Hitler. Occasionally a 'good' guard would have difficulty in holding back a smile, but they tried. It didn't take long for them to realise what we were doing and what it meant. However, the Polish civilians were slower at catching on to our meaning and would often ask the question to the guards in our presence.

"What does it mean when the English do this?"

With that, they would give the two-fingered 'V' sign.

"And what does 'F***'im' mean?"

The Germans in turn would become too embarrassed to say and would either ignore the question or become irate. The more daring Poles amongst them would follow our lead and when approached by a guard would actually repeat "F*** off" to them as well. It was most gratifying to know that we were teaching Johnny Foreigner so much educational Shakespearean English whilst disrespecting the beloved Führer, but I hoped the Poles didn't get into too much trouble.

We continued slaving on the wagons throughout the summer months. Each day I awoke with the image of Stacia's pure, youthful face on my mind. She filled my every waking moment and I so looked forward to our brief encounters.

Every morning, I would strip to the waist whilst working under that relentless summer sun. At first I thought it strange that my skin never got sunburnt, but I soon realised that it was due to the coal dust, which mixed with the greasy sweat that leaked from every pore of my body, forming a grey, emulsified sun screen that protected me. But as good as it was, I could see no long term commercial use for it.

~ PHOTOGRAPHS ~

At first I found it strange that the German authorities turned a blind eye to the cameras and film that were present in Stalag XXB. Possession of both was not a punishable offence and photographs were continually being taken of the men and them alone. The unofficial camp photographer was a Frenchman whose name escapes me. I, as 'Ma Minter', and the gang would often have our picture taken and copies duplicated to send home. I had no idea where 'Frenchy' got his camera from or how he acquired the many chemicals and equipment that he needed to produce the prints, probably much the same way as me, by stealing or bartering with the Poles. If you were brave, daring or stupid enough, you could always trade with the German guards. Of course, all photos that were posted home had to pass under the ever-watchful eye of the official camp sensor, who was stationed back at main camp, Stalag XXA. Unless the pictures depicted the prisoners badly by making them look dirty, unhappy or revealing some aspect of the camp that was forbidden such as a German guard or the oppressive-looking watchtowers and wire enclosures, the censor would pass them and they would be despatched to England. The four copies usually cost us a loaf of bread, which wasn't too much trouble for me to 'acquire'.

Towards the end of summer, our work on the coal wagons came to an abrupt end. Even though I knew that some day it would, I was mortified. I could no longer see my Stacia and with no way of passing a message to her, I was saddened. Our romance had lasted some four wonderful months. Heartbroken, I even contemplated escaping from the compound just so that I could explain, to say goodbye and tell her how much I loved her. Only after listening to the wise council of Jimmy, Bert and Johnny, did I put the idea out of my head.

~ A MATCH IS ORGANISED ~

Ever mindful of camp morale, McDowell had another idea as to how to lift the mood of the camp. The essential elements were already in place within Stalag XXB, so the idea appeared to be an immediate winner.
A good, old-fashioned boxing match was organised.

Before McDowell had been crowned camp leader, fighting was endemic. That ancient law, survival of the ones with the biggest fists and hardest punch, held the high ground, but not necessarily the moral ground. McDowell helped change that, although afterwards he was often threatened with violence, which was something he could handle extremely well. Having an almost inexhaustible pool of talented, bent-nosed brutes readily available and all too eager to knock ten tons of shit out of an opponent meant there were many volunteers.

A date was fixed, contestants identified, posters written and a ring hastily built. The stage was set to present 'The Stalag XXB Whatever Weight Boxing Championship of Europe'. As it was summer, the venue was held outside in the parade ground. Anybody who was in camp and who had a mind for gratuitous violence was welcome to attend, and they did, in droves.

On the day in question it was hot and sticky and there was standing room only, which is a bit misleading as there were no seats to speak of. The gladiatorial contest was brutal in the extreme. By now, most of the PoWs were much leaner than when they joined due to the starvation diet, so many were at lightweight or flyweight level, but there were still some muscle-bound individuals whom I would treat with respect if passing them in the streets of Glasgow after pub turn out. To inspire them, I believe most of those boxers imagined themselves in the ring with either the Camp Commandant, a German guard who had rifle-butted them or any other bugger who had upset them, including McDowell. Hence, each and every fight was nasty. With blood flowing freely, the referee seemed reluctant to step in to end any fight. The crowd, on the other hand, loved every gory second of it. Even the Germans came to watch and I caught many happy Kraut faces throughout the contest. One particularly witty PoW of ours even went up to one of the young Germans and asked him if he would like to fight him in the ring. The German just smiled and pointed to his rifle. I think his answer was a firm 'no'.

Afterwards, I heard a guard ask a pertinent question.

"Tell me," he said, "why do you British like to beat each other to a pulp and kill yourselves?"

We all knew the answer. The fights released a flood of in-built aggression that desperately wanted to be directed at our captors but nobody bothered to give our guard the explanation. The contest was another extremely popular event and was to become a major fixture on the Stalag XXB sports calendar.

At morning parade next day, many battered faces were in evidence but the mood was good. Volunteers were called for various working parties and mine was only slightly further afield, repairing and maintaining the rail track. I jumped at the chance for I already felt trapped.

1. Henry Minter (far left) as an upholsterer in Birmingham 1910.

2. After joining the Surrey Police Force 1912

3. Baby Dennis, 1920

4. Dennis & father, Broadstairs Beach, Kent, 1922

5. The fisherman's cottage, Dover, where his father, Henry Minter was born

6. Inspector Henry Minter

7. Dennis' brother Cyril & his lover
   Kathleen, 1935

8. Dennis, after riding to his parents house in
   Leatherhead, 1936

9. Dennis' mother, Helen Blanch Farr, 1918

1938

Last peacetime summer holiday

10. Flicker Johnson, Dennis,
    Joc Macavoy & Cyril Plumbridge at
    Rodin's Burghers of Calais statue

11. On the ferry to Calais.

12. Dennis & Cyril at Margate

13. Dennis & Flicker at Cliftonville

Officers of the 2nd/7th Battalion of The Queen's Royal Regiment who embarked for France on 21st April 1940
14. 2nd Lieutenant J. A. B. Mumford   15. Major J. W. Carr   16. Lieutenant Colonel F. E. B. Girling MC

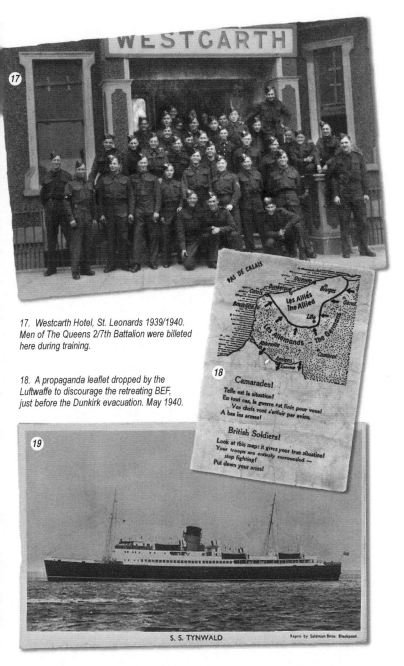

17. *Westcarth Hotel, St. Leonards 1939/1940. Men of The Queens 2/7th Battalion were billeted here during training.*

18. *A propaganda leaflet dropped by the Luftwaffe to discourage the retreating BEF, just before the Dunkirk evacuation. May 1940.*

Camarades!

Telle est la situation!
En tout cas, la guerre est finie pour vous!
    Vos chefs vont s'enfuir par avion.
A bas les armes!

British Soldiers!

Look at this map: it gives your true situation!
Your troops are entirely surrounded —
    stop fighting!
Put down your arms!

S. S. TYNWALD

19. *The S.S. Tynwald, peacetime ferry steamer that had been commandeered for the war effort and sailed with Dennis to Le Havre in France on 19th April 1940.*

While Our Men Give Battle in France and Fla

*Above: Original photo obtained from
The War Illustrated magazine*

Along this peaceful cobbled road in the northern war area British troops are marching
towards the battle zone. They are in open order, which considerably lessens the risk they
run from sudden swoops by enemy planes. Right are typical German prisoners captured
during the Nazi advance.

20. Dennis Minter, the only one wearing his forage cap. His platoon marching near Abbeville, France 12th May 1940.
Above picture was printed in The War Illustrated magazine 7th June 1040. Enlargement of Dennis from original photo obtained from the magazine

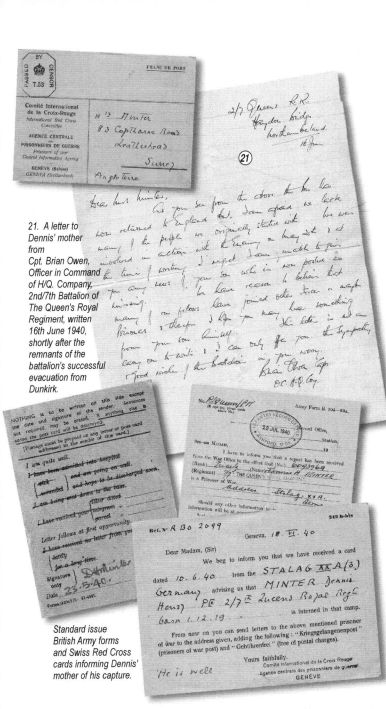

21. A letter to
Dennis' mother
from
Cpt. Brian Owen,
Officer in Command
of H.Q. Company,
2nd/7th Battalion of
The Queen's Royal
Regiment, written
16th June 1940,
shortly after the
remnants of the
battalion's successful
evacuation from
Dunkirk.

Standard issue
British Army forms
and Swiss Red Cross
cards informing Dennis'
mother of his capture.

Dear Mrs Minter,
As you see from the above that we have
now returned to England but, I am afraid we were
many of the people we originally started with
involved in action with the enemy on May 20th & at
for time of writing I regret I am unable to give
you any news of your son who in was posted as
missing. ... we have reason to believe that
he have ... many of our fellows have joined other ... or might
prisoner & therefore I hope you may hear something
from your son himself. This letter is all ...
easy on to write & I can only offer you the sympathy
& good wishes of the battalion in your worry.

Brian Owen Cpt.
O.C. H.Q. Coy.

FRANC DE PORT

Comité International
de la Croix-Rouge
*International Red Cross
Committee*

AGENCE CENTRALE
PRISONNIERS DE GUERRE
*Prisoners of war
Central Information Agency*

GENÈVE (Suisse)
GENEVA (Switzerland)

Mrs Minter
83 Copthorne Road
Leatherhead
Surrey
Angleterre

NOTHING is to be written on this side except
the date and signature of the sender. Sentences
not required may be erased. If anything else is
added the post card will be destroyed.

[Postage must be prepaid on any letter or post card
addressed to the sender of this card.]

I am quite well.

I have been admitted into hospital
{ sick } and am going on well.
{ wounded } and hope to be discharged soon.

I am being sent down to the base.

I have received your { letter dated
{ telegram "
{ parcel "

Letter follows at first opportunity.

I have received no letter from you
{ lately
{ for a long time.

Signature } D H Minter
only
Date 23.5.40.

No. P/Queens/P.W.

Army Form B. 104—83A.

INFANTRY RECORD OFFICE
22 JUL 1940
ASHFORD, MDX.

Record Office, ...Station,

Sir—or Madam,

I have to inform you that a report has been received
from the War Office to the effect that (No.) 6093909
(Rank) Private (Name) Dennis H. MINTER
(Regiment) 2/7 THE QUEEN'S ROYAL REGIMENT
is a Prisoner of War.
Stalag XX A.

Should any other information be received
information will be at once ...
...

242 b-bis

Ref. N^o R BO 2099

Geneva, 18. VI. 40.

Dear Madam, (Sir)
We beg to inform you that we have received a card
dated 10.6.40 from the STALAG XX A (3)
Germany advising us that MINTER Dennis
Henry PE 2/7th Queens Royal Regt
barn 1.12.19 is interned in that camp.

From now on you can send letters to the above mentioned prisoner
of war to the address given, adding the following : "Kriegsgefangenenpost"
(prisoners of war post) and "Gebührenfrei" (free of postal charges).

Yours faithfully,
Comité International de la Croix Rouge
Agence centrale des prisonniers de guerre
GENÈVE

He is well

22. *Generalmajor Erich von Manstein, brilliant architect of the successful lightning invasion of France and the low countries. Portrait taken in 1938, two years before Dennis' chance meeting.*

23. Shoulder flash from Dennis' old uniform and his Queen's Cap Badge.

24. Central picture,
Top left: Micky Phipps.
Top row, second from left: Dennis.

25. Below, two German tunic badges that Dennis acquired as souvenirs.

26. Dennis' Stalag XXB Identity Tag worn around his neck using string saved from parcels.

27. *Irena Dockendorf. The photograph she gave Dennis when he worked for her uncle.*
The back of the card reads: 'A reminder of war time (captivity).
To a colleague from friend Irena'. Marienburg 1st June 1941.

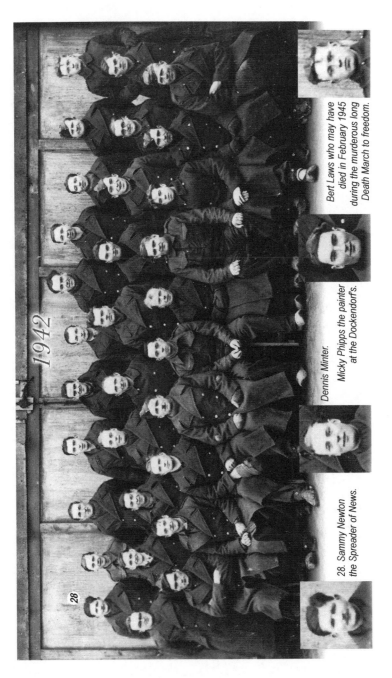

1942

28. Sammy Newton the Spreader of News.

Micky Phipps the painter at the Dockendorf's.

Dennis Minter.

Bert Laws who may have died in February 1945 during the murderous long Death March to freedom.

29. Ma Minter's Boys:
From top left to bottom right:
Bert Stupples, Johnny Dunbar, Dennis Minter
and Jimmy Farrington.

Above: A precious Stalag portion of bread, the like of which sustained
The Ghosts of Dunkirk for five long years.

"Ich fühle mich so frisch.
Es kommt der Frühling."

(ADOLF HITLER, 26.2.41.)

30. Front & back of propaganda
leaflet dropped by the US Air Force
after the the the raid shown below.
Heading reads:
'I feel so fresh. Spring is coming'.
A smiling Adolf Hitler is pictured
standing among frozen bodies of
dead German soldiers lying in the
snow. The ironic quote refers to
the fact that, during the invasion
of Poland, Hitler seemed oblivious to
the numbers of German casualties.

AN DIE SOLDATEN DER DEUTSCHEN WEHRMACHT!

EINEM GERECHTEN FRIEDEN!

31. The US B17 leaves the targeted Focke-Wulf plant at Marienburg. The blazing factory can
be seen in the background. Photo taken during the raid by 8th Air Force on 9.10.1943.

32. Above: The Hackbridge Factory complex in Hersham, Surrey where Dennis worked before and after the war as a draughtsman. Highlighted in the circle is the house where he rented a room, at No. 37 Claremont Close, until the winter of 1939.

33. Below: 1947. The Drawing Office staff at Hackbridge, after his return to work. From left to right: Dennis Minter, Mr. Boxall, unknown girl, Len Bewsy (or Bazley), Freddy Mills, Basil Hiscock and Alf Turner.

34. Dennis and his wartime Service Medals.

35. Left. Dennis Minter's wife Amy seen working in an Aircraft factory during the war.

36. Top: Dennis' Army Service Pay Book and his National Small-bore Rifle Association Certificate awarded for achieving the highest score possible of 100, 21st May 1952. A true marksman.

DOCKENDORF

Summary Turns to Autumn 1941

O ur group of nearly thirty PoWs were assembled and headed off towards the town and the rail yard once more, but found ourselves walking straight past the yard to a compound slightly further on. Here we picked up tools and were marched along rail lines until we reached a section of track about two kilometres from the yard.

As the interpreter, the Polish overseer turned to me with instructions to translate to my fellows. Unfortunately, he didn't speak German at all, only guttural, fast Polish and I couldn't understand a single word, which was not an ideal situation for an interpreter to find himself in. My face gave nothing away. Fortunately, the Pole waved a shovel about. As he called its name, he made a digging action, saying 'shovel' and 'dig' in Polish and pointed as he spoke. He then did the same with the scythe, naming and gesticulating with his arms, which finally helped me to 'interpret'. Phew! It was hard work but we got there. I thought my short career was over before it had really begun. Mind you, by now even the village idiot amongst us had grasped what he wanted us to do, but I sarcastically translated anyway with much derision and scoffing from the others. I had to laugh and regardless of the ridicule, I was the official interpreter and nothing could be done before I had slowly relayed in great detail what exactly was required of us to my audience of stupid English pigs.

We began to chop and dig away the undergrowth on the

embankments either side of the track, which continued for days until a huge swath had been cleared.

Once completed, we were given new labours: replacing old worn track, checking the joining bolts, under stopping (which meant underpinning the existing sleepers with stone chippings) and doing anything to keep the rail track safe and functioning within the Marienburg area of control.

At the end of the second week, the unfriendly Pole overseer chose to give us some really heavy work. It seemed to coincide with the hottest day that I can ever recall. After a long march under the baking sun, we arrived at the place where several sections of rail needed totally replacing. Unfortunately for us, the rails were already there, presumably brought out by train and dumped at the spot so we started work immediately, our overseer directing us. After stripping to the waist, we used huge, heavy, cast iron spanners to unbolt the fish plates that held the rails together. When freed we picked up the old rails using purpose-built long-handled clamps. When the handles were pushed together they gripped the rails tightly. Six of us stood either side and hauled the huge dead weights clear of the tracks. It was unbelievably strenuous, tough, thirsty, back-breaking drudgery and we were wilting under the oppressive heat. Working in relative isolation along the track afforded me no opportunity to fraternise with local Poles, therefore no chance to trade.

As our unrelenting toil continued, I began to wonder if I was ever going to benefit from this work party, but my wondering came to an end soon enough. One morning, just before leaving camp, I was handed the perfect opportunity to get out of this rut. Roll call had just finished when one of our guards approached my section.

"Wo is der Malermeister?" came the question.

Now this was a new phrase to me but I instantly grasped the essentials. I knew 'Maler' had something to do with painter, so I guessed that he meant "Where is the master painter?"

This really struck a chord with me. One of my new-found buddies in the camp was a fellow Brit called Mickey Fipps *(see picture reference 24 & 30)*. Both he and I shared the same hut but I didn't know him that well until we started work together on the rail lines. He was a good man with a broad, happy face and high cheekbones, and just a few years older than me. I soon discovered that he lived quite close to my home town in a beautiful little village called Albury, between Dorking and Guildford. He told me that he was a painter and decorator by profession before 'taking the King's shilling'.

Hastily returning to the guard's question I sensed the perfect opportunity, and thinking on the hoof, as I tended to do, I raised my arm.

"Over here," I shouted in response and pointed to Mickey.

Quickly, I added "and me,... we are the painters."

My reason for volunteering was obvious for painting was a doddle by comparison to what we were doing, and with Mickey to teach me it was a ticket to a veritable holiday. If the guard was pleased that I had resolved his quest for a painter, he didn't show it, which was not unusual, for most of them were not in the habit of showing gratitude. The only two emotions that they ever seemed to express were indifference or anger. Nothing else was said and he gave the order to get in line and march. I quietly explained the situation to Mickey and he responded with a wink and a smile. After a march of about two miles, we were ordered to halt in front of a pale, yellow bungalow. As ordered, Mickey and I 'fell out' and followed our guard through a gate in the old, weathered picket fence. We strode up to the front of the house, whereupon our guard knocked loudly on the front door before taking a step back. The door was opened by a tall, pale, over weight man with a very silly toothbrush moustache that reminded me of a mad, comical dictator, but I couldn't place his name.

This particular individual went by the name of Dockendorf. Unknowingly, we had been working for him over the last few weeks for he was in charge of this section of the Reichsbahn (German Reich Railway) network around the town of Marienburg and this was his home. Dockendorf had obviously just finished his breakfast as he still had his napkin tucked into his shirt. He looked down on us with disdain, examining us as if we were way down the evolutionary scale, lodged somewhere between cockroaches and bacteria. Reluctantly, he finished chewing, swallowed, removed his napkin and wiped the crumbs from his chubby face.

Our guard and Dockendorf exchanged a few words before he finally saluted the guard with an enthusiastic 'Heil Hitler' which was eagerly returned. Our guard spun round on his well-polished heels and addressed us with similar disdain. He ordered us to stay and work before rejoining the waiting prisoners and disappearing from view. Looking as though he had a turd stuck under his nose and didn't want the smell to enter his house, portly Dockendorf slammed the door shut and descended the three steps from his house. He couldn't

295

have looked more grumpy and ordered us to follow. We walked round to the back of his property, where we could see a large old barn, a summer house and another storage hut. Just like the house, they were all built of wood. He led us to the barn and pointed to several tins of paint, brushes and rags and told us to paint the lot, fence and all. It required little preparation or painting skills so it was ideal for me, but as I was a precise and organised person, careful painting was going to be easy. The wood was blisteringly dry after persistent long, hot summers and dry, cold winters so the wood absorbed the paint like a sponge.

We assumed that this arrangement was a 'trade' between Dockendorf and the German guards, our services in exchange for some contraband or other, over and above the arrangement between the Third Reich and the Polish farmers, mine and factory owners and leaders of industries who were all benefiting from our slave labour.

~ THE LUXURY OF LUNCH ~

Landing this undemanding job, painting woodwork for a few weeks whilst our unfortunate comrades continued to slave on the rails was marvellous for Mickey and I. Although we suffered with a very occasional twinge of guilt, we barely gave them a second's thought. Not only was the work effortless but we each received a substantial bowl of hot soup every lunchtime. This meant that our food ration had practically doubled overnight for normally, after our morning coffee, we received no food until we returned to camp and received our thin, watery soup with a portion of bread. This 'extra bowl of kindness' was brought to us by none other than Frau Dockendorf herself, a stern, pig-faced, real German sow.

My first encounter with her was on our first day. We had been busy all morning preparing the wood when we heard her rather loud, harsh bellow. She was summoning us both to the back door, which led straight into her kitchen. Her fat ruddy face was humourless and just darned-right nasty. She gave us no cordial greeting, just a ranting lecture and by her tone, I assumed that whatever she was saying certainly wasn't pleasant. Eventually she pronounced to us in no uncertain terms that, "alle Englisch sind grossmaul Lügner." ("all English are loud-mouth liars."), spitting the words out before grudgingly handing us the two bowls in her podgy hands.

Without wanting to appear paranoid, I was beginning to suspect that she hated us English.

Her soup was most welcome, even wonderful but on the other hand, anything would,... to a starving man. Mickey and I were not good enough to eat in the kitchen, so we ate in the shadow of the outhouse. Whilst I was licking the last traces from my upturned bowl, I noticed something above the roof of the Dockendorf's terracotta-tiled bungalow, on top of the tall brick chimney. Perched precariously on top, was a ragged collection of twigs and sticks, overhanging the clay chimney pots. On it stood a one legged stork, casually looking around. It could have been a scene from a Disney film. How on earth the nests did not fall off, must have been due to an amazing feat of bird engineering, especially during the windswept Polish winters. As the years passed, I was to discover that this was a common sight across Poland. I supposed that the nest enabled a safe location for the stork, giving them a commanding view of the surrounding countryside, and the heat from the house fires must have been very welcoming to them.

You will recall a paragraph ago, when describing Frau Dockendorf, that I used the words 'real German woman'. There was a reason for this and it relates to her husband, Herr Dockendorf. I found out from his niece that he was half-Pole, half-Prussian and called Zelinski. He changed his name to Dockendorf. If you read the complex history of Poland and the overlap of the German-speaking state of Prussia, you will have a better understanding as to why Poland was invaded, resulting in the start of World War II. As Zelinski had German/Prussian ancestry he was welcomed into the Greater Third Reich with open arms and Herr Dockendorf liked nothing more than to ingratiate himself to his new German masters, to such an extent that he even sported a Hitler moustache.

† As a result of the signing of the Treaty of Versailles on 28th June 1919, Germany lost most of West Prussia to the newly formed Polish state. For some time Marienburg (now Malbork) threatened to fall into Polish hands during the breakup. The argument for the inclusion of this area within the Polish state was primarily the fact that, according to the Poles, 80% of its people spoke the local variant of the Polish language - and thus, in line with the principle of the Treaty of Versailles'

creation of national states, this area should have been placed within Polish borders. However, the Treaty of Versailles did not grant the requested areas to Poland but left the decision to the local inhabitants. On 9th July 1920 the voting population of Powiśle took part in the plebiscite to decide the nationality of the Marienburg district (including the city). The 11th July outcome resulted in a victory on the German side with 17,805 votes cast to leave them within the limits of East Prussia, Germany and 191 for Poland.

Marienburg remained within Germany.

The negative result for Polish inclusion may have happened for a number of reasons: First, the German side had a huge material advantage, organisation and propaganda. Influencing the result of the plebiscite campaign were the terrorist activities of German militias, the somewhat biased attitude of the observers and the actual wording of the printed question. Moreover, the plebiscite was held at a very difficult period, during the general offensive of the Red Army during the Polish-Bolshevik war and the threatened imposition by force of the Soviet system. On the eve of the poll, the then Polish Prime Minister Wladyslaw Grabski formally asked for help against Soviet aggression.

Another important reason was the previous influx of German immigrants to the area, mostly from the Ruhr district. †

Mickey and I had been working at the Dockendorf's for a week and really enjoying (if that is the right word) the more sedate nature of our work. Under the blistering summer sun, the property was looking much improved for our labours, but all good things had to come to an end. We were unable to stretch the job out any longer and having come to its natural conclusion, we dreaded the return to the backbreaking work on the railway. However, such decisions were beyond our control. On our final day, I received a surprise. Dockendorf decided to retain my services. It might have been because I was a pleasant enough worker, but most probably because I was able to speak an increasing amount of German and Polish. He issued fresh orders in his usual stern manner, to the effect that I was to remain with him

† *Source: http://www.starymalbork.pl/stalag/ramka3uk.html and the The National Archives - The 1920 Plebiscite in Allenstein (East Prussia). Code 18 file 8441*

and become his 'Hofmeister' (Yardmaster) so I could not have been all that bad, in spite of being 'a loud-mouth English liar'.

Sadly, I had to say goodbye to Mickey each morning as he marched off back to the railways. Because of Dockendorf's job as the 'Fat Controller' of rail maintenance in the Marienburg district, overseeing miles of track in all directions, most of his back garden resembled a builder's yard. Stone, bricks, timber, sleepers and gravel were neatly piled all around. I was so delighted with my new appointment for I was outside the barbed wire, receiving extra food rations, the work was lighter and I had the opportunity to mix with the locals.

At the end of my second week as Hofmeister, I fell into line as the returning PoWs came to a halt at the front gate. Bert, Jimmy and Johnny, my new friends from my hut, were there to welcome me.

"Hope you haven't been overdoing it son?" was usually their first comment, sarcastically said, accompanied by a huge grin.

"Well, I've got a bit of wrist strain today when I lifted the brush, but I'll rest it tomorrow so don't worry," was my reply, or a variation of it.

"You jammy bastard," muttered Bert in his usual manner.

"How the hell do you do it, Mar (as they were beginning to called me), tell me, how the hell?" Johnny would ask, not really expecting an answer.

"Charm, pure charm," I replied.

It was all in good fun but on the march back to camp, I hoped I was not resented too much for landing such a plum job, but as I maintain, if you don't look after number one, no-one else will. As soon as we were back, I gave them a chunk of bread that I had managed to 'acquire' from the Dockendorfs. I continued to help my mates whenever I was able to with items of food and cigarettes that I obtained from my world outside the wire.

Inside camp, dysentery was making its unpleasant presence felt once more. Lacking any real medicines to alleviate the problem, the prisoners resorted to producing their own. Small amounts of wood were converted into charcoal brfore being crushed into a powder and then swallowed.

· · · § · · ·

~ I MEET A GIRL ~

There was a second reason for liking my new cushy job and it took the form of a wonderful distraction, a young lady. She appeared to be staying with the Dockendorfs and I soon learnt that she was Herr Dockendorf's niece. Her name was Irena.

When I first saw this rather beautiful girl at the house it was obvious by her manner that she was very wary of both Mickey and I. After Mickey left and I was left on my own, Irena slowly became more friendly, especially when she discovered that I was English and now regarded me, this friend of Poland, as a friend of hers.

My day began as usual, with barked instructions from my Lord and Master before commencing with the day's task. Today, I was in the barn tidying up, shovelling a pile of sand from one side to the other, when Irena came in. This had never happened before and was therefore unusual, given that both Dockendorfs hated the English, regarding us all as a totally untrustworthy, corrupt and spent nation. By her previous manner whilst in the company of the Dockendorfs, I was reasonably sure that she had been given strict instructions by her uncle not to associate with us on any account. Because of her presence today, I assumed that the two of them must be away from the house and that Irena was on her own.

I was delighted by her visit. As she stood in the doorway of the barn with the sun beaming down from behind, her long brown hair was adorned with a shimmering golden halo. She looked radiant and beautiful and I was already smitten. At first, she maintained a polite distance from me. She spoke to me by using a mixture of Polish and German. She was obviously highly educated and she told me that her father was a professor at Warsaw University. I was enjoying our conversation but it wasn't long before I became stuck. It took a while to realise that she was asking me if I was a Roman Catholic. I knew that Poland was a religious Catholic nation and I thought this might be an opportunity for some gain on my part that wouldn't hurt anybody, so without a moment's hesitation I started to lie through my teeth.

"Yes," I said, "of course I am Catholic," reaffirming my lie with a nod.

I would have said that I was a Hindu, a Buddhist, a Baptist or even a Martian if it would have helped my lust-driven situation, and what harm could there be in such a little white lie? She smiled nervously at me in a very sweet, naive way. Finally, she looked down at the ground and said a quiet goodbye before turning away and walking out of the barn back towards the house, and that was it. I thought nothing more about it, save for a wonderful fantasy that lasted for the rest of the day.

The following day, her uncle's presence was very evident, so when we met in the yard we passed like ships in the night. The following day, she casually walked over to me once more, cautiously checking that she could not be seen. We smiled once more and nodded a greeting in polite recognition.

Softly, she spoke to me.

"Do you smoke?".

I smiled, my face lighting up.

"Ja, ja, I do," I replied, again nodding my head as I desperately tried to think when I had last smoked a decent cigarette and not one of my home-made varieties. The prospect of what she had in mind was making me crave desperately. However, she just smiled again, turned and quickly walked away back to the house. I could not help wondering if she had misunderstood me.

But sure enough, the following day, she returned to the barn. Standing casually just outside the door, looking at me, she caught my eye and pointed to the wooden shelves beside me. I twigged what she meant and waited until she had turned and disappeared from view. I walked to the door to ensure that I could not be seen before hurrying back to search the shelves. They were full of dirty old pots, brown paper bags, packets and bottles, all covered with the thick dust of time. As I searched the first shelf at shoulder level, I lifted up a small wooden box. Hidden from casual view behind the box, I revealed a whole packet of German cigarettes. Smiling, I quickly grabbed my prize, less it be taken from me all too soon. This was a tremendously valuable present to me. When I had a moment to myself, I re-hid them carefully where nobody would discover them. I did not want to take them back to camp where I might lose them or have them stolen. Instead, each day, I would retrieve the pack, carefully remove one but only smoke half of it before pinching it out and returning it to the pack. That way, I was able to eke them out and make them last as long as I could. Although not as good as English ones, Irena's cigarettes still tasted heavenly.

Behind that small wooden box was to become our secret 'post box' as occasions like this continued, almost on a daily basis. Small items of food were her main gift, for which I was eternally grateful. Her kindness often used to make me cry, for I knew that she was taking a great risk to her future wellbeing by helping me and would probably receive a beating from her uncle, the fat Polish/German controller of rail maintenance, if he ever found out.

In time, I became aware that she had precious little of her own to give away for she was the poor relation, living off the charity of the Dockendorfs, and therefore in a very vulnerable position. I had seen the way both spoke to her and it was obvious there was little affection shown towards her.

I don't know how she knew but I suspect that it was my lack of knowledge of the ways of the Catholic Church, which often came up in conversations. However, one day, when she was sure we were alone, she came over to me with a rather sad face and asked me a question.

"You are not Catholic, are you?"

Instantly surprised, but unable to lie any longer to this delightful new friend of mine, I had to admit that I was not. I could not tell if she was upset but I thought that would be the end of our relationship. However, the next day we both greeted each other. It appeared that my religious preference didn't matter to her at all. She returned my smiles and we chatted as we had done a hundred times before.

Since meeting Irena, I had become aware of a change in my outlook of my present situation. My heart had softened since that terrible winter of last year and it was partially due to this girl.

One day in June, we found the time to snatch five minutes to talk alone and I asked her for a photograph of herself if she could manage it, for I had nothing of a personal nature on me, no pictures of my girlfriend or family, nothing to remind me of the former loving side of my life, and a picture of her would provide that need as she had given me a reason to live.

The following week, she came to me once more with a recent photograph of herself. We spoke a few words and she handed it to me, telling me that it was for me to keep. This simple act touched me and I felt a deeper, more loving intimacy with her than ever before. She was so good to me. It was never about the quantity of the things that she gave me but more about her friendship and the benevolence of a gentle female outside my life as a prisoner of war.

I still have that photograph with her message on the back and is still one of my most precious mementos from my years in captivity *(see picture reference 27)*.

We chatted for as long and as often as we could, during which time I learnt that she had been a student at Warsaw University when the Germans invaded. To protect her from harm, her father had immediately sent her to stay with his brother, Dockendorf, a Nazi sympathiser and an important member of the local Brown Shirts. Irena therefore came under his protection and obviously escaped the dreadful killings and destructions in Warsaw. With all the terrible horrors that were to befall their great capital city, the decision made by her parents to send her away may have saved her young life. Yet despite all of that, Irena detested Dockendorf and his wife. She hated them even more than she hated the invading Germans because he was the worst type of Pole - a traitor, a Pole turned German.

I had a growing suspicion that the Dockendorfs were aware of our friendship and they were keeping a closer eye on the both of us. He was probably aware that Irena was treating me kindly and respectfully and I don't think he liked it one bit. As a result, it became increasingly difficult to find the space to be alone and when we did, we had to be even more cautious. It was not that we wished to indulge ourselves in anything sexual, for that was not the nature of our relationship. I knew that she felt sorry for me and I loved her for her human kindness towards me and, although I did find her sexually attractive, I knew that I was not worthy of her love.

> *During one of our secretive, short conversations, Irena told me that she had another uncle, the brother of Dockendorf, who lived in a small town called Dundalk in County Louth, southern Ireland. During both wars with Germany, an 'understanding' between southern Ireland and Germany existed, which was reasonable, given that they shared a common enemy - England.*
>
> *Irena wanted to contact her uncle in Ireland to let him and his family know that since the German invasion both she and her family in Warsaw were well and unharmed, but she had no way of contacting them. So she asked me if I could send him a letter on her behalf to let him know. At that time, PoWs like us could only send two letters and two postcards home each month, but I was only too happy to repay her in some small way for her generosity and kindness.*
>
> *The following morning, when I went to our concealed 'postbox', there was a slip of paper. On it she had written her uncle's postal address in Ireland. I hid it in my deepest pocket and returned to my labours.*

That evening, as soon as I returned to camp and had time to myself, I retrieved her piece of paper and wrote the letter to her uncle, giving him scant, vague details of who I was, that I had met Irena and that she was alive and well. The information had to be carefully phrased so as to pass the German censor and to avoid trouble for Irena. Upon my eventual return to England, one of my first thoughts was to make contact with Irena as soon as I could. I wanted to try to bring her over to England, to help her and to try to repay her for her kindness.

Immediately after the war, Europe was awash with wandering refugees. Millions of displaced people were on the move, trying to return to their homes or to find a place of safety, people fleeing oppression once more, but this time from the Soviets. The International Red Cross had a sister organisation, set up in an attempt to co-ordinate the huge task of locating missing persons and re-uniting families. I wrote to them with as much information as I could recall about Irena. Unfortunately, the whole of Poland was then under brutal Soviet control and co-operation with them was practically impossible.

A short while later, I received a reply from the organisation saying that they could not look for her with the intention of bringing her to England unless I intended to marry her within one month of her arrival. At that point, I had no idea if she would have wanted to marry me, or indeed me marry her, however much I liked her. I wrote back to them, saying that I would dearly love to see her and to offer her my assistance and her freedom, but I could not definitely commit both of us to marriage. My attempt at finding her faltered at the first hurdle. I did not have the knowledge or resources to find an alternative method of contacting that sweet, generous girl, so I could do nothing. It saddened me to think what might have happened to her, given the terrible way that the barbaric Russian soldiers wreaked vengeance across the whole of their new-found empire, killing and raping during their relentless advance. To this day, I am still riddled with a certain guilt that I was unable and powerless to do anything to help her. In hindsight, maybe I should have lied and promised to marry her. They might have been lucky and located her in the Soviet satellite state, who knows. It might even have lasted. She was young, beautiful and very well educated. I was an inferior being to her in Poland, filthy, dirty and unshaven, an object of pity to her, or so I thought.

I never presumed that she would find me attractive or desirable in any way. I suppose I may have aroused the maternal instinct in her and for that I was pleased. Without doubt, Irena helped me to survive, and for that I will be eternally grateful.

I still had my photograph of Irena's and her uncle's address. Out of courtesy and a genuine desire to try to find her, I wrote to this uncle in Ireland again, updating him, asking if he had received my first letter and if he had any news as to her present whereabouts and circumstances. Some weeks later, I received a reply in which he briefly thanked me for the information with regards to his family but then launched into a bitter attack on the vile English and how they had betrayed Poland, with Churchill and Roosevelt allowing Stalin to take Poland after the war. He was not alone and thousands of Poles who had fought with the allies during the war were left feeling utterly betrayed. There was nothing else that we or the Americans could have done, except commence World War Three immediately after the defeat of Germany. I was hurt by this attack - after all, it was hardly my fault,... and what could any of us have done to stop the might of the Soviet Union? He even attacked me in person for not doing more to find her. I was incensed by his attitude and wrote a reply. In it, I vented my own anger at his response, saying how dare he attack me and anyway, what had HE done to find and help her? After all, he was her uncle, a blood relative, who had lived safely and comfortably in Ireland as a civilian during that evil and bitter war. What had he done? Absolutely nothing.

Needless to say, I never heard from him again.

The weeks passed and the more I saw of Herr Dockendorf, the more I grew to loathe him and the more comical he became.

Once a week, the local Nazi Brown Shirts held their meetings for the party faithful and Herr Dockendorf was very faithful. It was mid-summer and I happened to be in the outhouse collecting some tools. I was facing the door when I noticed movement in the house. At the back was a long conservatory stretching almost the whole width of the building. Inside there were two big, comfortable armchairs, one for each of the Dockendorfs. By one of the chairs stood a full-length free-standing mirror mounted on a frame that was centrally pivoted, so that it could swivel both up and down. Inside I could see Dockendorf. He was dressed in his full Nazi military uniform, peaked cap with

305

emblem, brown shirt, tie and red armband with a black swastika in a white circle, his huge, wide brown riding breeches held up with a Sam Brown type belt. On his feet, his big, shiny, knee-length leather boots completed the ridiculous ensemble. Bearing in mind that this overweight comedian wore the silly dictator's moustache, albeit on the ginger side, he looked positively hilarious.

Because he was a Germanic Pole, I suppose he had to appear and act even more German than a true German in order to emphasise his commitment to the Fatherland and to the party. To this day, I still laugh out loud as I recall the incident.

I watched from the safety of the outhouse as he walked over to the full-length mirror and presented himself to it, totally unaware that I was watching. He posed and postured as he turned to examine himself from every angle, adjusting his clothing continuously before deciding that he was perfect. He was a magnificently insipid and bloated buffoon. Finally he stood upright facing the mirror, watching himself as he gave a perfect Nazi salute to his own reflection. With a click of his heels he marched out through the front door. I assumed that he was off to attend the meeting.

The comedy was over so I returned to my many tasks. Four to five hours later, I became aware of the distant sound of someone singing, but on reflection, 'noise' would perhaps be a better description of what I heard. The realisation that somewhere in the distance a drunk was making a dreadful attempt at singing patriotic German military marching songs brought my smile back. As it got closer I suspected that the second instalment of the comedy was about to begin so I hid in the shadows of the outhouse and prepared myself accordingly. It was Dockendorf, returning home, very much the worse for drink. Quite simply he was as 'pissed as a fart' and as 'drunk as a skunk'. I questioned how he had managed to make it home. He eventually appeared, staggered around to the back of the house and lurched forward up the steps into his conservatory. With the doors left wide open, he flopped into his armchair. He then proceeded to belch loudly and forcefully a few times before collecting himself and bellowing at the top of his voice for his beloved.

"Frau!" he cried, and waited a moment for her to answer.

"Frau!" he bellowed once more, "come here".

In German society, as in many others at the time, the female was generally regarded as inferior to the male and Dockendorf treated his wife accordingly. You might not be surprised to learn that I had no sympathy for his sow. When Frau Dockendorf eventually emerged from the back of the house, he summoned her forward with his hand in an impatient manner whilst raising one of his boots into the air. She knew the procedure. She turned her considerable backside towards his face, straddled his leg and took hold of his boot in both her hands. He then raised his other boot and placed its sole onto her ample posterior before pushing against her big fat buttocks as she attempted to pull his boot off. Eventually there was an almighty burst of movement as the Frau was launched head first across to the other side of the room, boot in hand.

By now, I was in hysterics and having great difficulty trying to stifle the noise with my hand. The show did not disappoint. After repeating the process with the other boot, Dockendorf dismissed her in the same disparaging manner with which he had summoned her. Once more alone, he appeared to belch before settling back in his chair, whereupon he fell into a deep, drunken stupor, snoring like the ginger pig that he really was. (At this stage, I need to apologise to the true Polish pigs for insulting such a wonderful, intelligent breed of animal.)

I nearly wet myself with laughter. As soon as I returned to camp, I related the tale to my friends whilst repeating my hysterics all over again, with my audience joining in.

Every day I would start my labours with a visit to his newly-painted barn. It was sizeable and split into two halves by a simple length of fencing. On one side, the side I had to keep in order, Dockendorf kept most of his tools - picks and shovels and dry building materials such a wood, sand and cement. On the other side, he kept two great big fat pigs, which I suspected of being black market animals. The pigs were the spitting image of Dockendorf and they could have all come from the same litter. Twice a day, Frau would feed them with swill from the kitchen and later in the year, as Christmas approached, she increased their meals to three or four times a day. In my state of hunger, I was often tempted to taste the fine-smelling swill.

The following week, I was fortunate to see the whole absurd saga of Dockendorf preparing for his meeting - and his return. On this occasion, Dockendorf appeared to have had his usual vast quantity of alcohol as I watched his approach from the shelter of the barn. This time he made a zig-zagging beeline towards me instead of his usual arm chair. He did well to make it that far without falling flat on his fat Nazi face. He didn't even notice me in the shadows as he staggered through the door, taking hold of its frame to steady himself. Once composed, he lurched himself forward towards his brothers, the two pigs. He was swaying gently from side to side, having to steady himself on the rickety fence. Without warning he started to bellow at the two inoffensive animals for no apparent reason, save that he was absolutely pissed.

In almost incoherent German, he bellowed, "forward, forward," and "Left, right, left, keep going men, forward."

It was as if he was commanding his own army into battle. Soon his screaming reached fever pitch, ranting and raving at the poor beasts. He even managed to lift his leg through the railings of the fence, enabling him to land a hefty kick on the backside of one unfortunate beast that refused to obey his ramblings. But there was a snort of rebellion in the ranks as one of the pigs refused to stand his ground and take another kicking. He retreated from the battlefield. Dockendorf's boot missed the pig but his leg continued moving upwards. The idiot lost his precarious balance and fell backwards, hitting his large head on the dirt floor. I had to cover my mouth in order to stifle my joyous laughter. He lay there for a while, momentarily stunned, so I took my chance to sneak out and leave him to his headache. It was madness but brilliantly funny.

~ COATS AVAILABLE ~
ONLY ONE PREVIOUS DEAD OWNER
Autumn 1941

Days and months,... what relevance were they to us wretched prisoners? We had no calendars, no special occasions to look forward to and no change of routine, for what need had we of the precise passage of time and similar trappings of 20th century living?

I left the claustrophobic confinement of the camp each day and found myself looking around at nature's own more beautiful country calendar. I had watched the bare, skeletal arms of noble trees slowly push out their new buds of vibrant growth, eventually turning to the lush green leaves of summer, then watched as their canopies changed to glorious shades of yellow, orange and golden brown. Autumnal winds would start to blow, at first gently, gusting in from the east with that edge to them that was but a foretaste of winter's knife that would soon cut everything to the quick. Now was the start of autumn's own spectacular ticker tape display and often we would march in the thick of the parade. Memories of my first winter in the camp a year earlier came creeping back to me as I turned up the collar of my tunic against that chill wind. How I hated the cold above all else.

Back at the camp, it was morning parade. It was a chilling start to the day and all hands were thrust deep into our trouser pockets. However, this morning in particular, turned out to be a 'good morning'. Fritz had an announcement to make and we were all ears, even if they were cold ears.

A rather jolly overweight sergeant in his early fifties addressed our assembled rabble.

"Due to the kindness of the German people, we will start to issue you with winter coats."

Even though he was German, I could have kissed him. Coats,... and about time too. My grin stretched from ear to ear as I turned to share my joy with Freddy standing next to me. The smiles were everywhere to be seen.

Sure enough, over the next few days, those of us who did not possess a coat were issued with one. Unfortunately, they were not standard issue British Army greatcoats, which were made of good quality wool and lined inside. Instead, we were being issued with Polish or Russian Army coats, probably captured in bulk from stores and depots overrun during the German 'blitzkrieg'. The coats turned out to be of a much poorer quality than ours, paper thin by comparison, offering little protection against the harsh winter that was soon to follow. Many were second-hand and some bore the marks of battle, torn round holes with corresponding stains on the inside, but at least they were coats and were better than nothing, so I was grateful.

· · · § · · ·

~ OFFICERS SPOTTED ~
Autumn 1941

Johnny and I were sitting on the ground sharing a rare item together, an amazing, sweet-tasting real British cigarette, one of ten that I had acquired in a recent deal. We were both daydreaming, looking across the parade ground and the countryside beyond the wire, when we both caught sight of movement on the outside. We watched as a group of men walked towards us. We called over to the others and within seconds, a crowd had gathered in front of the wire, toes just behind the 'Dead Line'". Within minutes we could see their British uniforms as the twenty or so Officers strolled casually into view. They were on their own and free to roam.

"Hallo ducky, give us a kiss," shouted someone.

That was enough to open the flood gates. Before long we were a mass of baying beasts.

"Wooo!, don't they look nice."

"Got any food mate, any ciggies?"

"Look at those faggots, don't they look lovely."

"Done any work lately General?"

"Take it easy girls, wouldn't like to see your clothes get all filthy."

"Piss off back to your cosy beds," followed by wolf whistles and cat calls until all was drowned out by laughter.

One of them had the courage to look towards us, but all too soon they passed on by and sauntered off on their Sunday morning jaunt, disappearing in the direction from whence they came. As you can tell, our respect for our Officer Corps who had rushed us into captivity was still hovering above zero.

Intrigued, we spoke to one of the more friendly guards, who informed us that there was an Officer's camp nearby.

> *British Officers were allowed to leave camp of their own will, free to walk about unescorted. This was allowed by the Germans IF they gave their word not to escape. If any of them did try, the consequences were that this freedom would be withdrawn from them all.*

We all knew that captured British Officers were not expected to demean themselves by working like us, the common soldier, but I was bemused to discover that they were allowed to retain the services of their 'Batman' to help. If they didn't have one, then one was appointed, chosen from us lot. In the confines of camp and with all the time in the world at their disposal, I was not quite sure what they needed 'help' with, and perhaps it was best not to ask. Unbelievably, these privileged elite Officers were able to write home to their banks and pay for food, clothing and goods to be sent to them in camp.

~ RED CROSS INSPECTION ~
Stalag XXB Malbork (Marienburg) Visitation 19th Sep 1941

We had another visit from the Red Cross today after being briefed as to how we were to behave.

Author: Again, I have only included the report's conclusion here. The full text translation can be seen on page 591.

† *Report Conclusions:*
The representant of the prisoners together with the camp doctor state that Stalag XXB is a bad camp.

1) Over 50 % of the British prisoners do not have English uniforms, besides they have only one outfit - this also applies to the members of the work teams.

2) Over 50% have shoes in a very bad state.

3) No showers or installation for disinfection in the camp.

4) The number of beds in the sick room is insufficient.

5) The meeting rooms are too small.

6) The library is too poor, short of books, there is no football, and there are too small a number of board games.

7) The prisoners on the work teams work for too many hours.

8) Treatment of the prisoners on the work teams is often very bad.

9) NCOs were imprisoned because of refusal to work.

10) Soldier's pay is paid irregularly. †

---

† *Source: The Geneva International Red Cross Archives.*

~ THE 'UNTERMENSCH' ~
November 1941

Autumn did what it always did and turned into another dreaded winter. Today was an exceptional day because it wasn't raining for a change. The mud was still ankle deep, which made my walk to one of the other huts precarious to say the least. During the previous month, our camp had witnessed the arrival of bands of ragged, wretched prisoners. Several hundred at a time had been appearing during the autumn rains, accompanied by rifle-wielding guards and ferocious, baying Alsatians continually snapping at the prisoners, with the guards unable or unwilling to control them. They did not march in but merely crept and skulked along the muddy track until beaten and clubbed into more rapid movement. They were not allowed to join us in the 'relative luxury' of our section of the camp, for these poor men were the Untermensch, a heading that covered Jews, Slavs, Russians, Blacks, Indians, Gypsies, etc., or, more simply put, non-Aryans.

These particular new arrivals were just some of the millions of Soviet prisoners of war destined to receive the most appalling treatment that the Nazi state had to offer. Unfortunately for them, they were housed in our old, horrific earth huts.

As I neared their section of the camp, I looked through the two layers of wire that separated us from them. The new intake were herded into a confined area for counting and processing followed by another smaller one. Several armed guards accompanied the four pairs of Russians, each pair half carrying and half dragging four large barrels between them. The barbed wire gates were shut behind them as they made their way to the centre of the compound. At the instruction of a German, the Russians tipped the contents out onto the sodden ground and withdrew. This was the signal for the inmates to dash and slide forward and fight for the rotting scraps, the vegetable peelings and leftovers from the guard's dustbins that would normally have been offered to pigs. Only the fittest managed to secure even this insufficient waste from the German dustbins. I was appalled that men could treat other humans in this way. These emaciated beings were dressed in what remained of their uniforms and a collection of whatever rags they could muster. Some wore what remained of their inadequate boots or tattered shoes whilst others had to make do with rags wrapped around their suffering feet. They were pitiful and I thanked God for our 'preferential' treatment.

~ THE BEST OF NEWS - AMERICA'S IN ~
8th December 1941

As I returned to camp on that early December's evening, my friends told me that Sammy had been round earlier with both awful and good news. Apparently, Japan had launched an astonishing attack on an American naval base in the Pacific, a place called Pearl Harbour, news that had shocked America and the world. Having taking them completely by surprise, the raid was being described as unprovoked and cowardly. Roosevelt had spoken from America and his speech had been broadcast on the BBC World Service.

Not surprisingly, the following day, Roosevelt responded by declaring war on Japan.

Inside the camp, it came as no surprise to discover that it was the main topic of conversation. Speculation was rife that now America was at war with Japan it would somehow speed up our release. I was not so convinced by their arguments, so I delayed packing my bags for home.

Four days had passed. I had just walked into to my hut after another gentle day's graft at the Dockendorfs. I sat on the end of my 'sleeping shelf', chatting aimlessly at anybody who would listen and smoked one of Irena's cigarettes. It was wonderful. My head was spinning as I inhaled deeply. I lay back fully, savouring each wonderful draw of tobacco.

I was disturbed by a crash as the door flung open, smashing against the wall. It was little Sammy Newton, accompanied by an ice cold wind. He came running in as though his backside was on fire.

"Here comes Sammy!" came the instant melodic response, followed by another.

"Shut the bloody door!" cried Bert in the next bunk, less enthused by his appearance.

Sammy could barely control himself. He looked as though he needed to speak in order not to explode.

"News chaps, big news," he said, his eyes alight.

Without speaking another word, he walked down the centre aisle. The noise of his boots echoed on the bare boards. He was waiting for everybody to stop what they were doing and take notice, but could only contain himself for a moment.

"Listen up," he said sharply, as he reached the middle of our hut.

He waited, purposefully delaying his delivery for added effect, almost milking the tension as all eyes turned to him. Sammy seemed more persistent than usual and by now even I was actually getting impatient to hear what he had to say.

"Christ Sammy, get on with it for God's sake or we will find ourselves another reporter."

Sammy was getting good at this, relishing his role as the spreader of both good and bad tidings. After clearing his throat, he finally spoke. His timing could not have been better.

"Germany has declared war on America and America has done likewise. They're in boys, they're in."

The atmosphere was electric. People stood up and cheered, thumping each other on the back. We wanted to know more and he now had our undivided attention.

"About time," I muttered softly to myself whilst nodding my head, genuinely relieved and pleased. "About time."

Things were happening at a pace across the globe. After the sad news of Japan's attack on the American fleet, this latest news now ensured that it truly was a global war. No prizes for guessing what was the only topic of conversation. With both America and Russia in the war, we must now be assured of winning, weren't we? I finally allowed myself to dream of home, but in an instant put the thought to the back of my mind. It all seemed too much to hope for and we still had to be liberated from the heart of war-torn Europe, so once more I delayed packing my bags.

In the wider arena everything now changed, but for us, stuck in Poland, nothing changed. I continued to work at the Dockendorfs whilst the guards 'appeared' to be more miserable, but that was always a difficult one to gauge. Our food continued to leave us starving and Poland continued to get colder. Yep! Nothing had changed.

Herr Dockendorf kindly did his very best to keep me entertained once a week, returning from his party meetings in his usual inebriated state. The pigs were looking more and more like him as they grew fatter with every passing day, but I did feel sorry for them as they continued to receive a kicking if they did not parade properly or complete their manoeuvres as ordered by the very wobbly General Dockendorf, Fat Controller of Rail Maintenance in the Marienburg District of Prussia.

Unfortunately for the pigs, the manoeuvres all came to an abrupt end one very cold winter's day, when someone came to call. It was mid-December, about a week before Christmas. I watched him arrive from the corner of the house in his old, rusty, dented van that skidded along the ice-covered road. The door opened and the visitor emerged carrying a bag in his left hand as he struggled to remain upright on the icy path. The visitor knocked on the front door, to be greeted by Herr Dockendorf. Not even taking the trouble to invite the visitor in, Dockendorf picked up his coat and clambered into it ponderously. He closed the door behind him and led the way round to the back yard. I turned and walked away as they came towards me. I picked up a broom quickly and pretended to be busy brushing the sand into an even neater pile. I liked things to be shipshape,... when it suited me.

He ignoring me, as he always did, and the two of them made their way to the pig pen at the other end of the barn and leant over the sty's fence. They proceeded to chat over the heads of Dockendorf's relatives, probably planning something dark and dastardly. Eventually, I was summoned over to the pen by Dockendorf as he, in turn, walked over to the back wall of the barn. Leaning against a pile of planks was a large, wooden, trough-like object with two handles at both ends. It resembled an army field stretcher in many ways but instead of canvas, a shallow wooden trough was fixed. I had always noticed it but had never been unable to fathom its use.

Dockendorf opened the makeshift gate and we all entered the pigs' pen in turn, with me following on behind as always, to show my place in the hierarchy of the Dockendorf homestead. The swine seemed quite at ease with the two additional pigs and myself in their home. Dockendorf placed the handled trough onto the straw-covered floor. At this point I had my suspicions that this visitor to Dockendorf's home was in fact a butcher. From his bag he produced a heavy, gruesome-looking sledgehammer with a dark stained handle. I had a very good idea as to what was going to happen next, but I thought I had better keep my mouth shut in order not to warn the pigs as to their fate. The barn was beginning to resemble a scene from a horror film. There then followed a commotion as the butcher and I tried to grab one of the now very suspicious pigs as it appeared to sense that the butcher wanted to test out the hardness of his sledgehammer on his head. Suddenly all was uproar and chaos. I do not know if we had grabbed Pinky or Perky, but the first one was soon under the combined control of the two of us. The butcher raised his hammer high above his head and brought it crashing down onto the crown of the poor, defenceless swine. It gave an almighty screech as it dropped like a stone, but the blow had only stunned the pig. I was ordered to take a pair of legs whilst the butcher took the other two and we lifted the huge porky bulk onto the handled trough, which took some effort. With the animal still twitching uncontrollably, the butcher pulled a long knife from his bag, bent down and slit its throat. Deep red lifeblood pulsated from the wound, but all was carefully contained in the purpose-made wooden trough. The pig, slowly drained of its vital fluid, ceased moving altogether and died in front of us. As I stood over the carcass I smelt the sweet, sickly odour of fresh blood as the steam rose from it in the cold winter air.

I imagined Dockendorf lying there in its place and grinned.

Nothing of this pig was going to be wasted. The last drops of blood were drained and then poured from the trough into a bucket to be used by the Frau in the making of her sausages and black puddings.

By now, the second pig was understandably frantic and it took all three of us to overwhelm it. Within minutes, it suffered the same ignominious death. It didn't take long for both carcasses to be reduced to various, more manageable portions of meat, whilst the interior of the barn smelt like the slaughterhouse that it had now become. I carried most of the meat into the kitchen where Frau, the butcher and I salted it and placed it into wooden barrels for storage over the winter period. I don't know why, but somehow I doubted whether I would be getting my share of pork, despite all my help.

The considerable amount of meat that still remained was taken away by the butcher, as his payment or to sell?

A few days later, I was summoned to the kitchen by Frau Dockendorf. I had been working hard lugging heavy timbers across the yard and loading them onto a truck. The snow lay heavily on the ground all around the property and my efforts at removing it from the yard were still paying off, but if the falls got any heavier I was sure to lose the battle with nature. In spite of the cold, I was hot with the exertion. When I got to the door, the Frau ordered me to follow her. Inside, a fire was blazing away and the room felt stifling by comparison as I began to sweat even more profusely. In the middle of the room was the huge, heavy, old pine kitchen table. On it was a large industrial-size mincing machine, just like the ones I had seen in my local butcher's shop at home. Piled up by its side was a mountain of meat off-cuts, all that remained of Pinky and Perky. The Frau ordered me to start mincing, so I washed my dirty hands as best I could in the greasy water standing in the sink before flapping my hands about in order to dry them. I stuffed the meat into the machine, grabbed the large handle and turned it. Within minutes, the sweat was beginning to pour down my face. Within half an hour, my clothes were soaked with my arms no longer feeling a part of my body.

Just then, the door opened and the charming Irena walked into the kitchen, looking sweet and pure. Out of the corner of my eye, I saw the Frau signal to Irena, pointing to the back of her neck and then to me. So much sweat was pouring down my neck, leaving clean rivulets of flesh exposed on my dirty skin. I was so utterly embarrassed. Given how much crap I had endured as a prisoner and how low my spirits had sunk in the past, it surprised me to find that I was still capable of such deep embarrassment as this. I felt like a dirty, naked animal in front of my queen, less than human, a pathetic figure of fun in a foreign land.

As I finished off the last of the mincing, Irena returned to the kitchen once more and discreetly handed me a small bar of used soap, which was so kind but, in a way, made me feel even more humiliated.

When I returned to camp that night, I couldn't get the incident out of my head replaying it over and over again, feeling low, dirty and humiliated as never before. Somehow, standing in the presence of a beautiful young being like Irena seemed to sharpen the contrast between us, female and male, clean and unclean, free and captive, hope and without hope.

~ BITTER PUNISHMENT ~

Having finished my daily toil for the Polish Nazi pig and his sow, I joined Bert, Jimmy and Johnny and the others for the march back to camp. I blew into my cold, sore and chapped hands and rubbed them together and tried to put the indignity of the incident behind me.

"I heard something metallic drop on the ground today," I said, "I think it was one of my balls."

"Probably over using them Mar, so it's probably for the best."

We all laughed.

"These bloody coats are useless," complained Bert, as he pulled at the thin, greyish garment and he was right, they were.

"And remind me again gang, why the hell did I throw my greatcoat away?" For the umpteenth time, I had to ask for it was cathartic for me in the circumstances.

"Bars of chocolate, you greedy sod?" added Jimmy with a snigger.

"Hmmm!" I replied. "A few minutes of indulgence, stuffing my face with lovely, sweet, glorious, smooth milk chocolate that slowly melts in your mouth, fills your stomach and makes you smile... or a thick woollen army coat to stop me losing my manhood. Tough decision, really tough."

In spite of my sarcastic tone, at this precise moment in time, it still would have been a difficult choice for I dreamt of both food like chocolate and heat for my wretched body.

As we entered the snow-covered camp, we saw a British PoW ahead just inside the main gate, standing to attention in the freezing cold. I did not hear the offence or sentence being read out at morning parade, so this must have been a purely arbitrary punishment. Neither did I recognise the victim, for it was impossible to know every one of the thousands incarcerated inside our slave camp. As soon as I got back inside my hut, I was told that his heinous crime had been not saluting a German NCO. In the British Army, it is not necessary to salute ordinary ranks, only Officers, but for the Germans, even within their own Army, every senior NCO had to be saluted as a matter of course.

As we shuffled past I really pitied the poor bloke, standing in the thick snow. He was totally inappropriately dressed without a coat, and to intensify his pain and discomfort the Germans had removed his boots. He was slowly freezing to death. His eyes were shut and he was shaking uncontrollably. He had been made to stand there to attention for three hours and not allowed to move a muscle. When he did move, the sentry on guard duty screamed at him and stamped on his toes. It was pure, mindless brutality.

As I passed on by, I mumbled my chant.

"One day..."

By this time, my 22nd birthday had come and gone. There were no celebrations, no extra rations, nothing different, not even a cake from Mr. Hitler.

Two days before Christmas and we were all feeling dreadful; I hadn't even started to do my Christmas shopping!... Bert was worried about being under-dressed for the Commandant's Ball that he was sure to get invited to,... Jimmy couldn't decide which party to go to as he had so many tantalising invitations and Johnny was worried that he would not be allowed to take all his girlfriends to the Christmas Day banquet that was being held in Never Never Land!

Thank God we still had a sense of humour.

When Christmas 1941 did unceremoniously arrive the generous Germans gave us the day off work.

~ CHRISTMAS ~
LOVE AT FIRST SIGHT

There were those in the camp who were determined not to let this Christmas pass by without trying as hard as they could, to mark the festive season with some sort of celebration. They were the camp 'Entertainment Group', prompted into being by our master of ceremonies, Sergeant Major McDowell. In the never-ending search for ways of maintaining morale the camp panto was born. The show was written and rehearsed, costumes and wigs were created in the tailors' shops whilst soot from the stoves was put to good use and mascara and eye shadow were thus created. Musical instruments were acquired from somewhere, God only knows how, but I certainly would not have liked to have smuggled one of the trombones into camp tucked down my trouser leg. Unfortunately (or fortunately), I was away from camp, working at the Dockendorf's on the days they performed, but I heard they did a great job by putting on a commendable staged performance in one of the huts.

There was one person in our hut who did not want me to miss out completely and insisted on telling me every detail of the panto. His nickname was 'Nobby'. Don't ask why, but the clue's in the name.

There has always been a tradition for men to dress as women and women to dress as men in panto, but in a camp of over 10,000 men, no matter how hard we tried, no women could be found, so the show had to go on as an all-male production. Several 'ladies' wearing home-made bras, wigs and huge amounts of make-up applied with a trowel in bucketfuls, completed the illusion.

On the first night's performance, Nobby was in the audience and that's when it struck. Cupid was also present and aimed his arrow, causing Nobby to fall madly in love. Starved of female company, sent mad or just horny by his confinement, Nobby became obsessed with one particular 'lady'. He was there for every performance and began to follow 'her' everywhere. We tried to reason with him but he continued to pester 'her' every waking moment before eventually driving the poor 'lady' away. To escape his amorous advances, 'she' left the camp on the first available working party. The incident was both funny and tragic.

This first theatrical production brought to light yet another extraordinary pool of talent amongst our thousands of former fighting men; actors and performers. Like most fun events at Stalag XXB, the panto was a triumph for all involved.

· · · § · · ·

1942

STALAG XXB

The New Year came and went but I must have blinked for I missed that celebration too. There was nothing to mark its passing.

eather permitting, I worked at the Dockendorf's through the worst of that perishing Polish winter. After New Year, the snow worsened, which continued to add to our misery as there were no picture postcards with happy scenes of snowmen and toboggans. This part of Poland in 1942 was bleak beyond compare.

During January, the increasing snow started to pile up in un-clearable quantities. Fortunately, Dockendorf ordered me to stop attempting to clear it from the yard and to concentrate on forming clear passageways from the back door of the conservatory to the main barn, outhouse and to the road as these were the most frequently used routes. Using a large, flat, wooden shovel and whatever else I could find, I pushed the deep snow to both sides of my intended pathway, forming a wall on either side, thereby defining the passage. Every night, more snow would fall in abundance or the winds would blow, causing the existing snow to drift into ever-deepening patches. Every fresh fall or movements of snow determined my first job for the morning, to be repeated over and over again. Within a few days, the emerging snow walls had evolved into substantial bastions and buttresses against the Arctic conditions. Soon, the ice walls were as tall as me, and as the new winds blew throughout the winter months they did my work for me and piled up more snow on their outer sides, thickening them and protecting the passageway between. The walls had the effect of stopping new snow from building up within the two walls and provided a much-needed wind break against those agonising winds.

~ TEDIUM, TEARS, TOILET AND TOIL ~
DAY AFTER DAY AFTER DAY

Whenever I recall my experiences at Stalag XXB, it is the utter boredom of living in that prison camp that comes back to haunt me every time. Today was no different. The tedious cry awoke me to another day.

"Raus!"

The bang of a rifle butt on the hut door served to emphasise the call. Sometimes it was difficult to think positively but as my feet touched the cold floor, I somehow managed to thank providence that I had survived another night. During these freezing cold winter nights, we slept in our uniforms and coat with our blankets pulled tightly round our sleeping forms. Getting ready for roll call didn't take us long. We had only minutes to stagger onto the parade ground but if we were quick we had just enough time for a hasty visit to the open latrines. If anyone was late, they would incur the wrath of the guards and the displeasure of your fellow PoWs, for keeping us standing in the extreme cold for a moment longer than necessary was frowned upon.

To this day, whenever anybody asks me what the weather was like in Poland, I would say that they were only two variations, either bloody hot or bloody cold to the point that defies description.

I always considered myself more fortunate than others for I was outside the wire each day, mixing with others that I could trade with and acquiring life's little extras, not stagnating inside the camp and spiralling deeper down into the pit of despair. I was surviving and that is saying something.

When we first arrived, our latrines consisted of a huge open trench with a tree trunk positioned and supported each end by cross timbers. This was the toilet seat on which we all balanced. When in use, it resembled a perch with birds squatting on it.

Fortunately, there was some improvement during the summer of '41. The old latrine was filled in as it was full and was in danger of overflowing when the rains came. It was also a serious health hazard, attracting flies to the pit of human waste and excreta in plague-like proportions. But for me, it was the thought of the rats that existed and indeed thrived on and in our sea of filth. They really disgusted me so. Due to either the infinite wisdom of the Krauts or on the insistence of the International Red Cross, the Germans built a new latrine next to the old one, so we were still able to follow the old smell to find the new latrine. I say 'the Germans built', but rest assured they did not deprive us PoWs of the golden opportunity to lend a hand and thereby exercising our considerable labouring skills, for '99.9% of the occupants of the Stalags were labourers and the remainder were made up of lamp-lighters and their assistants'!

The new latrine was of a similar basic construction, but this time, a long, heavy, wooden plank replaced the shit coated tree trunk. Holes at regular intervals were strategically cut into the plank. In order to preserve a modicum of our decency, the puritanical Germans erected small 'modesty' walls between each hole and along the back. Finally a roof was added, thereby boosting the appeal of this establishment to such an extent that the prisoners would use it every day!

Unfortunately, even in the bitterness of winter, one still had to answer to the calls of nature. The modesty wall did well to protect the more demure and bashful amongst us but did little to stop those gale-force icy winds from freezing our tiny nuts off, so I tended to wait until the very last moment before pulling my trousers down and entering the 'hole'.

In all my time as a prisoner of war, I only ever seemed to pass sloppy faeces and the closest I ever got to delivering anything that remotely resembled a solid was during the harshest of winters, when the little 'jobby' would freeze on the way down before hitting the iced sewage.

Toilet paper was still conspicuously absent and we prisoners were forced to use whatever was available. Some used their hands and without anything to hand, wiped them on the walls. If you were very lucky, you might be able to beg, borrow or steal a page, a section or even a whole copy of the German newspaper Völkischer Beobachter (National Observer), readily available from all good German newsagents. The ultimate joy was to acquire a copy and then find a printed photograph of Herr Hitler. This provided one with the very best of wiping facilities, and with it a deep sense of satisfaction. When away from camp during winter, we had to rely on a handful of snow, and, in the summer, grass or leaves. Hardly ideal but needs must.

Today was cold, so one minute in the latrine was all I took.

~ PUNISHING PARADES & PLAYTIME ~

When the harshest of the winter weather struck in early January '42, it meant an end to my time at the Dockendorf's and the end of my friendship with the lovely, kind Irena. The camp went into almost total shutdown until the emergence of warmer temperatures. Occasionally we were called out to clear roads, but often, if the blizzards were too severe, even the Germans gave up on this task. However, one thing they never gave up on was calling us to morning parade. It was always a tedious affair with two counts as the norm. Often the numbers didn't tally and the count had to be repeated again and again and again until they did. It was usual for morning parades to be taken by a lowly German Feldwebel (Sergeant) before handing the proceedings over to Sergeant McDowell. It was unusual for a German Officer to attend, but with a certain regularity throughout the years punishments were announced during roll call to various poor souls. On such occasions, the Officer of the day was called upon to attend, and in the most serious of occasions, the exalted yet obscure Camp Commandant might make a rare appearance. Looking down upon the assembled PoWs before him, the Officer would read out names, reveal their dastardly crime and then the justifiable punishment that was to be administered. At each stage, he would stop and allow the interpreter to translate. The sentence usually involved a stay in the 'Punishment Block', affectionately known as 'Der Bunker'.

If there was nothing to be announced we were dismissed before descending on the cauldron of coffee and if snow permitted, we would join our work parties amid shouts of angry annoyance and intimidation from guards who were impatient to get going. Invariably their orders were answered with derision, grunts and informative instructions by us as to what they could do or where they could go, with references to their questionable parentage before culminating in a plain, old-fashioned 'F**k off Fritz!'

In the early days of our captivity, we could get away with the

'F' word, but by now they understood all to well what the phrase meant. The best you could hope to escape with was being called a 'Schweinhund!' However, if a particularly nasty guard heard you, he would remind you just how painful his rifle butt could be. If you were lucky you could dodge it; if not, you received a painful reminder of your lowly position.

After returning from work, we used the freedom that our captors allowed us to do whatever we wanted within the confines of our prison camp. Some would brave the bitter chill and walk around the camp in pairs, but often a lone figure could be seen stumbling around in the snow, knee-deep in depression and barely able to cope with the terrible burden of prison life, existing only until the kindly patron of death came to collect his willing soul.

Others chatted happily with each other, managing well. Like me, they sought humour in circumstances wherever they could as a means of surviving, grabbing what little life had to offer, thinking only of today and refusing to dwell on the horror of yesterday and the uncertainty of tomorrow.

Avid card-players spent every possible free hour engrossed in their addictive passion of gambling using insane amounts of IOU money and German playing cards, which had slightly different court cards, but otherwise, were identical.

From the very earliest of times at Stalag XXB, the ever-resourceful PoWs had established distractions to occupy their minds, pursuits such as singing, dancing photography, carving, drawing, painting, attending lectures, gymnastics or other commercial services.

As soon as the worst of the bleak winter was over, many took delight in playing football again on the central parade ground. There was no grass to play on, just a wet or frozen mess in winter and a rock-hard dust bowl in summer. I had no idea where the football came from but the goal nets were cleverly made by the prisoners themselves, 'woven' out of pieces of string collected from our parcels. I couldn't be bothered playing football or other sporty pursuits because I was utterly exhausted at the end of my working day and, I was not in the least bit interested.

At the day's end, we would queue up in a long single file to be greeted by the so-called 'cooks'. Standing in their dirty off-white aprons, they would drop a ladle full of the watery 'stuff' into your mess tin. The second would count through five men to share the loaf of bread that was handed to the first. Made from potato flour and roughly measuring 12 x 5 x 4 inches, the bread was solid and wouldn't crumble easily. We all inspected the portions very closely as it was down to you to make sure that your portion was identical to the next man's, which led to some heated disputes on many occasions. When no knife was available, one of us would use our sharpened Stalag identity disk, which eventually did the job.

Today, a nasty fight broke out as a result of one PoW running off with a whole loaf. He hoped to hide amongst the crowd already eating but was soon caught. He received a terrible beating for his selfish stupidity before the guards eventually broke up the fight, although they were in no immediate hurry to do so. Afterwards, I took my soup and ate it inside my hut in the relative warmth. Once finished, I spent what time was left talking with friends.

During the night the doors to our huts were never locked, which enabled us to pee into the strategically-placed wooden barrels. To use them, you had to stand on the steps leading up to the hut, which was OK for me as I was almost six feet in height. For the 'shorties' in the camp, it must have proved a tricky operation to say the least, unless, length-wise, you were extremely well endowed.

~ CAMP NEWSPAPERS ~
The Völkischer Beobachter

By early 1942, there were numerous sources of news, information and misinformation available to us in the camp, all of varying degrees of accuracy. Firstly, there was good, old-fashioned gossip, the most readily available source but more often wildly inaccurate and it had to be taken with a pinch of salt (that is, if we had any). Although sometimes erroneous, it was often interesting and hilarious but could also be most distressing.

Secondly, and probably the most inaccurate, was the official German newspaper the Völkischer Beobachter. This was the most widely circulated daily newspaper in Nazi Germany, with editions published in Berlin, Vienna and Munich. Naturally, the publishers only ever printed the truth,... as the Nazi party wanted their readers to see it. Once, whilst working at the marshalling yards at Marienburg, I was able to flip through a copy that one of the guards had accidentally 'mislaid'. Inside, I saw what I had always wanted to find, a picture of dear old Adolf, sitting down in a chair, actually reading a copy of the Völkischer Beobachter, thereby proving that even he read the damn thing. But there again, I suppose he would as it was owned by his party. There was nobody watching me at that time, so the newspaper quickly disappeared down into my trousers, for I had a use for it. That evening, after our watery dinner, I had occasion to use the latrine. When I finished, I took great delight in recovering my copy of the Völkischer Beobachter, tearing out the picture of Hitler and cleaning myself with it. I can assure you it was very satisfying and although it might be considered disgusting to do so, I left it stuck to the wall for all to see and enjoy.

As the Völkischer Beobachter was the mouthpiece of the Nazi Party, it was crammed full of brain-washing misinformation, which made the integrity of all its articles highly questionable. Every German battle fought was always 'A Glorious Victory for the Third Reich', and every tactical withdrawal for the Third Reich was also 'A Glorious Victory for the Third Reich'. (Their phrase 'tactical withdrawal' was actually a euphemism for 'an utter defeat'.) We all knew it was propaganda from cover to cover, but even so, it still made depressing reading for us PoWs, particularly in the early years of the war for we had precious little other information available to contradict it.

Thirdly, our camp was issued with copies of another official German newspaper, printed exclusively for the PoW camps throughout Germany and their occupied countries, the PoW Weekly. Why it was called a 'weekly' I am not sure for it was published and distributed intermittently. I believe that it was produced in several different languages - English, French, Greek, Russian and probably others. This was as equally inaccurate as the Völkischer Beobachter and bulging at the seams with propaganda. Surprisingly enough, I never did read of any German defeats, withdrawals or of Hitler's failures to 'crush the enemy' at every encounter. There was never any light relief from the relentless news speak but, as with all papers, it did have its uses!

The German guards were not adverse to a bit of gossip when in the mood and passed on news to us PoWs, but the value of such information was varied.

Information gleamed from the local Poles proved to be increasingly accurate and soul lifting.

Finally, there was dear old Sammy Newton. The news that he

supplied on a more regular basis turned out to be the most accurate, although initially we did not appreciate this.

~ A PARCEL FROM HOME ~
February 1942

When I eventually returned home to England, my mother told me that she had sent me many parcels of food, clothes and cigarettes. She could not buy and send the cigarettes to me directly but there was a method in place for doing so. She would post a request with payment to a specific department at The War Office, together with details of my name, number and PoW camp address. The department would, in turn, despatch the cigarettes to me in Poland. My favourites were Players Navy Cut, but Woodbines or Weights were more than acceptable. Unfortunately for me, like thousands of other PoWs across Europe, I rarely received them. Still, it cheered me up no end to know that some bastard, thieving German guards somewhere had smoked them and hopefully they had given the bastards terminal lung cancer.

In late February, I was lucky enough to receive a parcel directly from mother via 'McDowell's Mafia', about whom some were becoming increasingly sceptical. As the months went by, 'whispers' about missing parcels were circulating but, as far as I know, there was never any proof.

I took the parcel to my hut, sat down and opened it. It was carefully wrapped in string and brown paper, all of which I untied, unfolded and kept. Often, these items were as valuable as the contents. Inside, I found two pairs of socks and two of her knitted woollen pullovers but unfortunately no cigarettes. I was pleased and excited to receive the socks and pullovers; clothes were always well received, and even if I didn't need them, they always had a sale value inside, and more importantly, outside the camp. Amongst the items I found a little note from mum, filled with all the usual small talk from home.

I was desperate for some smokes and knew a soldier who was in need of a warm pullover so I popped out to see him. On the way, I saw that someone had built a large, round snowman with an outstretched arm as if saluting, and had stuck a Hitler moustache on it. I had to laugh. God, I loved British humour.

As I stared at the comical figure, it took me back to my childhood when I was nine years old during a cold and wonderful winter's afternoon. Thick snow greeted us when we came out from lessons after school. It was an amazing white winter wonderland and, as such, had to be celebrated with a snowball fight. Afterwards, Cyril and I took the same route back home across the covered green. Once past the smithy, we had to walk up an incline to our home at the police station. In front of the station, two brick pillars topped with large stone globes stood on both sides of the path.

During that first winter's evening covering, I built a snowball at the bottom of the slope. When it was a reasonable size I decided to take it home, and with increasing effort pushed it up the hill. As I rolled it, my snowball gathered still more snow until, puffing frantically, I reached the top and the two brick pillars. For an eight-year-old, I was suddenly faced with a huge dilemma. By this time, my snowball had grown to such a size that I was unable to push it through the gap. If I let go of the snowball, I feared that it would roll back over me and continue on down the hill at an ever-increasing speed, thereby causing untold damage to anything that got in its way.

I was stuck.

I shouted to father for help and then screamed at the top of my voice. Finally he heard my cries and came running. Immediately, he saw my predicament, quickly grabbed a shovel and rushed to my aid. In an instant, he sliced off the sides of my snowball and helped me push it through into our garden and onto the lawn. He went back to collect the chopped off pieces, using them to make a head and arms. Finally he got some small pieces of coal from the bunker. I pushed the pieces onto its face for eyes and a nose. My magnificent snowman was complete. This was one of the very few happy memories that I have of my father actually being with me and having fun!

The snowman remained on our front lawn for weeks after the snow had melted. I watched its demise until, finally, it ended up as a small patch of dirty grey slush before soaking away into the grass. All that was left were the three pieces of coal.

If only Hitler would disappear just as easily.

· · · § · · ·

~ SAD NEWS ~
Late February 1942

Towards the end of February, I heard some very sad news that had filtered back to me via a mutual friend.

Last year I had met up with a Londoner in the camp and, whilst telling his story he told me of his work on the farms where he had been the horseman. It was he who had given me the idea of 'faking' my qualifications some time later as his description of the job and the kudos that came with it really appealed to me, for it involved little work.

His name was Arthur and I believe his surname was Pearce.

He was older than me, in his mid-thirties. He worked on the London Underground and we shared a common interest in railways. I found him to be a thoroughly nice, decent chap. He had a child back in England but tragically his wife had died.

He was working on a German farm near Kwidzyn, some twenty miles south of Stalag XXB. Arthur had got into an argument with the owner who was a pig of a Prussian bully. The dispute had quickly become heated, for it was common for tempers to flare up in or outside the camp over what in normal circumstances, was a minor issue. On this occasion, the Prussian reported him to the guards. The guard sought out Arthur and shot him on the spot, at point-blank range and as a result, he died instantly. His body was brought back to camp before being buried in the local PoW cemetery in Marienburg.

However, the incident did not end there. A military inquiry ensued and both German and British witnesses were ordered to attend the court to give evidence at the regional military capital, Danzig (Gdańsk). After the court of inquiry, the German guard, who had effectively murdered Arthur was only sentenced to a derisory three months spell in prison. When I heard the outcome, we were supposed to be content with the fact that the Wehrmacht had taken the case seriously and punished him. Three months for the life of a decent Englishman.

"One day,..."

I had to pop over to see one of the guys, a chap called Willie. I never knew his second name. He didn't go out to work like I did, preferring to vegetate inside camp, as others did. Willie still had a silver lighter that had escaped the thieving hands of the German guards. He now wanted to sell it in exchange for food and had called on me to 'do a deal'. So he sent word to me. When I arrived at his hut, he was sitting at the table, doing a spot of reading from one of the books that was doing the rounds in the camp. I looked down at his feet. Willie was a skinny little chap, tough but scrawny. He only had clogs to wear as his boots had died long ago, but this did not seem to bother him too much.

"Hi Willie," I said, shaking his hand. He looked tired and I think I had caught him dozing between the pages of his book. Reading was usually only possible during daylight hours as lights out came early and the 'margarine lamps' were too weak for sustained reading.

"Hello Dennis," he said in his broad Scottish accent. "Grab a pew."

I climbed over the bench opposite him but before I had even sat down, he pleadingly asked a question.

"Have you got any bread I can buy? I'm so bloody hungry," Can't stop dreaming of the bloody stuff and it's driving me mad, morning, noon and night, food, food, food."

"Sorry Willie, whatever bread I bring in is eaten within the hour."

He searched his pockets and produced a shiny silver cigarette lighter with a flip top.

"Here, see what you can get me for this, would you?"

"What about your fags?" I replied, pointing to the lighter. "Won't you be needing that?"

"Haven't got any smokes and can't seem to get any so now seems as good a time as any to give the damn things up. Can't refill it anyway without fuel so what's the point?"

I was surprised to hear him say this as he was one of the heaviest smokers I knew. He would smoke almost anything that burnt and he was one of my best clients.

"Willie, you'll never be able to give them up. You always said to me you would prefer to starve to death than give up the ciggies. Remember,... keeps the hunger away."

He looked down at the lighter, twisting it through his fingers, watching it whilst harbouring the fond memories of a lifetime of tobacco.

"I haven't got neither smokes nor food. Toss up which is worse, the smokes or the hunger pains."

He paused for a moment, as though checking to see if that was still the case, whilst having second thoughts.

"Today, 'its the hunger pains I got. Tomorrow, who knows? War might be over by then anyway."

He handed the lighter to me and I placed it deep inside my breast pocket, which I secured with the button.

"Anyway, best you take it now and I eat the food before the bloody thing gets stolen and then I really will have bugger all."

"What do you mean?" I asked, slightly puzzled, not quite understanding the tone behind his remark. He looked straight at me and his face hardened, his previous smile having evaporated.

"Have you not heard? There's been a spate of thieving in the bloody hut. Mostly food and clothes. Some bugger stole a man's greatcoat t'other day. How low is that? Can't trust anyone. Been a terrible atmosphere in here."

"No, had no idea. Do you suspect anyone in particular?"

"Huh! We all do but can't prove it. Could be a couple. There's this guy called Harry and his mucker, 'Spanner', reckon they could be the ones."

Spanner was a hard nut, the name given to him not so much because he had been an engineering mechanic before the war but because he had a reputation for using a giant spanner in his inter-gang fights on the docks of Liverpool.

"Seen him lay into others for no apparent reason. We reckon he's running some sort'a protection business. Nobody likes 'em and they keep themselves to themselves. They never seem to be short of anything, food, smokes or clothes,... you name it, they seem to have it. No-one's seen the coat but nobody would be stupid enough to keep that hanging around. Probably already on the back of some other bloke in another hut by now. Could have been either of them, but that's the thing, can't be sure. The suspicion and not knowing is the worst,... bastards."

He nodded over to the other end of the hut but when I looked, I could only see a pair of boots sticking out of a bunk and didn't know if he was referring to his fellow PoW or the empty space on either side of him.

"Has anybody said anything to McDowell?" I asked, "if all else fails, he's your man."

"Yer, I know, but I think Tommy Lapherton may have already done so, as we can't find out who the bastard is."

Willie and I continued chatting for a while longer before I took my leave. It was always good to catch up with whatever was happening in the camp, but on hearing this news it just hardened my resolve to get out onto another work party as soon as I could. Stalag incarceration was not for me for any length of time. It was just too depressing.

Two days later, I had his food, a loaf of bread and a tin of meat. I popped over to him in his hut and passed them over. He gave me my share so we were both happy. Willie immediately took a bite off the loaf before continuing.

"If you'd come and asked me today what I wanted, smokes or food, today it would be smokes." He grinned and chewed.

I sat down whilst he continued. He wanted to talk, that I could tell, come to think of it, he always wanted to. He was a good man with an easy manner.

"Remember what I were saying other day,... about the thieving?"

"Yes, I remember. Did McDowell find out who it was?" I enquired, quickly looking around me, aware of the sensitivity of the subject.

"Appears we were right after all." Willie leaned forward and lowered his voice a little.

"Who was it then?" I enquired.

"Bastard turned out to be Spanner, big guy from Liverpool, or so we think."

He then went on to relate the full story.

"Do you remember yesterday at roll call, we were there for hours as they couldn't get the bloody numbers right. Turns out there was one missing." Willie paused, looking straight at me.

"Spanner?" I asked.

Willie nodded. "Couldn't find him anywhere. Jerrys came in here and looked through his bunk and then tore the place apart. Everything out the window. Bloody mess. God knows what's gone missing now."

He caught his breath before continuing.

"They'll be out there now, scouring the countryside looking for him. Reckon he's done a runner." He paused once more.

"Word is, they won't find him."

"What do you mean, why won't they?" I was really intrigued by now.

Willie smile broadened.

"He's minced meat by now, so goes the rumour. McDowell and his lads paid Spanner a visit. Seems he was not too co-operative at first, needed a bit of persuasion. Anyway, bloke got his coat back and some of the lads have got their fags and other bits back, so I guess McDowell got the right answers to the right questions after all... and from the right guy."

"So where is Spanner now?" My turn to pause and wait. Willie just looked at me with a blank stare.

"Where are they holding him Willie?"

On reflection, my question was naive. Slowly Willie smiled.

"Seems he was into all sorts. There was talk of him being very chummy with the Jerrys as well."

"But where are they keeping him?" was my only reply. "They can't keep him hidden forever."

"Won't need to," replied Willie.

Willie sat back, grinned once more, put his hands behind his head and stretched.

"Willie, stop pissing around and just tell me. What the hell have they done with him?" I was keen to get back, for I had some ciggies to collect and Willie seemed to be drawing out his story to maximise the drama, and he was succeeding. He didn't stop smiling and leaned forward again, folding his arms on the table.

"Nothing is for sure you understand, it's just talk."

He looked furtively around him and edged even closer.

"Word is they killed him and cut him. He's now in bits. Probably in the bottom of the latrines by now, in amongst the shit,... food for the rats."

Willie closed his mouth and just sat there.

"Bastard deserved it. Whoever it was did the right thing. I for one won't lose any sleep over him."

I left and walked back to my hut to join Johnny and the others. I hurriedly picked up the supply of ciggies for my next trade, eager to get back and enjoy the deliciously sweet English tobacco I had been without for too long.

As I crossed the parade ground, I felt the cold wind and thought of all the things that I had heard about McDowell and his gang. If it was true and Spanner did commit the crimes, I believed that the retribution dished out was justified. McDowell did seem to investigate issues when they were reported to him. Ultimately, there was nobody else to turn to. He was the camp leader and the closest thing we had to an allied police force. Conditions in the camp were tough. He was tough. Living at Stalag XXB was tough. Life was tough for us all, so it came as no surprise that the punishments had to be tough.

Nobody would shed a tear for a louse like him. Being guilty of theft was the bad enough, but a thieving turncoat collaborator?

If Spanner was a thief and in cahoots with the Germans, then the Jerrys would do nothing to stop him stealing from his fellows. These internal petty crimes were of no concern to them. I certainly couldn't see them searching through the tons of piss, shit and vomit in the bottom of the latrines, so the whole issue would probably die a natural death, eventually, but not before the Germans had wasted hundreds of military man hours scouring the countryside for the alleged escaped prisoner. At least in death, Spanner was of some small use to the war effort.

Next time I saw Willie, he told me that Spanner's mate Harry, the other suspect in his hut, had since gone. Once Spanner disappeared, it seemed he felt threatened and isolated for some reason and volunteered for some outside job.

The strange thing was their hut never suffered with a single case of theft again!

~ FIRST FARM ~
March 1942

I suppose that somewhere, out there amongst the dreary dampness that drifted in heavy waves from the river, there might have been a distant promise of spring threatening to replace the torment of winter,... but I couldn't see it.

More 'volunteers' were needed to work outside the camp once more and I didn't need to be asked twice. Camp existence was what I dreaded so I jumped at the opportunity of leaving it all behind, taking whatever the outside world had to offer, which was always more than what was on offer in our God-forsaken dump. Last year, I worked on the coal wagons, rail maintenance, painting and as yard master to Hitler's sycophantic disciple, Herr Dockendorf. This year was to start off with something new. I was to become a farm labourer.

After morning parade, I emptied my bedroom, collected all my worldly goods, packed my suitcase, said goodbye to all my family and friends, ate a hearty, farewell breakfast and waited for transportation to whisk me away to some heavenly location.

Unfortunately for me, 'fairyland' had also been invaded so my aspirations were no longer being granted and reality prevailed. Instead, I visited the latrines. My God, even in the depths of winter they stank. I was so cold. When I dropped my trousers, the chill hit me and I didn't linger longer than was absolutely necessary. I dashed back to my bunk to pick up a couple of pathetically small personal items and joined the squad already beginning to form just inside the gate for our march to wherever. Freddy and my old bunch of mates from 'The Queen's had all been sent away on another work detail whilst I stayed with my newish mates, Bert, Jimmy and Johnny.

We marched for two days, losing a few of our numbers at several farms along the way, where they were to be usefully employed digging for a German victory. We stopped for the night at a farm somewhere in the bleak Polish countryside, saving us from the horror of sleeping in the open. As was often the case, we were not given food and were locked inside a filthy pig sty for the first night. Fortunately, the pigs did not object too much to our smell. My unhappiness with our foul accommodation was tempered in the knowledge that at least our guards were spending a comfortable night in the warmth of the farmhouse.

We arrived at our destination late the following day, another farm in the middle of nowhere. By now we were ravenous and were fed well by the farm owner, a man in his fifties.

That night, I slept really well for we spent a more comfortable night locked in his large wooden barn. The following morning, I awoke to the usual aggressive rant for us to 'rise'. With acorn coffee and bread in our protesting guts, we assembled in front of our overseer and farm owner.

Both immediately walked amongst us and looked us up and down, examining us. I couldn't believe it. This was like a cattle market and we were the cattle. Presumably, if they liked the look of you and thought that you were capable of giving a good day's work, they chose you. I passed the visual test and became one of the chosen ones. Those rejected were sent away, back to camp I suppose.

Then came a question, in Polish.

"Who is the horseman?" This enquiry fell on deaf ears as usual, so he asked the same question again, this time in German.

As was normal, dumb insolence from us brought the usual abuse.

"English pigs!" was the guard's automatic response.

In an unashamed gesture designed to ingratiate myself with this important provider of food, but without any desire to enhance my own worth and secure more succour, I decided to assist the arse and offer my assistance as 'the interpreter'.

"He wishes to know which of you fine upstanding gentlemen

happens to be the horseman. Please indulge me and come hither to reveal yourself," I said as they all turned to face me.

Immediately, one of our number raised a hand in response.

"That will be me."

He was a short, stocky little Yorkshireman who had worked on the land all his life and was used to dealing with horses. His hands were enormous and covered with calluses through years of hard graft.

In order to prove my worth as 'the interpreter', I spoke the obvious and pointed.

"Here,... here is the horseman."

He was ordered to step forward and disappeared into the nearby stables. As for the rest of us, we were marched along mud tracks to a field where we were told to plant piles of seed potatoes. It was back-breaking work and we toiled all day until darkness descended and the last potato was taken from the wagon and laid to rest. That done, we climbed aboard and rode back to the farm in luxurious style. Our two escorts sat on the front bench with the Yorkshireman. Both seemed pleasant enough (for Germans). With work over, we were in high spirits.

Each and every day, the Yorkshireman sat on his backside, never lifting a finger whilst we continued with our planting. His job was regarded as skilled and, as such, he was not required to toil like us.

"Lucky bastard," I muttered to my workmates every time I saw him, whilst secretly envying him and his job. I logged the details of his covetous position into the recesses of my mind.

My eyes were everywhere, seeing what I could learn that could be my advantage in the future whilst always looking for 'things to borrow'. There was a saying in our camp that equally applied to any place that my fellow PoWs ever visited, I am sure: 'If it wasn't nailed down, it was thieved.' I did my utmost to keep that saying true to its core.

Although it was early March and the weather was supposed to be getting warmer, it didn't feel like it. We had been working on the farm for a week. This particular morning, the wind was blowing straight from the north-east, and it was painful. I was wearing my newly-issued Polish Army coat whilst our motley collection of PoWs were wearing the same or the Russian version, but neither could compare to the British coat. However, I concluded that the men who had previously worn them must have been stoic to have survived the bitter winter temperatures in them.

One of our two guards had proved himself to be reasonable and relatively fair and good-natured. His name was Tony and we called him 'German Tony'. My improved German vocabulary enabled me to piece together his story. After the French surrender, German Tony had been posted to France, and like many of the German troops he initially got on well with the local Parisians where he was billeted. According to him, there was little animosity immediately following the swift defeat of France. The slaughter on the battlefields of the last war had not materialised, Paris had been spared destruction and resentment and hatred had not yet sunk in. The resistance movement had not had time to organise itself into a viable force and most of the population were grateful that they had been spared and were relatively happy to befriend, or at least tolerate, their new Germanic masters.

Whilst undergoing his tour of duty, German Tony met a young French girl, fell in love and married her shortly after. Such close fraternisation was not altogether unusual. When he was eventually posted back to Germany, he took her with him. At this particular point, whilst he was relating the more wonderful aspects of his love-making, I found it difficult to concentrate on what he was saying, for he was smoking. Even though it was German tobacco and not a patch on ours, the beautiful smell of his cigarette was wafting past my rapidly inhaling nostrils. I moved towards him, trying to catch every exhaled waft of smoke and nicotine. Any closer and I would be kissing him. He reached into his trouser as I prepared myself, excitingly expecting him to offer me one. From his pocket, he pulled out his wallet and opened it to reveal a picture of his very pretty young wife. He smiled and was momentarily lost in the beauty of her countenance and the memory of her young body. Personally, I couldn't give a toss but tried to hide my disappointment, my mind concentrating solely on his rapidly diminishing cigarette, but on reflection, I did think her worthy of a dalliance. By the time he had replaced his wallet, he had smoked most of it. He looked at me, and passed me the other half to finish.

"Thank you very much," I said, "Thanks."

German Tony was no different from any of us, save for the fact that he was on the winning side. As a fellow soldier, he respected us and bore us no grudge for he knew we were only doing what we had to do, just like him - fighting for one's country. His philosophy was that we were all here in this hell hole together, bored and miserable, far away from home and our loved ones and with no control over our own destiny, so we'd better just get along together as best we could and make the most of a bad situation.

"You play balls with me and I will play balls with you," he loved to say, whilst we sniggered like school kids at his pluralisation of his reproductive glands. Two days later, we were still 'playing balls' and burying bloody potatoes in the cold, soggy ground. By now, we had established a working pattern with German Tony. As soon as we started our labours, he would allow us to keep our coats on for the first hour. After that, he would give the order for their removal. But a few days later our friendship was perilously stretched to breaking point. On this particular bum-numbing day, his order was ignored.

"Coats off, NOW!" he barked in a slightly raised voice.

Murmurs of 'F*** him' could be heard amongst our group as we chuckled to ourselves, continuing to ignore his increasingly impatient demands, working on regardless. I was standing close by and as I was the interpreter, he aggressively beckoned me over to him. I could see the rage on his face quickly developing. He was no longer the nice German Tony that we had come to know. .

"If they do not take their coats off now, I will shoot."
As he spoke he unslung his rifle, and holding it in both hands he raised the barrel and pointed it at my chest.

"Look lads," I said in a serious voice, "take your coats off."

Nothing. The lads were still ignoring the order as I heard the familiar click of metal on metal as he released the safety catch. I froze on the spot and my eyes followed the sound.

German Tony had withdrawn the bolt of his rifle, picked up the next bullet, re-engaged the bolt, pushed it into the chamber of the rifle and was ready to fire. A situation that had begun as a bit of a joke was no longer funny and was dangerously escalating out of control.

"I will count to five, then I will shoot you," was all he said to me. Swallowing hard, I panicked at being five seconds away from witnessing the end of my very short life.

"One..."

Shit, I thought.

"Two..."

My heart was racing and it kick-started me into action.

"For Christ's sake!" I screamed, frantically beginning to unbutton my coat. "Take your f***ing coats off. He's going to shoot me!"

Hitler could have heard me in Berlin

"Three..."

My coat was already on the ground. By the time he got to 'four', all nineteen coats had followed. He had easily won. Finally satisfied with his small victory, German Tony released the bolt and returned his rifle to its shouldered position... and we resumed our work. On that bitter day, we had dared to cross the Rubicon and as a consequence, his attitude towards us was never quite the same.

By the middle of March, the harsh winter was finally over but some snow remained, clinging stubbornly to the sheltered shadows, resisting to the bitter end before finally giving up the fight and soaking slowly away into the Polish soil. Spring was desperately forging its way to the fore. All the planting had been done and now we undertook any job that needed doing from digging out drainage ditches to cleaning out the pigsties.

The Polish farmer's job was to keep us working as hard as possible, to get as much work out of us as he could and reach his quota of production. With this in mind, he made sure that we were fed well, that is by PoW standards. There was a huge incentive for the Poles to maintain and improve production, thereby keeping their German overlords sweet. To help them achieve this, the German authorities often separated a farm owner from his spouse and relocated her to manage another farm, some distance away. If the farmer hit his target, he was allowed to visit his wife once every month, by which time he must have been desperate for sex. Come to think of it, so were we all.

You could almost admire the Germans for their intelligent interference at every level of life within Germany's Third Reich and their spheres of influence.

We toiled long and hard during the late spring and early summer. It was always crushingly arduous and I prayed for a rest. Whenever we could get away with it, we did as little as possible, whilst all the time looking as busy as a mindless worker ant. As time wore on I couldn't get the stocky little Yorkshire 'horseman' out of my mind. Although we were receiving better food than when we were in camp, his food was even better. Whilst we now received more food, he received even more. Whilst we were forced to eat locked in the barn, he was allowed to eat with the farm owner at his table. All day we slaved in the fields whilst he sat on his lofty perch atop his wagon. He lived a privileged life that I could only aspire to.

Jealousy is not an attractive trait but I really did envy the lucky little runt.

~ BACK TO STALAG XXB ~
May 1942

On our arrival back at camp, Bert, Jimmy, Johnny and I managed to find a billet together, just in time for the evening meal thank goodness, but in that short time away I had forgotten just how bad the Stalag food was by comparison to our gourmet farm cuisine.

The following day I picked up three letters, two from mother and unusually, one from father. They contained the usual local news updates but nothing of any interest with regards the war as this would have been removed by the censors. My mother's letter contained more tragic news about another of my three work friends - the disappearance of Peter Birch, who had gone into the Navy. He was missing, presumed drowned.

> *After the war, I went to visit Peter's parents, who filled in the details of his death. After his training, Peter was posted to HMS Prince of Wales, one of England's mightiest battleships. In 1941, she sailed to Singapore with the battle cruiser HMS Repulse. On 10th December 1941, both ships were on a mission about 50 miles from the coast of Kuantan in Malaya when they were attacked by a squadron of Japanese warplanes, armed with deadly torpedoes. The Prince of Wales was crippled after the first torpedo attack. Hit in the stern, her propeller shaft was twisted in the resulting explosion, making further avoidance manoeuvring impossible. To all intents and purposes, she became a sitting duck. The Japanese planes then turned their attention to HMS Repulse. She was hit by one or two bombs and an additional salvo of twelve torpedoes. Returning their remaining attention back to the Prince of Wales, they hit the ship with one additional bomb and ten torpedoes. Both mighty vessels were lost at a cost to the Japanese of only four aircraft. The few survivors were picked up by the escorting destroyers which returned them to Singapore. The loss of life was the greatest ever experienced by the Royal Navy in a single incident. Peter was pronounced dead, presumed drowned, along with over 840 Officers and men. His body was never found. To this day, his bones may still lie amongst the twisted, rusting wreckage of those once great ships. Of our happy band of four, two were now dead.*

We had been away from camp for a couple of months, so there was plenty of catching up to do and no end of bored PoWs only too willing to tell us every bit of gossip. Isolated as we were, news of the Singapore surrender to the Japanese and the subsequent capture of thousands of British troops during February had taken time to reach us and it was with a heavy heart that we listened to the tale. Not for the loss of that part of the Empire, but for the countless British Tommies suffering a similar fate to us. I pitied each and every one of them and rightly so, for their suffering was to be worse than I could have ever imagined.

It did not take me long to settle back into my mundane lifestyle. But things never stayed quiet for long.

~ RED CROSS INSPECTION ~
Stalag XXB Malbork (Marienburg)
Visitation 1st May 1942

They visited us again today, but their inspection didn't make a blind bit of difference to us, or so it seemed.

Author: Again, I have only included the report's conclusion here.
The full text obtained from The Geneva International Red Cross Archives translation can be seen on page 595.

> #### Report Conclusions:
> *Accommodation of prisoners in the camp leaves a lot to be desired. The barracks are overcrowded, old and badly ventilated and lighted. Sanitary systems are inadequate, especially in the latrines and camp infirmary. There remains a lack of showers in the camp, resulting in relapses of pediculosis (infestation of head, body and pubic lice, cooties and crabs). Departments in the infirmary and dental prostheses still leave much to be desired.*

~ ATTEMPTS TO TURN US ~
June 1942

Summer burst on the scene like a blazing inferno, I read an article in the camp newspaper heralding tales of great German advances across Russia. The German Army had unleashed their Blitzkrieg once more during the new summer offensive and although we were not privy to their objectives, they were heading for the rich oil fields of the Caucasus and routing all Soviet forces in their path - if the BBC news reports and our German guards were to be believed.

The Germans were unstoppable and victorious and the war seemed set to go on forever, with no chance of us being released and returning home. Germany was invincible with no end in sight to the 'Thousand Year Reich'. That being the case, I refused to think of my future.

During the heat of June, our camp was graced with a visit from the Nazi Recruitment Corps. Our visitors were not only Germans trying to recruit us but treacherous home-grown Englishmen who had 'turned'. Occupied Europe was full of prisoners of war, held for the duration. We must have numbered a million plus, and amongst these numbers it was probable there were some who were sympathetic to the Nazi cause for various reasons. Many may have been anti-Communist or anti-Russian, as the Soviets had invaded their countries, finding themselves drawn to the Germans against the common enemy Russia. Before the war there were many countries that 'boasted' a National Socialist Party, including our own, the British Union of Fascists, led by Oswald Mosley. He had many dedicated British followers, particularly in the East End of London. Likewise, across Europe were many parties and thousands of individuals who supported Hitler from as far afield as Portugal, Spain, France and Holland and on to Poland, Hungary, Romania, Bulgaria and Yugoslavia to Norway and the Baltic states. The ever-resourceful Germans were quick to realise that this pool of PoWs was a potential source of recruitment, hence their attempts to enlist them into their armed forces in the fight against the Allies. With some nationalities they were very successful, managing to muster thousands of volunteers. Those who joined were each given standard German uniforms, but with the small addition of their own particular shoulder emblem based on their country of origin. For example, the Belgian unit was called the Walloon Division and they wore the Belgian flag. There was even an Indian Legion, filled with anti-British Indian nationals, dedicated to the overthrow of the British Raj and acquiring self-rule for their homeland.

One day, four men appeared unannounced, dressed immaculately in their German uniforms. Two were British turncoats and each wore the Union Jack emblem, of the 'Legion of St. George'. The four proceeded from hut to hut, explaining to the occupants the hopelessness of the war situation for us. Britain's cause was obviously lost, Germany was unbeatable and the best thing that we could all do was to join them and help the Germans fight against the common enemy, Bolsheviks. A lot of propaganda and more hot air was expelled and consequently wasted. You might wonder why these traitors felt safe enough to come amongst their fellow Brits in this manner without fear of a lynching. Believe me, they would have been if it were not for the armed squad of Germans that accompanied their every move.

Over the years at Stalag XXB, they must have tried three or four times to recruit from our camp. To my knowledge, they never did manage to find a single PoW to join their gang of traitorous, misguided individuals.

† *The British Free Corps (Legion of St. George)*

Its founder, John Amery was the eldest son of Leopold Amery, Secretary of State for India in Churchill's wartime coalition government. Before the war, he drifted around Europe with seemingly little direction in his life. He called himself a socialist. However, Amery also believed that the world faced a Jewish/ Soviet plot to overthrow western civilisation. His views became known in Berlin. Minister of Propaganda, Joseph Goebbels, realised the importance Amery could play in the propaganda battle with Britain - a government minister's son supporting the cause of Nazi Germany. Amery received an invitation to visit Berlin. Initially, they gave Amery permission to raise a brigade of 1500 men who would all be POWs or internees. Amery started his recruiting campaign at once in Paris addressing internees there. He promised anyone who joined the Legion that they would be immediately released from their prison. The campaign was an embarrassing disaster. Invariably he was shouted down and verbally abused. In his first recruiting campaign, Amery got one volunteer - an elderly academic from Paris. Amery's efforts were so embarrassing that the Germans quietly eased him back to Berlin.

On 21 April 1943, he began a recruiting campaign at St Denis Internment camp near Paris for a "Legion of St. George". Prisoners were assured that the Legion was being formed to fight against Bolshevism, and would never be used against British or American troops. Apart from freedom from PoW camp and being treated like their soldiers, inducements also included the following lies:

That five colonels and a brigadier had already joined.
That unit numbers had already reached brigade level.
That it had the support of the British Government.
That joining would lead to promotion.

Only two recruits, a sixteen year old cabin boy and a eccentric professor, were gained by Amery, who soon lost interest in the scheme. Amery had already made a series of propaganda broadcasts (22nd Nov. 1942 - 8th Jan. 1943) for the Germans, and for the rest of the war was employed by them, giving lectures in the countries of occupied Europe.

The Germans, having had some success in recruiting legions from France, Norway, Denmark and the Low Countries, continued their efforts to recruit British PoWs for the Legion.

The following month they opened another camp, Stalag III D/517 at Genshagen. Immediately these camps were regarded with great mistrust by the prisoners, and were recognised as propaganda establishments to undermine the loyalty of the prisoners.

In May 1943 they established a 'holiday camp' for British prisoners-of-war in Berlin which was known as Stalag II D/999. With the Nazis taking more of a part in the recruiting campaign, the number in the Legion had risen to twelve. Those involved in Nazi propaganda believed that the idea was worth pursuing and with Amery side-lined, managed to increase the number to thirty by June 1943. The recruits were paid one mark a day.

In late 1943, the Nazis decided to re-name the unit the British Free Corps. The Germans thought that this name would make a greater appeal to Welsh, Scots and Commonwealth prisoners from all the services. Those in it were given a uniform - it was of German field grey colour, with the Union Jack on one sleeve, a collar patch of three lions or three leopards and a cuff with 'Britische Freikorps' on it. One of the British subjects who was first connected with the BFC was a civilian, Thomas Haller Cooper, born in England of an English father and German mother. He was on holiday in Germany when the war broke out, and voluntarily joined the "Leibstandarte SS Adolf Hitler" in 1940. He made a number of visits to the prisoner of war camps. On these visits the Germans, presumably having Amery in mind, presented Cooper as the son of yet another of Churchill's ministers, Alfred Duff Cooper, then Chancellor of the Duchy of Lancaster, and his wife, Lady Diana. The earliest recruits were taken to Berlin, given civilian clothes and housed in a villa in the Grünewald district of the city and in February 1944, the recruits were transferred to Hildesheim, and housed there at the Haus Germanien, a collection of buildings behind the St Michaelis Kloster, all very badly damaged during an air raid in March 1945.

The unit was affiliated to the SS and known as "Sonderkommando "E"". The uniform was the ordinary German field grey uniform with an embroidered Union Jack on the left arm. (It is an indication of the scale of German hopes that 800 of these Union Jack badges were made). Later, three Anglo-German Leopards were added to the collar and a service flash "The British Free Corps" in Gothic lettering was added to the cuff.

The military training at Nildesheim 'Holiday Camp' consisted only of a little drill and a daily parade. The mess was decorated with a portrait of the Duke of Windsor, who was regarded by the BFC as a 'fellow rebel' and whom they 'all recognised as the rightful King of England'. The men enjoyed an astonishing degree of freedom. Some of them were given passes and railway warrants and could travel unescorted in Germany on recruiting tours. As the BFC was a joint Foreign Office/SS venture the men did not therefore come under Wehrmacht control and discipline. At Hildesheim the men had no difficulty in obtaining late passes and were frequently out all night. Their behaviour in town was bad and led to difficulties with the town authorities, who were anxious to be rid of them.

However, early in 1945 military training was started in earnest, and a frantic effort was made to bring the strength up to 60, the smallest unit which could be employed in the front line. By this time every fighting man was needed, and in February/March 1945 an attempt was made to implement the original purpose of the BFC, namely to fight the Russians. This too failed, and finally the Germans called for recruits to join the 3rd SS Panzer division. Only eight men volunteered: these were subsequently withdrawn and the division was finally overrun by British troops near Schwerin.

Of all British prisoners in German hands, Navy, Army, Air Force, Merchant Seamen and civilian internees (including Dominion and Colonial troops) from a figure of some 165,252, only about 60 had any connection with the BFC. This must be considered a remarkable tribute to the spirit of the British prisoners as the temptations of comfort, liberty and pay offered to the men were great.

Arrested at the war's end in Italy and by Major Burt of the Intelligence Corps (Originally of the Metropolitan Police Special Branch attached MI 5), Amery was flown back to England and handed over to the Special Branch. He was put on trial in England on 28 November 1945 for high treason. Recognising that his case was hopeless, and wishing to spare his family the infamy of a protracted trial he pleaded guilty. He was hanged at Wandsworth Jail on 29 December 1945.

* A bizarre footnote to the history of the British Free Corps appeared in the "Sunday Express" 7 March 1976, when it was reported that a John Bechwith, who had served in the BFC, in 1944-1945, was seeking back pay and compensation from the West German Government. †

~ BRAND SPANKING NEW HUTS ~
Spring Turns to Summer 1942

When we arrived in the early winter of 1940, we were forced to sleep in the terrible Erdehütten, relics from the First World War. By the spring of '41, we were moved into old wooden huts vacated by the French. Although better, they were still far from ideal for there were no individual bunks as such, just three tiers of six-foot-deep shelving running from end to end. In the depths of winter, freezing cold blasts of wind sliced their way through the cracks and numerous gaps in the old weather-beaten timbers.

In the summer of '42, the Germans surprised us once more with brand new wooden huts for us British. Roughly the same size as our present ones, these were prefabricated and nailed together. We were

---

† *Sources: Extracts of this article were originally written in February 1993 from information stored in The National Archives at Kew, Ref: CRIM 5/14 indictment, 1945 and an article from The History Learning web site > World War Two > British Free Corps.*

For a bibliography of the British Free Corps see Imperial War Museum Booklist No. 1125.

all as excited as kids on Christmas Eve. Anything that occurred to make our lives more tolerable was most welcome. The authorities had decided to increase the size of the camp and a section was built behind our existing old huts and Erdehütten. The work took a couple of weeks and as was to be expected, the Germans supervised and we provided the labour. As before, we transferred from our old dwellings to the new ones on a hut-by-hut basis. As soon as one was completed, an old one emptied and us PoWs moved in. The timbers were tight fitting and gap free, having the wonderful smell of new pine. Quite simply, they were bloody marvellous. The main difference between old and new was inside, for instead of being one large open space, the interior was partitioned off into separate rooms. Each room slept twelve men, who occupied the three-tiered wooden bunks, of which there were four per room. Each room had a double window and, most importantly, a stove. An individual stove in each small room and wind-proof walls transformed our lives, but unless you were there suffering with us, it is difficult for anybody to appreciate the difference that this made. As far as I was concerned, we had arrived at the Ritz.

According to 'The Sammy News', Japan was conquering its way across the Pacific and in February, had captured Singapore. For most of us this was too far away for us to worry about. The whole island of Malta had been awarded the George Cross for bravery after almost continual enemy bombing. Elsewhere, a German Commander by the name of Rommel had become a dangerous thorn in the side of our boys in North Africa, threatening to take Egypt and the Suez Canal. Closer to home, there was the wonderfully received news that the Russians had resisted the German advances during the winter and had pushed them back, inflicting heavy losses on them. This 'fact', if true, had vast implications to us PoWs in Poland, for if they were pushing the Germans back, that meant the Russians were advancing towards us. As the news purported to come from the BBC via our radio and Sammy, it was regarded as reliable and gave us a grain of hope.

To top it all, during the previous month our wonderful RAF had apparently bombed Cologne to the ground and were now making continuous bombing raids across the industrial heartland of Germany. We wanted to believe it so the news lifted our spirits.

From the German point of view, the news that some Nazi butcher called Heydrich had been assassinated in Czechoslovakia was causing a huge rumpus, even in Poland. He had the ostentatious title of Deputy Reich Protector of Bohemia and Moravia and had been attacked by Czech assassins. The Germans were not happy, to say the least, and the repercussions for the local population were truly dreadful with thousands of innocent civilians being executed.

Then we heard opposing and less favourable news from the Poles and guards. According to them, the Germans were now starting their summer offensive in Russia and were swarming across the Ukrainian plains, pushing the Russians back once more.

That was always the trouble. On the one hand, we heard Sammy's reports from the hidden radio, filling us with hope, only to have them dashed when we heard or read the German reports. No matter how much we tried to convince ourselves that the German version was pure propaganda, we were always left with that nagging doubt in the back of our minds and all hope flew out of the window.

~ TYPHOID ~
End of May 1942

More Russians arrive. By now, their segregated section had been extended and the emaciated new arrivals were squashed into their already cramped accommodation. No contact with them was possible and the double barbed wire fence ensured that. At the end of May, we heard that typhoid had broken out in their section of the camp and that of the Serbs. The health-conscious Germans were petrified of such diseases and rightly so. We were informed of the outbreak and totally superfluous orders were quickly issued:

'Under no circumstances was there to be any contact or fraternisation with the Russians. Any allied PoW caught doing so would be shot'.

With the Russians in isolation under quarantine, no guards would enter their compound and no food was actually taken in to them. Instead, guards would simply throw a few loaves of bread over the wire. No compassion was shown to the sick of the 'Untermensch'. They were simply encouraged to die in their hundreds. After the disease had run its course, a mere handful somehow managed to survive.

Typhoid spreads easily from person to person through mucus and exchange of saliva with coughs or colds. This particular bacterium can only be spread by humans as it lives solely in people. However, the main reason for typhoid to occur is poor sanitation conditions, allowing the drinking water supply to become contaminated with bacteria from the faeces, so when people drink such water they contract the disease.

~ I RECOGNISE A FAMOUS FACE ~
Early July 1942

Today, I managed to get hold of another copy of the German newspaper the Völkischer Beobachter. I stuffed it quickly into my trouser pocket before I was noticed. I had no idea if the guards would mind if I took it but I did not want to take the risk of a beating. When I got back to camp, I went to my hut. My friends Bert and Jimmy were inside having a sleep. Outside, Johnny was sitting below the window, basking in the sun. I knew it was him, for being a member of the Gordon Highlander's he was singing his regimental ditty:

> *"A Gordon for me,*
> *A Gordon for me,*
> *If you're nay a Gordon,*
> *Then you're nay good to me."*

I lay down on my bunk and took out the paper. It was more than a week old but that was of no importance, paper is paper with so many uses. I flicked through the pages, looking at the pictures whilst trying to understand the printed German in a bid to improve my vocabulary. Suddenly, I stopped my reading. I had come across a picture of a man whom I recognised. I read parts of the story and pieced together the fact that he was a German Commander on the Russian Front. His name was General von Manstein *(see picture reference 22)*. He had just captured the strategically important Russian port of Sevastopol in the Crimea after heavy and bitter fighting and, as a reward, the General was being promoted to Field Marshall. I lay back staring at the photograph of him in his splendid uniform when it suddenly hit me.

"Christ!" I exclaimed, shattering the peace and quiet of our room, "it's him!"

Bert almost fell out of his bunk but Jimmy just carried on sleeping.

"What's up, what's all the noise about?" asked Bert.

"It's him Bert, it's him! You remember the bloke I told you about ages ago?"

I sprang up from my bunk and showed Bert the picture. Bert rubbed the sleep from his eyes and tried to focus on the photo, but with little interest.

"Who Mar, who are you on about?" he managed to say between yawns.

"This bloke," I said, poking the paper, "he's the one I met just after I was captured. He came over to me and spoke to me in perfect English and asked me who I was. You remember, I told you that he put me in a barn with all those smelly French colonials for the night."

It was indeed him. I suddenly felt quite elated to discover that I had actually met this important Officer who was a German war hero. Bert, however, was not so impressed and after responding with a rather curt and totally uninterested grunt, fell back on his bunk. I kept the page with the Manstein story for a while and 'used' the rest of the paper over the next week or so before finally, over time, losing the page altogether.

~ A PARCEL FROM A STRANGER ~
July 1942

There was a pleasant surprise shortly after returning from the farm. Apart from another priceless gift of cigarettes sent from my workmates at Hackbridge, McDowell's Mafia issued me with a parcel from a stranger, via the Red Cross. I think they were dished out at random, or in turn to whichever PoWs were present at the time of arrival. Mine contained a pair of really thick knitted socks, with a letter enclosed from a kind lady who had made them.

Within the harsh environment of camp, the generosity of this lady touched me deeply. It also reminded me of the benevolence of my father towards those less fortunate than himself, a generosity that nobody outside our immediate family ever knew about.

It was typified at Christmas each year, although it extended throughout his life. During the run up to Christmas, my father would decide which households on his 'patch' were poor, having a sustained period of misfortune and deserved better. But above all, they needed to be good, honest, decent human beings.

As Christmas approached, he would give my mother additional money each week with which to buy extra food, household items or, depending on the family involved, toys and books. Once bought, they were set aside and placed into large wicker hampers until full to bursting point. On Christmas Eve, my father would quietly visit the houses of the deserving families and leave the hamper on their doorstep, anonymously. He wanted no recognition for his good deeds; the pleasure he got from giving to less fortunate individuals was reward enough. Nobody ever found out that my father was the mysterious bearer of those Yuletide gifts.

In the letter, she hoped that the recipient of her gift would find a use for them and prayed that I was not involved in heavy fighting and that I would be safe. She signed the brief letter with her name, and at the top she had written her address. Back in England, there were tens of thousands of women across the land, just like this lady, who kindly sent what they could to servicemen, never to know who received them. My lady must have assumed that hers would be going to an active serviceman, but as far as our government were concerned the gifts went to all servicemen, whether active or PoWs like us.

As PoWs, we were only allowed to write two letters and four postcards a month. As I was starved of female company and their gentle ways, I became increasingly intrigued by this woman. As the days went by I couldn't get her out of my mind so I decided to write to her.

I thanked her for her kindness in sending me the socks and replied how useful they would be next winter when the snow returned. I explained that I was a PoW and how receiving any letters and parcels from home was such a wonderful treat for me. I enclosed my full name and Stalag XXB address, posted it off and waited.

For the next few weeks, I was sent out on several work parties, some local, others further away. Eventually upon my return to camp I received a reply from her. She seemed kind and interested in my plight, hoping that I had enough to eat. I was delighted to receive her letter, and although flattered at her warm, kind response I did not know this lady from Adam. I could not help but look upon her in a mercenary way, as a possible source of cigarettes, food and clothing.

I decided to continue to write to her in the hope of receiving more from her. We corresponded for a while but I hadn't received anything else from her so I decided that I needed to be a bit bolder. In my next letter I actually asked her to send me some of the precious items that we craved for. It took about six to eight weeks to get a reply.

> *"Dear Dennis,*
> *Thank you for your letter. Unfortunately, I feel I must make this letter my last. I have become engaged to a man and we are due to marry so I will be unable to correspond with you in the future."*

My little plan had failed miserably. It had been a long shot and, in ordinary circumstances, I should have felt guilty as to my avaricious attitude towards her, but as I didn't really know her and because of my desperate position in war-torn Europe, I think I could be forgiven for trying to use her.

~ SOMETHING SINISTER ABOUT THIS CAMP ~
Late July 1942

We journeyed north from Stalag XXB for over an hour before our small work party reached our destination. When we arrived, all we could see was the outside of a huge isolated camp hidden amongst the pine forest. Initially it looked just like any other prison camp, but as I viewed it from the outside its appearance became increasingly sinister for no tangible reason. There was something about the place that deeply unsettled me. It was different, for I could not see any inmates within the heavily barbed wired enclosure. The guards were there at the gates and in their watchtowers but there was not an inmate in sight. We could not see a single occupant, only the huts were visible, along with a scattering of filth and litter. As each breath of wind came and went, paper debris rolled across the dusty ground like tumbleweed. We were taken to the back of the camp where a single railway line could be seen approaching from the outlying countryside and running straight into the camp itself through a wire gate guarded by two Germans.

Sitting on the rails about four hundred yards from the camp was a row of about forty cattle wagons, just like the ones we had travelled in from Luxembourg. Our job was to clean them, remove the dirty straw onto one side of the rail line, stack it and then burn it. As I climbed in and set to work, I could see that it had been used by humans and not animals by the size and quantity of the faeces in the straw. Hidden amongst the filth I found many items of interest or value to me personally, small human possessions, a tiny sock, a pencil, a pair of glasses and military badges but mostly buttons and small coins from across Europe, including German coins. I also found a Russian Officer's metal cap or lapel badge and a German medal awarded to a wounded soldier. I slipped them quietly into my pocket.

Seagulls flew by, screeching noisily. I puzzled over the former occupants of the carriages, speculating as to their fate, but concluded nothing. There was nobody to ask except our guards, who were now chatting aimlessly with their counterparts from the camp whilst relaxing in the warm weather. At best, to ask would have been a waste of time, and at worst dangerous. Once emptied, we set fire to the straw before replacing it with fresh. This brief episode left me troubled and was to haunt me over the coming years.

Stutthof Concentration Camp

I pieced together what details Dennis could give me about the rough direction he travelled in, one hour's travelling distance, the presence of seagulls - indicating proximity to the Baltic Sea.

My research led me to believe the camp he refers to may have been Stutthof Concentration Camp. It was the first concentration camp built by the Nazis outside of Germany. Completed in September 1939, it was located in a secluded, wet, wooded area west of the small town of Sztutowo (German: Stutthof). The town is located close to the coast about 30 miles east of Gdańsk and 30 miles north of Marienburg. More than 85,000 victims died in the camp out of the 110,000 people deported to the hell hole.

The main gate was a narrow entrance located next to the German headquarters, allowing quick and easy access for the Germans. Most of those who were imprisoned there never entered through the small main gate since they were brought in by rail, and almost no-one inside the camp ever left. By early 1945, those still alive were force marched towards the port of Gdańsk to escape the advancing Russians.

~ LIVING WITH OUR OTHER UNINVITED GUESTS ~
Summer 1942

As summer '42 progressed, so did the temperature. Unexpectedly, I found myself briefly enjoying certain aspects of camp life; that is, until *they* arrived in abundance.

Unfortunately, I recalled only too easily that during the summer of last year, the vermin population had literally exploded. The rats, our first guests, invaded the camp from the River Nogat, enjoying the splendid food waste that littered our open latrines. This year, they returned once more but in lesser numbers, and the poison was immediately put to use.

Our second unwanted, blood-sucking, evil lodgers were a lot smaller and had been our constant companions for an age. They were our very own pet lice. We were all infested with them. No matter how many times I took off my clothes and 'popped' the little buggers, crushing the disgusting things between my finger nails in the manner that I had been shown, we could not rid our bodies of them. There were always plenty more lice waiting, in egg form, to take their place. Some prisoners tried other methods, such as opening up the folds and seams inside their tunics and torching the buggers with a flame, but whatever we did it seemed impossible for us to kill them off completely for they were prolific in their egg-laying, with new little critters infesting warm, moist crotches and arm pits within hours.

On top of our wooden bunks we continued to sleep on our palliasse. The cloth mattress was stuffed with straw, grass or whatever else you chose to fill it with to make it more comfortable to lie on. However, therein lay the drawback. The contents provided a wonderful housing opportunity for our third and final visitors who were very unwelcome. Creepy, crawling fleas and bed bugs added to our wretched lives along with our long-term favourites. As if things were not bad enough for us, these additional parasites were the bane of our lives. At night time, as I lay in my bunk trying to get to sleep, I can still recall the constant, soft, rasping background noise of men scratching,... everywhere.

I am sure that you have all heard of that old expression, 'necessity is the mother of invention'. In PoW land, that really did appear to be the case.

Stalag XXB had been built on the sandy soil that edged the river. The belief was that the soil around the camp was a breeding ground for these bugs, creepy crawlies and mites, so one day I tested the theory. I walked outside of the hut and under the heat of that sweltering summer sun, I lay on the ground by the side of the hut, resting my right cheek on the dirt, almost burning my skin. I looked across the sand at flea level and stretched out my arm, banging and disturbing the ground in front of my face. I couldn't believe what I saw. Hundreds of the little blighters jumped up into the air, dancing frantically. I picked up a handful of sand and allowed it to filter through my fingers and watched a host of other tiny creatures fall to the ground. These most unwanted guests were probably crawling up the supports into our huts and then up the bunk legs into our beds, joining the millions already in residence.

Over the course of the next few days, the best brains within Stalag XXB worked to come up with a solution. Other than body leavings, nothing in the camp ever went to waste, everything was recycled. Tin cans of any sort were acquired. Armed with four of these, each bunk support was placed into a tin and a liquid - any liquid but preferably a spirit or lime-based fluid - was poured into it and around the wooden legs, thereby isolating the bunks by standing each leg in its own liquid moat. Steps would then be taken to clean the place and even to take the bunks apart and pass each wooden post through a flame in order to burn the buggers and their eggs. Simplicity itself, but I am not sure if it actually worked for it was our infested palliasses that harboured the vast majority of parasites.

On reflection, we might have been better off if we had invited a troop of starving chimps into our huts for a parasitic feast!

~ AMAZINGLY RESOURCEFUL ~

Unless you have been in a similar confined situation, which I strongly doubt, nobody can ever appreciate just how bad things can get for prisoners of war. However, as bad as we thought our conditions were, they were even worse for Germany's concentration camp victims, detainees of the dreaded Gestapo and, as I later learnt, prisoners of the brutally barbaric and inhuman Japanese. At the time, none of us were aware of their tragic circumstances, for we might have found comfort in the dreadful knowledge there were others worse off than us.

From 1940 onwards, we were deprived of virtually every luxury known to civilized man. Consequently, this necessitated the 'mothers of invention' to secretly manufacture almost anything that was readily available in the outside world. The tinsmiths could turn every valuable tin can into cooking pots or utensils, or, by joining several together, they were able to make metal utensils, tubes or pipes. Wood could be whittled and modelled into most shapes and objects. Tin cigarette cases were flattened and joined together using a primitive but clever soldering method. Imprisoned jewellers amongst us made finger rings or other items of jewellery. Wall plaques were painted or engraved, depicting scenes from home, images of loved ones or favourite items. Clothing, bags and even leather shoes, if you had the money, would be made to your specification. Paintings and sculptures were produced and primitive cameras manufactured, the list was endless. The inventiveness and resourcefulness of mankind never ceased to amaze me, and by these methods, we survived.

~ GREAT JOY & ~
THE DEATH OF MY MOST INTIMATE NEIGHBOURS
(FOR A WHILE)

Our wardrobe did not extend to a regular change of clothing and Persil was not readily available to us, 'the great unwashed'. The occasional bar of peculiar, hard, German-supplied gritty 'soap' (and I use that word cautiously because it was more like an abrasive exfoliate) was still better than nothing.

Without the availability of detergents, boiling water, disinfectant or napalm, nothing was going to shift the tiny little parasitic buggers that plagued our lives. Once washed, drying clothes was not easy, for whilst they were being washed and dried most prisoners had nothing else to wear. Whatever the reason, neither clothes nor us got washed often enough, which was the main reason that we were infested.

During the hot summer, the parasite situation got painfully problematic. Through constant requests and the serious threat of disease, the Germans did eventually provide us with a solution. One morning, totally unexpectedly, we were lined up after morning parade for a little outing. Fortunately, on this occasion, I was not away working on one of the satellite farms, or I would have missed the fun.

We were marched towards Marienburg and after a short jaunt, we were brought to a halt outside at a long, cement-rendered building, not knowing where we were or why.

"Fall out and form an orderly queue."

Within minutes, word was passed along the line as to where we were. We had arrived at a delousing plant.

Our first treat was a visit to the hair stylist. A line of none too happy Polish barbers stood behind their wooden chairs, clippers at the ready.

Bert, Jimmy, Johnny and I sat down together. I couldn't resist it.

"Today, I think I will have a 'Clark Gable' cut my good man, but easy on the Brylcreem."

The others kept it up with dead pan faces.

"More of a full bouffant for me please," said Jimmy, indicating with his raised hand.

Bert turned enquiringly. "Got another hot date with Vivien?" he asked with exaggerated nonchalance.

> Vivien Leigh was an American screen goddess who co-stared Clark Gable in the Hollywood film 'Gone with the Wind', the last film we saw at our camp at Abancourt before engaging the Germans in May.

By this time, the bemused Poles had begun to shear our infested heads and Johnny just couldn't resist what he did next.

Whilst speaking in a rather severe Germanic accent, he picked up a lock of his black hair, put it under his nose and pinched his nose and top lip together to hold it in place.

"... and can you give me an Austrian parting and pull my fringe a little over my left eye lid?"

The whole group of us burst into fits of laughter as the guard came hurrying over, eager to find the source of our merriment. Johnny instantly released the pressure from under his nose as his false moustache fell back onto his lap, leaving the guard puzzled as to what had just happened.

"Quiet," he bellowed, "quiet."

But we continued and he had to endure a few more minutes of muted laughter and whispered banter before we rose from our barber's chairs. The Poles had totally disregarded our instructions, leaving us as bald as a billiard ball.

Once inside the main door, we entered the first unfurnished room. Apart from the crowd of never-ending prisoners filling the place, there was a large wheel suspended from the ceiling. From an opening high up in the interior wall came a chain, supported at intervals by rollers and brackets suspended from the ceiling. The chain entered our room, went around a large metal wheel and then ran back through the same opening. Hanging from this chain were open wire baskets. This was a conveyor belt operation. We were instructed to undress completely and to place our filthy garments in the hanging baskets.

"If only I had bloody known, I would have worn my clean underpants," came the retort from some wag.

We were relaxed and in good humour. What a sight we must have looked as we stripped unashamedly in front of each other, our tattered uniforms falling around our ankles. We placed our clothes into the baskets before moving forward into the next area, which happened to be the shower room. With the harsh German soap provided, we scrubbed ourselves almost raw, concentrating particularly on our hairy little places, where our abundant companions loved to dwell, in warmth and comfort. All this to the continuous hounding by the German guards.

"Schnell!"

"F*** him!" came the usual, almost obligatory muttered response.

Sometimes, we British can be so disrespectful.

I had not seen my fellow prisoners in such a happy mood since the 'cock contest', with voices and laughter filling the room. The water was warm and it was amazingly comforting to feel so clean. I felt almost decadent after being deprived of such luxuries for so long. I picked up a tiny paper-like towel with which to dry myself before going to the next room, still stark naked. On either side of the entrance into the next room were two civilians. Women. They were large, drably-dressed peasants and totally expressionless with scarves covering their heads. Each had a large bucket by their side filled with a thin, whitish-looking substance that I didn't like the look of - or the smell of for that matter. Each was armed with what looked like a short-handled mop. What I saw next made me laugh hysterically. Fortunately, the days of feeling embarrassed by standing naked in front of anybody, let alone two women, had long passed.

As I walked into the room, the woman on the left lifted her soggy mop from the bucket and proceeded to attack my 'John Thomas' with it, thrusting it forwards repeatedly, like a champion swordsman. It was left covered in the smelly liquid. Instinctively, I made a protective grab for my precious bits, at the same time stepping backwards, pushing my bottom back away from her. That precise response of mine seemed to be exactly what was required and was the prompt for the next stage.

The second woman behind me retrieved her soaked mop and stuck it up and down my backside and between my legs. Simple. The job of applying disinfectant had been done with typical German efficiency, but it was like a scene from a Carry On film. As I watched those who came after me, I almost collapsed into uncontrollable laughter. It was hilarious. Laughter is infectious and soon the place was in uproar. Those women must have seen a few willies that day, but by the blank expression on their faces they had probably been doing this for months and seen every shape and size of appendage known to man and appeared utterly oblivious to the whole proceedings.

From behind, I heard more laughter as someone spoke.

"That was 'orrid."

Within a split second came a reply. "Well, normally I wouldn't have minded having my balls played with, but we haven't even been introduced!"

"Well I rather liked that, think I'll go back and have it done again so she can give my 'old man' another bashing."

"Does that mean I'm no longer a virgin?"

I was in hysterics. As bad as things got, there was always some British soldier somewhere who could bring a breath of humour to any situation. Humour helped us to survive.

However, it didn't take long for us to lose our smiles. That thin white liquid was like Jeyes Fluid, salt, DDT with just a dab of napalm to give it an extra kick. Within seconds it was burning into the more sensitive skin of my not-so-private private parts, already made sore by my persistent scratching. Our tears of laughter were replaced with tears of flaming pain.

Still smarting from the experience and with my legs apart to stop any chafing, I fanned my lower bits whilst following the other prisoners to the end of the building. From the ceiling ran the other end of the conveyor belt carrying the baskets with our clothes. Whilst we had been moving slowly through the delousing plant, our garments had been shunting their way equally slowly through the hot house, where they were baked at a high temperature to kill off the lice. Finding my own clothes was relatively easy as I now had a few instantly recognisable non-military garments. Others were not so lucky and it was not until they climbed into their trousers and found them to be at half mast or lying on top of their feet that they realised theirs had become mixed up with another pair.

Baking our outfits did work. The lice did fry and that was

wonderful - for the rest of the day. Unfortunately, it did not kill their offspring. The oven was nice and cosy for the eggs and just the right sort of temperature for them to hatch. Within a few days, scratching was back to normal and we were 'popping' lice once more. On any given sunny day, scores of prisoners could be seen sitting in the open, stripped to their undies, 'popping' whilst nattering to their friends, passing the time of day. It was most surreal.

Upon our return to camp, we discovered that our German bastards had used our absence to carry out a search of our huts. Outside the windows were piles of our belongings. Anybody who had not hidden their most precious possessions now found them missing.

~ A PARCEL FROM HOME ~

Meanwhile, my mother had been busy. She sent me a knitted jumper and more socks that I was grateful to receive. My package arrived wrapped only in brown paper and string. It had travelled over a thousand miles to get to me. Looking at the battered parcel, I considered myself lucky to have received it at all. Thousands upon thousands of items from England and the colonies were being posted to troops and PoWs across the world. They were handled by hundreds of people before arriving at Marienburg goods yard. After being sorted by Germans, they were taken to camp for distribution to their lawfully intended recipients. With so many people handling the goods, pilfering was rife. Even our fellow PoWs were not averse to stealing from the rail trucks, regardless of who the parcels were intended for. 'Dog-eat-dog' and 'survival of the fittest' were still the underlying laws across occupied Europe.

~ A CAMP OF SHOPKEEPERS & TRADERS ~
Late Summer 1942

By now, camp life and procedure were well established. The Germans had it running like clockwork with the assistance of McDowell and his gang. Our slavish labours were in constant demand, allowing the majority of PoWs greater access to the outside world than ever before and, therefore, the ability to trade with the civilian populous.

As unbelievable as it may sound, the camp was actually prospering. Red Cross parcels were starting to arrive and packages from home were getting through, bringing in an abundance of merchandise. German guards could sometimes be 'befriended' and it was sometimes possible to carefully trade with them, at a price, for they loved our chocolate and English cigarettes. With my dealer's commission I, like others, had surplus spending power and a host of businesses and services sprang up to accommodate the needs of these nouveaux riches.

Tailors

Back in November 1940 when I first arrived, the Germans had a fledgling tailor's workshop in the camp, staffed by the resident French PoWs. The Germans later provided them with half a hut for their exclusive use, along with tables, sewing machines, yarn, scissors and everything else necessary. As time went by, they were joined by other nationalities.

After the defeat of our Army in Europe, the Germans had captured vast supplies of British ordnance, amongst which were vast stocks of uniforms. After a while, they were distributed to the various camps spread throughout their territories. Stalag XXB acquired such a batch. From 1942, the much-needed new uniforms were made available to us if you could prove to Sergeant McDowell that yours was worn out. Your old one would be processed or recycled by the tailors. If you were suitably rich by camp standards, you could employ the tailors to make you an exclusively-fitted uniform or whatever else you required, for the tailors made anything, for a price. I needed something in which to keep my valuables and the knickknacks I had found whilst cleaning the goods wagons several weeks earlier. Upon my return from a work party, I popped into the tailors. Their hut was always a hive of activity. Today, nine of them were busily working at their machines. A pile of British, Russian, Polish and French Army coats filled the back of their hut. I recognised one of the machinists, Arthur, and interrupted his labours. We chatted aimlessly for a while before getting down to business. I described that I wanted a small cloth bag, gave him the size and its purpose and left it to him. We agreed an exchange deal, half a loaf of bread, and I left with the promise that it would be ready in two days, for it would take me that long to get his bread.

· · · § · · ·

Photographer

Amongst the inmates was yet another Frenchman who was a professional photographer by trade. Why he and his fellow countrymen were still being held as PoWs, so long after the French surrender, I didn't know. 'Frenchy' had seen a business opportunity and opened a photography shop in the very early days of our captivity. He had his own camera and film in plentiful supply. He had sectioned off a portion of his room and fitted it out as a darkroom, complete with a Heath Robinson-style enlarger. Amazingly, he had also managed to acquire photographic paper and all the chemicals necessary to develop his films. The Germans were fully aware of what he was doing and may have actually sanctioned it, for Frenchy was quite open when applying his trade and it was common practice to see him taking photos of us inmates within the camp. As long as the backgrounds in his shots were harmlessly nondescript, the Germans didn't seem to mind and the censor at Stalag XXA would pass them for forwarding onwards to England.

The Germans also had their own camp photographer to take photos of us to send home. Every so often they would organise group shots, but we, their subjects would all be carefully vetted first. If any of us had a tattered uniform, he was issued with a decent one. Such was the caring attitude of our German hosts. To help confirm the lie that we PoWs were being treated in a respectable and appropriate manner, we were told to look happy, appear tidy and clean. If any of us didn't, then we knew that the pictures would not be allowed home, thereby depriving our loved ones of a precious memento and visual confirmation that we were alive. We had little option but to comply, for it was better for their peace of mind that they receive our staged pictures rather than none at all. Needless to say that once the photos were taken, the men had to hand back their borrowed attire and adorn themselves in their dirty old tat.

If more personal photos were needed such as pictures of you with your closest friends, then you could always pay Frenchy to take one.

By now, I was seeing less and less of Freddy and my other mates from The Queen's as we were assigned to differing work parties and I had already become very close to Bert Stupples, Jimmy Farrington and Johnny Dunbar. We decided to have our picture taken together by Frenchy and all send copies home to our respective parents. It was whilst writing the accompanying letters that we four came to a decision to help our relatives cope with our imprisonment and separation. We could never be absolutely sure if our correspondence arrived at its intended destination, so we created the 'Mar Minter Network'. We each supplied our respective families with contact details of each other's and as soon as one received a letter, they would in turn write to the others, keeping them all informed as to our well being.

After the war I found out this system worked perfectly and helped our families cope with our incarceration during those terrible war years, whilst we were guests of the Austrian Corporal.

Two days later, I returned to the tailors, armed with my payment of bread. As promised, the bag was ready. It was dirty grey-green in colour and made from a patch taken from a Russian coat, complete with drawstring.

Le Coiffeur

The barber's shop was well established before we arrived. Not surprisingly, it was run by another Frenchman, and as long as you did not want your louse-ridden locks coiffured into some outrageous Louis XIV Parisian beehive, he did his job admirably, for a Frenchman... and for a price.

Cobblers

New army boots were a rarity, so thank goodness for the cobblers. They patched again and again, thereby protecting the feet of many a grateful PoW, including my own. Even in PoW camps, capitalism and commerce flourished.

~ TO TOP IT ALL, THE GERMANS OPEN A JOKE SHOP ~
Mid-1942

Today, we received another visit from the Swiss Red Cross. During morning parade, we were briefed by the Germans as to when they would arrive and how we should conduct ourselves and assure the Swiss that we were being wonderfully treated and exceedingly well looked after by our hosts, who were complying fully with the Geneva Convention!

We had our first visit shortly after our arrival at the camp and I believed they may have been the instigators who prompted our move from the earth huts. Consequently, I assumed that the Swiss exchanged words with the German military authorities and brought to their attention the fact that they were employing us as slave labourers because they were not paying us for our work. By definition, if we were required to work and not being paid, we were slave labourers. Of course to the Germans, this was just a simple question of semantics and the solution was simple: they would pay us a wage. Problem solved.

So that is exactly what they did. However, instead of paying us in real money such as their German marks, they cunningly decided to print a special currency that could only be used within the camp. This 'money' was called 'Lagergeld', meaning camp money. But camp money is not money and becomes worthless if you cannot spend it in exchange for goods of some description. Again, the cunning Germans circumnavigated this irritating detail by opening the camp shop.

As was always the case when the Germans had good news (but more often than not, bad news) to announce, this was done after morning roll call. The Camp Commandant may have done it on this occasion, for the German looked fat and important enough. After his speech, his translator informed us in English.

"You will be glad to know that you will now be paid for your work."

He appeared to be loving his theatrical performance to us, his captive audience.

"But that is not all." With a smile, this comic presenter went on to announce even more exciting news.

"As a special act of generosity by The Third Reich, we will be opening a shop for you all."

German logic was infallible. I suppose this was the inevitable conclusion to the first announcement, for if there was nowhere to spend our precious wages the whole operation would have appeared very transparent, even to us stupid English.

You could almost hear the groans above the stifled sniggers.

"When, when?" came the chorus of responses to any announcement of a forthcoming treat.

"Tomorrow, tomorrow it will happen."

Sure enough, almost a week later, it did.

The Germans took over the front section of the Camp Medical Centre (or, to put it simply, it was the Polish doctor's hut) and converted it into the new shop. They, (or PoWs to be more precise) set about building shelves to house the goods and a counter behind which the German 'shopkeeper' was to stand and take our hard-earned lager geldt. The exterior of the hut looked no different, but it was now the designated Camp Shop, complete with sign. Within days, supplies came flooding in and the shelves were soon stacked high, almost straining under the sheer weight of goods. At the end of the following week, we received our first wages. I think the whole camp was there, forming an orderly queue. Eventually, I was handed my wedge of Lagergeld by a guard and a bureaucratic bookkeeper who made sure that we were not overpaid. Fat chance. The German anti-Soviet National Socialists were showing a remarkably 'communistic' side to themselves when it came to their wages philosophy for we all received the same wages, regardless of the job. There were some in the camp who did not work at all for various reasons so they naturally received no money. The Lagergeld was like Monopoly money in many ways, for physically the notes were small, in denominations of one, five, ten, twenty, etc., and much like Monopoly notes they were practically worthless. When my turn came to pick up my pay packet, I asked the same question that others had asked.

"When will the shop be open?"

"Tomorrow, tomorrow it will open," came the un-surprising answer.

Several days later, news spread like a fire in a match factory. The shop was about to open for business. I ran to the grand event, where I was joined by most of the camp. The scene was reminiscent of the January sales. By the time I crossed the threshold, the shelves were no longer straining under the weight. In fact, there was very little; a few tins of toothpaste, the strange German scouring soap, a razor blade or two, a few packs of playing cards, a fist full of pencils but no paper and a few other odds and ends littering the bare shelves. There was a noticeable absence of two items that could have been really useful food and clothing such as hats, boots and gloves for the coming winter. I was soon drawn to the only item that I was really desperate for - cigarettes. They were called 'Junaks' (Polish for boy cadets) and were made in Poland. They came in large boxes of two-hundred at a time. Inside, they were split up into smaller more manageable sizes of ten cigarettes in each thin paper pack. The most remarkable thing of note about them was that they were incredibly long, twice as long as a normal cigarette. However, all was not as it seemed. The first half of the ciggie was like a huge filter with no filling, just a thin cardboard tube inside the paper. The other half did contain a tobacco of sorts, for want of a better, more descriptive noun. If I had to hazard a guess as to what it was, I would say that it was filled with crushed acorn fibres, straw, chopped cardboard and cow pats, before being shown a Balkan tobacco leaf in order to give it a hint of flavour. Not only were we drinking coffee made from acorns but now we were smoking the bloody stuff.

As soon as I returned to my hut I lit one and inhaled. The first puff almost choked me to death. The cigarettes had a disturbing smell and were truly awful, but such was our nicotine craving and our desperation to smoke, anything that resembled tobacco was smoked. It was questionable whether there was actually a single particle of nicotine-saturated tobacco inside.

Within that first day, the shop had sold out of everything of any use and it was closed. And that was how it stayed, opening only briefly during every Red Cross visit. The Germans however, did leave a sign in the window, it simply read 'Aufmachen' ('Open'), but as they didn't have a sense of humour this must have been an oversight. However, we were stoic and used to such disappointments. On the plus side, losing the store probably saved the lives of many a young PoW like myself from contracting chronic ARLD (Acorn-Related Lung Disease).

Our captors persisted with the farce of issuing us with our wages each week for the remainder of the war, even though there was nothing to spend the money on. By continuing with our wages, the Germans paid lip service to the Geneva Convention.

The following pay day, Jimmy took his wages and turned to face us.

"Bloody notes are even too small to wipe my arse with."

"Shouldn't have such a big one then," came a shooting reply.

Another use was soon found for them. Gambling. With playing cards readily available, the money was used in games of poker and the like. Within only a few weeks, the camp boasted some very rich players and some exceedingly poor losers but there was absolutely no difference in the spending power of either groups, as the money was worthless.

· · · § · · ·

~ CLOGS ~
August 1942

We had been in captivity for over two years, and in that time we had marched across northern France into Luxembourg or via Belgium into Germany, and trampled across Poland. We had slaved in the fields, on the roads, the railways, mines, factories and coal yards whilst wearing the same British Army boots. Although they were good and substantial, they had taken a hammering and been repaired time after time but had reached the end of their lives. Obtaining replacements was not easy, but if you had enough money or alternative currency, you could buy almost anything. Captured supplies of British boots were being channelled into camp by the Germans for replacement purposes but stocks were limited. In addition, some new ones were getting through to individual prisoners after being sent from loved ones and were very well received.

Those who laboured outside the camp were in a more important category and for the most part received preferential treatment when it came to replacement boots. However, those who stayed in camp and shied away from slave labour did not qualify at all. Consequently, if these men couldn't trade for new boots on the open market, they had little option but to wear the wooden clogs of the farm peasant, issued courtesy of our German masters. They were extremely uncomfortable and cumbersome and, as one might imagine, they were painfully cold and wet in winter and prone to getting stuck in the mud and pulled off your feet. In the summer months they were marginally more tolerable, but the unforgiving wood rubbed on the skin, causing troublesome blisters that often turned septic in the filthy conditions that prevailed. Some Poles we saw didn't wear socks but instead wore something called a 'Fusschlappen'. This was fashioned from a large piece of square sacking cloth which was folded in half in the shape of a triangle. A foot was placed in the centre, pointing towards the apex of the triangle. The apex was folded back onto the bridge of the foot. The left side was then folded over to the right across the bridge and then the right side was folded over onto the left before tucking it into the left side angle and securing it. This had the effect of automatically bringing up the back of the cloth to lie against the back of the foot.

Those allied PoWs who had to endure this wooden footwear throughout their years in captivity and the marches were most likely crippled for the rest of their lives.

~ GOODBYE VIRGINITY ~
Late August 1942

I awoke to another heady Polish morning. During parade, Sergeant McDowell barked the order to stand to attention. Rightly or wrongly, many were increasingly perceiving him as part of the camp system and a stooge of the Germans, but there again, we, the lowest-of-the-low, tended to hate all NCOs, not just this particular Celt. A call went up for more volunteers to work outside the camp again. I hardly waited for the question to be asked before my hand shot up. I was determined to be beyond the wire as soon as possible.

I am guessing that the distance we were to travel was greater than usual as this time we had to wait for transportation. When it arrived I was a little surprised yet fascinated and looked on in some disbelief. The truck was not a conventional diesel or petrol-driven vehicle as I would have expected but an antiquated steam-driven lorry fuelled by coal or wood, complete with tall chimney belching forth smoke. We laughed as it chugged into view under its choking cloud of steam and watched as it hissed to a halt in front of the gates. We boarded.

Other than the sheer novelty of travelling on such a wonderful piece of history, our journey through the Polish countryside was uneventful, and apart from stopping to take on more much needed water and fuel at every opportunity, we travelled rather uncomfortably at speeds barely into double figures. Although no real distance from Stalag XXB, it was not surprising that we arrived at our destination later that afternoon and were immediately herded into a large, straw-filled barn which we rightfully assumed was to be our sleeping quarters. Within the hour I was feeling hungry, wondering if we were going to be fed when the barn door was unlocked and opened. I woke the others. A Polish farm worker came in accompanied by our guards, carrying several thick slices of bread with a thick covering of animal fat and dripping. It was most welcome and put us all in a better frame of mind. The temperature in the barn was comfortable as we lay within our blankets on the dry animal straw.

At first light, we collected the cup of statutory ersatz before assembling in the yard. The owner or manager quickly appeared. She just happened to be a woman. She was overweight but quite attractive with her blonde hair held in place with a neatly tied head scarf. She exchanged a few words with the guards before addressing us PoWs in Polish. No reaction so she tried German.

"I need a horseman, which one of you can do the job?"

I had heard this question on three previous farms, had seen what was needed, what was expected and the substantial benefits and knew what to do. Standing erect I braved my outrageous lie.

"I'm the horseman", I replied, before stepping forward.

Bert, Jimmy and Johnny didn't utter a sound. I stared straight ahead self-consciously. Time seemed to stand still as I waited for a reaction, but nobody challenged my ridiculous assertion or attempted to claim the coveted position. I must have looked particularly unprepossessing as the Frau took two steps towards me, looking me up and down as she approached. I felt like a prize piece of beef under inspection at a meat market or a working girl on offer in a brothel. Eventually she deemed me acceptable and I heaved a deep sigh, having overcome my first hurdle and passed that initial inspection. I was told to follow and obediently did, but turned and watched as the others were marched off to toil in the fields. I was excited to have had got away with it so far and grinned. The Frau took me to the stables, where several horses stood munching away on the fresh straw, tethered in their adjacent stalls in a line against the right-hand wall. To the left were several carts, ranging from small to large. On the far wall was the tack section, where harnesses and reins were on display. The barn had that unique 'horsey' smell. The horses themselves were slender, unlike the larger and stronger working cart and shire horses that we have at home. These slight animals appeared out of place and unsuited to a hard day's work pulling laden wagons over heavy soil. They would not have looked out of place on the parade ground, and indeed may have come from the now defunct Polish cavalry.

She turned and said something to me which I didn't understand. She was using words alien to me, but helpfully she pointed to the largest wagon whilst standing by the horses so I took an educated guess that she wanted the wagon and horses united somehow. I looked at the heavy wooden wagon. I had seen ones like this at work, delivering barrels of beer to the pubs back home. We would have called this a dray. It was tall, high off the ground, with its sides splayed out along its length above the wheels.

I looked back at the horse once more. I looked at the wagon. Finally my eyes came to rest on the quantity of leather items, ropes and chains that were meant to tether one to the other. My eyes repeated the previous scan, glancing over the three items, but no solution entered my vacuous head.

"Shit!" I mumbled under my breath, what do I do now?

I swallowed hard knowing that I had to act quickly or be found a liar. The wagon had one wooden shaft jutting out at the front, so I assumed that two horses stood either side of it. I looked at the tack again and recognised the row of heavy leather-clad oval items hanging from the barn wall. Horse collars. I walked over and took two down from the wall. They were heavy and I could only manage one at a time. I took the collar over to the nearest horse and placed it over its head. Common sense told me that they were to be connected to the shaft, but for the life of me I had absolutely no idea how to achieve this. I was stuck and it showed. I looked over at the Frau, who was standing close by with her arms folded under her ample chest. She simply stared back at me. I could tell she was irritated. In turn, she knew that I was flustered and puzzled. I was drowning in the brown stuff with no way of climbing out. I tried to explain myself in pidgin Polish.

"Things are different in England, we have different tackle, different ways. Everything is different in England."

My bluff had been easily exposed at the first hurdle and I fully expected to be thrown out into the fields with a flea in my ear. Shaking her head, she walked over to me, but instead of my fears materialising she softened, and for the next ten minutes she showed me what to do; how to dress the horses in their harnesses, traces and pole-straps and how to attach the lot to the correct parts of the horses' tackle. Feverishly, I logged every detail in my brain for I didn't want to go through all that again tomorrow... if there was going to be a tomorrow.

She had saved me. Briefly she smiled and I at her. Under her guidance, I hitched up the horses and led them into the yard. The Frau pointed, telling me to follow the others into the distant field and bring back the turnips.

The next stage was bound to be easy, surely. What could possibly go wrong?

I climbed onto the front of the wagon, which had a long, high bench seat and an angled wooden foot rest. The sides of the wagon were also angled upwards and outwards, being about four feet high. I unhitched the reins that the Frau had tied up onto a post by my side and I was ready. Remembering countless American westerns films that I had seen over the years, I knew exactly what to do next. With the horses already pointing in the right direction, I gave the reins a shake and a classic American-type cry that any self-respecting 1890s wagon train driver would have been proud of.

'Hey-hup!'

Off we went. Regardless of the obvious language barrier, 'Hey-hup!' must have been universally accepted amongst the worldwide equine population as the correct word for 'move off'. This was going to be a doddle. The horses instinctively understood me and knew what to do. It was fantastic as we made our way at a steady plod along the well-worn tracks to the fields. I was sitting high up and could easily see over the tops of the hedges into the fields beyond and soon spotted our working party some way ahead. Beginning to feel cocky by now and thoroughly enjoying this new experience, I then did something rather foolish. I lashed and flicked the reins once more and shouted 'Hup!' to the horses.

That proved to be one almighty mistake.

In an instant, they bolted. Had I not been holding securely onto the reins, the sudden burst of speed would have knocked me backwards onto the floor of the cart.

"Sshhhiiiiiiiiit!" I screamed as I fought to remain upright.

My heart was pounding as I tried to regaining my composure whilst fighting desperately to calm the horses and rein them in. Pulling as hard as I could with my feet almost pushing a hole through the wooden foot rest, I was unable to stop them, let alone gain any control. We were galloping at what seemed like breathtaking speed. I was helpless and panicking. No sooner had the two horses, the wagon and I reached full and furious galloping speed, I saw a break in the hedge and fence some hundred yards ahead on the right, just as the road gently curved away in the opposite direction. It was the open gate that led into the field where my fellows were hard at work. I did not even attempt to steer these two beasts from hell, for that would have been futile. The animals seemed to know what to do. They had probably done it a hundred times before and were running purely on instinct. At that instant, at a suicidal speed, they turned into the turnip field. The wagon pitched sharply to the left. How the old cart and I managed to stay upright, I will never know. I entered the field with the wagon still under me, its two left wheels driving firmly into the ground whilst the two right wheels spun wildly in mid-air. My heart was in my mouth.

And to think that we almost made it - almost. After the horses, the front two wheels and I made it through the gap and into the field, along with most of the wagon. Unfortunately, not the back right wheel. Suddenly, it made unfortunate contact with the gate post accompanied by an almighty bang. With a crash that could have been heard in London and a splintering of wood, everybody in the field had their eyes riveted on me and my wagon. But this was no time for embarrassment. If only that bloody gate had not been attached to that particular post, we might have cleverly avoided too much hassle and I could have bluffed it out, but it was not to be. Out came the post along with the old wooden gate which had now become firmly entangled in my wagon. Adversely, the horses gave no signs of slowing. In fact, the crash had caused the poor animals to panic as they continued to race across the deeply furrowed field. I tried as hard as I could to stop them, but my efforts were in vain.

By now, this Laurel and Hardy spectacle was being watched by nineteen hysterical PoWs, two furiously demented German guards and one hopelessly bemused Polish overseer. The extra weight of the gate, acting like an enormous anchor in that heavy earth, was slowly taking its toll as the horses began to tire. The wagon came to a gradual halt, fifty feet in front of the assembled audience. To say I was relieved might be an understatement - and then I saw the look on the guards' faces. As nervous as an errant schoolboy in front of a rabid headmaster I jumped down, eager to be free from my wayward chariot. Both Germans unslung their rifles and rushed over towards me, screaming as only they can do. In the background, my fellow PoWs were rolling in the aisles, laughing uncontrollably. One of the irate guards walked up to me, stared straight into my eyes, then brought the butt of his rifle up and sent it crashing into my left cheek. The force of the blow unbalanced me, sending me backwards into the side of the wagon, hitting it hard with my back. I was surprised then shocked by his action, not yet aware of the initial pain. He hurled every conceivable German swear word at me, 'English pig dog' being the least offensive.

"One day you bastards, you'll pay for this," I mouthed softly to myself as the throbbing in my cheekbone began. *"One day!..."*

I spat blood and fortunately for me, no teeth followed. I ran my tongue around my mouth and astonishingly, all still seemed firm. I wiped away the blood and cast a hate-filled glance in their direction, for which I could have received a second blow but fortunately they had turned back and were screaming for the others to return to work. The aching intensified.

The Frau had now arrived on the scene. She had seen my plight. Having watched the drama unfold, she had run down the track in hot pursuit. She panted as she examined the damage, which was not as bad as might have been expected. Both gate and gatepost were rotten which was fortunate for me, for had they not been, they would have been too strong, resulting in the more valuable wheel being smashed beyond repair. The Frau smoothed things over with the guards whilst I and another PoW disentangled the wagon from the gate before carrying it back to the hedgerow and flinging it to one side.

Drama over, the Frau remained whilst we resumed work and everything returned to a sort of normality but leaving me feeling stupid. The horses just sneezed, splattered and panted whilst they recovered from their exhausting trauma. I winced as I lent a hand and loaded the wagon with what had already been pulled. As soon as it was full, the Frau, four lads and I climbed aboard. I sat next to her and watched as she cautiously turned the wagon around with only the tiniest of encouragement and noise and made our way back to the farm. It was too much to hope for the lads to ignore my little accident. Immediately they began to rib me remorselessly about my horsemanship and driving skills, or to be more precise, lack of them. It wasn't long before we were all laughing, with tears running down my cheeks. I had to see the funny side despite the pain.

On arrival, the Frau climbed down and directed me to take the reins and steer the wagon to a place on the other side of the yard. I managed it quite easily under her watchful eye as the first batch of turnips were unloaded. They were to be laid down for the winter in what are called clamps. An excavation or long, shallow, rectangular depression had already been dug in the earth to make a base for the clamp. We then started to unloaded the turnips and spread them evenly across the straw-covered base. This method of storage was common practice amongst European farmers. As soon as we had unloaded, we returned to the field. We did this all day: loading, carrying and unloading, back and forth. Whilst we brought the crop in, the overseer covered the turnips with hay and by the end of the second day, we had built a long, high stack. The final task was to cover the sides and shovel back the earth, for this offered good protection from the worst that the winter weather had to offer. The method was simple but effective, and towards the end of the war, what I learnt was to be a life-saver to me and hundreds of other PoWs like me.

Whilst the lads covered the clamp, I led the horses back to the stables and removed their harnesses. Inside, the Frau was waiting for me. She smiled briefly whilst she told me what to do and watched as I tethered the horses in their stalls before watering and feeding them. Every so often I would look over at her for reassurance that all was well. She didn't seem to take her eyes off me, continuing to smile, so I smiled back.

Between each pair of horses next to their feed, I noticed a lump of glistening greyish rock held in an iron container. Both my horses were licking it with great fervour. I was puzzled but thought nothing more of it, but later learnt that it was a lump of rock salt for the horsed to lick.

My work done, I closed the barn door. The sun was low on the western horizon and the sky a blaze of flame. I watched my fellows being escorted to the farm house to collect their eagerly-awaited rations. I hurriedly joined them as they received their chunk of bread topped with a slice of sausage and washed down with ersatz. Whilst they walked to the barn, I waited just outside the door of the farmhouse, not sure what to expect. I had jealously seen what was on offer to previous horsemen on the other farms, so my hopes were high. The Frau approached and spoke, again in German.

"English" she said rather kindly, "come into the house."

Assuming that she was referring to me, I didn't need telling twice. I followed her inside, much to the irritation of the guard. I could see in his face that he thought I needed another smack for the gate incident. I followed the Frau sheepishly into the kitchen, a big, simply furnished room, typical of thousands of small farms right across this vast but poor, suffering country. In the centre stood a large old pine table, worn by time. Judging by its condition, it could have told many a tale going back over hundreds of years. Around it, several old and battered chairs stood, none of them matching. Against the walls stood cupboards and shelves. A pair of oil lamps supplied the only illumination, radiating a warm, cosy glow, but it was the smell that I really noticed.

On one side of the kitchen stood an old black range. On it, a large pot, black with soot, was smouldering away with steam steadily rising. But the smell? My mouth watered. I looked over at her as she reached for a ladle and stirred the contents of the pot. She looked at me.

"English, sit here."

I understood, drew up a chair and sat down, feeling rather uncomfortable. I had never been so luxuriously treated since joining the British Army. Not even my old platoon Sergeant had treated me so kindly. I smiled again and watched as she picked up a wooden bowl and filled it. Carefully, she carried it to the table and placed it before me. I inhaled and savoured every part of the wonderful-smelling steam that drifted lazily up and into my pleasured nostrils. The sides of my mouth ached as my saliva glands went into overdrive.

You might think I am over-reacting and being too flamboyant with my description of this far from lavish meal, but when you live through deprivation in these war years and you are hungry and starved of food for so long, I can assure you that no number of extravagant words can possibly describe the smell and taste of good, wholesome food.

Manners still held me in check until she brought her bowl to the table. She handed me bread and smiled. That was it. I dived in. It tasted beyond heavenly. She had cooked a stew of vegetables with grain of some sort and pieces of pork. Near the end, I took my piece of bread and cleaned my bowl. Oliver Twist would have been envious, for she insisted on giving me a second helping. I felt that I had died and gone to heaven.

We chatted using part German, part Polish, whilst we ate. After a few minutes I was more relaxed, and by the time I had finished my second bowl, my stomach was glowing with satisfaction. But all good things must come to an end, as they say, and it did. There was a sharp and unexpected knock on the door and in came one of the German guards, who took me back to the barn and locked me in with my fellows.

By now it was dark and I could not see the others properly and fell into the nearest space. I am sure I sensed their slight hostility towards me. In the morning, Bert, Jimmy and Johnny were fine with my luck but for a while, I was ostracised by the others, for they knew I had eaten better than them. Slowly that day they softened as we recalled the funny side of the previous day's 'crash' course in wagon driving. That night, I took the opportunity to explain to them that I had never been a horseman in my life before and that any of them could have volunteered for the vacancy if they had been quick (or stupid) enough. They seemed impressed with my brazen lie and my accident was therefore understandable in the circumstances, but still bloody funny. We recalled the incident several times more from differing perspectives before tiredness got the better of us and I and my contented stomach fell into a wonderfully deep sleep.

The following morning we awoke early as usual, and after coffee and bread with white sausage we went off to work. Fortunately,

I remembered what needed to be done and hitched up two new horses without help, albeit with some difficulty. I even managed to control the horses and the wagon without doing any further damage. Thank you God!

A relatively good day was rounded off with another splendid meal of potato and pork courtesy of the Frau, before I was returned to the barn.

On the third day, you could have been forgiven for thinking that I was an old hand at this horseman lark - if you were blind, that is, but I was slowly getting better.

That evening, the Frau assaulted my nostrils once more with another wonderful aroma of vegetable and potato stew. We continued with light conversation whilst I polished off a second portion, and I would have had a third had the Frau not left the table suddenly to disappear into one of the rooms beyond. As I sat there, looking at the sparse surroundings, I was half anticipating a knock on the door from my German minders, but instead I heard the Frau call to me.

"English, come here."

Her tone indicated that this was a gentle instruction from a woman in control. I left the table but could not resist just one more spoonful from the pot before following the sound of her voice. The farmhouse was a simple, single-storey building with two doors leading off from the kitchen, one closed and the other open. I walked through the open door and found myself entering the bedroom. Opposite stood her bed. I have no idea what else was in the room as my eyes were firmly fixed on her bed. Under the covers lay the Frau, grinning like a contented pussycat. Her bare shoulders and the top of her ample chest were visible above the bed clothes, so I assumed she was already naked. I swallowed as something between my thighs began to stir, something that had not stirred for a while as hormones, chemicals and emotions such as unadulterated lust surged through my body.

"Come here English," she growled seductively in a softened tone.

Far be it for me to disobey an order, but being a naive twenty-three, soon-to-be twenty-four-year-old virgin, I was still hesitant. I knew what was required of me but I just needed a bit of assistance. With eyes raised, I prayed.

'*Please Frau, take me,*' I heard my groin begging.

How was I to make this happen, for I wanted it to happen so badly. Over the years I had come close, but things were different in those days. Perhaps I still harboured an ingrained guilt associated with full sex through fear of fathers, unwanted pregnancies and so on. She must have seen the uncertainty in my eyes, if not terror on my inexperienced face. She threw back the covers. Unashamedly, she climbed out of bed naked and came towards me. This largish lady was now very, very, attractive. The buttons on my trousers were practically bursting as two ample bosoms came towards me. She flung her arms around my neck, pressing her soft, warm bust into my chest and drew my face down onto hers. Her eyes focused on my lips as she came closer. Then she kissed me. Her mouth was open and passionate. No tender embrace, just full of animal lust. The closeness of her unclothed body sent my head into a spin. I wasn't used to this surge of blood. Her warmth and the passion of the moment enveloped me. Hastily, she started to unbutton me, her hands feverishly yet expertly working to gain entrance. She slid her hand down the front of my pants until she easily found what she was searching for. The thought did not occur to me that I had practically been wearing the same clothes since leaving England in 1940, had little access to soap and washing facilities and was continuously troubled with pubic hair infestation. However, the Frau and I had scant regard for personal hygiene at this precise moment, for our ardour was now beyond control and our fervour was definitely in the ascendancy. Nothing, and I mean nothing, short of a ten-tonne bomb dropping directly on top of me was going to stop this erotic coupling.

My prayers had been answered. She flung me onto the bed and followed, falling on me to lock lips once more. Within seconds, she had turned me over to be on top and was frantically pulling me inside of her. It was the most wonderful feeling that I had ever experienced. So sensitive and so warm. The lustful manner of this experienced older woman's confident love-making was sending me wild. I believed I was doing something right, for it was not long before she was screaming with pleasure.

"Fest, fest, fest," she cried.

I assumed this meant 'faster' and consequently pumped away at a rate of knots that I didn't know I was capable of, only to discover that she was in fact saying 'steady'.

"Langsam, langsam Franz."

Now this one I knew so I went slower. Whatever she asked I did. I loved her taking control. She was wild. I had no idea what to expect but her moans and our raw, sexual act was driving me on like an unstoppable tidal wave.

"Quicker, quicker."

So I did.

"Hurry English, hurry!"

So I did.

Driven on even further by her expressions of lust, I too was rising to an almighty climax. A long cry of pleasure left her lips as she clung to me, pulling me down onto her, clawing at my exposed back and buttocks. I was now oblivious to her feelings, still going strong, trying desperately and selfishly to continue to my own culmination, but I was naive for she was spent. She composed herself and spoke firmly into my ear.

"English stop, pull out, pull out," she said, at the same time pushing me away, almost throwing me off. I understood the 'stop' command but was unsure of her other words. We uncoupled.

'Damn, damn, damn!' I thought.

Fearing pregnancy, she did not want me to ejaculate inside her, but having had her fun she demonstrated just how unselfish she was. Smiling tenderly, she kissed me once more before rolling me onto my back and finishing me off by hand. I was more than happy.

Now spent, we recouped side by side, happy with our labours. After what we had just done, I thought it only polite to ask her a question.

"What is your name?"

"Celestyna," she happily informed me and I repeated it. Celestial, a heavenly body?... Oh yes! most definitely.

After a brief pause, she asked for my name.

"Dennis."

"Den-nis," she repeated and nodded.

That was more than enough talking for she was not fully satisfied, and after several minutes rest she demanded more of the same. Given my appalling diet, weight loss and the physical demands of slave labour, I was amazed at how much staying power I still had. I felt like Adonis, the beautiful youth of Greek mythology, loved by the goddess Aphrodite. In reality, this was much too grand an analogy for a lust-filled youth like me, but losing my virginity seemed to warrant such rich terminology.

After a lengthier second round, she eventually seemed satisfied.

All too soon our intercourse was over and it was time to return to normality, to being a PoW and she to being the farm master. It had been a torrid act of mutual, lustful gratification and she was as happy and relaxed about it as she was with every other part of her bodily functions and daily routine. It meant nothing to her and that suited me. I wore my huge grin from ear to ear with pride for I was no longer a virgin and I had finally tasted the forbidden fruits of unbridled passion and was hooked. I happily shared the knowledge of my good fortune with my mates. They were sick with envy. I continued working for Celestyna as the horseman and her stud for several glorious weeks. I ate her wonderful food and, to use an appropriate equestrian term, 'covered' her almost every night before returning to the barn with smug contentment. I was a model student. As the nights progressed Celestyna showed me which buttons to press and I became a model button-presser.

One unfortunate morning, it all came to an abrupt end as all good things do. I had just hitched up the horses and was adjusting the wooden pin holding back the wagon's side when a large metal pitch-fork crashed onto the cobbled floor of the stable, causing the horses to lurch forward. My coat got caught in the moving wheel, pulling me forward with the wagon. I pushed my arm out to steady myself but it went straight through the wheel spokes with my hand coming to rest on the protruding floor of the wagon. The next spoke of the wheel continued forward and came smashing down on my trapped arm. My whole body twisted and I fell heavily to the floor, just missing being caught under the heavy wheel.
SNAP!

I wasn't aware of the pain initially but within seconds, I cried out and Celestyna came running in, steadied and secured the horses before bending down to help. The pain was intense although I tried to hide the fact, but my face must have said it all.

"Keep still Dennis, just sit there whilst I get help."

She ran to summon a guard who eventually came. By now my arm, wrist and hand were beginning to turn an interesting colour and blood oozed from an open wound. It looked a bloody mess. He showed no sense of urgency as Celestyna helped me up as I cradled my pulsating limb. Once inside the kitchen she sat me down in front of the stove and removed my coat and jacket. Every movement made me cringe. A sharp angry lump in my arm was clearly visible. Celestyna gathered three pieces of split wood, placing them around my arm and tying it all together with torn strips of cloth. Once the task was finished, she turned to address the guard who was hovered over me.

"He needs to go to *'lazarette'*. I'm sure it's broken."

At first I thought that sounds like an exotic holiday destination, only to discover that 'lazarette' meant Infirmary.

The guard didn't look overly pleased but decided it was the best option, telling her that we would have to use the wagon. She put on another coat and headscarf whilst the guard disappeared, presumably to speak to his colleague.

There now began another extremely uncomfortable return trip back to camp. Up until now, I had not really realised just how many potholes there were in the road network of this abandoned wasteland. I had stuffed my hand through the opening of my buttoned-up coat in the style of Napoleon, to support my arm and lay back on the pile of sacks that Celestyna had placed on the floor of the wagon. I closed my eyes and tried to blot out the pain. For over four long hours we bumped along in the direction of Marienburg before reaching the gates. I thanked Celestyna, heard her turn and head off, never to see her again.

Once inside, I was taken to the camp doctor. I say doctor, but I think he was a PoW who had once been hit with a medical book and a page of it had stuck. He soon decided that my problem was way out of his jurisdiction and I should be sent on to a proper doctor. The Germans were in no particular hurry but eventually I was escorted in a truck to the main hospital in Marienburg where there were real doctors and nurses. If I hadn't been in so much pain, I would have enjoyed the outing. I was seen by a Wehrmacht doctor who was actually human and spoke to me as such. Once my ragged bandages were removed he examined my arm and hand. I winced. By now, I was ready to crawl up the walls. He told me to relax. I muttered through clenched teeth.

"S*!!?**F.*,,*!^>*!!!," or words to that effect, for relaxation was not particularly easy at that point.

He felt, studied, felt again, gripped and SNAP!...

By now, I was halfway up the walls. At least in the cowboy films that I had seen as a child, somebody either gave the patient a piece of leather to bite on, a bottle of whisky to numb the pain or smashed a bottle over his head to render him unconscious,... but me, I got nothing.

My open wound was bathed in salt water and then iodine applied. As the chemicals burnt into the messy torn skin, I crawled to the top of the walls. An officious nurse took over but I couldn't understand a word of what she was saying. Her job was to sew my flesh together. Even before she began, I crawled from the walls onto the ceiling and tasted blood as I bit into my bottom lip. She finished off with another searing of iodine before my forearm, wrist and hand was put in a splint, bandaged and plastered. That was it. They actually did a good job but the after care was lacking. Without further ceremony, they turfed me out of the luxurious hospital and despatched me back to Stalag XXB where I was registered sick and excused work for the next few weeks.

~ NEW COATS ~
Early October 1942

Another year was slowly creeping to its inevitable conclusion through the miserable Polish autumn. Another year spent in captivity, now totalling two long years and four long months. How many more years would my captivity last?

I had survived the hospital and been back a week or two and was already bored, hungering to escape the claustrophobic confines of Stalag XXB once more. My mates were all off on their work parties so I had plenty of time on my hands. This allowed me to catch up with the bulletins, brought to us courtesy of Sammy Newton and the 'secret radio'.

Malta was still taking a hammering from German bombers but holding out bravely against all odds. Valiant Stalingrad was suffering greatly from the huge German onslaught, but they had finally halted their seemingly unstoppable advance.

In North Africa, a British General called Montgomery was turning the tide of defeat into a victory. There was fierce fighting at a place called El Alamein.

Finally, in the Pacific, the talk was of American and allied gains of islands somewhere or other, but that was still too far away for most of us to care.

My arm was healing well and I spent most of my days talking, reading, walking round the perimeter, writing as many letters as was permitted and listening to rehearsals. By now, the musicians and 'luvvies' of the camp had organised themselves into orchestras and theatre producers. I used to pop in to their hut and listen to the music. Norman Wylie was preparing for 'Swiss Spring', his latest production to hit the boards of The Willenberg Theatre (named after the nearby village just outside Marienburg). The quality of their musical renditions was amazing and utterly professional given the ad hoc collection of instruments they had acquired in recent times. But despite this holiday during convalescence, I was itching to get out.

What made the camp more unbearable than normal was the rain. We had entered a particularly wet period and the resulting quagmire made our lives hell. As unpleasant as it was for those with boots, the unfortunate prisoners who wore wooden clogs had to endure the hellish pain and discomfort of wearing wooden clogs that stuck fast in mud.

One such miserable morning, our jolly German jailers announced some rare good news.

"Winter is coming and soon we will give you warm new coats. We are very kind to you all, yes?"

"When?" came the expected catcall, all in jest.

"Tomorrow, you will get them tomorrow."

"Tomorrow, always tomorrow."

The muttered response from someone behind me was followed by murmurs of agreement and grunts of disbelief.

Tomorrow came and went as it always did, and so did the next day. Eventually, one damp afternoon some two weeks later, trucks turned up, sliding through the thick obstacle course of ooze that was the camp. Inside the trucks were the long-awaited coats. The following morning roll call was particularly long and the number count was repeated four times before the Germans finally accepted that nobody had escaped their clutches. We collected our coffee and our much-anticipated new winter coats. Unlike the previous coats, these were new or nearly new standard British Army issue, thick wool and properly lined. We were going to be warmer at last. I happily slipped off my old one and exchanged it.

· · · § · · ·

383

~ TRYING TO STAY WARM ~
Late October 1942

By now, the majority of PoWs had experienced two Polish winters. You really had to be with us to fully appreciate just how unbelievably cold it was. There was little to do in the dark, freezing winter months as farm work 'froze up' until the spring thaw, with snow clearing and rail maintenance our main occupation. Some of the inmates of Stalag XXB stagnated in camp, waiting for the winter to pass, whilst others filled their time with music, singing, acting and football. As for me, I was just desperate to get out.

Without adequate heating, the single-skinned wooden huts made inhospitable habitats during the winter months. Our ration of coal for our single stove was not enough to keep us warm. When our meagre supply ran out, we had to rely on the tried and tested methods of smuggling combustibles into camp hidden amongst our clothing. This helped a little, but when we couldn't get out of the camp, we had to resort to more inventive methods and our new three-tiered wooden bunks held the key. Under our straw palliasses was a hidden fuel, wooden slats that literally supported us at night. Someone had the bright idea of using this strictly limited and unrenewable resource to keep us warm. In the short term this did seem like a reasonable idea, but it did lead to problems. The first was obvious, for if we burnt too many we could all expect increasingly uncomfortable nights. Secondly, it was a punishable offence, for the Germans didn't take kindly to having their furniture burnt. Once we had burnt a limited number of slats, we were faced with the problem of concealing the crime. This was manageable because of one undeniable quality that the Germans possessed, that of being predictably methodical, and it was this characteristic that eventually helped us mask the crime. Every so often our guards would spring a surprise visit on us. Their arrival was an irritating expectation, for we could see them coming a mile off. Without hesitation the alarm was given and preparations made as the guards worked their way along the line of huts.

The first time I experienced such a search was one October day in '42, shortly before leaving for the sugar beet fields. We were sitting in our room when the guards came bursting in for a bunk inspection and, at the same time, searching our huts for contraband. Naturally, they would start by searching the rooms nearest to the main entrance and gradually work their way along the central corridor to the other end. All the bunks in these first four rooms would have their full complement of slats. As soon as the inspection of the first two rooms opposite each other was complete and the guards had entered the second pair, the first hut occupants would grab a few slats and shove them under their coats before walking down the corridor to the third set of rooms where they needed them. Quickly and quietly, they were handing over to the occupants to re-stock their bunks. Failing that method, they were shoved outside the windows to awaiting couriers, who took them to the next pair of rooms further along the corridor and so on. Using this method it was relatively easy to fool the systematic Germans. When the search was finally over and the Germans moved on, I realised just how hard my heart was pounding with the excitement of the little scam. Distractions like this were treated almost as a sport and they kept our spirits high, for in spite of our game-like attitude to the romp, there was always an underlying fear of being caught and subsequently punished. But that day we got away with it.

~ SLEEPING TOGETHER... AND SEX? ~

It was only late autumn but as winter approached, the night time temperature plummeted. One-hundred men sleeping inside the cold huts caused ice droplets to form on the walls. With just our clothing and a blanket for warmth, some of my fellow prisoners often took extreme steps to stay warm during the depths of the deepest winters. They would cuddle up in the one bunk, sharing their body heat under the combined comfort of their blankets. It made good sense I suppose, but it was not for me. I preferred to sleep alone with only my bed bugs, fleas and lice as my sleeping partners. I had no idea if the 'couples' ever got up to anything under the covers, neither did I really want to know, but I am sure that in some cases 'things' did happen. However, without doubt, actually sleeping huddled together did keep them warmer.

No matter how much I tried to resist the urge, I needed to go for a pee. The chill only making my condition worse. I couldn't hold it any longer, I was desperate. I folded back my blanket and quietly climbed into my boots. Even though McDowell's policing and campaign of law and order had considerably reduced incidents of theft within the camp, I still kept my precious boots tied firmly to my body whilst I slept.

My fear of having them stolen was still very real. I stood up and walked out into the central corridor and made my way towards the exit whilst wrapping myself in my coat. As I stepped through the open door, the icy Siberian wind made me shiver to my core. With the worst of winter yet to come, I faced the next few months with dismay. I stood in front of the piss pot and unbuttoned my flies. I was engrossed with the task in hand, so to speak, so I was hardly aware when a head appeared at crotch level.

"What the...!" I exclaimed, hastily shaking my todger before stuffing it back protectively from whence it came. Before me was the face of a stranger propositioning me for sex.

"Hey mate, fancy a bit of fun?" a distinctly male voice whispered. In the shadows, I could not see who he was, but I was sure of one thing, it was not Lana Turner.

Somewhat taken aback I replied. "No thanks mate, not my cup of tea," was all I could think to say. Apart from scaring the hell out of me, I was unable to properly carry out my business due to the strange circumstances. I quickly buttoned myself up and nipped back indoors. "Phew!" I sighed, "that was a narrow escape."

As time dragged on by, I grew tired of being pestered every time I needed to relieve myself, so 'piss off' became my personal choice of reply to such proposals. Apparently, sodomy, buggery, fraternity of every sort and just good old-fashioned hand jobs were available every night 'at a piss pot near you'. As for me, no thank you very much. Anyone touching my todger had at least have large bumps on her chest and not in possession of meat and two veg. However, I didn't judge those men, neither would I attempt to. We were all young, locked up together in the prime of our lives. Despite our appalling diet, inside the huts at night, testosterone was as rampant as our body lice. Therefore, it came as no great surprise to discover that in the absence of women, homosexuality was common place.

As I lay back in my bunk, I recalled my first confusing and reluctant brush with homosexuality,... and from an unlikely source;

> It was just before my twelfth birthday, shortly after moving to Hersham police station, that my parents decided it was time for me to be confirmed. Classes were being held at our local church of St. Peter's, next door to the police station. I had no great desire to be confirmed but it seemed to be expected of me, so I did what I was told. The classes were taken by

the Curate, a man with the flamboyant and amusing name of Mr. Ambrose Maryon-Watson. Dressed in his black cassock and dog collar he seemed friendly enough, and much to my surprise we thoroughly enjoyed his classes... at first. Very much aware that several of us boys, including myself, were interested in collecting postage stamps, he would gather us around the table when the class finished and produce his own collection of neatly presented stamps. On the pretext of viewing them properly, he would lift each of us up onto his lap in turn, whilst joking and laughing. Somehow, the experience always ended up with him 'accidentally' sliding his hands up the legs of our shorts. In our innocence, we were not fully aware of the perverse sexual nature of his actions. I could not verbalise my concerns, especially as it concerned a man of the cloth, but within a couple of weeks I felt increasingly uncomfortable with his behaviour so I decided not to attend his classes any more. As a result, he popped round to see my mother to enquire as to my non-attendance. Mother let him in and invited him into the lounge. We all sat down and after an initial chat, mother left us alone to talk the problem through. The moment she left the lounge his behaviour changed. I was still wearing shorts and he lent forward and began to touch me, inappropriately on my thigh. I stood up and backed away. He then stood up and moved towards me, so I ran around the room with him chasing after me, wanting to touch me. Eventually he managed to grab hold of me, most improperly. At that exact moment in time, my father entered the room via the other lounge door that connected our home directly with the police station. Father looked, saw and instantly knew what was happening. Within three paces, he had Mr. Maryon-Watson, pervert and Curate of the parish, in his big, powerful hands. He opened the front door and holding him roughly by his dog collar and the seat of his cassock, father dragged him unceremoniously across our small front garden and through the gate before launching him head-long into the road. He landed flat on his face for all to see.

As I recalled the image of the Curate lying face down in the road, I chuckled to myself, disturbing the man in the adjacent bunk who thought I had taken leave of my senses once more. From that moment on, whenever I needed to urinate at night, I always watched my front *and* back.

~ THE ONLY THING I GET TO PULL IS THE BEET ~
November 1942

My arm had healed with no unpleasant side effects and I was utterly delighted when I saw Bert, Jimmy and Johnny return from their work detail.

"Mar, good to see you again mate."

We smiled, patted each other on the backs and shook hands till they fell off. A twinge went through my arm.

"How was your holiday, "how's the arm, still got it I see?"

"We missed you,... or at least , we missed your shopping!"

"That sounds more like it, you rotten sods, how have you survived without me looking after you?"

"Easily thanks Mar and whilst you were away slacking, you missed the pleasure of the most beautiful ladies we have ever seen."

"Yes, forget your 'Celestyna'. Just after you left, a gang of Russian Dump trucks arrived."

"Yer!... made Betty Grable and Rita Hayworth look like scrawny witches."

"Piss off, you almost had me going there." It was great to have them back.

We spent the day catching up but I could not help rubbing in the fact that during my convalescence, I had basked in the delights of Red Cross parcels. They looked a little bit jealous so by way of compensation, I offered my cigarettes round, which was enough to please them.

By now I was finding the camp claustrophobic. It was time to get out, so off we went on the next working party. By this time, tens of thousands of prisoners like me were passing through Stalag XXB, working outside the wire. We had now acquired a nickname. We had become known as 'Cook's Tourists', a reference to the famous Thomas Cook travel agent's back home, with us working away from camp being the so-called tourists.

Immediately after morning parade, I collected my few belongings and ran back to join my group of 'Cook's Tourists' but a more accurate description would be slaves. The trucks took an age to arrive and we were kept waiting in the cold, making constant trips to the latrines just to keep warm and get out of the wind. When they eventually arrived, we boarded and settled down as comfortably as we could, not knowing how long our journey would take. As we passed the guard house, I watched through the open back as the camp drifted away into the distance. It felt good to be leaving the drabness of Stalag XXB once more, even if we were only swapping one shit hole for another.

The journey itself was bumpy and cold and would have been totally non-eventful had it not been for Taffy. It wasn't long before the first of our number needed to have a pee. Taffy, you might not be surprised to learn, was a stocky Welsh character and was now desperate. To even contemplate asking the German driver to stop was pointless, so Taffy announced to those present as to his intentions. The guards and those on either side of the benches nearest the opening slid back into the dry safety of the truck for fear of being caught in any back spray whilst Taffy prepared to unleash his hose. As if anticipating his action, the driver hit a huge pothole, causing the truck to bounce all over the road. In spite of Taffy's small stature and low centre of gravity, he was sent hurtling backwards onto the floor of the truck, his tool still firmly held in hand. We were all in uproar at his hilarious predicament. Now nursing an aching head (and his over-exposed todger), Taffy cautiously fought to resume his position whilst the truck continued to bounce over the rough surface. Now firmly holding onto the roof, he began to pee out of the back, and whilst doing so he came into full and glorious view of an unsuspecting pedestrian.

"Sorry love," shouted Taffy politely.

The startled woman was certainly shocked by what she was witnessing, which only added to our enjoyment of the show. Now even our guards were laughing. Before Taffy had a chance to finish his 'leak', the truck overtook an unfortunate cyclist who suffered the indignity of being hit by Taffy's urine shower. Unfortunately it wasn't a German soldier. The disgusted cyclist almost fell off his bike but managed to compose himself before shaking his fist and shouting what I assume to be obscenities as we sped off into the distance.

Things gradually returned to normal and we settled down. I buried myself in the warmth of my new coat and tried to get some sleep as best I could. It wasn't easy, but I eventually managed to drop off.

When I awoke, I saw that we had arrived at yet another farm just as the sun was sinking below the horizon. After the disappointment of no food washed down with a bucket of water, we were locked in the barn for the night, where I soon found my friend Johnny staring intently at a fat chicken. It wasn't long before his imagination got the better of him.

"Have any of you lot got some sausage and sage stuffing cos' I keep seeing a roast chicken jumping around in front of me."

We howled with laughter until someone stated that he thought it an excellent idea.

"Oh for f***s sake Johnny, shut up will you." Bert spat the words out. I wasn't sure if he was joking or not. All was quiet. Then Johnny started up again.

"How appetising that bird would look thinly sliced on a huge plate surrounded by crispy roast potatoes, peas, Yorkshire pudding and smothered in rich gravy washed down with a pint of beer..."

He hardly got the final word out before Bert jumped up with a crazed look on his face. Murder was about to take place. I looked across at the others. We all had a look of worried embarrassment coupled with an expression as if to say, 'I think you might have over-done it this time Johnny, prepare to die'. Bert fell on top of Johnny, grabbed him by the scruff of his scrawny neck and spat his words out, dripping with malice. Just as suddenly as it had all kicked off, Bert pressed his face to within an inch of Johnny's.

"Right you f***ing bastard. I'll get the chicken ready if you find the bloody Christmas Pud!" and gently squeezed his shrunken cheeks.

We fell about. It was side splitting time.

We continued to toy with the idea for a few wonderful moments until the cooking problem was explored. Unfortunately, the wonderful smell was bound to attract the unwarranted attention of the guards, the chicken would undoubtedly be missed and its disappearance soon realised. This would probably result in us being court martialled for grand theft, so the outcome for the chicken was favourable and it lived to tell the tale.

By now I was gasping for a fag as I hadn't been able to trade for any. Cigarettes for us were in constant short supply and to make matters even worse, I had already smoked the last of mine. It was with difficulty that I eventually fell into a nicotine-deprived sleep.

Dawn came all too soon but we were very glad that our resident chicken was a hen and not a cockerel for two reasons; the noise and the three eggs which we manage to spirit away.

After morning coffee and a generous chunk of bread and delicious dripping, we were escorted to the fields to start pulling sugar beet, which was usually one of the last crops to be harvested at the end of the farming year.

Boy, it was cold that morning. The wind was blowing bitterly from the north but at least we were more prepared for this winter. How I pitied the Russian troops fighting on the Eastern Front in this climate, let alone in the terrible winter to come. As we walked over the hard ground, I pulled down the side flaps of my cap and lifted high the collar of my coat, trying to bury my head into my neck and shoulders, eager to protect my ears. I felt the chill travel down the side of my neck to my body. I pushed my hands as far as I could into the depths of my coat pockets. As I walked, I looked around at my fellows as the sixteen of us continued to blindly follow our guards in a long single file. I saw the funny side of our line of identical-looking beings, short-necked specimens in long coats with all our heads leaning on the same side, into the wind, no hands visible, stumbling along the uneven ground towards a lone wagon on the edge of the field. A fine frost, like sprinkled icing sugar, covered the uneven mounds and furrows and limp tufts of sugar beet lay in untidy lines before us. The rows of beet seemed to extend forever across the vast open field. I had never seen such a great expanse of nothingness stretching away to the hazy horizon without interruption from trees, buildings or hills. It would take an eternity to prise this crop from the frozen ground. This must be what is meant by purgatory. Was I really that bad a human being that I would have to endure this toil until the end of time? The smile fell from my face.

We were each handed a 'dooker', a short-handled trowel with two straight metal prongs. The farm overseer or owner, for I knew not which, proceeded to show us how to lift the beet using the tool. Bending down, he took hold of the top leafy head with one hand and, holding the trowel in the other, he stuck it into the hard ground at the side of the plant before slowly forcing it out. Hey presto, one sugar beet lifted. Only another three-million-nine-hundred-and-ninety-nine-thousand-nine-hundred-and-ninety-nine to go. I could hardly contain my excitement at what was now in store for me. The overseer slung the beet down into the furrow at his side and then went on to the next plant, repeating the action several times before straightening himself up and telling us to begin.

In this exposed environment, I was frozen. Even our guards managed to look cold, dressed as they were in their thick coats, woollen gloves and knee-high boots. The most senior amongst them adjusted his rifle before screaming.

"Hurry shithead" he bellowed and turned to walk away, not going anywhere in particular, merely to get his circulation going. I suppose he needed to shout to emphasise that his side were the victors and we were the lowly captives.

"Oh please go away!" (or words to that effect) came the almost obligatory muttered response.

So we began our Herculean task. Our job was to each lift three rows, the length of which had already been predetermined and marked by the overseer. The ground was hard but we got stuck in, although the tubers were reluctant to leave their hard bed. By midday, my back was aching. It was a relief to stand up straight and arch my shoulders and spine in the opposite direction. As I looked around, I noticed a small group following in our wake. As they neared, I counted thirty of them, topping and tailing our discarded beet as they moved forward. The leaves fell into the left furrow whilst they dropped the roots to the right. Behind them came the horse-drawn wagon and another party of women who loaded the beet onto the wagon. Towards the end of the day they had almost caught up with us and I could see them more clearly. They were young like us and possessed the beauty that comes with youth. Even in their peasant clothes, with scarves tied tightly around their heads, you could see the fineness of their features. Every now and again I would stand up and look backwards towards them and smile, and in return they smiled back. Suddenly, the prospect of pulling the beet for an eternity didn't seem so bad.

As it grew dark, our very bored, very cold and very irritated guards called us over and counted us. Sixteen all present and correct. I don't know where they expected any of us to have disappeared to as we were surrounded by open nothingness. I felt exhausted and my back ached with the pain of my labours as we walked back along the dirt track. On our return, we took our chunk of bread and tin of wholesome soup to the shelter of the barn. What pleasure this basic food gave me. I cupped the warm tin in my hands, enjoying the comforting heat that radiated into my bones. I stared into the tin. Large chunks of fresh vegetables with oats and pieces of precious meat floating amongst the vegetables, albeit small. I held my tin close to my face and bathed in its steaming warmth. I could feel droplets of condensation form on my chilled face. I felt good. With the Polish girls now on site, I was actually feeling happier for the first time in a while. Bert, Jimmy, Johnny and I joked about our chances of romance, but Johnny insisted that if push came to shove he would prefer a cigarette. I, on the other hand, wanted both.

As I drained the last of my soup and ran my bread around the sides of the tin to collect every last tasty morsel, our guards returned in a much better frame of mind. They counted us one last time before slamming the barn door shut and placing the large wooden plank across the entrance door, returning to the farm house for their meal. Apart from the misery of standing in the cold for most of the day, I imagined the guards typically enjoyed this type of posting for they were safe, well fed and, once inside the house, were able to relax in front of a warm open fire. There they could drink, joke and relax before collapsing into their comfortable beds, all provided courtesy of the farm owner. A slight improvement to fighting on the Russian front.

Our guards were changed over on a regular basis, and I suppose it made perfect sense. Nearly all of them were active soldiers, fighting the Soviets. During the winter months the cold must have been appalling, for when they were transferred to us for rest and recuperation, many arrived with blackened lips and frost-bitten ends of noses and edges of ears. Sometimes I almost felt sorry for them, the poor bastards. Maybe being a PoW did have some advantages?

This same pattern followed day after day after day. We lifted the beet, the girls topped and tailed and others collected the trimmed beet. Fortunately, our three gangs were not the only working parties on the farm. Had we been so, then we really would have to serve a life sentence in order to clear the vast field. In the distance, I could see others dotted around, working on their allotted sections.

On the sixth day, my loins were aching and I had a germ of an idea that I was itching to implement. I slowed down and hung around waiting for the girls to catch up. As they neared, I saw the one who had previously smiled back at me and whom I particularly liked the look of. She was now only six feet away. I stood up, looked directly at her, smiled broadly and showed off my grasp of the Polish language with a swagger and a flourish that was meant to knock her off her feet and fall instantly in love with me. Such misplaced arrogance.

"Dzien dobry." ("Good morning").

She maintained her smile, nodded coyly and responded in the appropriate way.

Every day for the next three days, we repeated the same guarded greeting. I even managed to have a brief conversation with her and learnt that they came from Warsaw. All were young, pretty and well educated. Some came from the university whilst others had worked in

393

the beauty business before the war, but all had been forced out of the capital by the Germans to work as farm labourers. Collectively, they did look a fine bunch.

Within days, I had a desire to move my embryonic romance along a step further with my new Polish friend. I wanted to ask her 'How are you?' and by doing so impress her with my Polish, but I didn't know what words to use. Our Polish overseer was now working alongside us on a regular basis, encouraging us to work as quickly as we could. He seemed to be a decent enough person and we all got on well with him, for after all we both had a common enemy to hate. He was standing close by so I sauntered over to him, smiled and asked him the question.

"How do you say 'How are you?' in Polish?"

He smiled, casting a quick look back to the girls working behind me and instantly knew why I wanted to know.

He nodded knowingly, increased his smile and replied.

"Twoj cipa jest wilgotny i ocieka."

I repeated the phrase a couple of times to make sure that I had got it right, thanked him and returned to my duties, repeating the words to myself over and over again.

The following day my Polish girl appeared and as soon as I could engineer a close encounter, I greeted her.

"Dzien dobry," I said, and she responded as she always did, with her cute little smile.

Feeling confident, I repeated my newly learnt phrase.

"Twoj cipa jest wilgotny i ocieka"

Her countenance altered and a look of utter horror swept over her sweet, young, innocent face. She stopped dead in her tracks as her mouth dropped open, taking a couple of steps backwards before turning, almost tripping and fleeing to rejoin the safety of her group.

My mouth now dropped open as her wave of horror enveloped me. I was puzzled. What had I done but, more importantly, what had I said? My Polish girl had obviously spoken to her friends, for they were now staring at me with disgust. I looked about me, searching hopelessly for an explanation. All the others PoWs were still working, oblivious to my concerns. Then I saw the Polish overseer watching me. He seemed barely able to contain his smile. As the girls had now backed away completely, he had guessed that I had repeated his phrase. I smelt a rat as my face grew as red as the beetroot that we sometime harvested. I walked across to him.

"What does *Twoj cipa jest wilgotny i ocieka* really mean?" I enquired, deep suspicion etched in my weathered face.

He just kept smiling and shrugged his broad shoulders, suddenly seeming not to understand a single word of English. After pushing him further, he refused to reply, but at the same time denied any wrongdoing. However, the grin on his rugged face gave him away. This joker had caught me out, and whatever he had told me to say it certainly wasn't 'How are you?'. It was weeks before I managed to discover what his words meant. Unknowingly, I had deeply offended this beautiful, educated young girl by saying 'Your lower lady bits are dripping'.

(Even now, Dennis couldn't bring himself to use the swear word!)

The worst chat-up line in the world, I guess. Was it any wonder that we both coloured up and the girl disappeared from my life, never to speak to me again?

Every time I grabbed hold of the leaves to lift the beet, my hands became smeared with the sticky sweet sap, and day after day it etched deeper into the pores and creases of my skin. With inadequate washing facilities I couldn't easily remove it and consequently, in the cold conditions, my hands grew hard and brittle with the impregnated sugar. As I opened my palms each morning, the skin cracked and blood slowly oozed out. Likewise my fingers bled from every crease. After only a few days my bare hands were a sore, blooded mess. They soon became agonising. There was no elasticity or flexibility in the skin and they soon resembled old hardened leather. Of course, the Germans wouldn't issue us with gloves so we just had to grin and bear the pain.

We continued working through November and well into December before finally pulling the last of the cursed beet. I was relieved that our horrendous task was done, for there was a good covering of snow on the ground already and the worst of the Polish winter was about to hit.

Two days later, an old lorry arrived having been delayed by the snow. As usual, this was unannounced. We climbed into the back, having no idea what new miseries awaited us.

· · · § · · ·

~ FROM FARM TO FACTORY ~
Late December 1942

As the crow flies, it was a relatively short distance to our new place of work, but on the Polish roads, in our old canvas-covered truck, the painful journey was cold, uncomfortable and took forever. We travelled over ice-covered tracks, driven by a manic driver who seemed hell-bent on making our ride as disagreeable as possible, searching out every conceivable rut, pot hole and rock. He allowed us no stops. With no heating, food and more importantly, no cigarettes, we sat on the hard wooden flooboards whilst our backsides and bones took a hammering, accompanied by the melodic whistle of the arctic wind as it tore through the many gaps in the canvas cover.

We arrived at a huge, depressing-looking brick and concrete monolith set alone in the barren countryside of northern Poland. Running right past the building was a single-track rail line. On arrival, we were herded into the main building, which was the factory itself. Inside resembled a huge warehouse, cathedral-like in proportions. Although the interior of the building was only a few degrees above freezing, it felt good to escape the bitter wind that swept unhindered across the flat, open lands. This building was to become our home for the foreseeable future. We were taken to a quiet corner and shown our sleeping area: no bunks, just a collection of the usual straw-filled palliasses, dumped straight onto the cold, concrete floor. They had been well used but it was not wise to dwell on the previous occupants or what germs and parasites they might have left behind.

I flopped down onto the nearest spare mattress. I did consider ordering room service as I was feeling a little peckish, but after careful consideration I decided not to bother after watching a rather surly guard ram his rifle butt into the chest of another more blunt and unwise PoW.

The following morning heralded the dawn chorus.

"Raus".

How I hated to hear that word. I had no need to dress as I had slept in all my clothes, coat, boots and all. After morning coffee, we were counted and taken outside to where the rail line passed. To say it was cold was an understatement. In the light of a weak morning sun, I scanned the bleak landscape. All I could see was mile upon mile of flat, open wilderness littered with untidy coverings of snow on the vast open fields stretching as far as the eye could see. By the side of the rail line was a slightly raised platform. A long line of small, open wagons was waiting for us and filled with something that I prayed I would never, ever see again. Bloody sugar beet! Our factory was a centralised point for processing the beet!

Instinctively, I clenched my fists and felt the pain in my cracked hands. I picked up a huge fork with thick, blunted prongs. My instructions were to climb into the wagon and unload the beet by shovelling them into the broad metal trough running alongside the rail line. The trough was called 'Der Schwimmer'. It was on a slight decline that ran down into the factory itself. At the top end of the trough, water was pumped in and gravity dictated that it flowed down past us and into the factory, carrying the beet with it. This had the added advantage of washing the crop as it journeyed.

By now, the wind was howling, making the temperature appear well below freezing. I pulled down the flaps on my forage cap to cover my ears and began. Even with my new coat I still felt the bitter agony of the winter through to my bones, but after only a short time of labouring, sweat broke out and my coat came off. I carefully placed it by my side so that I could keep an eye on it, having learnt through bitter experience the stupidity of leaving anything of value unattended for even a second. To do so was to court disaster, being the difference between life and death in this agonising winter that was fast descending upon us.

As soon as we had emptied one train load, more arrived. It was looking like another unremitting hard slog. I knew I should be getting used to this toil by now, but it was still back-breaking. For the first time since my capture, I was made to work a twelve-hour shift and this became the norm. By the time it was over, I was absolutely drained. I climbed back into the shelter of my coat, having never allowed it to leave my sight.

The days limped on by. Whilst slaving at the factory, I was unable to refer to my diary and missed the opportunity of thanking the Germans for ignoring my birthday once more. It was probably a good thing because it would only have made me miserable by recalling my twenty-first birthday in the Erdehütte two years previously. God, was it really two years ago? Time was crawling by at a pace that only the young can understand.

As a child, each day took a year to pass. At school, the weekends seemed a month away. When I started my first job, each day

*lasted a week, but as a PoW, devoid of the most basic comforts
and without adequate food or clothing, every single painful day
dragged by as if it would never end. Now, in my old age, each day
draws to an end before it has even begun and I look back over my
life and wonder where all the time has gone. It is as though I have
been robbed of my youth and it pains me. A tear wells in my eyes
for I want to live... and be with my friends and loved ones forever.*

Today was Christmas day.

"Happy Christmas! Happy f***ing Christmas!"

This was the universal sarcastic greeting, followed by laughter,
for we still found humour wherever we could. Generous Fritz gave
us the day off, but that was more for their benefit as it allowed them
time to get merry and sing. For us, it looked like being yet another
miserable event, painfully reminding us of our separation from our
loved ones before passing on by. However, our Scottish partners in
misery would have none of it. Today was Christmas and, in a week's
time, Hogmanay, and it was a shame to ignore the former and a
mortal sin to ignore the latter. At midday, as if from nowhere, the
wonderful Scots revealed containers. Bread and Polish sausage were
produced and cigarettes were pooled in order for us to have what was
to be our own special Christmas dinner. We ate the food, smoked and
drank the contents of the containers and that was the last thing that I
remembered of Christmas Day 1942.

In the morning I grudgingly regained consciousness, surprised
that my body was still alive and wishing that my head belonged
to someone else, for I had the mother of all hangovers. Not even
the cold blast of that Siberian gale could shock me into life. I
simply needed to die. It was appropriate that today was Boxing
Day for my poor head was throbbing as though I had just fought
the American world heavyweight boxing champion Joe Louis.
That day, I took a solemn oath that I would never ever touch another
drop of that evil Scottish liquid.

· · · § · · ·

1943

Still at the Factory

January had arrived. Another birthday missed, another Christmas gone and another year of my young life squandered in captivity. How many more would I have to endure? But I dare not ask the question, scared of the answer. 'Live each day as it comes with no thought of yesterday or of tomorrow' was the only way I was going to survive this wretchedness in hell.

A flutter of winter's powder was falling as I looked on with displeasure, for by now I was hating this white offering sent from above with the express purpose of making our miserable lives even more intolerable. Through the eyes of my childhood, snow was always linked to happy memories, to sleighs and toboggans, to snowmen and snowball fights and to Christmas. It was special, it was different and it was fun. But here in Poland, it held no such charm. Work was hard enough, but in this white-out it made each labour many times harder, four times slower and eight times more painful. To top it all it froze your nuts off, but I suppose in the grand scheme of things that was no great loss to me at the time, for I had no present need for my testicles. However, I did need my feet, and at that precise moment I was losing what little feeling I had left in my toes. It was now too cold for my coat to ever come off until the spring.

I had just come inside after another twelve-hour stint. I collected my food and settled down on the floor as near to the stove as I could get, given the crowd of PoWs all wanting to do the same, for that stove was our only personal source of heating.

Apart from the grim weather, hunger and weariness, it had been an OK sort of a day because I had managed to steal an open pack of cigarettes from a guard who had left his army pack unattended for just a fleeting moment too long. Careless man. Immediately, I hid them and wisely so, for he soon discovered their disappearance. All PoWs under his charge were lined up and searched. Much to the annoyance of the guard, he found nothing and we were dismissed. Now in the quiet of the day was the moment to smoke one. I felt in my pocket, took one out, lit it and lay back on the floor. I inhaled deeply, holding the smoke in my lungs for a few seconds longer than normal before blowing out the spent smoke in a long, steady stream. My head spun as it always did when I had not smoked for a while. Even though it was German tobacco, it was heaven. I felt good and made myself more comfortable before inhaling again as I stared up at the rusty metal cross-members of the factory roof. It's funny how a small thing like a cigarette can bring so much comfort. As long as my cigarette lasted, I was in my own little paradise, dreaming of being back home and tucking into the biggest roast beef and Yorkshire pudding Sunday roast meal that I could imagine. With the cigarette spent and burnt down to my fingers tips, the pain abruptly propelled me back to the reality of my life as a PoW in war-torn Europe,... and back to misery.

~ THE VOICE OF AN ANGEL ~

Another day of toil and pain had come to an end, and with it another day nearer to the end of all this.

I was back in England again, with my mates from work on a Friday night, at the Kiwi pub in Walton having just finished our end of week treat of fish and chips. The bar was full with the sound of laughter. I stood amongst my friends, pint in hand. A tobacco haze hung in the air above our head.

I lay exhausted on the floor half asleep when, from nowhere, came the sound of an angel. At first I couldn't believe it. I thought I was still dreaming. Somewhere, somebody was singing. I opened my eyes and sat up. It was the sound of the most beautiful tenor voice that I had ever heard. He sang aria after aria. From where I was lying I couldn't see who it was but his melodies stirred me to my very soul.

By now, everybody in the building was perfectly still, awestruck and paying attention to every note. Even the German guards standing on the raised walkway that ran the length of the space, were standing still like statues, listening. Their appreciation of the male voice was well known and they seemed to be as delighted with this impromptu performance as we were. And who wouldn't be? His recital hit a chord with us all, for it caused us to reflect on our individual plight as prisoners, held in a foreign land, far from home and from those whom we held dear and loved. From young to old, rich or poor, victor or captive, of any nationality from any corner of the world, the power of song and music is beyond belief.

I closed my eyes and thought of my own father. He had a good voice too, similar to Paul Robeson and at Christmas time, he entertained us with his favourite songs like ' Ol' Man River', 'Shenandoah' and 'Were you there when they crucified my Lord? I felt both saddened yet exhilarated at the same time, if that makes sense, for my reflections were painful but my spirits were lifted briefly and my soul taken to places where it is good to go.

After some thirty minutes or more, he finished. It was over all too soon and I lay back down again, deep in thought. What had just happened seemed out of place in this bleak factory. Whoever just sang those amazing melodies certainly had a professionally-trained voice. I wondered who he was and how he came to be here with us. A volunteer like me I suppose, eager to do his bit for king and country. As my mind gently travelled this melancholy path, I drifted into a deep and peaceful sleep.

~ A ROASTING ~

The next morning, the drudgery started all over again. Every muscle in my body was still aching as I made my way to the toilets. The day began with the ever-awful mug of ersatz. It did not matter who made it or how it was brewed or if it was made from acorns or roasted barley - it tasted awful by whichever method. The only compliment that any sane British PoW could give this German beverage was that it was wet and warm... usually.

Whilst at the factory, we had sparse breakfasts, if any, before commencing work. As was the case throughout my time in captivity, we were only supplied with minimal meals unless we were assigned to a particularly heavy task or we worked on a farm. Our work here was not considered particularly heavy, so minimal rations were provided.

One day in very early January, as I walked through the factory, a delightful smell wafted past my nostrils and assaulted my senses. Food. I followed my nose and quickly found its source. In the middle of the building I saw a group of PoWs gathered around our pot-bellied stove. I knew the men and asked them what was going on.

"It's baking time," was the simple answer.

The top of the hot stove was covered with slices of something cooking. They were slices of sugar beet. I had tasted sugar beet before when I had dug one up in the fields a few weeks earlier when I was hungry. To me they tasted absolutely foul and they were cold. On the other hand, these were delicious-smelling slices of baked beet. A PoW standing by the stove took one of the hot, golden brown, oval slices and handed it to me to try. This act alone was unusual as, on the whole, we prisoners, short of food and clothing, were a pretty selfish lot. We had to be in order to survive. For another PoW to share food surprised and pleased me. I took the hot slice and placed it cautiously in my mouth, sinking my teeth into the soft flesh. It was fantastic, soft and sweet. I realised that the reason for his generosity was obvious, for this was a sugar beet factory. Surrounded by thousands of tonnes of the stuff, the Germans did not bat an eye to the odd beet finding its way into the belly of hungry British PoWs.

During my stay in the factory, roasted beet was to become the daily snack of choice for us PoWs. Come to think of it, this was the only snack available to us and it certainly helped to maintain our spirits.

~ SCOTTISH INVENTIVENESS ~

Speaking of spirits...

So far, I had spent weeks pulling up the sugar beet, then progressed to shovelling it into the factory and shown how to cook it to supplement our inadequate diet. Slowly, I was beginning to respect this little vegetable as I was about to be shown another way in which this versatile root could be used more inventively.

As anybody with a basic knowledge of our island history will know, within the British Army there have been Scottish regiments since the unification of our two nations some 300 years earlier.

In the summer of 1940, tens of thousands of soldiers from the finest Scottish regiments were captured, just like me. Scotland can also boast some of the most outstanding scientists and engineers that the British Empire, and indeed the world, has ever known. Maybe it is a particular trait of this canny nation to be able to use what God and nature provides on this amazing planet of ours and turn it to their advantage by using all of their inventive skills.

In the depths of our factory, the Scots had applied themselves and came up with what they always did best, an apparatus for distilling the fermented beet!

I think it can safely be said that our German hosts were, for the most part, unaware of the uncontrollable Scottish desire and need to maintain their ancient tradition of distilling and drinking. Trying to prevent this ingenious nation from doing what comes naturally to them would have been like trying to hold back the tides in the English Channel. It just wasn't going to happen.

Spirited away in corners of the factory were containers, old paint tins, food tins, even fire buckets (God forbid!), in fact anything that could hold quantities of liquid. These sons of Caledonia had mashed up the beet and left it to naturally ferment. Being packed with sugar, it did not take long. They brewed a basic sugar beet alcoholic beverage of some description, probably about 12-14% proof. That was the easy bit. Now came the transformation. Using old cylindrical food tins and somebody's tinsmith skills, they made pipes, containers and condensers and built a simple still. The beet wine went in one end to be heated and out of the other end came alcohol, pure, clear, lethal alcohol.

During my time in the factory, the process was in full production day in, day out and this enabled the Scottish workers slightly more than just a tipple after every shift. I had drunk this Satan's brew only the once. Despite its paint stripper taste, the distillers loved it and much to my surprise, were still capable of working the following day. To survive as a PoW often meant just getting by from day to day and burying your pain and troubles wherever you could, and if that meant in drink, then so be it.

At the risk of stereotyping, my war-time experience of Scottish soldiers confirmed the fact that they could drink. From my early days in France right up until Dunkirk, I had met groups from the Scottish regiments and most seemed to have a phenomenal capacity to out drink all other nationalities. That being the case, their incarceration without the benefit of a pub must have come as one hell of a shock.

~ BEETING OVER - BACK TO CAMP ~
Late February 1943

By the end of February, the beet processing was at an end, thank
goodness, and it was time to go 'home'. Not that it was any more
murderously harder work than the other slavish labouring jobs that we
were required to do. It was just that shovelling the damn beet day after
day after boring day was brain-numbing and a change was needed.
It was not only me that needed a break from the factory. By now, those
pickled Celtic livers required a rest, at least until the following year.
Upon returning, we entered a depressing Stalag XXB that was bleaker
than ever. Sleet was driving onto the grey snow, creating a dismal,
misty picture. How I hated this place.

Bert, Jimmy, Johnny and myself discovered that as soon as we
had left camp the previous November, our vacated bunks had been
re-occupied, even whilst the straw inside our palliasses was still
warm. I was so glad that the millions of my former bed bugs, fleas and
lice did not go cold or hungry for a moment longer than necessary.

We waited in the wet and cold before being assigned to a new hut.

~ SICK SENT HOME ~
1943

As time slowly ground on, we started to see more and more prisoners
suffering with life-threatening diseases such as TB and pneumonia.
The Polish camp doctor isolated them in the sick bay until, eventually,
a German doctor was called. He either rejected or confirmed
their illnesses, removing the most serious cases to the hospital in
Marienburg. As 1943 wore on and slid unstoppably towards '44, the
prisoner exchange scheme was up and running. Through the auspices
of the International Red Cross, very sick prisoners were exchanged
and repatriated back to England in exchange for German PoWs in
a similar condition. However, this method did not offer an easy
means of escape from the prisoner of war camp, for you had to be
seriously ill with a 99.9% certainty of impending death or a lifetime
of infirmity before they would send you home. I never felt envious of
the repatriated, for they were too close to death's ever-open door for
my liking.

A handful were returned from our camp, although I never knew them personally. Those who were sent back were deluged with letters from fellow PoWs to carry home to loved ones and addresses so that they could make contact with their relatives and pass on much sought-after news.

During my last few days at the factory, I had been increasingly troubled with more than my usual share of stomach cramps and diarrhoea so I was unusually pleased to return to camp and join the sick parade. The line of sick was as long as the surgery was sparse. The doctor had changed his room about since my last visit by rashly altering the positions of his only two medicines. The large glass tub containing massive white tablets and the tub containing the thick white antiseptic paste had been transferred to his desk, freeing up his shelves for no purpose at all as they were still empty. My explanation as to the reason for this year's visit prompted my doctor into choosing the tablets as my cure. I was directed to take two a day for a week.

Having visited him twice, I had now sampled all of the doctor's available treatments and could have been excused for regarding myself as a drug-addicted hypochondriac. I took the tablets as prescribed and thought no more about it until the following morning, when I needed to go outside for a pee. I was bursting to go and knew I couldn't make it to the latrines, so I did what was common practice in times of need: I relieved myself behind a hut. There was still plenty of snow, for this side of the building faced north and rarely received any of the sun's warming rays. Feeling childish, I decided to scribe my name with urine. I started with a broad stroke from left to right but was horrified at the varied pallet, for as I started to pee out came a deep orange that quickly turned to a vivid crimson. I nearly had a heart attack, believing that I had a really serious problem and was passing blood. As soon as I had finished, I rushed to tell the others. Of course, they all sympathised and hoped for my sake that my condition was not too dire. As the so-called camp doctor was unavailable, I had to wait and worry all night until morning sick parade.

As usual, we were rudely awoken. I jumped into my boots and hurried to the doctor with my dreadful discovery. After a brief consultation and diagnosis, you might imagine my surprise, which turned to utter relief, when he informed me that it was of no consequence and that this colouring of my urine was as a result of the tablets. I left his surgery with a huge sigh of relief. It was not yet my time to meet The Almighty. Upon my return, I told my so-called mates what the doctor had said, only to witness them burst into howls of laughter. The bastards knew the cause of my crimson waters all along, choosing not to share their knowledge for fear of spoiling their fun. Whilst the effects of the tablets lasted, I childishly continued to carve my name with a swagger and flourish, making the most of the last traces of winter's snow.

The camp was fine for the first week, meeting up with old chums, catching up with the gossip, local news and little Sammy Newton's 'secret' dispatches. Great things were beginning to happen in the outside world, which filled us with hope for the future. During January, the Russian Army had finally defeated the once invincible German invaders at the slaughterhouse that was Stalingrad.

In North Africa, Montgomery and his Eighth Army had swept into Tunisia. By all accounts, the tide seemed to be finally turning but I had to remind myself that as wonderful and pleasing as this information was, I was still a PoW in the hands of the Germans. Victories came and went on both sides as the battle fronts waned this way and that, so it was still far too early to start speculating as to when we would be released from captivity. With over a thousand miles between me and my homeland, I was getting used to the idea that Stalag XXB was going to continue to be my home for the foreseeable future.

A week later the sun made a rare appearance, which lifted our flagging spirits during the short winter days. Unfortunately it coincided with a raid. The window of our room was open and Johnny Dunbar was leaning out, staring into space. He was smoking and his mind was miles away, deep in thought. Casually, he called to me.

"Mar, come and look at this. Looks like trouble to me."

I took my time standing up, as suddenly rising often left me feeling faint. I went over to the window, rested my arm on Johnny's shoulder and looked out. An austere German Officer, who we assumed to be the current Camp Commandant, was strutting across the open parade ground in all his finery, careful to avoid the mass of puddles that threatened to dirty his mirror-finished boots. The hated NCO Posnanski and four armed guards were in tow. They barged straight into hut No.6 before forcibly ejecting the bemused occupants. We both watched with morbid fascination and waited whilst the six Germans remained inside.

"It must be a search of some sort."

"Come on Johnny boy," I said, patting him on his back. "Let's see what's going on."

We hurried over to hut No.6, where a small crowd had gathered. One minute was all it took. Out strode the Commandant with the devil's own disciple, Posnanski, at his side, holding something aloft in his hand, whereupon he made a brief announcement.

"We have found your radio. It is a waste of time. We always know what you are doing and we know where everything is."

With that he smiled arrogantly and was gone. I could have smacked him. Two of the guards forcibly ejected one of the residents before escorting him to the Punishment Block or 'Die Bunker' as it was affectionately known. It was the cell block where PoWs were imprisoned for 'crimes' against the Third Reich. I say Third Reich, as it sounds much more sensational than being imprisoned for crimes like blowing a raspberry at a German guard or telling him to 'go screw yourself', which was the most popular offence committed by guests of 'Die Bunker'. From the outside it was a standard wooden hut, much like any other accommodation block only smaller, but inside it was different. A corridor ran down its centre and on each side were punishment cells with heavy wooden doors.

In reality, the Germans had not even pretended to search for the secret radio, seeming to know precisely where to look and which floorboards to lift. As a result, rumours quickly circulated that a spy, a fifth columnist, was in our midst who had informed the authorities as to its whereabouts. That was a horrible prospect but how else would they have known precisely where to look?

Within camp, there were some guards who could at best be described as bastards, to a greater or lesser extent, but there was one f****ing bastard who was particularly cruel and, by late '43, he was at his worst. Feldwebel (Company Sergeant Major) Posnanski was his name. He was a German speaking Pole. The German Army was full of such men, Prussians who were trapped in the new Poland after the division of the German/Austro-Hungarian Empire after the First World War and the creation of the Polish state.

What may have made this particular Pole/Prussian even worse than the others was that Posnanski (a well-known Polish/Jewish name), would court favour from his Nazi masters (to possibly deflect any suspicions of a Jewish connection). Feldwebel Posnanski appeared more brutish than all the other guards put together. He had acquired a justified reputation as a sadistic bully. He was a tall, powerful man, over six feet and in his late thirties. He loved nothing more than to strut or cycle around the camp in his immaculate uniform with trousers tucked into his shiny, knee-length, black leather jackboots in a pompous, arrogant and threatening manner.

Following the 'discovery', McDowell was summoned by the Camp Commandant to participate in the subsequent enquiry by the Germans. Afterwards, McDowell launched his own more serious investigation as to who had talked and betrayed us all. Before I had time to hear the outcome of either exploration, 'Mar Minter's Gang' was on the move once more. By now, the snow was fast melting as winter was slowly withdrawing to the harsh north from whence it came. I had grown bored with being cooped up behind the wire, I was missing the farm rations and desperate for the opportunity to escape from the insular camp life. In addition, my thieving, dealing hands had an itch and were in need of some serious exercise.

Unfortunately the first trip out of the camp was not quite as I had expected, for the outing was but a short trip to a most welcome place, the delousing station. The drive was a slippery journey as, in places, the road was still covered with slush. As I queued outside the building I shivered in the chill wind, but once inside I could feel the warmth embrace me. The heat of the shower was wonderful and I wanted to remain there forever.

This time we all knew what to expect as we walked through to the final ordeal that awaited us in the 'pleasure room'. I could not be certain if they were the same poor old Polish women sitting at the end of the delousing process, attacking our 'bits' with their disinfectant-soaked mops. To me, they all looked the same, old, grey and bored to death. However desperate I was for sex at that precise moment, I was not tempted to linger a moment longer than was absolutely necessary to be pleasured by the Mrs. Mopskis. By the time we had made it through to the other side, we were all laughing once more with the 'joie de vivre' of it all.

Winter hadn't quite receded and the last dirty traces of compacted ice and snow still clung stubbornly to the deepest, darkest recesses of the camp. Now was the time for the Germans to put us to work once more. Bert, Jimmy, Johnny and I were on the very first working party out of that dump and away from the more unpleasant guards, 'McDowell's Mafia', disgruntled souls and the depressing drabness that prevailed within the camp.

Half a day's journeying was all it took for our party to arrive. I instantly recognised the place as being one of the farms that I had briefly worked at before. This time, I didn't volunteer to become the horseman. I just couldn't be bothered, mainly because the resident owner was male. This particular farm was relatively large and wealthy by Polish standards. As well as ourselves, there were other workers, some of whom were Polish girls and others Russian. The work was hard and laborious, as was to be expected. We started by clearing the drainage ditches, which needed unblocking after the prolonged winter havoc in readiness for the arrival of the rains. Whilst resting from this arduous task, I watched the Russian women in the fields. Unlike the Polish girls, these hardy peasants were built like prized oxen, big, incredibly strong and as wide as they were tall, like huge cubes covered in tattered layers of sackcloth. They would lift and shift huge loads of produce with the greatest of ease, but lookers they certainly weren't. Etched into their weathered faces was a story of endless pain through a lifetime of toil, suffering and inhumanity.

Food on the farm was adequate and the extra rations were most welcome. As soon as we had finished eating our evening meal, our considerate guards would usually ask us the same question they tended to ask before locking us in for the night.

"Which of you gentlemen would kindly like to partake of a trip and be escorted to the lavatories, for the express purpose of emptying your bowels?"... or words to that effect.

I decided to take them up on their generous offer. The days were still short and with no moon, it was blindingly dark. This particular Polish farmer had pigs that he kept in a sty at the furthest corner of the yard and that was where I was headed. Because the toilet was located over the sty, I had to climb some steps. I opened the door. Inside, were two separate toilet seats next to each other, which I knew off by heart. I call them toilet seats, but in fact I was sitting on a well-worn plank with two rough, circular holes cut through. The interior was blacker than a witch's arse, so I had to feel my way to the nearest seat before pulling down my pants and sticking my buttocks into the hole. A chill blast of winter air blew on my exposed behind.

I shuddered.

As was usual, I had no problem in going but the reaction to my actions always left me feeling very uncomfortable. As soon as I sat down I could hear the big porkers snuffling underneath my backside.

So close were they to my cheeks and hanging tackle that I swear I could feel the warmth of their breath on my nether regions. Whatever any of us did in that toilet fell straight down into the pig sty below, to be instantly gobbled up by the ravenous swines. I suppose you could regard these creatures as nature's ultimate recycling creations. No wonder neither Jews nor Muslims eat their flesh. In reality, I was not revolted by the pigs' eating habits, for this was the way it had been for hundreds of years, even in our own country. In fact, I tended to laugh when I heard the pigs fighting over my offerings. My worry was for the safety of my genitalia, for one day I hoped to find some use for them once more.

As I was finishing my business, I suddenly became aware of something or somebody other than the pigs breathing nearby, gently, very gently. I raised my right hand and came into contact with the wall, so I reached out with my left and almost jumped out of my skin when I came into contact with something soft and warm. It was a hand, and connected to the hand was a body. A woman spoke. Polish.

As casually as if speaking to my dear mother, I simply replied. "Dobri wieczór." ("Good evening").

As PoWs, we had all become accustomed to being dehumanised and living a humiliating lifestyle, sharing the most basic of human functions with anybody, animal, male and now female. Once I had overcome the initial shock and embarrassment of sharing a toilet with a stranger who just happened to be a woman, I relaxed and finished the task in hand.

The incident amused me, and as soon as I returned to the barn, Bert had a question for me.

"What are you so happy about?" he asked, causing both Jimmy and Johnny to look up, so I told them.

"I've just had a secret liaison with a local girl," I smugly replied.

"You big tart, we weren't born yesterday," chipped in Johnny.

"Well it's true, we sat together, I held her hand and we talked."

"How did you manage that, you lucky devil?"

"Charm and personality Jimmy."

"Come off it mate, the guard was with you so how come you got the chance?" continued Johnny.

"Do I detect a note of jealousy?" I replied and persisted with my slight exaggeration.

"Jealous of what, you heap of skin and bones?"

"Jealous of the fact that I really did sit next to a beautiful young

girl, held her hand and managed to chat to her for just long enough."
I was enjoying this innocent deception.

"Just long enough? he persisted. "What do you mean? Long enough for what?"

"Ahhh! That would be telling now, wouldn't it and a gent never tells,"I replied, tapping the side of my nose in a knowing way.

"Come on now, long enough for what?"

By this time I'd got him. He was hooked and my great grin was almost split my face in half.

"Long enough for me to finish my shit, 'cos, unbeknown to me, she was sitting in the dark on the toilet next to me."

They roared with laughter as I filled in the gaps by giving them a full account of my not-so-romantic encounter. Jimmy added that it might have been a blessing in disguise if the pigs had forcefully removed my tackle, thereby saving scores of innocent Polish girls from the lecherous advances of a rampant British Tommy.

By the following week we had finished our tasks and we were no longer required, so we returned to the greyness that was Stalag XXB.

~ WE ATE LIKE WEALTHY SCAVENGERS ~
April 1943

On that first evening back, we smoked and chatted well into the night with the other occupants of our new hut, exchanging stories of our capture and details of home life. I re-told the comical tale of my romantic encounter with the Polish girl in the toilet with the pigs as chaperones. They all seemed suitably impressed, with just a hint of mockery.

Today, I received another letter from mother. It always filled my heart with joy to know that my family were safe and that my home was still there, a focus of my hope for tomorrow and the one stable thing in my life. As I read her letter, I came to a reference concerning my last close work friend, Alan Hores, who went into The Royal Engineers. She had received a letter from Alan's father. My heart sank and I feared the worst. I had always assumed that his posting to The Royal Engineers was relatively safe, for a soldier. As I read on, I discovered that even he had not escaped tragedy in this long war. He had lost a leg but was alive, and to think that we could all have been exempt had we not been so naive and keen to serve our country. I was the only one left whole from our brave band of recruits. I felt alone and brooded with sadness for the rest of the day.

By morning, I had turned the sad news around and now I viewed my present predicament as a PoW almost with a sense of relief for at least I was alive, not wounded and, at the moment, out of danger and relatively safe.

At morning parade I received some good news; we were to receive Red Cross parcels. My return to camp could not have been timed better. In all my years at Stalag XXB, I never did understand how the parcels were allocated. As I was away on work parties for much of the time, I seemed to miss out on my fair share of Red Cross goodies, but today my mates and I were going to be unusually lucky. We were hoping that we would finally be allocated one each, but our hopes were soon dashed. We collected the parcel from McDowell's hut and carried it back to our room to share between the twelve of us. Inside, I could hardly contain myself with excitement. Carefully removing the valuable string and opening the box, I was delighted to find a tin of Morton's marmalade, two boxes of McVities and Price biscuits, Morton's steak and tomato pudding, a Huntley and Palmer empire cake, some Maypole tea, Lusty's roast meat, a very belated Chivers Christmas pudding, a bar of chocolate, a tin of margarine, a bag of sugar, a tin of Nestlé condensed milk and perhaps the most precious commodity of all, a tin box of 50 Players Naval Cut cigarettes. Only God knew where the parcel had been kept all this time for it was now early April, but the Christmas pudding was welcome whatever the time of year.

We ate like lords for the next few days, being grateful that neither the thieving Germans nor our own light-fingered fellows had pilfered the food for themselves, as was often the case.

The pleasure of smoking the British cigarettes had to be inhaled to be believed. I treated the occasion almost as a devout ceremony, opening my box and taking out the first of my share. I lifted it, savouring the rich, sweet smell of the fine Virginia tobacco, lay back on my bunk, closed the lid and struck the match, lighting the wonderful white stick. I inhaled deeply, so deeply, and kept the sweet smoke inside my lungs for as long as possible. This first puff always made my head spin, until I slowly released the smoke in a thin, constant stream of white mist, concentrating on its soothing powers whilst drifting off into another world.

~ SPRING IS HERE, TIME FOR OTHER MATTERS ~
April 1943

By the end of the first week of April, the weather had improved considerably and spring had well and truly established itself. It was now time. My mind was turning to matters of the heart, or, to be more precise, my groin, for I still had wonderful memories of losing my virginity the previous year and I was eager to lose it again and again and again.

Spring is a time of rebirth, fresh growth and thoughts of summer, but at Stalag XXB it was grey and as the years progressed, the grey was getting greyer.

I could have guessed that warmer weather was on the way because it was time for 'roll call manoeuvres' to begin. This involved the tried and tested game of annoying the Germans. As the guards moved amongst us counting our numbers, men would hop between rows, screwing up their calculations. As it was a nice sunny morning, we knew this was going to go on for a while, or until the children amongst us had had enough.

We had just finished our forth recount when a familiar and much hated figure emerged through the gate. A guard ran across to speak to the evil Posnanski. The two of them talked for a moment before the guard stood back, saluted and ran back to the gate house. Meanwhile Posnanski joined us and gave commands for the guards to come to order behind him. Rifles were unslung and a more threatening pose was taken. From the gate house, three guards ran forward, each carrying something. They stopped just in front of Posnanski and set about their task, mounting a machine gun on its stand right before us. A strained silence filled the parade ground as a metallic click of the bolt action disturbed the air.

Posnanski's bellowing voice carried across the camp "Well, enough of this stupidity. Let's do this ONE MORE TIME, shall we?"

Nobody moved, for if there was one person who you never, ever dare to cross, it was Posnanski. Within minutes, he had the numbers that he required.

"Unfortunately stupid pig dogs, your delaying tactics have caused a problem in the kitchen,... which means you will not be receiving your meal this evening. Enjoy the remainder of your day."

He shot a twisted smile, turned on his heels and disappeared. The ensuing silence said it all.

After morning parade came the 'request' for working party volunteers. Within the hour I was off once more. There was no sadness as I always felt I was stagnating and suffocating inside the confines of Greylag XXB. Outside, I felt alive.

We marched through the blooming Polish countryside to a destination yet unknown. The light breeze intensified at times, blowing away the greyness, cleansing everything. The trees were in early leaf, their top boughs danced back and forth, threatening at any moment to break from their mother trunk and take flight and seek their destiny wherever the wind took them. Above, the sky was a wonderful shade of blue. Billowing white clouds, forever changing, sped across the vast expanse in the strong, refreshing breeze. Nature's artists had finally emerged from their slumber, to repaint winter's landscape. Now awash with colour, it was wonderful to behold. It was cathartic and so good to be on the move once more.

We had a two-day march to this particular farm, and as we trudged our way along the dirt roads, I wondered if there was going to be an obliging Frau to continue my education. We rested the first night in a cow shed, fortunately without the presence of the cows. However, they had left a few reminders of their previous occupancy, for which we were less than grateful. That night and the next morning, there was only water, for unlike our guards, we went hungry and resumed the march.

We arrived at dusk and were eventually fed. The morning afforded me my first opportunity to view our new 'home'. The place looked larger, better organised, tidier and more prosperous than the previous farm, with bigger outbuildings and generally in a better state of repair. The main house was two storeys high, the upper floor having windows set into the roof.

As we waited in the yard for instructions, I caught sight of the owner or manager. Excellent, at least she is female. I was impatient for the question to be asked, *'who is the horseman?'* - but it never came. She simply looked us over and spoke to her assistant before returning to her house.

"Shit!" was my disappointed reaction.

We collected our tools and set off for work. In the distance, I could see a horse driven cart and cursed that she already had a drayman. We did everything that was required of us, from clearing ditches to weeding and preparing the fields. There were no Polish girls on this farm, just more Russian women than ever before, the new slave labour from the conquered Soviet territories. They were kept completely segregated from us and any contact was forbidden. If these women were fearful of being molested by us Brits then their worries were unfounded, for what I had seen of the cube-shaped Amazonians, they had more balls than any of us.

We were two weeks into our arduous toils, the weather was improving by the day, the food was good and our two German guards were only partial bastards. One morning, from out of the blue, the Frau walked over to us whilst we were planting in the fields. She spoke to the guard first before addressing us.

"Deutsche bla, bla, bla, bla,...?" and then I heard her utter the magical word *'horseman'*!.... My chance to escape the drudgery had finally come. The question posed by her had hardly left her sweet Polish lips when my hand shot up into the air, beating any competitors to the prize.

"Oh bloody hell,... here we go again, Don Juan and his trusty dick are off," muttered Bert in his rough Ulster brogue, accompanied by a huge suggestion of jealousy.

I refused to sink so low as to even acknowledge his crude comment, but blew a rather childish raspberry anyway. She indicated for me to follow without any change of expression on her blank face.

As I left, Johnny muttered, "give her one from me, will you."

I turned and laughed. Once inside the stables, I easily managed to hitch the horses to the wagon. I had forgotten nothing. I led the horses into the yard, where the Frau was waiting. She issued her instructions to me and I grovellingly thanked her, for I was grateful for the privileged job. For her part, she did not respond in either a positive or a negative way, just a frosty glare before turning and walking back to her cottage. Maybe I wasn't going to be so lucky in the *Schlafzimmer* department this time round.

My first task was straightforward enough and I even managed to keep the horses under control but I was still pleased that she accompanied me, showing me where to go and what to do.

At the end of the working day and putting the horses to bed, I joined my fellows who seemed at ease with my appointment as horseman. We rested and chatted a while, aimlessly recalling things back home, but I could not help feeling a tad guilty as I noticed that the fingers of my fellow PoWs were already looking blistered and dirty after their day's grind, whilst mine could have graced the hands of the highest courtier in Tsarist's Imperial Russia.

Just after dusk we were called into the farmhouse to collect our meal. We walked through the front door and into the hallway. There were four doors leading off on both sides. The Frau was leading us into her kitchen at the far end of the hall. In the middle of the passageway was a stepladder leading to the upper floor, presumably where the bedrooms were?... well, it was just a thought. We were greeted by the comforting smell of boiled vegetable and whatever-meat-she-had stew. Each contented man collected his generous ration and chunk of heavy German black bread and carried it back to the barn. I, on the other hand, was overjoyed to see that the habit of allowing me, the highly skilled worker who was held in high esteem, to sit and eat at her table. Almost bursting with pent up relish, I collected a second portion of leftovers. In her difficult to understand East Prussian-German-cum-Polish dialect, we tried to talk, but with some difficulty. I got the ball rolling and introduced myself.

Pointing at myself, "I A M D E N N I S," was my initial offering, speaking as though to a half-wit. Suspecting that at any moment she might strike me with her ladle, I watched for her response. The blank, almost disinterested glare from her gave it all away, so I repeated my statement,... twice, before finally getting the correct response.

"Ahhhhhh!...D E N N I S,... tak,... ja".

Contact.

"And you,... your name?" I continued in Pole-German, pointing to her for I was now on a roll.

"My name is Krystyna."

It was my turn to repeat it and I told her it was a good name, for which she thanked me and smiled. I continued to eat as we continued exchanging both words and smiles. I was soon flirting with her, probably in a seemingly desperate way but, who cares.

All too soon, the guards returned to escort me back. No rumpy-pumpy for me tonight. The guard could barely hide his impatience, eager to discharge his final duty for the night and lock us in. Now their time was their own. It was common knowledge that they would usually try to find the nearest local Polish equivalent to a pub, where they could meet up with other guards in the area, get drunk, raise their glasses to Adolf *Bloody* Hitler, sing a few bawdy songs and hopefully get laid.

> *Now that last wish might surprise you but, personally, I hoped and prayed that they did get laid, and with it, acquire a massive dose of incurable pox!*

Things continued nicely for several days and although each day was as dull as the previous, at least I had my comfortable job and was rewarded with ample portions of Krystyna's tasty stews I hasten to add. She was 'more woman' altogether than my first, virgin busting Celestyna. By that I simply mean quantity wise; there was just so much more of her. Every time she moved a muscle, she had trouble controlling her more than ample bosom. This rather amused me for as a child, we had a neighbour who helped a local farmer with his wild rabbit problem. To assist, he took with him two of his frisky ferrets in a sack. Krystyna's over-burdened blouse reminded me of that sack. She often caught my eye as I watched them, but I simply smiled whilst continuing to lust after her.

It was the fifth day of my new appointment. I was seated at her table, waiting for my evening meal. As always it smelt delicious and as always, I was drooling, for more than just the food. She filled my bowl from the simmering cauldron that hung over the fire and placed it before me on the table. In so doing she leant forward, offering me a generous view of an enormous cleavage that had not been so evident until now. Had she undone a button or two? I thanked her (not only for the food but for the view), and then I began to eat. She had cooked her usual pork and vegetable stew. I ate as much as I could as quickly as I could and as well mannered as I could in the hope of being offered more. Halfway through my meal she still had not joined me but continued with her pottering about the kitchen. As I watched, she turned her head slightly to look at me. With a rather suggestive half smile, she walked into the hallway. As soon as she had disappeared, I quietly got up and went over to the cauldron and helped myself to another bowlful. Well,... our lives were always uncertain and when she eventually returned, she might not be in the mood to give me another portion. I threw my second helping down my throat and heard her muffled voice calling to me from another room.

"Dennis, come upstairs, come to the bedroom."

I hesitated, thought,... 'did she really say that,' but took another ladle full instead, desperately trying to down more of the delicious stew. She called again, louder this time and more forcefully.

"DENNIS,... come upstairs, come to the bedroom."

Wow! My good fortune hadn't escaped me but surely, I couldn't be this lucky? I threw down the last mouthful and wiped my mouth on my grubby sleeve and tried to make myself as clean and tidy as possible whilst following the sound of her voice. What a joke. I chuckled at the ridiculous notion that I could erase nearly three years of PoW stench, filth and stubble with the wipe of a hand. I walked out into the hall combing my hair with the fingers of my left hand and climbed the ladder that ran from the hallway to the upper floor. Ahead was a small passageway but off this gloomy corridor I could see four doors, one of which was ajar. A warm, glowing light filtered from the room, offering the only illumination. I walked to the doorway and stopped, peering into a bed chamber. I pushed the door gently. Against the far wall stood a big old pine bed with thick pillows and a deep, great duvet. Standing next to the bed was Krystyna. My heart quickened a pace as I crossed the floor. She really was all woman, barely dressed in a skimpy yet practical cream chemise (or whatever it was called, but it was a womanly bed garment of some sort). The only problem was that she was having great difficulty in maintaining her modesty. The material around her bust was under considerable tension. The sight triggered a stirring in my nether regions as my heart went into overdrive. It was reassuring to feel those old familiar twinges and to know that it was still working. As I neared her, I unbuttoned my jacket and let it fall to the ground. I stumbled a little, hastily kicking my boots off and then my trousers and pants. Oblivious to the fact that I was skinny and undernourished, I stood in front of her, butt naked, just as nature intended, except for my socks of course.

After all, I am British!

Krystyna's chemise was hopelessly inadequate and incapable of containing her massive chest for much longer and had to be removed for fear of tearing her top asunder. The word 'splendid' sprang to mind and I couldn't take my eyes off them.

Knowing what she wanted, Krystyna took control of the situation, pulling back the duvet in an inviting way. She lay down, pulling me with her. I was immediately engulfed in a cocoon of fluffiness. Her bed was the softest that I had ever experienced, for on top of her ordinary mattress was a thinner covering filled with soft insulating down, as were the pillows and huge duvet. I was soon engulfed in a sea of warm doughy flesh. I was loving it, but unfortunately, my wallowing was about to get raunchy. Being a virile young man in my prime, my loins were afire. During this dark period in the history of Europe, life was about as uncertain as it could get and I couldn't afford the luxury of thoughts of tomorrow, only of today. Presumably, her philosophy was much the same. Whilst our mouths quickly sealed in a lust-driven kiss, our hands were everywhere. We were not going to make love by any stretch of the imagination. This was going to be sex, desperately needed raw sex. In our heightened state of passion, she rolled me over and sat on top of me, impaling herself. She purred with delight and desire. As she worked on me, her great pendulous breasts hung down over my face, almost smothering me alive. What a way to go! As she moved up and down my face took a beating, each breast hitting me in turn, swaying to and fro. I could have howled in triumph.

> *Whilst Dennis related this story, he had to put down his coffee as he shrieked with laughter, recalling every wonderful battering slap. Tears of joy ran down his face.*
> *"You know Pat, maybe it wasn't all bad," he recalled.*
> *At which point we both collapsed with laughter.*
> *The passage of time is a wonderful healer to a tortured soul.*

That night, the guards left me for longer than was usual. Inside the barn, all were asleep, exhausted by their day's labours. That night, I too slept the sleep of the contented dead, but for a different reason and with a huge grin on my smug but 'battered' face.

The pattern of relentless work on the farm continued in this manner for the following eight weeks, with no events of any real interest to break the toil, save for the kindness of Krystyna. I indulged in countless bouts of very physical sex whenever her urges needed satisfying. I must confess that I never resented or blamed her for inflicting her base animal instincts upon me. The awful fact that she took full, diabolical advantage of a poor, defenceless British Tommy and corrupted me, week after week, forcing me to be her sex slave, was something that I will have to endure, suffering in silence and taking the recollection to my grave.

For those months in late spring, I did my duty, for king and for country, and I wouldn't have had it any other way.

~ THE DIRE CONSEQUENCES OF SEX ~
Summer of 1943

I awoke to another hot summer's morn. I had awoken naturally, without pressure from the guards. The sun, being well up in its firmament, meant that beams of sunlight were bursting through the small, inaccessible window high up in the rafters of our wooden barn and through the multitude of cracks and holes that peppered the dry old timbers.

Inside it was already baking as I got up and looked about me, beads of perspiration forming on my brow. I was desperate for a pee but we were still locked in and the bucket was full to overflowing. The others in my party were, for the most part, still asleep. I was puzzled, for we should have been woken at the crack of dawn and dragged off to work ages since. Last Sunday was our rest day, so we were not due another for a month.

It was no good, I could not hold it any longer. I crept over to a corner of the barn and urinated through a hole in the wall so as not to cause too much of a stink inside. I hoped no person, or even worse, no dog was on the other side to witness my exposed appendage poking through. Bert and Johnny were semi-awake whilst Jimmy slept on, lost in his world back home in the Scottish Lowlands. Soon, we were all wondering why we had not been ousted. In the increasing heat we waited for a further hour before the door was finally flung open and the full glory of fresh air and the sun's rays came bursting in, filling our humble quarters. We were eager for our breakfast, but unfortunately our two German goons had other plans for us and we were ordered outside with instructed to fall in. Krystyna was nowhere to be seen either. They told us nothing, but that was not unusual and within minutes, we were marched along the dusty dirt road, following the track between fields, past the lush green hedgerows on either side. With subdued voices we speculated as to where we were being taken but couldn't come to any conclusion.

Soon, the countryside opened up and we could see well into the distance without the hindrance of trees. After half an hour we spotted figures in a field some distance away. They appeared to be standing under a large, solitary, mature tree. Increasingly I became aware of other small groups such as ours scattered around. Like us, they too appeared to be converging on the tree in the middle of the vast field. By now we were all intrigued, for anything out of the ordinary that broke the boredom of life as a PoW was always of particular interest.

As we approached, I could make out the uniforms of six German Officers in their immaculate attire and mirror-finished jackboots. They chatted amongst themselves whilst our guards directed us towards them before finally coming to a halt. 'Heil Hitlers' were exchanged before we were ordered to 'stand easy' and join the motley collection of other PoWs, local civilians, peasants and Germans already in waiting. In total, we must have numbered a hundred or more. This was strange!

For the next hour, we stood waiting until the last of the straggling bands joined us, swelling our numbers. We were all ordered to spread ourselves around the tree and wait patiently. By now, all focus was on the horse-drawn cart directly underneath the tree and the two individuals who stood by its side. One of them was a young male civilian in his twenties, whom I took to be a Pole, dressed in shabby shirt and trousers. He appeared to be in a sorry state, barely able to stand. To me, he looked as though he had been beaten, or even worse. Expressionless, he stared vacantly ahead into space, seeming oblivious of his surroundings. The other was a young woman, about the same age. Her hair had been cropped off, patches of untidy chunks remained. She too was in a daze. She was dressed in a dull grey and brown dress of sack cloth. Around her neck was tied a rope, from which was suspended a heavy wooden board. On it were painted some words in German script:

'Ich habe einem polnischen Mann meinen Körper gegeben'.

I knew enough German to understand its meaning. Quite simply and tragically it read, 'I gave my body to a Polish man'.

I had not seen such a gaggle of German Officers since my capture. Sensing that the time was now right, the Senior Officer spoke softly to a junior subaltern who was clutching a clipboard, turned towards him and saluted before turning away once more and moving forward a few paces. He raised his clipboard, and from it began to address us all in swiftly-spoken German. It was far too speedily delivered for me to understand every word, but I need not have worried. When he finished, another Officer came forward for the benefit of us and translated his speech into English.

Whilst we had been gathered, clouds had begun to fill the once blue sky and cut across the summer sun. Occasionally, contrasting shadows were cast, rolling quietly over this troubled landscape. The timing was ominous and the hushed scene was full of foreboding.

There followed a brief crime and punishment reading mixed with a deluge of Nazi racial propaganda. The girl before us was a German in her early twenties who had been found guilty of having sexual relations with a young Pole. This was against German law and, as such, was punishable by death for the Pole and a long prison sentence for the woman. There was no reaction whatsoever from either of the

421

accused and nobody stirred or commented. Our sole purpose for being there was to witness the horrific event, add to their humiliation and ultimately serve as a warning to others not to do likewise, or face a similar fate.

The Officer stood back and an order was given. Two soldiers climbed aboard and took hold of his arms which were tied behind his back and dragged the helpless Pole upwards like a sack of potatoes, onto the wagon which now served as a platform. The poor being looked on the verge of collapse. Whilst one of the troops held him, another picked up the length of rope that had already been prepared. The noose was placed over his head and tightened, just enough. The other length was thrown over the stout branch immediately above their heads and then passed to another on the ground who then secured it to the trunk. The two Krauts then jumped down.

At that point, junior officer moved forward towards the girl who was standing a few paces away, head downcast. He took hold of her forcefully and turned her to face the wagon. Without a shred of compassion, he pushed her chin skywards, thereby forcing her watch the ensuing horror.

The poor Pole continued to show no reaction, just swaying unsteadily from side to side. His facial expression remaining blank, seeming resigned to his terrible fate. It was almost illusory, like watching a lynching on an American western movie, yet the horror was that it was all too real. With a curt order from an Officer, a soldier slapped the old horse on the backside. Instead of bolting, thereby bringing the execution to a speedy conclusion, the horse jerked his head up in surprise and slowly walked forward. He was in no rush. Such was the sluggish progress of the old horse that the unfortunate Pole was forced to walk the four steps along the cart platform until he reached the back end, whereupon, with nowhere else to go, the horse gently took the flooring away from him, leaving him walking off into space. There was no sudden drop, thereby severing the vertebrae in his neck and killing him instantly. His full body weight was simply taken up by the tight rope at the noose. Painstakingly slowly, it tightened around his neck. His feet and legs kicked out wildly whilst his face reddened. His eyes began to bulge as the rope gradually cut into his neck, garrotting him. Finally, his legs and body gave a final violent dance as the last breath was strangled from his wretched body whilst the countryside fell into shadow. It had taken two agonising minutes for the young man's troubled life to end.

My fingers were hurting. My fists were clenched so tightly that I had drawn blood as my long nails dug deeply into the palms of my hands. I was so angry and frustrated. I had just witnessed a murder, a cold-blooded, brutal murder and I could do nothing about it and it hurt. It ate me up inside, but angry didn't even begin to describe my emotions. It was just another cruel reminder of what our German oppressors were capable of doing at any given moment of their choosing, to anybody.

"To hell with you, to hell with you all," I whispered to myself as I relaxed my fists.

"One day, when this is over,..."

> *So often throughout my years as a PoW, and contrary to my Christian upbringing, I came to the conclusion that it was this hatred that I felt for my captors that helped to keep me going. The hatred and belief that one day my turn would come. I so desperately needed to survive in order for me to witness the change of circumstances and to have my turn, our turn, anybody's turn as long as they were enemies of Germany. Love and human decency were playing no part in my survival, only a burning hatred for all things German and a desire to live long enough to have that revenge.*

The Officers were the first to break away. Immediately the victim stopped dancing, they left the field and returned to their army vehicles parked on a track nearby. We were ordered to return to the farm to resume our work as if nothing had happened. As I marched away, I could not help wonder what was to become of the young woman who had only fallen in love.

In spite of the brutal killing we had been forced to witness, we now had to readjust to the sickening world we were in and continue as though it had never happened. As soon as we returned to the farm, Krystyna emerged and issued us with our instructions.

A few days later, I got the chance to talk to two Polish men, drivers who had stopped at the farm to deliver some sacks of fertiliser. I had with me a spare short-sleeve jumper and wanted to trade it for desperately needed cigarettes, but preferably not Polish ones. Whilst we talked they told me news about the death of their leader in exile, General Sikorski. He was leaving on a flight from Gibraltar when his plane crashed on take-off. German saboteurs were the obvious suspects, but the two Poles had a more disturbing explanation

The dreaded Russian Secret Police were prime suspects. Regardless of who was actually responsible, both men considered the Russians just as much of a threat and an enemy of their country as the hated Germans.

We stayed on that farm for two more weeks before returning once again to our mother camp.

~ BACK TO CAMP ~
Beginning of September 1943

I had enjoyed my stay on the farm, if 'enjoyed' is the right word, only because of my fling with Krystyna. The death of the poor young Pole that we had witnessed, executed for having dared to love a German girl, was still playing heavily on my mind. I thought of my own situation, of my earlier platonic relationship with both Stacia and Irena and my subsequent liaison with Celestyna and finally Krystyna. But I was not a Pole and the Frau was not a German farmer. If the relationships had ever come to light, I assumed, rightly or wrongly, my punishment would have been less severe.

~ I SEE THE LONE LOVER ~

Within days of my return, I had the opportunity to join a local work detail. Along with the others in my group, we were ordered into Marienburg to undertake road maintenance and general labouring, which meant that I was based in the camp for a few weeks. As we marched through the streets of the town one morning, I saw something up ahead that both saddened and then angered me. Walking towards our column was a German soldier escorting a young woman whom I instantly recognised. Still with her shaven head, she was walking slowly ahead of him. She approached with her eyes downcast, staring at the road. The soldier walked on the pavement but she was forced to walk in the gutter. Her feet were filthy for she was shoeless. Around her neck hung the same painted wooden board that I had seen her wear back in the summer when we were called to witness the death of her lover.

'Ich habe einem polnischen Mann meinen Körper gegeben'.

A major part of her continuing punishment seemed to be her very public humiliation, thereby adding to her suffering. It saddened us all to see her as we marched past. Such punishments also served as a very obvious warning and deterrent to others. I was later to learn that there was a prison in Marienburg and it was suspected that the girl had been sent there to serve her long sentence. From subsequent sightings it seemed that she was paraded through the streets of the town on a daily basis and on into winter. The resulting damage to her feet must eventually have become insufferable.

~ ITALY INVADED & SURRENDERS ~
3rd September 1943

It was another hot, oppressive day. Johnny and I were lying on our bunks, chatting about topics that were closest to our hearts: endless quantities of food, chilled lemonade and beer, pretty girls, dancing, smoking forty cigarettes a day and all supplied courtesy of our grateful government upon our triumphant return home.

It was late in the afternoon when the main door burst open. Then came the now familiar cry.

"Here comes Sammy!"

He was full of his usual excited enthusiasm as he stood in the doorway of the first room and delivered his latest news.

"The Allies have invaded Italy!"

This was big and it was exciting. All through our time at Greylag XXB, Sammy had drip fed us snippets of information about Allied achievements and enemy failures. Initially we were not sure if he was making it up, but he insisted that the news came directly from the BBC World Service. Unfortunately, during the summer, the guards had discovered yet another radio in one of the huts and for a while poor Sammy was out of a job. However, within weeks, the flow of news resumed. We assumed that another radio had somehow been acquired or built by some clever boffin, so we ceased to question the authenticity of his reports.

The invasion of mainland Europe by the Allies was the best news so far and it electrified the camp but within the week, Sammy was back with another more explosive bombshell.

"Italy has surrendered and declared war on Germany!"

The invasion, subsequent surrender and future progress of the war now allowed us all to speculate once more as to the timetable of progress of the allied fight back in Europe, along with the unheard of possibility of a German defeat, and finally our eventual liberation. The news spread like wildfire and lifted the spirits of even the most sceptical of prisoners.

The camp now played host to an increasing number of Italian PoWs who had been imprisoned here for reasons that I was never quite sure of as I didn't speak any Italian and they spoke no English, but they appeared delighted when news reached them of the invasion and subsequent surrender. Italy had become an ally of ours once more, which caused much hilarity amongst us Brits. However, the Boche appeared not so amused with their former allies.

The following day I saw a *friendly* guard, more mature than the others, who often spoke to us prisoners. He was almost human. I couldn't resist raising the question of the turncoat Italians.

"They are useless and always were," was his simplified comment. "They have no backbone, no courage and can never be trusted. We are better off without them."

I smiled and looked at him.

"Well, it's only proper. We had them in the First World War so it's only fair that you have them in this one."

He understood the joke, which was rare and even managed a smile.

~ POLISH PEAS IN A POD ~
5th September 1943

In spite of the wave of euphoria that prevailed, it dawned on me that southern Italy was one hell of a long way off from us, stuck in these wastelands of northern Poland. To my mind, we were likely to be here a while longer, if not forever. Personally, I dared not think about the probability of liberation. To survive, I still had to concentrate on the here and now by getting through today and with no thought of tomorrow. To that end, Ma Minter's Gang volunteered for the next work detail. On this occasion, we were marched to that same old elusive place, F***knowswhere, in the middle of Godonlyknows. All these different farms and factories were beginning to merge into one grey, completely forgettable mass of misery, only made acceptable by the extra rations (and the slim chance of sex). This time, we were being sent off to work on a pea farm.

Regardless of whether we were pulling beet, potatoes, turnips or peas, it was all painfully back-breaking. If I could have been bothered to indulge myself in sarcasm, I might have consoled myself in the sure and certain knowledge that at least we were getting paid for our hours, months and years of slave labour by the Germans in the form of their precious and lucrative Lagergeld (i.e. totally worthless camp money).

To be shown another bloody field stretching to the far horizon and bursting with crops and then to be told to harvest and clear the lot is the stuff of nightmares and remains the most soul-destroying and demoralising task that I can ever recall. Even with the help of my thirty fellow PoWs, this was a daunting task. As I entered the vast field, my mind screamed a question.

"Where the hell do we start?"

Fortunately, the overseer took that decision away from us and we began. The pods had reached their optimum size, turned blackish and were now ready to be harvested - pods, leaves, stalks, roots and all. We harvested the whole plant and stacked them in piles on the ground ready for collection. By the end of our first day, we seemed to have made little impression on the enormous field about us, but what the hell. We had our whole lives ahead of us in which to complete the task. By comparison, the labours of Hercules seemed far less daunting.

Within minutes of our arrival, others had joined us and more were to follow in the coming days. In the main, they were Russian women. With scarves framing their wide faces they appeared as peasants from the Middle Ages. Since occupying vast areas of the Soviet Union, they were an almost inexhaustible commodity. They constantly came to our attention for one not-so-endearing habit of theirs. Whenever they needed to go to the toilet, they would just stop where they were, stand up straight, pull up their ample skirts and, without further ado, urinate and defecate where they stood, showing no modesty. Without knickers to hinder them, I suppose it was easy. Initially we were all taken aback by their crude toilet habits, primitive by our standards, but we soon grew accustomed to their ways.

After a day's toil, I discovered that peas were one of the better crops to harvest, being relatively pain free to gather as opposed to pulling sugar beet. I was surprised to learn that they were not intended for human consumption but were to be used as animal feed. However, that did not stop us from trying them. They were edible and nourishing and that was good enough. We had to take care not to get caught, as anyone found eating the crops of any sort could expect a thump with a rifle butt for his sins.

Our seemingly never-ending labours continued unabated. The days were already chilling and shortening as the sun retreated southwards. I often took a few moments to look up and watch the frequent flights of birds, travelling in untidy flocks, following the waning daystar. How I fantasised about following, migrating with the birds to escape the creeping onslaught of winter.

Finally, one morning, we were offered a break from our drudgery and instead of being taken to the fields we were diverted to pastures new.

We ended up at a pea processing plant, not too many miles from the main camp, consisting of a collection of buildings set amongst the never-ending plains of northern Poland. From the moment we arrived, a steady stream of wagons and trucks loaded with tonnes of pea plants followed us in. I was about to learn an entirely new skill; how to unload pea plants and move them into the factory's threshing machines, a useful skill that did me no bloody good at all. Throughout the working day, varied open carts and vehicles of every description would arrive at the main entrance. One of us would climb on board and, with the aid of a pitchfork, throw the pea plants down onto the ground just inside the door. Others would form a human chain, passing the plants along to the threshing machine. This would go on all day for days and then weeks. It was mind-numbingly boring and we were forever searching for any diversion of any sort from any source.

However, there were a couple of very positive aspects to our new found work; The factory employed more of the young Polish women that we had met throughout the last two years, well educated and attractive. The Nazi occupiers and war machine had no need of their service skills, and consequently they were redeployed, forced to uproot and adjust to their new working lives on the land and factories for the greater good of Third Reich. They were employed to do all manner of jobs from cleaning, planting, labouring, packing and labelling. In our factory, there were over fifty girls employed; fortunately for us few were built like Russian dump trucks.

At this point, the writer feels that it is a good a time as any to mention but not apologise for the un-PC language used at times throughout this book. The men of that war spoke as they thought and saw, with a refreshing honesty unhindered by today's political correctness. As shallow and bigoted as it may sound to today's reader, these soldiers lived in a different era. No offence is intended, just an honesty spoken when witnessing foreign cultures that were as alien to them as men from Mars would be to us today.

Another wonderful aspect was that our guards were far less strict and officious here. Seeming to equally enjoy their new posting, they were far more relaxed. Within days of our arrival, we were on nodding terms with the girls. Still regarding us as allies, deprived of their own men and for the most part nurturing a deep hatred for the occupiers, they still looked upon us Brits with some affection. Even though they were brought up as good Catholic girls, the war had changed the way that many regarded relationships and sexual contact. Uncertainty in their lives and the ever-present threat of death and deportation at the hands of their masters, brought with it a certain amount of promiscuity. 'Live for today for tomorrow may never come' was a phrase often recited in the minds of the young civilians, soldiers and PoWs alike throughout war torn Europe.

Before long, all of us had got to know at least one girl quite well, becoming girlfriend and boyfriend. I had already set my sights on a pretty little thing called Stasha, a year younger than me. She was fresh faced with long blonde hair. Throughout the working day, each one of us would take it in turn to leave the chain gang, search out our 'beloveds' and sneak off somewhere to be alone. Our chosen place was usually the loft of an outbuilding. What the others got up to was of no particular interest to me, but Stasha and I had a very firm idea as to what we wanted to do and we did it as often as we could.

Naturally, condoms were unavailable to us, so my first sex tutor on the farm had taught me the 'withdrawal method' of contraception, for the last thing that she needed from me was another mouth to feed, coupled with the difficulty of explaining a new addition to her absent husband.

Stasha, on the other hand, was different. One day whilst making love, she asked why I pulled out every time I climaxed. Her question surprised me so I told her. She smiled sweetly and then asked me not to, so I didn't. I came inside her, which for me was a first and the experience was far more satisfying. Afterwards, we rested in each others arms on the sacking and talked. But now I was curious.

"Stasha, why did you ask me to come inside you and risk a pregnancy?"

She gently pulled away and sat up, resting on her elbow and turned to me.

"I am very happy to risk getting pregnant because I want a baby."

With my own limited experience before the war, the one thing that scared us over sexed-young men was getting a girl pregnant.

"But why, why now,... why not wait until the war is over and you are married, when you have someone to look after you,... and your baby,... surely that would be better for you both?"

She looked down, rather uncomfortably for a moment, as though not sure whether to continue or not.

"If I get pregnant, I will go to the Bürgermeister and tell him."

I suddenly felt more than a little uncomfortable at the prospect of being reported to the authorities for having sex with a Polish girl and making her pregnant, given what I had been made to witness back in the summer.

"Do you have to?" I asked defensively.

She could probably see the worry written over my face.

"Don't worry," she giggled, "it will be alright. The Bürgermeister will fill in the paperwork and when it comes to the bit about 'who the father is', I will tell him."

"What, tell him it was me?"

Stasha looked down at me, expressionless. Then her face cracked and she burst out laughing and slapped my chest.

"No stupid, not you. I will tell him that it was a German soldier and that I don't know his name,... or where he is. The Bürgermeister will simply enter 'Unknown German Soldier' and that will be the end of it."

"But why, how will that help you?"

"The Nazis want their filthy soldiers to breed freely with us, they want us to become baby machines and produce as many as we can. That way, Germany will have a never ending supply of fresh new recruits in the future. So you see, me having a baby is all for the greater good of their beloved Fatherland."

Wow! I was slightly taken aback. So Adolf needed millions of German-born for his master race, to fight and colonise his vast, newly-acquired eastern empire, new recruits for his Thousand Year Reich Army.

"And you want to help them do that?" I still didn't understand why she would do it.

"No, of course not. I hope it's a girl anyway. No,... as soon as I am pregnant and he fills in the paperwork, I will be rewarded with extra generous food rations and not be required to work. That's got to be better than this. That's why I don't mind getting pregnant with you."

Personally, I wasn't sure it was better, but said nothing. It was her decision and to be honest, I was enjoying helping her.

> † *This was all part of The Lebensborn Project, one of many secret and terrifying Nazi projects founded by Heinrich Himmler on 12th December 1935. "Lebensborn" translates to "The Fountain of Life."*
>
> *The purpose of this society was to offer to young girls who were deemed "racially pure" the possibility to give birth to a child in secret. The child was then given to the SS organisation which took charge of the child's education and adoption. Both mother and father needed to pass a "racial purity" test. Blond hair and blue eyes were preferred, and family lineage had to be traced back at least three generations.*
>
> *As the war continued, more 'suitable babies' were needed to replace the dead and The Lebensborn Project was expanded to welcome non-German mothers. In a policy formed by Hitler in 1942, German soldiers were encouraged to fraternize with native women, with the understanding that any children they produced would be provided for by the state. In return, the children and their mothers wanted for nothing, with the finest food, homes and clothes supplied to ensure the next generation of Nazis. Others were taken to orphanages, then farmed out to rich Nazi families. But this programme went far further. The cruellest aspect of the scheme involved stealing children who fitted the Nazi racial stereotype of blond, supposedly 'super-beings' who could be 'Germanised' with Nazi families. †*

Although I didn't know it at the time, Stasha did eventually become pregnant by me before the end of my time at the factory. It saddened me greatly to have to leave her and it tore a piece of my heart out, for I believe I was falling in love with her.

---

† *Source: ABC News 20/20 Special Report — Hitler's "Master Race:" The Daily Mail news article, Stolen by the Nazis, The Tragic Tale, www.jewishvirtuallibrary.org*

~ RETURN TO STALAG XXB ~
Late September 1943

We drove straight into camp, waved through the gate by the elderly guard. By now, there were no young guards as they had been withdrawn over time and replaced by increasingly older men, either veterans of the First World War or conscripts too old or infirm to fight on the front line.

Graylag XXB was looking as grey as ever in the dull drizzle of that September evening. As soon as the truck halted, we jumped down into the squelching ooze and formed up on the parade ground to be counted. We were soon counted and ticked off, confirming that nobody had gone AWOL. Whilst I lumbered awkwardly through the thick mud towards our huts, Bert suddenly appeared out of the greyness and came running over to greet me. The other members of the gang had not gone with me on that occasion and I was pleased to see his friendly face once more. He shook my hand warmly.

"Great to see you again Dennis. We missed you."

"You too mate. How are the others?"

"We're all fine. What with all this sun, food and resting since you've been gone on your little jolly, we've had a ball."

I turned and saw the glint in his eye.

"I suppose they've laid on some showgirls for you as well?"

"Yer! to be honest, we're getting a bit bored with all this lavish attention and luxury. Every time we see some of the boys return, we always check to see if you've come back, finally decided to grace us with your presence, your lordship."

With that, he pulled his forelock and bowed.

As we walked, I thought I could hear music. I stopped, and sure enough I heard it more clearly, coming from somewhere, along with loud voices. The sound reverberated across the open ground. However, the accompanying noise was not voices raised in anger but utterances attempting to follow the melodic sound - all be it badly. Bert saw my interest and elaborated.

"That's the actors and orchestra rehearsing for the Christmas panto," he added matter-of-factly. "Don't know how they got hold of so many instruments."

I turned to him and smiled. "Didn't know we had so many musicians in the camp."

"You'd be surprised what we've got in here mate."

"Oh no I wouldn't," I retorted with a knowing wink. It was his turn to smile and we both burst out laughing.

I suppose that given the thousands of prisoners from every walk of life inside our camp, it should have been no surprise there was an amazing wealth of musicians and amateur actors in our midst.

As we neared, the singers came in on cue to accompany them. It didn't sound too good to me but maybe that's why they were rehearsing so early before Christmas.

"Even got themselves a recreation hut, or theatre as they insist on calling it." He paused before continuing.

"Wonder if we'll get to see it this Christmas?"

"Bloody hell Bert, I hope I won't be in camp that long. Yes, it would be good to see them but I'll go potty if I am still here by then."

"See what I can do Dennis. If you go, I'll have a word with the Commandant and see if he will chauffeur you back from the beet factory, just so you don't miss the show."

"Piss off!" I answered. "Think I would prefer slave labour than listening to that lot attempting to sing."

We entered our hut. Two other chaps were in the room lying down. One was holding a book. I had attempted to read it myself, a couple of farms ago. It was a copy of Gibbon's Rise and Fall of the Roman Empire, a thick book from the camp 'library'. Hardly an easy read but at least one had the time here to digest such a volume.

"Hello, I'm Harry, but most people call me ''Enry'."

'Enry' sat up and slipped off his top bunk deftly. He had bare feet and took a couple of steps towards me before offering his hand.

"Hello 'Enry', good to meet you. I'm Dennis, but my mates call me Mar. I just got back."

"Been on 'oliday mate?"

I liked this man.

We chatted for a while before I asked him which bunk was free. He pointed to the empty bunk opposite. Needless to say, it was on the bottom of the three tiers, my least favourite position, but it was that or nothing. Nobody really liked to sleep on the lower bunks because of 'droppage'. This came in the form of a steady sprinkling of living or dead bed bugs, lice and fleas from the straw-filled palliasses above. Stalag XXB was still infested and it was impossible to rid oneself of them. I was already beginning to scratch just thinking about them.

I lifted the palliasse and decided that it looked even worse than I imagined. I removed it and shook it outside the window before slinging it in the corridor. The thought of sleeping on a million revolting bugs that had only just finished gorging on the body of the previous occupant filled me with revulsion. After all, I had more than enough of my own to contend with.

That night I slept on the bare boards whilst picturing the filthy scroungers showering down upon me. I prayed that I kept my mouth shut to avoid swallowing them, but such was my discomfort, the following night I abandoned my foibles and recovered the mattress, preferring the company of more bed bugs to another night of cold and misery.

My roommates told me they hadn't seen little Sammy Newton for a couple of weeks, which surprised me. Whether this meant that he had no news to tell, was unwell or the radio had been discovered yet again was not clear. However, there were tales sweeping the camp, rumours of German defeats and Russian victories in the east, but nothing official. That sort of news could have come from Sammy or from the Poles via returning working parties. The guards didn't seem any more miserable and unpleasant than usual, so there was no indication one way or the other from that quarter.

The men who shared my new quarters proved to be a good enough crowd. Three of them were from the Royal Northumberland Fusiliers attached to the 51st Highland Division, captured at St. Valéry-en-Caux, where they lost so many of their comrades in the bloodiest of battles. They had experienced a similar nightmare journey to Stalag XXA by rail and overcrowded, dank river barges before being transferred to this shit hole. They had some pretty harsh words to say about the High Command and many carried that feeling of having been badly led, failed by the authorities and abandoned by those safely back home in England. It was a story all too familiar to me, having heard similar reports throughout the last three long years. If there was a bigger picture, we were not aware of it.

Soon Jimmy and Johnny entered the hut. Their faces said it all as they greeted me cheerfully and we spent the next hour catching up, laughing and smoking. It actually felt great to be back for once.

Today, my guts were playing up and I had to make a desperate dash to the latrines. I had heard the noises a thousand times but I never got used to it and it made me shudder. In the stinking pit below me, I could hear the scuttling of rats in the sewage. I hoped my latest contribution landed smack on their disgusting little heads.

Upon my return, I was almost at the door of my hut near the entrance gate when I saw a squad of about two-hundred men standing on the other side of the wire. Escorted by guards and dogs, they looked a sorry bunch. I thought nothing more of it until the following day when we learnt that they were Serbs. I hadn't met any Serbs before and I wondered if they would be of any benefit to us.

We only stayed in the camp for a few days before McDowell got us onto the next big work party out of the camp. For me, our departure came none too soon.

~ ANOTHER FACTORY ~
Early October 1943

Once on our way, it didn't take us long to exhaust our conversation, so we settled back on the floor of the truck. There is nothing like a sleep to shorten a journey, and by now we were all very good at it.

It turned out to be a short but bumpy ride. I was not too surprised to see that we had returned once more to a familiar huge building in the middle of nowhere, the sugar beet factory. As we ran through the pouring rain, I subconsciously rubbed my hands over the healed scars of last winter.

It was too late to commence work, so we ate a meagre meal and began our slave labours the following morning. Bert, Jimmy, Johnny and I heaved a sigh of relief as we realised we were to bypass the field work this year, which was excellent news for my back and hands. Instead, we were assigned outside work which was going to be grim if this wet weather continued.

At the double, we were escorted by a particularly aggressive, gaunt and miserable-looking guard with a wrinkled, weather-beaten face. He shouted at us to hurry to the back of the building, where we passed a group of surly looking emaciated beings dressed in rags that bore some resemblance to uniforms. I took them to be Russians. We were confronted by huge mountains of coal that had been brought in and stockpiled during the summer months in order to keep the furnaces going through the coming winter. At the base stood another group of prisoners already working.

We set to work straight away, shovelling the dirty, dark brown rock into the small wagons that ran into the factory on the narrow gauge tracks from the slag heaps. In no time at all, we were sweating like pigs. As soon as the small wagons were full, we pushed and pulled them towards the factory and, once inside, tipped out the coal into the hole above the boiler room. The coal ran the steam engines that powered the machinery that shredded then mashed the beet into pulp before it was processed. Our work schedule was arranged in two punishing twelve-hour shifts. Between us, we agreed to swop jobs every week, just to try and fairly share the misery evenly amongst ourselves.

After my first session I collapsed into an exhausted deep sleep and awoke so stiff that I had great difficulty getting up at all. Ignoring the initial pain, I commenced work, as we all had to do. We settled down to the monotonous pattern with inadequate food for such hard labour. Fortunately, as in the previous year, we were able to supplement our insufficient diet with home-cooked slices of delicious roasted beet.

A few days into the task, I heard a commotion coming from inside the factory building, angry shouting barely audible above the clatter of the machinery. Then all went quiet as first the shredder shut down and then the conveyor belt. Now I could clearly hear the ruckus.

"Who turned it off? Who is responsible, get out of the way," came a shout from an irate German.

As the belt stopped, our immediate guard who had been sheltering from the continuous drizzle, unslung his rifle and ran inside. Curiosity got the better of me. I turned to make sure that I was not being watched and cautiously sauntered inside and followed the sounds of excited voices. Quickly I sidestepped back round a corner and watched discreetly as a guard gave hurried orders.

"Climb up and get him out, quickly."

"Move, " another screamed, pushing back the small crowd of PoWs that had gathered around the machinery,

"Get him out of there," the first guard bellowed. I then saw two men pulling something from the trough of the shredder. It wouldn't budge so a third grabbed another part and pulled. Slowly a blooded mass of clothing was lowered without ceremony to the factory floor with a body or what was left. The guard climbed up to take a closer look. He was not happy.

"Get the rest out and you,...." pointing to some other prisoners, "get a hose and clean this shit up."

Suddenly, I felt a sharp jab in my back. Half expecting a rifle butt to smash into my face as I turned, I instinctively ducked.

"Minter, get back to work you lazy bastard!"

I could have killed Jimmy had I not been so relieved to see him instead and not be spitting out my bleeding teeth. He just laughed but I was not quite in the mood.

"Somebody has just sabotaged the Third Reich's shredder by jumping into it," I glumly answered.

Jimmy's smile vanished as he took a peep at what was going on before quickly turning and pushing me away.

"Hurry Dennis, bloody German's heading this way."

We bolted back outside and started to push our empty wagon back towards the pile of coal.

The conveyor belt was stationary and remained so. Being forced to take an unexpected break, I instantly became jealous of the beet loaders until my envy gremlin was banished by our guard when he impolitely informed them that they would be joining us on the coal run for the duration of the belt's inactivity. The announcement of a return to normality was sudden as the conveyor belt sprang into action and the men returned to their allotted tasks. Late into the evening as we sat around the boiler, all talk was of the body in the shredder.

"He was a Russian, not one of ours," was the considered opinion of Sid Harland, who announced it in his broad Yorkshire accent. He was one of the lads who came with us from our home, Stalag XXB.

"Yer! Guards have had a check and we're all accounted for," Bert confirmed.

"Poor Ivan, couldn't have been easy to slip up into a shredder?"

"Maybe he leaned over too far?"

"Might 'ave 'ad enough of this place and jumped in?"

"Cor!.. what a bloody end, must have been a mess?"

"Well I hope next time Hitler puts a couple of lumps of sugar into his tea, he ends up with one of Ivan's eye balls staring up at him.'

That raised a restrained snigger, but even after what we had been through and what we had seen, any death at the hands of the Germans deserved some mark of respect.

~ LEAFLETS FROM THE SKIES ~
9th October 1943

Finally the rain stopped, enabling us to slave through the night under the clear, chilling sky until the end of our shift. Somebody had the presence of mind to start cooking the slices of beet which I was now

437

eating with relish whilst recovering with the others around the stove. I bathed in the relaxing warmth that radiated from its blackened sides. I leaned back and lazed against a stack of crates, gazing up at the windows set high in the factory walls. I watched as daybreak burst upon the ever changing sky, revealing first a purple and amber canvas before turning a pale blue. The effect upon me was wonderfully soporific and my eyelids grew heavier with each passing second until they gave up the fight and fell shut. My mind and soul drifted easily and gently away, across the continent of northern Europe and over the sea, back home to England.

I was pulled back into my body with a jolt, as shouting violently interrupted my slumbers. In the sleep-hazed distance, I could see my fellow PoWs running towards the door of the factory and out into the daylight beyond. It was then I felt the first vibrations and deep, distant boom. I jumped up to follow them, slowing a second or two to grab a few slices of roasting beet from the top of the stove. Well, life was uncertain, and whatever the reason for this sudden mayhem, my stomach thought it prudent to stock up, just in case. In a few seconds I was through the factory and out the other side with the others. All were looking skywards, some pointing whilst others just stared, shielding their eyes with their hands from the bright glare of the morning sun that was still low in the sky. Another set of dull, distant explosions were followed by more deep vibrations, which were stronger now but all set against a background drone of heavy aircraft engines. As I raised my eyes, I was met by an amazing sight. High above flew a glittering formation of giant American bombers, silver Flying Fortresses. They filled the sky, each trailing four neatly cut white lines of vapour from their mighty engines. It was an awesome spectacle and the first time I had seen any sign of an active allied military presence since my capture some three years before. Our bemused guards had now joined us and they, in turn, watched as the aircraft soared above their target some few miles away and released their first batch of bombs. Their presence triggered a patriotic outburst of cheering from us, sending our spirits soaring skywards in joyous pursuit of the American machines. Our mood contrasted greatly with those of our guards, who were somewhat angry. Above, bombers circled and returned to their target, followed shortly by another round of more tumultuous explosions. The ground shook once more as our guards dived for cover prompting us to follow suit. But really there was no need, for the bombs were not straying too far from their intended targets.

† After crippling bombing raids on the Bremen factories, production was transferred out of reach of British bombers to Marienburg (see picture reference 38). Here, ten F-W 190 fighters a month were being produced, representing 47% of Nazi production.

According to General Henry Arnold, Chief of the US Army Air Force,...

'the Oct. 9 attack on the Focke-Wulf plane factory at Marienburg, East Prussia, was the best example yet of successful precision bombing. On this mission, American heavy bombers based in England flew a 1,800 miles round trip to hit their target, 400 miles from the Russian battle line of Vitebsk. Although losing 29 planes in sky battles that day, they not only damaged every building in the Focke-Wulf plant at Marienburg, but went on to batter the German Naval bases at Gdynia, Poland, Danzig and Anklam, Pomerania.

After the raid, Air Chief Marshal Sir Charles Portal called it "the most perfect example in history of the accurate distribution of bombs over a target."

The USAAF B-17s apparently did a very good job of disrupting production, for a while, but not ending it and all at great personal loss to the Americans in terms of both aircraft and men. Concentrated attacks like this often employed as many as 400 Fortresses and 4000 men. †

As I stared skywards, I wondered how these aircraft could have flown so far with such a heavy payload and still have enough fuel to return to their bases, wherever that might be. We continued to watch the spectacle as the B-17s continued to circle and return. Some of the guys jumped up and down, waving - an empty gesture I know, but it was more a show of empathy with the airmen than a realistic desire to make contact.

As they flew overhead, we became aware of something falling from the skies. Soon we could see thousands upon thousands of pieces of paper slowly drifting down from the American bombers, falling like snowflakes, scattering themselves across the vast, open countryside. It was magical to watch as they finally came to rest,

---

† *Source: An extract from Life Magazine Vol. 15, No 19, page 119. Dated 8th November 1943.*

littering the ground. The guards immediately became agitated, running around like headless chickens.

"Don't touch them, don't touch!" barked our demented gaolers.

"Reading is strictly forbidden!"

With rifles underlining their verbal threats, we were ordered back inside the factory building, but to me their orders were like a red rag to a bull. I could not help myself. After a cautionary look around and with no guards watching, I swiftly bent down and picked up one of the leaflets and stuffed it into my tunic as I ran back inside *(see picture reference 37)*, where things quickly returned to normal. I found my buddies, Bert, Johnny and Jimmy, before retrieving my leaflet.

"You don't want to get caught with that" was the short response from Jimmy for unlike me, he could not have been less interested in my piece of paper.

Printed on the front was a picture of a smiling Adolf Hitler standing amongst the frozen bodies of dead German soldiers as they lay in the snow of a harsh Polish winter. Hitler is seen to say:

'Ich fühle mich so frisch. Es kommt der Frühling.'

('I feel so fresh. Spring is coming.')

Apparently, the quote was an ironic referral to the fact that, during the invasion and occupation of Poland, Hitler seemed oblivious to the numbers of German casualties, which were higher than expected. German casualty statistics were vastly under-recorded due to countless thousands being attributed as 'missing' rather than the more accurate description: 'dead'.

I suppose that if the B-17s had dropped slices of bread, my fellows might have been a lot more interested, but a piece of paper accompanied by a death threat from the guards? I suppose I could see their point of view. My problem was that I was a natural collector and had been ever since I was a boy, be it lead soldiers, model trains, stamps, letters, postcards or other little things. This leaflet appealed to my collector's instinct. Even in the camp I still managed to save stamps, collected from other PoWs' letters.

I took off my tunic jacket and folded the paper neatly and carefully before inserting it into the lining of my right epaulette, as the left one held my carefully concealed money. For me, this was a great start to a wonderfully exciting day.

Two days later, the furnace at the beet plant broke down but nobody could be found to fix the problem so our guards were forced to return us all to camp.

~ ITALY DECLARES WAR ON GERMANY ~
13th October 1943

We had only been away for two weeks and I was deeply disappointed to be back so soon. We arrived at a most inopportune time to a very unwelcoming reception. The camp was in turmoil as dreaded typhoid had found its way into our camp, apparently brought in by the newly-arrived Serb prisoners. Germans with face masks were milling through the compound, moving from hut to hut, forcing out the occupants before disinfecting each hut as thoroughly as possible. A mass hair-cutting and delousing operation was instigated in the hope of stopping the spread of the disease and thereby save their lives.

I had not seen or heard from the camp's ace reporter since he brought us news of the allied invasion of Italy and it was a sign that everything was still normal when one afternoon the doors around the camp burst open again, to the sing-along cry of,

"Heeeeeerrrrrrrreeee comes Sammy!"

These days, we looked forward to seeing him as his news was usually upbeat as opposed to his depressing news during the early days of our incarceration.

He bent down, breathing heavily, hands resting on his knees and his thick mop of dark hair hanging down over his face. He had been running. Overflowing with enthusiasm, Sammy could hardly contain himself whilst trying to catch his breath.

"Italy has joined the Allies and declared war on Germany. We just got word from the BBC, it's official," he blurted out in one go.

Indeed this was good news. The fight back had been gaining momentum but I couldn't help but wish that the Allies had invaded a little closer to us in Poland. Italy still seemed a hell of a distance away. Also, I wondered if the news of Italy joining us would shorten the war or prolong it, for although our new Latin allies had a reputation, it certainly wasn't as fierce fighters.

~ COLD-BLOODED MURDER ~
16th October 1943

Since the end of the Second World War, film-makers have enabled the general population to become familiar with the general layout of the German PoW camps spread across Europe. Each camp's boundary was defined by its watchtowers. Each watchtower housed at least one guard equipped with a spotlight and often a mounted machine gun. Along its margin ran a single, high, barbed wire fence or two parallel fences separated by a metre gap. Sometimes the fence was electrified, sometimes not, depending on the security classification of each camp. In our camp, set one metre in from the perimeter fence and parallel to it ran a single wire, one metre above the ground. Because it was only a single strand of wire, anybody could cross it if they so wished, but at a price. Anybody who did so faced the prospect of being immediately cut down by a hail of machine-gun fire from the ever vigilant watchtower guards.

'Do not cross the death wire' was the message drummed into us on entry to the camp, reinforced with notices that read 'EINGANG VERBOTEN'.

Stalag XXB had become 'home' to several Italian PoWs, even whilst they were allies of the Nazis. This fact surprised me as they were fighting alongside the Germans on the Russian front. However, there were some amongst them who apparently wanted no part in that terrible campaign that tested men to breaking point and beyond. Starved of supplies and adequate clothing and over a thousand miles from their warm homeland, many did not embrace the struggle and refused to fight, ending up in camps like ours. Hence their early imprisonment at Stalag XXB, before their country's change of loyalty. After that, our camp started to receive more Italians in ever-increasing numbers. Now regarded as cowardly traitors, there were not many Germans who were willing to show them kindness. To me, they were always reluctant partners and ineffectual aggressors and,... just Italian.

This particular day was a rare warm and sunny October day. Taking full advantage of the sun, I washed a few of my clothes and hung them outside. I was chatting to some of the men when I spotted Feldwebel Posnanski walking in our general direction. I thought nothing more about it until he got closer. Fortunately for me, our paths had never crossed, but I had the misfortune to see him in action on two previous occasions during my captivity. This third occurrence was to be his most savage to date that I witnessed.

Nearby, a small group of newly-arrived Italians had gathered. When he reached them he stopped, and with his hands clasped tightly behind his back he stood bolt upright, drawing himself up to his full, towering height. He rocked back and forth on the balls of his feet, looking more German than bloody Hitler himself.

Posnanski stood between the Italians and the wire perimeter 'dead line', staring at one particularly small Italian, the closest one to him. Somehow I felt as though something was going to happen. I watched intently as he began to speak. Slowly he unclasped his hands, grabbed hold of the unsuspecting Italian and pointed with his other hand towards the wire behind him, drawing the bewildered Italian's attention to a single piece of paper littering the ground on the other side of the 'death wire'. Our group was close enough to see and hear all that was being said. The tension was now palpable and the situation worrying. En masse, we all began to gently drift closer. The Italian said and did nothing but looked back at Posnanski, at the paper and then back at Posnanski again. Posnanski repeated his order in a stronger but still precise manner. This time the Italian shook his head and pleaded, "No, per favore, no."

I could feel a knot in my stomach beginning to form, my fist tightening and my anger rising. Posnanski let go of his collar. He then placed his left hand on his gun holster and undid the cover. With his right hand stretching across his body, he deliberately and slowly withdrew his pistol, cocked it with his left hand and pointed it directly at the Italian's head.

"Pick ... it ... up," he simply repeated.

The blood had drained from the poor Italian's face. As white as a ghost, he slowly edged towards the wire and paper before stopping a few inches away from the wire. He looked back at Posnanski, who still had his pistol drawn and pointing directly at him. The Italian sank slowly onto the ground by the side of the wire. His attention now turned to the closest watchtower, well within firing range. From his lofty perch, the tower guard was watching. By now, there was total silence. Even the birds seemed to have stopped singing, and in that still autumn air I heard the metal on metal 'click' of the machine-gun's firing pin as it was slid into the engaged position. It was as if I was watching a film slowly unfolding before my eyes. I could scarcely believe what I was seeing. The Italian's gaze darted back and forth between the eyes of Posnanski and the tower guard as inch by inch the poor sod slowly stretched his arm forward under the wire, towards the piece of paper, now almost within touching distance... but not quite. His eyes were fixed rigidly on the guard in the tower.

By now, a large group had gathered. The atmosphere was tangible. I gazed up to see the watchtower guard clasp hold of the butt of his machine gun, tucking it tightly into his shoulder before bringing the barrel down to bear on the Italian. Posnanski's pistol was also still aimed at him. Both players seemed to know the 'game' and the poor victim was the pawn, stuck between a rock and a hard place. The Italian was just a hand stretch away from the paper. Ever so slowly, he edged forward again, his fingers walking the last inch across the dirt. He could stretch no further from the safety of his tenuous position before finally placing his head under the wire.

Even though I was expecting it, I still jumped. The noise of gun fire from the watchtower shattered the almost overpowering intensity of that day. The hail of bullets peppered the ground before tearing into the Italian's body. He died instantly. Posnanski continued to stare as blood oozed from his lifeless form and drained into the dusty Polish sand. Having feasted his eyes on the corpse for an indecent length of time, he leisurely turned away, pistol still drawn, whilst he scanned the semi-circle of PoWs who were eyeing him with utter contempt. It was as if he was willing someone, anyone, to come forward, to protest or have a go, thereby giving him an excuse to use his weapon once more. A smirk spread across his face as he slowly and deliberately replaced his pistol with all the aplomb of a seasoned actor. He adjusted his tunic before turning once more and walking away, straight through our ranks and towards the main gate, without a care in his rotten, stinking world.

The sad thing was that here in 1943 Europe, life was that cheap.

~ BOILER MENDED - BACK TO THE FACTORY ~
16th October 1943

We arrived back at the factory to find that unfortunately, the furnace had been fixed. The Polish foreman told me that if this hadn't been a war situation, the furnace would have been scrapped years ago, but his factory was low priority so he was required to maintain it with an escalating succession of 'sticking plaster' repairs plus a kiss and a prayer.

Throughout the bleak winter of 1943 and into 1944, we slaved at the factory. We were given a day off for Christmas, courtesy of the generous Third Reich. This allowed the guards to indulge themselves in their Christmas festivities, whilst we foolishly consumed the fearsome beet alcohol, courtesy of the ever-brewing Scots. So much for my promise to never touch another drop again. I think we had a good time!

1944

DRUDGERY

After days, weeks and months of toil, I stood back and looked up at the fruits of our labours. That huge slag heap of a coal mountain still looked just as tall, which of course could not have been true, but the sight was soul-destroying. We laboured twelve hours a day on a never-ending treadmill of hellish despair, and all the time in the perishing cold. The bitterness of those Arctic winds will remain with me and haunt me to my grave. It was not until early March '44, when the last of the beet was finally processed, that we eventually returned to the drabness that was Greylag XXB.

By now, leaked tales of Russian advances and German defeats were flooding into camp. This was confirmed by Sammy, but the geographic location of the Russian towns and cities that were quoted as falling back into Russian hands meant nothing to us. However, when I was told of the rumours that the Russians were about three or four-hundred miles from Warsaw, my excitement rose a gnat's whisker above rock bottom. News of the Italian campaign and the allied advance through the boot end of Europe seemed slow but steady. There was speculation amongst some that the Allies might move directly north and liberate us first, but such a long slog over the Alps to join the fight on the Russian front in preference to taking France first was soon dismissed out of hand. With no imminent change in sight to our position as Hitler's guests, our life within the camp settled back down into its familiar, mundane pattern.

The few Serbs who had survived last year's typhoid outbreak had now been joined by others. They seemed to be a decent but emaciated lot and soon settled in well amongst us. In the main, they were tall, good-looking and trustworthy and had a very endearing habit of saluting every Brit they passed, regardless of rank. For some reason, which I never quite understood, they had a deep-seated hatred towards the remaining Frenchmen within the camp. On the other hand, we seemed to be the only nationality that the Serbs actually did like, which was fine with me.

By the middle of '43, our little gang of four were relatively prosperous, as was the camp in general. Pilfering from the Germans, trading with the Poles and more Red Cross parcels meant we were doing alright, comparatively speaking. We were more affluent than at any other time since our captivity, but the downside was that, like the Germans, our fortunes had reached their zenith and since then, it had been downhill all the way, mirroring the misfortunes of our not-so-conquering masters.

In the spring we were approached by a Serb called Dusan. Since joining us we had got to know him quite well and genuinely liked him. He spoke pidgin English, which was a relief because our knowledge of his language was nonexistent. We found him willing to do anything to help us, as long as we paid him. At first, he offered to do our washing. None of us liked doing this job at the best of times but our clothes definitely needed his help. We still had enough surplus 'currency' to pay for his services, so we negotiated a price, using Lagergeld, bread or cigarettes, whichever was available at the time. From then on, Dusan did our washing, using the only place available for washing everything and anything, the trough in the wash house. He did a good job, and whatever else we wanted done, Dusan or one of the other Serbs would be only too happy to oblige.

Following wash days, our hut resembled a laundry room with string washing lines hung from wall to wall and home-made pegs holding our clean clothes. No matter how well Dusan washed them, he could never rid us of our pet lice, for without boiling water, detergents, disinfectants, dynamite or the furious fires of hell, their eggs were beyond destruction. If only our tanks had been made of lice casing in 1940! On the whole, the Serbs proved to be a great addition to life within the confines of the camp.

I had not had a parcel or letter from home for a while, and to date I had only received one whole Red Cross parcel when in hospital whilst recovering from my broken arm. One day I mentioned the latter to a fellow in the room next door. He didn't seem surprised at all, adding that there were plenty of them in the store room adjoining McDowell's hut. He knew this for a fact because he had seen them. At first, I couldn't understand why this should be and it made me angry, but I didn't have the nerve to ask McDowell the reason why. I suppose he could have been keeping some back for a future emergency or to give them to the sick in our camp. He may also have used them to 'bribe' the guards or trade with them for quite legitimate reasons. Unfortunately, there were many rumours flying round the camp concerning McDowell's honesty and I had no idea as to where the truth lay, for only the man himself knew the real reason, and without proof of any wrongdoing his innocence had to be assumed.

Camp food had not improved, and with few Red Cross parcels reaching us to supplement our rations we needed outside food more than ever. For the next couple of months, 'Mar Minter's Boys' continued to toil in the surrounding farms where we stole, begged and traded with the locals for both food and cigarettes, even the revolting Polish variety.

At the end of May, we returned to camp for a short holiday and luckily, with a bit of persuasion, we managed to get a billet together. Immediately, we brought ourselves up to date with the news. Abroad, the Allies were advancing slowly up through Italy and the Russians were pushing the enemy back from whence they came and therefore getting closer to us. Closer to home, I discovered that McDowell had been replaced some time ago and now, R.S.M. Singleton was in charge. I didn't really care who held that lofty position as long as they kept out of my way and passed on the Red Cross Parcels.

During yet another beautiful, warm May, followed by a blazing June, we spent our time working on the surrounding farms. Summer was here, and by comparison with the Polish winter we accepted the sweltering heat inside our sauna-like huts with a stoic resignation.

As far as I was concerned, anything was preferable to prolonged exposure to sub-zero temperatures. The once new pine walls of the huts were now weathered, bone dry and grey. Such was the sun's intensity that on the hottest of days, the walls emitted a wonderful, heavy odour of smouldering wood, which was good for it covered up a multitude of less pleasant aromas.

At the end of June, another group of British Officers were spotted walking past our camp, accompanied by their escorts of guards. Again, none of the Officers attempted to make any form of contact with us, which I still regarded as strange and distant of them.

· · · § · · ·

6th JUNE 1944

THEY CALLED IT D-DAY

6th June was arguably the most momentous day in modern history and was to herald the end of the Second World War. We saw it as revenge for Dunkirk.
Within a week Hitler unleashed his V1 Flying Bombs on an unsuspecting England and a war-weary London and my parents were under threat from their destructive powers.

Shortly after dawn, we found ourselves driving into town in the back of several trucks to the goods yard. It took a couple of hours of waiting in line for our turn and then loading a hundred or so boxes of long-anticipated Red Cross parcels. These were the first I had seen for a long while. I calculated that they wouldn't go far when shared amongst the thousands of PoWs back at camp. In the process, I managed to sneak away to trade and returned with two loaves of bread and a pack of British cigarettes from a friendly Polish civilian, which brought a smile to my gang back in camp.

By late afternoon, the heat was oppressive. Anybody unlucky enough to look round the corner into our room would have caught me lying down flat on my back on top of my bunk, dressed in nothing but my shabby, discoloured underpants, scratching at the irritating little parasitic bastards that still occupied my warm, comfortable crotch.

Sammy Newton, still with his big, thick, bottle spectacles, ginger moustache and amazing enthusiasm for his chosen task, came crashing into our hut with the excitement of a child who had just been told that Father Christmas was here. His sudden entrance was accompanied by silence, not the usual response, for we were all too hot to bother. It had been almost three long years since Sammy had brought us news of the German invasion of the Soviet Union and now he was about to shatter the dullness of our miserable existence once more. He stood in the central corridor. All the doors to our rooms were left permanently open during summer in a vain attempt to lower the internal temperature. A few heads popped out of rooms to greet him but most stayed hidden, quite unconcerned.

"Listen up chaps, listen up. This is important. It has finally happened. The Allies have landed in France. The invasion has begun."

Inside our hut was utter silence. You could have heard the bed bugs moving. Then came the chaotic noise of men scrambling to their feet and rushing into the corridor to listen to his news in earnest, unsure if they had heard it correctly.

Aware that he now held everyone's attention, Sammy spoke again in a slow, almost solemn tone, such was the importance of his broadcast.

"It's true, the Allies have invaded," he repeated. "Started at dawn this morning, a massive army of British, Yanks and allied forces have landed in France. This is it lads, the end is in sight."

The news was indeed momentous and instantly Sammy was bombarded with questions from all directions. He told us what he could but he had no finer details to add so he left in order to spread his earth-shaking news to the rest of the camp. We were in shock. This was the most pivotal news story since the beginning of the war. Suddenly a couple of the guys screamed and jumped into the air, elated. Now I could finally allow my mind to wander, to dream, to imagine what liberation would mean and how soon it would become a reality. Thoughts of home raced through my mind.

By the end of the day, the mood throughout the whole camp was electric. Everybody knew, and by the attitude and expressions of the guards, they knew too. In the days that followed, the mood of the guards changed, with many becoming openly aggressive and downbeat, whilst a precious few appeared kinder and even compassionate. I was immediately reminded that with the end of our captivity now an eventual possibility, the thought that the Germans might have to account for their actions might have had some bearing on this change in attitude, or was I being too sceptical?

~ HIMMLER PUT IN CHARGE OF ALL POWS ~
20th July 1944

Whilst Hitler was at the 'Wolf's Lair' (his command post for the Eastern Front), disillusioned Officers of the Wehrmacht made a failed attempt on his life. An army general in charge of us PoWs happened to be one of the conspirators. Consequently, all trust in his army generals evaporated and Hitler turned to his 'loyal and trustworthy' Reichsführer, Heinrich Himmler, for support. One such problem for him was a solution to the PoW issues. After too many escapes from the camps, (and in particular the now famous Great Escape, on the night of 23rd/24th March 1944, by 76 PoWs from the practically escape-proof Stalag Luft III) Hitler had had enough and Himmler was nominally put in overall charge of PoWs and the bureaucracy that ran the camps. Himmler had argued the point that it was only the SS and Gestapo who could make the camps secure. On 25th September, Hitler formalised the position and Himmler appointed his underling, SS Generalleutnant Gottlob Berger, to the unenviable task of supervising all PoWs and internees, as well as the PoW camps.

This deeply concerned the Army and Air Force Officers who were actually running the camps at the time, fearing that the intervention of the SS and Gestapo would have disastrous consequences for their prisoners. With the defeat of Germany now a distinct probability, repercussions by the allies threatened, and those responsible for any mistreatment of PoWs would naturally be held accountable by the allies.

Fortunately for us all, we did not know of this development and the SS never actually attempted to take over the administration of the camps and impose their own particular brutal treatment. One must assume that at that point in the war, both Hitler and Himmler had more pressing and urgent matters to worry about.

~ TANSI THE SERIAL ESCAPIST ~
11th July 1944

The general exuberance over the long-awaited D-Day landings could not be maintained. Once we realised that our liberation was dependent upon the strength of resistance of the still formidable German war machine, it quickly dawned that it could still take many months, possibly years for the British or Americans to reach us, so life soon reverted to a sort of normality once more.

I had just received another parcel from the lads at Hackbridge back home. Since shortly after my arrival at Greylag XXB, they had been sending me much appreciated cigarettes. That same day, I wrote a sincere 'Thank You' card to them all.

Even though the allies had landed, the majority of us thought that the escape route across Europe to dear old Blighty was still too difficult a task and was not worth contemplating for even a second. But the camp did hold some who thought that it was a great idea. Over the years, escapes were planned and some made, but most failed. Getting out of camp was the easy part; staying free was another matter entirely.

Within the confines of Greylag XXB, there were several individuals who had attempted escape. One such person was a young man from Liverpool. His name was Tansi, but I never did discover if this was his real name or nickname. He was a 'professional' escapee and was not put off by a mere 1,000 mile journey, but on every occasion he was re-captured and returned to camp and punished in 'Die Bunker'. He was regarded as a bit of a hero, for each time a prisoner such as he escaped, it cost the Germans time, effort and precious troop resources to scour the vast countryside for one lone British soldier. Added to that, such successful escapes did not look good on the Commandants' reports. Inevitably he would be castigated by his superiors. As a result, I suppose you could see the Germans' slightly biased and negative attitude to escape attempts.

For persistent escapees, there was only one answer. After Tansi's last abortive endeavour in the spring of 1944, the Commandant and army authorities wanted to be rid of him once and for all. It was decided to send him somewhere out of harm's way, to a special harsh punishment camp designed to be escape-proof.

A few days before he was destined to leave, word went round that one last final effort was to be made to get him out of camp and away before the German authorities could collect him. To this end, a plea went out for as many cigarettes as possible to be donated for his benefit. Runners were sent to scour the huts and beg for as many as could be given. I and five others volunteered and the majority of my own recently received cigarettes went in the pot.

I have to admit that it was exciting to be involved in such a brazen escape. It was all a bit 'Boy's Own Comic Book' and I was loving it. Eventually we managed to collect several thousand cigarettes. I didn't know that there were that many in Europe, let alone our camp.

The plan itself was not elaborate by any stretch of the imagination, for there was no time for a sophisticated plot. Quite simply, under cover of early morning darkness, someone would quickly dig a shallow trench under the perimeter wire halfway between the watchtowers. Tansi would then crawl under the wire and run off. In order to avoid a patrolling German foiling his escape, it was necessary to enlist the help of one such guard on the outside of the wire. This could only be achieved by bribing him to look the other way. It was easy enough to discover who would be on guard duty at that time of the morning and on that section of wire as the methodical Germans never varied the rota. And that was where the thousands of cigarettes came in, a bribe to enable Tansi to escape. Simplicity itself. Almost too simple. Escape attempts were few and far between, and the Germans felt quite confident that most would not even bother, and to a greater extent, they were right.

One morning in early July, the 'reliable' guard had been identified, the bribe paid and the plan for Tansi's departure implemented. Two hours before dawn, the shallow trench was hastily dug and under the wire he went, scuttling off to freedom. At least, that was the plan. Unfortunately, the Germans had other ideas. A welcoming committee was waiting for him just out of view on the other side of the fence. The 'not-so-reliable' guard had informed the camp authorities. Consequently, the escape plan was foiled. Tansi was immediately apprehended and held in the cells until his escorts arrived, before being carted off to his new camp for naughty boys. That was the last we ever saw of him.

But that was not the end of the incident by any means, for there were repercussions.

The ever-efficient German investigative branch swung into action as the incident had to be fully probed and the accomplices brought to account. The whole camp was interviewed and questioned about who exactly gave what, how many cigarettes were collected and from whom and which person actually bribed the guard. At the end of the enquiry and as soon as the paperwork was completed and correlated, the German authorities discovered that the 'reliable' German guard had been less than honest with them. In fact over six-thousand cigarettes had been collected and paid to him. This came as a revelation to the camp authorities and was an unfortunate disclosure for the guard, as he had only declared three-thousand cigarettes, keeping very quiet about the rest. As a result, not only was the person who bribed the guard punished, but the guard himself was given twenty-eight days solitary for 'embezzlement' and a free trip to the Russian Front. I had no idea if the prisoners were accurate with their statements or if they just wanted to throw a huge spanner in the investigator's works and, at the same time, stitch up the guard, but no matter for at least we felt the guard got his just desserts.

The fallout from the escape attempt spread even further. Shortly after, the new Camp Commandant and his interpreter made a rare appearance and addressed us at morning parade. It was obvious that something significant was about to happen. Commandant Theodor Lorentzen was a fifty-year-old veteran Officer of the First World War. He stood before us in his best uniform, but other more senior Officers from outside the camp were there also, dripping with braid and menace.

Tansi had already gone, along with the greedy guard and the PoW who handed him the bribe. Now it was the turn of those who had assisted in collecting the cigarettes from the inmates. Because almost the whole camp had contributed to the bribe, the shock announcement was that unless those directly responsible for the actual collection of the cigarettes came forward and identified themselves, then reprisals would be taken against the whole camp. I and the other five responsible suspected that this was going to be the most likely scenario, and consequently, we had already discussed our course of action beforehand and knew what we were going to do. By now, my heart was pounding and my hands sweating. The Commandant, flanked by other Officers, addressed the camp in German and then the English translation was read out by his interpreter.

"All those responsible, take one step forward."
There was barely a moment's delay. All six of us stepped forward en masse. An order was given and guards came to collect us and march us to the side where we gathered. The rest of the camp was dismissed and all six of us were escorted to 'Die Bunker'.

~ DANZIG ~

Once inside, I was taken to my cell and the door slammed shut and locked. I was now alone. Like my fellow prisoners , I had no idea how long we would be detained or what was going to happen to us. I sat down on the wooden bunk and looked around. Unlike our huts, my small cell had an internal wooden wall. The cavity was filled with wood chip, shredded paper or the like, not to insulate it from the cold but to keep the internal room as quiet and isolated as possible. The cell was about two metres square. My only furniture was a wooden bunk, without a mattress but with one thin blanket. I looked up to see a narrow hole cut in the side of the wall, about the size of a letterbox and open to the elements, being just large enough to let in some fresh air at least. The overhanging eaves of the roof allowed only a faint trace of light to filter through. Suspended from above was a lone light bulb hanging precariously by a wire from the ceiling. I spent the whole day without food or water, heard nothing, saw no-one, and it was as boring as waiting for the sea to evaporate.

Without warning, my cell was plunged into total darkness as the single bulb was switched off. I tried to sleep, but without a palliasse the bunk was uncomfortably hard, making for an extremely restless night, if indeed it was nightfall, for there was no sure way of knowing. I awoke as soon as I realised that the light had been switched back on, only to have it extinguished again shortly afterwards. This disturbing pattern continued at irregular intervals, supposedly with the intention of disorientating us prisoners within a prison. If that was their aim, then they succeeded.

Minutes, hours or days ticked on by; all measure of time had disappeared. My cell door was suddenly opened and I was handed a mug of lukewarm coffee and a hunk of bread by a glum and uncommunicative guard, which proved to be the highlight of my new prison life.

Eventually, I was reunited with my fellow transgressors and taken out into the blinding, unfamiliar sunlight. We squinted painfully until our eyes grew accustomed to the daylight. We greeted each other with a nod of the head and a shrug of the shoulders, thereby indicating that we hadn't got a clue as to what was on the agenda, but by now we were used to the surprise element, being kept in the dark in more ways than one by the army authorities. All part of being a soldier, I guess.

In the blistering heat we were taken to the camp clothing store, stuffed to the rafters with British, French, Yugoslavian and other nations' livery. We were each handed a clean, new uniform to change into. In exchange, we handed over our old ones, which were bagged and labelled before being stored away.

We dressed in silence, nervous with uncertainty. It occurred to me that we were probably not about to be shot, for why clothe us in new uniforms only to have them peppered by a volley of bullets and subsequent blood stains? That was the collective thinking amongst us six and I desperately wanted it to be true.

We were driven the relatively short distance to Marienburg's main passenger rail station, where we eventually boarded a train. Unlike my last train journey, this time our carriage had seats. What luxury! We followed the leading guard who entered a compartment and forcefully ejected the two civilian incumbents, before the eight of us sat down and made ourselves comfortable. Few words were spoken as we were all suffering from varying degrees of anxiety, but at least we were together which did give us a collective strength, helping to maintain our spirits. The journey didn't take too long, some two-and-a-half hours. It was mid-afternoon when we pulled into our final destination. The signs at the platform read 'DANZIG'.

The knot in my stomach twisted and tightened as I rose from my seat and stepped down from the train. Doors opened along its length and a crowd spilled out onto the platform. Whistles blew and engines hissed with exhausted steam. People busied themselves with urgency whilst others stood searching the faces of passing strangers, looking for friends and loved ones. Despite the fact that it was the height of summer, all about was still a sea of grey drabness, no doubt as a result of my trepidation.

Our guard barked an order, which snapped me back to my present situation, as a PoW on a charge on our way to somewhere as yet unknown. All my concerns returned with a vengeance. We walked from the station to a waiting truck. The tailgate was lowered before we were ordered to board. Our two guards followed. They sat down on either side of the tailgate before unslinging their rifles and nestling them between their legs, barrels pointing skywards. The traffic on the road was heavy as we drove the short journey to the city centre. German military vehicles were everywhere, moving with urgency. Occasional black cars and animal-powered carts vibrated past on the cobbled stones. We came to a halt briefly outside an important-looking stone building, cold and official in appearance. Above and either side of the main entrance, a pair of red, white and black German Swastikas hung in all their terrifying glory whilst a huge golden eagle of the Third Reich adorned the dull, grey face of the sombre building above the door. What little conversation there had been between us stopped; our combined bravado had evaporated. We slowly drove on past the entrance. Two sentries were guarding the portal. Around their necks hung a decorative metal plate, rather like symbolic miniature breast plates. A sneaky smile quickly flashed across my face as I imagined seeing the words 'FIDO' neatly engraved on each. We took a right turn through a side entrance, halting in front of the security gates. After an initial delay we entered an open square at the rear of the building and alighted. Once inside, we were processed by the military authorities and taken below ground. We found ourselves in a gloomy passageway leading to the holding cells of the German Army Headquarters, formerly the official Polish Police Headquarters before the occupation. My brick-lined cell was about three metres long by two metres wide. The only furniture was the low wooden bunk with straw-filled palliasse and a single blanket. In the corner was a bucket, for our personal use. As I turned round, the guard slammed the heavy metal door shut. I walked to the door and for a brief moment, looked through the small metal grid covering the glass window until the guard released the catch that sent a flap crashing down to cover my only view of the outside world. Above me, a single dim bulb provided the only source of light. It was indeed grim. This place was a proper gaol.

I spent a restless night imagining what was going to be the outcome of our ordeal.

The following day, a guard handed me a mug of water and a chunk of bread. I ate in silence. A while later, he returned and ordered me out of my cell and into the corridor. My other five partners in crime were there waiting for me. We could only greet each other with a weak smile and a simple nod before being led up a plain stone staircase and along a short corridor into a large and imposing but plain room. Inside were an array of chairs and polished desks with various army personnel waiting for our arrival. Smart NCOs busied themselves with quiet efficiency whilst others turned to watch our arrival. At the end of the room, a high-ranking German Officer sat behind a long, grand table in an ornate chair. He seemed to be busy, reading his way through a wad of papers and files. On both sides of him, two other more junior Officers sat patiently waiting for the theatricals to commence. In front of each of the five Officers, their smart peaked caps were neatly placed in a row facing towards the front of the heavy wooden table. We were led to a row of utilitarian seats in front of the Officers' table but ordered to remain standing but at ease.

The Officers studied each of us in their own time whilst reading prepared typed documents and speaking quietly amongst themselves. The room had taken on an even more sombre atmosphere as my heart thumped hard against my chest. The proceedings came to life suddenly as the senior Officer spoke in a stern authoritative voice and then translated it into impeccable English. Naturally, he remained seated. He was a large man in his mid-forties. He was courteous and polite yet totally professional in every sense. This was, after all, a military court and had to be conducted in a proper military manner. He turned and spoke to the NCO seated to the side of him, who sprang smartly to attention before addressing us, the prisoners, in German.

The NCO ordered us to stand to attention before sitting back down again at his desk and returning to his paperwork.

It was then the turn of a junior Officer, one of the prosecuting team. He stood to attention and acknowledged the most senior Officer before turning and addressing us in German for several minutes. He read out the charges levied against all six of us before sitting back down again. The most senior Officer of the court then spoke a few words to another Officer at the side of us. This Officer was our defence lawyer. He in turn spoke to the court before turning to us and again, in perfect English, translated the charges,... of bribing a guard and aiding a PoW in his attempt to escape contrary to blar, blar, blar section, military law, etc.,etc. After which he addressed us all in turn, asking if we wished to plead guilty or not guilty. There was no point in denying the charges, for we had already admitted our guilt to the heinous crime. As each of us replied 'guilty', the Officer repeated the question until we had all answered. He then addressed the Officers at some length before returning to his desk. The senior Officer then spoke a few more words before our two German guards behind us sprang to attention and ordered us 'about turn', and marched us out of the court room and back to our cells.

The whole process had taken less than half-an-hour but we still had no idea as to our fate. Within the hour, our guard returned and marched us back into the court room. This time, we remained standing to attention in front of the senior Officer and his associates. He held up a piece of paper and read from it before looking at us and sentencing us all, first in German and then in English.

"Six months imprisonment in a 'Sträflager' (punishment camp)."

Our defence lawyer then spoke to us all, telling us that he would automatically appeal to the court for leniency, and until our appeal was heard by the court we would continue to be held in the cells below.

So for the next week, we remained in solitary. Time dragged through every waking moment as never before, but at least we knew the worst-case scenario.

~ THE WOLF'S LAIR ~
RASTENBURG
19th July 1944

Whilst we waited in our cells in Danzig for our appeal verdict, 200 kilometres to the east of us, Hitler was at his "Wolf's Lair" field headquarters, deep within the forest near Rastenburg, East Prussia. It was the day before the failed assassination attempt on his miserable life. From there he gave orders to Field-Marshal Keitel (of Army High Command) with regards to the evacuation of all PoWs from the eastern territories, to stop them falling into the hands of the advancing Soviet forces, for reasons that were uncertain. Were we to be used as hostages when dealing with the enemy? Did Hitler believe that it was inevitable that the western Allies could be persuaded to join with him against the Red Army? We will never know.

At some time during the night of the 19th and the early hours of the 20th, our Commandant, Theodor Lorentzen, received Keitel's directive, to 'make extensive preparations for the mass evacuation of all PoWs under your control at Stalag XXB'. The Soviets had already captured Minsk at the beginning of July. The Commandant of Stalag Luft VI near the border of East Prussia and Lithuania had received his instructions a week earlier and had already begun the implementation of his evacuation instructions. By the end of the month, the Soviet Army was within 12 miles of Warsaw.

~ MEANWHILE, AT DANZIG ~
August 1944

Eventually we were collected and marched back to the court room, which we quietly entered, for those inside were busy in conversation. This time, we were shown to some seats at the back of the court because there was another trial still in progress. We would have to wait before our case could be attended to.

On this occasion a stocky, powerful-looking British soldier, well over six feet tall, was at the centre of the proceedings. We settled back in our seats and listened as the case unfolded in both German and English. Soon, I was engrossed.

The British soldier standing to attention in front of the court had been working on a farm, just like us and untold thousands of other PoWs spread across the continent. He had entered the farmer's house, but whether this was by invitation or by forced entry was unclear. Very soon afterwards the British soldier got into a blazing row with the farm owner, which got progressively more and more heated. At the height of his anger, the British soldier lost all control, grabbed the nearest object, which just happened to be a portrait hanging on the wall, and brought it smashing down upon the head of the farmer, smashing the picture, glass and frame to pieces and, in the process, hurting the farmer.

By this time, all six of us 'convicts' felt like cheering as we eagerly awaited the next part of this absorbing little tale.

It was now that the prosecution lawyer delivered his punch line, thereby allowing the full horror of the dastardly crime to come to light. It was bad enough that the British soldier had smashed this picture over the head of the German/Polish farmer, but rather unfortunately the picture had been a large portrait of their beloved Führer.

As the German Officer spoke the words, all of us looked at each other with huge grins creeping across our faces. We were barely able to contain our chortling, but I was glad that it was not me standing there in the dock at that precise moment.

As prisoners, we did not have many opportunities to laugh but this was one of those magical moments when life presented itself as a comedy of errors and we were loving it. The outcome of the trial was that the poor British soldier was sentenced to three years' imprisonment.

Now it was our turn. I was grateful that we had all managed to control our amusement; had we not, then I am sure the senior Officer in charge of reviewing our sentence would have been most reluctant to look at our case with any compassion. We had enjoyed one hell of a good time and now we were more relaxed.

We were called to the front of the court room and ordered to remain standing. Why they bothered with our seats remained a mystery. The senior Officer briefly read the charge again, followed by a long, drawn-out speech. Combined with the translation into English, his oration seemed to go on for an age. Finally, he said the court had gone over all the evidence and decided to reduce the sentence from six to three months. Coming on the back of the previous show, we were jubilant and exchanged smiles and handshakes as we were led back down to our cells.

We spent our final night at Danzig in a far better frame of mind than when we had arrived. The following day, we left and made the reverse train journey to Marienburg and 'home', to Greylag XXB.

~ SOLITARY ONCE MORE ~

It was as though we were leaving school at the end of term with our spirits high for we chatted easily and joked continuously, relieved that it was all over.

As soon as we entered the camp, we were taken directly to the clothes store, to hand back our nice new uniforms in return for our filthy old rags. Inside was one of the men from our hut. In the briefest of moments whilst left unattended by the Germans and changing back into our lice-infested uniforms, he speedily managed to update us on news of the war. Whilst we had been away, little Sammy had obviously continued to spread the word. We all knew that things were not going well for Hitler's beloved Thousand Year Reich and now looked likely to be re-named the Ten Year Reich.

It occurred to me that so far I had not seen any of our old guards. Those I had seen so far were strangers and even older than the previous. It was like being guarded by our granddads!

Ever since the invasion of Russia back in 1940, battle-weary combat troops were pulled back from the front and given a rest in the form of guard duty at camps across Europe. But all that had changed. Weary or not, they remained at the front in an increasingly desperate attempt by the Wehrmacht to halt the unstoppable flood of the Soviet hordes, hell-bent on ridding their country of the jackboot. Far older soldiers, fifty plus years of age, had been drafted in to guard us, thereby freeing up every able-bodied man.

We had been told we would spend our sentence in the German Military Prison at Graudenz, where both allied and German military

461

prisoners were incarcerated. Once dressed, we were immediately escorted back to 'Die Bunker' and locked up. I wish I could say it was nice to be home again, but I couldn't quite manage it. All we could do now was await for our transfer to the 'Sträflager'.

And then we waited, hours, a day, a night? To me, it felt like an awfully protracted period before my first meal, so when I eventually heard the metallic sound of the key unlocking my door and the tiny squeak of the hinges, I jumped off my bunk. It was the first sound of human activity that I had heard and I was glad of it. The armed guard entered, looked at me, handed over my lump of bread and mug of water before closing the door and disappearing without a word. Room service had not improved since I had been away. Prison food was really no different from the barely palatable slops that we were given in camp and never varied. There was little to gauge the passage of time, which was the worst aspect of my incarceration as time dragged relentlessly. The tiny opening set high up under the rafters allowed insufficient daylight to seep through into my room and was insufficient to mark the switch from night to day as the flood lights were turned on at night to illuminate 'Die Bunker'. My single meal of the day seemed to come at irregular spells so that was no indication, for the Germans might come twice within six hours and then leave a gap of thirty-six hours for all I knew, all designed to further disorientate us and increase our discomfort, as was the switching on and off of our internal light at irregular intervals.

I must have dozed. After a period of sleep, I awoke to the strange sound of fluttering and noticed movement high up above my head. I looked up to see that a small bird had appeared from nowhere and was standing in the tiny ventilation slot. He flapped his little feathers as if to straighten them and then looked down at me as I lay on my bunk bed. We stared at each other for a few seconds. He cocked his head from side to side as if puzzled by my presence. He twittered his little song for a few moments as if talking to me, so in turn, I replied.

"And where have you come from, little fellah?"

He didn't understand English so I spoke 'birdy', whistled a few notes and received a satisfying musical response. My new feathered friend was a wonderful distraction and so brightened my day that I felt happy again for the first time since leaving the court. The bird dallied all too briefly before taking his leave. I was sorry to see him go but he did eventually return. I tried chucking a few crumbs from my minuscule ration of bread up into the tiny opening to encourage the bird to come and visit me more often and I succeeded. His visits also indicated to me that it was daytime. With nothing else to do, I began to look forward to his daily visits, which lasted for the duration of my stay in the cell. I spoke to him of my troubles, my reflections and my dreams for the future. He was a very good listener.

Between the bird's visits, I attempted to sleep whilst thinking of fabulous banquets in cosy restaurants, imagining the taste of sweet Virginian tobacco wafting through my nostrils. Then I would wake up with nothing to occupy my mind. Waiting for my one meal and the arrival of 'Birdy' and my toilet routine were the highlights of my existence. Twice a day, I was escorted across the parade ground to the toilet block. Being isolated from the rest of the camp and starved of any visual stimuli, what time I had sitting on the toilet I spent soaking up every detail of the camp and latrines whilst the guard waited impatiently. Although the latrines had improved since the first crude construction back in 1940, they were still grim. Now there was a roof and they were semi-enclosed on three sides, but the open fronts remained. The place still stank to high heaven, especially in summer, but no amount of ventilation was ever going to stop that. Fortunately, I was no longer sick with the stench. Every so often, the Germans gave us large barrels of a white chemical disinfectant, which was poured into the deep pit below. What horrors lay floating in the revolting quagmire played on my vivid imagination. I pictured the rotting corpse of the camp thief and the rats feeding off his bones and toyed with the image of forcing the head of the evil Posnanski into the filth until his lungs filled with excrement.

I finished my business but still there was no paper.

Afterwards, I was escorted to the wash house for a splash around under the cold taps, which was refreshing in the summer but torture in the dead of winter. Whilst attending to my ablutions, I was forbidden to talk to anybody who might walk in, but in the circumstances I could hardly regard this as a major punishment for I had my new feathered friend to talk to.

· · · § · · ·

~ MY RELEASE ~
24th August 1944

One morning, afternoon or night, for I knew not which, an elderly guard opened my cell door. His visit was most welcome, as was any interruption to my isolation. I was ordered into the corridor, where I found my fellow criminals. We were taken to the Commandant's office, presumably to be transferred to a German Military Prison at Graudenz, some sixty miles away. An officer whom I had never seen before sat behind a desk as we stood to attention, waiting.

"You are to be transferred to Stalag XXA to complete your sentence. Meanwhile you will be allowed back into camp whilst the necessary arrangements are made. That is all."

We saluted and marched out, released back into camp without explanation. Now we were really confused, but we soon learnt that life outside the camp was also becoming more and more confusing and chaotic. The Russians were pushing relentlessly westward towards Germany. British and allied forces were advancing across France, giving the German military authorities bigger issues to deal with. We therefore assumed that the question of our transfer and sentence was just a minor, irritating detail, to be put on hold until things improved for them.

Our fellow PoWs welcomed us back into the fold as mini heroes and the next few weeks were a good period for us six. We had tried to help Tansi escape and been subsequently punished and so everybody indulged us. The only one conspicuous by his absence was our current camp leader, R.S.M. Singleton. However, I had an even better greeting, another cigarette parcel from the lads at Hackbridge. Over the years as a PoW, they had really been supportive. I took the opportunity to write another 'Thank You' card and had to tell them that for the foreseeable future, my new address would be Stalag XXA.

~ POSNANSKI AGAIN ~
August 1944

Central Poland in mid-summer was hell on earth but without the fun, as the temperature soared to well above 90° Fahrenheit, with a humidity to match.

Sammy's continuing news of the allied push, away from the

Normandy landing area and their progress across France, gave us all great hope, as did the more relevant Russian advance westward, towards us.

It had been another long, sweltering night in our room. The thin wooden walls offered no insulation from the oppressive summer heat or the freezing conditions in winter. At seven in the morning we were subjected to another long morning parade, another two long hours of suffering as our numbers did not tally again and again and again. To make matters worse, Feldwebel Posnanski was present. He had just ridden up on his bike, his preferred method of transportation when touring the camp before any parade. He was doing what he did best, strutting around the parade ground in his immaculate uniform, trousers tucked into his knee-length leather jackboots. Moving through our ranks in his pompous, arrogant manner, hands clasped behind his back, you could tell he was bored, and that was potentially dangerous. He drifted between the lines, casually inspecting the men. The bully was about to find a particular favourite of his amongst us PoWs, a man called Willy Moir. Willy was a very short and insignificant-looking Scotsman, a fraction over five feet tall. The tall Posnanski liked nothing more than humiliating him whenever the opportunity arose. This particular morning, I was able to watch out of the corner of my eye as he approached. Willy was standing to attention almost directly in front of me. As he reached Willy, Posnanski drew himself up to his full, overbearing height, turned slowly to face him and smirked. Willy had no option but to stand there and wait for the inevitable. Posnanski looked down his nose directly at him. His face showed utter contempt as his eyes crawled down Willy's short body to his tattered boots and slowly back up again. He now started to 'tut'. He looked him up and down once more whilst shaking his head from side to side. Finally he spoke.

"In the last war, I remember when Scottish soldiers were great and tall, very good with the rifle and bayonet."

Then followed more 'tutting' whilst turning his head from side to side, before continued his sarcastic tirade.

"What has happened, what has Scotland become with this nothing worm of a soldier? What a terrible state Scotland must now be."

With that, Posnanski shook his head one more time, gave a final 'tut' and walked away, leaving Little Willy humiliated and, at the same time, absolutely fuming mad. I knew Willy and under normal circumstances this wiry Scotsman would have disregarded the height difference and torn into the man like a pitbull terrier. All Willy could do was stand and take it, for to have retaliated would have given Posnanski an excuse to shoot him. Posnanski enjoyed this sport so much that whenever he saw an opportunity, he would try to humiliate anybody.

During that summer and autumn, work on the surrounding farms continued unabated and we ate accordingly, making brief returns to camp. By now, trading opportunities were becoming increasingly scarce as deliveries of Red Cross parcels and our post from home were becoming more erratic. This may have been due to transportation difficulties across German territory as allied bombing took its toll or due to the fact that some Germans were diverting them for their own purposes. On the whole, it was obvious things were getting worse.

~ ALLIES CAPTURE PARIS ~
Late August 1944

Sweltering, humid August was about to melt into September. We met Sammy outside, running along in front of the huts. He was wearing his broad grin, so we guessed he was the bearer of good news.

"They've taken Paris," was his first remark. "Paris has fallen."

I couldn't resist the sarcasm.

"Hi Sammy, that's wonderful news. Did the BBC say when our boys would be arriving to unlock the gates?"

Sammy looked slightly puzzled. He didn't really do humour for that would be frivolous and his news was too important a subject to joke about. He turned to walk away but not without a departing salvo of informative text.

"French troops have marched in with little resistance. Won't be long now chaps, won't be long."

With that, Sammy ran off to spread his glad tidings.

Bert, Jimmy, Johnny and I carried on walking back to our room, deep in thought, discussing the increasing speed of the allied advance.

My thoughts raced back to an earlier time, of towns where we stayed when we first arrived in France as raw recruits. Places such as Abancourt, Amiens and Abbeville popped into my mind once more. The area around Calais and Dunkirk where we were captured four years ago. I had not thought of them these last four years. I had mixed feelings in the knowledge they were now being fought for all over again, swarming with British and allied forces, but this time they were winning. Now it was the turn of the once invincible Germans to be on the receiving end of an immense force, to be pushed back to where it had all begun, back to Poland and the declaration of war in September 1939 and the subsequent assault of Belgium and the low countries and the once mighty France.

What a waste, what a bloody and terrible waste.

We decided to celebrate the good news by all having a smoke. We were down to our last few packets as even these important items were now in short supply. As a result of the deficiency, market forces prevailed and the exchange rate for cigarettes shot through the roof. Johnny casually let slip his thoughts on the shortage.

"I think it's time Mar Minter started to look after us a bit better, don't you lads?" he said as he nodded in my direction and winked.

"Ok then Johnny, I'll just nip down to the corner shop to get a few packets," I replied sarcastically.

"Anybody got a half a crown?" I asked, holding out my hand.

"No need to go that far Mar, pop over to the Camp Shop and put them on my tab," intervened Bert.

"Oh, to hell with it, tell them I'll settle up when I collect my wages," Johnny replied, waving me away with his hand.

We ended up telephoning Hitler and asking him to get them!

Two days later there was a surprise in store: a cart load of parcels from home arrived, which delighted us all. A Scottish Corporal handed them out. We were all eager to see if there were any for us but it was not to be.

We were 'Cook's Tourists' again, leaving camp for a few days or weeks at a time, harvesting early potatoes and the like on the surrounding farms. Amongst the populace, shortages of every description were now commonplace, especially clothing, but within the farming community there was invariably an abundance of black market food, kept back from the Germans, but potentially a dangerous activity. I was constantly on the lookout for farmers who needed clothing, one commodity of ours that we were willing to exchange for anything, whether or not we had a surplus. During the sweltering heat of summer there was often a temptation to forget about winter and the need for our warm clothes from home, so I was asked to exploit this mutually beneficial trading situation that existed, advantageous to both PoWs and farmers alike.

~ A CHILD IS BORN ~
September 1944

I do not know the Polish equivalent of our Indian summer, but in September 1944 we were experiencing one, unbearably hot and sticky. There was still no word of my six months imprisonment in a 'Sträflager' for which I was relieved,... no news is good news!

I was on a working party headed for the other side of Marienburg. We had been marching for a while and were in the centre of town when my attention was caught by a girl pushing what looked like a home-made wooden pram. I immediately recognised the owner as being Stasha, my girlfriend from the pea factory. I quickly did my maths and realised that inside the pram could be my new-born child. Reservedly I called out to her and waved, much to the irritation of our miserable guard who ordered me to be quiet. She heard me and instantly recognised me, smiled broadly and pointed at the baby. Wow! So it was mine. I felt a strange emotion, one of excitement and pride. She had what she desperately wanted, and with it the financial benefits courtesy of the Third Reich, but for how much longer?

I turned to Johnny, who was marching next to me, and told him my news. Johnny then told the next person in the column, and so on. Before long, they all knew that I was a daddy, as did all my mates back at camp shortly afterwards. For days I was congratulated but nobody produced a bottle of champagne with which to celebrate, not even the Commandant.

During the course of the next few weeks, I was lucky enough to see them on several occasions, for Stasha seemed to make a point of being in the same spot each day. She would stand by the roadside, her new-born held high, to face me. Every time our column passed them, the boys would cheer and call out in a light-hearted manner.

"Baby Dennis,... hello baby Dennis" and comments like "the baby's not as ugly as you mate."

Stasha always smiled and waved.

Within two weeks, our work was finished and I never saw Stasha or our child again, but if the child survived the tough times that lay ahead, somewhere in Poland there might now be a line of the Minter family.

· · · § · · ·

~ I NEED TO SHOP ~
October 1944

After my release from 'Die Bunker', I was free again to take up my post as 'Mar Minter' the trader. I was reasonably flush with goodies. My army boots had served me well during my years in captivity and now this latest pair were dying on my feet, developing holes in the soles and splits around the toes. My feet would not have looked out of place on a tramp. With winter fast approaching, I thought it best to go shopping for a new pair. As prisoners in the heart of occupied Poland, this was not a straightforward task. The cobblers and shoe menders didn't have any, having given away the last of their stock a while hence. Although I couldn't pop down to the local high street shoe store, our camp did have its fair share of unofficial shops. I put the word around that I was in the market for a new pair of British Army regulation boots, size 9, give or take a size, for somewhere among the thousands of prisoners, there would be someone willing to trade. Sure enough, a couple of days later, word got back to me that someone had a pair of surplus boots. This chap had been one of the lucky PoWs to have received a parcel from his dear old mum, containing the boots and some other personal items. He had no need for them as he had already been given a pair in May. I met up with him in his billet. We haggled for a few minutes before agreeing on two loaves of bread and smokes in exchange for his boots. So the deal was done. The boots unfortunately did not have metal studs set into the soles, but they were new and exactly my size and I was very relieved to be facing the Polish winter in them.

At first the leather was its usual unforgiving self, so I thought it prudent to break them in gradually, only wearing them for an hour or so at a time. I remembered a conversation I had when I first joined up, when handed my first pair of boots. The kind, understanding NCO issuing them to me had said: "You don't wear the boots in to fit your feet soldier, your feet are worn in until they take the shape of the boot."

That was painfully true at the time and my feet certainly didn't relish a repeat experience, but I was concerned that if they were not on my feet, some thieving bastard would relieve me of them, so I withstood the pain.

I also had no gloves as such and with the approach of winter I made myself a pair as I did every year. Using whatever rags I had to hand, I wrapped strips around my hands and each finger, but leaving the tips exposed. I cut a square cloth and made five holes down its centre before pushing my fingers and thumb through. To finish them off, I tied the corners together either side of my wrists.

~ PULLING BLOODY BEET AGAIN ~
Late October 1944

Another winter was approaching and I was off to another bloody field on another bloody farm full of endless rows of bloody sugar beet stretching to the bloody horizon. I make no excuse for swearing for bloody was how our hands always ended up, cracked open and blooded. It was too early for the snow but not for the unfaltering wind that raced across the open land, stinging and freezing our exposed skin. I was in my usual jovial mood, trying to make the most of a bad situation. I wanted to sing again, and get my fellows to join in with the Disney classic from Snow White and the Seven Dwarfs, *'Hi ho, hi ho, it's off to work we go...'* I think it would have been therapeutic, although I do believe I would have been strung up from the nearest tree.

The night had left a dusting of frost across the inhospitable landscape. By now, the sun was somewhat reluctantly clawing its way up from the horizon, half hidden behind clouds. We knew that we would be working until it finally disappeared below the bleak western horizon. With similar reluctance, we began the arduous task of pulling the beet. It didn't take long for the horror of the previous years to awaken painful memories of the cold, the back pain and the agony and re-open old scars. I was now allowing myself the luxury of thoughts, of the end of this war and the end of our suffering. I took an oath, swearing that when this was all over, when I got back home to England, if I ever saw another sugar beet again I would have to burn it in hell.

~ THE RUSSIANS ARE COMING ~
Late December 1944

There were almost forty of us from camp working on the farm. We joined an existing group of Russian mamas already slaving feverishly. As I watched them, I wondered if they knew how close their fellow countrymen were to us and if they could taste the sweetness of impending freedom, or the bitter foretaste of reprisals and possibly execution.

On our second night, locked up once more in our overcrowded barn, I decided to climb up into the lofty rafters above, for I needed to be alone. Whether it was the sudden realisation that yet another birthday of mine had slipped past without acknowledgement or I was suffering from a momentarily yet understandable lapse in my usual sunny disposition, was of no great importance, I simply needed to be alone. I sat down in the far corner of the loft and drew my knees up under my chin. At the edge of the old cladding I found a small hole in the woodwork caused by a large knot that had dried out and fallen away. I now had a window to a world that was beyond the beet fields.

I took a cigarette from the pack that I had 'liberated' from a guard some time earlier. Its discovery had angered me because it was an English pack, probably from a Red Cross parcel that had been stolen by some thieving Kraut.

I looked out through the gap onto an amazing night sky, rich, unpolluted and blue-black in colour, littered with clusters of twinkling diamonds. I saw a shooting star. It only lasted a second or two, racing from right to left before burning itself out. In a childlike manner, I closed my eyes and quickly made a wish... for this war to end and to be home by next Christmas.

I rubbed my eyes. They were dry and pained me as I blinked, blasted by winter's biting breath as it softly whistled through that tiny hole, cutting into my optic orb. I turned away and reached into the breast pocket and retrieved my matches. I had difficulty parting my lips, which were momentarily glued together by frozen spit. I cupped my hands around the flaring match, its wonderful warmth caressing my palms and face, causing me to shiver. Briefly blinded by the bright light, I inhaled. The soporific warm smoke invaded my lungs. I savoured the nicotine mist before allowing it to leave my body. I am sure I speak for all smokers when I say that after suffering from nicotine famine, that first cigarette transports you into a parallel utopian universe and your woes are left far behind. I instantly felt better and my gaze returned to the outside world once more. I looked upon the heavenly sky before allowing my eyes to lazily drift from left to right and back again, to the distant horizon. In doing so I became aware of an orange glow that at first glance went almost undetected. Dawn already, I thought briefly, but no, it couldn't be, the night had only just begun. I continued to stare, more intently now. Every so often, a part of the horizon pulsated, flared up and then subsided. A few seconds later another section did the same, the thin, warm, orange glow contrasting with the blue-black of the night sky that weighed down heavily on this disparity.

I wasn't sure at first so I turned my ear to face the opening and in the dead of night, in that clear, still air, I heard a noise that could only be the distant boom of explosions. Someplace, somewhere was being pounded.

The Russians were coming.

Working all through November and into December was yet another painful hand-cracking experience in the bleak fields of north-eastern Poland. After harvesting the hated crop, we were expecting to move on to the beet factory to process the little buggers and meet up again with the Scottish brewers as we had done in previous years. I was actually looking forward to it as I stared down at my chapped hands, feeling the cutting polar winds paining every inch of accessible flesh. I knew they would heal once the harvesting was over.

At the end of the working day, I found what comfort I could inside the barn. The ashen walls had not seen a coat of paint for a generation. The planks of aging wood that were its walls barely protected us from the harsh winds that winter threw at us. Countless sweltering hot summers, contrasting with the extreme cold of winter, with soaking rains between, had taken their toll on the old timbers which were now as dry, broken, twisted and inflexible as an ancient witch's claw. No tight-fitting shiplap walls here to keep out the Arctic gusts. There were more holes in the wood than in a slice of Emmental.

As the night temperatures plummeted, we buried ourselves deeper into the piles of old straw that littered the barn and huddled together. Although plagues of mites and other insects were already in residence, we were grateful to share in its protection, and in it we survived the worst of that winter.

Several nights had passed. The dark winter's air was particularly inert and as cold as it could get. The stillness all about allowed sound to travel over great distances. As I lay in the heavily-populated straw, a sudden muffled series of booms vibrated through the hard, cold earth, followed by several more. Thought processes ground ponderously into sluggish mobility. Thunder perhaps? No, its source was man-made, the distant thud of artillery. How distant? German or Russian? I knew not, but it gave us all food for thought. One thing was for sure: the Russians were getting closer with each passing day.

1945

ONE LAST ASSIGNMENT

We had just been dragged into a new year.
Someone in our hut shouted "Happy 1945".
"Piss off," was followed by a salvo of other responses accompanied by
a barrage of missiles aimed in his general direction. I knew not whether
to laugh or cry.

It was 8th January and I took the opportunity to write a couple of letters to my mother, Freddy Mills and my old work mates at Hersham. As usual, there was little I could say without falling foul of the German censor. It was more to inform them that I was still alive, so I just wished Fred and his wife Molly a happy new year and sincerely hoped that I would be seeing them soon.

> *Little did I realise these were to be my last letters home and that*
> *despite the chaos that was now engulfing the Third Reich, I later*
> *learned that amazingly, they were delivered to their intended*
> *recipients.*

Two days later, we were ordered out of our 'Ritz Hotel' accommodation in the tried and tested manner.

"Raus!"

These old guards of ours had no conversational people skills. Breakfast that day was a little rushed and the service was not quite up to scratch. The crushed roasted acorn coffee was barely lukewarm mud and the freshness of the rock hard potato bread with its coating of glutinous pork dripping fell well below Michelin star rating, but I kept my own council and chucked it down my throat with relish.

Breakfast over, we packed our meagre belongings, in the minute in which we were given to do so, before gathering outside the barn in the winter snow. I pulled the flaps of my forage cap around my ears and thrust my neck down into what protection there was on offer from my coat collar, gave my troublesome crotch a well deserved scratch before joining the others. I had with me my bag of worldly goods slung over my shoulder. I felt like Dick Whittington, off to seek my fame and fortune, but the misery of my predicament soon brought me back to reality.

Within a moment we were off without any explanation. None of us now expected to be informed of anything, ever. We marched north all of that first day through the freezing snow-covered wastelands, with nothing to break the monotonous boredom of that bleak winter countryside. We tramped along frozen dirt tracks and pathways before ending up at yet another God-forsaken place that was no different from any other frozen hovel in occupied northern Europe.

We arrived at the very small rural village of Wossitz (now called Osice). As the crow flies, it stood about 25 miles north-west of Marienburg, in the heart of the sugar beet countryside of East Prussia, but on the twisting, winding country tracks it was more like 40. Dusk had well and truly fallen as we were corralled into one of the few buildings in the tiny village which just happened to be a small local school. The Germans had long regarded the Poles as an under-race who did not warrant an education. The smell of dampness and decay, thick dust and neglect was ample evidence that the school had stood empty for years. But at least it provided protection from the icy wind that was howling across the flat, bleak, surrounding farmlands. We slumped to the floor, huddled together and made ourselves as comfortable as was possible, wondering what was going to happen next, although not expecting an answer. Unexpectedly, our guards entered our room bearing welcoming loaves of bread, not just one between five as was the German way but one loaf each. Surprisingly, they also brought jam and coffee.

The next day, we were taken to a barn nearby, where we were allowed to fill our palliasses with fresh straw. I decided on the deluxe mattress and stuffed in as much straw as I could possibly manage as it never took long to flatten and reduce. Once outside, I looked about me and saw a few other buildings close by. Those nearest were formerly peasants' homes but were now occupied by our guards. Some of the buildings had corrugated iron roofs whilst others were crudely thatched or covered with sods of earth and grass. Many of the buildings had a small fenced area alongside the main building for livestock, probably pigs. No toilets were to be seen, and if this village was like the others, urinating in the garden and feeding solid waste to the pigs was the norm. The village was inhospitable, primitive and feudal-looking. If this was all there was of Wossitz, then this was a desperate place.

There were two ways by which this isolated community was linked to the outside world. These were the ice-covered trail that we had marched along the previous day and the small narrow gauge railway that ran through the village. The railway's main purpose was to enable the small steam engine to collect the vast quantities of sugar beet from the surrounding farms and transport them to the centralised beet factory for processing.

For whatever reason, the Germans had decided that Wossitz was to be made more accessible and connected to the disintegrating Third Reich via a new arterial road network. Thanks to Adolf, we were to be given the opportunity to make it happen. We would provide the unskilled labour whilst a group of Polish civilian workers took care of the more skilled aspect. The project had begun some while ago as we were taken along a completed section of the road, to one of its ends, to continue with its construction. We arrived to find the Poles already busy, squatting down on their knees on the frozen ground, laying large cobble stones before knocking them into place with mallets. Each stone was about 20cm square by 30cm deep.

There then followed the usual staged confusion and chaos that prevailed at the start of any task until I, as the official translator, managed to glean what was required and explain to the other uneducated, unskilled English pig-dogs exactly what was required. It was still the most enjoyable aspect of our guard baiting.

Having been handed shovels and pick-axes, we set to work. First, we had to scrape away the overnight fall of thick snow before proceeding to dig out the foundations in the frozen mud. Throughout the day, old wood-burning lorries arrived laden with sand, which was dumped behind us and just ahead of the following Poles. We spread the sand over the foundations, into which the Poles would lay the stones. This was all that was required to build the road. The work continued relentlessly throughout the day. The whole process was painfully slow, and when I stood back after the day's toil to survey our labours, the unfinished end of the road contrasted with the sand and snow and reminded me of a row of gappy teeth. That first day we only progressed some twenty metres. I could not help but think at this rate, building a road to anywhere was going to take us the rest of our unnatural lives. Each stone came to symbolise a day in my life as a prisoner of this cruel nation, a nation that had once more brought death and destruction to the world.

As we quickly settled into our new labours, each day that followed was identical to the previous. Laboriously it went on, day after laborious day with practically nothing to break the monotony.

Working with us was a fellow PoW called Rupert Pratt. He was a lot older than any of us, being about forty years of age. He was a frail man and couldn't work like us, suffering a lot through ill health. We tried to look after him as best we could, covering for him whilst he sheltered and rested. Rupert was a lover of opera, and in particular Gilbert and Sullivan. He knew every one of their operas by heart and could recite them word perfectly, which he constantly did. Each night, we returned to the school to be fed and watered. Once inside, with all the doors, window and shutters secured, Rupert happily entertained us until his voice tired. He repaid us many times over, with his moving songs, helping us through those bleak and lonely nights. I grew to love hearing him.

Unbeknown to me at the time, I had heard him sing for the first time last year, January '43, at the beet factory, but I didn't see him or know him then. He was inspirational.

To this day, I still remember his renditions, and Gilbert and Sullivan remains one of the loves of my life.

Often on the way to or from work on that awful road, I would watch the small, narrow gauge railway and the little engine chug its way grudgingly across the bleak countryside, through the village and on again, only stopping if there was a need to deliver goods or for passengers to embark or disembark. Apart from being a collector of stamps, I also have a huge fascination with model railways and this mini train fired my passion, giving me something else to occupy my bored mind whilst toiling and surviving.

Our column was on a section of road that passed close to the rail line. As we marched off to work on this particular dark and bleak January morning, the train seemed to strain under the weight of sacks being carried in the open wagons, presumably for delivery to the surrounding farms. At the back were two small squat carriages, inside which a few lonely passengers sat. The carriages had a roof to protect the occupants from the worst that the severe Polish weather had to offer, but had no side or end covering, allowing the wind to cut through without mercy. It must have been torture. The heads of the seated passengers touched the low carriage ceilings but their faces were completely hidden from view, wrapped in anything that would provide protection from winter's blast. The men, with their cloth caps pulled down tightly, and the women with scarves and rags wrapped tightly around their heads, all sat huddled into tight bundles. The hunched figures looked drab and depressed, reflecting the inhospitable greyness of that ashen, cheerless day. The train clattered on slowly by until it disappeared into the distant foggy gloom. First-class travel this most definitely wasn't.

As the days and nights wore on, we were becoming increasingly aware of the growing intensity of the still distant artillery bombardments. Whoever was firing was slowly fighting their way closer.

My three friends and I were still together and for that I was grateful, for their companionship was comforting. We still looked after each other as best we could, sharing, covering and supporting one another. Since the incredible news of the D-Day landings last June, we knew that the tide had irreversibly turned against our captors. Six months had elapsed and we were still well and truly detainees, but with the British and Americans in the west still fighting their way through France, it was the approach of the Russians from the east that we were now focusing on for our deliverance. The trouble was that this particular prospect opened up a can of worms that did not sit well with any of us for two main reasons. Firstly, if the Russians did overrun our working party or our main camp of Stalag XXB, would they mistake us for Germans and kill us as well, for none of us could protest our innocence as we spoke no Russian?

Secondly, if the Germans feared that they would be overrun by the Russians, would they perhaps slaughter us out of frustration and bitterness before we could be liberated? Suddenly, the approach of these allies was not such a rosy prospect after all. With that thought playing on my mind, I drifted into a rather troubled sleep.

~ DENTISTRY, POLISH STYLE ~
January 1944

We had only been in Wossitz a few days when there came a rare interlude in our normally humdrum existence. Amongst our work party was a chap called George. He was thirty years old and only five feet four inches above ground level. His surname escapes me but this omission is of no great consequence. The poor man had been suffering with chronic toothache for several days and it was getting worse with each passing day. With no distraction during those long winter nights, his pain was at its most excruciating. Consequently, he was soon unable to work and spent the day lying on his palliasse, clutching his face in unmitigated agony. Strangely enough, and in spite of several pleas to their better nature, our German guards refused to allow him to return home to England to consult with his dentist!

Several days into George's pain, we returned to our school to see him rolling on the ground, groaning quietly, almost unconscious. He was sweating profusely, muttering indiscernible words and rolling his head from side to side. At first we all thought he was delirious, but when Bert laid his hand on him, we discovered he was still with us and he managed to raise a pain-filled greeting. Out of the darkness a German guard emerged, accompanied by a numbing blast of biting wind that chilled me to the marrow and swept forth a mound of snow. Wearing a toothy grin on his smug face, the guard approached George and spoke.

"We have a man called Herr Tierarzt, der Zahnarzt. He is a dentist and he is here to help your friend."

Germans who care for our welfare? This was uncharacteristically kind. At that point the guard stood aside and ushered in a tall, slim man who had been hiding in the background. He was carrying a bag. He wore a rather battered trilby hat and bulky long overcoat with his face almost concealed behind his brown scarf. It was still scant protection against the frozen outdoors. He wasted no time and asked for the patient. I immediately pointed at poor old George, still lying on the floor. With the side of his face swollen for all the world to see, any further intimation was unnecessary. George managed to sit up with a little encouragement. He opened his mouth, allowing the dentist to examine him. George pointed to his upper jaw and tried to speak but only managed to emit a guttural noise. The dentist had difficulty in seeing the offending tooth as George was so short.

Speaking in Polish, which I translated, he asked for the bench to be pulled under the light and for George to stand on the bench itself. In this elevated position, the dentist could now clearly see the problem. He bent down and gathered a few items from his case, one of which was a piece of twine. Given our unexciting existence, this drama was now beginning to intrigue us all. We formed a semi-circle behind the dentist and watched his every action. This had all the makings of the best entertainment that we'd seen for a long time, even if it was at George's expense.

The dentist proceeded to loop a piece of twine around George's bad tooth, before grasping both ends through the centre of his right hand. He then took up the slack by wrapping the remainder around the outside of his hand before resting the lower part of his now clenched fist on top of George's chin. Using his chin as a fulcrum, the dentist made a sharp twisting movement with his fist. Something flew out of George's mouth, into the air behind us. At that point, George let out an almighty scream that could have been heard in Berlin. Suddenly startled, we all jumped. After that split second of silence following his howl, there followed a universal cheer and praise for George's bravery. Our attention was now drawn to the door, where a group of German guards now stood, also watching the show. They were laughing. I could not see the funny side and was shocked by what I regarded as their callous attitude, but we didn't know the full facts. The senior guard, therefore, gave us a much-needed explanation. Through the tears of laughter, using a mixture of German English with a mimicking of animal noises, the guards managed to convey that Herr Tierarzt was not actually a dentist after all. In fact he was the local vet, and on many occasions was called upon to remove troublesome teeth. Then we learnt that Herr Tierarzt was not his real name, 'Tierarzt' being German for 'veterinary surgeon'. Now we understood, we all burst out laughing. This was a rare but wonderful example of communal hilarity with our captors, and once all was explained to a still very confused George, even he finally managed to see the funny side.

The following day, his pain had begun to subside and he expressed his gratitude to the guard who sought out 'Herr Tierarzt', even if this 'dentist' was actually a vet.

Construction of the road continued to progress on its ponderous journey to nowhere whilst Rupert provided the music as we worked - that is, until one morning it all came to an abrupt halt.

At some ungodly hour the guards entered our room. They appeared jumpy, irritable and detached. It didn't take a genius to conclude that something was disturbing them, but in our isolation away from camp and the secret news broadcasts, intelligence of any sort was no longer available to us. The frozen moisture from our collective breath stuck stubbornly to the windows, obscuring our view of the inhospitable outside world as the new day threatened. The dull thud of the distant bombardments could be heard, creeping ever closer. The elderly guard who had called 'Herr Tierarzt' to attend to George stood before us. He looked weary. He was wearing full uniform with forage cap and greatcoat, scarf and full kit with extra packs he normally didn't wear. We were instructed to assemble outside, immediately. Nobody smiled. We all looked more morose than ever. I was growing apprehensive and so were the others. After four years in captivity, we had become totally institutionalised. Our lives were run for us like clockwork by the Third Reich and their strictly imposed system.

Despite our British recalcitrance, we still did as we were told when we were told (most of the time) following their imposed routine, daily, weekly, monthly, year after sodding year. We assumed that we were being called out to start work early and, as usual, we left our few precious possessions and blankets behind in the old school. Once outside, Bert, Jimmy, Johnny and I gave each other a nervous half smile, as though we were walking into 'the valley of the shadow of death'... and not too bravely either. The piercing easterly wind hit us with all its bitter fury as we formed ourselves into a column. At the same time, the guards appeared from their billets and surprised us for they were cradling loaves of still warm bread in their arms. We were each handed one and I smiled with gratitude, heaving a sigh of relief. I instantly felt more comfortable, reasoning that the Germans were less likely to give us bread if they intended to shoot us. With our guards forming up alongside us, rifles slung over their shoulders, we began to march.

It was the morning of 20th January 1945.

> *According to historic archives, during the previous night of the 19th, the guards had received a telephone call from Stalag XXB with orders from Commandant Lorentzen to evacuate all prisoners and take them west, ahead of the fast-approaching Russians.*
> *I believe Commandant Lorentzen was still the Commandant.*

· · · § · · ·

THE
DEATH MARCH

20th January 1945

Thank goodness we were all totally unaware as to the extent of our unfolding plight. It was the 18th century English poet Thomas Gray who was quoted as saying 'ignorance is bliss'. The man clearly knew what he was talking about!
Exactly four years ago, in the winter of 1940, during my training at St. Leonards, I had already experienced one of the coldest winters on record. This January and February were to be amongst the coldest winters of the 20th century, with temperatures plummeting as low as -25°C (–13°F). Even in March, temperatures stayed well below freezing. Most of the PoWs were totally unprepared for the evacuation that was to follow, and the appalling winter conditions they were about to face.

t first, we attempted to march like British soldiers, disciplined and as best we could on the snow-covered track, trying to maintain a pride in our tattered uniform and in ourselves, but not for long. Within minutes we settled into a shuffle and apart from the occasional slip, we moved without any idea as to where we were going. The only thing we knew with any certainty was that we were moving in the opposite direction to the sound of the constant but still distant bombardment.

Dawn arrived and stayed a whilst as we walked. Fresh snow began to drift down and settle. The best we could manage was slide and walk. All too rapidly the sun departed, ushering in an inhospitable night.

Without rest, we continued on through the darkness under a clear deep blue, star-studded sky. With no cloud cover, tonight was going to be a bitter one. Previous traffic, pedestrians, horse-drawn and motor vehicles had compacted the snow and formed a hard, icy layer more reminiscent of an ice rink than a road. With care we continued until ahead, in the distance, we saw the lights of a town. As our group of forty plus approached, I became aware that it was bigger than Wossitz. We marched straight into a small central square about half the size of a football pitch. It was crammed to capacity, filled with PoWs and with the menacing Germans standing around the perimeter, rifles at the ready. The prisoners all appeared to be British, and as we talked amongst ourselves we soon learnt that they had gathered from the outlying farms, factories and working parties. We numbered about two to three-hundred. Whilst some were milling around aimlessly, others jumped up and down and practised the well-known 'Stalag Shuffle' in their attempt to keep warm. Most were resting wherever they could find shelter or space, but there was little of the former. As Bert, Jimmy, Johnny and I walked amongst them, we all asked the same questions.

"Excuse me mate, any idea what's going on?"

"Any idea where we're going?"

"Do you know anything?"

None of us knew diddly-squat, but I had my own method of sensing if there was tribulation ahead - twinges in the pit of my stomach and a troublesome sphincter. The latter now told me that somewhere up ahead, there was trouble in abundance, patiently waiting.

It was late, gone eight, and we assumed we would be stopping here for the night. We desperately needed to bed down, but where? There was no space in any of the buildings, which were, for the most part, occupied by guards. We had no option but to settle down where we were. The cobble stones of the village square were cold and unforgiving as we sat back-to-back in a huddle, resting as best we could. I was indescribably cold, and for the most part I found sleep an impossibility. Our only pleasure was to gnaw on our fast-diminishing loaves.

I was relieved when morning eventually came, but without meaningful sleep I felt dreadful; my backside was numb and my whole being chilled deep beyond my bones to the very core of my soul.

"Raus!"

Guards milled amongst us, kicking the occasional foot if its owner was slow to respond, as most were. Sadly, some seemed unable to rise, even with the threat of a menacing rifle prodding their bodies. I stood up slowly and bent backwards, stretching, rubbing my buttocks as I tried to get my blood circulating and some life back into my dead extremities. No smiles today from anyone, just a look of misery and bewilderment at our continuing plight. However, I did manage to utter thanks for surviving the night's ordeal and to be alive to witness another day, but it was tough. I looked about me and I could see that several of the men were still lying about on the ground. Their comrades were trying to help them up but without much success. I watched as a lone German went over to them, pushing the helpers away, ordering them to leave their stricken friends and join the column, all with the help of a rifle thrust hard across their chests.

Before dawn, we were back on the road again without our usual cup of ersatz. If I had known that yesterday's cup of that familiar brew was going to be my last in captivity, I might have taken the unusual step of savouring every last drop and requesting a second.

I turned my head sideways and stared at the handful of PoWs still on the ground. For those lying helpless in the snow, whom we were forced to abandon, I did have grave concerns, wondering if they would get the help they so desperately needed. We could do nothing more for them. Sadly, we had to push all thought of them out of our minds and concentrate on ourselves, for in their terrible condition, we had neither the stamina nor the medical facilities to carry them nor care for them over the treacherous terrain.

We quickly settled into an unsteady stride. Under foot, the road surface was a nightmare. Walking on wet glass might have been easier. Unfortunately, I had never learnt to ice skate. I was soon made all too aware of the obvious dangers. With no metal studs on the soles of my boots with which to find any purchase on the ice I fell over backwards, not once but many times.

As the morning progressed, the first group of Russian PoWs joined us from a side road. They were in a far worse shape than us. Gradually, I began to warm up, although 'becoming slightly less cold' would be a more accurate description. The first pangs of hunger soon began gnawing at my stomach as I remembered the bread still buried deep in my coat pocket. I took it out and broke off a piece, the solid lump nearly cracking my teeth. I chewed it for a while until it mixed with my saliva, softening it into a manageable mash. Cautiously, for I knew not when we would be provided with another meal, I rationed myself.

We journeyed on throughout the short winter's day into nightfall under a grey, overcast sky, threatening more snow at any time. Our guards on both sides looked as jaded as us but continued to 'encourage' us to speed up with their threats. Finally, freezing, tired and hungry, we were ordered off the road and into an open field where we bedded down for the night. At a guess, I would say that we had walked about 25 kilometres that day. The field was covered with a crusty layer of crisp snow, hardened by the previous night's frost. As I stared up at the night sky, I felt the first flutter. Another miserable night was in store for us and I wondered how we were going to survive more exposure to sub-zero conditions. We huddled together, back-to-back, as close as we could to each other with arms folded into our bodies. None of us spoke much as we were all too deeply immersed in our own misery. Throughout the long hours of darkness, my guts churned with protestations at the lack of body fuel but I was desperate to keep the remainder of my bread until the following day. I reached out and scooped up a handful of snow before placing it in my mouth and drinking the resulting chilled water. Again, sleep tried every trick in its book to avoid me whilst the night attempted to keep the day at bay, so I was surprised when I did eventually wake. Although we were still waiting for dawn, the reflective moonlight from the covering snow meant we were able to see quite clearly. It was gratifying when the sun finally made its long-awaited appearance over the eastern horizon and the subsequent sporadic dawn chorus heralded the start of another harsh day.

"Raus!"

"Change the bloody tune you square-headed bastard," was the welcome response from a jovial wag.

I was pleased to get up and move around, to test my limbs and see if they were still functioning or if they had succumbed to frostbite. Just as we were about to set off, I heard a commotion. I turned to see a guard shouting at a PoW in a Russian uniform who was either a bit slow or refusing to get up. I couldn't tell if he was ill, had just given up or was already dead. As I watched them, the guard shouted and then kicked the side of his thigh, but there was no response from the prostrate body. As a result, he raised his rifle and shot him. The bullet passed clean through his skull, making his head twitch with a single shudder. I couldn't believe it and turned away, clenching my fists, causing my long, dirty nails to dig into the palms of my hands.

"One day,..."

Within minutes, my mind had switched off again. It had to. I was back home in England once more, languishing in The Kiwi pub at Walton-on-Thames with my mates from Hackbridge on a Friday night eating a lavish banquet of steaming steak & kidney pie washed down with ale. I would run through a full menu and dream of eating every single item on the list whilst my robotic legs just did what they had to do without any instructions from me. I was running on auto.

The air was clear and still as we trekked along the well-trodden path. I instantly recognised the bagpipes as a lone piper played from somewhere up ahead of me. I wondered if he was the same piper who had led the Seaforths in the early days of captivity. I firmly believe there is nothing more stirring on God's earth than the sound of the bagpipes. It seems to be in tune with your very soul, regardless of nationality, for even though I am not Scottish I instantly stiffened my posture, as did we all. On that day, we walked with pride once more whilst the piper played his best.

For the next few days, our straggling column continued on its relentless shuffle north, south and then westward along quiet country roads, tracks and paths, over open farmland and through numerous pine forests. My loaf had long gone and the only food available was that which I could beg, borrow or steal, so I went hungry and ate snow.

It was the fourth day since leaving Wossitz, some 20 kilometres south-east of Danzig... or was it the fifth? I couldn't be sure for the cold was already numbing my mind. In that time we had probably covered a hundred kilometres. Now we found ourselves wandering into another town. This one was packed with PoWs from all the other camps and isolated work places that came under the jurisdiction of the main camp, Stalag XXA. Amongst their numbers were British Officers. I could not fail to notice that many of these more fortunate British prisoners were wearing hats, balaclavas, scarves or gloves and were carrying blankets slung over their shoulders, tied together with string. Some even possessed roughly made sledges piled with possessions. Unlike us, they had obviously been given time to prepare for the march westward. Jealousy and anger flooded over me. Why hadn't we?

To the side of the town centre, my eyes were drawn to a half-hidden German field kitchen that was in the process of being set up on the edge of the square. Many seemed unaware of its presence so I pulled on Bert's sleeve and grabbed the attention of the others. We casually manoeuvred ourselves nearer to ensure that we stood a good chance of receiving whatever might be on offer. Two hours later it opened, and within seconds of it being apparent, a fevered excitement spread amongst the hungry as the realisation sunk in. Fearing a sudden riot, the rifle-wielding guards moved in to assert control and maintain order, for after all, this land was still German controlled and order had to be maintained at all times. Eventually we were rewarded and the four of us secured a meagre portion of watery stew and bread. Despite the fact this was our first warmish meal since leaving Wossitz, it hardly prepared us for the bitterness of the coming night. It proved to be another terrible one, and by morning my buttocks were numb. I was not surprised to discover we were covered with a thin blanket, not one of wool but of frost and snow.

With the usual 'encouragement' from our irritable guards, we set off. Our numbers had swelled to eight-hundred Brits and two-thousand Russians, all unhappy souls, and still we kept moving, only occasionally speaking for there was little to comment upon that had not been said a hundred times before.

Hunger and exposure were beginning to take their toll as more and more failed to respond to the morning 'raus'. Many were literally falling by the wayside. I had never experienced such a prolonged cold environment with such little protection and without food. I believe that I only managed to subsist and keep going for most of the day by immersing myself in the depths and shelter of my own troubled mind.

As a consequence of this near 'sleepwalking' habit amongst many of us, towards the end of the seventh day's march I suddenly found I was alone. In my dazed state, I had lost Bert, Jimmy and Johnny somewhere along the long, ragged, drawn-out line of miserable beings. As soon as I realised, I panicked. I desperately looked about me and turned to face the sea of advancing PoW refugees. I started to walk back through them, frantically scanning every face that passed me by, bumping into others who appeared in a similar stupor. I pushed and squeezed through larger groups but there was no sign of any of them. A puzzled German guard shouted at me, unslinging his rifle and walking hurriedly towards me.

"Turn back, turn round...NOW!", he screamed, causing those nearby to jump out their trance-like shamble. He came to a halt in front of me and raised his rifle horizontally before crashing it into my chest. I looked straight into his pale blue eyes. Although old, he meant business.

"Go back."

In the freezing air, I could see his hot breath as he bellowed, spitting the words into my face. I blinked and came to my senses. I did not resist, allowing him to push me back until, finally, I realised that it was futile; there was no hope of finding them now. I may have been drifting along alone for hours. They could be anywhere, in front or behind, so I turned back with the flow but glanced back just one more time in some forlorn hope. The guard responded immediately by crashing his rifle into my back. I momentarily stumbled forward and fell to my knees.

"Get up, move," he shouted once more.

Slowly, I stood up and continued walking, head bowed. I was alone. I had never felt so isolated and abandoned since the theft of my bread on my 21st birthday back in 1940.

At that moment in time and unbeknown to us all, one of the biggest migrations that Europe had ever seen was now underway. Not only were thousands of allied PoWs on the march trekking westward, but hundreds of thousands of German civilians were on the move, towards the perceived relative safety of their German heartland. They would prefer to fall into the hands of the advancing British and Americans and be at their mercy than face the ultimate horror of falling captive to the all-conquering and much-feared Russians. That unfolding nightmare was to become another abomination in itself.

~ THE CULLING SQUAD ~
WAS FULLY EMPLOYED
Late January 1945

I awoke. My feet were in pain as they were freezing. I had not eaten for days but my stomach was learning to protest less. After each and every step, the other foot would follow on its own accord without any conscious effort on my part. Was I still alive? Was I a figment of my own nightmare? My mind was drifting all over the place as I heard the shot. It came from behind, the muffled crack that a single shot makes in the quiet of a foggy winter's day. I jumped, momentarily disorientated and bewildered. We were in a forest, journeying along a narrow track, but it could easily have been a road as the surface was hidden under the compacted ice. Snow lay heavily on the dark, oppressive branches of the fir trees, causing them to hang down like the arms of dejected monsters. Once I realised what I had heard, I turned to see who had fired but I could see nothing except our line of dishevelled misery, spread out as far as the eye could see. I didn't really need to see who it was as I could make a guess, having witnessed the execution of the Russian. I suspected that the guards were probably shooting prisoners who were falling by the wayside, for by now the 'culling squad' seemed fully employed for there was much work to be done. However, I may have been wrong, maybe the Russian was an isolated incident and the shots were a warning, maybe. I hoped so but I suspected otherwise and even wondered if they saw these as mercy killings.

Eventually we left the dismal gloom of the forest and were back into more open countryside. We had just passed a farmer's cottage set well back from the track when something in my head finally clicked into place. My days of slaving on the farms flashed back into my mind and the root vegetables that I had so often laid down for the winter. In other words, here was food. On the other side of the leafless hedge was a mound that could only have been a clam. I could have kicked myself. Over the last four-and-a-half years of captivity, I had forgotten all the lessons that I had learnt on my march across northern France and Luxembourg and onwards into captivity: living off the land. Why had I not thought of it before? How stupid of me. Food hidden under a layer of dirt and straw. I did not even care if it was bloody sugar beet as, by now, I was almost beyond hunger. I knew I had to get sustenance from somewhere and this offered my best chance.

Nobody seemed to be watching as I made the short dash through the open gate into the farm. I ran low and made it to the clam without being detected by the guards. I kicked at the base of the mound with my boots until I had broken through the protective covering of frozen earth and straw to expose the crop. I had found turnips. I picked up as many as I could manage to stuff into my coat and trouser pockets and anywhere there was space. Holding others in my hands, I carefully rejoined the column. I had not been missed but I had been seen. Behind, others were now storming the mound with scant regard for what the guards might do. As I hurried away, I picked up a handful of snow and washed off as much grit and dirt as I could before sinking my teeth into the cold, hard root. By the time I had finished gnawing, my stomach ceased complaining. From now on, I must remain more alert and be watchful for any other opportunity to acquire food that presented itself to me. That moment was another turning point. I had finally come to terms with the loss of my friends and re-found the will to live, the desire to survive this last great trial and what must surely be my final ordeal.

Within the hour, I was desperate. The parsnips had gone straight through me and I needed to go. I ran forward, took my trousers down and squatted in a ditch, just like so many others that I had witnessed. A fat lot of good that root did. It ran like water. I used snow to clean myself and jumped back in line before the 'culling squad' caught me in my compromising position. What a way to meet one's death,... a bullet through my skull with my backside and tackle on display as the whole world shuffled on by!

Days had passed and the turnips had been eaten, I was sinking back into despair, so during the previous night, I had literally given myself a good talking to.

"Dennis, pull yourself together. You can get through this. Remember, one day at a time. You have to survive this, to get even with these bastards for all the misery they've caused you,... one day at a time."

That day was getting closer, I could almost see it, but talking to myself did beg the question: Had I finally flipped? Was I mad, schizophrenic? I chatted to myself to find out whilst laughing.

The following morning, after another torturous night in the open huddled against anybody who would have me. I was up early, kicking my feet trying to restore circulation. I blew into my cupped hands, rubbing them vigorously and dancing the 'Stalag shuffle' whilst others reluctantly joined me. Today I was going to eat, come hell or high water. They say you should never underestimate the power of positive thinking, and just maybe that is what got me my loaf of bread and smoked sausage that day.

It was nearly midday when I noticed a thin grey line of smoke lazily rising into the clear blue sky. Through the trees I could see a single-storey building, an isolated cottage. I cast a good look round to check for watchful guards before jumping into the roadside ditch and scrambling out the other side. Crouching, I ran to the side of the building and then behind into the yard beyond. By this time, I had no idea if we were still trawling through Poland or trekking through

Germany so I could not be certain as to the loyalty of the occupants. The house was obviously occupied, but when I saw the owner chopping wood I decided to take the risk. I went back to the front of the cottage and tried the door. The handle turned and the door opened. The hallway was dark with no visible sign of life and no sound reaching my ears. I crept inside, leaving the door open for a quick getaway. At the end of the hall and to the right-hand side a door opened into the kitchen. The sight that greeted me left my mouth watering. Without hesitation and with my heart pounding, I swiftly grabbed the loaf and smoked sausage and apples on the kitchen table and was out in the twinkling of an eye, stuffing my ill gotten booty into my pockets. I felt no shame for my crime; my very existence depended on my cunning in whatever form that took, and today I was an opportunist thief. My emancipated feast lasted two days, revitalising my spirits. What idiot said crime doesn't pay?

~ THE UTTER JOY OF SEEING ~
A FAMILIAR FACE
End of January 1945

That night we had found some form of shelter, under an uncertain roof, held up by four corner posts but without the benefit of walls. But still, by morning I could barely feel my limbs as I arose in response to the wake-up call. I was shaking and my head was muddled.

How could any of us continue to live through this exposure to such a hostile environment. Yet, every morning, I was amazed and eternally grateful that I had, along with most others. Within minutes, the track was filled with the weary and hungry kicking life into their suffering feet. Little white clouds of water vapour hung momentarily in the air above the heads of every PoW as each warm breath emitted from their chilled bodies condensed in the cold January air. I grabbed a handful of snow to quench my thirst before setting off on our relentless shuffle westward. Occasional conversations were struck but soon died - for we were all too engrossed in our own misery. Sometimes I would picture myself greeting my dear mother as I arrived back in England after the war. At other times I would dream of smashing the face of some guard who had been particularly cruel in the past. On occasions, I would dream of nothing in particular, just letting my mind wander aimlessly wherever it decided to drift. It was the only way to cope with the pain and misery of this endless trudge.

Another day of constantly walking along never-ending country roads. Every so often, the sight of an abandoned vehicle caught my attention. Some had obviously been strafed by fighter aircraft, presumably Russian, their roofs and sides peppered with neat rows of puncture holes. Others lay blackened, broken and twisted, victims of bombs or artillery shells, broken carts, a stranded car, a lorry, the debris of war.

I was always on the lookout for food and cigarettes, quickly scouring the inside of each vehicle before moving on. Every now and then, that single shot would shatter the otherwise peaceful day as another wretched PoW fell victim to the 'culling squad', forever following our long, meandering column of destitution. They were the very vultures of death.

It was nearing the end of the day when I saw a vehicle ahead. A small Wehrmacht staff car lay partially in a ditch on the right-hand side of the narrow road. I could see no obvious sign as to the cause of its fate. One might have been forgiven for thinking that it had merely run out of petrol as it raced from the advancing Russians had it not been for the precarious angle at which it lay and the open door. As I neared, I saw an arm dangling at an awkward angle from behind the door. It was a German soldier. I could see from his insignia that he was a Feldwebel. The body was twisted on the driver's seat, with his boots still resting on the pedals in the well of the car. His upper body and head were hanging out through the open door, his neatly cut hair almost touching the ground. Lifeless eyes stared at the sky above whilst his mouth hung open in a grizzly grimace. There were no visible wounds that I could initially see, but on closer inspection I saw the neat line of punctured holes, probably aircraft cannon shells, that led to a deep crimson stain on the right hand side of his body, darkening his uniform. I thought he was just another anonymous casualty of this war until it hit me. I moved my position to get a closer look. I could see that it was a familiar face, the German bastard Sergeant Posnanski from our camp. He was dead but I wanted to be sure. I looked about me for any sign of our guards. All was clear so I aimed a kick at his collar bone. Yes, he was definitely dead. I was so pleased, so utterly delighted that I smiled. It could not have happened to a better person and I hoped that his death had not been too quick or pain-free and then I felt cheated. I wished he could have been brought to account, openly punished by the judiciary and hung for his crimes. Death so early, by whatever means, had been far too good for him. There was no terror in his eyes, no expression of having suffered, no recognition of having met his maker or having faced his own hell. Here was just the frozen, glazed expression of the dead, a soon-to-be-forgotten corpse. I spat at his face and watched as my spittle froze where it landed on his forehead. I prayed that he had already arrived at the Golden Gates, had met St. Peter and come face-to-face with those whom he had murdered, before being banished to hell itself for all eternity.

· · · § · · ·

OUR RUSSIAN SAVIOURS?

February 1945

A blizzard was raging all around. We had dug a hollow in the three feet of snow and built a circular wind break around us. The days and nights were drifting by in a haze. I was early February, another freezing night spent in another open field, but this one felt like no other at -20°C. I couldn't stop shivering. My toes, fingers and nose were in agony but my group told me that the pain was a good sign, for it showed they were still alive. Those who had a blanket shared with others, using them like a tent to wrap their warmth in. I had to keep one thought in my head, forsaking all others - another day gone and a day closer to freedom. How many nights had I slept like this? How many more would I have to endure? I didn't really want to know, but I was one day nearer to the end.

There were no familiar faces within our bedraggled army of wretchedness as we spilled out onto the track. I didn't know any of them and yet by now, every single face was familiar. All were pale and drawn, faces prematurely aged and lined with pain. Sunken cheeks smeared with dirt, covered by stubble and mangy beards. Faces that had lived a whole lifetime in a few years. Faces that had lost hope. They were downcast with their heads drawn into their coats away from the bitter air, each one hoping that today would be their last in captivity, but fearing the worst. I knew and understood every one of those faces, for they were as one.

As the night prepared to hand over stewardship of the earth to the welcome dawn, we moved off. Our column bore scant resemblance to our regimented column that had begun some weeks ago. In the distance I heard the first rifle shot. Its echo was dulled by the surrounding snow-covered trees, but I knew what it was. A minute later came another, shortly followed by a third. The cull had begun.

The previous day I had managed to find another clam, this time swedes and potatoes. Others had been there before me and behind were many more, all eager to grab their share of this plunder, richer than any pirate's gold. I filled my pockets with what remained of the mound, which was soon immersed in a sea of scavengers, like vultures feasting on carrion.

As I walked I ate, but only one, deciding to wait until nightfall before gnawing on another. My stomach was in turmoil, and whatever I ate only added to my problems. Dysentery was increasingly spreading amongst us.

We had been moving westward for several hours, blindly placing one foot in front of the other with the body having no option but to follow. Every so often I needed, or felt I needed, to defecate. Each time I raced ahead, to put as much distance between me and the tail-end 'culling squad', before dropping my trousers and doing whatever I could do. Afterwards, I put the snow to good use and rejoined the ever-moving column of desperadoes whilst heaving a sigh of relief, for I was still ahead of the 'culling squad'.

~ LIBERATION, RUSSIAN STYLE ~

I don't know how I knew but I did. It might have been the sound of a church bell tolling in the distance, the word of a knowledgeable PoW or just a spiritual presence in the peaceful, desolate winter wonderland, but I was in no doubt that this particular morning was a Sunday.

The sky was as clear as could be with not a cloud in sight. Had it not been for this war, I could have lain down and admired the beauty of the azure firmament. I could actually feel the feeble warmth of the winter's sun shining on my face, and a rare moment of serenity flowed through my aching body. Eventually, the trees gave way and I could see scattered patches of white rolling countryside. Ahead, a small town some several miles away came into view. I pushed my hand deep into my pocket, found the remaining swede and tested my resolve once more. Would I eat it or save it? Save it was still winning so I kept my eyes peeled for anything else that resembled food.

Before midday, we reached the outskirts of the town. There was an old, weather-battered wooden sign placed on its perimeter. Its condition made it difficult to read but I think it read †*Innenheim*.

† *The author has tried but is unable to confirm the town's identity.*

Something told me that we were over the border and into Germany. We soon reached a large central square. The population had promptly swollen with the arrival of thousands of us prisoners, both British and the poor wretched Russians, distinguishable by their lamentable condition and uniforms that hung in tatters from frames of bone. Many had no footwear and shuffled painfully along, their feet wrapped in layers of sodden rags. Those who had arrived earlier were either standing or lying slumped where they fell, waiting. This is what we had done best, ever since our capture four-and-a-half long, pain-filled years ago; we had learnt well to wait.
I walked into the densely packed town, one amongst a tardy meandering column of fellows. However, amongst this huge throng of torment, I felt utterly alone, a microscopic droplet in a tidal wave of despair. I wandered amongst the crowd in the forlorn hope of finding both food and a friendly face, in particular Bert, Jimmy or Johnny, but to no avail. I had agonised over what had happened to them, 'Mar Minter's Boys', bitterly regretting having lost them. The pain came flooding back to me, but this time it was more emotional.

Why had we stopped here? I doubt if it was to rest for there were still plenty of marching hours left in the day. It would have been uncharacteristically charitable of our Aryan escorts to show such compassion. Maybe they knew something that we didn't, such as what lay ahead?

The explosion that shook me to the core was muffled by the snow. Its echo boomed in the distance, followed rapidly by a chain of others. Everyone looked concerned. Our horde of newly arrived prisoners had only been in town for an hour. We were made aware of a distant clattering. As the seconds ticked by, it grew louder. Whatever was causing it was coming our way. Many of those who had been lying down were now standing, looking for the source of the old, familiar sound that we had not heard for four long years.

You could almost touch the tension hanging heavily in the air. The guards were tense and obviously concerned and stood, bracing themselves, facing the oncoming sound. To a man, we probably knew it was the clatter of metal tracks on cobbled streets accompanied by the throb of powerful engines.

To me, it was unmistakable. In spite of the warning, it still came as a shock when the first vehicle drove into view, bursting into the square from a side street. It took a moment for its significance to sink in. Those closest reacted first before the panic infected us all. We turned and ran. The guards, however, looked on, standing motionless for a second or two before reality dawned. With unslung rifles they dived for cover, scant match for the intrusive metal monsters. Slowly, a tall stubby vehicle, an American-made Sherman M4 tank entered the square. It was followed by a second and then a third. But American they most certainly weren't. My eyes were drawn to the red stars of the Soviets painted proudly on their turrets.
Shit!

† *For several years, both America and Britain had been shipping tanks, arms and ammunition to Russia via the Arctic waters of Northern Russia, all part of the Lend Lease Agreement. In this way, some 3600 Shermans became part of the Soviet arsenal, along with 1200 General Lees, 1233 General Stuarts, and from Britain 301 Chuchills, 832 Matildas and 3487 Valentines.*

Then it got serious. A single shot echoed around the square, followed by volleys in rapid response. As the lead tank neared the centre of the square, it jerked to a halt before responding by opening up with its mounted machine-gun, spraying everything and anybody that came into view, with no thought for whom they hit. The panic was blind and spread like wildfire. The other tanks moved forward, guns ablaze. They could not be sure exactly who they were firing at for their gunners were running on nothing short of pure adrenaline and a killer instinct. All about, men were dropping like flies in front of their continuous onslaught, German, British or Russian and whoever else got in the way. Their bullets were great levellers and didn't differentiate between nations. By now, men had scattered in all directions, to anywhere just as long as it was away from those tanks.

† *Source: www.theeasternfront.co.uk.*

I too turned and ran. A hundred yards in front of me I saw a barn, its doors open. I ran as fast as I could and burst in, nearly tripping over the uneven cobbles in my desperation to escape the flying hot metal projectiles. I reached a pile of straw at the back of the barn and dived headlong into it, burying myself as deeply as I could, out of sight. In my rush for cover, I was barely aware of the other body that had accompanied me.

Another round of gunfire.

I dug myself in deeper, lying as low as I could. Then came the sound of an explosive hammering. It filled my ears as I realised that the barn walls were being sprayed with machine-gun fire. I closed my eyes again and ducked. Absurd, I know,... as if hiding deep inside this heap of straw could protect me from a hail of bullets. I guess I was just relying on 'out of sight, out of mind'. After a few minutes the initial onslaught subsided, allowing me to relax a moment. I sensed somebody next to me, lifted my head and turned to establish with whom I was sharing my hideaway. He had the same idea. If I had not been so scared, I might have laughed out loud as we both lifted our heads above the straw mound, straw dangling from our matted hair. I turned towards him. He did likewise and our eyes met. He was Latin-looking with a thick mop of dark, wavy hair, dark eyes and a pale olive complexion. I looked at his uniform and was relieved to see that it was British. Sitting chest-deep in straw, I extended my hand and smiled.

"Hello, I'm Mar,... sorry,... Dennis,... Dennis Minter."

He shook my hand, exposing a toothy grin and in a Mediterranean accent, he responded.

"Hello too mate. My name is Feodras Karas," he replied in a sing-song voice.

With straw hanging from our heads, we must have looked comical. Simultaneously, we instinctively ducked down as another volley of gunfire pierced the air.

"Bloody hell mate!" he continued "this is not good."

His use and pronunciation of the word 'mate' made me laugh,

"Tell me, where are you from?"

"I come from Cyprus mate, my friends call me Feo."

"Well Feo it is then. I'm pleased to meet you."

At which point, there was another round of explosive hammering, in front of us and above. That burst shot through the front wooden panels and out the other side. Daylight punctuated the inner gloom of the barn's interior. The vibrations to the old wooden building had disturbed the dust of ages, which now drifted down like fairy dust, illuminated by the shards of sunlight that pierced the gaping holes.

"Shit!" I screamed, ducking back down out of harm's way. This saga was beginning to resemble 'The Gun Fight at the OK Corral'. The firing intensified for some time. When it eventually ceased, we waited several minutes before finding the courage to prudently venture forth from our wholly inadequate sanctuary. We turned to face each other for some indication as to what we should do next, but nothing was forthcoming. I crawled sheepishly to the open doorway, taking cover behind the side walls, and peered out to see what was happening. My new Cypriot friend followed, crawling to the other side of the doorway. From this position we could see most of the square. Bodies littered the cobbles. Those Germans who had stayed to fight were either dead or dying. They must have been easy pickings for the tank's machine-guns. The only moving figures were swarms of Russian PoWs who were emerging from their hiding places, running towards the tanks, cheering and waving. I was mesmerised by the unfolding spectacle as the tank commanders emerged from their hatches to warmly greet their liberated comrades.

The crew looked resplendent in their warm leather helmets and black uniforms. Soon all three commanders and crew had joined their comrades in the square. The freed Russians were jubilant, somehow finding the strength to jump with joy, kissing and hugging their liberating heroes. My mind was too confused. I was still pumping adrenaline as I watched this 'happy' scene and sudden change of circumstance.

This was the liberation that we had waited nearly five years for.

The war's finally over for us.

After several weeks of horrendous foot-slogging ahead of the advancing Soviet army, I had not even thought what it would really be like to be free from captivity. It had all happened so quickly and our liberation seemed almost an anti-climax, having come so suddenly. From the relative safety of our hideaway, we heard a tank commander addressing the Russian ex-prisoners in a stern manner. When he had finished, the crew returned to their tanks before handing out rifles and ammunition to their liberated countrymen who were now surrounding them. For their part, the baying crowd were clamouring for them, eager to snatch a weapon. The senior tank commander now addressed the men, often punctuating his speech by smashing his clenched fist into his other open hand. Each blow seemed to arouse his audience, galvanising them into a heightened state. I wished I could have understood what was being said.

Now armed, the emaciated men were intoxicated with the power of their new-found situation. Someone fired wildly into the air, shouting and dancing, drunk with joy. The liberated Russians now fanned out in all directions. These prisoners of war had always been treated far more harshly by the Germans than us, regarding them as inferior beings that needed to be eliminated. Years of harsh, brutal treatment inflicted on these tough, oppressed, desperate, poorly-educated peasants had taken its toll. Now this particular batch of the 'under-race' was fired up, they set off in search of anything that was remotely German, with revenge clearly on their minds. But first, there was looting to be done.

~ SHAMEFUL, BUT UNDERSTANDABLE? ~
Later that same day

† *The advancing Soviet Army were testing and probing the teetering German front line by sending forward tank squadrons through vast gaps in their inadequate defences to cause havoc behind their lines.*

Since crossing into Poland, the Soviets would often stumble upon some of what remained of the five million Russian PoWs taken captive by the Nazis. For them, the war was far from over. The liberated Russians had a frightening future in store for them. Regarded as deserters by the Stalanist Soviets, these men were expected to have died fighting instead of 'allowing' themselves to be captured. Now they were compelled to fight as soon as they were liberated, regardless of their deplorable condition or circumstances. But after the war, an even worse fate awaited them. They were not trusted in case they had been brainwashed and turned. Branded as traitors, they were held in captivity once more, brutally tortured amidst questions as to their loyalty, before being executed or at best, condemned to 'The Gulags' of Siberia, to slave away their lives in appalling conditions, equally as brutal as the years already spent at the hands of the Nazis. No other set of prisoners could have been so badly treated by an enemy or their own country. †

---

† *Source: The Works of Anthony Beevor,*
Historian of the Second World War.

Feo and I toured the square, chatting with other PoWs that we met. As we passed the bloodied body of a guard, I quickly searched his pockets and found what I was looking for, a tin of English Player's Navy Cut cigarettes that could have only come from a Tommy like me or a stolen Red Cross parcel. I felt no remorse or shame. In his pack was a paper bag with bread and cheese. That too went into my pocket as Feo looked on. We searched several other bodies and removed more scraps of food and cigarettes before moving away.

With our backs to a building and partially hidden from view, we shared the booty 50-50. We smoked then watched as the town was plundered on a grand scale. Every door that was closed was kicked in. Every kitchen they stumbled into was ransacked. Every house was pillaged. Every item of value that was small enough to be carried was looted and every bottle of alcohol that was found was drained. Within the hour, the Russians were either plastered or comatosed. After years without, it did not require much to turn them into intoxicated monsters. Now every living German was in danger... mortal danger. Guards who had not taken flight, who had stood their ground to engage the enemy, were either wounded, dying or dead. Without mercy, the Russians took their revenge. The wounded were immediately dispatched as they moved amongst them, executing those barely alive by whatever means. Even the dead were not spared mutilation, corpses had their faces kicked to a pulp. Accompanied by sporadic gunfire, they now turned their attention to the civilians. People were dragged from the surrounding buildings by the rampaging Russians, eager to wreak vengeance on anybody remotely Aryan. The first to be brought forth could have been anyone the Russians didn't like the look of, but I suspect they included the local town officials such as the elderly Bürgermeister and police chief. Their victims looked prosperous and well to do as they were dragged unceremoniously from the shelter of their homes and offices and brought into the town square. Ropes were found and thrown over the brackets of the wooden telegraph poles. We watched the spectacle slowly unravel before our eyes as if we were watching the latest movie release. I knew what was going to happen and, as the plot unfolded, I felt no sorrow or remorse for these victims. Like my fellows, I had witnessed too many acts of mindless cruelty and brutality by the Nazis. Now I was incapable of feelings of compassion towards them.

The officials did not appear to struggle as they were led to the base of the poles, seemingly resigned to their fate. The ropes were hastily tied around their necks. The Bürgermeister was fatter than the rest. We watched a Russian attempt to place the hastily tied noose around his fat head and neck without success. His legs buckled from under him, causing him to sink to the ground. For his sins, he received a kick in his back from the Russian standing behind him, accompanied by shouts of abuse. Others roughly grabbed hold of his arms and hair, hauling him onto his feet once more whilst another adjusted the noose and tried again. This time, it was forced over his fat head and tightened in a less than gentle manner.

By now, the first German had already left the ground. It was with some difficulty from a team of Russians, that the overweight Bürgermeister was hauled into the air, rapidly followed by others. Some struggled violently for several minutes, fighting for breath, feet kicking wildly as if dancing a demented jig, whilst all the time slowly strangling to death. Others died more easily.

> *I find it strange how easily people seemed to accept the inevitable path to execution in such terrifying circumstances. After all, what else could the vengeful Russians or murderous Germans do to punish you for not walking peacefully to your death? Kill you? I make no judgement. This is just an observation, for I am sure I could be led peacefully to my own execution in similar circumstances.*

After the town's dignitaries had ceased to twitch and they had gasped their final breaths, it was the turn of any remaining battered guards. With hands tied behind their backs, some suffered the same ignominious fate but there were neither enough telegraph poles nor rope for all their victims. This was the very symbolic face of retribution for all to witness. Further revenge was to follow.

Any remaining guards were either shot during further intermittent skirmishes, had their heads smashed with rifle butts, bayonetted or if lucky, shot in cold blood at close range before their bodies were butchered and mutilated. No prisoners were taken, no mercy given, no compassion shown and none expected. This was war at its worst and payback was long overdue.

Whilst this summary justice was being administered, individual Russian PoWs, who were now completely intoxicated with alcohol or drunk on their new-found power, fired their recently acquired weapons indiscriminately wherever they desired. All was pandemonium.

After all we had witnessed, Feo and I thought it best to stay where we were for the time being, whilst these early excesses ran their course. Nearly an hour had passed before we decided that it might be safe enough to leave our hideaway and venture forth, knowing that we could not stay inside the barn forever.

I do not know if this particular town was susceptible to flooding on a regular basis or if it was just common practice, but many of the houses were built on raised foundations and could only be accessed by climbing the short flight of steps to their front doors. As we walked we saw a line of Russian PoWs standing, some swaying, in a long queue in front of one such building. Some were armed and admiring their new weapons whilst others nursed bottles of schnapps or tucked into whatever food they had managed to steal. I had no idea why they were queuing but all were in high spirits. They stared at us momentarily, but these former PoWs knew who we were just by looking at us and nodded accordingly. They could smell that we were indeed one of them.

At first, I wondered what was happening and why they were queuing at the door of the unassuming building. What was so special about that house? At first I thought that they might be queuing for food or for some precious supplies that were being handed out. My inquisitive mind required me to take a closer look, for if there was food on offer I wanted my share. As we neared the front of the queue, the reason became abundantly clear. At the top of the steps stood two Russians on either side of the closed door. Between them stood a local woman, stripped naked in the freezing cold winter air. Each of them held an arm. They literally had her pinned against the door. In front of her was another Russian, his trousers hanging round his ankles whilst his white buttocks moved rhythmically back and forth. He was raping her. She was old, possibly a grandmother, at least sixty years of age. Behind him, the remaining Russians waited patiently for their turn. I stared up at her, unable or unwilling to do or say anything. Her eyes were shut, her mind having taken refuge whilst her body was being violated. I was horrified, yet I wasn't surprised. Elsewhere throughout the town similar scenes were repeating themselves. Screams from open windows echoed around the town. A woman (or young girl for I wasn't sure), her top clothes torn from her body wearing only a skirt, ran screaming from a building, chased by several men. She was soon caught and carried back, spread eagled, into the house by four men. Her fate was sealed and I suspect that every female that day suffered the same horror of violation and murder.

After years of barbaric treatment, it made perfect sense to me that these desperate, poorly-educated peasants-turned-soldiers might want to vent their anger on anything German, just like me. Unfortunately, revenge was now a grim reality and it was the innocent who were suffering. Feeling slightly ashamed at the behaviour of our fellow men, we both looked at each other, turned and walked the other way without uttering a word. With no weapons to support our protestations any interference from us would have been futile, but deep down I knew that after everything that millions like us had been through, neither of us were willing to become Good Samaritans to the Germans that day.

Every few minutes we made contact with other British PoWs who were slowly emerging from hiding. I was still searching for a friendly face, anybody that I knew from the camp. As we talked, it soon became apparent that we were all clueless as to what to do next. After years in captivity, we seemed incapable of making a decision for ourselves. Without orders we were lost, as infants without their parents.

After a brief tour of the town to the accompaniment of sporadic gunfire, we found ourselves re-entering the square. Now several naked women were evident, nailed to the fronts of houses, crucified. I felt utterly sick.

We made our way over to the Russian tanks and met the crew. These were the first Soviet troops in active service we had seen. Their uniforms were simple and clean. They grinned at us as we tried to explain that we were British. I think they grasped the essentials and came forward to shake our hands and hug us. I was uncertain about the hugging, for such practice between men was alien to me. We were joined by more Brits, who were greeted by our liberators in a similar fashion. The tank commander returned to his tank, whereupon he produced a few more weapons and now offered them to us. We were reluctant to take his arms. At first he looked puzzled, but then he became angry as a rifle was thrust in our direction. I looked back at him and shook my head, raising the flattened palms of my hands to him in a gesture of 'no bloody thanks mate' whilst taking one step backwards.

Whilst the earlier arms distribution was taking place, Feo and I had discussed the dilemma of taking up arms at this stage and we had both agreed there was little point for we knew not where we were, how far away we were from the British and American lines, where the official Russian lines were and what support we could expect. We were not even confident that the Germans had gone. There were too many questions and not enough answers and we were therefore fearful of the repercussions. My decision had been arrived at when I viewed this situation as a competition. I considered placing an imaginary wager, betting on the outcome of a battle between this increasingly drunken rabble and a sober, vengeful, German division, one that I had experienced four- and-a-half years ago. To me, there was no contest - no thanks mate. The tank commander hurled abuse and returned to his duties, disgusted at our refusal and cowardly stance.

We did not join the Russians in their vengeful slaughter, in their quest for sex or alcohol, we simply walked away.

I was aware that I was not hungry. Whether it was the excitement, the fear, the brutality or simply the surge of adrenaline through my body on top of weeks of starvation, I did not know. In short, cleverly surviving this immediate predicament was more important to us than eating our newly acquired rations so they stayed in our pockets. Smoking, however, was another matter.

~ OUR WORLD DESCEND DEEPER INTO DARKNESS ~

In the aftermath that followed the short battle, we drifted about. I suspected by now that most of the population were either dead, dying, had been raped, had fled or were wisely hiding somewhere inaccessible. Most of the houses that we passed had their doors kicked in and we chose one at random and entered. Inside was chaotic, having obviously been ransacked. Despite not feeling hungry, we thought it prudent to search for whatever food we could find, whilst we still had the opportunity. In the kitchen, we discovered some fatty remains in a pot, scooping it out with our fingers and spreading it onto bread that had been overlooked by the Russians. I forced the food down but had to admit this humble fodder tasted like a king's banquet.

Darkness was approaching as we went outside, smoking. What a hell of a day so far. Now it felt good to wander freely and settle down to our unexpected deliverance. My bowels had experienced enough excitement to last a lifetime and they were enjoying the rest, but they were about to start work again.

Feo and I were still chatting with other Brits when we heard the first deafening explosion. Instinctively we ducked quickly, falling to the ground. There was no sound, no pre-warning, just a sudden eruption in the square. Accompanying the deafening sound was a deadly shower of debris and stones and hot tearing metal hurtled through the air, landing all around us with a thumping great clatter, followed by the random patter of smaller particles. A plume of dirty smoke billowed skyward.

This heralded the start of the German counter-attack.

Despite the fact that one had always been possible, it took us by surprise. Another explosion followed. Hoping to avoid the flying shrapnel, I instinctively covered the back of my head with my hands (fat lot of good that would have done). More mortar bombs detonated around us. We waited for any slight pause in the bombardment before jumping up together and running as fast as our mercurial feet could carry us, back to our refuge, back to the old wooden barn with the protective armour of the pile of straw. Behind us, panic ensued. PoWs were scattering, trying to seek cover wherever they could. Several of the drunk Russians had sobered up enough to take some kind of evasive action, whilst others were too far gone to care. Above the noise of the explosions, I heard the sound of the Sherman engine spluttering into life. I turned momentarily to see the tank commander slam shut the hatch of his armoured vehicle as his comrades did the same.

Out of breath, Feo and I managed to make it back to our sanctuary just as the second bombardment shattered the all too fleeting peace. We dived onto the floor of the barn and tried to push ourselves into the unforgiving stone floor. During the next bombardment, I had a compulsion to turn round so that I could see what was going on outside. Two tanks had already made their getaway, whilst the third one could just be seen tearing off down a side street in jerking movements, trailing a cloud of dense diesel smoke that hung in the winter air.

Five minutes and three bombardments later all went deadly quiet once more, but only for a moment. Then someone opened the gates of Hades. From every direction, troops poured into the square. We watched as fast-moving, well-trained German infantry edged forward around the perimeter of the square, taking protective firing positions in the doorways and recesses of the buildings before entering to do their work. Others in turn provided effective covering fire for their advancing comrades. Slowly but surely, they crept forward. Without the protection of the Russian tanks, the battle was bloody.

I was now watching a turkey shoot as drunken Russians burst forth from hiding, firing wildly in all directions, incapable of seeing straight let alone focusing down the barrel of their Soviet rifles. Scores of them dropped like flies. All resistance was futile and short-lived. Against these overwhelming odds, some Russians tried to go-to-ground wherever they could, but many more were incapable of hiding themselves anywhere or even identifying the danger they now faced. We British were nowhere to be seen, having already sought refuge the moment the first bombardment struck. With the main attack all but over, the mopping-up operation now began.

~ LIBERATION IS SHORT LIVED ~

It was like a re-run of the movie that I had witnessed an hour or so earlier. From the imperfect safety of our barn, we watched in the approaching twilight as the drama continued to unfold before our eyes. The fear in our bellies added an extra dimension, giving an alarming edge to the performance.

Several hundred German troops stormed efficiently through the town, moving from house to house, searching for their quarry. They were soon unearthed. Those found lying in a stupor proved easy prey and were either executed on the spot, beaten to death or dragged out at gunpoint in a bloody state. From the outset, their orders appeared clear and they did their work with typical Germanic efficiency. Twenty or more at a time were rounded up, set against a wall and dispatched with a volley from their awesome Schmeissers. Officers and NCOs went amongst the bodies, Lugers drawn. A bullet through the skull ensured there were no survivors. This went on for half-an-hour. At the start of that day, there had been two-thousand Russian prisoners with us. The vast majority were unarmed, but now they were all paying the ultimate price for their actions.

Before long, German troops wandered over to our barn.

"My friend, I think it is time we surrendered," Feo commented.

I nodded in agreement. We sprang up with our hands raised as high above our heads as we could, and believe me you have no idea just how high my hands could go. Just as suddenly as it had begun, our all too brief hours of freedom had ebbed away, back into the frozen, inhospitable, war-torn terrain.

Our sudden appearance startled them. The troops looked angry and menacing as they brought their rifles to bear upon us, bellowing in a language that I didn't understand, but their message was clear: get out of the barn and into the street. Several moved behind us to search for others, paying particular attention to the stack of hay that had been our refuge, probing every part with bayonets and jackboots. At this point I looked at their national insignia on their shoulders and noticed they were not German. but were Lithuanian troops, probably volunteers who were not necessarily pro-Nazi but more anti-Russian. Therefore, anyone who was an enemy of the Russians was automatically a friend of theirs. Faced with this latest revelation I grew more concerned, for neither of us could speak their language and they certainly couldn't speak ours. They appeared barely able to control their murderous desires to avenge the latest debacle. I naturally assumed the worse and was sure that within minutes, Feo and I would both end our young lives under a volley of bullets. We were pushed at gunpoint back towards the town square as other groups of captured British and Russian PoWs joined us. All remaining Russians were dealt with swiftly and without mercy, forced up against the wall of a house before the eager troops took quick aim and... bang! Six more bedraggled Russians slumped to the ground to join the ever-growing pile of dead. I jumped at the sharp crackle of each volley. Us next. God, I was scared. After all that I had been through, this was not the way I expected it all to end. Please, please, please don't let me die.

More Brits were joining us by the second as others were discovered. Still the shots rang out all through the town as a sweeping search of the town was made and brought back under German control. And still, the executions continued. With our backs against a wall, hundreds of us were herded together, nervously awaiting our turn. Our predicament seemed dire.

The majority of the Russians were now dead, their bodies piling up, silhouetted sharply against the snow-covered cobbles and litter of battle. Mortar craters, dirt and body parts defiled the once peaceful square whilst congealed pools and splatters of crimson lifeblood contaminated the scene. More Lithuanians gathered in front of us, their fingers twitching impatiently on their triggers. Most were smoking during the lull in executions, seeming to wonder what to do with us, whilst all the while looking on menacingly. I kept trying to reassure myself that I had done nothing wrong. We had only been doing what we were told to do, just marching. It wasn't our fault the Russian tanks attacked. It wasn't our fault that their comrades had been killed by the Russians. We hadn't taken up arms. I wanted to scream, *it wasn't my time to die!*

As desperately as I tried to talk myself into the possibility of surviving this latest test, I had to admit that inside my head my arguments sounded absurdly unconvincing. Without a common language, how could we make them understand that we were innocent British soldiers caught up in this death-dealing storm?

From across the square, an Officer was fast approaching, pistol drawn. The senior NCO stiffened as he neared before finally standing to attention and saluting. As the Officer spoke quietly, several troops looked over at us as the Officer gesticulated. I believed an order was being given, without explanation. Finally, as the Officer finished, the NCO lowered his arm and barked his own orders. Immediately, the tension ebbed away. The NCO gestured whilst ordering us into squad formation. Collectively we heaved a sigh of relief, for today, it seemed, we were not going to meet our maker.

To this day, I firmly believe we would have been shot had it not been for the intervention of that Officer. With the late afternoon air chilling by the second, the square was once more crowded as the remaining British were brought in. Our elderly guards, who had been with us since leaving Wossitz, lay dead. As a result we were forced to wait as a detachment of local Deutcher Volkssturm (the German equivalent of our Home Guard) were mustered to escort us on our onward journey. Those in the Volkssturm were far too old or infirm to fight, contrasting with younger Lithuanians who were front-line troops and had more serious things to attend to.

Darkness finally descended on the slaughter yard. As we exited the town, I surveyed the scene of carnage for the last time. Bodies were everywhere. Every one of the two-thousand Russian PoWs that had been with us were now dead. All that fighting and death for what? What a waste, what a bloody waste!

My body easily slipped into auto mode, one foot in front of the other, left, right, left, right, left, right, allowing my mind to revisit the bloodbath and reflect. It's always so easy to spout wise words in hindsight, but somehow I knew it would all end in tears as soon as the first salvo of mortars heralded the German counter-offensive, causing the Russian tank crew to duck back inside the safety of their tanks and bolt. How could they just leave their countrymen, drunk and in total disorder and disarray, to end up as mere cannon fodder against a highly-trained enemy? I jerked in mid step, suddenly turning to check that my new Cypriot buddy Feo, was still by my side. He was.

With the last traces of adrenaline in my body now spent, what had just happened left me utterly exhausted. I was both physically and emotionally shattered. Initially I was relieved to get away from that town, but unfortunately the guards were eager to put as much distance between the Soviets and ourselves by quickening the pace and marching throughout the long night. The disappointment of our brief, premature liberation was obvious, but after four-and-a-half years of distress and pain I could still afford to be philosophical. Once more I had survived and now I had to go on, to come through at all costs. I felt that we were all facing the final and the greatest test of our endurance. Surely I had not come all this way to fall at the last hurdle and die! I was convinced that my freedom would come... and soon.

Even though it was dark, the clear, star-studded sky, moon and snow provided sufficient reflected light to guide our path. Three hours before dawn we were finally ordered off the road and into another field. Utter weariness enveloped my mind and body. I couldn't remember how long it had been since I had last slept under cover and out of the freezing night air. The blue-black sky was always my bedroom ceiling. It was with utter relief that I finally collapsed onto the cold, hard ground. Eagerly, Feo and I ate the last scraps of food we had found in the town but I couldn't stop shivering. I closed my eyes and huddled with Feo and others for communal warmth and fell into a deep, exhausted slumber. Our metabolism was grinding to a halt as our bodies tried to conserve every ounce of energy.

For days, we survived on melting snow and for the most part, food was almost nonexistent. What became available was often dirty and contaminated to some extent. Even though my stomach was more resilient after so many years of bad food, I was still troubled with constant stomach cramps. My dysentery was just getting worse.

After only two hours rest, we were on our feet again, just as the sun prepared to show itself. I felt like death. By late morning something caught my eye just ahead of me. On the side of the road, five British PoWs were gathered. Two were kneeling in the snow whilst the other two stood over them and stared intently at something hidden from view.

Feo was as curious as I. "Let's take a look mate!"

As we approached, I saw two legs twitching in the air, just visible over the shoulders of one of the figures. I stood in silence. One of the men held a home-made knife and was attempting to cut off a piece from the body, causing the legs to twitch. I was not disgusted for the body in question was a small lifeless pig. Its body, and in particular its belly, were bloated, unnaturally so. The 'butcher' looked back over his shoulder towards me. His dark sunken eyes looked manic. He tried to block my vision in a gesture that clearly said 'bugger off, this is ours'. By now, most of our stomachs were in turmoil, but to eat this flesh would be to invite dire (and I do mean dire) consequences. No blood flowed from the pig as he cut deep into its hind legs. The meat looked discoloured, strange and sickly. Let them take the risk of eating a raw, rotting carcass that may have been lying there for days or even weeks. To me they were foolhardy, but I could not blame them for their actions, for desperate men do desperate things. I had no interest in their 'find' and walked off, knowing what a terrible price those men could pay in the hours and days ahead.

· · · § · · ·

HEAVENLY SCULPTURES

2nd Week February 1945

The time of marching as a proud, self-respecting body of men had long gone. Our miserable bodies suffered from varying degrees of exposure, disease and starvation. Our progress had slowed to a shuffle and I found myself trailing a long way behind the others. I was reminded of the dangers of lagging behind by the sharp crack of a rifle. Was that the murder of another poor PoW? Was the 'culling squad' still following? I shuffled on as fast as the ice, snow, blistering feet and aching limbs would allow.

f I were to hazard a guess as to where I was, over three hundred miles west of Danzig would be as close as I could manage, somewhere up near the Baltic Sea. The wind was blowing so bitterly now its iced fingers stabbing at me, slicing through my clothes to my bones. It was as though I was naked. As I stumbled on in a daze, I thought I could smell the sea. I noticed a gap in the trees ahead. As I approached the clearing the air grew more chilled, the breeze more penetrating. I felt the full power of the howling wind as I left the protection of the wall of trees. I believed us to be in the area of Swinemünde (Polish Name - Świnoujście), a small a port and seaside resort in extreme north west of Poland on the Polish-German Border north of the town of Stettin (Polish Name - Szczecin), located on the Oder River.

My mind came out of hibernation and by so doing, I witnessed one of the most spectacular sights I have ever seen in my short life. I am not a religious man by any means. Maybe I have seen too much wanton cruelty and suffering to believe in anything more than the supreme barbaric nature of mankind. In the last five years I had not seen enough of the power and wisdom of God, only the brutal power of his opposite number. However, what I now saw before me was enough to turn a hardened sinner into a devout Christian. Beyond the clearing, the snow-covered earth sloped down to meet the waters of the Baltic Sea. Despite the wind, its once turbulent surface was still and frozen, but not with a flat, calm covering of ice such as I had seen as a child on the ponds and lakes of England. Not a smooth surface on which to slide and skate. This sea was in utter turmoil, a twisted, ice-bound, troubled form. Dynamic waves that had been swept up by the forceful blasts of the Arctic winds had become frozen in time, as if caught on camera in a single snapshot, locked in this beautiful, suspended form until the arrival of warmer weather. I was confronted with one of the most wonderful sculptured creations of nature that, to this very day, I had ever seen. I had never looked upon a frozen sea before and my eyes were riveted. I stopped in my tracks and stood mesmerised, transfixed and in awe as others walked on by. I could clearly see the nearest waves; the chilling, glutinous, brackish liquid had begun to roll in and break on the bleak beach, just as the risen waves had begun to curl over before crashing down onto the shore. Click! The cold did its job and the moment was captured as the wave froze, time after time, forming an amazing collection of ragged, curled, scalloped shapes that tapered into thin, spindly strands, all at the same obtuse angle, blown in the same direction. Bubbles and spray were still attached to the crests, delicately hanging, suspended in space. As far as the eye could see there stretched this enchanting entanglement of ice.

Even the tall grasses on the sand dunes near the water's edge were covered with the chilling spray of the Baltic, now bent and frozen in unison, pointing permanently inland until the chill abated with the inevitable approach of spring, allowing this strange, still scene to unlock and melt away, returning everything to its former, more accustomed state.

I felt the eyes of passing prisoners staring at me as they shuffled to the side of the track to avoid bumping into me. Perhaps they were wondering if I was alright, if the cold, pain and hunger had finally got to me and turned my addled mind to a point of no return.

They probably had a point. After all, why would anybody just stop on this death march, in the harsh winter chill, glued to the same spot, staring out across a frozen sea?

How long I stood there I have no idea. Circumstances were playing strange tricks on me. I became aware of a pain in my eyes. I had been staring so intently that my eyelids had frozen open. I couldn't even blink. I placed my cold fingers on top of my eyelids and rubbed them until they thawed. For a moment, it was agonising.

Bang! A rifle butt across the shoulder blade brought me painfully back to February 1945. I was propelled forward by a pig of a German who was walking beside a horse and cart. In the cart were five other guards. The horse was just skin and bones. They were enjoying a 'well-earned rest'. Whilst we had walked and shuffled the whole length of northern Poland and then on into Germany, our guards took it in turns to rest in what started out as one of hundreds of horse-drawn vehicles. This was probably the last horse remaining, if appearances were anything to go by. How it had any strength left in its poor, emaciated body to pull those bastards was beyond me. Within a day, it looked as though it would be horse meat. There would be no dignified death for this particular beast of burden but its overworked body would not be wasted.

As I left the clearing and bade farewell to the Baltic, I let my consciousness retreat into the comforting safety of my addled mind as we trudged on into the darkness that was creeping over the horizon. I had no idea how I managed to keep going; the pain of total fatigue was all consuming and engulfed us all. That night, I joined a group who took refuge under a huge fir tree and lay upon a thick bedding of fallen needles before slipping into the deepest of sleeps.

~ SANCTUARY ~
UNDER COVER AT LONG LAST

I had been walking for weeks. As soon as my feet hit the road, my thoughts became safely detached from my bitterly cold body, from the dampness, from my odour, my lice and the harsh reality and horror of what was happening all around me, of the dead and the dying. I moved when ordered to and dropped to the ground to sleep when instructed. Every day was the same. Fortunately, Feo was still with me but I missed the companionship of Bert, Jimmy and Johnny and the support we once gave to each other, especially the warmth of their bodies against the ever-present cold as we huddled together in those early days of our agonising, long, death march. This had become a never-ending nightmare in which I was trapped, an unfolding horror that would hold me till the end of time. I would never wake and escape from this black incubus.

Without even knowing it, I had arrived like a zombie at a farm in the middle of nowhere. The snow covering merged everything into an ill-defined dirty white sculpture. There were hundreds already there and we found refuge from the cold where we could. Like many others I was with, I ended up in a barn. The place stank of cows, but at that point I could not be sure which smell was worse, the cows or us. Tonight we would rest under cover.

I walked quickly to the back of the barn, my bowels protesting. When I had finished, I started to walk back. Ahead of me, two guards were wrestling with a pair of scrawny chickens. In turn, they hung them over a log and quickly despatched them before being taken into the farm house to be eaten. I ran forward and picked up the severed heads and sucked the still warm blood from each head. I tore at its neck flesh and ate whatever came away. The eyes slid easily down my throat. I sucked and chewed until there was nothing left. I even tried to eat the red comb on top of the head and the wattle, but it proved too tough. It wasn't much but it did provide me with some sustenance and just goes to show how desperate we all were,... forced to eat anything in order to stay alive.

This was the first time that I had been under shelter from the perilous elements for an age, however many days or weeks that had been. Walk and live was all I could manage. For tonight at least, I could relax.

I lay back and immersed myself in the warmth. The cows had obviously just left, and whilst I was grateful for their newly vacated bed I was envious of the bloody guards who must now be preparing to tuck into their cooked chicken, but for the first time on this march, I felt at ease. Was I delirious? Closer to death than I realised? I removed my boots for the first time. My once thick socks had holes, worn by hundreds of miles of trekking. My feet were dirty, sore and rotting. The extremities of my toes looked frost-bitten. They were in desperate need of medical attention. Using the laces, I tied my boots to my hands for they were priceless and could be the difference between life and death. Many of my fellows were journeying in their unforgiving wooden clogs with damp sack cloth for socks. Others wore what remained of their boots, split or in tatters, and these desperate times could even make thieves of the saints.

The sounds of distant explosions came as a welcome distraction from the itching in my crotch. I was spent, too weak to tackle my parasites. Within minutes, I drifted into a deep and restful sleep, delighting in the shelter.

Dawn came all too early. Like the call of the morning cockerel, the guards disturbed the peace of the countryside.

"Raus!"

It was not morning proper - it was another two hours till dawn. My boots were still with me, thank God. I moved to don the first one, but as much as I tried I could not force my foot inside, no matter how hard I tried. Overnight, the leather had frozen and would not accommodate my swollen foot. I loosened the laces even more and tried to flex the rigid leather, battling for several minutes. Eventually I prised a battered foot inside. It was agonising. My second foot fared no better. I cursed my folly for having removed them in the first place and swore never to make the same mistake again. I stood and hobbled forward. The boots felt more like concrete than leather. The next few hours were going to be tough. I walked outside into the bitter air and tried kicking them into comfort. As I scanned the surrounding yard, I noticed a familiar-looking mound some distance behind the barn.

It looked two metres tall and flatish on top. I dashed over to investigate. After a kick with my unforgiving boot, the pain stopped me in my tracks. I bent down to clear away the snow and almost cheered when my suspicions were confirmed, for here was another clam. I picked up as many turnips as I could and bit into the cold, tough root but it was food and nourishment and helped us to stay alive. Within seconds, the mound was crawling with my fellows, eager to share at my table as Feo and I took our leave.

The boots took all morning to warm and soften, causing painful blisters. Along this trail of death and suffering, men were as autumnal leaves littering the wayside, there to rot. Starvation, pneumonia, diphtheria, pellagra, typhus, trench foot, tuberculosis, hypothermia and a host of other illnesses ran rampant through our midst, but there was no medical assistance of any kind.

The only relief available to those poor PoWs was the 'culling squad', although I had not heard any shots since leaving the embattled town some days hence.

The most ubiquitous medical problem of all was dysentery. We were all desperately hungry, ready to eat almost anything. We drank adulterated water, if not from polluted streams then from urine-tainted snow that was inadvertently drunk, resulting in the further spread of this illness. It made our bowel movements constant, uncontrollable and bloody whilst slowly sapping our strength and gradually causing acute dehydration. In addition, men were often forced to sleep on ground covered with the faeces of those who had passed before them. Cross contamination was unavoidable. During every halt, little fires in specially adapted tins were in evidence as men made their charcoal in order to eat to help combat this debilitating illness.

~ SANCTUARY ~

More days crawled by. Our meandering forest trek went on forever. The Germans seemed hell-bent on diverting us off the main roads, just as they had done on our march into captivity, enabling scarce reinforcements and increasingly rare supplies to reach their wilting eastern front. We had already seen evidence of a mass exodus of German civilians living in the east, fleeing west towards their Nazi heartland, seeking refuge from the vengeful Soviet hordes.

This morning was bitter but it was the dampness that left me praying for warmth. We left the confines of the dense forest, where the mist hung stubbornly to the floor, refusing to disperse. Its presence muffled the sounds. Trees, like sentinels that had walled us in for days, appeared to be standing in water. Arising from the freezing fog, a huge church slowly defined itself, the first sign of human habitation for more than a week. It may even have been a cathedral, such were its proportions, dominating its location. As I approached, it seemed strange to me that there were no buildings surrounding this House of God. It really was in the middle of nowhere. From whence the worshippers came is anybody's guess.

Our guards gathered by the impressive entrance whilst we were funnelled towards the huge open portal and into the once majestic building. Once inside the vast space, I was momentarily stunned by the beauty of the interior. It looked more like a Catholic church than a more austere Protestant place of worship. The building itself was still in perfect order, as though prepared for the next Sunday service and we were the expectant congregation. As we entered, Feo made the sign of the cross. At the far end stood the raised altar with the figure of Christ on the holy cross, watching over the central nave. The spectacle was debased by the multitude of suffering PoWs already there. Many were making use of the church candles, holding them close and enjoying what little warmth they had to offer whilst men continued to file in after me. Behind the altar, the magnificent stained-glass windows, depicting biblical scenes, allowed the weak winter light to filter through into the gloomy interior. The richly carved raised pulpit caught my attention, for it was one of the few areas still unoccupied. An open bible was still in its place. I wondered for how long that would remain the case, for during the early days of our captivity the fine paper of our own pocket bibles had proved to be very useful in the preparation of hand-rolled cigarettes. This bible was a whole lot bigger, and in the hours to come the pages may have proved too tempting to the less religious members of our sad, motley, God-forsaken flock.

Downstairs was full to capacity. Late arrivals such as us were ushered up the stairs and into a surprisingly large area with an open gallery, overlooking the ground floor. At least here there was still some space. I carefully stepped over the weary bodies of the prostrate half dead. Through the remainder of the day, more were herded inside until late into the evening, when the huge wooden doors were slammed shut and the guards did what they did best... stood guard.

We remained there for three long days and nights with no food and little water, our bodies in lock down. Now we were under cover, our spirits had lifted and were hovering just above rock bottom.

Fortunately, the pangs of hunger were almost nonexistent, such is the remarkable way in which the body copes with famine. However, this did not mean that other less pleasant bodily functions stopped. For many of us, including me, diarrhoea was a constant companion. To combat mine, I took the opportunity of making some charcoal from the easily sourced wood and ate some, as this was the only remedy available. Within twenty-four hours the whole building was a stinking hole of dejection with men going in the many designated places. To desecrate the building in this manner seemed sacrilegious to me, but what could any of us do about it? When eventually it was necessary for me to go, I did the same. Goodness knows where it all came from. Input never seemed to equate to output!

I lay down on the limited floor space and tried to sleep. I must have succeeded, but it was a restless sleep. I was used to every manner of smells but the following day, I awoke to an even greater stench that was assaulting my nostrils to such an extent, I was feeling physically sick. I looked at Feo, but he was blissfully unaware of it and still in the land of the fairies. I sat up to discover a British PoW sitting next to me. He had removed his wooden clogs and the sack cloth around his feet to expose his toes. Half of his right foot was black and putrid. A foul-smelling discharge was seeping from the open sores between his toes. Gangrene was slowly creeping up his limb. I knew that without drugs or amputation, he would die. We had no medical personnel with us who could help him in any way.

"Christ mate, if I were you I would show that to the guards and tell them you demand to see a doctor," his friend uttered, in all innocence. Fat chance, I thought, but if he didn't, he would never see home again, so what had he to lose?

I got up and scanned the crowd below but I could see no familiar faces. After years as a prisoner at Stalag XXB and the surrounding 'working hostels', I was surprised not to see anybody that I knew, but on the other hand, there were so many of us.

There was nothing to do except talk and sleep, but even talking became too much of an effort. The loudest sounds to be heard were the constant coughing, sniffing and frequent violent outbursts of swearing, which were more intense than usual. Given our crowded circumstances, however, it came as no surprise. For the most part we slept, tired beyond belief, but at least we were under cover, away from the dank and dangerous chill of winter. With a thousand sinners crammed inside God's house, the collective body heat allowed our filthy clothes to gradually dry for the first time in weeks.

Early on the morning of the fourth day, the doors were finally flung open and orders were bellowed in German.

"Everyone outside, quickly!"

The stench that greeted our guards must have been truly awful and for that, I was overjoyed. As I waited to embrace the light and the fresh, clean air of the outside world I turned and viewed the full length of the building towards the high altar for the last time. I could see the pulpit, but I could no longer see that bible!

518

I was still suffering with 'gut gripe', but less so, as we left the fetid stench behind. What a relief. We scooped up handfuls of clean snow to satisfy our thirst and wash away the taste of stale filth, but still there was no food. It took a while for us all to vacate the once beautiful House of God as we snaked back onto the forest track that apparently led westward, to continue our relentless wanderings through this dirty, white wilderness. I wondered why we had stopped here in the first place. With hunger, fatigue and suffering as our chaperones, it was a relief. An additional four days without food had weakened us further, but at least we were dry.

The following day I finally saw a familiar face but one that horrified me. He was the same age as me but it was his sandy-coloured hair that I instantly recognised. Underneath the stubble and dirt, his face was still kind and handsome. Despite the inadequate camp diet, he managed to maintain a sturdy frame even though it was not covered by any meat. At Stalag XXB, he played football and exercised and none could have failed to notice his physique. We first met at Stalag XXB in 1941. I had lost track of him in the latter days of the war, working at different locations. The last time I had seen him, he was still beaming with relative health and always had a joke to share, even if I had heard it a thousand times. Now I looked down upon his lifeless form. He was gaunt and drawn, like us all, but still recognisable. He was lying face up on the side of the road, where he had been placed with some dignity, hands folded on each other. How he died I will never know. I saw no signs of a violent end. If he had died of hunger, an illness or the cold, it no longer mattered. He looked at peace now. He had no more cares in this world. He was dead at twenty-six years of age and one thing was certain. Directly or indirectly, the Germans had killed him, as sure as my left foot followed my right. This young, beautiful man was one of millions who would never find their way home and his parents would never be able to say farewell and never be able to grieve at his grave-side.

~ WILL THIS MISERY NEVER END? ~

Eight weeks of agonising existence. As much as I try to describe my suffering, it is really beyond words. My cold, unwashed, blistered, crotch-infested, wretched body of rag and bones felt like it had been through enough. Tiredness was causing constant pain. Only by concentrating on my hatred for those who were causing all this could I find the strength to continue.

I saw clusters of swedes and turnips today. An army of desperate beings were kicking them free whilst a lone guard half-heartedly attempted to move them on. I ran to join them and managed to get my share. Eventually the guard lost his patience and fired his rifle into the air. Such was our hunger that few took any notice, sure in the uncertain knowledge that he had insufficient bullets to shoot us all. We continued along country roads, shuffling and sliding on the treacherous surface, made worse by the thousands of weary feet that had trod this path before. Progress was pitifully slow. The tranquillity of the cheerless, desolate forest was shattered once more by a single shot. The interval before the next shot was all too brief as I pictured another poor Tommy being dispatched to a better place. The 'culling squad' were busy today! Then all went quiet. Presumably their work was done. Along the road today I passed more bodies. The lack of evident wounds indicated they too had died from exposure, disease, sheer exhaustion or hunger. Whichever way mattered not for I knew who was responsible.

I quickened my pace. We had seen few signs of civilisation and the fir trees on either side of the track were still heavily laden with old snow that was sticking stubbornly to the branches. No fresh snow had fallen for two days. I pulled the flaps of my forage cap down tightly over my ears as a cold blast lifted them, making them dance in the bitter winter's air. I am sure that my cap would have been lifted from the top of my head had it not been weighed down by four-and-a-half years of accumulated sweat, dirt and grease that had soaked into every fibre. The biting wind stayed with us for several days, but it was to be the last bitter breath of winter. The worst was over, and with its departure came renewed hope that those of us still alive might just make it.

~ REUNITED ~

Two days later my section of this never-ending column came upon a building. The unmistakable hand-painted logo on the wall indicated that this was a Red Cross depot. A detachment of fresh-faced, young-looking German troops, barely capable of shaving, were preparing to leave, re-assembling on the road outside the abandoned building.

As they marched by, presumably to engage the rapidly-advancing enemy, I saw that each carried two Red Cross parcels, parcels meant for us. I took a moment to step into the shell of the building. All remaining parcels had been ripped open, their contents littering the floor or looted.

I now received the shock of my life and so did he. Ahead I saw my friend Jimmy Farrington with no sign of Johnny or Bert, whom I had lost some six weeks ago. He had joined with a group of fellow Scots, some of whom I recognised as coming from our camp, men who had carved a very comfortable niche for themselves in the Scottish hierarchy. Jimmy's new-found friends had somehow acquired a sledge and were busy piling it with anything that had not already been pillaged by earlier looters. British food items such as marmite and gravy cubes still littered the floor, products that the Germans discarded. Such was our desperation that even these items were regarded as a feast. Jimmy and I exchanged a glance and nodded but it was strangely awkward. Something had radically changed and disappeared from our relationship. He made no effort to offer me anything from his booty and I was saddened. I felt troubled and betrayed. We had spent almost four years together and I had helped provide for him and my other two friends, Bert and Johnny, in my role as Mar Minter. Now he was distant and unwilling to share with me. He seemed only too keen to stay with his fellows and abandon me once more, his buddy with whom he had been through so many tough and difficult times and enjoyed many contrasting, rare and precious moments of happiness. It hurts me to say we finally parted that day and I have never seen him since.

~ 'FRIENDLY' FIRE ~
March 1945

Trudging, sliding, call it what you will, we advanced like the walking dead, plodding on, having little option other than to drop and die. The ice and snow was beginning to thaw in places, inevitably giving way to the accursed mud. What a relief to leave the confines of the gloomy forest for the more open farmlands. Our ever-present guards no longer travelled in luxury for their cart had been discarded when the poor horse had been flogged to death before being butchered. They didn't even share its skinny carcase.

Every day, the sound of artillery fire and explosions punctuated the otherwise quiet of the German countryside and by now, even our elderly guards were nearing the end of their tether. I was convinced their numbers were reducing as each day passed. None of us knew where they were disappearing to but it did not take a genius to hazard a guess - their dwindling numbers was a clear indication they had long since accepted defeat and self-preservation was the unofficial order of the day.

A shot rang out loud and clear. At first I thought it might be the culling squad whom I had not seen or witnessed for weeks, but as I turned I saw several prisoners running, making a break for freedom. A guard was kneeling in the snow, firing. First one then two fell. The other three stopped in their tracks, raising their arms high. Why were they preventing them from fleeing when the war was clearly lost? What purpose did it serve? Why couldn't the bastards just let them go? Why put a bullet through them at this late stage, after all they had gone through? In my anger, I ground my teeth and clenched my fists.

"Bastards,... one day and one day soon...?"

We only existed by living off the sparse resources the land had to offer and stealing whenever the opportunity arose. Today I found nothing, causing my guts to grumble whilst my personal little army of parasites continued to irritate my crotch. I might have been starving but my exasperating little companions were not. Just how many generations of ugly, grey, bloated lice I had nurtured in all my years in captivity, I hated to imagine.

It was mid-morning. The sky was bright and clear but it was ice cold. High above our heads, those who heard the drone of the engines would have seen the formation of Flying Fortresses flying westward, their white vapour trails marking the blue sky. I was probably somewhere in the middle of our long meandering column, stretching for miles in both directions. The whine was unmistakable but nobody could fully understand the significance until the first explosion. We responded slowly before diving for cover. Three bombs hit the area somewhere to the front of the column. It was one thing to be targeted by the enemy, but to be bombed by your own side was a bitter pill to swallow. In their defence, I suppose from their height, the airmen would have had no idea who we were. All they could see was a dark line of movement silhouetted against the snow. As only three bombs fell, it may possibly have been a lone pilot jettisoning his payload onto anything that moved within enemy territory.

When I reached the carnage I saw that only one bomb had neared its target, landing close enough to inflict death and destruction on innocent PoWs. A pair of legs and trousers hung from a roadside tree. Other body parts were scattered across the ground. Some barely alive were tended by their fellows whilst the walking wounded walked, forced to continue, aided by friends. We had come so far and how terribly tragic it was to have been killed by our own side. There was nothing I or anybody else could do but continue to walk. The guards ordered them to leave their wounded comrades and continue. Several brave PoWs stubbornly and recklessly refused to leave the and no amount of intimidation could force him. In the end, the guard gave up without carrying out his threat to shoot and simply walked away. Maybe he had finally realised it was all so utterly pointless. Brave men's lives had been spared that day.

Night slowly descended, our straggling column ground to a halt and we collapsed on the ground at the sides of the track as we had been doing for weeks. Behind us on the other side of the bordering ditches were the open fields. As was the custom every night, I cuddled up against total strangers for warmth and what little comfort was on offer. Sleep was a troubled affair but exhaustion always helped. During the night the dampness permeated through my trousers to my skin and I was miserable with the chill. Before dawn came in earnest to this hell of ours, I watched the period of strange half light as the sun's light crept around the curvature of the earth, reflecting off the swathes of winter's snow that were determined to remain as long as possible, to blight our lives still further. This was usually the time the guards started to arouse us from our slumbers, but today all was quiet. Deathly quiet. I slowly rose and stood up, gazing at the road in both directions and observed other PoWs scattered along its length, some standing, others still resting, but I could not see a single German. After months of the same miserable, monotonous routine, this unexpected occurrence caused me some anxiety, as was always the case when the unexpected happened. I sat back down and waited with the others. Something was wrong, very wrong.

The morning air was cold and still. There was not a sound to be heard; no sound of distant artillery fire nor sound of screaming

German soldiers. As the minutes ticked on by, I felt increasingly uneasy. This made no sense to me, no sense at all. We should have been continuing our remorseless, unrelenting march westward. I was now so conditioned to this routine that I could have continued till the end of time, but not now,... not today. As time passed, others woke and joined the scores of PoWs just waiting. Even though I was surrounded by hundreds of fellows stretched along the road, I felt utterly alone, on a ship without its captain. Our winding snake of disorientated souls was without its head.

I had no friends with me, nobody to consult. My self-preservation instincts were screaming at me to do something, anything. My paranoia could not have been more acute. Slowly, in case I was being watched by an unseen German guard, I backed away from the track where my comrades waited, across the ditch and into the field beyond. I sensed fear and smelt death, but was it coming from me alone? I was still not ready to meet my maker. I had come this far and I still had to make it to the bitter - but hopefully sweet - end.

By now, prisoners were gathering in smaller groups, questioning our plight. As for me, I still feared a bloody massacre in the quiet of that morning. I was suspicious of the unnatural silence, believing that at any moment it would be smashed to pieces by merciless machine-gun fire from a myriad of vengeful, executing Germans. They were certainly capable of it, as I had seen from their treatment of others, not to mention the activities of the 'culling squad'.

Inch by slow inch, I retreated across the field. By now, I was fifty yards away from the road and still moving. How far could I get before the shit hit the fan? I stopped moving and just stood there, waiting. I watched those on the road chatting amongst themselves before they moved on to other groups to exchange views. I looked about me as the distant boom of several explosions thundered across the landscape, but they were distant battles. As the sun reluctantly dragged itself higher in the cloud-filled sky, everything before me looked so peaceful. Eventually my paranoia subsided ang my fear of a bloodbath proved unfounded. Now it was my isolation that filled me with dread so I hurried back to the road and joined the others, taking comfort in their numbers.

"What to do now" were the only words on everyone's lips.
I joined the nearest group of eight, who like me hadn't a clue what to do next. By midday, small parties of men began to drift off along the track in the direction that the column had been going all along -

westward, or was it south? It was so difficult to keep track, but for many days now I felt that we had been moving south. With only an often masked sun for guidance, we appeared to have travelled in all directions of the compass since leaving the Baltic coast.

My feet pained me. A hole had appeared in my worn sole. I re-tightened the rags around my boots and legs before beginning the 'Stalag shuffle' to get some blood flowing through their veins. A discussion within our faction ensued, and to a man we decided to follow the others.

All that day we walked and without guards on either side, we felt strange. We could have gone anywhere, done anything, but we didn't. Although I was now free to wander, I did not feel free. I simply felt lost, insecure, weak and vulnerable, for I was still institutionalised. However, without guards to keep us in line, it did offer us the option to loot any dwelling that we came across, and for the rest of that day we were on extra alert for any likely-looking targets.

As evening approached, we turned a corner in the road and came across a small village ahead, consisting of twenty to thirty houses. On the outskirts we stopped dead in our tracks, almost bumping into each other. From the tiny chimneys we could see thin trails of smoke drifting lazily up into the clear evening sky. Not a sound could be heard. The scene was still, almost picturesque. Apart from the smoke, there were no other signs of activity. None of us was sure whether to enter the village and see what we could find in the way of food and shelter or be sensible and skirt round it to avoid any potential problems and dangerous encounters. Our decision-making was painfully indecisive but eventually it was decided that perhaps one of us should go into the village alone, to reconnoitre and report back. At least that way, if there was trouble only one of us would get killed. Great idea, but I thought it prudent not to volunteer. I had not come this far to die a foolhardy hero. Eventually, one of our small group got bored with the dithering and volunteered himself.

"Rather you than me mate," I thought.

I relaxed, thankful it was not me.

The first small house facing us stood alone. It was a single-storey building some twenty yards away. The eight of us stood and watched as our brave, impetuous companion walked towards it. His short journey seemed to take an age. He walked straight past the first building and headed towards the house that had smoke trailing from its chimney. He came to a halt right outside the front door. He stood there for a brief moment, turning back to look at us sheepishly, before cautiously raising his arm and banging on the door. He took two steps back and looked at us again, almost in a forlorn plea for help. We offered him none.

And nothing happened!

He took another step forward, supposedly to knock again, raised his fist when suddenly, the door swung open, flooding him and the road outside with light. A visible cloud of cigarette smoke wafted out of the cottage and caressed the top of the door frame and eaves before dispersing into the chilled night air. Silhouetted in the doorway stood a lone German soldier with his sleeves rolled up, his braces hanging down by the sides of his breeches and a cigarette hanging from his mouth. We couldn't see further inside the house but our heroic companion could. Behind the lone German at the door lounged a house full of German soldiers, sitting around relaxing, drinking, smoking and laughing in front of a roaring log fire. Our hero slowly backed away. Within a second he turned and ran as fast as his weary legs could carry him, back towards us. We were already way ahead of him, sprinting. I glanced back over my shoulder to see our hero gaining on us. He was alone. There were no Germans following behind him, no shots, no pursuit. I don't know where the energy came from but we didn't stop running until we were well clear of that village. I was ready to collapse. I bent down, hands on my knees, feeling sick at the sudden exertion, my heart pounding and my sphincter muscle working overtime.

We put a mile between us and the village before deciding to rest for the night. We were back in the countryside once more but soon found shelter in an old cow shed in the middle of a field. It was pretty open to the elements but it was better than nothing. With the end of the big freeze came the damp, so the relative dryness of the shelter was very welcoming. Although still cold and hungry, we were increasingly more cheerful than we had been for a long time. We could almost taste our freedom, despite our uncertainty. We laughed aloud as our reluctant hero re-told his tale, of the look of surprise on the German at the door after he managed to refocus his confused, drunken eyes and realise who his visitor was. He either didn't care or was too drunk to act. We imagined those same Germans telling their side of the story and how they might have reacted. By now, our spirits were high.

LIBERATION

March or April 1945 ?
I wasn't sure

The following morning we walked with renewed vigour but didn't come across any signs of civilisation during the hours of daylight. However, as soon as sunset threatened we saw lights twinkling ahead as a small town came into view.

I sensed a repeat performance of yesterday. This time, we all kept together and approached it en masse. No lone heroics this time. As we got closer, we could see army vehicles parked up alongside the buildings, small armoured cars and a lorry. A white five-pointed star was painted on the door of the lorry and then I saw the jeeps. Tears welled in my eyes and then a smile slowly crept across my face. I couldn't believe it. Americans! They were Yanks, wonderful bloody Yanks!

> *We had stumbled upon a Reconnaissance Unit of the American Army. As to where we were at that particular moment, I could only guess. On reflection, and knowing what I do now about the approximate whereabouts of the American and Russian troops, I would estimate that we were in a small village somewhere on the west bank of the River Elbe. We must have been moving south for some time. During our long trek, the temperatures had been so low that I had not even been aware of crossing the Oder and Elbe rivers for they were frozen over and covered with snow.*

The village we now found ourselves in was typically German, seemingly untouched by the horrors of war, looking prosperous, even quaint and well maintained without obvious scars. We walked up to the nearest group of Americans before noticing that the first soldier was black. In fact, the whole unit was made up of black soldiers save for one white American, an Officer, whom we had yet to meet.

The men seemed to be an undisciplined bunch, congregated around the twenty or so vehicles that lined the road out of the village. Some had their engines still running for some unknown reason. Clearly fuel was not in short supply. It amazed me that in spite of the fact that this was a war zone, these soldiers seemed relaxed and totally unaware of any possible danger whilst casually leaning against their vehicles, headlights beaming straight ahead, illuminating the uncertain surrounding countryside. No cautious blackout in operation here.

To a man, the black Americans were smoking, some talking amongst themselves or lying on top of the warm bonnets of their vehicles. To me, their reluctance to post sentries was dangerously negligent; after all, we could have been Germans intent on continuing the war in their own back yard.

I suppose I was foolishly expecting some sort of heroes' welcoming committee from our Allies, or at the very least a warm greeting from these troops. Considering what we had all suffered and gone through, some sort of recognition as to what we had endured for so many years would have been appreciated, but it wasn't to be. These men couldn't give a stuff. Like me, millions of PoWs and political prisoners across the globe had all clung to the hope of eventual freedom, often the only hope that kept them alive, praying for their day of liberation. All I wanted or needed was a smile, a warm greeting, a sincere reception, but no. Our liberation was a major anti-climax and a disappointment for us all.

By contrast to these troops, we looked dreadful. Over our starved, emaciated frames our uniforms hung, old, badly-fitting and filthy. Those of us who still had forage caps wore them with their flaps pulled down over their ears. My matted blonde hair was long, hanging down in a dirty, greasy mess over my face. Shaving was not a luxury available to us on our long, torturous march to freedom so we all sported varying lengths of beard. We probably stank to high heaven as well, but I certainly couldn't tell for I had been living with my own stench for too long to notice and I certainly didn't care.

By contrast the Americans, in combat uniforms that had yet to see action, were squeaky clean. Their helmets had been replaced with woollen hats and their weapons were casually discarded. As some of them looked up from their pressing games of cards or dice with an expression of utter indifference, there was nothing friendly in their greeting. In fact, there was no greeting at all and they couldn't have been less interested if they'd tried. They didn't even wish to know who the hell we were and where we had come from but we introduced ourselves anyway, addressing the senior NCO. We explained we were British soldiers who had been held as PoWs since 1940 and had just walked across Europe ahead of the Russians for the last three months. Nothing. No response at all.

We then told them we had not eaten or drunk properly for weeks. Nothing. Still no response whilst the Sergeant simply continued with his chewing, gum presumably. For some strange reason, I recalled the old western movies of my youth, thinking this black American could have been munching on a mouthful of chewing tobacco. The other Americans didn't listen to us either. Eventually we had to ask if they could give us something to eat. There was a curt response from the driver of the nearest jeep.

"Go help your f***ing selves," pointing with his thumb to the back of the jeep.

None of us bothered to give him a 'thank you'. Such courtesy and basic communication skills somehow seemed inappropriate here. It wasn't the swearing that got to me, it was just the totally unsympathetic, hostile indifference to us that pissed me off. It hurt.

We all shuffled past him to the back of his vehicle and looked inside his canvas-covered jeep. My eyes lit up, as a child's on Christmas Day after Santa's night-time call. The jeep was filled to the gunnels with food. Bread, tins of beef, wine, whiskey and champagne - much of it looted no doubt. I wasn't as surprised as I had once been, over four years ago in northern France, just before my capture. Then, our Commanding Officer would buy provisions from the locals for us, his hungry charges, rather than just take food. If he had no money with him to purchase food, we went hungry. By now, even I accepted that looting was the universal soldiers' way and had been since the dawn of time.

None of us had seen any real food like this for years and we didn't need telling twice. We dived in and loaded our pockets before managing to coax a few words out of the bored driver. They had been in the village for a couple of days and were awaiting further instructions, and that was the full extent of his verbose outburst. We tried once more to explain to them who we were and that we had finally escaped from the Germans and now didn't know what to do next.

"Please your f***ing selves what you do," replied the same guy, still chewing and not even having the decency to look up at us.

By now, I thought it was about time I had my turn in saying something.

"We would all feel a lot better if we were armed."

As soon as I had finished speaking, I could almost guess what his response was going to be and I was right.

'Chewey', as I now referred to him, responded.

"Help your f***ing selves."

"With what?" I replied.

"In the village, just go help your f***ing selves," he said, at the same time pointing back down the road with his thumb without even turning his head.

I was not sure exactly what was in the village or how this would help us arm ourselves, but it seemed unlikely we would get much more information out of him, or anybody else for that matter, even though this American was the most talkative in his squad. We looked at one another, stared and shrugged a shoulder here and there before silently agreeing to leave. We turned to walk away but I had one more request to make before leaving.

"Have you got a cigarette?"

The other eight of our party stopped dead in their tracks. Their eyes lit up and we all looked at the American, as if our lives depended on him conjuring up these magical white sticks. This did cause 'Chewey' to turn his head, but he was still devoid of any expression, save that of utter apathy. Almost reluctantly, he opened his left breast pocket, took out an unopened pack and gave them to me. He then gave me a box of matches before reaching down to the floor of his jeep and retrieving eight more packs to distribute. This act alone was worthy of huge thanks.

With food in our pockets and a pack of cigarettes, I opened a bar of delicious chocolate. To say it was unbelievably fantastic was an utter understatement. We all tucked in to whatever food we had been given and instantly felt the better for it as we walked off, down the road in the slowly progressing twilight. Amongst the small houses, individual shops were scattered about, not grouped together as in other larger villages. From what I could see there were no visible signs of damage to the buildings and no bomb craters as one might have expected.

After eating came the moment to light up. The taste was beyond belief and totally beyond words. How can something so simple bring so much pleasure? I inhaled deeply and held the smoke for a couple of seconds before ever so slowly exhaling, drawing every ounce of satisfaction and gratification that I could from that first puff. As usual, I felt dizzy as the nicotine surged through my bloodstream,... but I also felt good. After years of untold damage to our lungs through smoking dry leaves, grass, occasionally nicked Balkan tobacco, German dog ends, terrible Polish cigarettes and the forgotten taste of English Red Cross ciggies, this American ciggie filled with strong, sweet Virginian tobacco hit the spot. My head was swimming and I felt happy and content for the first time since leaving Wossitz in early January.

By now, the lights were being turned on in some of the surrounding buildings and all seemed peaceful, far removed from the storms of war still raging all around. In the central square lay a stack of weapons and ammunition that had been captured from Germans or removed from the dead. Lugers and other pistols, rifles, machine-guns, anti-tank weapons, grenades, bayonets and boxes of ammunition were piled high like some modern-day sculpture depicting a cryptic anti-war message. Scattered randomly all around the square were the odd bodies of Germans, soldiers and civilians alike. I had no idea as to how long they had been there but no attempt had, as yet, been made to clear them up. More telling was that nobody in control really cared.

We stood amongst the weapons examining them before bending down to select our choice. My travelling companions picked up rifles and ammunition. However, I chose something that I had always wanted and admired, a 'Schmeisser', a 'Maschinenpistole MP40' to give it its full name. It was a weapon of beauty, a powerful sub-machine-gun, much prized and feared by anybody on the receiving end of one. I had often seen German troops carrying these awesome weapons and now I had one. I found the release mechanism and checked the long, thin, rectangular magazine. It was nearly empty, so I searched around for the ammunition and found boxes of 9mm bullets with which I reloaded the magazine. I also found several spare magazines in a German army pack which I kept, filling the rest of the available space with more ammo. I picked up a magazine, checked that it was full, and clipped it into the weapon. I bent down and stuffed a further four magazine clips into my pockets. Each clip held about forty rounds, so I figured I was now adequately armed.

Satisfied with my choice of weapon, I made ready to leave when something else caught my eye. I leant forward. Almost hidden amongst the weapons I spotted what looked like a scope. I pushed other arms aside and saw a marksman's rifle with the telescopic sight attached. It was a German K43, a sniper's rifle. I lifted it out and inspected it. It was in fine condition, looking as though it had been lovingly cared for by its previous owner. I had only heard scraps of information about them and had yet to see one being used. Like many German rifles I had seen, it had no bolt action and was gas-operated, which meant that the high-pressure gas expelled when the cartridge is fired is not lost but channelled to power a mechanism to extract and eject the spent case and to chamber a new cartridge, so it is immediately ready for action again, thereby increasing its rate of fire.

> *My interest in rifles stemmed from my membership of a local rifle club before the war, where I had been a marksman of some repute. (see picture reference 44)*

I removed the magazine and recovered a bullet. It was a 7.92mm x 5mm Mauser. I searched for additional ammunition, there in abundance, before reloading the magazine which held ten rounds. I took another full pack containing several boxes. Finally, as if I was not armed enough, I pocketed an interesting-looking small pocket pistol whilst my companions watched me with incredulity.

"Are you ready to start another bloody war all over again Dennis?" commented the one who had disturbed the Germans in their cottage.

"I'm not ever going to be a victim again and I've got things to do."

> *If only I had been thinking into the future, as was the case amongst the troops we were to meet later, I could have made a killing. There were trophies of war just lying around for the taking, the Luger pistols for example. If only I had realised...*

I was weighed down with my newly-acquired weapons. As a result, I no longer felt naked as we strolled back to the Americans. However, we were still without direction. 'Chewey' seemed almost irritated at our all too quick return, not even waiting to hear the next question.

"If you want something to f***ing do, go and round up some f***ing square heads and bring them in. They're a pretty docile bunch now they know they're defeated and have all but given up, so they shouldn't be no trouble."

By now, it was dark. Although we had spent the last three winter months sleeping in the open, in terrible exposed conditions, we thought we now deserved some decent shelter after what we had endured.

The timidity of my thought reflected how very subservient and totally institutionalised I still was after years in captivity. We were incapable of thinking in more demonstrative terms. How to go about finding accommodation was verbalised by one of my companions to the American.

"Where can we find somewhere to sleep for the night?"

We should have guessed his response.

"Help your f***ing selves, just go and take over any house you like the look of," was 'Chewey's' answer.

Then another of our group chirped in with his two penny's worth.

"But the doors seemed to be locked."

By now, I think 'Chewey' was a bit pissed off.

"Well go and kick the f***ing door down then!" he shouted, as if the solution was abundantly obvious.

It was time to leave.

We walked back to the village centre with the express purpose of obtaining a billet for the night, spurred on by the forthright attitude of 'Chewey'. As we wandered aimlessly around, trying to decide at which house to 'kick the f***ing door down', we were delighted to come across two scruffy British PoWs walking towards us, one behind the other. Between them, they were carrying what looked like a stretcher. As we passed we looked down to see that the 'stretcher' was, in fact, a long, wooden tray with four carrying handles. Cut into the tray were rows of holes and each hole held a single egg safely cradled. In all, they must have been carrying a hundred eggs. I couldn't remember the last time I had seen an egg, let alone tasted one.

"Hello mate, good to see a friendly face, been here long?"

"Na, just drifted in this morning."

"Excuse me chaps, where did you get those delicious eggs from?" came the instant question.

"Back there," one of the Brits said, flicking his head back over his shoulder, thereby causing his long, lanky hair to fall over his eyes.

"Just stumbled across this warehouse full of 'em."

I looked past him and sure enough, in the distance, we could make out a huge, low building on the edge of the village, its double doors open to the world. A thin line of men were walking towards it and returning from it. I turned to look at the others. None of us needed telling. We all sprang into action and joined the line.

Once inside I could see that it was almost full to capacity and now in desperate need of emptying... by us. We picked up a tray and walked back into the village, hell-bent on cooking the biggest fried egg the world had ever seen. For a few moments we stood rather sheepishly looking at each other, wondering what to do next.

One of the guys eventually said something.

"I guess we'd better do as the Yank told us and go kick a door in." Although we had been authorised to do so and had the firearms to 'legitimise' our actions, none of us could actually kick a door in. It wasn't so much that we lacked the strength (however true that was), it was more to do with the fact that, even in a war situation, such vandalism went completely against the grain. So, purely at random we chose a house, walked up to the door and politely knocked. The lights inside were flickering so we knew somebody was at home. Slowly, the door was opened a fraction and in the gloomy half light stood a man in his sixties. Half hiding behind what little protection the door had to offer him, he looked frightened, whilst his wife stared out at us from deep inside the perceived safety of the hall's dimness. Despite the obvious alarm in their eyes, I felt little pity for them for they were German, and by now I hated all things German. Both looked petrified. I told them to move aside and we all trudged in with our eggs, leaving the old man to close the door behind us. My German language skills made it easy for me to make myself understood.

Having found our courage, I pointed to the trays and barked an order.

"We want beds and we want you to cook these."

Boiled, poached, fried or scrambled, it didn't matter to me one jot. The two, barely able to contain their fear, led us into their kitchen. As far as we were concerned, we just wanted a place offering a bed and cooking facilities. The small house had a rustic and rural appearance, was immaculate, clean and tidy. This humble place was a stately home by comparison to the bleak huts of Stalag XXB and a palace beyond compare to our early earth huts. More seating was brought in to accommodate us as we sat in the spacious, warm kitchen, making ourselves at home. Someone asked for coffee, hoping for the real thing, but, as expected, we received ersatz instead.

It didn't take long for the first batch of eggs to be cooked.

The smell alone was enough to make me drool. As the husband poured the coffee, the wife placed a loaf of bread on the table and we tucked into our feast. Now was not the time to remember our manners, and with our mouths full, we asked for more. Immediately, a second batch was prepared. The taste was the most delicate and delicious that I could ever recall. With a full belly of proper food inside me for the first time in three months, I felt marvellous. Smiles stretched from ear to ear. In the warmth of the couple's home it was not long before tiredness overwhelmed me, and by the looks of the others' faces, we all had the same idea.

"Sleep, where are the beds"? was all the conversation I could be bothered to muster to our increasingly relaxed hosts, who had now decided that in spite of the arsenal of weaponry that we carried, we were not going to shoot them. We were shown to the bedrooms and four of us immediately barged straight into our host's, not waiting for the invitation, whilst the others moved into a second bedroom. I pulled back the sumptuous feather-filled duvet as we kicked off our filthy boots and discarded our coats. Still fully clothed, we jumped into bed. I sank into the soft mattress, my smile broadening by the second. Within minutes, I, my fellow PoWs and our ever-present pubic lice, were all far away in the land of nod. Heaven!

We slept the sleep of the contented dead, the best night's kip I had experienced since leaving England. Nobody moved a muscle until morning. I awoke feeling in good spirits, for we were still free and it hadn't all been a cruel dream. Then I remembered the eggs. I jumped out of bed and in spite of the groans of my stomach, I was desperate for more, and more was what I was going to have. I woke our reluctant hosts, who were still sound asleep in their lounge. I ordered our meal. The choice was not too demanding, and every mouthful of my fried eggs, with what remained of the bread, tasted just as good as the previous night's feast. I was pleased to discover my new-found diet was also having a wonderfully calming impact on my bowels and the 'runs' had almost stopped running. Given the binding effect of two-dozen eggs, I suppose this news was not surprising, but I did have to admit that I was feeling sick.

The smell of fried eggs woke the others and by the time we had finished, the vomiting and runs began.

We offered all the remaining eggs to the old couple.

"Have as many as you want."

Primarily, this was not so much an act of kindness, for we were still short on compassion to squander food liberally on members of the German race. No, it was purely that we still had so many of them left, and at the edge of the village there remained a warehouse overflowing with eggs, that would probably all go to waste anyway and waste of any kind, especially food, was abhorrent to all of us PoWs. However, their reaction quite surprised me for they declined.

"Nein, nein, for if we are caught, we will be severely punished."

Somehow, even now, they did not believe or did not want to believe that Germany was defeated and their police state was dead.

Initially, the woman and her husband seemed more relaxed that morning, in the certain knowledge that they were at least going to survive our intrusion. As we ate, the husband stood nearer, hovering awkwardly with some expectancy. He nervously began to rub his hands together before he eventually plucked up enough courage to ask a question to which they were both desperate for answers.

"Are the Russians coming?" he timidly enquired in his native tongue.

At that time, we had no idea what had been planned by the allies with regards the carve-up of the former Nazi state and where the border between east and west was to be drawn

None of us were in any mood to placate these Germans, or any others for that matter, so I gave them the straight answer.

"Yes, the Russians are coming. We will be leaving soon, but the Russians will be coming after we're gone."

We left them in no doubt. They looked shaken, visibly petrified. No matter how many times or ways they asked the same question they got the same answer. The man then went to a drawer and took out a piece of paper and pencil and offered it to all around the table.

"Please," he said, "please, write down that you are British PoWs who are fleeing back to your home and that my wife and I helped you and fed you and treated you well."

Their plan was both desperate and utterly futile, foolishly believing that when the Russians eventually arrived, all they had to do was show them our note and somehow, it alone would be viewed as a

Note of Immunity from Retribution, and consequently, the Russians would spare them and leave them in peace. We knew the idea was dead in the water from its very inception. To a man we felt that mercy was not to be shown to this evil nation at this stage; it was too soon for a show of compassion and forgiveness from us and the victims of the Nazis who had all suffered so much.

Even if we had written the note, no Russian soldiers would have been able to read it, let alone understand it. Its only use would have been as toilet paper. If the experience of what had happened a few weeks ago, when we had witnessed the actions of the vengeful Russian prisoners, was anything to go by, then every German the Russians came into contact with was in fear of their lives and more. We had all witnessed first-hand the inhuman treatment the Germans had administered to the Russians throughout our internment, and I for one could not blame them for what they were about to do. Accordingly, we refused to write the letter.

I now turned my attention as to what to do next. All I could think of was the rage burning inside me and my weapons. The food and our new-found freedom was giving me renewed strength and the arms upstairs gave me a power that I had never experienced before. Hatred gave me a purpose and as I thought about my situation further, I knew that I had now discovered the desire and ability to kick a door in.

For the next ten minutes we talked over the kitchen table about the American's suggestion of hunting out any remaining German troops, but it appeared that I was the only one that wanted, or needed, to go 'hunting'. The others argued they had been to hell and back for the last five years and just come through the most painful and terrible of forced marches that was in reality, a March of Death. 'So why endanger our lives now?' The war was all but over and we could be home in a week or so. For them, it seemed foolhardy to rejoin the fight now. I could of course see their point of view, it all made common sense, but I knew that I couldn't let it rest. The pain and torture of the last five years was too fresh in my memory and it had only been this hatred for my brutish and sadistic captors that had kept me going. I was not about to forgive or forget.

"Dennis, sorry mate, but I have a wife and children to think of," answered Harry, his face full of sorrow.

"Me too,... well a girlfriend actually," replied another.

"Dennis, what's the point? We have played our part and paid a hell of a price for doing our job. Let these others clean up the mess and let's go home."

I knew I was getting nowhere, no matter how much I argued.

"Sorry chaps, I just can't let it drop," I responded. "Someone has to pay for my suffering and there is still a war on, so if you don't want to come with me, then I will go on my own."

"What do you plan to do?" Harry asked, concerned for my wellbeing.

"I'll collect my guns, walk back and take it from there," was all I could say for I had not really thought it through. I was just burning up with an inner rage that would not be quenched. I had no dependents waiting for me and nothing to lose... except my life of course, but my mission took precedence. I gathered my Schmeisser, rifle and ammunition, some biscuits from the couple and some hard boiled eggs. I loaded both weapons and once again familiarised myself with them before making my way downstairs. All the lads were there to see me off as I bade them a fond farewell.

"Can we persuade you to change your mind Dennis?" asked the eldest of our band.

"Sorry Jack, I need to do this."

With that, I shook them by the hand, and feeling rather lonely I left, turning just once to wave them good-bye.

It was still early in the day as I followed the road on which we had first entered the village and said goodbye to the Americans. They were not surprised or unduly concerned as to why I was leaving and wished me well, but not without insisting that I first look through a pile of German army boots that had been liberated. I looked down at the sorry state of my footwear that had only just survived the terrible journey to freedom. They were literally on their last legs, so I gladly took up the Americans' offer. I found a pair that fitted and begged a pair of socks from them.

"Just one last thing Sergeant, I need to try out these weapons. I don't want to find out they don't work at the wrong time."

"Go ahead, be my guest."

For once, he didn't swear.

· · · § · · ·

VENGEANCE
IS MINE

Beginning of April 1945

Just ahead was a gate at the side of the road. In the grounds of a house in front of me was a small outbuilding some distance away, with a bucket hanging near the side window. It looked deserted. I rested the Schmeisser beside the gate and prepared my rifle, setting the range to 50 metres. I steadied myself against the gate, took careful aim and fired. It had been five years since I had last fired a gun. The metallic clang confirmed my hit as the bucket swayed briefly to and fro. I had lost none of my marksman's skills.

I fired a second shot. Even though it was still swaying, the shot hit its mark. Now it was the turn of my beloved Schmeisser. I unfolded the handle, locking it into place, and checked the long magazine. Gripping the bolt, I pulled it back and cocked it ready for action. I took aim at the same target, releasing a hail of bullets. The gun recoiled into my shoulder as I fought to steady it. The bucket took a hammering as did its surroundings, and flew into the air. Once it hit the ground I released another short burst, sending it spinning into the wall of the barn.

By now, confused and anxious Americans had come running from the warmth of their surrounding billets to see what the hell was happening. I turned to see the Sergeant raising his hand to them, calming their concerns. My weapons were fit for purpose.

I thanked them all. The black Sergeant stepped forward, handing me more food, a waterproof cape and pushed another batch of cigarettes into my pockets before pointing me in the direction of the German lines. I put on the cape, uttered a last farewell and walked off with conflicting emotions gnawing away in the pit of my stomach: excitement, dread, fear and loneliness.

Tired snow still clung to the ground in the surrounding countryside, heavy in places, as I retraced my journey. The exodus from eastern Germany continued as isolated bands of civilians walked hurriedly past, casting furtive glances in my direction. All seemed headed for the American lines.

My 'new' boots were pretty comfortable, considering they had been worn in by another's feet. Hours went by before I reached the outskirts of the village that we had stumbled across yesterday, where I knew German troops were housed. It was late afternoon. I unslung my Schmeisser, hoped for the best but prepared for the worst, just in case. From the edge of the village I stared down on the few civilians that passed through past the small houses and cottages, before finally focusing on the third house. Smoke still trailed from its chimney. I was suddenly conscious of the fact that I was wearing German boots and the thought came to me that if I was recaptured by fanatical SS, or even Wehrmacht troops, I could expect no mercy. However, my desire for revenge overrode any concerns lurking in the recesses of my unforgiving mind.

I left the road and carefully made my way round the back of the buildings opposite, remaining hidden from their view, if indeed they were still there. Just before I reached the house, I casually walked off the road to a shed that stood at the back of a cottage facing the house. I opened the weathered door and walked in. The shed was full of drying vegetables, logs and dusty old household furniture. I turned to the right and stared at the house through the broken glass window. A sack curtain hung from one corner, acting as an anchor point for a dust-covered web. It was perfect.

I made myself at home, preparing for my task ahead by moving an old bench in front of the window in order to rest my weapons on. I opened my food bag and took out three of the hard boiled eggs and ate them, one after the other. Before I had finished, the door of the house opposite swung open. A lone German soldier walked out and headed down towards the village centre. He was unarmed. Now my heart was pounding with anticipation, for this confirmed they were still there. I pulled over a stout wooden box, picked up my rifle and sat down. I estimated the distance to be 100 metres, made the adjustment to the sights and trained the K43 on the house. Through the scope, I could see the door in fine detail. I scanned across to the window on the left and then on the right. Inside, the dull glow of a weak light was visible and I could clearly see figures moving. They were Wehrmacht. I rested the rifle and made sure that it was fully loaded and that my Schmeisser and ammunition were to hand. I raised the barrel, looked and took aim at a figure in the room, finger resting on the cold trigger. I began to squeeze. A woman suddenly appeared and walked across my line of vision. My heart missed a beat.

"Shit."

I raised my head and heaved a sigh of relief. A second later and I would have shot her and killing innocent civilians was not my intention. My hands were shaking so I put down the rifle and took out my cigarettes. I needed a smoke to calm my nerves. As I did so I stared through the window. All I could visualise were the German guards on our march into captivity as they screamed abuse and kicked over buckets of precious drinking water to prevent us satisfying our torturous thirst. I saw the face of the guard that had mocked me as I begged for a drag of his cigarette. The rifle butt that smashed into my face on the farm. I saw the look of fear and hopelessness on the faces of the PoWs in the sweltering wagon as we journeyed across Germany and on into Poland. I saw the sentry at the gate as he stamped on the bare feet of the frozen Tommy as he stood in the deep snow. I saw Posnanski laughing as he forced the Italian to cross under the 'death wire', only to be racked with machine-gun fire. Five years of pain and suffering flashed before my eyes, and all this to the sounds of rifle shots as the 'culling squad' did their worst.

By the time I had finished my smoke, my nerves had calmed and the ice cold hatred flowed through my body once more, focusing my mind. I lifted my rifle once more, took aim, found my target and paused, breathed heavily, paused again and fired a single shot through the broken window. Across the 100 metres of open space, the window shattered and momentarily, I lost sight of my intended victim, but I knew I had not missed. Even after all this time, my marksman's skills had not deserted me. There was pandemonium in the building opposite. I took aim once more and gently squeezed the trigger. This time I saw a German take a head shot and fall against the back wall. Someone inside killed the light and the room was plunged into gloom. I could only imagine the chaos. From behind the house I caught sight of a trooper making a dash across the open ground towards the next building, rifle in hand. I swung my rifle round and fired but missed my target as he dived behind the protection of the house. As another attempted to follow, I quickly took aim and fired again. He went down, but as I watched through the powerful scope I could see that he was only wounded. I fired again at his head. This time he ceased to move. As a third ran from the building, I heard the first volley hit my shed. They had found my hideaway. I ducked then lifted my head again. More shots followed and whilst firing, others made a bid to escape on the other side of the house. It wouldn't be long before they realised that the shots were coming from a lone rifleman.

"Shit and double shit!" It was time to go.

I picked up the Schmeisser and turned towards the door but in that one horrifying moment, it dawned on me that the door was in full view of the angry Germans. How could I have been so stupid as to not check my escape route? I focused on the wooden planks at the back of the shed and thought I could manage it. Returning to the window once more I fired a withering hail of bullets towards the house and either side until the magazine was empty. I put on the ammunition pouches and quickly reloaded. By now, more troops were exiting in both directions so I fired a longer burst, first to the left and then to the right. Some collapsed, but I had no way of knowing if they were hit or just diving for cover. I reloaded the Schmeisser once more, grabbed hold of the K43 and remaining ammunition and ran to the rear of the hut, raising my boot as I reached the back wall. Several of the old planks gave way. I kicked again and created a gap big enough to break through whilst a withering hail of bullets peppered the walls.

Once outside, I ran as fast as my skinny legs could carry me. I couldn't remember ever being so scared. I was alone and behind me were a hive of angry, pissed-off Wehrmacht, with me as their sole quarry. I ran straight, conscious of keeping the shed in their line of fire. I struggled over the back fence before reaching the wooded area on the edge of the village and did not stop until I collapsed in the snow, utterly exhausted. The firing had stopped, but I wasn't sure if they were following my rather obvious footprints or not. After the briefest of rests, I hurried away from the immediate area. Then it hit me. In my desperate attempt to escape, I cursed at the realisation that I had left my food supplies behind, but at least I still had my ammunition and cigarettes.

Eventually, I found a road and followed it, hopefully heading eastwards. More desperate civilians were tramping along its length, trying to get to somewhere, anywhere that was not here. I could see no German troops so I joined the road, travelling in the opposite direction, assuming that I was heading towards the Russians. Weary, fearful faces stared back at me as I passed. In my filthy uniform of no discernible origin, wearing a British but unmarked forage cap and draped in a US army cape, with two weapons and pouches of ammunition, I must have cut a frightful figure. Dusk was fast approaching and I needed to find shelter, for I had no intention of ever sleeping under the stars again. After passing through a small hamlet, I left the road to follow a wide path with fresh cart tracks clearly visible. Before long I came upon a small farmhouse standing alone. Its quiet location seemed ideal. Cautiously I edged closer, my Schmeisser at the ready. One by one, I looked through each window but the occupants were nowhere to be seen. Slowly I opened the back door and entered. A quick search confirmed that the place was empty. At the same time I looked out through each window to make sure that nobody had followed me. I was all alone. The lack of any small furniture and personal belongings suggested that the owners had fled so I made myself at home, butterflies still circling inside my stomach.

I began a thorough search of the house, for food, bedding and anything else that might be of benefit to me, but found nothing. I cursed again at having left my food behind, but this wouldn't be the first time I had tasted hunger. Now it was dark and I felt cold and uneasy. Under the lean-to at the back of the house I found what I was looking for, dry firewood. With paper and kindling, I soon had a roaring fire in the kitchen stove.

After closing the window shutters and locking the door, I felt more secure. I filled an old pan with water and let it boil to make a drink that I swore I would never, ever drink again once I was free - German ersatz coffee. It was the only item remotely useful that I had found in the kitchen. Using my ammo pack as a pillow, I settled down on the wooden floor and nursed my coffee. It still tasted awful but at least it was hot.

The following morning I awoke early, eager for the daylight and to be on the move. After a final cup of ersatz, I picked up my belongings and once outside, I made my way back along the track to rejoin the road. As I neared the junction I saw movement, a platoon of German soldiers heading away from the American lines. I ducked out of sight and waited till they passed. To my right ran a wall and trench that disappeared into a wooded area. To my left, a similar wall stretched across open fields. Behind, from whence I had come, the track curved as it twisted between the trees of a thicket. I slung my beloved machine-gun securely over my shoulder, checked my rifle and moved to the right, into the ditch and behind the stone wall. I soon found what I was looking for, an ideal gap in the stones with a commanding view of the road,... and waited but I didn't have to wait long. Seven more German troops walked into view, hurrying by in the same direction as their comrades. This was too good an opportunity to miss. I altered the range, stuck my rifle through the hole and took aim. Bang! One fell as I released another bullet. Bang! The second dropped onto the road. The remaining five fell to the ground or ran for cover. Bang! Another failed to make the relative safety of a nearby house and fell forward. Four left.

Returning fire caused me to withdraw my rifle and remain hidden as I leaned back against the wall. But I needn't have worried for the troops were firing wildly, still uncertain as to where my deadly fire was coming from. By now, the few refugees had scattered amid screams and panic. My position was still secure. Cautiously, I turned and looked through the gap and decided to risk another shot. I could see two firing from where they lay. They were not an easy target as they faced me, but through the scope I knew I could do it. Bang! The shot missed, but I saw the bullet ricochet as it hit the road just to the side of the figure. Bang! I fired again. His head went down, he stopped firing. I knew I had hit him but at a price for I had been spotted. Bullets began smashing into the wall. For the last time I took careful aim and Bang! I fired at the remaining figure on the road. It only took the one shot before he too lay silent. The troops were probably young and inexperienced but they were still German. Five kills was enough. I withdrew as hurriedly as I could, running along the ditch towards the wood as sporadic firing continued. I kept moving as quickly as I could in case the two remaining soldiers gave chase, although I suspected they wouldn't. Adrenalin surged through my body with the thrill of the danger, an experience that I had never known before. This was totally unlike my first kill in 1940 which had left me shaken and feeling physically sick, This had pleased me like nothing else I had experienced in my life. A feeling of joy enveloped me as I justified my actions as virtuous retribution, vengeance on behalf of prisoners everywhere and, more importantly, my payback.

I was overjoyed with my sniper's rifle, I felt empowered. Had I been issued with such a weapon in 1940, I felt sure I could have won the bloody war single-handed.

I followed the general direction of the road from a safe distance, within the protection of the woods. By now I was ravenous and desperate to find food. There were only two alternatives, for I was not prepared to scavenge for raw vegetables again. They were; finding a likely house and taking some, probably at gunpoint, or retracing my steps and walking back to the safety of the American lines. I had been lucky in as much as I had escaped after engaging the enemy without consequences. It was certainly safer to return, and by the time I had recalled the warmth of the elderly couple's house and bed, I had made up my mind. I argued that once back at the American village, I could replenish my food supplies and ammunition and return to 'hunt the Hun'.

It was still morning, and I estimated that I could be back soon after nightfall, so I turned and retraced my steps. Occasional breaks in the trees showed me there was still much activity on the road, but all civilian. I was eager to avoid coming face-to-face with the two survivors of my earlier confrontation but assumed they would have gone by now, so I decided to join the road. Nobody seemed to take any notice of the lone, ragged individual who joined their ranks, for all seemed too engrossed in their own misery. With German boots and weapons and a cape covering my barely recognisable British greatcoat, I was not challenged. I now made quicker progress and before too long, past the junction where I had ambushed the troops earlier. Blood stained the ice-covered road in several places and tracks led to an adjacent house. Although I could see no sign of the survivors, I kept my head down and hurried on. The muscles in my face tensed as I half expected a voice to call out 'halt!', but it never came.

Once free of the hamlet I made good progress. I overtook pathetic groups of elderly and young alike, carrying their most precious worldly goods in suitcases, hand-drawn sledges, prams and carts. No-one spoke. A British Typhoon, flying low over the treetops, suddenly burst into view. Panic ensued and people scattered to the road sides, but it was too late. The plane was upon us and luckily passed without raining death and destruction into our midst. Flying so low, the pilot must have easily identified the civilians for what they were - or he had another more pressing goal.

It was the unmistakable sound of jackboots marching in step that alerted me. I had failed to notice the squad of German troops heading towards me. There were civilians in front and around and I quickly moved to the right-hand side of the road, burying myself amongst them. My heart was racing once more and I feared for the worst. Slowly, I readied my Schmeisser, which was hanging across my chest, my finger on the trigger. People moved aside to allow the soldiers to pass unhindered, and within seconds they were upon us. From the corner of my eye I watched them pass, the first row, second, third. Their passing took forever as they marched on past, eyes focused ahead. They were all boys and old men, Hitler's desperate scraping from the last rotten barrel to be flung at the advancing Russians, probably destined to die during the remaining weeks of their lost war. As the last rows approached, I sensed the eyes of one of their number staring at me. Inadvertently, I met his gaze. He could have been no more than fourteen. Every fibre in my body tensed.

"Calm, calm, stay calm Dennis," I muttered to myself.

He drew level and stared at me as we passed each other. My blank expression gave nothing away. Did he realise who I was? If he smelt my fear through the stench of my clothes, then I would be in trouble. The column had almost passed. I prepared to dive for cover whilst listening intently for any break in the rhythmic sound of their footsteps. I counted every step as they disappeared down the road. My intestines were in knots. I turned round and heaved a huge sigh of relief. They had gone. I left the road and hid behind a shed. My hands were shaking. I slid to the ground and sat there a while, recovering before rejoining the road to continue my journey, but this time I stayed alert.

As the day wore on, I could hear the boom of occasional explosions behind me. Everyone jumped but continued onwards; they were all used to the noise of war by now.

Night approached and the column of refugees started to thin out as some looked for shelter wherever they could find it, but I kept moving, eager to return to the allied lines, the warmth and, more importantly, the food. After walking for five or six hours through darkness, I felt that I should have made contact with the Americans again and was beginning to worry that I had somehow lost my way. Sounds of artillery and gun fire often shattered the otherwise quiet countryside. On the horizon I could see the glow of destructive flames as they consumed whatever lay in their path. I was nervous, and in my isolation I felt uneasy. As I approached a bend in the road, I saw the twinkle of lights ahead and knew that I had reached the village. Cautiously, I walked forward in the centre of the road with my arms raised as I didn't want to be mistaken for the enemy and shot. I need not have worried for the Americans seemed still to ignore the necessity to place sentries. All seemed quiet and peaceful, almost surreal, as I walked on past the sleeping Yanks towards the centre. Only one lone American acknowledged me.

"Hold up there buddy, not so fast." He held his rifle at the ready. I turned towards him with my arms outstretched and smiled.

"Hi buddy, back so soon?"

I shook his hand, pleased to be back.

"Yer, I lost all my food. I'm starving, otherwise I wouldn't have come back so soon."

"Better come inside, got a coffee pot on the go if you could do with a cup?"

Inside, their billet was warm and inviting. With his thumb, he indicated to his comrade.

"Look who I found strolling into town, our limey friend returning from his little war. Can you take the watch now, I need to warm up."

His friend nodded in recognition, picked up his rifle and lazily ambled to the door. My friendly GI poured us both a cup and offered me the obligatory cigarette, for which I was happy to take.

"You like a hot dog?"

At first, I hadn't a clue what he meant until I saw the bread roll and sausage sitting in the pan on the hot stove. He didn't have to ask me twice.

We talked about where I had been but I kept the details vague for some reason unbeknown to me before I took my leave.

"I need to get some sleep, it's been a long day."

I thanked him and left with a passing goodbye to the American who stood at the entrance, intent on smoking himself to an early grave.

I easily found the cottage where my newly-acquired comrades were billeted and knocked on the door. I knocked again before hearing the bolt slide back and the door cautiously open. The elderly man was still there and I let myself in. He made no attempt to stop me. The whole house was quiet, and not wanting to disturb anyone I told the old man to leave me and made my way to the kitchen. The range fire had gone out, but warmth still radiated from its dying embers. With food in my belly, I lay on the floor and soon fell into a deep and contented sleep.

I was awoken by the old man tending to the fire. Reluctantly, I arose and went upstairs in search for the others.

"Wakey wakey!" I bellowed as I entered the first bedroom.

Bodies reluctantly stirred until they saw that it was me, whereupon I was greeted warmly, even though I had only been gone a couple of days. We all went downstairs and were soon joined by the others, where upon I was subjected to a barrage of questions.

"Well Den, have you won the war? Is it over?"

"Where have you been, what did you see?"

"Did you find your Germans?"

It was strange. Although I was back and wanted to talk to the men, once again, I had no desire to tell them what I had done, so I omitted the gory details.

After breakfast we left the cottage and spent the morning wandering the streets which were becoming increasingly free of snow. We were enjoying our newly-found freedom and wherever we met the Americans, we stopped and chatted to them with an increasing confidence. As uncompassionate as they at first appeared, their generosity showed no bounds as they continued to hand over food and ciggies as if desperate to be rid of them. They appeared to possess unlimited supplies of their 'C' rations; fabulously rich gourmet meals the like of which we had not seen in our lifetime. There were tins of meat, beans and stews with the name 'McConikies' stamped proudly on the sides and other delicious recipes, and unimaginable sweet biscuits and what they called candy, but we knew simply as sweets. They gave us packs of a concentrated beverage powder, along with packets of gum, but it was their strong Chesterfield cigarettes and real coffee, both of which we craved for and those particular commodities, courtesy of the US military, appeared inexhaustible.

Then came the most luxurious, self-indulgent item of all - toilet paper. Not the torn up sheets of newspaper that was in common usage at home, nor the nonabsorbent crinkly paper, but a softer, more wonderful American toilet tissue that felt as soft as a rabbit's ear.

What a difference the last few days had made to our lives. We now had freedom and security, a full belly, cigarettes in abundance and toilet paper, things that until recently we could only dream of. Life surely couldn't get much better. It all seemed so decadent.

We ended up at the American's billet and asked to speak to their officer who seemed pleasant enough (for an officer). We saluted and stood to attention.

"At ease men, what can I do for you?"

"Could you help us please? Have you heard from anybody as to what we PoWs are meant to do now?"

"Yer! all we really want to know is how do we get home to England.?"

"I haven't been told anything about that," replied the fresh faced Lieutenant, "but if you like, I will ask a few questions at company command and get back to you. Come back later today and I'll let you know."

"Thank you sir." We saluted and left.

After our American supplied lunch that our recently over worked stomachs could barely cope with, we walked back to our billet and reluctant hosts.

We had left the bulk of our firearms and ammunition in one of the bedrooms and locked the door, with strict instructions to the owners that they were not to enter. After a brief consultation we decided on a tour of the village, combining some sight-seeing with a search for any 'square heads' who might still be in hiding. As we walked down a cobbled street towards the outskirts of the town, I was several yards ahead of the others with my beloved Schmeisser at the ready. I felt good for I had come through. I was not hungry, I was no longer cold and I was no longer afraid. However, as I reflected on my great fortune at having survived, my smouldering anger had not fully abated. We approached a junction with a side road running off to the right. As I neared the blind turning, I could hear shouts and a disturbance of sorts, followed by the sound of people running. As to how many they numbered I could not be sure - more than two was my nearest guess. I knew they were not American troops because of the unmistakable sound of their studded boots on the cobble stones. The Americans had rubber soles and this was a sound that I knew only too well. The sound of German jackboots.

I moved to the right-hand side of the road and with my Schmeisser at the ready, I crept forward. I signalled to the others, who were still several paces behind, that there was trouble off to the right. By now, I was at the junction of the two roads. I looked up, and for some reason my eyes travelled up the side of the corner building on my right. I noted that it had suffered superficial damage, probably caused by small arms fire and shrapnel, the first that I had seen in this peaceful town. I jumped to the right, pushing my back flat against the wall. By now the running sound was very close. Such was the thumping

549

of my heart it seemed that I was in danger of alerting my quarry to my presence. Now was the time for me to act. I stepped forward and released the safety catch before raising my weapon into a firing position. I turned to face my nemesis, before stepping away from the protection offered by the building and out into the road.

There they were, four of them only yards away.

Instinctively, in that same split second, my finger squeezed the trigger and I fired, releasing a torrent of withering death. I did not relax my trigger finger until the whole magazine was empty. If the runners had been German civilians, or even children, I could not have stopped what I was doing. By now, I was a spring under pressure that had just been released. My face was a distorted grimace, teeth bared to the world. On the receiving end of my gun were four German soldiers. I fired for what seemed an eternity. In the fantasy world of my vengeful mind I was actually killing every bastard German whom I had ever encountered. Every bastard German who had ever brutalised me and my comrades. Every bastard German who I had ever seen mistreating fellow PoWs. In fact, every bastard German in the whole of bloody Germany. I loved every satisfying, bullet-spitting, bone-shattering, blood-letting second of it. The years of hatred flowed from my brain down through my arm and hand, through my gun and straight into their guts in one, long, satisfying stream of retribution. They died instantly in my devastating volley, cut down in a second. As if in slow motion, I watched their bodies contort and their knees buckle. Like discarded rag dolls, the momentum caused each to tumble forward before hitting the hard cobbles, rolling for what seemed like an eternity until all movement finally ceased.

A heavy silence followed. In that oh-so-brief moment of gratifying retribution it was done. I walked to where the bodies lay, an Officer and three other ranks. Only two were armed, but killing the other unarmed soldiers didn't bother me in the slightest. I stared down at them for half a minute, satisfied with my handiwork, for these four epitomised the stinking German nation whose pernicious cruelty had permeated through Europe for far too long. The senseless brutality that we had encountered had been so unnecessary. The shouting, threats and the rifle butt to encourage compliance, were unnecessary. They stole our dignity and took too many of our young lives. Cold-blooded systematic killing of unarmed PoWs, let alone wholesale murder of millions of innocent civilians, had been committed across this occupied, supposedly civilised continent. Others had been killed indirectly through suicide, like the young British PoW in the winter of 1940-41. Already driven to despair with news from home, his hopeless condition compounded by starvation, cold and hunger, verbal abuse and assaults from the guards, he hung himself from a rafter in the latrine. The tragic circumstances of his young death will forever haunt me.

I shut my eyes to reveal the faces of all those callous guards who had laughed in my face when I had asked for the last puff of their cigarette, watching my reaction as they threw their half-finished smoke onto the frozen ground, crushing it under foot; the face of the guard who had made sure that his half-eaten slice of sausage was offered to his dog in preference to me. So many faces of hateful inhumanity flooded through my consciousness in a kaleidoscopic montage of evil Teutonic apparitions. My head was spinning. I opened my eyes and stared once more at the bodies, two with their faces exposed and two lying face down. More dead Germans, four less of this stinking race. I wanted to laugh, but suddenly I couldn't. As I stood over them, I became aware that my anger was leaving me, flowing from my being, just as the deep crimson blood slowly seeped from under the bodies before me, through the gaps between the cobbles, draining into the cold earth below. Unlike the other killings, seeing these bodies close up made them personal, and now I saw something else. The body of the young soldier who had been my first kill. My mood changed in a heartbeat. The feeling of elation evaporated and was replaced by a slow, deepening sense of sadness. My anger, nurtured over four-and-a-half stinking years as a prisoner of this finished nation, was ebbing away. From that first dreadful killing in the woods to these four, it was all a waste, such a bloody waste. Four-and-a-half years of my life wasted. I had seen so much, too much death and destruction, too much suffering, too much inhuman cruelty, too many bad things, more than any young man should. I paused to breathe.

My fury had evaporated. It was spent. I threw my beloved Schmeisser to the ground next to the four bodies, almost in disgust. That was enough for me. I now knew that it was all over and it was time to go home.

I turned and walked away.

· · · § · · ·

THE FINAL ODYSSEY

9th April 1945

spent another restful night under the snug duvet, only occasionally disturbed by my persistent crotch-munching parasites. Unbeknown to me, that night was to be our last as guests of our elderly German hosts.

Whilst our final breakfast was being prepared, we drank copious amounts of beautiful, smoky smooth coffee and were in serious danger of suffering a caffeine-induced heart attack. Combined with its fitting companion, a Chesterfield cigarette, which we possessed in abundance, we were blissfully unaware that if a heart attack didn't kill us, then lung cancer would almost certainly despatch us. But in these times of limited enlightenment, there was no danger in smoking 60 a day and caffeine had yet to make an appearance on the doctor's radar.

These heaven sent aromas must have been enough to cause our German couple to salivate uncontrollably. Sensing this, and with my attitude towards the Germans mellowing, we shared both food and coffee with them. But the one item that the old man and his wife still refused to share, were the stolen eggs.

During and after breakfast, the Frau kept her pans busy. We ate the last of the bread and although there was a bakery just down the road, like all the other businesses in the village, it was not operating.

We left the house, leaving them to decide what to do with the remainder. Outside, the day was chilly, wet and overcast as we made our way to the American's billet for any information.

What a lovely quiet war they were having. On this occasion, we easily found the white American Officer.

"Come in men, I have news for you. Your instructions are to make your way to Brussels Airport. There, you are to present yourselves for repatriation and your flight home."

The prospect of our imminent return home thrilled us and we beamed with delight.

"How do we get to Brussels Airport?" I enquired light-heartedly.

It could have been on the other side of the world for all I knew, but after our death-defying slog across half of Europe, this task had to be a doddle.

The Officer shrugged his shoulders and gave a less helpful reply.

"I've no idea." came the immediate response before continuing.

"But you guys should have no problem hitching a ride. The road's crawling with thousands of supply trucks, moving back and forth from the coast to the front line. Any of them would give you a lift in that general direction."

Life can be uncertain, and not wanting to subject my stomach to any more deprivation we scrounged more supplies before leaving the Americans for the last time and thanking them all for their help.

With patches of snow still clinging stubbornly to the wet earth, we abandoned our firearms, collected our few belongings from our lodgings and prepared for the last leg of our journey, across newly-occupied Germany to liberated Belgium and finally onwards to home.

The American Officer was true to his word, and by early afternoon we had secured our first lift, in the back of an American army supply truck on the wet open roads. At times our journey was definitely not as the proverbial crow flies, but a rather torturous zig-zagging route. It soon proved impossible to scrounge a lift whilst journeying in such a large group. Gradually we split up into smaller and smaller groups until 'we' became one, me on my own once more. This didn't bother me at all. In fact, I found it quicker to cadge a lift and easier to scrounge additional supplies on my own. I was still painfully thin, probably seven stone, but I was now a very well fed scarecrow, which must have been satisfying for my still irritating parasitic travelling companions, now getting fat on this new intake of rich nutrients.

The American drivers were a friendly bunch on the whole. I soon came to realise that every supply driver appeared to have 'secured' an abundant quantity of liberated produce, be it from the enemy or their own army, which they shared generously. Contraband and looted alcohol in the form of beers, wines and champagne by the case load seemed to be forever on tap. I was not interested in the alcohol but I did happily chain-smoke all the way from the River Elbe to Brussels. The British drivers were equally engaging, but it was evident from the start just how few supplies they had to share by comparison with their richer American counterparts and I often found myself sharing my Chesterfields with the British drivers.

During the week to ten days that it took me to passage, I saw for myself the destruction that war inevitably brings to families, property and vehicles alike. We always attempted to skirt round the major towns and cities where the damage was most intense, but often it was unavoidable. I was then able to witness first hand the total devastation of these centres of population. There were eerie skeletal remains of tall buildings surrounded by rubble, standing like whale bones on a barren shore or gravestones on clear fields, silhouetted against a troubled sky. Attempts had been made to clear the roads of debris by the civilian population working together, the worker ants, collecting piles of broken bricks in wheel barrows or hand carts and then stacking the reclaimed bricks in preparation for the massive reconstruction that would eventually follow. Roadblocks diverted us away from the worst areas where the devastation caused by the justifiable allied carpet bombing or vengeful Germans would have slowed our progress to a snail's pace. Even in the small towns it was impossible to avoid the carnage littering the highways. One could not help be shocked by the almost total ruination of Europe.

As the hours drifted by, I grew more silent. With my grubby hand, I wiped away the fog of condensation from the window and stared out into the late winter gloom. I became mesmerised by the vast convoys of heavily-laden supplies heading east. They seemed never-ending.

As the Allies prepared for this invasion of Europe, the British Isles, standing alone on the western edge of Europe, had become a vast arsenal and food depot. Ever since D-Day, its doors had been flung open, spilling its contents across the Channel in an unfaltering flood of resources.

I slept wherever and whenever I could, often in the trucks whilst being driven through the grey, depressing landscape or at supply depots on route.

One rare sunny afternoon, whilst sitting in the passenger seat of another British truck, I finally arrived at the gates of Brussels Airport. The complex was huge. Having never seen a working airport before, the sheer size of the place left me aghast. As soon as it had fallen into allied hands, I suspected it had rapidly expanded to receive the unimaginably vast supplies of ordnance that were required to sustain the Allies in their final victorious thrust to end this war.

As we approached the security barriers on the perimeter, we were waved through on a quick visual inspection without stopping. The whole complex appeared as one huge car park. A myriad of bombers and American Dakota 54 cargo aircraft, the workhorse of the armed forces, littered the sprawling air base, bearing the alternate white and black striped markings of the D-Day invasion to distinguish them as allied aircraft. Around the edge of the runways, military trucks swarmed over the ground, from plane to warehouse and from warehouse eastward, like a giant swarm of bees delivering precious nectar to the newly-acquired hive of Europe. Some were in neat, straight lines whilst others scurried around seemingly without purpose.

My driver brought his truck to a sudden halt amongst a collection of others, adjacent to one of the warehouses, awaiting another load. I thanked him for the ride before jumping down onto the tarmac.

"Good luck mate," he cheerfully called out in a broad London accent as I slammed the door shut.

I looked around me, slightly bewildered, trying to fathom out where I should report to as I scratched, just a little reminder that I still had my lousy companions with me. After searching and questioning, I discovered a British Lieutenant who looked as young and as clean as a new-born baby. He emerged from a hut. The Officer was able to semi-officially update me, informing me that at present there was little organisation in place for the repatriation of allied prisoners and so it was left to each individual to negotiate directly with the pilots of the Dakotas for a lift home.

"Have you had any food yet?" he enquired kindly.

Having learnt never to pass up the opportunity of a meal, I replied in the negative.

"Pretty hungry though sir."

"See the low building next to the hangar on the right," pointing with his clipboard, "that's the NAAFI. They will sort you out."

"Thank you sir." With that, I saluted and went on my way.

Inside was bedlam, with noise levels to match. I was not used to such crowds of seemingly happy, boisterous people. The majority seemed to be American airmen, complete with pencil-thin moustaches. Almost to a man, they wore leather flying jackets and peaked caps at a jaunty angle, à la mode Hollywood film stars. Although I felt embarrassingly out of place in my tatty, filthy rags, it was still recognisable as a British uniform. I collected a plate of scrambled eggs of the powdered variety, sausages and beans and bread, all washed down with the most truly amazing drink that I had ever tasted, a mug of beautiful English tea with milk and loads of sugar, my first for five long years.

I joined a group of similarly scruffy individuals, a mix of Army and Air Force ex-PoWs, who I soon learnt had made the same deadly trek across northern Poland and Germany. I felt pity for them for they all looked to be in a dreadfully sorry state, until I realised that as yet I had not seen a reflection of myself in a mirror, and probably, I had fared no better.

"Hello chaps, mind if I join you?" I asked timidly, but eager for company.

They all looked up and instantly recognised a fellow sufferer of the Nazi state system, one of them. I smiled a warm greeting that only comes from men who have shared a common hell. Their bony backsides shuffled along the bench to make room for one of their own. The nearest man extended his hand.

"I'm Chas, have you just arrived?"

I took hold of his hand and noticed his blackened fingertips. Frost-bite was a common affliction amongst the survivors of the death march.

"Yes, just now. I'm Dennis, pleased to meet you lot."

A cacophony of names assaulted my ears and hands were waved all about me. I quickly acknowledged the occupants at the table before taking my seat.

"Where were you held mate?" was the first of a succession of questions.

"Stalag XXA briefly in 1940, before transferring to XXB."

There then followed an hour or so of talk that flowed easily between us as each shared brief highlights from their own tragedies. As each finished eating, cigarettes were lit, adding to the white fog that hung like a false ceiling above our heads whilst endless mugs of tea were brought to the table. I was eager to learn how to get back home as quickly as possible and I sought to share what information they had, but I was soon disappointed. Brussels Airport was the magnet for every British PoW and each man was expected to find his own seat or space on any aircraft heading for England. Availability was limited and competition was intense. Consequently, every time a plane landed the men would flock towards it like vultures to a carcass.

During the following week, I saw hundreds of flights come and go on their taxi run, back and forth to England. Thousands of tons of supplies were being landed from these winged transporters, which turned round as soon as they had been refuelled to continue with their relentless shuttle service. I would spend each day searching out the pilots and every time ask the same question.

"Excuse me, are you flying to England? Could I scrounge a lift please?"

Every day, my enquiry was met with the same answer.

"Sorry mate, full load."

Often they would try to help by identifying an aircraft they knew was leaving shortly by its number and we would rush off to find it. After several days of fruitless searching, I became increasingly disappointed that our government could not have put more effort into arranging for their PoWs to be repatriated. Abandoned at Dunkirk, and now, after five long years in captivity in appalling conditions, and a death march across Europe through atrocious winter weather, it all seemed so unfair. There was no welcoming committee or co-ordinated services simply to organise our transportation home. As individuals we could all have been forgiven for feeling that Britain had abandoned us yet again, but to be generous, in the grander scheme of things it had to be assumed that the military authorities were still focusing on the ongoing war and had not yet the structural resources in place to see to our needs.

After trying for almost a week to catch a flight and having been rejected for the umpteenth time, I leant back against a wall and lit another Chesterfield, blowing smoke rings up into the sky whilst doing what I did best, waiting.

My eyes drifted to my right and came to rest upon a nearby aircraft sitting on the runway with its doors open. From across the tarmac, I saw what was to me, a familiar sight. A German army dispatch rider's motorbike approached the craft but was ridden by an American soldier. He drew up alongside, dismounted, walked to the open cargo doors and pulled out two large planks of wood to form a ramp. This done, he released the throttle and drove the bike noisily up into the body of the aircraft. Although thousands of tons of supplies were being flown into Europe on the Dakotas, it appeared that equally, tons of looted booty, such as this motorbike, were being airlifted back. It was amusing to see that the entrepreneurial spirit of so many individuals had not been forgotten in any way by this inconvenient little war. I smiled and wished that I had taken more than the small items that were hidden in the inside pockets of my army greatcoat.

The following day was a fine spring morning. After a week of trying to emerge from behind a barricade of grey, rain-laden clouds, the sun shone down. It was a glorious day, and to top it all I found a pilot who finally said "yes".

"We are just leaving, so make it quick. Find a space in the back."

I was going home. With mounting excitement, I boarded the aircraft through the open side door just behind the main wing. As I placed my foot onto the single metal step, I pulled myself up and into the Dakota. Inside, I was greeted by a gathering of forty other lucky Brits. There were no seats inside as this was purely a transport aircraft. In the middle of the floor was a large rectangular opening. I assumed this was for parachuting supplies where no landing was possible. I nodded a casual greeting to those nearby and made myself as comfortable as possible by sitting on some of the small wooden crates that lined the sides of the fuselage, waiting patiently for departure with increasing anticipation. Eventually, the pilot appeared and closed the side door before returning to his cockpit in preparation for the off. I spoke to the scruffy soldier next to me. Unlike me, he had been a prisoner in Germany itself and not had to endure the long, murderous march that had resulted in the death of many of my fellows. Our brief conversation was interrupted by the deafening noise of the twin engines coughing and spluttering into life. One after the other, they finally caught and exploded into action before settling down to a smoother rhythm. Without further ado, the aircraft crept forward, turning and moving into position for take-off. The metal bird was rattling and vibrating so loudly that it felt as if its rivets would be shaken free from their holes. This was going to be anything but a smooth ride.

After taxiing to the main runway, there was a brief pause before we began to speed down its length. For some mechanical reason the drop hole in the floor remained open, and through it I was able to watch as the ground raced by until it became a blur. Slowly, we bumped and then rose into the air. We were off. A whirring noise followed by a dull thud could be heard as the wheels raised themselves into the wing space behind the engines. Once airborne, I watched as the ground fell away, causing me to smile like an overjoyed child, for this was my inaugural flight. I had dreamt of such an occasion since I was a child, obsessed with the heroic activities of the biplane pilots of World War I.

Slowly we gained height and I was loving it.

Because of the aircraft noise conversation was all but impossible, so I sat back and enjoyed the ride. With the open door it rapidly became bitterly cold inside the Dakota, but having spent the winter months marching and then shuffling across the snow-covered wastes of eastern Europe, I was used to being cold. As if the person next to me could read my mind, he verbalised my thoughts exactly.

"I feel on the warm side of death."

I pulled my greatcoat snugly round my body and lifted my collar around my neck, still relishing the ride. Our speed was not great, but all too soon we left war-ravaged mainland Europe behind as one of the passengers pointed out the beaches of Dunkirk. How strange it felt to be flying over those same beaches again, where my ordeal began all those years ago, and were now heralding its ending.

We crossed the English Channel, skimming over the sea. I watched the choppy waters and white horses race past in a blur. Once more I buried myself in my thoughts, recalling events that had befallen me during my internment, the pain, the cold, the suffering, the cruelty, the fear. Then speculating about my imminent return home.

Within no time of leaving the French coast I was jolted out of my reflective contemplation by a shout from one of the passengers as he stood in the front of the aircraft.

"There, look, over there! I can see the white cliffs of Dover!"

Instantly, we all jumped up and rushed forward towards the nose of the aircraft, eager to catch sight through the pilot's windscreen of the famous landmark that heralded our return. Suddenly, without warning, the tail shot up and the nose of the aircraft dipped down, just as I caught my first glimpse of Old Blighty. The whine of the aircraft suddenly changed as we began to nose-dive and bank steeply towards the distinguished cliffs and grey-looking sea.

"For f***'s sake get back, get back will you, get the hell back!" screamed the agitated American pilot.

With all forty of us rushing forward, the Dakota had instantly become unbalanced. To a man, we rushed back to our boxes, assuming that none of us wanted to make a closer inspection of those cliffs.

The plane responded to the pilot's will and righted itself, signalling the ending of our little emergency. We cast a collective sigh of relief as our eyes scoured the aircraft, catching the attention of anybody whilst exchanging smiles of relief. Embarrassed laughter followed.

We landed with a bump, braked and rolled along the full length of the runway before coming to a halt at an RAF station near Wotton Underwood, a few miles from Aylesbury in Buckinghamshire.

Dennis Henry Minter, raw recruit, young soldier of misfortune and ex-PoW, had finally come home.

· · · § · · ·

SWEET
ENGLAND

21st April 1945

The passenger door opened. I stood up and walked, unsteadily at first, and joined the queue eagerly waiting to clamber out. I reached the door and stood with my head outside, breathing the wonderful sweet air of freedom. At long last, my beloved homeland.

During my darkest hours, there had been occasions, too numerous to mention, when I thought that I would never see England again. I cast appreciative eyes around the aerodrome, savouring my first breathtaking views of my homeland, as I stood on the threshold of the aircraft. I needed this brief moment of contemplation to fully appreciate my deliverance from the hell from whence I had come, a spiritual moment that I could not share with anyone, my moment and mine alone.

Oblivious to those behind me patiently waiting, and to their consternation, I stood, blocking their exit. Finally, my epiphany passed. I jumped down to be met by a group of RAF personnel that had gathered around the plane's door. At first I thought they were the welcoming committee, but soon learnt otherwise. As I passed each of them, they all asked variations of the same question.

"Have you got any Lugers, Nazi Daggers, flags, medals?"

That's when it hit me. What was probably the best currency in peacetime England? Luger pistols. Bugger! I had none. If only I had filled my bag and pockets with the stockpile of weaponry and pistols

I saw in the village occupied by the black American Reconnaissance Unit. If only. I shook my head at a missed golden opportunity.

"Sorry, I have nothing," were the only words that I could muster as I followed our procession of liberated souls, like sheep. If only I hadn't been understandably preoccupied with food and cigarettes, been a bit more forward-thinking, I could have made a small fortune. It was unlike me to have missed such an opportunity to make some money, but, in my defence, it spoke volumes about my lamentable state of mind.

As I walked away, I searched for a cigarette, thrusting my hands deep inside my greatcoat pockets, feeling something hard and cold. I took hold of it, half withdrew it before realising what it was: the small Italian pistol that had taken my fancy some two weeks earlier. Having pocketed it, I had thought no more about it until now. It was only a .22mm hand gun, but it was very neat. The trigger mechanism folded up into the body of the pistol for easy concealment in one's clothing whilst allowing easy release when firing was required. However nice as it was, it wasn't a Luger.

> As such, the pistol was to remain one of my PoW mementos marking my years in captivity, thereby gathering dust in a bottom drawer for half a century. I was to re-discover the pistol some fifty-seven years later, hidden in a box in the shed of my garden. At that time the police were holding one of their many firearms amnesties, so like a model citizen, I took the antiquated pistol to my local police station at Woking. Now I wish that I hadn't bothered, for it has done nothing to combat the spiralling gun crime that plagues our society today.

We climbed aboard our waiting Bedford army truck, out through the gates past the armed sentry and out onto the beautifully quiet, winding roads. Save for the occasional trucks heading for the airbase, weighed down with much-needed supplies destined for Europe, the country lanes were quiet. Early spring sunshine bathed the fresh countryside that was looking better than I could ever recall. The budding green leaves of springtime were forcing their way through whilst early cherry blossom was tossed onto the breeze, causing a floral snowstorm. Mass clusters of daffodils waved at us as we sped past and so delighted me, I struggled to hold back the tears. I couldn't recall a time in my short life before this war when my country had looked so wonderful. We were driven to a large army camp some thirty minutes away. As we drove up to the barrier, I looked out and saw row upon row of half cylindrical, corrugated iron military Nissen huts on the other side of the barbed wire enclosure. At the entrance, the paperwork was examined before we were allowed through the gate and onwards into the camp. The truck pulled up in front of a small collection of buildings where a surly little Corporal stood watching our arrival. As we disembarked, I was forced to accept the worrying realisation that Hitler had not yet been eliminated but had somehow been transported and relocated back to my new home in the guise of this jumped up little tyrant of an NCO. He immediately launched into aggressive army mode, barking orders that were reminiscent of the meanest guards that Stalag XXB had to offer. We were marched to a nearby hut, where we waited until, one by one, we were taken inside. When it came to my turn, I was escorted in by our quasi-Nazi NCO and brought to attention before two Officers seated behind the desk. After saluting, I gave my name, rank and serial number. They failed to look up and their utter indifference gradually angered me until I was seething. Stuck up, arrogant, pen-pushing, desk jockey, toffee-nosed bastards. After almost five years away as PoWs, there was no gentle greeting to be had here.

'Welcome back home Minter. I am sorry for I understand that you have had a tough time over there', or something similar would have been nice! Fat chance. Whilst one Officer busied himself with his pen the other began asking me a series of questions. By the tone of his voice, he had probably asked them a thousand times before and it showed. He appeared bored to tears which prompted my anger to bubble and fester just below the surface.

"Name?"

"Dennis Henry Minter, Sir."

"Rank?"

"Private, Sir."

"Number?"

"6093969, Sir."

"Unit?"

"2nd/7th The Queen's Royal Regiment, Sir."

"Where were you captured?"

"Near Dunkirk, Sir."

"When?"

"Not entirely certain, Sir, sometime, early June perhaps, Sir."

"Where were you held as a prisoner of war?"

"Stalag XXB, Marienburg in Poland, Sir."

"Were you required to work by the Germans whilst captive?"

"Yes Sir."

"And what exactly was the nature of the work that you undertook?"

"General labouring." I then went on to list all the differing jobs that I was forced to do. He questioned me in more detail about my work on the railways, noting everything. Other quick questions followed before the final ones.

"Did you bring back any weapons?"

"No, Sir." I lied so easily.

"Any injuries?"

I mentioned my broken arm and contemplating wasting the next hour whilst I bored him with minute details of five years of every ailment that I suffered with from the shits to frostbite and crutch infestation, beatings, starvation,... but decided against wasting my valuable time.

"Are you alright?"

By now, my annoyance and anger had been building and suddenly, that one question threw me and I pondered it for a while. My delay in answering this straightforward enquiry caused him to raise his head for the very first time and acknowledge me. I stared into his cold, disinterested eyes, set above his ever-so-neatly trimmed Hollywood, pencil-thin moustache as he waited impatiently for my reply.

Hmmm! Was I alright? Let's just see a moment, shall we?

I, like so many, was sent to France by you lot, totally unprepared, told to fight without the necessary training or equipment to do the job, abandoned in a foreign war zone by Army Command and the government, starved, deprived of water and held in a moving oven of a train for three days, thrown into a hell hole of an underground hovel in the depths of the worst winter that I had ever known, without adequate clothing and heating, held captive for almost five years without sufficient food or medical care, made to undertake gruelling slave labour for the whole period of my internment,... bullied, beaten, forced to footslog for three months from near the Polish/Russian border into central Germany, across a thousand miles of bleak, freezing, inhospitable land without thought for my wellbeing, watch whilst my fellow PoWs dropped dead around me, made to suffer the indignity of my own filth and lice. Hmmm!... Now let me think,

Sir, am I alright? Am I bloody alright? You must be joking, you uncaring, stuck-up, pompous arse! At that moment, I pictured my fist embedding itself in his clean, skinny, well-chiselled face as I smashed it to a pulp, a picture that brought pleasure to me. My mouth opened to spit out my reply.

"Yes, Sir, fine, Sir" was all I managed!

My self-discipline and natural respect for authority was still intact and amazingly uncompromised. Such was my timidity, I was surprised that I had not actually apologised to the arrogant, pen-pushing bastard for having wasted his time with my trivial presence. I could have kicked myself for my reserve.

The cold interview continued.

"Do you have any German currency?"

"Yes, Sir," I replied.

He held out his hand. Should I shake it? As I didn't immediately respond to this action,, he jiggled his fingers up and down impatiently and looked at me once more. I assumed that he wanted me to hand it over, so I retrieved the notes in my pocket and the ones still hidden in my epaulettes and handed them to him. He unfolded and counted them as his associate noted the Deutsche Reich Marks and Lagergeld.

"You will be compensated for this money later, in pounds," said the Officer after telling me what the current exchange rate was.

I was then dismissed and marched out.

> *'To date, some sixty-five years later, I am still waiting for my money from those at the War Office. I am a patient man but even I might have to accept that I will probably never hear from them. Maybe I will get my reward in heaven?'... Dennis laughed at that point.*

I was billeted with other returnees in a hut that was to be my new home. By now, thousands of us were collecting in transit camps like this for the long, drawn-out process of debriefing. The following day I went before the medical officer. After years of inadequate medical attention and having to survive on starvation rations with only limited nutrients, I felt confident that this was going to be a more thorough assessment of my wellbeing. I entered the officer's hut and stood to attention, awaiting the lengthy examination, preparing to get my kit off and cough, just as I had done when I enlisted. The officer, who was seated in front of me, looked up from his desk and asked me for my rank, name and serial number before uttering the immortal words that I had been asked the previous day.

"Are you alright?"

What could I say?

"Yes, Sir," I simply replied.

With that, he dismissed me. So much for the thorough examination!

To my mind, today's society is smothered in cotton wool and pampered to the point of suffocation.

When we returned home in April after those years in punishing captivity, we receiving no counselling, no particularly gentle understanding and little sympathy from those in overall command and care of us. I believe attitudes may have changed slightly by the time later arrivals returned, but for us, we just had to get on with it as best we could, unlike now.

Today, for example, an employee of any local council might be offered counselling by wet woolly-minded, liberal do-gooders because, he or she befriended an illegal immigrant who had a gay son that was bitten by a homophobic flea from a cat belonging to an indigenous white person!

Or am I being cynical in my old age?'

For the rest of the afternoon, I passed my time smoking, eating, scratching, sleeping, chatting and playing snooker but all the while, I felt rather subdued, bemused and overwhelmed!

I was relieved when the following morning, we were taken to the 'cleansing shed', where we stripped. Since the death march to freedom my clothes had become welded to my body with dirt, sweat and bodily fluids. There was no sadness as they were taken away to be unceremoniously cremated, along with my parasitic companions, the last in a long line of countless generations of blood-sucking cadgers that I had nurtured since my capture. However, it was with dismay when the time came to hand over my old forage cap. Its metal regimental cap badge featuring a horned ram holding a flag had long gone, having been 'liberated' by a German souvenir-hunting soldier shortly after my capture. We had been together constantly throughout my long ordeal, serving as both sun hat and head warmer. Inside, the material was black with years of gathered sweat, grease and grime.

Our cleansing process had finally begun.

After being given a bar of luxurious carbolic soap and shaving equipment, I walked into the hot, communal showers and soaked away the stench of war and captivity. I bathed in the blissful torrent of steaming water, a simple pleasure that could only have been surpassed by my preferred cleansing method of choice, a really decadent, deep, steaming bath. I washed and washed again every weary part of my neglected body until the bar of soap disintegrated.

Then came the finale. Clouds of DDT was puffed over every tiny part, nook, cranny and crevice of my cleansed body, with particular attention being paid to my personal bits and my more congenial armpits, where the eggs of my parasitic companions might still be lurking. Just to make totally sure that none would survive this mass extermination, what was left of my body hair was sprayed with another killing potion. This process was far more gentle and civilised than the delousing house in Poland, but not so hilarious.

Finally, I emerged and went to the basins. God I looked a mess, albeit a thin mess. Slowly, my naked face emerged as my beard disappeared down the plug hole. I stared back at my newly revealed features. The face was obviously mine but it appeared strange as I studied it in fine detail for the first time in an age. It was an older, wiser, a more lined image that stared back at me now. I dried myself and moved to the next room. Time for stage three and a meeting with my stylist. There were two of them. Mine presented himself as a surly cuss, armed menacingly with a trimmer.

"Morning!" I greeting him cheerfully. "I've been away and I'm not familiar with the latest Hollywood style, what would you suggest?"

I received a blank stare by way of a response. This shearer of heads was as uncommunicative as an automaton in an Orwellian factory. I sat and bowed my head as though in servitude to this barber deity and watched as wave after wave of my locks cascaded unceremoniously to the floor. I was a new man, and for the first time in five years I actually felt as clean as a shiny new pin, an apt simile as I was as thin as one. Fortunately, the army saw fit to re-cloth this 'pin' from head to foot and issued me with a brand spanking new uniform, which hid my bony frame.

Now re-clothed, I genuinely felt better. I was shown into my new accommodation block, with fresh beds and bedding so there would be no re-infestation. I had finally said farewell to my blood-sucking, leech-like parasitic creepy crawlers.

The days that followed were luxurious beyond compare. Even though we were still under military discipline, with morning parades, etc., our billet was more like a holiday camp where we were able to relax and return to some sort of normality. Three wonderful hot meals every day in the mess hut were bliss. Maybe somebody did care for us after all.

We idled away our time playing cards, darts, snooker or reading whilst continuing relentlessly with our lifelong ambition - smoking ourselves into premature graves. Conversations often took the form of exchanging stories and recounting experiences whilst in captivity, but for some this was too painful a conversation to have. The door to their particular nightmare was slammed shut, locked, bolted and sealed within their minds forever, as soon as they had touched down on English soil. For many, including me, our real nightmares would manifest themselves later.

Our camp was eleven miles from Aylesbury. So far I had not left its confines, although others had already journeyed unofficially beyond the wire. Initially, I was content to remain within the reassuring boundaries of the camp after years of confinement as a PoW, not yet ready to venture forth because of some as yet undiscovered phobia.

Late one afternoon of our second week, a group from my hut returned to camp full of the joys of spring. Earlier in the day they had decided to walk to town and chose to follow the railway line, assuming that it ran all the way to Aylesbury and was the most direct route. After years of internment and enforced sexual restraint, many of these pent-up young men were hell-bent on finding some action, which roughly translated to drink and girls, but not necessarily in that order. After a mile or so of walking along the line, they came to a junction where a spur line ran off to one side. Choosing to follow the latter they came upon a compound nestling conveniently alongside the track. As they stared through the boundary wire, the lads believed they had finally arrived at heaven's gates for the enclosure was bursting with WACs (The Women's Army Corps). This body of heavenly maidens were employed to re-package equipment and supplies once destined for Europe. The European war was rapidly drawing to its conclusion and it was only a matter of time before Germany's total capitulation. Thousands of tons of ordnance, no longer required on the continent, was stockpiled here. However, the continuing bloody war against the fanatical Japanese was still raging through the Pacific islands and Asian mainland with no imminent cessation in sight. Consequently, these much-needed supplies had to be reassessed for suitability in this tropical environment and re-packed by the WACs before being diverted to the Far East. The presence of WACs so close by was compelling and a discovery of this magnitude could not be contained. That night, word spread like the proverbial pox in a front-line brothel that hundreds of these beautiful, buxom, sex-starved girls were readily available for the picking, begging for super studs like us. So desperate were they that they waited with their groundsheets under their arms 'for the use of'. The reality was a lot less colourful but there may have been a grain of truth somewhere, and by the law of averages somebody might have got lucky with someone, sometime, surely,... wouldn't they?

After hearing this tale, I thought it prudent to see for myself what all the fuss was about. The following afternoon, I overcame my unfamiliar reticence in the ladies department and popped down the line to have a look with a few of the others. Unusually for me, I was not in the mood for sex, even if it was on offer. I simply needed a therapeutic chat with a friendly female before returning back to the comfort of camp. I discovered that promiscuous, unlimited sex was not readily on offer but it was wonderful to socialise with the charming English girls once more. Day after day these jaunts continued, with columns of highly-charged, testosterone-filled lads harbouring massive expectations, who stomped along the granite chippings on their journey to 'heaven's gates'.

~ HOMEWARD BOUND ~

I had been in the camp a while when it all came to an abrupt end. One morning, we were deemed ready, handed our papers and travel vouchers, told to pack our new kit and given our long-awaited home leave. I was delighted to finally be going home, almost five long, unforgettable years to the day since leaving for France at the start of the war on the western front.

We were driven in army trucks to Aylesbury railway station to disperse across the country, making our own separate ways.

How strange it was beginning to feel. Unbeknown to me, my parents had already been informed via a postcard from the War Office in London that I had arrived back safely in England, but they had no idea when they would see me. That time had now arrived.

The extensive war damage suffered by all of London had yet to be fully revealed to me, but enough was evident as I passed along the rail line.

The rail system along with every other building had been constantly targeted by the Germans. The civilian population had suffered terribly, as their ruined houses bore witness. I had to change lines in central London and as I disembarked, the station heaved with people - civilians and servicemen alike. The mood of the population seemed jovial and upbeat, in marked contrast to when I left for France all those memories ago.

I crossed through the large, covered entrance lobby, past walls of sandbags and tape-covered windows before transferring to my connecting train bound for Leatherhead. The train pulled in at nine-thirty in pitch darkness.

With my kit bag slung over my shoulder, I followed the same half mile path that I had trod with my father in January 1940, to where my parents still lived. Inside, no lights were visible but I knew they were home. I walked round the side of the house to the back door and knocked. Soon I heard the sound of footsteps on the stairs and then the door opened. Light flooded out to engulf me. In front of me stood my mother, father and Frank, my younger brother, surprised and shocked. I hardly recognised Frank, the man that stood before me, for the last time I saw him, he was only thirteen. My mother's face shone, whilst a rare smile broke out across my father's face. Mother, with tears welling in her eyes, was the first to speak. She flung her arms around me.

"Oh ducky, you're home."

· · · § · · ·

HOMECOMING

F***ING RULES AND
F***ING REGULATIONS

I had dreamt of hugging my mother,... and of my homecoming for so long, but the reality was that it felt very strange. So much had happened and I had changed, grown up out of all recognition. I felt I no longer belonged.

My sleep was troubled and I awoke in my old bed feeling utterly exhausted. The Army had given me six week's home leave. I had lost so much weight that all my old clothes fell from me as if I was just a hanger. Money was tight and rationing was still very much in force so I continued to wear my new military uniform. After breakfast, my father left for work. Mother and I talked for a while for she was so happy and lively, as I always remembered her to be. Although she had aged, she also looked more frail and I suspected that her health had suffered during my incarceration. I thought no more about it as we revelled in each other's company. I caught up with local gossip and family news, but with regards to all aspects of my ordeal I kept my counsel. It was lovely to see her again and I was glad to be alone with her whilst father was out fighting crime and policing the sedate streets of leafy Surrey.

I stood at the bathroom sink with my top off whilst I washed and shaved. Without warning mother walked in, not realising that I was there. I could see her reflection in the mirror. She looked at my naked back and gasped, quickly covering her mouth with her hand. She was horrified at seeing my emaciated state, with all my ribs showing and without an ounce of fat to hide my bones. She burst into tears and ran from the room. I had already put on a pound since my release, but I still only weighed just over seven stone.

After lunch, I told mother that I was going over to see an old friend of mine, a chap called Bill Mackey. He owned Burvale Farm, off Seven Hills Road in Hersham, close to where I had my digs before the war. My bike was still in the garden shed where I had left it. The lack of dust and cobwebs suggested to me that mother had lovingly nurtured it in anticipation of my safe return. I reflected how little here seemed to have changed, but for me everything was different.

I arrived at Bill's and saw the initial shock on his face as he saw me for the first time since 1940, but his expression quickly turned to one of joy. His big, beaming smile said it all as he welcomed me, as only a great friend can. To see him once more was a tonic.

I spent the following weeks making contact with my old chums and toasting my safe return in our old haunts. On a more sober note, we followed our greeting with a toast to the memory of former friends and relatives who were not as fortunate as me and would never see the end of the war or their loved ones again.

Within two days of my return, my legs started to swell up to such an extent that I could not remove my trousers, so the local GP was called out to examine me. I was delighted when he immediately diagnosed a vitamin deficiency, typical of many PoWs who were now returning home. He simply prescribed a double ration of vitamins to return my strength to normality, which it eventually did.

After several days of inactivity I was bored to distraction and becoming increasingly irritable; readjusting to my old life was difficult. I asked Bill if I could do some work with him, unpaid of course, such was my desperation. He was delighted, and from then on he and I would drive round in his small open van to the outlying business establishments, hospitals and schools collecting swill for his pigs. After years on starvation rations, I was appalled at the waste from people's plates. Once back at the farm, millet was added to the swill and boiled in a cauldron and the resulting concoction smelt absolutely delicious.

One particular morning, Bill turned off the main road to collect from the nearby Burhill Golf Course. As we drove up the long tree-lined drive, we happened upon a group of Italian PoWs who were working on site. They were unguarded, save for the lone efforts of an unarmed civilian 'minder' who was nowhere to be seen. The prisoners had wheeled the large swill bins across the gravel drive ready for collection. Having decided that this was too strenuous to be achieved in one movement, they had chosen to rest, leaving their bins scattered across the drive and blocking our path. Bill was forced to come to a halt. Just to the side, the Italians were sitting back, smoking and bathing in the warmth of the late spring sun. Surprisingly, they made no move to clear the road, forcing Bill to sound his horn.

There was no response.

He repeated his 'honking' twice more but still there was no sign of any co-operation. We could both see one particular Italian muttering conspiratorially to another, a comment clearly aimed at us. I found myself clenching my fists and felt my face redden and my temper rose. The others returned belligerent stares of dumb insolence that I recognised only too well, the stare that simply said 'F*** off'. The lead Italian then jumped up onto a closed bin with his cigarette hanging from his smug mouth. Once settled on his lofty perch, he kicked his heels against the sides of the bin and grinned in a blatant act of defiance. The Italians were now quite content to sit back and watch the stalemate.

By now I was seething and I was unable to control my anger. I simply snapped, feeling a return of the rage that I had last experienced just days after my liberation. I was out of the van like the proverbial 'shit off a shovel', covering the five yards to the insolent Italian soldier in a wink of an eye. Without any hesitation, and in one flowing movement, I mustered all my strength and punched him in the mouth, knocking the mocking smile clean off his smug face and sending his cigarette flying. He fell backwards, landing heavily on the ground whilst the other PoWs sprang into animation, clearing the bins from the road in record time.

The contrast between myself as a PoW and these Italians was all too evident and it outraged me even more. They were free to come and go with minimum civilian security, looked well fed, were given the same food as our troops or better, as stated in the Geneva Convention, paid real money for their labours and had access to English cigarettes, welfare and untold privileges unknown to their British counterparts in the country of their former allies in Nazi-occupied Europe. They were living a life of luxury *in my bloody homeland*.

I managed to restrain myself from killing them all, turned round and walked back to the van only to find Bill laughing uncontrollably with tears streaming down his cheeks. Slowly, I softened, saw the funny side and laughed, but I still felt that anger deep within.

As I climbed back into the van, I heard a voice from behind. I turned to see a man hurrying towards me. The fifty-something-year-old rotund civilian, dressed in a neat but rather small navy suit, confronted me. Having just witnessed the whole heinous crime, this feckless toff just happened to be their 'minder'. In his best BBC accent, he let it be known that he was, as he put it, "very upset indeed with me for striking HIS prisoner-of-war."

"Excuse me,..." I muttered incredulously.

"I want your name and service number."

His foppish voice and manner instantly irritated me.

I was seething as I in turn approached him, my nose only inches from his and my fists clenched tightly, forced against my thighs.

"What for?" I angrily retorted, almost bowling him over with the ferocity of each word.

"You have just struck a PoW, which is strictly against the Geneva Convention, and I demand that you give me your name and number."

"Oh just piss off you f***ing idiot!" I replied angrily. "Where was your f***ing Geneva Convention for me and all the other PoWs for the last five years?"

By now, Bill was unable to breathe through laughter. I, however, was not so amused and was ready to kill again, with this civilian looking increasingly like my next victim. He continued to argue his point and press me for my details again and again. Eventually, for reasons unknown to me, I did give him my name, regiment and number, bidding him to do his worst, for at that precise moment, I couldn't give a damn.

I turned away and walked back to the van, whilst the petty, officious little jobsworth noted my details in his little notebook with his little pencil, to keep his precious little paperwork in order.

Eventually Bill managed to stem his tears of laughter and we were able to collect the discarded food remains but I remained enraged for the remainder of the day. As we drove away I stared menacingly at the Italians, who averted their eyes. Later that evening, as Bill and I relaxed in the pub with a group of locals, we recalled the day's events with increasing hilarity - and in the end even I too sniggered as Bill retold the tale again and again with ever increasing embellishments.

I soon forgot about the ridiculous incident, but early one morning almost a full week later I was painfully reminded of it once more. I was still staying with my parents and my father had just gone off to work, leaving my mother downstairs attending to her household chores. I was upstairs washing and shaving at the time when there came a knock on the door. My mother opened it. Outside were two men dressed in uniform. They were Redcaps, Army police, both wearing side arms. They asked to speak to me and mother called up.

"Son, there are two soldiers here to see you."

Assuming them to be comrades of mine, I ran happily down the stairs, still mopping my face. What I saw instantly wiped the smile from my face. The nearest Redcap addressed me in a stern, monotone voice.

"Private Minter?"

I was initially taken aback but confirmed my name nevertheless.

"You are under arrest. Get dressed and come with us."

I was utterly speechless and returned upstairs, dressing as quickly as I could, wondering what on earth I had done. When I went back down, they were still waiting for me in the hallway. The same Redcap spoke again.

"You are charged with violation of Section blah, blah, blah of the Army blah, blah, blah Code... in that you blah, blah, blah..." And so he went on.

By this time, my mother was becoming increasingly agitated. As for me, I was utterly indignant, almost unable to believe what was happening to me as I was led out and bundled into the back of an open-topped jeep. My poor mother could only stand and watch from the doorstep, crying as I disappeared round the bend in the road. As far as she was concerned, she was losing me all over again and her distress only deepened my sense of outrage and resentment.

We drove the few miles to Dorking, to a church hall that had been taken over by the Army, where I was escorted inside and told to wait my turn amongst a host of other 'Army criminals'. After several hours had elapsed, I was marched into a cold, bleak room that bore the smell of dust and dampness. I came face to face with the military judicial process, to stand trial. A waiting panel of three Officers was seated before me. My crime? 'Striking a prisoner of war in contravention of blah, blah, blah...'

A defending Counsel was appointed by the Court to speak and act on my behalf, which left me wondering how he would have had enough time to prepare my case as the trial was to begin immediately and I had not even spoken to him yet. This was going to be rough justice, Army style. Already, I could feel my anger rise. Fortunately, after a few words were spoken, I was dismissed and left the Court with my defending Officer. Within the hour, I outlined to him exactly what had happened whilst he indicated what would happen next. That done, we returned to commence my trial.

The charge was read to me once more and I was asked for my plea: guilty or not guilty? I saw no reason to deny the charge and responded accordingly, proud as to what I had done but seething with anger once more.

"Guilty."

The facts of my case were stated, questions asked by both the Court and my defence, and my disgruntled answers given. After ten minutes, it was the turn of my defence lawyer to outline the provocation and mitigating circumstances for my actions before his summing up. Details such as *where I had been for the last five years* were offered as an excuse but seemed to be falling on deaf Army Officers' ears. My case was debated and legal arguments pleaded. Claims and contentions passed this way and that. To a certain extent I held my temper, but after half an hour my restraint was wearing thin and I began to swear at given opportunities. For me as a PoW, this 'colourful' language had become commonplace and was now proving difficult to control. Tourette's Syndrome was still waiting to be invented, so I couldn't use that as a valid excuse. Every time I blasphemed, the words "watch your language soldier" were barked at me by the fresh young duty Sergeant.

Finally I could hold my temper no longer. My exasperation boiled over and I exploded. 'Irate' inadequately summed up my mood.

"I have just spent the last five f***ing years of hell as a bloody prisoner of war and I come home to this time-wasting SHIT."

I was ordered to leave the room in no uncertain terms and escorted out by the NCO. I could have sworn he was trying to hide a smile. I counldn't resist one final tirade.

"To hell with you and to hell with your f***ing army," for they were the same officer corps that sent me into battle totally unprepared in the first place and whom I still blamed for the last five wasted years.

The Officers considered their verdict and after several minutes, I was marched back in to hear the senior Officer begin his speech.

"You have been found guilty and you have been awarded..."

Instantly, my mood improved.

"Wow," I thought, that's alright then. They are going to give me some reward. Such was my ignorance of these proceedings, I had ceased to listen and understand.

"... days lost,... royal warrant,...?" the officer continued. "Dismissed."

I was escorted out of Court, followed by my defending Councillor. As I got outside, I turned to him and asked him what it all meant. Apparently it was Army legal jargon which translated to eight days loss of pay. Immediately, my blood pressure hit the ceiling and I was spitting blood. Barely able to control myself, I addressed my defending Officer.

"It's just not right, where's the bloody justice?"

He sympathised but offered nothing in return, except that I could now go.

"And how am I expected to get back home to Leatherhead?"

"That's up to you," was his simple but blunt reply.

Still in a bolshy mood and now not caring what happened to me, I replied.

"In that case, I am not leaving here until some arrangements are made for me to return home."

I could see from the compassionate look on the Officer's face that he was considering my plight.

"Wait here and I will see what I can do," he answered.

I stood kicking my heels and pacing for fifteen minutes whilst trying to calm down, chain smoking as I waited. I had just lit my third cigarette when the Officer returned.

"There is a jeep waiting outside for you to take you back home."

With that, he handed me a carton of cigarettes with a wry smile on his face and shook my hand. He at least had accepted that I was aggrieved. Given my understandable mitigating circumstances, he accepted that I had been treated harshly, but that was the Army and it could often seem blind and insensitive. Rules and regulations. It always boiled down to rules and bloody regulations!

Author: The sole reason that I reveal this episode in this last chapter is simply to highlight the difference between the hell of Dennis' life as a PoW under the Nazis and the comparative soft-handling and gentle touch shown to the axis PoWs held by the British.

True to the Officer's word, I was driven back to Leatherhead.

A few weeks later, my war effectively came to an end amid tumultuous celebrations, the like of which I have never seen before and I doubt I will ever see again.

It was 8th May 1945. VE Day was declared, Victory in Europe. After five seemingly never-ending years, peace had finally returned, but for some reason, I didn't feel the happiness!

· · · § · · ·

CLOSURE

Dennis Minter

lthough I and thousands like me received our campaign medals for serving in Europe *(see picture reference 41)*, our terrible march into captivity, our suffering as PoWs at the hands of the Nazis for five long years and the terrible march of death in 1945 were never acknowledged. There was no recognition of the part played by the 68,000 British men of the BEF, including those who ultimately gave their lives and those who gave their freedom in order to ensure the successful evacuation of so many men, an act that saved Britain from invasion and eventually led to the winning of the war. Recognition that the best years of our young lives had been taken from us because our government had sent us into battle under-trained, under-strength and with outdated 1918 equipment to pitch against the superior German war machine. No bloody recognition of our part, played out of duty and patriotism to save our country, to save our loved ones and to save theirs. No recognition of the bravery and self sacrifice of whole sections of the BEF, epitomised by the heroic stand of the 51st Highland Division and the men who gave their lives. Surely, a simple medal commemorating their sacrifice would have been a cheap but symbolic gesture to say 'thank you for sacrificing your young lives and playing your part'.

To top it all, we suffered financially at the hands of the mean, penny pinching accountants in government, who had played no part in winning the war from the safety of their cosy offices in Whitehall, who deducted from us the so called pay that we had received from the Germans for our slave labours in the form of their utterly worthless Lagergeld.

Mean does not even begin to describe their lack of awareness and any recognition.

I remained a member of the Queen's Regiment, working as a cook until 8th September 1946. It was a cushy little number and with rationing still in force, I employed some of my questionable skills acquired as a PoW. This allowed me to pull off a few lucrative deals with the local hotels, pubs and restaurants, which proved beneficial to both parties. Consequently, I was able to supply my parents and friends with food items that were impossible to acquire with their limited food vouchers. However, when my father found out, he refused to take any more food and ordered me to stop forthwith, an order I found impossible to obey. His reaction was understandable and predictable, for he could never take off his policeman's hat.

It took me a while to find the willingness to return to my shooting club. A warm welcome greeted me when I eventually did and I practised as much as possible, for I loved the sport, increasing my scores and qualifications as the years rolled by.

Not knowing what else to do in terms of employment I successfully re-applied for my old job at Hackbridge *(see picture reference 40)*. Engineering and manufacturing was booming as everything in post war Britain needed to be rebuilt. I returned to the drawing office where I was welcomed back with open arms by the old crowd and heartily thanked them for supporting me during the war. Initially pleased to be back amongst old friends, I found it very difficult to slot back into mundane civilian life.

Over the coming years, I had many stories to tell to a room full of men who had wisely missed 'The Great Adventure', but in my more quiet moments working overtime at my drawing board as the factory slept or when I was alone in my bed, I could see the ghosts of my three work friends who had not been as lucky as I, and not returned to their boards. I would see them turn and walk over to me, each with a cigarette in their mouths and a cup of tea. They would gather round my board. We would laugh... and plan 'The Great Adventure'. Percy Studwick, Peter Birch and Alan Hores - all good, brave young men.

I would cry. I missed them. Behind them were the legions of fellow soldiers and PoWs who had come into my life and shared in the horror and pain of prison life for so long. They had each left footsteps and treasured memories burnt into the very composition of my troubled and often tortured mind. You never quite get over such a horror, you just learn to live with it.

That same year I married my girlfriend, Amy Louisa *(see picture reference 42)*. However, after I married, my 'troubles' began and the trauma of my years in captivity manifested itself in some unpleasant behaviour and an embarrassing series of problems befell me. During the nights, I would get up in my sleep and urinate in the wardrobe, over all the clothes, and in the morning remember nothing about it. It was most upsetting for my new wife, but now I can laugh about it and often do. On other occasions, in my sleep, I would climb out of bed and urinate outside from the bedroom window. On one occasion whilst staying with friends, I removed Amy's shoes from under the bed and urinated in both. Being her only shoes, you can imagine that she was not well pleased. In spite of government guidelines for the mental care of returning PoWs, like other thousands I received no counselling or special treatment and neither did I seek it. It took a long, long time without treatment or help from the Army or Government, for my anti-social habit to stop altogether but I am not sure that my seething bitterness and anger ever did. Some scars go too deep to ever heal.

Amy and I only had one child, Michael, who was born in 1951. He was destined to join the local fire service, where he forged a successful career.
I was eventually demobbed, but my Army connection remained, for like thousands of fellows I was kept in the Army Reserves until my final release on 10th February 1954.

After the war, my dear, sweet mother's health slowly deteriorated. When my father retired, he made them move away from friends and family to a bungalow that he bought in Louvine Avenue, Wickford, Essex. I rarely saw them as travelling on public transport was both expensive, long-winded and laborious, involving a bus journey, five different train journeys and a two-mile walk there and back.

In 1956, dear mother died from her illness. She was only 61.

My father, always a bit of a loner, took the news badly and isolated himself even more. He befriended a couple, Mr. and Mrs. Gobey who lived two doors away. When he died, my father helped his widow with the gardening and odd jobs around the house. Gradually, they became very close, and one day on a family visit, my father took my brother Cyril and I for a walk up the garden and asked us what we would think if he were to marry Mrs. Gobey.

"Dad," I replied, "I know you have been very lonely since mum died and I think you should marry her."

So he did.

On 29th November 1966, my father died at the age of 75. He left £300 for us, his three children.

On 12th June 1984, after thirty-eight years of happy marriage in our house in Cobham, Surrey, my dear wife Amy died of cancer.

A couple of lonely years later I met up with a previous neighbour of mine, a lady by the name of Ruth Osborne, who used to live two doors from me. Ruth was German and a wonderful lady who had married her husband, George Osborne, just after the war in 1946. They met after his release from a PoW camp in Germany. Sadly, George died suddenly of a brain embolism in 1974. Subsequently, Ruth and I became good friends once more. History repeated itself, for like my father before me, I partnered my former neighbour Ruth for another fifteen years of happiness and companionship until her sad demise through cancer in 1997.

As for me, in 2010, I am still alive to tell my soldier's tale. My body is slowly failing me, which really annoys me, but my mind, humour and sense of enjoyment of life are just as active and mischievous as they were seventy years ago. I still drive, work one day a week as a gardener, and on other days I help out at our day centre looking after the 'old folk' - those younger than me. I go dancing at least once a week, love the theatre and socialise as much as humanly possible, and I still have a twinkle in my eye. Not bad for an old boy.

Every morning, as I awake from my slumbers, I still thank God for giving me one more day on this wonderful earth of ours. I have had a good life and met some lovely people along the way. Each day, I have tried to find some means of enjoying every second as if it were my last, with the exception of a few years in the 1940s, of which I have said enough and finally laid to rest.

· · · § · · ·

At 90ish years of age I have survived Dunkirk
it's aftermath and all of life's traumas and dramas
and I am still smiling,...
so make sure you do
for this truly is a wonderful world,
but when it is eventually time for me to meet my maker,
I still won't be ready, so
I will fight Him,
or the devil
for the reluctant possession of my happy soul.

THE END

Every effort has been made to verify all material published in this book.
If the reader discovers any error or glaring omissions in this book,
please contact the author at
email: ghostsofdunkirk@talktalk.net
and he will be only too happy to correct the inaccuracy or add such facts where possible
at the earliest opportunity.

or

To learn more about this book, add your own information or interact
please visit me on **FACEBOOK** at
www.facebook.com/ghostsofdunkirk

A BRIEF OUTLINE OF THE GERMAN'S FORCES AND
BATTLE PLAN - 18th MAY to 5th JUNE 1940

The area around Abancourt, Arras, Vauchelles-les-Quesnoy, Bellancourt and Abbeville:

Overall commander of German Army Group A was Generalfeldmarschall Karl Rudolf Gerd von Rundstedt.

His Panzer Group numbered seven panzer divisions, three motorised divisions, and 35 infantry divisions.

One Korps Commander was

Generaloberst Heinz Guderian who served under General Paul von Kleist of Panzer Group Kleist.

Order of battle (18th May to 21st May 1940)
HQ

1st Panzer Division
2nd Panzer Division
10th Panzer Division
20th (Mot.) Infantry Division
Infantry Regiment Gross-Deutchland
1st SS Division Leibstandarte Adolf Hitler

18th May
Korps Headquarters: Villers-le-Sec

Korps Boundaries: Boundary with XLI Armeekorps; St. Gobert-Neuvillette-Navroy-Gouzeaucourt-Bapaume.

Korps Orders:

2nd Panzer Division will attack from the Origny and Ribemont bridgeheads and capture the crossing points over the Somme. It should also occupy the bridge in St. Quentin by surprise.

2nd Panzer Division captures St. Quentin; it is ordered to seize the Somme crossings at Morcourt.

19 May 1940
Korps Headquarters: St. Marleville

Korps Boundaries: Boundary with XLI Armeekorps; St. Gobert-Neuvillette-Levergies-Gouzeaucourt-Bapaume-Berles-au-Bois-Sombrien-Magnicourt.
Korps Orders:

The Korps will reach the line Fins-Peronne with 1st and 2nd Panzer Divisions. It will then cross the Canal du Nord, establish a bridgehead and continue the attack towards the line Le Mesnil-Clery.

2nd Panzer Division's crossing point will be between Equancourt and Manancourt. After the establishment of the bridgeheads both divisions will advance to Peronne.
Daily Operations:

2nd Panzer Division pushes through Albert to Abbeville.

20 May 1940
Korps Headquarters: Querrieu

Korps Orders: 1st Panzer Division's left boundary will be the Somme. It will capture Amiens at 09.00hrs.

2nd Panzer Division is given Abbeville as its main point of effort.
Daily Operations:

The Korps units cross the Somme. 1st Panzer-Division takes Amiens at 09.00hrs and sets up a bridgehead while the 2nd Panzer-Division takes Abbeville at 19.00hrs and suffers some losses due to enemy bomber attacks.

During the night a battalion of the 2nd Panzer Division breaks through Noyelles and is the first German unit to reach the Atlantic coast. After the capture of Abbeville, the 2nd Panzer Division then turns right and advances north-west. At the end of the day the divisions established bridgeheads at Abbeville, Condefolie, Corbie, Bray and Peronne. The bridges and crossings are prepared for demolition if absolutely necessary but are not blown, since they will be used in the second phase of the French Campaign.

21 May 1940
Korps Headquarters: Querrieu
Korps Daily Operations:
2nd Panzer Division is also on the defensive and covers the line Nievres-Doullens.

28 May 1940
The 1st SS Division Leibstandarte Adolf Hitler was operating in the general area in and around Arras, Beaumetz-les-Loges and Ficheux and were responsible for the murder of French civilians. After their surrender, soldiers from the 2nd Battalion Royal Warwickshire Regiment, the Cheshire Regiment, and Royal Artillery as well as French soldiers in charge of a military depot were taken to a barn in La Plaine au Bois near Wormhout and Esquelbecq. When there were nearly 100 men inside, up to 12 soldiers from the 1st SS Division Leibstandarte SS Adolf Hitler threw stick-grenades into the building. Two groups of five survivors were taken outside and shot in the back as the grenades had failed to kill everyone. A total of 80 men were killed, 15 men were eventually found by a regular German Army unit. Their wounds were treated before they were sent to prisoner of war camps in occupied Europe.
Also operating in the area were the fanatical German 3rd SS Division Totenkopf, attached to Rommel's 7th Panzer Division, who were ready to commitment their first war crime.

17 May 1940: *north and east of Cambrai were the 16,000 French prisoners were captured by the division, including 200 French-Moroccan troops who they executed on the spot.*

27 May 1940: *In the Le Cateau and Cambrai area they were engaged in "mopping up" operations against Allied forces. At Le Paradis village SS-Obersturmführer Fritz Knöchlein unit machine-gunned 97 out of 99 British officers and members of 2nd Battalion of the Royal Norfolks and the 8th Lancashire Fusiliers after they had surrendered. Only two survived their injuries. After the war, Knöchlein was tried by a British Court and convicted for war crimes in 1948. He was sentenced to death and hanged.*
Rommel's 7th Panzer Division became known as the Gespensterdivision, (Ghost Division) because of its rapid movements leading few to know exactly where the division was, including the German High Command. On 15th May he reached Philippeville and continued Westward passing Avesnes and Le Cateau.

21 May, *he reached Arras where he was counter attacked by 2 British Tank Regiments. British tank advance stopped by feared Flak 88 "Tank Killers".*

5 June 1940 *- Positioned near Abbeville.*

Source:
axishistory.com.
François de Lannoy & Josef Charita - Panzertruppen: German armoured troops 1935-1945
David Westwood - The German Army 1939-1945 Vol 1: Higher Formations
Florian K. Rothbrust - Guderian's XIX Panzer Corps and the Battle of France: Breakthrough in the Ardennes May 1940.

THE GENEVA CONVENTION

The principles of the Convention were as follows:

Countries participating in a war are bound to offer nominal medical aid to injured soldiers of either side of the conflict.

People who have surrendered may not be injured further by another side and must be treated humanely.

Those who are not actively engaged in combat cannot be murdered, raped, tortured or mutilated.

Any sentencing of a person accused of crimes must be done before a court.

When possible, armistice or ceasefire should be called in order to collect the dead and wounded, especially after a battle or engagement.

A person from the opposing side should keep a record of an injured soldier's death to be forwarded to the country for which he/she fought.

Establishments for the medical treatment of soldiers should never be attacked.

Primarily these treaties exist so that captured or wounded soldiers can be treated humanely, and without prejudice.

With regard to specific reference to prisoners of war:

PoWs have the right to honour and respect.

Allowed to notify their next of kin and the International Red Cross of their capture.

Allowed to correspond with relatives and to receive relief parcels.

Given adequate food and clothing.

Provided with shelter equivalent to those of their captor's troops.

Given medical care.

Paid for any work they do.

Sent home if seriously ill or wounded provided they agree not to resume active military duties afterwards.

Quickly released and sent home when the war is over.

Prisoners of war must not be:

Forced to give any information except their name, rank and number.

Deprived of money or valuables without a receipt and guaranteed they will be returned at the time of release.

Given individual privileges other than on grounds of health, sex, age or military rank.

Held in close confinement, e.g. solitary confinement, unless they have broken any laws. They can, however, have their freedom restricted for security reasons.

Be forced to do military or dangerous or unhealthy work.

Not all countries signed the Convention, but in 1929 the main players involved in the Second World War who did were:

Australia, Austria, Belgium, Bulgaria, Canada, China, Czechoslovakia, Denmark, Estonia, Finland, France, Germany, Greece, Hungary, Italy, Japan, Latvia, Liechtenstein, Lithuania, the Netherlands, New Zealand, Norway, Poland, Portugal, Romania, the Russian Federation but not the USSR, the Republic of Serbia, Slovakia, Spain, Sweden, Switzerland, the United Kingdom and the United States of America.

From this point on, you will see that for ALL of us who were unfortunate to be captured by the Nazis, the principles of the Convention never lived up to expectations during the troubled times that lay ahead. In the event, it seemed largely non-applicable to PoWs whose countries did sign up to it and completely failed to protect those whose countries didn't.

THE RED CROSS REPORT ON THE INSPECTION OF STALAG XXB
MALBORK (MARIENBURG), 22/23rd NOVEMBER 1940

Source: The Geneva International Red Cross Archives

Camp Commander: Oberst Bollman

Personal status:
The total number of 14,000 men, about 2/3 are French. In addition, 550 Belgians are also housed. The camp has 400 working teams (in the surrounding countryside).

Camp:
Located on Wielbark, a few kilometres south of Malbork, dominates the valley Nogat. The climate seems to be healthy. The camps location is very dry and sandy, situated next to a large pine forests. The camp was opened in August 1940 after the installation and completion of drainage works (sewers).

Accommodation:
The wooden huts are spacious and well furnished: tables and chairs set in a way that offers a lot of free space. The beds bunks are three stories high. Electricity is available to each hut. Heating will later be supplied using tiled stoves. During our visit, not all of the ordered stoves had arrived.

Some barrack huts were built in the Polish way, ie, the floor is about one meter below ground level outside and made of beaten earth. The roof is partially covered with turf. This type of construction, after all, does not cause any inconvenience as the area is very dry and sandy. Soon, these barracks will close. Around them, new, more spacious barracks are under construction now.

Throughout the camp, many fire hydrants are located. In addition, the manual fire extinguishers (buckets of water) are located in each barrack (hut). Each hut is built at a considerable distance from one another, so the risk of fire spreading seems to be minimal.

Food:
Rations are the same as in other camps. Members of the working teams also receive the same allowance as civilian employees. Our delegation interviewed several prisoners. Everyone is happy with the food.

Attire:
The camp has a stock of clothing to allow for worn ones to be replacemed with new ones. This also applies to underwear, with each prisoner having two pairs.

There are no replacement boots in stock. When worn through, they are replaced with wooden clogs, of which the prisoners are happy. Workshops have been created for shoemaker's and sewing.

Canteen (Shop):
The main camp has a canteen. During our visit, the canteen sold:
beer (25 pfennigs), lemonade (20 pfennigs), gherkins, molasses, artificial honey, lemon, toiletries, soap, various brushes, harnesses, etc., at cheap prices.

Hygiene:
Every prisoner who comes to the camp is immediately disinfected (deloused) and may be allowed delousing again if necessary. Thirty to forty people can be disinfected within a half hour. Prisoners use the washroom in a single hut which is not yet fully completed, and which will be heated by two large brick ovens. Two large troughs provide A sufficient amount of hot water which will eventually flow into the cement troughs. Installation of showers should be completed a few days after our visit.

Exercise:
Prisoners can play football and organise matches on Saturday afternoons and Sundays. These groups are very large and well attended.

The sick room:
It is well led by French and British doctors under the supervision of a German military doctor. More serious cases are referred to a military field hospital in the neighbouring town, where the German doctor works, moreover, there are several French physicians there. Tuberculosis cases are sent to a special camp in Tangerhütte.

Intellectual and moral needs:
Mass is celebrated every Sunday by a German priest.

Discipline:
Is provided by several noncommissioned officers (NCOs), both in camp and in the work crews.

Abstractions:
Prisoners who work in the working crews receive from 70 pfennigs to 1 reichsmark each day. The food they receive is good. Those who work in small crews as peasants are particularly well treated, becoming part of the family life and are less supervised. We have encountered several such teams on the road or in the fields, taken by carts or walking to work.

Correspondence:
Prisoner's private parcels are opened and inspected before being sent to the recipients. Collective delivery of the Red Cross parcels are opened and shared in the presence of two representatives of the prisoners.

Attempts to escape:
During these two months 14 prisoners, including two Frenchmen tried to escape. All but two were caught. Those caught were punished, serving for 14 to 21 days in solitary confinement.

Conclusions:
Everything suggests that the conditions in the camp will be perfect.
Food is good and possibly corresponds to the tastes of the prisoners.
Thee prisoners themselves are happy.
In turn, when it comes to clothing, especially underwear, it seems that there are still some shortages.

Paul Glogowski

Authors Note: *There are some inconsistencies between these reports and Dennis' recollections. This is totally understandable. In part possibly due to his inability to accurately recall those events of 70 years ago, but more likely because of the Swiss Red Cross Inspectors inaccurate interpretation of misleading and false evidence presented to them by the German administrators of Stalag XXB.*

THE RED CROSS REPORT ON THE INSPECTION OF STALAG XXB MALBORK (MARIENBURG), 19th SEPTEMBER 1941

Source: The Geneva International Red Cross Archives

This large camp consists of 36 wooden barracks. The neighbourhood is flat, the ground is very sandy and is covered with only a very thin layer of grass. The barracks are built around a wide sports square, about 150 m long and 80 m wide. The camp is surrounded by barbed-wire entanglements, in each corner there is a watchtower. Within the camp there are bedrooms, kitchens, lavatories, canteens, meeting rooms, etc.

This camp, in which the number of prisoners changes constantly, is in fact a Gulag. About 650 working teams operate from it, and the teams are employed on the farms, in factories, road works, etc. The numbers within each work team varies from 5 to 250 people.

Staffing:
9.371 British
8.920 Frenchmen
301 Belgians.
On the day of our visit in the camp there were about 700 British present, among them was a doctor and 6 medical staff.

Camp representative: *C.S.M.J. Fulton, No 14.830*
Camp doctor: *Alexander Lundie, No 318*

Accommodation:
Each hut may house from 20 to 200 people. The prisoners sleep on the wooden 2 storied bunk-beds, each of them has two blankets. All straw mattresses were burned because of the vermin plague which infested the camp. We observed that there is overcrowding with too many prisoners in some huts; we saw a room assigned for 60 people, in which 75 prisoners lived. Each room has 2 wooden tables and 4 benches; we observed that during lunch many prisoners ate standing, due to the lack of seats.

Food:
Meals are prepared by a French cook, who has British helpers as per a request of the British representant. According to what is said by the prisoners, food is of good quality, but of insufficient amount, so the canned food, which the prisoners may receive in parcels from home or the Red Cross, are of great importance. The prisoners have no opportunity to prepare the food individually, for they can only make hot water for their condensed milk and cocoa drinks.

Attire:
The prisoners are lacking in uniforms and shoes. Only half of them have English uniforms, which are mostly in a bad state. The prisoners' representative complained about this and confirmed that his companions are very rarely provided with any replacements. Every prisoner has only one uniform, which is especially bothersome for those who are employed in working parties. We saw that those who returned from these parties had badly worn-out clothing. The same applies to the footwear which is in an equally bad state of repair. The prisoners returning from work parties often had shoes hardly fit for wearing. The prisoners' representative complained that they get neither clothing nor footwear from the camp's reserves and he was not allowed to send those who most desperately needed new clothing to the camp

storehouse. The representatives of the Red Cross, who visited the camp several weeks before us, were assured by the German authorities that this issue will be settled, but until now has not been addressed. The prisoners working in the work groups were supposed to get two uniforms each. The German authorities indicated that about 5,000 English prisoners do not have the English uniform and gave us the number of clothes in the camp's reserves on the 5th of September 1941:

Coats 3,343	Work clothing 2,934
Trousers 1,500	Shoes 2,070
Socks 5,674	Shirts 3,300
Underwear 12,722	Sweater 1,872
Blankets 1,456	Pyjamas 1,014

The German authorities informed us that the prisoners have enough underwear, shirts and socks and are satisfied. We were told by the representative of the prisoners that they wanted to send a British sergeant, who was a tailor, to work in the tailor's workshop. This request was refused.

Canteen (Shop):
The camp has a well supplied canteen, selling all everyday items as well as apple juice, lemons, but there is no beer or fresh vegetables. What is very much requested is shoe polish. The prisoners' representative complained about not receiving requested information about canteen's profits.

Hygiene:
The camp does not have an installation for delousing; such an installation is available in the neighbouring town's field hospital, which is about 30 minutes from the camp. We are told that there are a lot of bedbugs in the camp. The prisoners kill them by burning the mattresses. Even those in the sick room have these bugs. Vermin (such as rats) are annoying, especially in winter. A delousing facility seems to be especially necessary. Cold and hot water is insufficient. However there are still no showers in the camp itself, but they are also in the town's field hospital, which is very inconvenient. The prisoners are allowed a shower every 15 days, more or less. In summer they can bathe in the river.
The number of latrines is also insufficient.

The sick room:
The camp sick room consists of two rooms; there are 17 beds in one, 36 in the second; all were occupied during our visit. They lay on timber bunk beds, which seems to hinder the care for sick, and besides, there are too many sick in each room. Each prisoner has a quilted coverlet sent by the Turkish Red Cross and two bed linen sheets. There seems to be no lack of medications and dressing materials, nevertheless the camp doctor submitted a demand for vitamins, quinine, calcium, tonics of all kinds, condensed milk, as well as dressing materials; also he demanded priority in assigning packages to the sick.
Seriously sick are sent to the field hospital in the neighbouring town, and those in need of surgery are sent to the civil hospital. Most of the sick belong to the work teams, and are most often afflicted with periodontitis (a gum disease that can progress to affect the jaw bones), skin diseases, as well as victims of industrial accidents.
There are neither prisoners unfit for work, nor tuberculotic patients. There haven't been any contagious diseases so far. According to the camp doctor, the overall health condition of the prisoners is satisfactory.

The doctor together with 6 assistant medics are healing their companions.
Only the doctor himself has the right to walk outside the camp area.

Intellectual and moral needs:
The library has only 150 books. A small orchestra and a theatre group are active in
the camp. The groups unfortunately are never complete because of the fact that the
members are often away on the work teams outside the camp. Their board games
are insufficient and the representative of the prisoners made a request about this to
the International Red Cross. The camp has no internal newspaper.
There is no vicar for the Protestant prisoners. One British warrant officer presides
over the prayers every Sunday. Catholics can also participate in the services every
Sunday.

Work:
Most of the prisoners are employed on the farms and work on the roads as well as
working in factories. Some have light work; however some have very hard work.
The prisoners' representative receives many complaints concerning bad treatment,
living quarters and food, etc. Many prisoners are made to work on Sundays without
any equivalent day off during the week. We were able to read a prisoner's letter
addressed to the prisoners' representative:
"There is a lack of drinking water, save the dirty pond in the vicinity, we can't wash
our stuff. Our quarters are in a very bad state and dirty. We have only one blanket
each. There are many vermin, rats and mice. The German soldiers often threaten
us and interfere with our allocation of Red Cross packages".

Reportedly one British prisoner was shot for refusing to work on Sunday.

In another camp the guards were apparently afraid that the prisoners were
escaping and fired over the barracks. As a result, one British soldier was killed
and another badly wounded. During the visit to the field hospital, we met a British
prisoner from the working team, wounded in his chest by his employer.
We want to indicate: 36 British NCOs who refused to work were punished and
locked up for 15 days before our visit, in a little hut surrounded with barbed wire
entanglements situated within the camp. The hut is too small for the 36 persons.
Those prisoners are permitted to read and are allowed to receive half of the
contents of the packages sent by the British Red Cross. They do not receive any
cigarettes, and only in the morning are they allowed to go to the toilet or bathroom.
They are not allowed to communicate with their companions on the other side of
the barbed wire.

Soldier's pay:
All soldier's pay is very irregular and delayed. Every week the representant of the
prisoners receives many complaints.
Also the camp doctor only received his soldier's pay in January, April and July,
that is every three months.

Correspondence:
Almost all prisoners received news from their families. Every person may write
two letters and four post cards per month; this also applies to the members of
the medical staff. Only the doctor can write twice as many. Private packages are
received very irregularly. Every prisoner receives one package a week with 50
cigarettes from the British Red Cross, for which everyone is very grateful.
(Authors note: That was never the case).

Conclusions:

The representative of the prisoners, together with the camp doctor, state that Stalag XXB is a bad camp.

1) *Over 50 % of the British prisoners do not have English uniforms, besides they have only one outfit - this also applies to the members of the work teams.*

2 *Over 50 % have shoes in a very bad state of repair.*

3) *No showers or installation for disinfection are available in the camp.*

4) *The number of beds in the sick room is insufficient.*

5) *The meeting rooms are too small.*

6) *The library is too poor, short of books, there is no football, and there are too small a number of board games.*

7) *The prisoners on the work teams work for too many hours per day.*

8) *Treatment of the prisoners on the work teams is often very bad.*

9) *NCOs were imprisoned because of their refusal to work.*

10) *Soldier's wages are paid irregularly.*

Dr. Schirmer

Authors Note: *There are some inconsistencies between these reports and Dennis' recollections. This is totally understandable. In part possibly due to his inability to accurately recall those events of 70 years ago, but more likely because of the Swiss Red Cross Inspectors inaccurate interpretation of misleading and false evidence presented to them by the German administrators of Stalag XXB.*

· · · § · · ·

THE RED CROSS REPORT ON THE INSPECTION OF STALAG XXB MALBORK (MARIENBURG), 1st MAY 1942

Source: The Geneva International Red Cross Archives

Spokesman of the camp: *the Frenchman Marcel Boruta, No. 21 409*
Belgian: *Robert Duchesne, No. 51 230*

The doctor of the camp: *(French) Adolphe Keller, No. 4078*

The strength of:
French 8331 (of which 664 in the camp)
288 Belgians (of which 62 in the camp)
9729 prisoners (including 850 in the camp)

Sanitary and medical staff:
Doctors - 8 French (one in the camp)
6 Serbs

Members of the medical personnel:
55 French (of which 11 are in the camp)
Two Belgians (of which one is in the camp)
19 Serbs (of which 3 are in the camp)

Number of working teams: *approximately 704*

Location: *See the previous report.*

Accommodation:
The whole camp covers about 38 wooden huts, of which nine are inhabited by the French and Belgians. The camp still has about 8 dugouts ('Erdbaracken or Erdehütte'), in which live many of the French. They are hollows dug in the ground and from the outside, you can only see their roof tops. In winter they are very warm, and cool in summer, like an ordinary wooden barracks. They are much smaller than the other huts, and especially much lower, so that prisoners can only sleep on a single tiered bunk of one storey). At the entrance and at the back is only one window, and we conclude that the interior has not sufficiently lighted. The prisoners can only read and write by this one window. These dugouts are inhabited by any number of prisoners from 8 to 25.
Prisoners living in the other barracks sleep on bunks of two-and three-tiers, depending on the size of the hut. All beds have mattresses but they are empty due to lack of straw. In the Autumn of 1941, the prisoners received only sawdust to fill mattresses, but they all prefer to sleep on empty mattresses, since sawdust hides too many bugs (bedbugs). The prisoners argue that by doing this, the plague of bed bugs is very quickly eliminated. Naturally, sleeping on empty mattresses is not very comfortable, but at least the bugs and insects do not bother them. There are also fleas present. Each prisoner has two blankets and extra blankets can be obtained by their own methods. They can also obtain private clothing from the "Zahlmeister" (Paymaster) as well as the clothing sent by their families.

Conclusion:
In our opinion, the barracks are often too crowded, which means for example, that the prisoners in one barrack did not have enough places to sit. This is wrong as

they only have one meeting room, which serves as a library, theatre, reading room and chapel, and has a limited number of places.

Since our last visit to the camp in September 1941, nothing has been done about this problems. The camp commandant explained repeatedly as to his willingness to help with this matter, but still in vain, so the project was rejected due to lack of building materials.

Electric light is weak and there is no possibility of reading and writing by all the inhabitants of the barrack huts. Ventilation is good.

Heating is provided. According to the words of the advocates and prisoners during last winter, and despite sometimes having heated stoves - they were not sufficient for heating the barracks. Often there is a lack of fuel because the prisoners are forced to prolong the limites supplies. We were told that one morning it was so cold inside the barracks that the water froze in the dishes. Since 1st May and on the day of our visi, the heating has ceased altogether. Overall, the barracks and buildings inside Stalag XXB are still fairly primitive, but the arrangement of beds in a row, in two or three tiers is the best way to gain space.

Food:

According to the words of advocates, the food is good, but not in sufficient quantity. Prisoners are happiest when they receive parcels and additional foods. The kitchen is good, run by chefs of different nationalities. The French have a representative in the kitchen, who is also their boss. We talked at length with the latter who confirmed to us that he is unable to control the amount of allocated food to each prisoner because he cannot weigh it. This has escalated from time to time but for now he will be able to weigh the food in the presence of advocates.

Prisoners receive the following allocation: one loaf between five for five days and one loaf between six for two days a week (one loaf = 1.500 gram).

Daily Rations:
Tea: 2 g
Sugar: 25 g
Potatoes: 750 g
50 g barley
Swede 650 g
Cabbage 70 g

Rations for the week:
Meat 300 g
Fat: 62.5 g
Margarine 143 g
Cheese 125 g
Marmalade 150 g

Prisoners often have barley, turnips and cabbage in place of potatoes.

Previously, prisoners were able to cook meals for themselves privately on the stoves in the barracks. Currently, this is not possible. However, during our conversation, the camp commandant assured us that this ability IS PROVIDED in each barrack hut. Overall, the food in the Stalag is good and it looks healthy and nutritious.

Attorneys told us that they receive complaints about insufficient food in one or another branch of work. In this case, such an action is reported immediately to the camp commandant, who sends an officer to investigate.

The distribution of collective consignments from Geneva is well settled. Shipment in January and February were found to have no irregularities. This was done by the following method:

The whole area of the camp is divided into "Bezirke" (Districts) and a head of each District is appointed. Ours is a French speaking spokesman. When a shipment arrives from Geneva, part is retained by the Marienburg District, and the rest sent to the other Districts. Each District Spokesman can then splits this share amongst the individual Working Teams. Overall control and verification is done using a card attached to each shipment. The Working Team Spokesman then acknowledges receipt of each shipment on the card. Then all the cards are sent back to the main District Spokesman of the camp This can show them exactly what the various Working Teams have received in recent months. Lost packages are extremely rare and in such cases, the District Spokesman will inform the camp commandant, who will immediately initiated a serious investigation.

Attire:

Proponents argue that all prisoners have a complete set of clothing, but the state of uniforms is very variable, depending on the operating circumstances in which they work. The camp uniforms are good because this is where their stores are located. Every prisoner has a double set of underwear, and if you get a shirt or pants from family members, the prisoners may retain them to wear. Some prisoners have 5 or 7 shirts and pants also.

Footwear is a problem as all deliveries are transferred to the Working Teams and there is currently no provision for footwear in the camp. The same applies to uniforms, everyone is happy if they get something new from Geneva. Trousers wear out quickly during work times and currently there ae none in store. A Spokesman for the French has already written several times about this case to the Red Cross in Geneva, but has had no response.

Most Belgians prisoners are missing clothing, especially when it comes to trousers, pants, jackets and coats.

Distribution of uniforms sent from Geneva are dealt with through a Spokesperson, in a similar fashion to collective consignments of food as already described. The main District Spokesman in the camp sends clothing to each District

On 27th December 1941, Geneva sent:
555 woollen blankets to the French in the camp, but the French spokesman reported that they only received 510. This was reported to the German administration, which began the search for missing 45 blankets, so far without success.

The camp has a new laundry room, which works flawlessly. All the prisoners use it and they can change clothes every week. Underwear is collected and washed in the barracks. Soap is delivered directly to the laundry camp, but prisoners do not get a soap allocation to wash themselves individually, unless soap is sent from their family. Prisoners confirmed that the laundry is very clean.

In the tailor's workshop, a lot of work is done and is very well organised.

Canteen (Shop):

The existing canteen offers virtually nothing for sale. Last year, the prisoners could still buy tomatoes, lemons, cucumbers and carrots.

Hygiene:

As has already been pointed out in our last report of September 1941, the camp itself still does not have showers installed, . The prisoners are deloused and take to a shower in the infirmary located about 4 km from Malbork. Civilians employed by the camp, who work in the office and those who work in the camp are able to use the shower in the bathroom of the German guards. Of all the prisoners, no more than

250 a week are able to have a shower. The others do not have the opportunity to take a hot shower for several weeks, which explains fully why the camp is plagued by insects (fleas and bedbugs during both winter and summer). A German Camp Officer said that the installation for disinfecting and showers will be launched soon, in about fifteen days. Washbasins for the camp are in a big washhouse, which is situated roughly in the middle of the camp. If water flows continuously, ie, if the building was open all the time, this would be sufficient. But it is only open from 05.30 to 07.00, then from 11.00 to 14.00 and from 18.30 to 21.00 to save water. According to the words of the Camp Officer, the use of so much water in the area was never envisaged.

Various attorneys have asked us for the washroom to be open all day. This has been promised by the Camp Officer.

Water flows along three long pipes and out through holes at regular intervals into long concrete basins or troughs. Anything from 80 to 100 prisoners could wash here at one time.

Latrines are very primitive and totally unhygienic. During our visit in spring, they were absolutely filthy. We can only imagine what the conditions must be like during the summer. Our delegation asked for immediate construction of new latrines. Currently, the latrines consists of several open huts made of wooden boards, at some distance from the camp, inside which are two long rows of seats, separated by only a single partition of board with no side walls. Seats, as we have said, are very dirty. The seats are over a long pit.

For sports, an area is set aside, located between the barracks. The prisoners can play soccer, handball and basketball. But the terrain is not suitable for very much sport, as it is very sandy and the prisoner's feet sink into it up to their ankles. The whole area is sandy.

The Sick Room:

Nothing has changed in the infirmary since our last visit. All we found were the same old condition (see previous report). The infirmary is located in a wooden hut, consisting of several rooms, one of which is used as a Research Office. The other patients' rooms (split into nationalities) are treated by non-paramedics. The rooms for patients are far too small for the size of the camp and the rooms for the sick are always overcrowded. Patients lie on a set of three-story bunks. You can only imagine the difficulty in treating them in such conditions, especially in a crowded room and those on the top bunk bed. Just as in the whole camp, the sick lie on the bare boards, with only two or three blankets available. The hut has a depressing effect, because it is very dark, poorly lit and the walls and the beds are painted in dark colours. When we went to the infirmary we could hardly believe it. They had no signs on the door. The patients do not have sheets, which is unhygienic, especially for patients with fever. The Research Office is also used as an operating room, is very primitive and lacking essential medical tools. These instruments have been ordered long ago, but still to are not available.

Patients:

The infirmary currently houses 24 Frenchmen patients and a few Belgians. These are the mild cases, because the other more serious patients are transferred to the town's German hospital. Most commonly ailments are arthritis, boils, struts(?), bronchitis, etc. One room contains patients permanently unfit for work who are waiting to be repatriated. At present, this is the case for 104 French and 8 Belgians. The infirmary also houses 56 French and 5 of Belgians unfit for work. The camp commander will be happy if these prisoners were all repatriated as soon as possible to their own countries because they take up space and must be fed the same as prisoners who do work.

Doctors have a sufficient supply of drugs, most of which come from the medical reserve ("Sanitatspark") which are produced in France. To date, the lack of a dentist and dentures means that dentistry is conducted in the German field hospital, by a German dentist after presentation of an authority issued by a German doctor. At the moment there is no possibility of getting a camp dentist, the German dentist treats all. We talked about it with the commandant of the camp and he promised to make efforts to install a dental clinic in the camp. It is mainly the French who have teeth in a deplorable condition.

Intellectual and moral needs:

In this area, a lot has been done in the camp, especially for the working teams. The French Library has several thousand books. These books are shipped in small boxes for various working teams for about 4 to 6 weeks, after which they are exchanged.

The orchestra and theatre productions are operating at a high level, although their room is too small, which has already been reported. The Germans would do well to build a new hut specifically for these entertainers.

The sports ground is big enough for all prisoners.

The camp has a priest, who is also one of the attorneys. Mass is celebrated every Sunday. Almost every Working Team has been assigned a working priest who supports them if necessary. This is all well settled.

Correspondence:

Prisoners of all nationalities receive a designated number of forms. Post cards are regularly distributed. In addition, letters and packages arrive without problems, and all prisoners receive their mail regularly.

Collective shipments:

The French receive Red Cross packages and everything is in order. A District Spokesman for the camp controls their arrival and is personally involved in the distribution of the packages. Belgians generally receive too little and we would be grateful if you could send them more shipments.

Work:

Overall, work at the camp, with some exceptions is well organised. Our Controlling Officers received explicit orders to track down cases of workers doing too much overtime or too heavy work. If such cases, the Advocate will be informed and will immediately intervened and inform the Camp Commandant. During our last visit in September we raised the question of this problem and a Spokesman told us that after our visit, such cases become very rare.

The situation in the camp has now changed and the prisoners are taken to employers without any explanation. If prisoners on a Working Team complain about the bad treatment, bad food, etc., the Spokesman for the camp, along with an officer, go there immediately to resolve the situation, which usually works. Moreover, the Spokesman for the camp has already visited a few Teams and is kept informed of everything that happens to the Working Teams, and can give them advice.

Soldiers Pay:

Wages are paid regularly, no complaints

Marienburg Hospital:
(See report) Accommodation and treatment of patients is good. According to the words of a French physician, patients usually come to a military hospital too late and with advanced diseases. Since most have a high fever they must be allowed to go to the doctor immediately when they are in Working Teams. We talked about this issue for a long time with the Commandant of the camp and he promised to address the issue.

Doctors have told us of two recent cases, who were sent too late to a military hospital:

1) Felix Domecq, No. 53 702, *went to the infirmary with dual tuberculosis. The prisoner was reported to a civilian doctor on 17th December 1941 due to coughing blood. This doctor recommended he have two days in bed. Then the prisoner was sent back. He was weak and exhausted, but still had to work. 5th January, 1942 he began to cough blood again and the same day a civilian doctor (Dr. Schöneberg) took him to a military hospital, where shortly after his arrival he began to spit blood once more. There he had a blood transfusion and given X-rays and found to have extensive tuberculous cavities on both sides of his lungs. His condition is very serious.*

2) Fernand Pages, No. 52 966, *was dealt with by the same doctor. For six days the prisoner was in his Work Team lying and suffering from abdominal pain. He was transported to the military hospital in Malbork for an emergency Laparotomy, where he died an hour after surgery. Diagnosis: Peritonitis.*
In our opinion, the doctor should have taken appropriate action. The German military hospital doctor has informed his superior, and we hope that this doctor will in future supply medical care for the prisoners.

Conversation without witnesses with the advocates of the camp:
Since our last visit to the camp, many things have improved, especially in the working brigades, and ill treatment of prisoners is now very rare. We are very grateful. Distribution of collective shipments, food and clothing is made without reservation, wholly in the hands of attorneys.
In the camp there are no new concerns.

Conclusions:
Accommodation of prisoners in the camp leaves a lot to be desired. The barracks are overcrowded, old and badly ventilated and light. Sanitary systems are inadequate, especially in the latrines and camp infirmary. There remains a lack of showers in the camp, resulting in relapses of pediculosis (infestations of head, body and pubic lice, cooties and crabs.

Departments in the infirmary and dental prostheses still leave much to be desired.

Dr. Schirmer

Authors Note: *There are some inconsistencies between these reports and Dennis' recollections. This is totally understandable. In part possibly due to his inability to accurately recall those events of 70 years ago, but more likely because of the Swiss Red Cross Inspectors inaccurate interpretation of misleading and false evidence presented to them by the German administrators of Stalag XXB.*

ACKNOWLEDGEMENTS

My wife Angelika Gibbon - thanks.

Bianca Rose, daughter, proof reader, advisor and encouragement officer.

Tobias Gibbon, son, for his help & great knowledge of the SS divisions during WW2 and for modelling and the use of his uniform on some of the chapter headings.

Nick Galt, friend and reader.

Gary Tidbury, friend and reader.

David Butcher, Historian, friend and proof reader.

Rachel Pearson, editing, proof reading and translator, a huge thanks.

Matthew White, editing and proof reader.

David Roberts of POPPUBLISHING, friend, established author and advisor who encouraged me to keep going.

Vivian Marciandi, for his assistance in bringing this book to print

Joshua Collins & Colin Reilley from The Queen's Royal Regiment - Living History Group

Jordan Toovey, also from The Queen's Royal Regiment - Living History Group for modelling and the use of his authentic uniform and weapons for use on the front & back covers and the chapter headings.

www.allthequeensmen.co.uk

Bundesarchiv - Federal Archives, Division B6.
Potsdamer Str. 1, D-56075 Koblenz, Germany.
www.bild.bundesarchiv.de

Getty Images, 101 Bayham Street, London NW1 0AG, England.
www.gettyimages.co.uk

CICR International Committee of the Red Cross, Geneva, Switzerland.

Surrey History Centre, 130 Goldsworth Road, Woking, Surrey GU21 6ND, England.
www.surreycc.gov.uk/recreation-heritage-and-culture/archives-and-history/surrey-history-centre

The National Archives, Kew, Richmond, Surrey TW9 4DU, England.
www.nationalarchives.gov.uk

The National Ex-Prisoner of War Association is a member of the Council of British Service and Ex-Service Organisations.
www.prisonerofwar.org.uk

Book sources, information & verification:

'The Second World War, Volume 1, The Gathering Storm' by Winston Churchill.

'Dunkirk, Fight to the Last Man' by Hugh Sebag-Montefiore.

'Lost Victories' by Field Marshal Eric von Manstein.

'Dunkirk, The Men they Left Behind' by Sean Longden.

'The Last Escape' by John Nichole & Tony Rennell.

'Prisoner of War' by Charles Rollings

'Hitler's British Slaves' by Sean Longden.

'The History of The Queen's Royal Regiment 1939 - 1945' by Roy E Bollenn, 1958.

'No Cheese After Dinner' by Fred Kennington.

I really hope you enjoyed reading my book.
I hope you have learnt a great deal and can now
appreciate the sacrifice that these men made
all those years ago, who heard the call to arms and
went to war in order to protect
Britain and her people from
the evil of Hitler and his Nazis.

Every effort has been made to verify all material
published in this book.
If the reader discovers any error or glaring
omissions in this book,
please contact the author at
email: ghostsofdunkirk@talktalk.net
and he will be only too happy to correct the
inaccuracy or add such facts
where possible at the earliest opportunity.

Your comments are welcome and appreciated.

To comment, learn more about this book,
add your own information that the author can use
or to interact with other followers,
please visit me on **FACEBOOK** at
www.facebook.com/ghostsofdunkirk

Thank you.